Peter Norton's

Complete Guide to Microsoft® Office 2000

Peter Norton
Jill T. Freeze
Wayne S. Freeze

SAMS

A Division of Macmillan Computer Publishing
201 West 103rd Street, Indianapolis, Indiana 46290 USA

Peter Norton's Complete Guide to Microsoft® Office 2000

Copyright © 1999 by Peter Norton

International Standard Book Number: 0-672-31174-7

Library of Congress Catalog Card Number: 97-67998

Printed in the United States of America

First Printing: April 1999

02   01   00   4   3

Trademarks

Warning and Disclaimer

Executive Editor
Jim Minatel

Acquisitions Editors
Jill Byus
Don Essig

Development Editor
Jill Hayden

Managing Editor
Brice Gosnell

Project Editors
Natalie Harris
Kevin Laseau

Copy Editor
Chuck Hutchinson

Indexer
Kevin Kent

Proofreader
Andy Beaster

Technical Editor
Jim Grey
Mitch Milam

Interior Design
Gary Adair

Cover Design
Aren Howell

Layout Technicians
Brandon Allen
Stacey DeRome
Tim Osborn
Staci Somers

Contents at a Glance

Table of Contents

About the Authors

Computer software entrepreneur and writer **Peter Norton** established his technical expertise and accessible style from the earliest days of the PC. His Norton Utilities was the first product of its kind, giving early computer owners control over their hardware and protection against myriad problems. His flagship titles, *Peter Norton's DOS Guide* and *Peter Norton's Inside the PC* (Sams Publishing), have provided the same insight and education to computer users worldwide for nearly two decades. Peter's books, like his many software products, are among the best-selling and most-respected in the history of personal computing.

Peter Norton's former column in *PC Week* was among the highest-regarded in that magazine's history. His expanding series of computer books continues to bring superior education to users, always in Peter's trademark style, which is never condescending nor pedantic. From their earliest days, changing the "black box" into a "glass box," Peter's books, like his software, remain among the most powerful tools available to beginners and experienced users alike.

In 1990, Peter sold his software development business to Symantec Corporation, allowing him to devote more time to his family, civic affairs, philanthropy, and art collecting. He lives with his wife, Eileen, and two children in Santa Monica, California.

Jill T. Freeze is a freelance management consultant who has worked with such organizations as the John F. Kennedy Center for the Performing Arts, the National Endowment for the Arts, The Smithsonian Institute, and the White House. Having used computers extensively over the past decade for work and play, Jill finally decided to put her experience to good use writing computer books. Aside from *Peter Norton's Complete Guide to Microsoft Office 2000* (Sams, 1999), she authored *Sams Teach Yourself Internet Explorer 5 in 24 Hours* (Sams, 1999), *Sams Teach Yourself Computer Basics in 24 Hours* (Sams, 1998), *Using Microsoft Office 97* (Que, 1997), and *Introducing WebTV* (Microsoft Press, 1997). Her formal education includes a bachelor's degree magna cum laude from the University of Massachusetts at Amherst (in Arts Administration and Writing) and a master's degree from George Washington University (in Nonprofit Administration). For fun, Jill likes listening to music, writing fiction, watching NASCAR races (Go Terry Labonte!), surfing the Net, playing her flute, and playing with her two children, Christopher and Samantha. Jill can be reached at JFreeze@JustPC.com.

Wayne S. Freeze is a full-time computer book author, software developer, and technology consultant. Having worked with computers for over 25 years, Wayne has seen computers grow from room-sized machines to palm-top devices. In addition to collaborating with his wife on *Peter Norton's Complete Guide to Microsoft Office 2000* (Sams, 1999), Wayne has written many advanced computer programming titles, including *Hands On SQL Server 7 and Visual Basic 6* (Prima, 1999), *Expert Guide to Visual Basic 6* (Sybex, 1998), *The SQL Programmer's Reference* (Ventana, 1998), *The Visual Basic 5 Programmer's Reference* (Ventana, 1997), *Programming ISAPI with Visual Basic 5* (Prima Publishing, 1997), and *Leveraging Visual Basic with ActiveX Controls* (Prima Publishing, 1996). Several of these titles have been featured on Microsoft's Web site or have been reviewed in *Dr. Dobbs* magazine. In his spare time, he likes to photograph warbirds at air shows, read (and write) science fiction, play with his two children (Christopher and Samantha), tinker with his aquarium, and play with his collection of cars in varying sizes. Wayne's formal education includes degrees in electrical engineering, computer science, and business management. He can be reached at WFreeze@JustPC.com.

Dedication

This one's for my father, Bucky Heyer, who bounced back from a heart attack with his sense of humor intact. I feel so blessed that Christopher and Samantha have been given many more years to get to know "Grampa Buck." And I know I don't say it often enough, but I love you, Dad.

Jill T. Freeze

Acknowledgments

Much like Oscar-winning movies are a result of the work of a cast of thousands, so too are computer books. Maybe there aren't thousands of people involved, but there are definitely dozens.

First, I would like to thank Peter Norton, whose outstanding work and reputation in the field is recognized by millions around the world. Thanks for giving me the opportunity to work on such an invigorating project! And to Scott Clark, thanks for helping us achieve a style that is consistent to this series of books.

At Macmillan, a number of folks have contributed greatly to the fine product you see before you. Jill Byus, you've been a pleasure to work with—an outstanding professional and a kind (and patient) soul. Thank you for your kindness and generosity during my father's illness. Jill Hayden, your powers of observation and concrete suggestions have contributed more to the quality of this book than you can ever imagine. Thank you! Jim Grey, you are the finest, most thorough tech editor I've ever worked with. Can I keep you <grin>? And to Jim Minatel, thank you for taking the time to discuss every issue under the sun with me. You say some authors think you're scary to work with, but you don't scare me. I like working with editors who really know the product and can offer up a good challenge. Thanks for having me back! Then there's John Pierce with whom I've probably played more telephone tag than I have with any other person in the world. Thanks for the long chat; now whatever you do, don't forget it <grin>! Mandie Rowell, have I finally gotten the hang of formatting chapters yet? Thank you so much for all your hard work and patience! And finally to all those behind the scenes who have dotted every *i* and crossed every *t*, my heartfelt thanks. Yours is the toughest job of all—turning tens of thousands of words into a real book!

And this book would never have been written without the love, patience, and support of my family. My husband, Wayne, juggled book projects so he could lend his database and programming expertise to this book. Thanks for your help and for putting up with my weird work schedule. Christopher and Samantha, my only regret about this project is that it ate into a lot of our Christmas fun time. But just so you'll know for future reference, no matter what I'm working on, Christmas Eve and Christmas will always be yours! And to my parents (all four of you), thank you for helping us through the worst of times. Here's hoping 1999 will be *much* better!

Jill T. Freeze

Beltsville, Maryland

1 February 1999

Tell Us What You Think!

As the reader of this book, *you* are our most important critic and commentator. We value your opinion and want to know what we're doing right, what we could do better, what areas you'd like to see us publish in, and any other words of wisdom you're willing to pass our way.

As an executive editor for the Desktop Applications team at Macmillan Computer Publishing, I welcome your comments. You can fax, email, or write me directly to let me know what you did or didn't like about this book—as well as what we can do to make our books stronger.

Please note that I cannot help you with technical problems related to the topic of this book, and that due to the high volume of mail I receive, I might not be able to reply to every message.

When you write, please be sure to include this book's title and author as well as your name and phone or fax number. I will carefully review your comments and share them with the author and editors who worked on the book.

Fax: 317.581.4663

Email: `office_que@mcp.com`

Mail: Executive Editor
            Desktop Applications
            Macmillan Computer Publishing
            201 West 103rd Street
            Indianapolis, IN 46290 USA

xx

Introduction

You have a busy life, so who has time for a book on Office 2000 that covers every conceivable way to do something in excruciating detail? Wouldn't it be nice to have a volume that cuts to the chase and gives you one way to do the job? And what if that book could also help you decide which features would help or hinder your work? Too many books tout one-size-fits-all solutions. Not this book. We recognize that everyone's needs are different and that one corporation's favorite new Office 2000 feature could be virtually useless to its small business counterpart. Rather than bombard you with endless sets of steps for using a new feature, we take a little time to tell you when it may and may not be useful to use. Remember, Office evolved over a long period of time. Often you'll find a new feature or enhancement whose purpose duplicates a function found in earlier versions of Office. Rather than strip the old way of doing things, Microsoft many times just leaves well enough alone so that veteran Office users need not start from scratch in learning the applications.

Who Should Read This Book?

Rather than us giving you some song and dance about how useful this book can be to virtually anyone, why don't you be the judge? If you answer yes to any of the following questions, then you'll gain a lot from this book:

- Do you already know the basics of Office but want to learn how to use some of the more complex features?

- Are you looking for an Office 2000 book that not only tells you how to do things but tells you when they work best or when to avoid them as well?

- Would you like to reduce the amount of time you spend at the keyboard so that you can spend your precious time interacting with coworkers, playing with your kids, or doing other things you enjoy?

- Is generating professional-looking output important to you or your company?

- Would you like to discover how various Office 2000 features can help you conserve paper, toner, and other resources?

Although this book assumes that you have some degree of familiarity with Office-like applications—you know how to work with the mouse, select text, change fonts; you know the difference between cells, menus, and so on—you by no means need to be an Office guru to follow the content.

How This Book Is Organized

For your convenience, the book is divided into the following nine logical parts:

- Part I, "Office 2000 Essentials"—This part covers all kinds of common Office material, including new Office 2000 installation options, customized menus and toolbars, file management, common tools and applets such as the Clip Gallery, as well as an Internet Explorer 5 quick course.

- Part II, "Using Word 2000"—This part takes a look at how Word 2000 can help you achieve a more professional result while saving time at the keyboard. You'll discover why style codes and templates are so useful, how to tackle mail merge and envelope printing head-on, and how to build a Web page using Word 2000.

- Part III, "Using Excel 2000"—In addition to learning some of the tips and tricks of using Excel on a daily basis, you'll find in-depth coverage of charting data, using PivotCharts and PivotTables, and putting the new Office 2000 Web components to the task.

- Part IV, "Using Outlook 2000"—Discover the ins and outs of emailng with Outlook in this part. You'll learn the differences between IMAP and POP mail servers, discover the ability to automate tasks using the powerful new Rules Wizard, and gain the know-how to personalize your messages using stationery and signature files. You also will be introduced to the concept of using Outlook 2000 as a personal information manager (or PIM).

- Part V, "PowerPoint Essentials"—Learn about the new PowerPoint workspace, add pizzazz to your presentations by making use of a variety of multimedia options, and even schedule live broadcasts of your presentation over the Internet.

- Part VI, "Publisher Essentials"—Get acquainted with Publisher 2000's catalog of valuable templates and wizards as well as learn how to create the documents you want from scratch. You'll even learn how to take your Publisher documents to the Web

- Part VII, "Access Essentials"—Learn everything you need to know about building a database and generating charts, forms, and reports.

- Part VIII, "Advanced Integration"—Even if you consider yourself only an intermediate Office user, you'll discover how to put Visual Basic for Applications (VBA) to work for you. One chapter in this part deals with VBA issues in general, and the other takes a look at VBA in the context of specific applications.

- Part IX, "Appendices"—Here is where you'll find useful tidbits such as free stuff from Microsoft, tips on Web graphics, a glossary, and more.

Throughout the text, you'll find a number of notes and tips designed to help you get more from Office 2000. You'll even find special elements called *Peter's Principles* that tie our years of personal experience with the product together with sound advice for making the most of your time at the keyboard. In addition, you'll find an appendix that points you to many of Microsoft's free resources on the Web.

Other Important Facts About This Book

Note that this book is written based on using Office 2000 Professional with the standard Windows 98 desktop. Results and screens may vary slightly for Windows 95 users and/or those using the Active Desktop, but in general, you will notice few differences.

While you're flipping through the table of contents, you might notice that FrontPage 2000 and PhotoDraw 2000 are not covered in this book. The reason for this is twofold. First, these applications are included with the Office 2000 Premium Edition only. Although the applications would be a tremendous asset to any user, few people may actually acquire them. Historically, computer manufacturers have included Office Professional or the Small Business Edition as part of their systems. As a result, we've found that the majority of prospective readers will be working with those versions of Office for that very reason; there's no out-of-pocket expense to upgrade.

Of course, not covering these additional applications has yet another positive side effect: The applications included here are given the rich, insightful coverage you deserve both as a consumer and as a professional computer user.

PART I

Office 2000 Essentials

Overview of the Office 2000 Architecture

What if your boss suddenly came up to you and said, "Gee, you've really gotten a lot of work done lately; why don't you take the afternoon off?" You would be overjoyed, right? Although I can't promise that your efforts will be rewarded in such a way, I can promise that after reading this book, you'll be a far more productive Office user than you've been in the past. Part of the key to unleashing this productivity is to have a firm grounding in what each Office application does and to understand which product is best used for what purpose. In this chapter, I'll introduce you to each of the components of Office 2000 and will explain how each of the programs works.

> **Note: What's this architecture stuff?** Techies use the word *architecture* to describe how a program works and, in the case of Office 2000, how each application fits in with the others in the set. This terminology makes sense if you carry through the analogy between buildings and computer programs because architecture in both cases refers to a blueprint of how something's put together—be it a skyscraper or a word processing program.

Office 2000 is one of the most complex products ever written by Microsoft. Although it was designed to be easy to use, it has many features and functions that most people never use simply because they don't know these features exist. It's a shame, too, because many of these features can dramatically increase your personal productivity and enhance the professionalism of your output—be it a proposal for funding, a Web page, or a slide presentation.

Interestingly, Microsoft found that over 25 percent of the features requested for Office 2000 were already in Office 97. So what about the other features Microsoft chose to include in this latest version of the popular Office suite? Are they worth using and investing countless hours to master?

It's my job in this book to show you how to use these less commonly known features and functions because you already know the basics. And along the way, I'll tell you which features work best when.

What Is Office 2000?

Six major Office applications are included in the Office 2000 Professional package. Although you'll find more applications in the Premium and Developer editions of Office 2000 (such as FrontPage 2000 and PhotoDraw 2000), I've focused my attention on the applications included with the Office 2000 Professional on down because that's what a vast majority of users will have installed on their machines.

These core applications provide capabilities such as document processing, spreadsheet analysis, contact management, and graphic design. And they all have a common look and feel as well, which makes switching from using one application to another a whole lot easier. The applications included with every configuration of Office include the following:

- Microsoft Word 2000—Helps you build documents from very simple letters to comprehensive manuscripts.
- Microsoft Excel 2000—Enables you to build spreadsheets and charts to help you analyze your data.
- Microsoft Outlook 2000—Provides a complete solution for such personnel management functions as email, calendar scheduling, and contact management.
- Microsoft PowerPoint 2000—Helps you create professional presentations complete with vivid color, text animation, and a variety of output options. You can even broadcast these presentations over the Internet or intranet.
- Microsoft Access 2000—Helps you build complete database applications with minimal programming thanks to the extensive use of wizards. Using Access is a great way for major corporations to enable employees to access data stored on a large server.
- Microsoft Publisher 2000—Makes it easy to create newsletters, brochures, and other documents that will be published in print or over the Internet.

Even though Internet Explorer 5 is not an official member of the Office family, each of the Office applications is now woven tightly around it. Also included are many small applications (also known as *applets*) that work behind the scenes to provide value to all the applications. For example, you can use the Clip Gallery to import categorized clips no matter what application you're working in, and you can use WordArt to turn plain old text into works of art.

You can easily use Microsoft Office 2000 with other Microsoft applications such as MapPoint 2000 and Microsoft Project. Also, Microsoft Office is designed to work with many of the services provided by Windows NT Server, such as Exchange, SQL Server, and the Internet Information Server. In these cases, the whole is much more than merely the sum of its parts. And best of all, this tremendous scalability potential makes Office 2000 a great choice whether you're a home user who designs a monthly newsletter for your local Porsche owner club or the president of a multinational corporation who plans to deploy the suite to desktops throughout the company.

The Flavors of Office 2000

In the preceding section, I touched on some of the flavors of Office 2000. Figuring out what's what can be a bit complicated (and locating the information on Microsoft's Web site is like embarking on a virtual treasure hunt), so I've spelled it out here for your convenience.

Because everyone might not need all the applications in the Microsoft Office 2000 suite, Microsoft has created five different editions containing different combinations of the six main applications and two sets of tools.

Table 1.1   Major Applications by Office 2000 Edition

Application	Standard	Small Business	Professional	Premiere	Developer
Word	yes	yes	yes	yes	yes
Excel	yes	yes	yes	yes	yes
Outlook	yes	yes	yes	yes	yes
PowerPoint	yes	no	yes	yes	yes
Access	no	no	yes	yes	yes
Publisher	no	yes	yes	yes	yes
FrontPage	no	no	no	yes	yes
PhotoDraw	no	no	no	yes	yes
Small Business Tools	no	yes	yes	yes	yes
Developer Tools	no	no	no	no	yes

How Office 2000 Works?

Although you might think that Office 2000 is merely a collection of applications (you know, the "buy two and get four free" syndrome), it really is one super application with many integrated components. Over 70 percent of the code is shared among the various Office applications. Therefore, when you learn how to use one feature in one application (such as the Clip Gallery or the File Open dialog box), you will know how to use it for all the other applications.

Because Office 2000 is highly integrated, all the components are designed to work with each other. You therefore can embed a Word document inside a PowerPoint presentation, for example, or an Excel spreadsheet inside a Publisher document quickly and easily.

What Are Documents and Templates?

Each Office application stores its information in a specially formatted file or set of files. These files are technically known as *documents*, *workbooks*, *presentations*, *databases*, or by other names depending on the application. When talking about Office 2000 in general terms, I'll often use the term *document* to refer to any file that contains Office 2000 information.

Often you will find yourself in a situation in which you have to create multiple documents that are similar in nature. For instance, you might want to include a standard logo at the top of each page or include a predefined set of style codes so that the text of all documents originating from your company looks the same. If you can create a standard document that contains this information, you merely have to open the specially formatted document each time you want to use it. Of course, you have to remember to save the new document with a new name, or you risk destroying your standard document. However, you could instead create a template from that document and use it to create a new document each time you need it. Templates are merely skeleton documents used to create blank documents. In some cases, these templates may also contain boilerplate text that users are to include in the newly created document. The big advantage of creating a template is that you needn't worry about inadvertently blowing away the stock document; you are prompted to name the document when you start to save it just as you are when you create any ordinary document.

What's New in Office 2000?

Any new version of software must have a bunch of new features that justify buying the latest version of the software. And if those new features aren't immediately recognized as useful by the consumers, the software company has its work cut out for it. The software company needs to persuade the prospective users that they really do have a need for these features, that they could get their work done faster or conserve system resources by applying the new features, or that at the very least the features are fun or cool to use.

Office 2000 is not the exception to this rule. Although many of the new features are specific to one of the applications, a few key features can be found throughout the entire Office suite. With these new features, you can now do any of the following:

- Save your documents using a new HTML/XML format that preserves all the information that was previously lost when you created an HTML copy of your document

- Use enhanced Open and Save dialog boxes that remember more about where you store your files and give you more flexibility and power for finding the files you need

- Collaborate with other users over the Internet by using the new Office 2000 Server Extensions
- Improve your productivity by using the new style menus and toolbars
- Collect and paste multiple chunks of text with the new multi-item Clipboard
- Build documents that contain words and phrases from multiple languages and have the proofing tools such as the spell checker and grammar checker automatically switch languages
- Select a common visual design theme for your documents
- Get improved help from the enhanced Office Assistants
- Customize your installation of Office 2000 using the new setup process

In the following sections, I'll go into a bit more detail about these new features and discuss why they may or may not be of value to you.

View Any Document in a Web Browser by Saving It in HTML/XML Format

Probably the most visible change to Office 2000 is the integrated Web support. You can save documents either in their old proprietary format or as an HTML/XML document. This capability makes it easy to publish the document to the Web because the document is now a Web page.

> **Note: XML is not HTML!** Don't confuse XML with HTML. Each has its own purpose, and one doesn't replace the other. HTML is used to create the visible component of a Web page. XML is used to hold the invisible data, such as document properties and special formatting requirements that aren't visible on a Web page.

Unlike Office 97, where saving a document as an HTML file and loading it back in resulted in a loss of formatting information, Office 2000 can save and load Office 2000-created HTML documents without any loss of information.

Find What You Need Using Enhanced File Open and Save Dialog Boxes

The File Open and Save dialog boxes have been significantly improved. They now provide an easy way to switch the view of your files to the history of the files you have accessed, your personal folder of documents, the desktop, your list of favorite documents, and your list of Web folders. These easy-to-access buttons are collectively referred to as the Places Bar. The Places Bar makes it easier to locate the file you want than the Office 97 way of presenting the list of the four most recently accessed files. You even have a Back button now, just like you have on a Web browser. This button returns you to the previous file view as opposed to bumping you up a directory level.

> **Tip: A Favorite document may not be your favorite.** You may already be aware of this point, but it bears repeating for those who might not have experience with creating Favorites in Microsoft products. Saving a document to your Favorites folder doesn't necessarily mean you find the document fun to work with. In this case, any document you use repeatedly on a regular basis may be a good candidate for the Favorites folder. If you name it a Favorite, retrieving it is easier when you need it.

Enhanced Collaboration Potential Using the Office 2000 Server Extensions

Supporting HTML/XML documents is fine; however, being able to share them through a Web server is even better. The Microsoft Office 2000 Server Extensions (OSE) are a collection of utilities that transform an Internet Information Server on a Windows NT machine into a rich workgroup environment. With an OSE-enabled server at your disposal, you can do the following:

- Store and retrieve your documents in Web folders on the server
- Browse Web folders or use a search engine to help you find the document you want to access
- Use the Web Discussions feature to let multiple people insert comments into a Web page at the same time
- Subscribe to documents on the Web server and receive automatic notification when the document is changed

Multiple users can also browse and edit documents over the Internet. For instance, you can let users access a spreadsheet over the Web to create different charts of the data. You can even use the Internet to deliver presentations, complete with real-time voice and video.

New Menus and Toolbars

Probably the most noticeable feature of the Office 2000 applications is a change to the menu bar, which Microsoft has dubbed *personalized menus*. You'll either love them or hate them; there doesn't seem to be a whole lot of middle ground where this feature is concerned. With personalized menus, only the most common menu items are listed. Leaving the cursor over the menu for about three or four seconds displays the entire menu, including all the missing items. If you select one of the missing items, it is added to the list of common items for that menu. You can also click the arrow button at the bottom of the menu to display all the menu items immediately.

> **Tip: I hate them!** Working with these personalized menus can be very distracting because the location of menu items suddenly shifts when the rest of the menu options appear. It seems I was constantly clicking the wrong thing by mistake when they were enabled. To turn off personalized menus, select Tools|Customize to display the Customize dialog box. Choose the Options tab, and then uncheck Menus show recently used commands first. If you like the shorter menus, don't mind clicking the arrow button, but hate the automatic timer, leave that option checked, but uncheck the Show Full menus after a short delay option.

Toolbars are also improved (or for those of us who are cynical and/or resistant to change, "enhanced"). Buttons that would not have been visible on Office 97 applications can be found on Office 2000 applications by clicking the small arrow button at the end of the button group. Even when all the other buttons are missing from a toolbar, clicking the arrow at the end of the toolbar shows the Add or Remove Buttons choice. All the missing buttons are displayed with an option to change the toolbar's configuration. Clicking Add or Remove Buttons produces a drop-down menu where you can choose which buttons you want displayed on the toolbar; plus it provides options to reset the toolbar to its default values or invoke the toolbar customization menus. You can also save real estate on your workspace by having the Menu and Standard toolbars share a line.

Holding Multiple Items in the Office 2000 Clipboard

Office 2000 now has a Clipboard that can hold up to 12 items at the same time. Each item you copy is added to the end of the Clipboard. When you copy the thirteenth item, Office prompts you to decide whether you want to discard the first item on the Clipboard. When you need to paste something from the Office Clipboard, you merely select the item from the Clipboard toolbar and use the familiar paste function.

The Office 2000 Clipboard is independent of the Windows Clipboard, except for the fact that the last item in the Office 2000 Clipboard is always copied to the Windows Clipboard. You therefore can continue to use the Clipboard to copy and paste into non-Office applications. The Office Clipboard is available to all Office applications, and is closed only when no Office applications are running.

Support for Multiple Languages

Most users won't see one of the biggest changes in Office. In Office 97, each language had its own particular version of the software with its own unique set of code. In Office 2000, Microsoft uses just one set of code to handle all languages. Using one set of code makes it easy to support different languages and allows you the opportunity to use multiple languages in a single document without losing any language-dependent functions such as the spell checker or grammar checker.

Although this feature isn't used by everyone, it is an interesting feature for multinational corporations and companies that employ people from a variety of countries. With it, you can identify which parts of the document are written in a particular language. In some cases, the Office application may be smart enough to recognize that the text is in a particular language and automatically mark that text, thus enabling the proper spell checker and grammar checker. This capability makes it easy to create and manage multilingual documents.

Common Themes

First introduced in FrontPage 97, *themes* are a set of templates and graphic images that you can use to provide a common look to all your documents. Themes include such coordinated design elements as document backgrounds, color definitions, graphical bullets, font type, and size. You can even choose the default color mix or a vivid color mix that makes a bolder statement.

New Help and Office Assistants

Office 2000 has replaced the old help files with new HTML-formatted help files containing better information than in the previous version of Office, plus help now includes an improved search facility that allows users to ask a question of the Answer Wizard in plain English as opposed to technobabble.

The Office Assistants (which you'll see in figures throughout this chapter) have been upgraded to use the newest Microsoft Agent technology. The new assistants no longer live in a fixed box but float on top of the open windows. You can choose from many new assistants, such as Rocky, the dog; Links, the cat; and F1, the robot; plus many of your old favorites, such as Clippit (with a new 3D look), The Dot, The Genius, Mother Nature, and the Office Logo.

New Setup Process

In the new setup program, like the old setup program, you can choose exactly what features of Office you want loaded during installation. With this setup, unlike the old setup program, however, you can also identify features that should be loaded the first time you use them or features that should be run from the CD-ROM. This way, you can load only as much software as you need, which is helpful in situations in which disk space is usually tight, such as on a laptop computer.

A side effect of this new setup process is that Office 2000 applications can detect and correct problems such as missing files when the application starts. The most that might happen is that the application prompts you to insert the installation disks.

> **Tip: Keep those CDs handy!** When Office 2000 is installed, many of the features are not installed by default on your hard disk but may be installed the first time you try to use them.

What Is Word 2000?

If I polled 1,000 Office users, I bet I would find that 995 of the users have worked with Word, and that a majority of them use the application almost daily in their work. Word is easily the most popular and commonly used component of the Office suite (see Figure 1.1). In addition to producing typical letters and reports, you can create Web pages from within Word and even use it as your email editor.

FIGURE 1.1

View a sample Word 2000 session with the Genius, the Office Assistant.

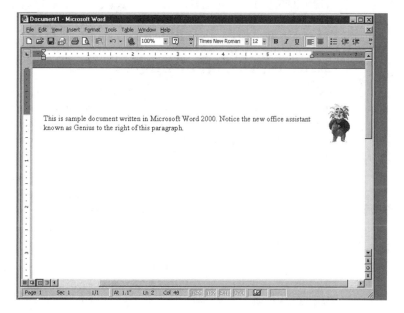

When Should You Use Word 2000?

Word is not the only tool in Office that can create print and Web documents. Most Office 2000 applications have this capability. However, Word is targeted to a diverse set of users who need to produce documents ranging from simple business letters to complex manuscripts such as this book. If you want to use only one tool in Office for both Web page development and document creation, then Word is the tool for you.

That last statement may leave you wondering when you should choose Word over any of the other applications. If you want to produce a complex report with a table of contents and an index, Word 2000 is the application of choice. With a few simple mouse clicks, these elements basically produce themselves.

Do you need to make use of footnotes or endnotes in your documents? Many scientists, lawyers, and researchers—among others—do, and Word is the only Office application with this capability. And although other applications can produce outlines, Word 2000 is by far the most powerful tool. You can manipulate Word outlines with ease, so reorganizing a document is little more than a drag-and-drop effort. And, of course, you can easily import these outlines into applications such as PowerPoint 2000, so you can make complementary slide presentations with minimal effort.

Basically, any time you plan to work with text (as opposed to data, which you might want to add in Excel or perform analysis in Access), you should turn to Word. For specialized documents such as newsletters, brochures, and flyers, you might want to consider using a tool such as Publisher 2000. It can build these types of documents easier and faster than Word can, and you don't need to fight with uneven column lengths.

How Word 2000 Works

Word 2000 is a document processor with many (and I do mean *many*) tools to help you format your documents. Besides the normal tools that let you change text alignment and font styles, along with other basic options, you can easily create multicolumn documents, insert graphic art, build tables, generate indexes and tables of contents…you name it, if you can do it with text, so can Word.

Because Word is a *What You See Is What You Get* (*WYSIWYG*, pronounced *wiz-e-wig*) word processor, you don't have to worry about how your document is going to look. Thus, if it looks right on your display, it will look right on paper or the Internet. And if you're still not convinced, you can easily access the Word 2000 Print Preview tool to verify that everything appears as you want it to.

Templates and wizards also play an important part in Word, helping you create documents such as résumés, legal briefings, and the like quicker than if you had to create them from scratch. When you create a new document, simply choose the template or wizard to give you the proper starting point. Then all you have to do is replace the sample text in the document. You can also create your own templates to help promote use of a common stationery within your organization.

Word also has many automatic tools that can make your life easier. The spell checker flags misspelled words as you type, whereas the grammar checker offers suggestions to improve how your document reads. Using AutoComplete means that you have to type fewer characters, and AutoCorrect can fix common spelling errors without asking.

Using Word 2000 with Other Office Applications

I've already touched on some of the ways you can use Word with other Office applications, but here's a more comprehensive list:

- Use Word 2000 with Outlook 2000 to create and view your email (though I much prefer using one of the Outlook products for this purpose).

- Cut or copy and paste text from Word, and include it in any other Office application you can think of. No need to rekey an existing article for your Publisher newsletter or your company Web page.

- Build an outline in Word, and use it as a basis for a PowerPoint presentation.

- Embed an Excel spreadsheet in Word to add Excel functionality while producing one combined text/data document.

- Produce a data source that can be used for mail merges in either Word or Publisher.

- Print mailing labels so that you can affix them to Publisher documents for mailing. You can also print envelopes in Word with ease for mailing any type of Office document.

See what a versatile application Word is? Now let's take a closer look at how Word accomplishes all these tasks.

What's New in Word 2000

Besides the capability to perform roundtrip editing of Word Web documents saved as HTML, Word 2000 also includes a Click-n-type interface. With it, you click on the screen anywhere you want to enter text, and Word automatically adjusts the formatting to match. Word even shows what kind of formatting will be applied through *cursor hinting*, in which a left, right, or center alignment icon is attached to the cursor. This is a marked change from previous versions of Word in which you had to press the Enter key or reset the margins to start typing lower on the page.

Probably the most notable change in Word 2000 is the switch from a Multiple Document Interface (MDI) to a Single Document Interface (SDI). Although this change might not seem like a big deal, it has a dramatic effect on the behavior of the application's windows.

In MDI (the way Word used to be), each document is displayed inside the application's main window, and all the documents share a common menu and toolbar. In SDI, each open document has its own window and menu and toolbar. Internet Explorer works this way when you open multiple Web pages. A side effect of this change to SDI is that each document has its own entry in the taskbar, making it easier to switch among multiple documents.

Note: Pros and cons of SDI. Whether SDI is better than MDI has sparked a religious war among Office users. Many people (including me) like the new user interface, but many people still prefer the old way because they feel the new way needlessly clutters up the taskbar. Also, if you try to close an open document by double-clicking its program icon in the upper-left corner of the screen, all the active Word documents are closed.

Table formatting has had many enhancements in Word 2000. You can now nest tables and adjust the whitespace and border settings like you can on a Web page. You can even allow text to flow around a table without putting the table into a text box or frame. Also, table cells now automatically adjust to the proper size when graphics are inserted.

The spell checker and grammar checker have been improved as well. More words and names have been added to the dictionary to reduce the number of incorrectly flagged misspelled words. Fewer false problems are now identified by the grammar checker. Also, fewer critiques without suggestions (for example, "Your sentence is too long") are made. And with the new multilanguage support, these tools "speak" more than the user's primary language (provided multilanguage support has been installed, of course).

Other enhancements to Word 2000 include the capability turn off features that aren't present in older versions of Word—great if you constantly work with others using previous versions of Word. And you can now use pictures as bullets in bullet lists. Printing multiple pages on a single sheet of paper is also supported, as is the capability to zoom a page at print time to fit any size piece of paper.

What Is Excel 2000?

Excel 2000 is one of the most versatile tools available for data analysis (see Figure 1.2). You can analyze your data in three main ways in Excel: spreadsheets, charts, and PivotTables.

Spreadsheets allow you to enter data into a series of rows and columns. Then you can perform calculations on the data, sort the data, or filter the data. This data can be printed or used to create charts using the Charting component.

Charts take data from the Spreadsheet or PivotTable components and produce various types of charts. They range from simple bar charts to complex radar and scatter diagrams.

PivotTables enable you to analyze data through different views. You can dynamically sort the data, filter the data, or summarize the data by different rows and columns. You can also drill down into the data to understand how it was created.

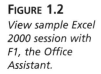

Figure 1.2
View sample Excel 2000 session with F1, the Office Assistant.

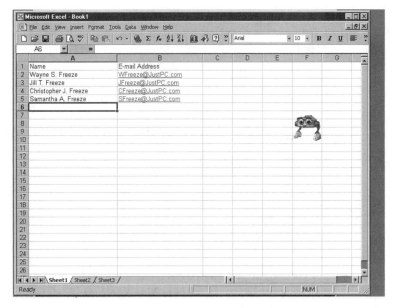

When Should You Use Excel 2000?

Excel is one of those tools that nearly everyone should know how to use. It's great for performing simple calculations, such as adding a column of numbers. It's great for tasks such as budgeting and forecasting. It's also great for keeping track of a list of things, especially if you need to sort the list. Think of Excel as a lightweight database without the intimidation of using Access. It's also great for creating charts and looking at the results of a database query.

Basically, any numbers-based document is a good candidate for Excel, as are lists (like a club's members, the audio CDs in your collection, and so on) that you might want to sort and re-sort in various ways.

How Excel 2000 Works

Excel 2000 is a data processor with tools to help you format, calculate, and analyze your data. Each *worksheet* you create consists of a series of rows and columns. A row and column intersect in a *cell*, which can contain a text value, a numeric value, a formula, or an object. A *formula* is merely a mathematical equation that includes numeric values, function calls, and references to other cells. The result of the calculation is displayed as the value of the cell.

The Charting tool takes data from your worksheet and creates a chart from it. You can choose from bar charts, pie charts, area charts, surface charts, stock charts, and others. You can add legends, labels, titles, and other elements that will make the chart easier to read and interpret by its viewers. You can also choose the colors for each series, choose to display gridlines in the background, and even include the data used to create the chart as part of the legend. All these capabilities work together to produce a meaningful chart.

A PivotTable is a special type of worksheet, in that the data it contains can be viewed in many different ways. This feature allows you to look for relationships between various data values. You can summarize or drill down to see different data values.

Using Excel 2000 with Other Office Applications

Excel 2000 can generate tables and charts that can be embedded in other Office 2000 applications, such as Word and PowerPoint. You can also populate a worksheet with the information from an Access database. More specifically, you can insert an Excel worksheet into Word or PowerPoint, or you can create an interactive Web page from an Excel table; this Web page can be manipulated by others using their Web browser, whether or not they have Excel installed. Even PivotTables and charts can be used in this manner.

Although SQL Server isn't technically an Office application (it's included in Microsoft BackOffice), Excel 2000 has been enhanced to work with SQL Server's Decision Support Services (also known as OnLine Analytical Processing, or OLAP) as a source for PivotTable information.

What's New in Excel 2000

PivotChart, which is a new facility in Excel 2000, allows you to create a chart linked to a PivotTable. You can explore the chart interactively to see more details and to pivot the data just like in a PivotTable.

And now importing data into Excel 2000 is even easier than it was in the past. You can add columns to your spreadsheet containing formulas that reference data in the database columns that were imported. These columns are retained when you refresh the data retrieved from the database. Also, any formats that you have applied to the database columns remain unchanged after refreshing your data.

Web queries have been enhanced over what existed in Excel 97. The new Web Query dialog box helps you build your Web queries by taking you through the steps necessary to retrieve the data from a Web site and store it into a spreadsheet.

Now you can refresh text data that you import from outside Excel without having to go through all the steps to import the file again. This way, you can preserve any formatting and calculations that you may have added to the imported text file.

You can reference SQL Server's OLAP facility to get data for a PivotTable. Using this approach, you can access larger amounts of data than was previously possible. Only the data you want to see is transferred from the OLAP server, not the entire data set. Performance is improved because now the processing is split between the Excel client and the OLAP server.

Other enhancements to Excel 2000 include support for displaying four-digit dates (Year 2000 support), the new Euro Currency symbol, and new cursors that prompt you for the type of information required. Excel now displays selected cells with a light-colored background, rather than in black on white. This feature makes it easier to see details such as formatting and borders than was previously possible.

Excel also supports the capability to publish documents in HTML format so that others can view them over the Internet. In addition to publishing static documents, users of Internet Explorer 4 or newer can even manipulate them using the new Office Server Extensions.

What Is Outlook 2000?

For large companies needing a way to keep their activities in order and communicate with one another, Outlook 2000 is a great all-in-one tool. Outlook 2000 falls into a class of products called *Personal Information Managers* (*PIMs*); see Figure 1.3. These products perform a variety of tasks that are aimed at improving your productivity. Outlook 2000 enables you to do the following:

- Send and receive electronic mail over the Internet and with Exchange Server
- Maintain your personal calendar
- Schedule meetings and appointments with others
- Participate in discussion groups
- Maintain an Address Book with email addresses, post office addresses, and other contact information
- Maintain a list of tasks and other work assignments
- Record summaries of telephone calls, meetings, and other contacts

Note: Look out, there's another Outlook! Microsoft has two Outlook products: Outlook 2000 and Outlook Express. Even though their names are similar, the products aren't. Outlook 2000 is a comprehensive Personal Information Manager, whereas Outlook Express is designed primarily as an Internet email and newsreader program. Note that in many cases you will need both programs because Outlook 2000 can't read newsgroups, though it can launch Outlook Express to read newsgroups.

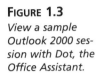

FIGURE 1.3
View a sample Outlook 2000 session with Dot, the Office Assistant.

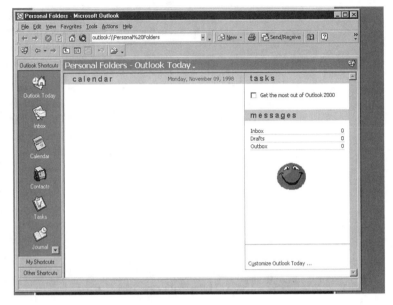

When Should You Use Outlook 2000?

This section could easily have been titled "When to Use Outlook 2000 as Opposed to Outlook Express." If all you want to do is read your email, you have two good products to choose from, Outlook 2000 and Outlook Express, which comes with the Internet Explorer 5 suite of applications that is now packaged with Office 2000. Both do the job very well. However, if you need features beyond email, that's how you should choose whether you need one or both Outlooks.

Peter's Principle: So do I need both Outlooks?

In this section, I tend to look at the need for one or the other Outlook based solely on the functions you want to take advantage of. That's not the complete story, however. You also need to consider whether your coworkers have access to Outlook 2000 and a common Exchange Server as well. If they don't, what good is being able to schedule a meeting with yourself? You can do that the old-fashioned way with a calendar or daytimer. Whenever my work environment changes, I often take the opportunity to re-evaluate my software needs. If no one else uses Outlook and my peers and I aren't linked by an Exchange Server, I often remove Outlook from my system and get along on Outlook Express alone. Before you make a decision about which one to use (or whether you really need both), just be sure to factor in all aspects of your particular situation. I know I often find that Outlook Express is more than enough to meet my personal needs. I only wish that in the past I had worked for companies that had access to such powerful tools as Outlook and Exchange Server.

If Outlook 2000's calendars and contact management system might be useful to you, then you should choose Outlook 2000. If you only want to read newsgroups and handle email, Outlook Express should be your choice. Unfortunately, if you need the contact management system and want to read newsgroups, you need to use both applications.

> **Tip: More on Outlook Express, please.** Because Outlook Express is not an integral part of the Office 2000 suite, I've given it minimal coverage in this book. If you want to learn more about it, pick up *Teach Yourself Internet Explorer 5 in 24 Hours* by Jill T. Freeze (Sams). It takes an in-depth look at Internet Explorer as well as Outlook Express.

How Outlook 2000 Works

You can use Outlook 2000 in three different modes: No Email usage, Internet Only usage, and Corporate/Workgroup. No Email means that only the contact, task, and calendar features of Outlook are enabled. Internet Only usage adds support for sending and receiving mail over the Internet. Corporate/Workgroup adds support for Exchange Server (or other MAPI-compliant mail server). This third option exists because many of the group-oriented features of Outlook 2000 require access to an Exchange Server. However, Exchange Server is not necessary for most common features such as email and contact management. It comes into play most when you want to access other users' calendars and participate in group discussions.

Outlook works by saving information in specially formatted files called *personal folder files*, which the file type .pst. You can easily import data into Outlook from other applications, which makes it easy to migrate your mail messages from other applications. You can also export data into formats used by other applications such as Excel and Access.

Besides accessing Exchange Server, Outlook 2000 can also access POP3, IMAP4, and SMTP servers, so you can send and receive email via the Internet. Mail stored in a POP3 server is automatically downloaded into your Outlook Inbox. Mail stored in an IMAP4 server remains on the server but can be accessed through a series of folders similar to the standard Outlook folders. The SMTP server is accessed only when you want to send mail to others on the Internet.

Using Outlook 2000 with Other Office Applications

Outlook 2000 is the ideal front end to Microsoft Exchange Server. In fact, many of the more advanced features work only with Exchange Server.

You also have the option of using Word 2000 in place of the standard Outlook 2000 mail editor. This way, you can easily build complex messages with different fonts, colors, and even embedded images. You can even use different colors to highlight parts of a forwarded email message.

Outlook Express is a viable alternative to Outlook 2000 if you don't need the scheduling and contact management facilities. It lets you access both POP3 and IMAP4 Internet mail servers and any standard NNTP news server as well.

> **Note: Alphabet soup.** You'll find two types of mail servers on the Internet. The most common is POP3 (Post Office Protocol, version 3), which holds your mail until you can download it to your local machine. After the mail is downloaded, it is deleted from the remote mail server. POP3 is the most common Internet mail protocol in use today.
>
> IMAP4 (Internet Mail Access Protocol, version 4) also holds your mail on the server. But it also lets you file your mail into different folders on the server. This capability is ideal when you access your mail from multiple computers.
>
> NNTP (Network News Transport Protocol) is a way to talk to a news server. You can access the list of available newsgroups using an NNTP server. Then, after selecting a newsgroup, you can read messages from the newsgroup and post your own messages to the newsgroup.

What's New in Outlook 2000

Outlook 2000 is based on Outlook 98, which was a complete rewrite of Outlook 97. Most of the new features in Outlook 2000 can also be found in Outlook 98. You can now access multiple Internet mail servers in a single Outlook client. Read receipts are automatically generated upon request for Internet mail servers (but only if the message recipient's program is capable of sending those receipts).

Users can exchange contact information using the vCard standard. This information is automatically added to the Contacts list. Also, limited calendar support is available over the Internet using the new iCalendar standard. Also, because all the Office 2000 applications can generate HTML documents, you can email these documents and let the receiver view them without the corresponding application.

Using Microsoft's Expedia travel service Web site, you can download maps and directions to a particular contact. You can also automatically add information about a message's sender to your contact list just by setting a single option.

In Office 97, all the applications except Outlook supported Visual Basic for Applications (VBA) as a macro programming language. Outlook 2000 corrects this problem by replacing VBScript with VBA as a macro programming language.

What Is PowerPoint 2000?

PowerPoint 2000 is an easy-to-use program with which you can create and show graphic presentations (see Figure 1.4). The presentations can include features such as animation, sound clips, background music, and full motion video. You can choose from many design wizards to give you as much or as little help as you want. Presentations can be shown both face to face and over the Internet.

FIGURE 1.4

View a sample PowerPoint 2000 session with Clippit, the Office Assistant.

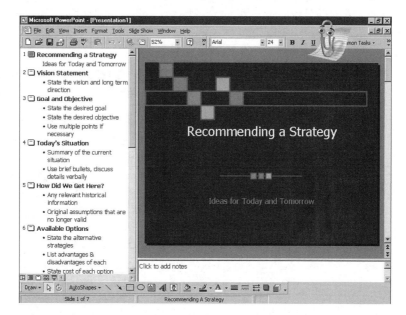

When Should You Use PowerPoint 2000?

PowerPoint 2000 is a much better alternative for making presentations than the traditional overhead projector. It is designed to create interesting full-color presentations complete with animation and sounds. What's more, presenters can generate printed handouts based on the slide show with minimal effort.

You might use PowerPoint on a laptop to make presentations to small audiences, such as a salesperson making a presentation to a potential customer. Or if a computer is available at your destination, you can use PowerPoint's Pack and Go Wizard to put the entire demonstration on disk to take along with you. PowerPoint can also be used in a more structured environment such as a classroom. The capability to produce handouts from the presentation makes it easy for the students to take notes while the class is being taught.

Multinational corporations might find PowerPoint's capability to broadcast presentations across the Internet or intranet in real-time–a tremendous tool. Just think, the company's president could narrate the slides illustrating a major reorganization so that all parties concerned could hear it at the same time.

How PowerPoint 2000 Works

PowerPoint allows you to create a series of slides. Each slide is a document that can contain text, static or animated graphics, video, and sound. The complete presentation is stored in a presentation file, which can be easily distributed. All you need to do is run PowerPoint to present the slides. You can also save the slides on the Web so that Web users can view your PowerPoint presentation.

Using PowerPoint 2000 with Other Office Applications

You can use PowerPoint 2000 with NetShow and NetMeeting to show your presentations over the Internet. You can also schedule your presentations using Outlook 2000 and have them automatically begin using the same tools.

PowerPoint users also can call on other Office 2000 applications to help design their presentation. For instance, you might import a Word 2000 outline as a basis for the order of the slide show, or you might incorporate an Excel chart into the presentation.

What's New in PowerPoint 2000

If you use the Presentation Broadcast feature, users can view presentations over the Internet by using Internet Explorer version 4 or newer. You can use Outlook 2000 to schedule the broadcast and use an Event Web page to allow users to tune in to the broadcast or get information about the broadcast before it begins. You can even store the presentation so that users can view it on demand. What a super tool for corporate human resource personnel—you can create presentations on company benefits and policies, and archive them for viewing at any time!

With this newest version, PowerPoint is more flexible than ever before. Slides can now automatically adjust to the size of the display. Voice narration is now synchronized with the original presentation, including the slide transitions. You have even more options to choose from when you're creating handouts for the presentation, so you have many more options than just one slide per page.

In the past, having to switch from one PowerPoint view to another to accomplish various tasks made the application much more intimidating (not to mention confusing) than it needed to be. A new Tri-Pane view is available in PowerPoint 2000; this view combines the Slide, Outline, and Notes views into one for ease of editing. You can use graphic images as bullets, and AutoNumbered bullets automatically adjust their values as you add and delete items in the list. Choosing AutoFormat as You Type changes your text to ordinals, fractions, em dashes and en dashes, rich text AutoCorrect entries, and smart quotes just like in Word 2000. Microsoft has even built in basic table capabilities, so if you're faced with a simple task, you needn't format a table in Excel and import it into

PowerPoint; you can just do it all in PowerPoint, provided no calculations or special formulas are needed.

PowerPoint 2000 can also exploit the multiple monitor feature found in the latest versions of Windows by allowing you to drag your slide show to a secondary monitor. You can disable the screen saver from a laptop's low power screen mode during a presentation.

What Is Access 2000?

Access 2000 is a desktop database management system (see Figure 1.5). It is targeted at small- to medium-sized organizations; plus, it can also act as a front end for SQL Server databases in the case of large corporations. It includes features that allow users to design databases using wizards, so even novice users can create useful database applications.

FIGURE 1.5

View a sample Access 2000 session with the Logo Office Assistant.

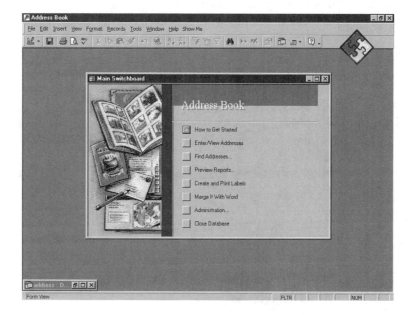

When Should You Use Access 2000?

With Office 2000, you have two approaches for storing database information in a computer. You can create a very simple database using an Excel spreadsheet, or you can use Access 2000 to create a more complex database with a user-friendly set of forms to access the data.

Which approach you choose depends on the type of data you have to input and the number of people who need to access the data. Excel 2000 is great when you have a set of data that you can store as a single list of information. For example, entering information about your personal Barbie doll collection into Excel will more than do the job because you can still sort the dolls by name, price you paid for them, and so on. And it's not like dozens of people will be entering information about your collection, so you needn't worry about several people trying to access the database at one time.

Using Excel probably isn't a good idea, however, if you have several people who need to update (and view) the information it contains. Consider a company that uses Access to have its phone operators track merchandise orders or a nonprofit service organization that relies on Access to store its membership data. In these situations, you definitely need to provide for access by multiple users.

Mega-sized corporations or institutes may have even greater needs that require them to turn to what Microsoft often calls *enterprise solutions*. Visual Studio and SQL Server are great for developing these enterprise applications. They can be scaled to manage even the largest applications. However, using these tools requires an experienced programmer and possibly an experienced database administrator. These options are probably overkill if all you need to manage is a couple of hundred entries in your database.

The gap between where an Excel database is acceptable and Visual Studio is necessary is the place for Access databases. It is great at handling small to moderate amounts of data with small numbers of users. You can easily design databases in Access 2000 using database wizards and then use other wizards to create forms to enter the data and to create reports containing your information. You can even build nice, clean data entry forms that will help you ensure consistency in elements such as state abbreviations.

How Access 2000 Works

Access 2000 is a true relational database management system with an integrated development environment based on Visual Basic for Applications. At design time, you merely design the forms, reports, and other objects to be used in the application. This information is stored in the database file along with the application's data.

Using Access 2000 with Other Office Applications

Now that you can access the SQL Server database directly from Access 2000, you might want to use Access 2000 as a front-end development tool. It enables nonprogrammers to create database applications.

You can now drag and drop access databases into an Excel 2000 spreadsheet and use an Access database as the source of data for a Word or Publisher 2000 mail merge. And don't forget the possibility of mapping Access data and including it on a Web page or in a PowerPoint presentation.

What's New in Access 2000

The biggest change for the average Access user is the new database window. It brings all the pieces of your Access database together in one easily used window. You can also drag and drop your database into Excel to populate a worksheet. Other enhancements to Access include conditional formatting, name AutoCorrect, and the capability to save your Access 2000 database in Access 97 format to maintain compatibility with previous versions of Access.

The biggest change for the serious application developer in Access 2000 is that you now have a choice of data engines. You can choose from the Microsoft Jet database engine that has been associated with Access since the beginning, or you can use a version of SQL Server known as the Microsoft Data Engine that has been optimized for the desktop. You can also use Access as an application development tool for your enterprise SQL Server database.

The Microsoft Jet database system now supports Unicode character sets. This means that you can create databases containing non-English characters. Although you would expect that conversion tools exist to convert Access 97 databases into databases compatible with Access 2000, you can also convert Access 2000 Jet databases to Access 97 databases. This capability helps to ease the transition from Access 97 to Access 2000.

Visual Basic for Applications 6 is included to bring many of the new features from Visual Basic 6 into Access 2000. The Database window now exposes the new objects available in Access 2000. You can use subdatasheets to present a spreadsheet-like view of hierarchical data. Each row in the table is displayed as a single line in the datasheet, and you can expand that row to see another datasheet containing the detail information behind the displayed row. You can repeat this process as many times as necessary until you can see the lowest level of the data.

Data Access Pages are available to make your database available over the Internet. Using these pages offers an alternative to using the traditional Access 2000 forms and reports.

What Is Publisher 2000?

If you operate your own new or small business, chances are you know how expensive getting a professional-quality newsletter, form, or brochure can be. Or if you volunteer to create the monthly newsletter for your daughter's nursery school, being able to put one together that looks great right from the start would be nice.

Publisher 2000 is aimed at users with little or no design experience who need to create professional-looking publications such as newsletters, flyers, and invitations (see Figure 1.6) inexpensively and many times in a hurry. The key to this application is the extensive use of wizards and templates. It can also use the themes that are common to most Office applications to create a consistent look to all your documents, whether they're brochures, Web pages, or letters.

FIGURE **1.6**

*View a sample
Publisher 2000
session.*

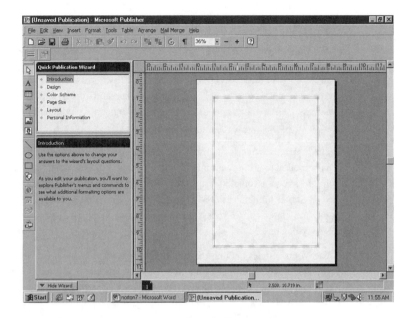

When Should You Use Publisher 2000?

There is nothing you can do in Publisher 2000 that you can't do in Word 2000, at least from a text standpoint. However, when you're trying to create newsletters, brochures, and other specialized documents, Publisher 2000 can't be beat. Publisher's reliance on frames for text as well as images dramatically reduces the headaches you frequently encounter dealing with column length in Word. Publisher, like Word, comes with a large number of templates, so all you need to do is replace the default text and graphics with your own.

So what's the big deal about Publisher? Take a look at this compelling list of tasks you can do best in Publisher 2000:

- Design French-folded greeting cards without the hassle of worrying about proper text orientation when the paper is folded.

- Create a poster with tear stubs containing your phone number—great for selling items or advertising a room for rent on a bulletin board!

- Produce your own layout of a full-color catalog in-house, perform the color separations using Publisher, and then use Publisher's Pack and Go Wizard to get all the necessary files together to take them to a commercial printer so that you can produce more economical output.

- Produce a coordinated set of business stationery for your new company, including letterhead, business cards, and tri-fold brochures.

- Convert a printed newsletter to a Web site of its own with a few simple mouse clicks.

The list of useful tasks you can accomplish with Publisher 2000 goes on and on. You can even have a little fun with your son building paper airplanes or trying your hand at origami. (Yes, you'll find templates for these in Publisher as well as a host of incredibly useful goodies.)

How Publisher 2000 Works

Publisher 2000 is a wizard-driven tool. You use wizards to create the basic layout of the document; then you replace the sample text with your own material. You do so visually by manipulating areas known as *frames* on the page. An area can contain text or graphics, and areas can overlap each other. Whether you use the dozens of wizards Microsoft includes, or you venture out on your own, you need to be familiar with the concept of frames. Publisher also lets you build your own templates (in addition to using ones they provide), so you can get the quality you desire time and time again.

Using Publisher 2000 with Other Office Applications

Like the rest of the Office 2000 family, Publisher works exceptionally well with other applications in the suite. With Publisher, unlike other applications, however, items seem to get imported as opposed to exported. For example, you can use standard Windows cut, copy, and paste commands to extract text from any other application and include it in a Publisher document.

In addition, Publisher can easily make use of address source data stored in Word, Outlook, Excel, or Access to perform mail merges. And like the other Office 2000 applications, Publisher has access to shared tools such as the Clip Gallery, WordArt, and so on.

What's New in Publisher 2000

Publisher 2000 includes over 2,000 templates for you to choose from. These professionally developed templates include newsletters, flyers, brochures, catalogs, and Web sites. In addition, over 200 different fonts and thousands of pieces of clip art are available on the CD-ROM that ships with Office. If that's not enough, you can browse and download even more from Microsoft's Web site through the Clip Gallery applet.

The new Quick Publications feature in Publisher 2000 allows you to quickly build one-page publications. The Logo Creation Wizard helps you use existing logos or create your own professional-looking logos. Publisher 2000 can also prepare your document for professional four-color printing, pack up all necessary files to take to a commercial printer, and make changes to wizard selections (that is, go from a two-column newsletter to a three-column newsletter) as you work.

What Is Internet Explorer 5?

Internet Explorer 5 is a suite of tools that provide the features that you need to access the Internet. It contains the following components:

- Internet Explorer—Allows you to browse the World Wide Web and display HTML-formatted documents
- Outlook Express—Allows you to access email and newsgroup servers over the Internet
- FrontPage Express—Provides a basic tool that can create Web pages
- Microsoft Chat—Allows you to participate in real-time chats with other users on the Internet
- NetMeeting—Allows you to talk to other NetMeeting users in real-time while optionally sharing a whiteboard, Office documents, or exchanging live video and audio streams
- Web Publishing Wizard—Helps you publish documents to a Web server

When Should You Use Internet Explorer 5?

The most obvious time to use Internet Explorer is when you need to browse the World Wide Web and display HTML-formatted documents. Because Internet Explorer is an entire suite of applications, you will find yourself using it for more than you ever expected. Use the Internet Explorer tools as follows:

- Use Outlook Express to access electronic mail and newsgroups. You can even maintain basic contact information on your clients, friends, and family.
- Use FrontPage Express any time you need to create a Web page. FrontPage Express enables you to build Web pages the easy way—no need to learn HTML programming.
- Use Microsoft Chat when you want to access chat and discussion groups in real-time. You can even assume the identity of an array of comic strip characters to liven things up if you like.
- Use NetMeeting when you need to communicate and exchange ideas with others over the Internet. You can communicate by voice, by text chat, by drawing on a shared whiteboard, and you can even collaborate on Office documents with people across the globe.

Many Office 2000 tools automatically use Internet Explorer 5 to display HTML information. In some cases, you can even use Internet Explorer to preview your document as a Web page before you even save it as a Web page. Internet Explorer 5 is also integrated into the Office 2000 help files, so you'll be using it even if you're not aware of it.

How Internet Explorer 5 Works

If you think that just because you're not connected to the Internet you won't be needing Internet Explorer, you're wrong. With the shift to an HTML-based Office environment, Internet Explorer shows up even if you never connect to the Internet. Internet Explorer's rendering engine (the feature that translates cryptic, text-based HTML statements into the graphical Web page you see) is used throughout the Office suite of applications.

Using Internet Explorer with Other Office Applications

Although Internet Explorer is not technically a member of the Office 2000 family, many of the features found in Office 2000 applications rely on Internet Explorer.

Although both Outlook 2000 and Outlook Express can send and receive email, Outlook 2000 can't read newsgroups. (Microsoft claims Outlook 2000 can read newsgroups, but it does so by launching Outlook Express, so I don't consider this to be a function of Outlook 2000.)

NetMeeting adds value to many other Office applications by providing real-time communications facilities between multiple machines and the capability to work on Office 2000 documents with others.

What's New in Internet Explorer 5

Although the newest version of Internet Explorer 5 was initially touted as a release geared primarily for Web page developers, it turned out to be so much more!

Microsoft has improved the ease with which you can organize all your favorite Web sites. Now many once complex operations are a mere mouse click·away. And sharing those Favorites with others has never been easier. You can email a link to a page, email the Web page itself, and attach a folder of Favorites that a friend can import to his or her browser (even if it's Netscape). You can also export your Favorites to disk so that you can move them to another machine. And if you're always competing over a phone line for Internet access, you'll love the ability to browse your favorite sites offline.

Internet Explorer 5 also makes finding things more convenient thanks to its new Search Assistant. Best of all, the search results are displayed in a separate pane on the left side of the screen, so you can scan your search results and view pages simultaneously. The Search Assistant is totally customizable, too, so you can choose your preferred search engine as the default.

Finally, a host of new AutoComplete features makes surfing the Internet a breeze. AutoComplete for Web Addresses presents a list of previously viewed sites with URLs close to the one you started entering in a scrollable drop-down box. Just double-click your selection. AutoComplete for Forms "remembers" your input to a specific form, so performing repeat searches is effortless. Lastly, AutoComplete for Passwords and User IDs lets the Web browser remember those things for you, so you needn't bother yourself with memorizing dozens of passwords for various sites.

On Your Own

By now, you should have a good understanding of the basic services found in each of the Office 2000 applications. You should remember that all the applications might not be present on your machine. Which applications you have depends on which edition of Office 2000 you have selected and/or which applications your network administrator has chosen to make available to you.

Take a few moments to walk over to your machine, and ask yourself the following questions:

- Which of the applications listed here are installed on your computer?
- Which one do you use most frequently?
- Given what you've read here, can you think of items or information you'd like to see in some kind of database (think about both work and home)?
- Which application—Excel or Access—is best suited for each task?
- Which Outlook is best suited for your needs at home? On the job?

Office 2000 Installation, Configuration, and Maintenance

Okay, so maybe you don't need step-by-step guidance through the software installation, but Microsoft has made some subtle changes to the process you'll want to know about. Although these changes were made with the intention of increasing overall productivity and ease of use, those same changes can cause a lot of grief down the road if you're not prepared to deal with them.

When installing Office 2000, you're faced with more decisions than ever before. In fact, it's kind of like going to an all-you-can-eat buffet instead of a sit-down dinner—you can pick what you want instead of having to take what's offered without substitutions. Although this increased flexibility might appeal to some, for others it can mean confusion and countless headaches. And interestingly, knowing which category you fit into depends more on your personal work style than on individual preferences.

In this chapter, we'll examine some of the issues you'll want to take into account before making the big move to Office 2000. My mission is to make the upgrade or installation as painless as possible because, frankly, you've got more important things to do than worry about your software! And even if Office 2000 was preinstalled on your new computer, you might want to go back and change what was or wasn't installed to better meet your needs.

Preinstallation Hardware Considerations

According to Microsoft, if your machine runs Windows 95, Windows 98, or Windows NT, you should be home free when it comes to running Office 2000. Although technically that might be true, it's a whole different story when it comes to practicality.

If you're a fan of flight simulators or car racing computer games, you've undoubtedly experienced this deviation between what the box says will run the game versus what in actuality will run the game in a playable form. Sure the game will run with the minimum setup, but the performance is often so painfully slow that it's all you can do to keep from throwing your computer out the window!

And when you think about it, Office 2000 is an unusual beast. One user might rely on Word as his or her sole application of choice. Another user might perform complex statistical analysis in Excel while drafting a proposal in Word, preparing accompanying PowerPoint slides, and surfing the Net for supporting statistics. The first user might be fine with the minimum configuration, whereas the second power user might tax even some of the high-end souped-up machines on the market today.

So what exactly is the minimum system requirement for Office 2000? The published minimum CPU speed is a 90MHz Pentium machine or faster with at least 32MB or more of RAM. If you're a person who consistently uses one application at a time, you should be fine with this configuration. If, on the other hand, you're more like the power user described previously, the more power you can muster with your hardware, the better. I will tell you this: the minimum configuration gives the power user sluggish performance at best; some would even consider it unacceptable. So if you want or need to upgrade your computer, now would be a good time to do it. If you must live with what you've got, you'll want to take special note of any performance optimization tips you'll find throughout this book. Little tweaks here and there can go a long way to increase your system's performance.

As far as hard disk space goes, you'll need roughly 250MB of free space for the entire Office suite not counting your data files, clip art, or any special language support files. So how can you tell whether you have enough free space before you start working with the installation process itself?

Fire up Windows Explorer (Start|Programs|Windows Explorer) and click the name of the drive on which you plan to install Office 2000 (the C: drive in the majority of cases). Next, choose Properties from the File menu. The General tab of the Properties dialog box (as shown in Figure 2.1) gives you a clear picture of just how much free space there is on your machine.

And of course you'll need a CD-ROM drive from which to install the software. A sound card and speakers might also be desirable if you hope to experience the full personality of Microsoft's new Office Assistants.

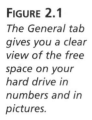

FIGURE 2.1

The General tab gives you a clear view of the free space on your hard drive in numbers and in pictures.

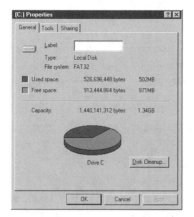

Decisions to Make Before You Begin the Installation Process

Before you pop the disk into the CD-ROM drive, there are some things you'll want to resolve before you're forced to make a snap decision during installation. These issues revolve around three basic areas:

- Hardware availability
- Which of the applications you use
- Your personal work style and situation

Hardware Availability

All things considered, the hardware availability issue is one of the easiest to deal with—if you haven't got the disk space, you either have to clean up unnecessary files or install only parts of Office 2000. As for CPU speed or RAM, if you haven't got the muscle needed to run the suite, you can expect some grief on the performance front when it comes to doing more than one thing at a time. Take the time to evaluate your hardware in addition to the other two areas listed previously. Your findings after reflecting on all three issues will be immensely helpful come installation time.

Application Usage

Next, you should think about which applications you use on a regular basis (or even at all for that matter). If you've never touched Access in your life, maybe it's not worth wasting the hard drive space on it. And remember, there's a lot more to Office than there used to be. In addition to the basics of Word, Excel, PowerPoint, Access, and Outlook, there's Internet Explorer, Publisher 2000, and in some cases FrontPage 2000 and PhotoDraw 2000. Since updated versions of Web browsers frequently become available for free download over the Internet, it's entirely possible that the version of Internet Explorer already loaded on your system is even newer than the one included with your Office disks; therefore you won't need to include it in the installation. Think carefully about each application and how often you use it (or how likely you are to try to use it) because it will have a direct effect on which installation option you choose for that given application.

Personal Work Style and Situation

Lastly, your personal work style or situation can dictate some of your installation choices. For example if you need to share your Office 2000 disk with a colleague several offices down, the last thing you want to do is have a bunch of features that you've designated to install on demand. Imagine this scenario: you're knee-deep in putting the final touches on an important report and decide to apply a fancy theme to it since you'll be publishing it on the Web as well. You press the button to select the chosen theme. Office 2000 sets your hard drive into motion. Seconds later comes the message telling you to insert your Office 2000 disk. The coworker with the disk is out to lunch…you get the picture. Some of the more impromptu installation options are great if you'll always have the disks readily available, but if there's a chance you won't (either because your site license for five came with one set of disks, or because the disks might be buried deep beneath the mounds of papers on your desk), they can be a nightmare. However, if you're connected to a LAN/intranet and your network administrator has made all the Office 2000 components available on the server, you might not mind the brief delay of the installation itself.

> **Caution: Okay, so maybe "caution" is a bit strong, but it's important nonetheless.** If your company or organization accesses Office 2000 on a network, you'll want to check with your computer support staff before making any changes with regards to installation options. They might have a preferred way of setting things up.

Let's face it, doing an on-the-fly installation can derail your train of thought. It doesn't take long in the scheme of things, but it can be long enough to destroy any flow you might be experiencing while writing a document. That can obviously present a major problem in terms of your personal productivity. But before you rule out installing on demand altogether, consider this. I've found that what's most disruptive to the flow is not the few seconds it takes to install a new template or theme. Rather, it's the rooting around for the disks. So if the disks are readily available or all the components are accessible via a network server, installation on demand can work very well at conserving system resources.

It All Makes a Difference

All these factors work together to create your optimal Office 2000 installation choices, as you'll see in the following sections.

You'll also need to decide which applications from previous versions of Office you'll want to keep around (if any). There shouldn't really be a need to keep old versions of Office applications around since Office 2000 lets you easily save files to earlier versions of Office. But if you decide you want them anyway, I'll show you how to preserve them later in the "Customizing Your Office 2000 Installation" section near the middle of this chapter.

Introducing the New Office 2000 Installation States

Installing Office is no longer as simple as deciding which applications to keep or not to keep. Now there are degrees of installation, so to speak. In fact there are four installation states which can greatly increase system resources if used appropriately. The four installation states are:

- Run from My Computer—This state installs the selected application or feature to your hard drive so it can be run immediately without needing to access the Office 2000 CD. Obviously you'll want to use this option for Word and other applications you might use frequently.

- Run from CD/Network—Selecting this option requires you to insert the Office CD (or have your machine fetch the necessary files from the network) each time you use the respective feature/application. It's a good choice for those who are light on disk space or who have sole custody of the Office 2000 CD. Clip Gallery elements are good candidates for this installation option.

- Install on First Use—This installation option means you'll see the feature in question on all your menus, but when you attempt to use it for the first time, you will be prompted to insert the CD (or access your company's network) to install it. Of course each subsequent time you try to use the feature, it will be treated as a regular Run from My Computer feature. It's a good way to conserve disk space until you really need to use it, but again it can be a hassle if you might not be able to put your hands on the Office 2000 disks when you need them.

> **Tip: Never say "never"!** Install on First Use is a great choice if you seriously doubt you'll use a given feature. After all, why clutter up the hard drive when you don't have to, right?

- Not Available—Choosing this option "hides" the given feature from your Office 2000 menus. That doesn't mean, however, that you can't install the feature at a later date.

So which option is best for you? Only you know what works best for you given your situation. That's why it's so important to factor in each of the three issues presented earlier.

Peter's Principle: A few megabytes might not be worth the headaches.

It's true that installing the whole Office 2000 suite can gobble up disk space faster than an old muscle car burns up gas, but you might not save much disk space by excluding smaller components from the installation. In fact, attempts to conserve disk space can backfire in the long run as you fumble for the disk then wait for the element to install properly, thus losing precious work time. Disk space is cheap and plentiful these days; if you have a fairly new system, try to install the whole suite up front if you can (or at least the components you know you'll use sooner or later). That way you can work straight through a project without unexpected interruptions (at least from your computer).

Upgrade or Customize?

As you will see in the sections that follow, Microsoft at some point will ask you whether you want to Upgrade or Customize your Office suite. If you already have a previous version of Office on your system and don't mind replacing it with Office 2000, you can use the Upgrade option to install the same applications and elements you currently have on your machine. Office will migrate as many of your old settings and preferences as possible to Office 2000. And since Office 2000 contains a number of new features, these will be treated with the Install on First Use option. This serves a dual purpose of letting you know that the option exists without taking up more disk space than anticipated.

If, on the other hand, you want to pick and choose what's installed or want to leave previous versions of an application intact, you'll need to customize your installation.

Note: When you're hard at work on an important document, there are times when the words really begin to flow. You've established a rhythm and tone, and any little interruption is capable of wrecking your train of thought. Installing a feature on-the-fly can be more than a little interruption. First off, you might have forgotten which features you did or didn't install, and there's no good way to tell unless you attempt to use the feature. Now if you decide to actually install the feature, you need to launch a full-scale search of your workspace for the Office 2000 disk. That's easier for some of us than others (the saying "a messy desk is a sign of genius" comes to mind). Then you have to perform the installation, which might not take long in and of itself, but is still additional time away from the task at hand. Sure, not everyone's made of money for enormous disk drives, but the features you're likely to hold back for later use shouldn't be huge in the scheme of things. In fact, if you're running that tight on disk space, you run the risk of experiencing non–Office 2000 performance problems and system instability.

Upgrading to Office 2000

You can expect the upgrade to take between a half-hour and an hour depending on system speed and whether you're present the entire time to respond to prompts and such. At certain points, the Installation Wizard might ask you to do certain things along the way such as click OK to restart your system and so on. Naturally if you've stepped out of the room and miss the request, it'll take the installation and setup that much longer to finish.

Follow these steps to begin upgrading Office on your computer:

1. Make sure no other applications are running on your computer. By shutting everything down, you minimize the chance of any other program interfering with the installation, and maximize the system resources that can be allocated to the task.

2. If the Office 2000 CD is not already in your computer's CD-ROM drive, insert it now. The Installation Wizard screen shown in Figure 2.2 should appear automatically. If it doesn't, you'll need to run Setup.exe from the CD (Start|Run, and then browse to the Setup file on the Office 2000 CD).

3. When the Office 2000 Installation Wizard appears, it asks for a variety of user information including your name, initials, organization name, and the key code for your Office 2000 CD (see Figure 2.2). When you've finished filling in the requested information, click the Next button.

FIGURE 2.2
The opening screen of the Installation Wizard will ask you to provide some user information.

4. Next, you'll see the License and Support screen that presents a long-winded EULA (End User License Agreement). Use the scrollbars to browse the document, and then tell the wizard whether you accept the terms. Keep in mind, however, that if you don't accept the terms, you'll be tossed out of the Installation Wizard on the spot. That means no Office 2000 for you until you say "Yes"! Click Next after your selection to continue.

5. This brings us to the Ready to Install screen where you must tell the Wizard whether you want to Upgrade or Customize. Choose Upgrade. If you want to Customize the installation, you may skip ahead to the next section in the chapter. Click Next to set the upgrade in motion.

Caution: Are you sure you want to do this? Remember that upgrading replaces all previous versions of the software on your machine. Proceeding with the upgrade might mean you'll end up reinstalling the previous version of the application should you decide you need it. I don't see why you would need it, but having the old version of the software around until they get adept at using the new one comforts some people.

6. A status bar appears, showing you the progress of the upgrade (see Figure 2.3). Be forewarned that it might not always look like your system is at work. Before taking any drastic action such as aborting the upgrade or restarting your computer, give things a few minutes to settle out. In a majority of cases, the brief delay is self-correcting.

FIGURE 2.3
The Installation Wizard's status bar shows you how far you've come.

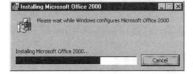

7. When the status bar has reached 100%, you will see a message box that gives you the option of restarting your machine to complete the setup. Click Yes to restart your machine and continue with the setup.

8. After the system has rebooted, you'll see a Windows Installer message box that says your system settings are being updated. This might take awhile, so don't be surprised. Eventually, you'll see a Completing Office 2000 Installation box in the upper-left corner of your screen. It basically says that the Windows Registry and Startup menu are being prepared for their first run with Office 2000. That, too, will run for awhile, so be prepared to wait a bit longer.

9. Finally, a message box appears saying that the setup completed successfully. Click OK to acknowledge the message. Now all should be well in the world of Office 2000; you can start using the applications any time you want.

Tip: If at first you don't succeed... Performing an installation on multiple applications at once is a complex task. Things can—and sometimes do—go wrong. If something doesn't work quite right when you attempt to launch an Office application for the first time, reboot your system; there might be some setup loose ends to tie up. Often a simple reboot will clear things up in no time.

Customizing Your Office 2000 Installation

Customized installation options run the gamut from the default "Give me the works" option which loads all applications onto your local machine to the more selective "Hold the pickles, hold the lettuce" installation where you select only a few of the suite's applications for installation.

Note: Custom installation might also help previous Office users. It is suggested that the Upgrade installation be used for those with a previous version of Office already on their system, but what if you really don't want to keep all the programs you had on your system before? You can make great use of the Customize Installation option, which helps you install what you want and uninstall the old stuff you don't want. And if your new computer came with Office 2000 preinstalled, you'll be happy to know that Microsoft has made adding and removing Office 2000 features a snap. Take a look at the "Adding and Removing Office 2000 Features" section near the end of the chapter to see just how quick and easy it really is!

You should allow anywhere from a half-hour to an hour for a custom installation depending on how much you install and how long it takes you to select the options you want to install. Follow these steps to get started with your custom installation:

1. Shut down any other applications that might be running on your computer. This minimizes the chance of any other program interfering with the installation and maximizes the system resources that can be allocated to the task.

2. If the Office 2000 CD is not already in your computer's CD-ROM drive, insert it now. The Installation Wizard screen you saw back in Figure 2.2 should appear automatically. If it doesn't, you'll need to run Setup.exe from the CD (Start|Run, and then browse to the Setup file on the Office 2000 CD).

3. When the Office 2000 Installation Wizard appears, it asks for a variety of user information including your name, initials, organization name, and the key code for your Office 2000 CD. Fill in the requested information, and then click the Next button.

4. Next, you'll see the License and Support screen that presents a long-winded EULA (End User License Agreement). Browse the document if desired, and then tell the Wizard whether you accept the terms. Note that if you don't accept the terms, you'll immediately be tossed out of the Installation Wizard. That means no Office 2000 for you until you say "Yes"! Click Next after your selection to continue.

5. If you've accepted the terms, you'll see the Ready to Install screen where you must tell the Wizard whether you want to upgrade or customize. Choose Customize.

6. The first thing you'll need to do is tell the Wizard where you want to place Office 2000 (see Figure 2.4). The default location should be fine unless you want to preserve your previous version of Office as well. Click Next to continue.

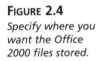

FIGURE 2.4

Specify where you want the Office 2000 files stored.

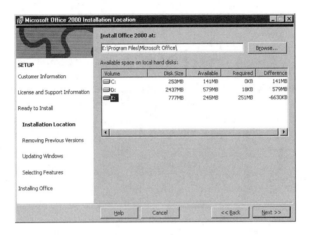

7. The Installation Wizard then goes out and detects any previous versions of Office applications residing on your system. It displays them alphabetically by name, and gives you the opportunity to remove them on the spot. Click the Next button when you've finished dealing with or have decided to keep the listed applications.

8. Next comes the Web Browsing Support screen. Since many of Office 2000's nifty new Web features rely on the latest version of Internet Explorer, you will be asked to upgrade to Internet Explorer 5.0 if you haven't already done so. Although it's entirely up to you whether you do it or not, keep in mind that many of the new Web features will be unavailable without it. You are given three options. After you've selected one, click the Next button.

Caution: When it comes to browsers, newer is better. Before going any further, you might want to verify which version of Internet Explorer is installed on your machine by launching Internet Explorer and clicking Help|About Internet Explorer. The very first version released of a Web browser (or any other software product for that matter) can often be buggy thus prompting a new release (or in the case of operating systems and office suites, service release patches). If you surf the Net much, the possibility exists that you might have a newer version of the Web browser on your machine than that which was shipped on the Office 2000 disks. If the version on your machine is newer, the last thing you want to do is replace it with something older and potentially less stable.

- Typical—By default, the most common configuration of the Internet Explorer 5.0 suite of applications will be installed.

- Minimal—This option will give you the least you need to make use of Office 2000's Web features.

- Do Not Upgrade—Forego the upgrade for now.

9. The Select Features screen (see Figure 2.5) is where the customized installation gets real interesting and potentially tricky. Each of Office 2000's major applications is listed. By default, they will all be loaded onto your computer. To pick and choose your desired features, you'll need to click the plus (+) sign next to the application you want to work with. This expands the application's list of features. To select options for a given feature, click the drop-down arrow right next to its name as shown in Figure 2.5 and then select the desired installation state for that item. Work your way through each application, enabling and disabling features as necessary.

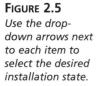

FIGURE 2.5
Use the drop-down arrows next to each item to select the desired installation state.

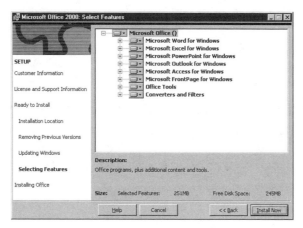

Caution: It's not all or nothing with Office 2000. If you elect to store one element on your computer, don't automatically assume that all the items listed underneath it will be installed in the same installation state. Take the Office Assistant as an example. If you load the Office Assistant onto your machine, only the default Office Assistant (Clippit, the bug-eyed paper clip) will be installed along with its "brain" so to speak. If you anticipate using any other Office Assistants, you'll need to manually select them for installation at this stage, or plan to produce the disk and take the time to install them when you want them. The same goes for Word and its themes, and so on. Make sure you click the plus sign to expand each category fully before you make your decisions.

10. After you've set the installation options for each of the features, click the Install Now button.

11. A status bar appears, showing you the progress of the installation (refer back to Figure 2.3). Again, be forewarned that it might not always look like your system is at work. Before taking any drastic action such as aborting the upgrade or restarting your computer, give things a few minutes to settle out. In a majority of cases, the brief delay is self-correcting.

12. When the status bar has reached 100%, you will see a message box that gives you the option of restarting your machine to complete the setup. Click Yes to restart your machine and continue with the setup of Office 2000.

13. After the system has rebooted, you'll see a Windows Installer message box that says your system settings are being updated. This might take awhile, so don't be surprised. Eventually, you'll see a Completing Office 2000 Installation box in the upper-left corner of your screen. It basically says that the applications are being registered with Windows in preparation for their first run. The Windows Startup menu is also updated at this point. That, too, will run for awhile, so be prepared to wait.

14. Finally, a message box appears saying the setup completed successfully. Click OK to close the message box. Now all the wonders of Office 2000 are available to you (or at least the features you chose to install)!

Using the Windows Add/Remove Program Utility

As you perform your customized installation, the Installation Wizard might uncover a number of previous versions of Office applications on your machine. It is suggested that you use the Add/Remove Programs utility to remove them if you so desire.

Tip: There's more to it than that. For those who aren't familiar with this utility, you'll want to pay extra attention to these steps since you can follow them to remove virtually any program from your system.

To remove a program using the Windows Add/Remove Programs utility, follow these simple steps:

1. To access the utility, click the Start button, and then point to Settings|Control Panel. In the Control Panel window, you'll see a number of folders. Double-click the Add/Remove Programs folder. The Add/Remove Programs Properties box shown in Figure 2.6 opens.

FIGURE 2.6

A list of the programs currently installed on your computer will appear.

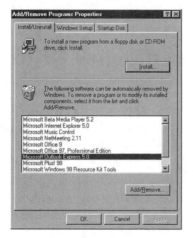

2. Before doing anything, verify that the Install/Uninstall tab is showing. This tab displays a list of all the applications residing on your computer. If it's on this list, you can easily remove it with the Add/Remove Programs utility.

Caution: Not all that glitters is gold. Just because an application appears on this list doesn't mean it's really still there. For instance if you decided to go in and manually clean up your system before installing Office 2000, the application's name might still appear until you attempt to remove it again using this utility. Windows 98 will respond saying the application was not found, and might give you the chance to remove it from the list. Also keep in mind that although this method of removing programs is quick and easy, it's not always thorough. Bits and pieces of program files might remain unless you go in to the specific application's folder and delete everything by hand.

3. Click the program you want to remove, and then press the Add/Remove button near the lower right corner of the window. If it's a simple application, or applet as they're sometimes called, the program might simply disappear from the list before you even know what hit you. In the case of more complex applications, you might be asked a few questions before you actually delete the file or files. And in other cases still, you might actually be asked to insert the Office 2000 CD.

Caution: I can't believe I just did that... Before you press the Add/Remove button, double- and triple-check the name of the application you selected to make sure it's really the one you want to delete. Unlike many other operations in Windows programs that ask you multiple times if you really want to perform the specified action, the Add/Remove Programs utility frequently does its thing on the first try without requesting confirmation. You can never be too careful.

Adding and Removing Office 2000 Features

What happens if you completed your installation and find there's something you wish you would have done differently? Or what if you find yourself in the middle of a new project that could benefit from using an application you never installed? If either of these situations describes you, adding the program before you have to start working with it might be the way to go.

To do this, you'll need to pop in your Office 2000 CD and run the Setup program. The Installation Wizard will detect that the Office suite has already been installed, and will cut over to what's referred to as Maintenance Mode (see Figure 2.7).

FIGURE 2.7

The Microsoft Office 2000 Maintenance Mode lets you fix up, customize, or remove your Office 2000 components.

You can perform three major operations from Maintenance Mode:

- Repair Office
- Add or Remove Features
- Remove Office

Prepare to add or remove files by clicking the Add and Remove Programs button. The screen in Figure 2.8 appears. Look familiar? If you performed a custom installation of Office 2000, you'll recall that this was the exact screen used to select which features you wanted installed in the first place.

FIGURE 2.8
This familiar screen lets you add and remove Office 2000 features with ease.

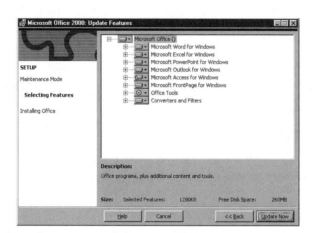

Be sure to click the plus (+) signs next to each feature category to expand its listing. Then you'll use the drop-down arrows to access available installation states for each feature. Rather than seeing an Uninstall option as you might expect, you'll need to choose Not Available from the list to remove a feature or program. Other then that, all the other options are pretty self-explanatory. When you've made all your selections, click the Update button, and within minutes you'll have a newly customized version of Office 2000 on your computer!

Performing Maintenance on Office 2000

Your computer is like a finely tuned Porsche—it needs occasional tweaking to keep running smoothly. When you launch an Office 2000 application, you've undoubtedly seen the message box shown in Figure 2.9.

FIGURE 2.9
This message box indicates that some pre-launch cleanup is being performed on your computer.

This message box is brought to you courtesy of the new Office 2000 Self-Repairing Application tool. Microsoft added this tool to the new office suite to increase reliability and enhance performance. Basically this tool monitors the launch of an application and, if necessary, rearranges and/or fixes files on your hard drive. Microsoft admits that it doesn't increase the speed of Office applications' launches on every system out there; it's of maximum benefit to FAT32 systems, though I've noticed a delay as opposed to an improvement in performance even then.

> **Note:** If your system gets messed up to the point where you need to reboot it to recover, you might see a more elaborate Tuneup Wizard message box. This box gives you the option to abort the Tuneup Wizard, but hurry—there's a running countdown of the seconds until it fires off onscreen!

Using the Detect and Repair Feature

Then there are the times your programs might start acting a little flaky. Executing a certain command can cause the application to crash, or a template might give you unexpected results. This might happen because somewhere along the line one of the program's files got deleted, became corrupt, or something similar happened. We might not be able to figure out exactly how or why it happened, but the important thing is that we can fix it. With the new Office 2000 Detect and Repair feature, recovering from such problems doesn't require years of computer programming experience. In fact, you can fix it from within the affected Office 2000 program. Open the Help menu and select the Detect and Repair item. A dialog box such as the one shown in Figure 2.10 opens. You can either start or cancel the Detect and Repair command, but should you decide to run it, be prepared to provide your Office 2000 CD. The process can take awhile, but the utility will go in and attempt to repair any files related to the application from which you ran the utility.

FIGURE 2.10
The new Detect and Repair feature helps keep your Office 2000 applications running smoothly.

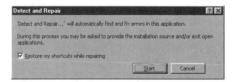

Repairing Office 2000

As I mentioned previously, the Detect and Repair feature within each application is best used when you can isolate a problem to that application and that application only. When the problem spills over to multiple members of the Office 2000 suite, it's time to turn to the Installation Wizard's Maintenance Mode—the Repair Office 2000 option to be specific.

To begin repairing Office 2000, click the Repair Office 2000 button. When doing so, you'll see the screen in Figure 2.11. From here, you can opt to reinstall Office 2000 the way it was originally installed or you can tell the wizard to repair any damaged Office 2000 files. And don't forget to check the Restore my Shortcuts box if you want the wizard to do so.

> **Note: Don't worry; you're in the right place.** As the Installation Wizard performs all its file detections to see whether or not Office 2000 has already been installed on your machine, you might feel uneasy about seeing all these "Preparing to install Office 2000" messages. Although it might not feel right, rest assured that you'll eventually kick over to Maintenance Mode if your installation of Office 2000 is intact.

FIGURE 2.11
Using this option, you can either seek out and repair damaged files only or reinstall your previous configuration of the entire suite.

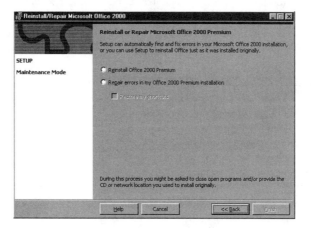

After you've selected the desired option, click the Repair button and wait for the wizard to finish its job. When the wizard has done its thing, open the problem application(s) to see whether the issue was resolved by the repair.

Uninstalling Office 2000

Suppose your company works with highly specialized software and your tech support people discover a conflict between that software and Office 2000. It might then become necessary for you to temporarily remove Office 2000 from your system until a workaround has been figured out.

To perform a clean uninstall of Office 2000 files, enter Maintenance Mode of the Installation Wizard, and click the Uninstall Office 2000 button. You will see a dialog box such as the one shown in Figure 2.12 that asks you whether you're sure you want to remove all the Office 2000 files. Click Yes or No as appropriate.

FIGURE 2.12
Before uninstalling the Office 2000 suite, you have one last chance to change your mind.

Installing Features on Demand

If you've marked features as Install on First Use, you can easily install them from within an application when you're ready to use them. Access the feature as you normally would. You'll see a message much like the one shown in Figure 2.13. Simply click the Install button and wait—the feature will become available in a few short moments. Although most smaller features such as Word 2000 themes don't take very long to install, others (especially entire applications such as Excel) can take significantly longer.

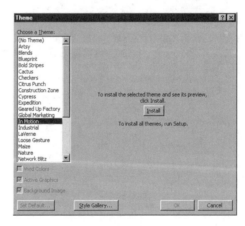

FIGURE 2.13
Installing a feature on-the-fly is as simple as clicking the Install button.

Peter's Principle: Install on demand can be quick, but is it quick enough?

This is another case where your personal work style comes into play. If you usually have ample time in which to prepare a document, spreadsheet, or whatever, you might not find the slight delay caused by installing a feature on demand bothersome. If, on the other hand, you're always rushed, you might find it worth your while to do a complete installation up front.

On Your Own

As you can see, Microsoft has given us more flexibility than ever before when it comes to installing the Office suite of applications. But it's also true that although some of these features look great in marketing paraphernalia and White Papers, they can pose significant headaches in the real world.

I urge you to skim through the chapter one more time while thinking about how you use Office 2000 applications. Everything from the type of document to the timeframe in which you have to prepare them can influence your choices. Factor in your PC resources, and you should easily be able to come up with the Office 2000 installation and configuration that works best for you.

Toolbars, Menus, and Ways to Get Help in Office 2000

If you thought Office 2000's installation flexibility was amazing, wait until you see the new toolbars, menus, and Office Assistants.

The Standard and Formatting toolbars are now optimized for display on a single line, which leaves more workspace visible onscreen. How is it possible to fit two long toolbars on one line? Because the toolbars have become smarter with age—they now boost the buttons you use a majority of the time to the prime location onscreen, while nesting less frequently used buttons underneath a visible drop-down arrow.

And the intelligence doesn't stop there; Microsoft has also created personalized menus, designed to "learn" your favorite commands and push them to the top of the list while temporarily hiding the others.

Finally, while we're on the topic of intelligence, you may be happy to know the Office Assistant has gotten smarter, too. The Answer Wizard (the brain behind the body, so to speak) has been tweaked up a bit to better understand users' questions. Just type in a question as you would ask a friend or colleague, and the Answer Wizard sifts through all the help files to find the most likely matches. And thanks to the latest in Microsoft Agent technology, these characters are no longer confined to special windows that rob you of precious workspace. They can literally move around the screen to provide valuable visual cues while blending in with the scenery.

Each of these new features is designed to make Office 2000 more friendly and responsive to users' needs. It is also hoped that they will enhance productivity.

In this chapter, we will look at each of these new features in depth. You'll learn how to customize them, alter their appearance, and, in case you're feeling nostalgic for Office 97, learn how to disable them altogether.

Introducing the New Office 2000 Personalized Toolbars

Compact but smart, these new toolbars will take some getting used to for veteran Office users (see Figures 3.1 and 3.2).

FIGURE 3.1

Word 97's toolbars held nearly every button you would ever need.

FIGURE 3.2

Word 2000 tries to squish only the most commonly used buttons on its toolbars.

As noted earlier, commonly used toolbar buttons are promoted to the main toolbar line. You can access other buttons by clicking the drop-down arrows at the end of each toolbar, as shown in Figure 3.3. The process works the same way no matter which Office 2000 application you're in.

FIGURE 3.3

Access even more toolbar buttons by using the drop-down arrow at the end of each toolbar.

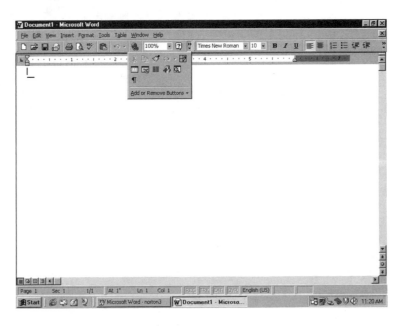

To add or remove buttons from this drop-down button list, click the Add or Remove Buttons button while viewing this list, and then check or uncheck items on the list of options provided, as shown in Figure 3.4.

FIGURE 3.4

Remove the clutter by eliminating buttons you never use, or add obscure buttons you occasionally use.

You can also increase or decrease the amount of space taken up by each toolbar by placing the mouse pointer on the line between the toolbars until it becomes a crosshair pointer. Click and drag the line in the desired direction.

> **Note: Now you see it, now you don't.** If you're making extensive use of one toolbar and not the other, Office 2000 automatically increases the size of the toolbar you're working with so that all the buttons you need are easy to find. Although this feature is a great testament as to just how intelligent these toolbars really are, it also makes finding the commands you need a bit of a challenge because you never know what you're going to see when. In time, you'll either learn to adapt, will become a master at using keyboard shortcuts, or will scrap the intelligence in favor of more traditional toolbars like those in Office 97.

Disabling the Personalized Toolbars

If you've tried all these new-fangled features and have decided that you don't like them, moving back to something a bit more traditional is not impossible. By tweaking just a single setting, you can restore some degree of normalcy and consistency to your Office 2000 toolbars.

Choose Tools|Customize. A dialog box with three tabs appears. Select the Options tab to see the screen shown in Figure 3.5. By default, the Standard and Formatting toolbars share one row. You can give each toolbar its own row a la Office 97 by simply removing the check mark next to the Standard and Formatting Toolbars Share One Row option. You have to repeat this process for each Office 2000 application you want to apply the change to.

FIGURE 3.5

Use the Options tab of the Customize dialog box to remove the personality in Office 2000's toolbars.

With each toolbar occupying its own row, you can now customize the toolbars to appear the way you want them to, not the way Office 2000 thinks you'll want them to.

Customizing Office 2000 Application Toolbars

With toolbars set into separate rows, putting things where you want them is a snap. Right-click any toolbar to see a lengthy list of toolbars available to you. Is the one you plan to work with already visible onscreen? If not, take this opportunity to place a check mark next to it. Next, you need to select the Customize button from the bottom of the same shortcut menu. Open the Commands tab; there you can find all sorts of commands to add to your toolbar. Click the type of command you want to browse in the Categories window; the corresponding commands (along with their icons) appear in the Commands window.

> **Tip: Making room for change.** Because you'll be dragging and dropping buttons to and from the toolbars onscreen, you might need to get the Customize dialog box out of your way. To move it, just click its title bar (the dark blue bar across the top of the box) and drag and drop it away from the toolbars you'll be working with.

After you've located a button you want to add to your toolbar, click it, drag it up to the toolbar, and drop it into place, as shown in Figure 3.6.

FIGURE 3.6

Simply drag and drop the desired button into position.

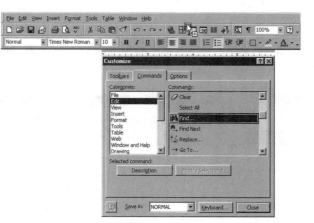

Deleting buttons you rarely use is equally easy. Just click them while the Commands tab of the Customize dialog box is open, and drag them off the toolbar. You can even reposition all the buttons currently residing on the toolbar by clicking them and dragging them wherever you want to put them.

After you've finished making all your changes, click the Close button in the bottom-right corner of the dialog box. Your changes are not only instantly available, but they are preserved for later use as well.

Peter's Principle: Make a new toolbar, or fix up the old one?

You may already know that Microsoft lets you create and name your own toolbars as well, but is it really necessary? Let's face it, Microsoft has already put many of the more popular functions in easy-to-find locations, and odds are you'll find yourself adding or removing far fewer buttons from an existing toolbar than you would have to if you created the toolbar from scratch.

That's not to say there isn't a time and a place for a totally customized toolbar. If your company relies heavily on customized templates and/or macros, you might find creating a custom toolbar immensely worthwhile. To make one, open the Toolbar tab of the Customize dialog box, and click the New button. Name the toolbar, and then use the drop-down arrow to tell Office 2000 which template or document to make the new toolbar available in. Click OK when you're done. The beginning of a tiny toolbar appears onscreen. Open the Commands tab to begin adding the desired buttons and commands to it as you learned previously.

Introducing Office 2000's Personalized Menus

When it comes to producing intelligent tools, Microsoft doesn't discriminate—the Office 2000 menus are smart, too! Instead of showing you the entire list of options as you saw in previous versions of Office (see Figure 3.7), Office 2000 menus display only your most commonly used choices first (see Figure 3.8). To expand the menu so that it includes all your options, run your mouse pointer over the double arrow at the bottom of the menu. The menu will pop up to full size in no time.

FIGURE 3.7
Word 97's Edit menu holds every option available.

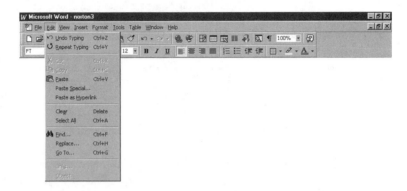

FIGURE 3.8
Word 2000's personalized Edit menu temporarily "hides" some of the less commonly used menu items.

> **Caution: Make sure you know what you're getting into.** If you unintentionally let your mouse pointer rest over a grayed-out menu option for a few seconds, the menu expansion may activate when you're not expecting it to. Suddenly seeing all the options can really be disorienting when you're about to make a selection. Before you make any potentially irreversible or damaging choices, be sure to verify your menu selection one last time. Even if it doesn't hurt your document, an incorrect choice could cause you extra work—not to mention headaches. To counteract some of these potential problems, you can disable the feature by opening the Options tab of the Customize dialog box and deselecting the Show Full Menus After Short Delay option.

Disabling Personalized Menus

If all these constantly changing menus are more trouble than they're worth to you, you'll be happy to hear that they can easily be tamed. With just a few mouse clicks, your Office 2000 menus can lose their dynamic appearance in favor of something a bit more traditional. Just revisit the Options tab of the Customize dialog box, and deselect the Menus

Show Recently Used Commands First option. The menus will instantly look like others you've worked with in the past (with the possible exception of a new feature or two listed in the menu).

People either seem to love these new intelligent features or hate them; there doesn't appear to be much in between. But in all fairness, try to give them some time before rushing to disable them. People have a natural tendency to resist change, especially when it's as radical as this. But who knows, you might be one of the people who starts raving about the personalized toolbars and menus.

Customizing Office 2000 Menus

Do you constantly look for certain commands under the wrong menu? Perhaps customizing the menu(s) in question will help you out. In fact, adding items to a menu is just as easy as adding them to a toolbar. Just follow these simple steps:

1. Make sure the menu you want to modify is visible onscreen.
2. Click Tools|Customize, and then open the Commands tab.
3. Select the category for the command you want to add in the Categories box.
4. Drag the icon of the command you want from the Commands box over the top of the menu in which you want to place it.
5. When the menu expands to show its list of commands, point to the location where you want the new command to appear on the menu, and then release the mouse button.
6. Repeat as needed until all the desired commands have been added to the menu.

> **Tip: Can't find the command you want?** If you don't see the command you want under a particular category, click All Commands in the Categories box.

Quick Launching an Office 2000 Application or Document

Because the underlying theme of this chapter revolves around enhancing personal productivity and making your life with Office 2000 easier, here's a tidbit I think you'll love. Unfortunately, it's only for users of Windows 98 (or users of Windows 95 who have installed Internet Explorer version 4 or later.)

You know that Quick Launch bar at the far-left end of your Windows 98 taskbar? Wouldn't it be nice if you could launch something from it other than Internet Explorer or Outlook Express? Well, you can! Imagine instantly being able to fire off Word 2000 or even a specific document all with one click, and you don't even have to clear your desktop to do it! Sure, you could drag an icon to the Start menu and launch it from there, but that's a three-step process: click Start, hunt for the item, and then click it. With the Quick Launch bar, it's all right there at the left end of your taskbar, accessible with a single click. If you've been relying on shortcuts to avoid navigating through the hierarchy of the Start menu, Quick Launch offers a clutter-free alternative. Just follow these simple steps to create your own Quick Launch shortcut:

1. Navigate to the application or document you want to add to the Quick Launch bar using the My Documents folders, Windows Explorer, or the Start menu.

2. Click and drag the item down to the Quick Launch bar where the mouse pointer turns into an I-beam.

3. Using the I-beam as a guide, drag the item into the desired location, and then release the button.

A great tip for users with 800×600 or better resolution is to increase the taskbar to two rows high, leaving the entire bottom row open for the Quick Launch bar. That way, the means for launching all of your applications is always visible and quickly accessible. And it doesn't take up very much screen real estate—especially at 1024×768 or better resolution.

Launching a Favorite Application or Document When Windows Boots

Now for a neat trick everyone can use...Does your work require you to access the same application or document day after day? Are you tired of starting your day waiting an eternity for Windows to boot and then having to plow through an assortment of folders looking for what you need to work with?

Maybe you're a data entry person who uses an Access front end for input or a corporate executive who's always fiddling with numbers in Excel. If you find yourself launching the same applications or documents every time you sit down to work, you might want to try this trick to save yourself some time and mouse clicks: Have the desired application or document fire off automatically when Windows does. Now you can go grab a cup of coffee and a doughnut while your computer does the work for you.

Just follow these steps to set up an application or document for automatic launching with Windows:

1. Right-click the Start button, and then select Open from the shortcut menu. The Start Menu window appears.

2. Double-click the Programs icon, and then double-click the StartUp icon. In the StartUp window, you see icons for each application (or document) set to launch automatically with Windows (see Figure 3.9).

FIGURE 3.9

In the window shown here, you see that the Word document "norton3" is programmed to open with Windows. When you specify a certain document, Windows automatically adds its respective application to the StartUp window.

3. Keeping the StartUp window open, you need to find the icon for the application or document you want to have launched with Windows. You can do so using either the Windows Programs or Documents menu, or by browsing Windows Explorer or any other standard file dialog box. And for Windows 98 users, you can even drag items over directly from the Start menu.

4. After you've located the desired file or application, right-click its corresponding icon, and then choose Copy from the shortcut menu.

5. Make your way back to the StartUp window, and right-click inside it. Choose Paste Shortcut from the shortcut menu, and within moments you'll see the icon of the item you programmed to launch with Windows.

6. Still don't believe it works? Reboot your system and try it for yourself.

Finding Help in Office 2000

When you're driving around looking for an unfamiliar place, and you get lost, what do you do? Pull over and pull out a map? Get on the cell phone and call someone at your destination for better directions? Drive to the nearest gas station and ask for help? Continue to wander around, sure that you'll uncover a clue at some point?

The fact is, there is no right or wrong answer here; we all have different ways of handling the same situation. Realizing this, Microsoft has given us more ways to seek help in Office 2000 than we can imagine. The choices run the gamut from an absent-minded professor who wanders across the screen offering context-sensitive advice to searchable indices to up-to-the-minute Web content.

In the sections that follow, we'll take an in-depth look at each help tool. You'll learn how to use them, how to customize them, and in some cases how to disable them.

Using the New Office 2000 Office Assistants

Who says "man's best friend" can't help you at the computer? Meet Rocky, one of Microsoft's newest Office Assistants (see Figure 3.10). Rocky joins a whole group of new and improved Office Assistants from which you can choose. Among those new and improved Office Assistants is a bit more subdued Clippit, who continues in his role of default Assistant.

Rocky may not be able to fetch your morning paper, but he can sure fetch some good help advice.

FIGURE 3.10
Rocky the dog—Microsoft's star Office Assistant.

When you launch an Office 2000 application, Rocky or whichever Assistant you've chosen (Clippit the paper clip is the default) appears along with an Assistant balloon (see Figure 3.11). In this balloon are a series of topics related to getting started with the current application. You can either click one of them to learn more, or you can type your own question into the text box at the bottom of the balloon and then click the Search button. Rocky returns a list of relevant links from which you can choose.

FIGURE 3.11
Use the Assistant balloon to ask your help-related questions.

Powered by Microsoft's Answer Wizard technology, the Office Assistants attempt to answer your questions as you would normally ask them. For example, you can enter How do I create a Web page?, click the Search button, and the Office Assistant will come back with a set of applicable links. If you use the Internet a lot and have become accustomed to performing more traditional searches, rest assured that that method works here as well.

For those who cringed at Clippit's annoying interruptions in Office 97, you might want to consider giving him a second chance in Office 2000. Microsoft has tamed him a bit, so he interrupts your work less frequently and is, on the whole, significantly less annoying now.

While you're working within your Office 2000 applications, your chosen Office Assistant basically hangs out onscreen until you need him (unless, of course, you've disabled him). For the most part, you won't even know that he's there. This doesn't mean the Office Assistant is totally passive, however. If he has a useful tip to share that's related to what you're doing onscreen, a yellow light bulb appears above his head. Simply click it to review the context-sensitive advice.

Should you need help at any other point, just click the Office Assistant to make the yellow search balloon appear. Enter your question or the desired search terms, and then click Search. The set of related links described previously appears. To close the balloon to return to work, just click the Office Assistant. Think of the Office Assistant as one big search balloon toggle switch.

If you're used to using menus or keyboard shortcuts, you should know that any of these actions will be successful at opening your Office Assistant's search balloon as well:

- Choosing Microsoft ___ Help from an application's Help menu (where ___ stands for the name of the application in which you're working)
- Pressing the F1 key (only if the option was not turned off previously)
- Clicking the Help button on the Standard toolbar

Turning the Office Assistant Off and On

If you've attempted to use Office Assistants in the past and want them out of your life before you go any further, just right-click the Assistant, choose Options, and then remove the check mark in the Use the Office Assistant check box. The Assistant disappears, giving you full access to the traditional Office help files. In Office 2000, however, these files include full text access to the Answer Wizard, so you can ask your natural language questions even without the imposition of an Office Assistant.

Should you decide to call your Assistant back into duty, choose Help|Show Office Assistant from any Office 2000 application, and you're set to go.

Changing Your Office Assistant

Find the default Office Assistant annoying, or simply want to look at a fresh face? Changing your selected Office Assistant may be just the ticket. Follow these simple steps to select a new helper:

1. Right-click your Office Assistant, and select Choose Assistant from the shortcut menu. The Office Assistant window shown in Figure 3.12 opens.

FIGURE 3.12
Preview all the available Office Assistants in this window.

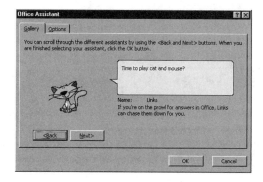

2. On the Gallery tab, use the Back and Next buttons to browse the available Office Assistants, and after you've chosen one, click OK.

3. If the Assistant you selected is installed on your machine, the change is made on the spot. If, however, the Assistant is not available, your old Office Assistant pops on to the scene asking whether you want to install the necessary file now. Click Yes or No as desired. If you click Yes, you need to insert your Office 2000 CD or, if applicable, verify the connection to your company's local area network (LAN).

Note: Thanks for asking. If you disabled the Display Alerts option in Office 97, the setting carries over in the upgrade; thus, you might not see the request to install the desired Office Assistant.

4. Your new Assistant is ready to serve you. Should you decide to return to your old one, just repeat the preceding steps.

Tip: Finding new Assistants... Several new Office Assistants may be on the way. If you haven't yet adopted one as your own (or are always game to try something new), keep an eye on Office on the Web (establish a link to the Internet and choose Help|Office on the Web from any Office application). You should find them there ready to be downloaded and added to your Office Assistant Gallery.

Customizing Your Office Assistant Settings

When it comes to what your Office Assistant can and can't do, you have more control than you might think. By right-clicking the Assistant and selecting Options from the shortcut menu, you can enable and disable a variety of Office Assistant options, as shown in Table 3.1. With a simple mouse click, your Office Assistant can give you as much (or as little) help as you want. Just click the check box next to each option to insert or delete the check mark as desired.

Table 3.1 Office Assistant Use Options

Option	Description
Use the Office Assistant	This box is checked by default and remains checked until you turn off the Assistant as described earlier, or you remove the check mark in its option box on this screen.
Respond to F1 Key	Activated by default, this option makes the Office Assistant launch when the F1 key is pressed.

continues

Option	Description
Help with Wizards	By default, the Office Assistant assists you through any of the special Office 2000 wizards you might want to use.
Display Alerts	When this default option is on, the Office Assistant appears with advice when trouble occurs.
Search for Both Product and Programming Help When Programming	Because working with Visual Basic for Applications isn't considered a common activity, the Office Assistant doesn't provide this kind of help unless you specifically tell it to do so.
Move When in the Way	This option, which is activated by default, sees to it that the Office Assistant stays out of your way when you're working.
Guess Help Topics	By default, this option tells the Office Assistant to guess what you might need help with as opposed to going strictly by the presence of a certain word or phrase in the documentation.
Make Sounds	Your Office Assistants make some pretty interesting sounds by default. Although they may be endearing at home or in a private office, they may be bothersome to others (not to mention even potentially embarrassing by their "cuteness") in the workplace.

In addition to defining how the Office Assistant is used, you can also tell it what kinds of tips to offer when. Table 3.2 shows you the range of available tips. Keep in mind that these options are not only located on the same dialog box as the options in the preceding table, but they are also enabled and disabled in the same manner—with a single mouse click.

Table 3.2   Office Assistant Tip Options

Tip Option	What They Provide
Using Features More Effectively	One of only two tip options set by default, this option tells your Office Assistant to point out when a certain feature could be used more efficiently. For example, if you attempt to set up a table-like text block using multiple tab stops, this option calls upon the Office Assistant to create a table to hold the data.

continues

Tip Option	What They Provide
Using the Mouse More Effectively	The second option enabled by default asks the Office Assistant to show you how to use your mouse better. Say, for example, you try to use your mouse to select an entire document using the old click-and-drag method. With this option enabled, the Assistant prompts you to try putting the mouse pointer in the left margin until it turns into an inward-pointing arrow and then clicking three times in rapid succession to select the whole document.
Keyboard Shortcuts	Enable this option if you want the Office Assistant to alert you to possible keyboard shortcuts when they're available.
Only Show High Priority Tips	Believe it or not, Office 2000 tips actually have differing priority levels. By enabling this option, you can greatly reduce the number of tips offered by the Assistant. This option may be useful to Office veterans who already know all the ins and outs of using the applications.
Show Tip of the Day on Start-up	What a great way to get acquainted with a new application—have it launch with a new tip of the day. Experienced Office users might find that this option takes up more time than it's worth, but novices might appreciate the insights.

Tip: Real (wo)men don't use Office Assistants! Because Office Assistants can be almost too cute, many users shy away from them. In some circles, these animated helpers are considered security blankets for new users. Don't let other people's opinions get to you. For starters, using Office Assistants is a great way to get to know an application and can radically reduce the amount of time you need to get comfortable with and even learn a new program. And for every vocal computer user who makes fun of the Assistants, you'll find at least one veteran computer user who finds them fun and entertaining. The choice all goes back to your preferences and personal learning style. Whether you should use the Office Assistants is your decision, and don't let anyone tell you otherwise. If they help you get the job done quickly and more efficiently, then more power to you.

Note: Fun with Office Assistants. If you're experiencing writer's block or simply need a break from work, you might find playing with your Office Assistants to be an interesting alternative to playing solitaire. Simply right-click the Office Assistant onscreen, and select Animate! from the shortcut menu. Sit back and see what your character has in store. Below, Rocky dons protection and blows away a document in this random animation.

Turning to the Help Files

Long before Office Assistants came on the scene, people had to rely on simple text-based help files. Although you occasionally see graphics in these files where appropriate, they still are, for the most part, text-based. Even so, some people still take great comfort in working with these old friends.

Before you can do anything with the Office 2000 help files, you need to turn off the Office Assistant, as described earlier. After it's turned off, you can access the help files by using either the Help menu or by pressing F1.

When you launch the help files for the first time, you might be surprised to find that your application's workspace shrinks to the right side of the screen, and the help files open over the top of it. As was the case in the past, you have three separate ways to seek assistance from the help files: Contents, Answer Wizard (which replaces the Find tab), and Index. If you don't see these tabs on the left side of the help file pane, you might need to click the Show button on the help file's toolbar to make them appear.

Tip: Shrink it down to size. If you're viewing your Word 2000 document or Excel 2000 worksheet at 100 percent size, you might want to back it down to, say, 75 percent using the Zoom drop-down box so that you can see everything onscreen at once. If 75 percent proves to be too hard on the eyes, remember you can always add a value somewhere in between manually. Just type it in, and press Enter.

Before we explore each tab, you should know about some general help file functions. For example, you can move backward and forward through the files using Back and Forward buttons just as you would use in a Web browser. Using these buttons makes revisiting help topics a breeze. These subtle changes are what's referred to as *HTML-based help files*. You'll even find hyperlinks to closely related topics, so additional help is a single mouse click away.

You can always print help files by simply clicking the Print button. This action opens either the standard Print dialog box (in the Answer Wizard or Index tabs) or a smaller dialog box (while you're viewing topics in the Contents tab) that gives you the option of only printing the current page or all the help topics underneath the selected heading.

Which tool should you use when? I'll give you some additional ideas in the sections that follow. But generally speaking, if you carry through the "help tabs are roughly equivalent to their printed book counterparts" analogy, you'll discover the following: If you're learning about something for the first time, you might start by skimming the table of contents (the Contents tab). It gives you some basic starting points whether or not you know the lingo, so to speak. If, on the other hand, you're a pro and know that you want to do something very specific—such as publish pivot tables to the Web—then the Index tab might get you the information you want quickly. If you have a general question you want answered even if you don't know the exact terms, the Answer Wizard may be just the kind of help you need.

The Contents Tab

The Contents tab can be likened to the Table of Contents you find in a book: It contains a list of general topics that you can expand to hone in on more specific topics of interest. To see all the topics that appear underneath a general heading, just double-click the heading's title. The choice of topics expands, as shown in Figure 3.13.

Figure 3.13
Double-click a heading to see a list of topics nested within it.

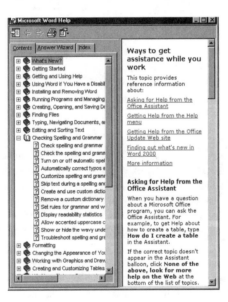

Click the topic you want to learn more about to see its information displayed in the Help file pane. Flip through the Help file pages just as you would a chapter in a book.

The Contents tab is a great place to start if you kind of know what you want to learn more about but maybe aren't sure of the exact terminology. It's also a good place to begin browsing if you want to learn more about an application but don't have a specific task in mind.

The Answer Wizard Tab

Microsoft has put a lot of time and energy (not to mention money) into developing intelligent software. Earlier in the chapter, you saw how smart the Office 2000 Office Assistants have become. This intelligence is due, in part, to the sophisticated Answer Wizard technology.

By clicking the Answer Wizard tab in the Office 2000 help files, you can type in a question as if you were asking it to a human being. Instead of browsing Contents topics or entering a specific word in the Index tab, you can enter a general question; for example, you can enter How do I save a Word document as a Web page? The Answer Wizard comes back with a list of relevant topics from which you can choose (see Figure 3.14).

FIGURE 3.14

Type in your question, and then click Search to see the results.

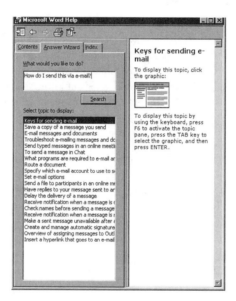

Just double-click the desired topic in the Select Topic to Display window to view it in the Help pane. You can then click inside the application's workspace to see the document you're working on and the applicable help topic side-by-side. No more toggling back and forth between your document and the help screen!

The Answer Wizard tab is the tool of choice for users who aren't necessarily familiar with all the technical terms but who have a fixed idea of what they want to learn more about.

The Index Tab

The final help tool is the Index tab. Like the index of this book, the Index tab houses every Office 2000 word you can think of and then some. You can either type in the desired keyword or words, or use the scrollbars to browse the help index manually.

Should you decide to enter your keywords, you should note how the index moves with each letter you type. This modified AutoComplete feature often helps you jump to the desired term after pressing as few as two or three keys. When the desired word appears onscreen, double-click it to see a list of related topics. When you've found the topic you want, double-click it to make its text appear in the Help pane.

The Index tab is the perfect choice if you know what you want to do and need to "cut to the chase" to get the job done quickly. Those unfamiliar with Office 2000 terminology might find this tab a bit more intimidating than the others because of its reliance on specific words as opposed to concepts.

Using "What's This?"

If you see something unusual onscreen and aren't quite sure what it is or what it does, use the What's This feature to get the whole story. In various dialog boxes, you'll see a little question mark icon in the upper-right corner of the box. When you click it, the mouse pointer turns into an arrow with a question mark beside it. Click the object in question to view ScreenTip boxes of information about it. If the question mark button is not visible, press Shift+F1 or click Help|What's This? to access the feature.

Getting Help on the Web

Occasionally, the answer to a software problem is discovered, but because all the application's disks have been created and distributed to a number of people in a variety of locations, keeping everyone current is virtually impossible. At this point, Office on the Web comes in. By clicking Help|Office on the Web, you can get up-to-the-minute help with any Office 2000 quirks that might arise.

On Your Own

In this chapter, you learned about a lot of exciting ways you can customize your work environment using some of Office 2000's newest features. Before you disable every dynamic feature you can find (hey, I know some of you have had horrible experiences in the past with the plethora of Auto features), try going about your work with all the new features enabled. As you find one totally intolerable, disable it, and then go about your business. Eliminate only one feature at a time, allowing some work time in between. That way, you can efficiently isolate the features that make you crazy while getting acquainted with the ones that can actually make your life with Office 2000 easier.

Peter Norton

Managing Office 2000 Files Productively

File management (or a lack thereof) can be one of the primary causes of grief to computer users. I've seen highly paid computer center managers let all their files accumulate in the My Documents directory and then panic six months later when they can't find something they need. No matter how well you name a document, it's going to take you awhile to track it down amidst hundreds, if not thousands, of files. Sound file management techniques will not only make you more productive in the long run, but they help reduce your stress level as well, because you can quickly put your hands on the data you need.

In this chapter, we'll take a look at all kinds of file management issues, including where to store your files, how to find the files you need, how to work with others using previous versions of the same software (or even people using non-Microsoft applications), and how to work with multiple documents at once in the same application, among other topics.

Getting to Know Your Office File Extensions

Before you can successfully manage your Office 2000 files, you need to know which of the files on your system are, in fact, Office 2000 files. With all the new Web capabilities in Office 2000, that's not as easy as it may sound. Although some of the extensions may appear to be a bit exotic at first glance (like the PowerPoint Web template [.pothtml] file extension), you might find yourself using them later as you get acquainted with some of the product's newest features.

In the tables in this chapter, you'll see three columns of information for each Office 2000 application. In the first column, you'll see a picture of the icon that represents the file type in question. Seeing the icon is especially useful because an icon may be the only visual clue you have as to a file's type. The second column presents the name of the file type represented by the preceding icon. The last column gives you the file type's actual file extension. For simplicity's sake, I have opted to include only file types that you can open and/or manipulate, not file types that may be unique to the program files them-selves. Admittedly, this information doesn't make real compelling reading, but you will find it extremely helpful as you begin taking charge of file management on your PC. You should also be aware that the types of files you actually see on your machine may vary depending on what Office components you have installed, how they've been configured, and whether you've used previous versions of the applications.

> **Note: Bookmark this page!** If you don't think you'll be needing the informa-tion contained in these tables, consider the following: If you're poking around in Windows Explorer trying to figure out which files you can delete to make more room on your hard disk, you'll find these tables extremely helpful. You wouldn't want to delete that special template it took you hours to put together. Or if someone emails you a file, you may see only the corresponding file type icon or the filename along with an unrecognizable file extension. These tables will help you know what you're getting into before you double-click to open those files.

In addition to Office 2000 file types, I'll present some of the more common non-Office file types you might encounter elsewhere.

Recognizing Office 2000 File Types

Word is undeniably the most commonly—and frequently—used member of the Office suite of applications. As you begin to push Word 2000's features to the limit, you'll start to encounter some new file types. Take a look at Table 4.1 to see what they are and to familiarize yourself with their respective icons.

Table 4.1   Word 2000 File Types and Their Respective Icons

Icon	File Type	Extension
	Word 2000 document	.doc
	Word 2000 document template	.dot
	Word 2000 HTML file	.dochtml
	Word 2000 HTML template	.dothtml
	Word 2000 rich text format	.rtf
	Word 2000 backup file	.wbk

If you spend a lot of time working with spreadsheets and numbers, you should be familiar with the file types presented in Table 4.2. Although Excel itself generates the majority of them, at least one of them can come from any number of alternative sources.

Table 4.2   Excel 2000 File Types and Their Corresponding Icons

Icon	File Type	Extension
	Excel 2000 worksheet	.xls or.xlb
	Excel 2000 template	.xlt
	Excel 2000 workspace	.xlw
	Excel 2000 HTML file	.xlshtml
	Excel 2000 HTML template	.xlthtml
	Excel 2000 backup file	.xlk
	Excel 2000 Web query file	.iqy
	Comma-separated value file	.csv

When people think of email programs and personal information management software, very rarely do they think in terms of file types. Email files, for the most part, get moved around from within the application as do Address Book files. But if you need to move vitally important email messages and contact files to another machine, would you know what to look for? In Table 4.3, you can find the file types commonly associated with Outlook 2000 functions.

Table 4.3   Outlook 2000 File Types and Their Corresponding Icons

Icon	File Type	Extension
	Outlook 2000 item	.msg
	Outlook 2000 template	.oft
	Address Book file	.wab

As you can see in Table 4.4, PowerPoint 2000 has multiple file types as well. With the recent addition of Publisher 2000 to multiple Office suite configurations, you should be familiar with the file type listed last in Table 4.4.

Table 4.4 PowerPoint 2000 and Publisher 2000 File Types and Their Corresponding Icons

Icon	File Type	Extension
	PowerPoint 2000 presentation	.ppt
	PowerPoint 2000 slide show	.pps
	PowerPoint 2000 template	.pot
	PowerPoint 2000 HTML file	.ppthtml
	PowerPoint 2000 HTML template	.pothtml
	Publisher 2000 file	.pub

In Access 2000, you can work with a variety of file types, which run the gamut from simple database files to project files to Access HTML files. Table 4.5 presents the file types you're most likely to encounter while working with your personal data files.

Table 4.5 Access 2000 File Types and Their Corresponding Icons

Icon	File Type	Extension
	Access project file	.adp
	Access 2000 data access page	.maw
	Access 2000 database file	.mda
	Access 2000 database file	.mdb
	Access 2000 HTML file	.mdbhtml
	Access 2000 HTML template	.wizhtml
	Access 2000 blank database	.mdn

Recognizing Other Random Bits and Pieces

In addition to the file types that are native to certain applications in the preceding tables, you might encounter a host of other file types in a variety of situations. Perhaps you have embedded a sound file into your Word 2000 Web page and need to move it to the Web server. The same holds true for image files.

Take a look at Table 4.6 to see various file types you encounter on (and perhaps even download from) the Web or in your email.

Table 4.6 Assorted File Types and Their Corresponding Icons

Icon	File Type	Extension
	Microsoft organization chart	.opx
	Microsoft Graph 2000 chart	.gra
	Microsoft Office Search	.oss
	Microsoft HTML document 4.0	.htm, .html, .stm, .htw
	Microsoft XML document 4.0	.xml, .xsl
	Text file	.txt
	JPEG image file	.jpg
	GIF image file	.gif
	Bitmap image	.bmp
	NetMeeting whiteboard file	.wht
	MIDI sequence file	.rmi, .mid
	Outlook Express email file	.eml

continues

Icon	File Type	Extension
	Outlook Express newsgroup file	.nws
	PCX image file	.pcx
	RealMedia file	.ra, .rm, .ram, .rmm
	Sound clip—AU	.au
	Sound clip—AIF, AIFF, AIFC	.aif, .aiff, .aifc
	Sound clip—Basic	.snd
	TIF graphic image	.tiff, .tif
	WAV sound file	.wav

Note: A difference you can see... The appearance of graphic images such as JPEG, GIF, PCX, TIF, and bitmap can vary depending on what kind of graphic software you have installed on your computer. Although the icons shown in Table 4.6 are the standard defaults for Windows, they may look significantly different if you have Paint Shop Pro, LView Pro, or a similar program installed.

There you have it—all the grungy details that form the basis of file management on your computer. Now that you know what the file types are, both by name and by icon, you're ready to begin tackling file management head-on. If you've been using your current machine for a while, think of file management as spring cleaning for your computer. With the tips and techniques outlined in this chapter, not only will you be able to find what you want when you want it, but at the end, you should have a lot less clutter to sift through. If you're just getting started with a new PC, consider yourself among the lucky few who'll never have to deal with the evils of a cluttered machine firsthand. Finally, if you've been using your machine for some time and are so organized that you can find what you need in seconds, you are to be applauded. But I hope you'll stay on for the remainder of the chapter anyway because I'll describe some wonderful new Office 2000 file management options and techniques you might find useful in your quest to maintain an organized PC environment.

Organizing Your Files for Maximum Ease of Use

If I were to come to your home or office and launch Windows Explorer, what would I see? Would I see the standard My Documents folder along with all the other standard folders only, or would I see a network of self-defined folders similar to what's shown in Figure 4.1?

FIGURE 4.1

The more folders you have, the more easily you can find that lone document amidst hundreds (if not thousands) of other documents.

Obviously, the complexity of your network of folders varies depending on the frequency with which you use your computer. If you use it once a month to write Aunt Julie a letter, that's one thing; but if you produce document after document for various projects at work or school, then you may benefit greatly from a highly organized system.

> **Tip: Find the happy medium for you.** Be careful not to create too many folders in proportion to the documents you have to keep organized. If you have too many folders, you'll find yourself experiencing the very same problem that prompted you to get organized in the first place. I wish I could give you an exact rule of thumb for the optimal number of folders, but what you need really does depend on a number of factors. Just consider this: If each folder houses a tiny number of items (and I'm talking the less-than-five-items range here), then multiple folders may hinder, not help, your productivity.

Back in Figure 4.1, you saw a bit of my personal machine's structure. Generally, I have a folder for each book I've written, with subfolders for screenshots, material I've submitted to the editors, chapters the editors want me to review one last time, and so on. In addition, I have separate folders for each consulting client, dream house plans I found on the Net, Web page design goodies I've categorized even further with subfolders...you get the idea. Although this system might seem overly complicated on the surface, you need it when you start dealing with high volumes of material.

> **Tip: It's more than a name...**Because you could find yourself staring at two or more files with the same name (you could have both a Word document and an Excel worksheet called Budget, for example), you might want to call your knowledge of the different file types into action to decide which file goes where in your network of folders. You can also group the files by type when you have multiple file types in your view. From within the desired directory in Windows Explorer, click View|Arrange Icons|By Type. If you're looking at the files from within any Office 2000 application's standard Open or Save As dialog boxes, then click the Views drop-down arrow, and then select Arrange Icons|By Type. Then the filenames appear together in alphabetical order grouped by type of file.

Have you ever had the opportunity to work with or see a substantial collection of paper files up close? I'm not talking about the two lateral file cabinets you see in many smaller offices; I'm talking about the banks of ceiling-high cabinets you see lining the walls of many doctors' offices. Literally thousands of files are crammed in there. For example, to find a patient's test results from his or her last visit, an assistant would have to first find the correct file cabinet among those lining the walls, then look for the proper drawer in the cabinet, browse for the proper hanging folder, flip through the hanging folder to find the correct manila folder, and then skim the contents of the folder for the necessary document. Although that process looks like a lot of work in and of itself, think of how difficult it would be to find those results without this nested structure? Talk about searching for the proverbial needle in the haystack!

> **Caution: Be careful what you move!** Obviously, all this file organization applies only to the files you work with, not to the program files that actually drive the applications. These program files live in their own Programs directory (or folder), so it's not likely you'll end up moving them by mistake. However, you should be aware that if you do move such a file, it could potentially result in the "breaking" of the application whose file was moved. This "breaking" simply means the application won't run. Granted, Office 2000's new Detect and Repair feature makes such fixes a whole lot easier than they used to be, but still this situation can—and should—be avoided.

A structured environment can be beneficial in other ways as well. Putting documents together in a special folder can make copying them to a disk, archiving them on a ZIP drive, or emailing them to a coworker a snap.

Exploring the New Open and Save As Dialog Boxes

Sound file management practices begin with the manner in which you save your files. Given that, we'll turn our attention to the Save As dialog boxes and their nearly identical twin, the Open dialog box.

When you first launch an Office 2000 application, you might not immediately see the differences between it and its predecessor. If you try to open or save a document, though, the change should hit you instantly. The simple dialog boxes found in Office 97 (see Figure 4.2) have been replaced by more feature-rich counterparts in Office 2000 (see Figure 4.3).

FIGURE 4.2
The typical Office 97 Save As dialog box was fairly simple in appearance.

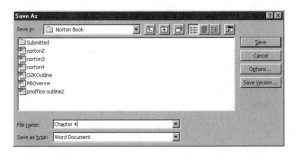

FIGURE 4.3
The Office 2000 Save As dialog box looks different but behaves in much the same way as its Office 97 counterpart.

Notice the new Outlook-like bar down the left side of the Office 2000 Save As or Open dialog box. Although it has minimal relevance to saving a document, this Places Bar does have a major impact on how you locate files you want to open. (More about this topic later in the chapter.) Beyond that, not much is new when it comes to saving a document. The same old tips apply.

It's All in a Filename...

As you create a document, think about a name for it that fully (and accurately) describes its contents. Use the following tips as a guide for coming up with that all-important document name:

- A good filename can make a world of difference. Make the name as short yet descriptive as possible.

- If you tend to include your company's name in every filename as well as the document's title (for example, a spreadsheet named CBCNS Budget, a Word document named CBCNS Grant Application, and so on), consider creating a folder for the company (in which case, the document could simply be called Budget or Grant App.). Of course, if you work with only one company, you might not need to place the company's name on the document at all. If every document has the same word(s) in front of it, think how difficult it would be to sort through them in a hurry! The objective is to make each document's name as distinctive as possible.

- Consider using a date or year somewhere in the filename if it's relevant. For instance, documents with names like Budget, New Budget, and Projected Budget mean less than Fall 98 Budget or 99 Projected Budget.

- Name the way you work. If your work involves creating many kinds of documents for a single entity, then you should emphasize a document's contents in its filename. If, on the other hand, you're a consultant who does feasibility studies for multiple entities, you'll want the entity's name to appear prominently in the file's name.

Peter's Principle: Life's full of contradictions...

Some of these tips may seem to clash with one another at first glance. For instance, how can you have a short, descriptive filename when you're trying to incorporate a date, a company name, and the type of document? The answer is simpler than you might think. For starters, try combining file-naming and folder-placement strategies. The two strategies are not mutually exclusive. In fact, they should—and do—work hand in hand to get the job done.

Remember, the goal here is to keep the number of entries in a given folder—or directory—to a minimum. Given that, it's imperative that you take a long, hard look at the way you work. Every little detail—from the total number of documents you create over the span of a year to the types of documents they are—influences how you store things on your machine. Although sophisticated file-searching tools make finding things a lot easier than it used to be, nothing beats good file organization from the ground up.

Knowing Where to Store It

The proper placement of a file in your computer's network of folders goes hand-in-hand with the document's name when it comes to enhancing your ability to find the file again when you need it.

Consider the following as you develop your computer's filing system:

- Don't just let all your documents accumulate in the My Documents folder; that's just begging for trouble!

- If you tend to include your company's name in a filename as well as the document's title (for example, a spreadsheet named CBCNS Budget), consider creating a folder for the company (in which case, the document could simply be called Budget). Or if that idea is still too broad, under the company's name, make a sub-folder called Finances that could then store the Budget document. Having large numbers of documents with similar names like CBCNS Budget, CBCNS Newsletter, and CBCNS Reg Form can make finding what you need much harder than it needs to be.

- If you know the types of documents you usually generate up front, sitting down and sketching out a list of applicable directory names may be worthwhile. With a little forethought, you can avoid having grossly unbalanced folders where some contain a handful of entries, and others contain dozens.

- Microsoft has always made it easy to create new folders on-the-fly. If you don't see a category that fits the document when you start to save it, don't hesitate to create a new folder at that exact moment. Doing so as you save the document eliminates the hassle of having to go through scads of entries later and manually moving them to more logical locations.

- Don't overdo it! Just because you see the logic in creating multiple folders doesn't mean it's the right thing for you. If you produce very few documents, storing them in multiple locations can actually cost you more time than it saves.

Although I would love to give you the definitive answer when it comes to the best way to organize your files, attempting to do so would be a gross deception. You deserve the truth, and as wishy-washy as it sounds, "it depends" really is the best answer. As long as you employ the guidelines presented in this section, though, you'll be in great shape.

Creating a New Folder as You Work

As mentioned earlier, one time-effective file management technique is to define an appropriate folder when you start to save the document for the first time. To do so, follow these steps:

1. With the document you want to save onscreen, click the Save button. If the document was previously named and saved, you need to click the File menu item and then choose Save As.

2. Click the Create New Folder button  at the top of the Save As dialog box. A New Folder dialog box like the one shown in Figure 4.4 appears.

3. Type in the name you want to give the folder, and then click OK. Notice that the name of the new folder now appears in the Save In text box. In previous versions of Office, you had to double-click the new folder for it to become the active folder. In Office 2000, the new folder is automatically moved to the Save In text box, so the document is instantly ready to be saved where you intended it to be saved—the newly defined folder.

4. The next order of business involves giving the document a meaningful name. Think back to all the tips you learned earlier in the chapter, and then factor in the name of the folder in which you saved the document. After you've entered a document name that fits the bill, just click the Save button at the bottom-right corner of the Save As dialog box. The document is then safely stored in its new location.

Saving a Document as a Favorite

Perhaps you have a document or two that you work with on a regular basis. If that's the case, you might want to consider yet another file-saving strategy: saving a document as a Favorite. By doing so, you can quickly access the document from the Favorites section of the Windows Start menu. All you have to do is select the document's name from the list, and Windows launches the necessary Office 2000 application.

> **Tip: This strategy may not be for you if...**If you're like me and have gobs of goodies in your Favorites list, the strategy in the preceding paragraph may not help you much. You could manually click your way to the desired document in the time it would take you to wade through the dozens of Favorites in the list.

Saving a document as a Favorite is simple; just do the following:

1. Open the Save As dialog box from within any Office 2000 application, as described earlier.

2. Click the Favorites button on the Places Bar. A list of all your Favorites appears. You see the same folders when organizing or saving your favorite Web pages in Internet Explorer.

3. From here, you have two options. You can either save the document to the Favorites list so that it appears by itself, or you can save it to the predefined My Documents folder.

> **Caution: Hey, don't put that there!** If you still have a bunch of random documents cluttering up your default My Documents folder, you should avoid saving the current document in the My Documents folder as well. Either find an appropriate home as you create the documents, or if you need to create a bunch of documents for a single project, consider changing the default Save As folder, as demonstrated in the following section.

4. After you've chosen the best location to store the document and have named it, click the Save button. From that point on, you can open the desired document from the Favorites section of the Windows Start menu.

Changing the Default Save As Folder

Do you have a major project coming up that will spawn a number of related documents? If so, you might want to consider changing your default working folder. That way, when you start to save one of the documents, you can just name it and click the Save button as opposed to having to create a new folder or, worse yet, browsing your entire computer for the proper folder. Of course, that means you have to be a bit more careful when saving documents you may have otherwise let accumulate in the My Documents folder. Under this plan, these documents might inadvertently end up getting stuck with a project folder, never to be seen again. You should also know that changing the default save as location in one application does not affect the others, so you need to address each one separately.

...in Word 2000

To change your default working folder in Word 2000, follow these simple steps:

1. From within Word 2000, click Tools|Options.

2. When the Options dialog box appears, click the File Locations tab.

3. Because you want to change the default folder in which documents are saved, click Documents under the File Types column, as shown in Figure 4.5. (This item may be highlighted by default when you open the File Locations tab.)

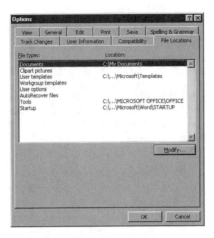

FIGURE 4.5
Select the file type whose default storage folder you want to change.

4. Click the Modify button. A Modify Location dialog box appears. It bears a striking resemblance to the normal Save As and Open dialog boxes.

5. Browse to the folder you want to define as the default, or create a new folder if needed.

6. After you've chosen the desired folder, click OK to save the file path. Notice the document's file location has changed to reflect your selection.

7. Click OK one last time to close the Options dialog box. From that point on, all new documents will be saved to the new location by default. You can rest assured that existing documents will continue to be saved in the location previously specified unless you specify otherwise. It's that easy!

> **Caution: Get a fresh start.** To make sure the new default takes properly, close any other Word documents before creating the new document to be saved in the new location. Failure to do so may result in the new document being saved to the same location as the last saved document.

...in Excel 2000

Changing the default save as location in Excel 2000 requires you to open the application, click Tools|Options, select the General tab, and then enter the desired location in the Default File Location text box near the bottom of the dialog box. Click OK to save your change and dismiss the dialog box.

Tip: Start anywhere you want to. If you're working on a project containing a number of files in a single folder, you might find it useful to give Excel 2000 an alternate startup file location. That way, when you click File|Open, you don't need to click your way to the desired directory because you'll already be there. To change this setting from the default My Documents location, simply type the full pathname to the desired file location in the Alternate Startup File Location text box on the General tab of the Options dialog box.

...in PowerPoint 2000

In PowerPoint 2000, you can change the default save as location by clicking Tools|Options, selecting the Save tab, and entering the desired file location in the Default File Location box at the bottom of the tab. Click OK to save the setting and close the dialog box.

...in Access 2000

Click Tools|Options, open the General tab, and then enter the desired file location in the Default Database Folder text box to change the default location in Access 2000.

...in Publisher 2000

Changing the default save as location in Publisher 2000 requires a few more steps because the publications and images are stored in separate locations.

1. From within Publisher 2000, click Tools|Options, and select the General tab if it's not already in view.

2. In the File Location box at the bottom of the tab, click the item—Publications or Pictures—for which you want to change the default location.

3. Click the Modify button to browse to the desired location.

4. When you're in the desired folder, click the OK button to close the Modify Location dialog box, which closely resembles a typical Open or Save As dialog box. The name of the new location then appears in the File Location box next to the element you modified.

5. Repeat the steps if necessary to change the default save as location for the Publisher 2000 item you didn't modify.

6. When you're done, click OK to save the changes and close the dialog box.

Sharing Files Compatible with Previous Versions of Office

Do you need to share documents with people using Office 97 or earlier? Or what if you got a new computer at home complete with Office 2000 preinstalled, but have only Office 97 at work (or vice versa)? Obviously, if you just plan to print the output or publish it to the Web, it doesn't matter if you incorporate new Office 2000 features that aren't supported elsewhere. Your readers will just see a great-looking document. The issue of version compatibility generally comes into play only when others must work on a document with you, or when others must view your work using previous versions of the software you used.

The solution to the potential version incompatibility dilemma is not as overwhelming as it may seem. In fact, Microsoft has given us multiple ways to deal with it.

One way involves saving the document in a previous version's format. You do so by clicking the drop-down arrow next to the Save As Type text box in the Save As dialog box and then choosing the applicable version from the list. You can also convert an Excel spreadsheet to Lotus 1-2-3 format or a Word document to a WordPerfect document using the same procedure.

Another option is to simply disable features that are incompatible with earlier versions of Office. You can easily do so in Word 2000 by accessing the Compatibility tab of the Options dialog box. For other applications, you need to be familiar with which features are supported in earlier versions and which are not. For example, angled text is supported in later versions of Excel but could produce horrendously ugly results in earlier versions.

> **Tip: Okay, that advice makes sense, but how do I find out what features are supported in which versions of an application?** Each Office 2000 application has its own set of chapters within this book. In those dedicated chapters, I will give you the low-down on what works where, as well as what to avoid. You also need to learn the difference between features that may just look slightly different in other versions versus those that really screw up the way a document looks. You'll discover all that information in the chapters devoted to the application of your choice.

If version compatibility is an ongoing consideration for you (as in the case of your having Office 2000 at home and Office 97 or earlier at work or vice versa), then you might want to consider a more fundamental solution: setting your applications to be saved as another version by default. Saving them this way doesn't mean you can't later bring them up in Office 2000 to incorporate new formatting features or Web publishing options. To save an Office 2000 document as another version by default, use the applicable drop-down list in the following locations:

- Word 2000—Choose Tools|Options and then open the Save tab.

- Excel 2000—Choose Tools|Options and then open the Transition tab.

- PowerPoint 2000—Choose Tools|Options and then open the Save tab.

- Publisher 2000—Choose this setting each time you save a publication using the Save As Type drop-down box in the Save As dialog box.

- Access 2000—Saving a database as a non-Access 2000 database is not a trivial task. Turn to Chapter 24, "Creating Access Applications."

Of course, the simplest solution of all is to avoid using all the funky new features altogether. To learn which features to avoid, turn to the section of this book that covers the application in question.

Peter's Principle: Avoid collaboration discrimination from the start.

Having numerous people collaborate on a large-scale document such as a proposal for funding, a business plan, or budget projections is not uncommon. To complicate matters further, each of these people might be working with a different version of Office. So what should you do to make everyone's life easier?

I know you might be tempted to make the document look good from the start with fancy formatting, unusual fonts, and such, but I strongly urge you to work with the document in as basic a form as possible while in the collaborative stages. Save the final touches for the very end of the project. That way, you don't run the risk of losing your Office 2000-specific formatting. And working this way has the added benefit of giving the workgroup a real sense of accomplishment as the document evolves from a grungy single-font document with colorful revision marks and comments throughout to a polished, professional-looking document.

If you've upgraded your Office suite in the past, you might have experienced some rough times when making the big move. Well, there's great news on the migration front when it comes to Office 2000. First, all the applications (with the exception of Access) have retained their old file types, which means you should see no difference when opening your old Office 97 documents in Office 2000. If you're ultra-concerned about the changes, you can make backup copies of your Office 97 files on a floppy or ZIP disk before you inadvertently open them in Office 2000.

Working with Multiple Open Files at Once

When you need to work with a Word document, an Excel spreadsheet, a PowerPoint presentation, and email all at once, Windows makes switching from one task to another a breeze: Just click the applicable button on the Windows taskbar, and you instantly go to the desired location. What happens if you're working with multiple files in the same application, though?

Some significant changes have been made in this regard with Office 2000. In Office 97, all documents were stored under a single application icon on the Windows taskbar. In other words, all Word documents were stored under a single Word button on the Windows taskbar. To access the various documents within an application, you either had to press Alt+Esc to cycle through everything on your Windows desktop, or you had to click the desired application icon and then click the Windows menu item and choose the desired item from the bottom section of the list. This is known as a *Multiple Document Interface*, or *MDI*, because multiple documents are stored under one taskbar icon. In Office 2000, things have changed for virtually all the applications. The most dramatic change is in Word, which has moved to a *Single Document Interface*, or *SDI*. This means that each open document in Word now has its own button on the Windows taskbar, making it nearly effortless for you to hop directly to the document you need.

Note: The pros and cons of SDI. Not everyone is as enthusiastic about the move to SDI as I am. Opponents argue that an SDI needlessly clutters the Windows taskbar. My counter is, "Hey, if you don't need to get to the document eventually, why do you have it open in the first place?" To me, the MDI approach requires far too many steps to get where I want to go. And unless you have the memory of an elephant, you'll need at least two keystroke attempts to discover which key sequence cycles you through all the open documents and applications on your desktop.

As for the cluttered taskbar, most people don't have an outrageous number of windows open at once, so they can easily see what's what. And those who do work with lots of windows are most likely power users who either have all the shortcuts engrained in their brains, are running at a higher screen resolution on a larger monitor that allows more legible taskbar buttons, or they've rearranged and/or resized the taskbar to make room for everything. Of course, if the folks at Microsoft wanted to make everyone happy, they would let you turn SDI on and off, but that's no simple feat—at least from a programming standpoint.

To make things even more complicated in Office 2000, the remaining applications are neither MDI nor SDI. They're something that can best be referred to as "simulated SDI." Each document has its own button on the Windows taskbar, yet when you click the application's Close button (the "X" in the uppermost right corner of the application), all the documents and the application close. This new flavor of document interface will definitely take some getting used to because most users are familiar either with straight SDI or MDI. And if you used the old Alt+Tab trick to cycle between applications in Office 97's MDI environment, you'll be interested to know that in Office 2000, the command now cycles you through applications as well as documents. This difference is a direct side effect of Word 2000's SDI and the other applications' simulated SDI.

Increasing Your Taskbar Viewing Area

With 17 windows open, you can see little more than the icons on the Windows 98 taskbar shown in Figure 4.6.

Figure 4.6
When displayed in the traditional way, the Windows taskbar can occasionally appear overcrowded.

If you're concerned about not being able to see enough on your Windows taskbar, you'll find the following workaround helpful. It involves moving the taskbar to the left side of your screen, widening its viewing area, and then setting it to AutoHide when you're not using it.

> **Caution: Stay to the left!** In America, we're used to doing everything on the right. We drive our cars there. We walk there in school halls. But in this one instance, you'll want to avoid the right. Putting your Windows taskbar there might interfere with the use of scrollbars commonly found on the right side of the screen. When you attempt to use a scrollbar, the taskbar might slip into view instead. Keeping the taskbar on the left eliminates that problem. Of course, if you select several rows in Excel, frequently use Word's style bar, or seldom use scrollbars to scroll, you may have an alternative placement preference. As is often the case, efficient taskbar placement is a matter of personal preference. It is also highly dependent on your work habits.

To gain more taskbar viewing area, just follow these steps:

1. Click inside an empty gray area of the Windows taskbar, and move the mouse pointer to the left side of the screen. A line appears from the top to the bottom of the screen, showing you where the taskbar will be positioned. Release the mouse button to set the taskbar in its new location. The setup may take a little while to complete.

2. To further increase the viewing area, run your mouse pointer over the right border of the taskbar until you see the resize marks (the two-sided arrow). Click and then drag the border to the right. With just a little adjusting, you can gain significant taskbar space (see Figure 4.7).

FIGURE 4.7
With this setup, you have plenty of room for expansion.

3. As is, the larger taskbar robs potentially valuable workspace. But that can be changed, too, by telling the taskbar to hide when you're not using it. To set up the taskbar to respond to the AutoHide feature, right-click inside an empty gray area inside the taskbar, and then select Properties from the shortcut menu.

4. On the Taskbar options tab of the Properties dialog box, make sure the AutoHide box is checked, click Apply to save the change, and then click OK to exit the dialog box.

5. To call your taskbar into action, simply run your mouse pointer over the left edge of the screen. The taskbar then slides into view.

Finding Files When You Need Them

Microsoft gives you more ways to locate a file than you can possibly imagine. In the sections that follow, we'll explore a variety of tools and techniques you can use to find what you need so that you can spend your valuable time doing something more important than hunting for documents. Of course, the success of many of these methods depends on how well you've employed the file-naming and folder management tips presented earlier. If everything's in order on your machine, you should be able to find what you need in no time.

Starting with the Start Menu

If you're looking for a file you've used recently but can't remember the name of it, you might want to try clicking the Windows Start button and then pointing to Documents. Your 15 most recently accessed files appear on the Documents list that slides into view. Just double-click an entry to launch the desired document along with its native application. If the document doesn't appear here, don't worry; you still have plenty of other strategies to try.

> **Tip: A slight variation on the theme.** In addition to looking in the Documents list, you might try launching the application that produced the needed document and then opening the File menu to see the most recently created or modified files for that application. Obviously, this strategy may not be useful for Word, in which you might produce dozens of documents a month. For Publisher, PowerPoint, or any of your less frequently used applications, however, you might be able to jump right to the document you're looking for. In Word 2000, you can even adjust the number of most recently used files that appear on the File menu by clicking Tools|Options, opening the General tab, and changing the value in the Recently Used File List box.

Using the Find Tool

Windows has another tool to help you locate files: Find. To begin using the Find tool (which is available in Windows 95, 98, and NT), click the Start button and choose Find from the menu. By default, the Name & Location tab of the Find: All Files dialog box shown in Figure 4.8 appears, but you actually can work with three tabs: the Name & Location tab, the Date tab, and the Advanced tab.

FIGURE 4.8
The Find tool helps you find anything on your computer.

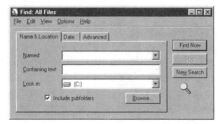

Searching by Name & Location

To begin using Find to search for a file by its name and location, do the following from within the dialog box shown in Figure 4.8:

1. If you know the name of the document you're looking for, enter it in the Named text box. You can narrow the search further by adding the file extension if you know it (for example, newsletter.pub).

2. Don't know the name of the document? You can have Find search the text of the documents instead. Just enter the terms you want to search on in the Containing Text field.

3. Tell the Find tool where to look using either the drop-down arrow or the Browse button. Just click your way to the desired folder or disk drive. If the selected folder has subfolders that you want searched as well, make sure that the Include Subfolders item is checked.

> **Tip: Give it some thought...** You might be tempted to search, say, your entire C: drive and its subfolders if you really have no clue as to the whereabouts of the document, but if you have an older machine (say a Pentium 133 or slower), you should think twice before doing so. Setting off such a broadscale search could take an eternity because the tool has to work its way through hundreds, if not thousands, of program files and such. Try focusing the search on a narrower area if possible, preferably a descriptive parent folder with a few subfolders.

4. Click Find Now to set the search in motion. Depending on the size of the area you want searched and whether the search is on a filename or document text, the search could take anywhere from a few seconds to several minutes.

5. The results of your search are returned (see Figure 4.9) with the following information displayed:

   • Name—The document's filename

   • In Folder—The location where the document is stored

   • Size—The document's size

   • Type—The name of the document's native application

FIGURE 4.9

The status bar at the bottom left of the Find results window tells you how many documents match your search.

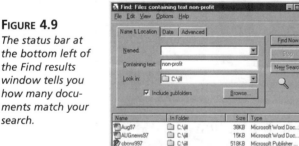

6. To open a document that appears on the list, double-click its name. The document then appears along with its native application.

7. If the search does not produce the results you need, click the New Search button and enter the desired search criteria.

Searching by Date

The Date tab of the Find tool (see Figure 4.10) can be extremely helpful in locating files created, modified, or accessed within certain date criteria.

FIGURE 4.10
If you want to locate a file that you worked on during a particular time frame, the Date tab could be the answer you've been looking for.

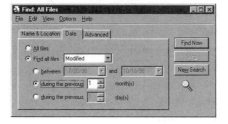

To begin using this tab for date-specific searches, do the following:

1. Launch the Find tool as directed in the preceding section, and then click the Date tab.

2. Click the Find All Files item, and then use the drop-down arrow next to it to tell Find whether you want to locate files that were Modified, Created, or Last Accessed on the date criteria you're about to provide.

3. Check one of the following three items to search on any of these date criteria:

   • Between Two Dates—Click the drop-down arrows next to each text box to reveal a calendar from which you can select the desired date.

   • During the Previous ___ Month(s)—Use the arrow buttons to move the number up or down as needed.

   • During the Previous ___ Day(s)—Click the arrow buttons to shift the date up or down.

4. Click the Find Now button after you've entered the information on which you want to search. The results then are displayed, as shown in Figure 4.9.

Tip: Mix it all up! You don't have to use each tab on its own. In fact, combining them can give you even more power and precision to find what you need quickly. To use all the tabs (or any combination of them), just fill in the necessary information in each tab, and then click Find Now.

Searching by Type with the Advanced Tab

Don't be intimidated by the name of Advanced tab in the Find tool. It's little more than a way to search by a file's type or size. Although you might find the capability to search by a certain file type handy, typical Office 2000 users don't search by size very often. If you know the file type's extension, you can include it in the Name box as described previously. That way, you needn't even bother with the Advanced tab.

Browsing for the Document

If you're working in the application in which the desired document was created, consider simply opening the Open dialog box (by choosing File|Open) and looking through the folders you think you may have placed it in. Don't overlook the default folder, either. You can easily forget to save a document in its place when you're snowed under at work.

Office 2000 gives you even more ways to track down the files you need. By simply changing the file views in any Open dialog box, you can gain access to a wealth of useful information. To change the file view, just click the View drop-down arrow, as shown in Figure 4.11, and make your selection.

> **Tip: Sample the goods.** When you're getting to know these file views, you might find it helpful to cycle through them one at a time to see just what they have to offer. The best way to sample the goods is to select a familiar document, click it to select it, and then click the View button to cycle through each view in turn. It won't take you long to discover some favorite views!

Browsing Through the List View

By default, the List view is the file view you see when you open an Office 2000 Open or Save As dialog box. The List view (see Figure 4.11) is a modest view, displaying only the file's name and the corresponding application icon. For computers housing a minimal number of files, this view is often all that's needed to find a document.

FIGURE 4.11

The List view is Office 2000's default file view.

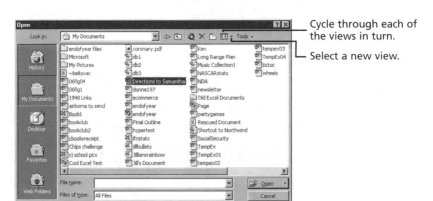

Cycle through each of the views in turn.

Select a new view.

Browsing Through the Details View

The Details view (see Figure 4.12) gives you access to a file's name, its size, its application type, and the date and time at which it was last modified. If you have two similarly named documents and need to track down the freshest one, this view can help. A file's respective application icon is also displayed at the beginning of its entry, so you can quickly look for the desired type of file.

FIGURE 4.12
The Details view can help you find the freshest copy of similar documents.

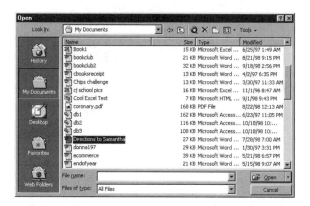

Browsing Through the Properties View

Still don't have enough information to find what you're looking for? Surely, the Properties view (see Figure 4.13) will have what you need. From the author of the document to the size of the document expressed in paragraphs and lines, it's all here. Using this view is a great way to browse your company's intranet for documents written by a certain person.

FIGURE 4.13
Learn all the vital statistics about a document using the Properties view.

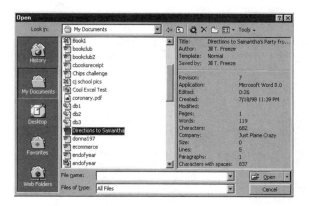

Caution: Hey, I didn't write that! Keep in mind that documents written by multiple people using the same computer may carry the same author name even if the same person didn't write them all. For example, interns sharing a machine at a local arts organization may author documents that all carry the name of a former intern who was on staff when the computer was set up. Or worse yet, if your new computer came with Office 2000 pre-installed, all your documents may be written by "Valued Gateway Customer." Unless someone takes the time to change this information, it may not be 100 percent reliable.

Another issue you may or may not be aware of is the title on the Summary tab of your document's properties. This title, by default, is generated from the first few words in the document, not from the filename as you might assume. What's more, when you save a file for the first time, the first few words of that version of the document are used for the title, no matter what subsequent changes you make to the leading text. Just think of the trouble and misunderstandings that naming convention could potentially cause! If you really want to be security conscious, your best bet is to enter the title manually by clicking File|Properties, opening the Summary tab, typing the desired title in the Title box, and then clicking OK.

Browsing Through the Preview View

Sometimes a file may look like it's the one you want, but you aren't sure it is the right one. Who wants to take the time to open each file one-by-one only to have to go back and close all the unwanted items? With the Preview view, you can click a file's name and see a small picture of the document, spreadsheet, or whatever in the preview window at the right side of the dialog box (see Figure 4.14). And just because you access the Preview view from within Word 2000 doesn't mean you can't see an Excel spreadsheet, for example. That's right. It doesn't matter which application you're working in; you can see any Office file from anywhere.

FIGURE 4.14
Using the Preview view, you can look at a file without even having to open it.

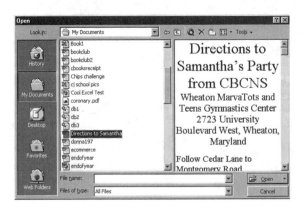

Using the Places Bar to Find the Documents You Need

Remember the Places Bar I pointed out earlier in the chapter when we were taking a look at the new Open and Save As dialog boxes? Well, here you can get a good look at its value and usefulness when you want to find things on your system.

As you may recall, five buttons down the left side of the screen make up the Places Bar. These buttons are History, My Documents, Desktop, Favorites, and Web Folders. Clicking the various buttons does the following:

- History—Clicking this button grants you access to between 20 and 50 of the documents you most recently worked on. In one document, Microsoft actually referred to this display as a "Most Recently Used (MRU) list on steroids" because it lets you see up to 10 times the number of entries you'll find in any application's MRU list. (You remember application MRU lists, the four or five documents you see listed at the bottom of a application's File menu, right?)

- My Documents—By default, this view comes up when you access an Open or Save As dialog box. Although it's useful if you tend to dump all your files in the default location, it's actually of minimal use for those who place their documents into specific folders or who have named a new default working folder, as discussed earlier in the chapter.

- Desktop—This button lets you move quickly to another hard drive on your system, to a public folder on your company's intranet, and so on. Unless you have multiple hard drives or your computer is hooked to a local area network (LAN) or other type of network, you might not find this button very helpful.

- Favorites—If you've specifically saved a document as a favorite, using this button is yet another way to track down that file. Note that you see your Web Favorites folders and sites listed here as well.

- Web Folders—Files that have been saved in special Web folders can be viewed with this button. Keep in mind, however, that only users who have Office Server Extension capabilities can make full use of these folders.

The Office 2000 File Search Tool

You should be aware that Office 2000 has its own tool with which you can search for files. Personally, I find the Windows Find tool much more user friendly. But should you discover Find does not fully meet your needs, and you decide to take a look at this tool, just open an Open or Save As dialog box inside any application. Click the drop-down arrow next to the Tools button, and select Find from the list. A Find dialog box like the one shown in Figure 4.15 appears.

FIGURE 4.15
Office 2000's Find
tool is a little
more powerful
than the Windows
Find tool.

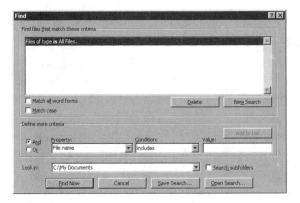

FIGURE 4.15
Office 2000's Find tool is a little more powerful than the Windows Find tool.

Although Office 2000's Find tool appears more intimidating on the surface than Find, it's even more powerful. For instance, you can search for documents by author, by company, by the date it was last printed...the list is seemingly endless. What's more, you can search on multiple criteria and even save the search in case you need to repeat it later.

Truly appreciating the extent of this tool's power may be hard without playing with it a bit first, so I invite you to open it and take a look around. To perform your own complex search, follow these general steps:

1. Open the Office 2000 search tool as described earlier.

2. All searches are expressed using the Property, Condition, and Value drop-down lists. Click the drop-down arrow next to each text box to make a selection, and then click the Add To List button. Notice that the proper syntax for the criteria you defined appears in the Find Files That Match These Criteria window.

3. Repeat step 2 as many times as necessary to narrow your search, clicking Add to List after each set of definitions.

> **Tip: When a Bill isn't a bill...**It doesn't happen very often, but occasionally you meet someone whose name is also a common noun. Consider the name *Bill*, for example. A search that is not case sensitive could return a huge number of documents, including billsdue.xls, Bill's Resume.doc, billdispute.doc, and so on. In cases in which a search value could potentially mean two very different things, you should make sure the Match Case box is checked.

4. After you've entered all your search criteria, use the Look In drop-down list to select a location for the tool to search. If that location has subfolders you want to search as well, you need to check the Search Subfolders box.

5. To save a complex search for later or repeated use, click the Save Search button, and give the search a descriptive name. (To use it later, you click the Open Search button.)

6. Click Find Now to set the search in motion.

On Your Own

Whew, this chapter definitely gave you a lot to consider. This information is a lot to digest at one time, but good file management practices combined with a thorough knowledge of the many file-finding techniques available can increase your productivity tenfold both on the job and at home.

Do yourself a favor, and take some time to explore these file-finding tools to see what they have to offer. Reading about them is one thing, but actually being able to go out and pluck a sought-after file from thousands is truly amazing.

And although I vowed not to make this book a "let's-show-the-reader-every-possible-way-to-do-this" kind of book, I thought the time was well spent on ways to find a file. Although the various search tools and file views may appear to overlap, you will find subtle differences in the way they operate and return results. One thing is certain: With the plethora of options out there, there's literally something for everyone. So what are you waiting for; go check them out!

Shared Applets and Tools Available in Office 2000

With all the new Web capabilities available in Office 2000, creating documents with visual appeal is more important than ever before. Whether you have a scanned photo of your corporate headquarters or some nifty-shaped text for a Web site, you can use it all thanks to the many shared applets and tools available in Office 2000. Table 5.1 shows a list of these applets and their functions.

Table 5.1 Applets and Tools Available in Office 2000

Applet/Tool	Purpose
Clip Gallery	Use this applet to insert clip art, sounds, and video into your documents.
AutoShapes	So what if you can't draw; let AutoShapes render the perfect shapes for you.
WordArt	Add pizzazz to your text with these unusual, easy-to-create effects.
Chart	Create professional-looking charts similar to those found in Excel from within Word 2000 or other Office 2000 applications.
Organization Chart	Illustrate your organization's hierarchy using this powerful, easy-to-use tool.

In addition to all the functions listed in Table 5.1, Office 2000 lets you insert a graphic file residing on your computer, a MIDI sequence, a freehand drawing, and so on.

Each of the elements produced by the tools described in this table is known as an *object*. Before we get into how to use each of these tools, let's take a look at some basic rules of thumb with regard to working with objects.

First, objects are generally confined to their own box—or *frame*—onscreen. You therefore can see their size and position in relation to any other objects or text you may have in the document. Objects are also generally easy to move and resize after you learn all the tips and tricks. You'll see just how easily you can manipulate them later in the chapter. And no matter what application you're working in, you can add one of the object types described in the table.

In the next few sections, you'll learn the specifics of creating each object type, and then we'll move on to a more general discussion about working with objects.

Working with the Clip Gallery

If you've used the Clip Gallery in past versions of Office (or in Publisher before it was included as part of Office), you're in for some pleasant surprises. In this latest version, the Gallery does not close the instant you insert a piece of clip art or other clip; it remains open, thus saving the location you clicked your way to. And if you think the default size of the Clip Gallery covers up too much of your document, you'll love the Change to Small Screen button shown in Figure 5.1. It turns the Clip Gallery into a compact little tool (see Figure 5.2) that you can move anywhere onscreen by clicking and dragging its title bar.

FIGURE 5.1
The new Clip Gallery can be large...

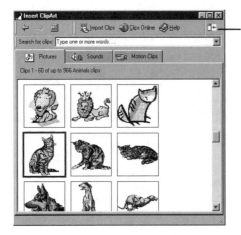

Click here to shrink the screen.

FIGURE 5.2
...or small.

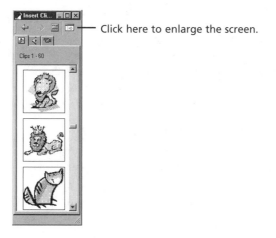

Click here to enlarge the screen.

In the sections that follow, you'll learn how to maximize your productivity by taking advantage of all the neat new Clip Gallery features.

Inserting Clip Art from the Clip Gallery

Although you can insert sound and video files with the Clip Gallery as well, let's focus on clip art for a moment. With the new Clip Gallery, you can insert clip art into your document in multiple ways. But first, you need to launch the tool. Do so by selecting Insert|Picture|Clip Art from an application's menu bar. Click your way through each of the categories until you find the image you want, and then do either of the following:

- Set the insertion point in the desired location in the document, and then click the desired image. Click the Insert Clip button at the top of the menu (Insert Clip appears when you click an image in the Clip Gallery).

- Click the desired image, and then drag it into place on the document.

> **Tip: To clip art or not to clip art...** Clip art does wonders for the look of a printed newsletter or other paper document, but it can come across as unprofessional on Web pages. For Web page design, consider using .gif or .jpeg images, WordArt objects for neat text effects, or any of the professional graphic arts tools such as PhotoShop. Unless you're artistically inclined, try to avoid freehand (or draw-it-yourself) objects at all costs. Bad art is often worse than no art at all. For a glimpse at including images on a Web page, turn to Chapter 12, "Building a Web Page with Word 2000."

Replacing One Clip Gallery Image with Another

It happens when I least expect it. I'm putting the finishing touches on a newsletter I edit, and then it happens—I see a piece of clip art in the gallery that I like even better than the one I used. Replacing it is a major pain in the neck, right? Not so, though I occasionally may need to do a bit of resizing after I make the swap. (You'll find more details about resizing and moving objects later in this chapter.)

To replace one Clip Gallery image with another, just follow these easy steps:

1. Double-click the image you want to replace to launch the Clip Gallery. Notice that the clips displayed by the Clip Gallery are similar in nature to the clip you clicked.

2. Click the desired image in the Clip Gallery, and then select Insert Clip from the pop-up menu that appears. The original image is replaced with the one you just chose from the gallery.

3. If the image you chose cannot be found on your machine, you are prompted to insert the necessary CD.

That's all there is to it. Just remember, some resizing may be necessary to help the image fit in better with your text or other objects.

Adding a Piece of Clip Art to the Gallery

With so much great clip art available around the Net, you're bound to stumble onto images you would like to include in your Clip Gallery. Sure, you could use the images in Office 2000 by inserting a picture from a file (by choosing Insert|Picture|From File), but wouldn't it be a whole lot easier to be able to access the images from the Clip Gallery with all your other clip art?

To add a piece of clip art, a sound file, or a video clip residing on your computer (or essentially any peripheral device you can hook up to your machine like a CD, a floppy, or a ZIP drive) to the Clip Gallery, just do the following:

1. Launch the Clip Gallery from within any Office 2000 application.

2. Click the Import Clips button at the top of the Clip Gallery window. The Add Clip to Clip Gallery dialog box shown in Figure 5.3 appears.

Figure 5.3

Use this dialog box to click your way to the desired piece of clip art.

3. Browse your computer and its peripherals until you find the name of the file you want to import to the Clip Gallery. When you see the file's name onscreen, click it once. Clicking it places the file's name in the File Name text box.

4. You need to decide how you want the file dealt with. By default, the Clip Gallery makes a second copy of the clip and keeps it in the default Clip Gallery file directory. You have other options as well. You can move the file from its current location to the Clip Gallery, thus extracting the file from its original source, or you can tell Clip Gallery to locate the file wherever it is stored. Make your selection by clicking the appropriate option button.

> **Caution: Now you see it, now you don't!** Use extreme caution when exercising either of the alternative clip import options. If you move the file from a Web folder to the Clip Gallery, the image won't be available the next time you update your Web page. And if you tell Clip Gallery to access it from its current location, well, that's fine if the item resides on your hard drive, but what if it's on a floppy or ZIP drive? In the vast majority of cases, the default option is your best bet.

5. Click the Import button to set the process in motion.

6. After a few seconds, the Clip Properties dialog box shown in Figure 5.4 appears. In the Description tab, you are asked to enter a word or phrase that best describes the clip. This description can be anything you think will jog your memory if needed. Notice that a preview of the clip appears in the top-right corner of the dialog box in case you can't remember the clip specifically by name.

FIGURE 5.4
Give yourself some clues as to the contents of the clip.

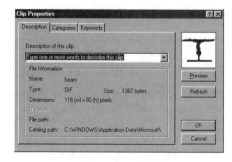

7. Click the Categories tab. You then see a list of all the Clip Gallery categories with check boxes next to them. Click the category or categories you feel the clip best fits into.

Tip: Pigeon-holing clips... Although you can create your own category by clicking the New Category button, I wouldn't bother unless you plan to have a large number of specialized clips in that same category. If you're making the new category simply because you think it'll make the clip easier to find when you need it, you now have the option to save clips as Favorites, which can make a big difference. To add a Clip Gallery clip to your Favorites list, launch Clip Gallery, click the image you want to include, click the Add Clip to Favorites or Other Category button on the pop-up menu, and then click the Add button. This way, the clip will always be within easy reach.

8. If you want to be able to search for a clip using a keyword, click the Keyword tab, and then click the New Keyword button. You are asked to type the keyword into a special text box, and then click OK to add it to the list. Deleting a keyword is as simple as clicking it to select it and then clicking the Remove Keyword button.

9. After you've filled out all the tabs, click the OK button to perform the clip import. The newly added clip appears on a screen by itself.

10. To verify that the clip has been successfully imported to the categories you specified, click the All Categories button (third from the left) at the top of the Clip Gallery window, and then select one of the categories you chose for the clip. If all went well, you should see the clip you just added displayed alongside the rest of the items in the category.

Adding to Your Clip Gallery from Microsoft's Web Site

Doing a special document with a holiday theme and have pretty much exhausted your choices in the Clip Gallery? Try going to Microsoft's Clip Gallery Live Web site. There you can often find a host of new clips in a variety of categories, including ones dedicated to upcoming holidays.

Note: You can do it either way, but be prepared. It's true that you can save the Clip Gallery Live Web page as a Favorite so that you can easily visit later from your Web browser, but doing so poses some distinct drawbacks. When you access the site from within the Clip Gallery, clips are effortlessly imported to the gallery. If you visit the Clip Gallery Live Web site from your browser (or save the clip to disk instead of just opening it), you need to go through all the import clip steps presented earlier as well.

To visit Microsoft's site and add an image to your Clip Gallery, follow these steps (you'll learn how to add multiple images in a separate set of steps):

1. With a live connection to the Internet and the Clip Gallery window open, click the Clips Online button. A message box appears saying that if you have access to the Web, click OK to go to Microsoft's site. Any clips you select there will automatically be added to your Clip Gallery.

2. Within moments after you click OK, Internet Explorer 5 launches and takes you to the Microsoft Clip Gallery Live EULA (End User Licensing Agreement). After you've scanned the agreement, click Accept if you agree to the terms.

3. You then go to the opening page of Clip Gallery Live. From here, you can jump to the desired items in a number of ways:

    - Select a tab at the top-left edge of the page to jump to clip art.

    - Perform a keyword search by typing the desired term into the text box provided and then clicking the Go button.

    - Use the drop-down arrow next to the Category text box to select from the list Microsoft provides. Note that you need not do anything more than select the desired category to be transported to the new location. The chosen category's Web page loads automatically.

    - Each time you visit the Clip Gallery Live site, you'll see some links to featured clips. Most likely, one of the items will be a link to new clips. The other links may take you to unique categories such as Storefronts, Vintage Fashion, or Halloween.

4. After you've reached the desired page, a number of clip images are displayed. Move to the next set of clips or the previous set of clips using the navigation buttons provided at the top of the clip previews. Under each clip are three bits of information: the size of the clip, a button you can click to download the desired clip instantly, or a check box you can use to gather all the clips you want (see Figure 5.5).

5. To download the file on the spot, click its download icon. A download status box quickly flashes onscreen as the file is downloaded. When the download is complete, the newly downloaded clip appears in the Downloaded Clips section of your local Clip Gallery. You can resume this set of steps with step 9. If, however, you want to download a group of images at one time, place a check mark next to any clips you want to download. Notice that the number of items in the Selection Basket display (the top-right corner of the page) increases by the number of check marks you place.

6. To begin downloading the items in your basket, click the Selection Basket link. A Web page displaying the clips you've selected appears. This is your last chance to delete an unwanted clip from the download by removing its check mark.

Click here to download the clip immediately.

Click here to store the clip in your Selection Basket.

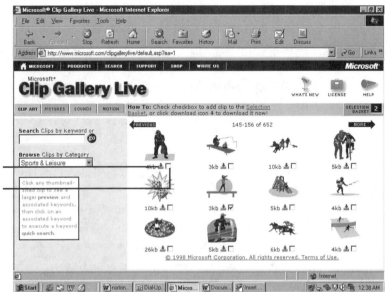

7. When you're satisfied with the images that appear, click the Download link, as shown in Figure 5.6.

Click here to begin download-ing the clips.

The Selection Basket

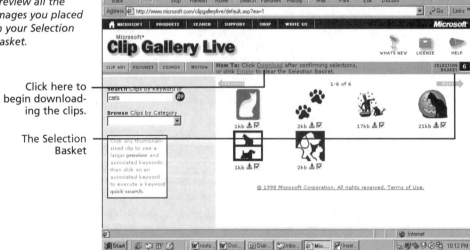

8. You then see a Web page describing the download process. It also tells you how large the group download is and gives you an estimate of how much time it'll take to download. Click the Download Now! link to get started. The usual Download dialog box appears with its status bar. When the download is complete, you might need to click the Close button to close the dialog box.

9. You then go back to the Clip Gallery Live Web page, where you can resume your clip gathering. For the sake of these steps, return to your local Clip Gallery window. Verify that you're in the All Categories view, and then look for the Download Clips category. Click it to see previews of clips you've downloaded from Microsoft's site.

10. Right-click a clip, and select Properties from the shortcut list to define its properties, as described in the "Adding a Piece of Clip Art to the Gallery" section earlier in the chapter.

> **Tip: How badly do you need properties?** Technically, you really don't need to define the properties if you're in a hurry. You can easily get to the clips by clicking the Download Clips category in your Clip Gallery. But what happens when you have a couple hundred clips in that download list? If you have as many as a couple dozen clips in the category, you might still be fine, but a larger number may quickly start eating into your work time as you take extra time to browse the list. At that point, you should strongly consider defining the properties so that you can search for the clip by keyword, or at least find it in a logical category.

Creating Flowcharts and Callouts with AutoShapes

Who has time to explore every nook and cranny of Office 2000 between all the meetings, reports to write, and so on? Given that, you might be wondering what in the world a person does with AutoShapes besides draw perfect circles and squares in a document.

Well, two functions buried within AutoShapes could be extremely useful to the busy professional. Not only do they add another level of functionality to Office 2000, but they can give your documents and presentations that extra bit of professionalism as well. Even though I don't have expensive project management software on my machine, I was able to produce a terrific flowchart to outline a plan of action for my workgroup. And then there was the time I used callouts in an Excel spreadsheet to highlight a particular statistic. Are you interested in learning how to incorporate these elements in your work as well? Read on to find out how to make your own flowcharts and callouts using AutoShapes.

Building Your Own Flowchart with AutoShapes

With a little bit of patience and some know-how about how flowcharts work, you can create a stellar flowchart similar to the ones you can design with expensive specialty software packages. Figure 5.7 illustrates a very simple flowchart.

FIGURE 5.7

Produce quick-and-cheap flow-charts like the one shown here, or go for the gusto and add color, special fonts...the works!

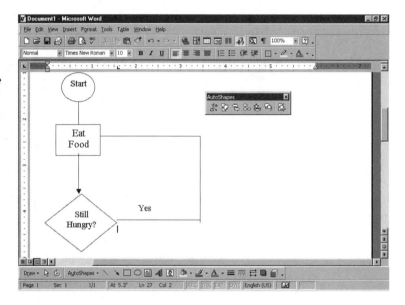

To begin creating your flowchart, do the following:

1. Launch the application in which you want to create the flowchart. Use Word 2000 if you plan to print the flowchart on paper or include it as part of a report. Use PowerPoint 2000 if you want to use it as part of a presentation (slides, overhead transparencies, or live Net meetings).

2. Click Insert|Picture|AutoShapes to launch the AutoShapes toolbar shown in Figure 5.8.

3. To begin constructing the flowchart, click the Flowchart button on the AutoShapes toolbar, and then select the desired shape from the resulting menu.

> **Note: You can take it with you!** Rather than watch the various AutoShapes menus pop in and out of view, you'll be relieved to know that all the AutoShapes menus are tear-off menus. That means when the menu opens, you can click the bar across the top (it resembles a title bar) and then drag it into position where it will stay anchored until you deliberately close it.

FIGURE **5.8**

Using this toolbar, you can begin creating flowcharts and callouts.

 — Click here to begin adding callouts.

Click here to begin making a flowchart.

4. After you've clicked the shape you want, the flowchart menu disappears. To place the shape, just click the desired location onscreen.

5. With the object in place, you can add text to the object. To do so, right-click inside the object, and select Add Text from the shortcut menu. The insertion point blinks inside the object, prompting you to enter the text. Note that you can style, color, and size object text in the same ways you can alter text in general.

6. Connect the various AutoShapes objects with lines or arrows to illustrate the flow of the elements. To add these elements, click the AutoShapes Lines button at the left end of the AutoShapes toolbar. A menu much like the flowchart menu appears. Select the line or arrow style you want to use, and then click the location in which you would like to initiate the line or arrow. While you're holding down the left mouse button, drag the line to the desired endpoint and then release the button. You can move your newly created line just like any other object, as you'll learn later in the chapter.

7. Repeat the preceding steps as necessary until your flowchart is complete.

> **Note: Hey, how'd you do that?** Near the end of the chapter in a section titled "Working with Objects," I'll show you all kinds of fun and useful things you can do with an object, such as turn it into a link to a supporting document or Web site, colorize it, or define how text surrounds it.

Applying Callouts to Your Documents

For those who aren't familiar with the term, a *callout* is a word or string of words that make reference to a specific object or other item on your document. Consider this book as an example. Callouts are used in Figure 5.8 to show you exactly where to click to complete a task. In comic strips, thought bubbles above a character's head can technically be referred to as callouts.

Consider using callouts to draw attention to a certain cell in an Excel spreadsheet (see Figure 5.9), or use them to add character to photos on a Web page. And how about accenting a certain PowerPoint element in a presentation?

To add a callout to an Office 2000 document, follow these simple steps:

1. Open or create the document in which you want to incorporate a callout.

2. Access the AutoShapes menu by clicking Insert|Picture|AutoShapes.

3. Click the Callout button, as shown back in Figure 5.8. Choose the style of callout you want from the resulting menu by clicking it.

FIGURE 5.9
With the AutoShapes Callout feature, you can create scenes like this.

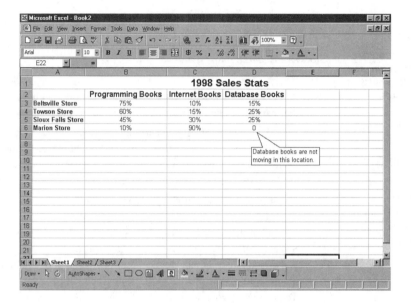

4. Click inside the document's workspace in the approximate location you want the callout to appear.

5. Add a message to your callout by clicking inside its text area and typing in text when you see the blinking insertion point. Note that you can format, color, style, and size the text just as you can any other text.

6. Because all callouts are created in a uniform size, the amount of text you typed (along with the size of the element that the callout is referring to) may warrant resizing the callout. To resize, click inside the callout, and drag any of the white sizing handles in the desired direction.

7. When you see the full callout onscreen, you might want and/or need to reposition it a bit. The first step is to get the callout's text area where you want it. Do so by clicking the center of the callout's text area. Eight sizing handles should appear in a box around the callout. Next, move the mouse pointer toward the edge of the callout's border until you see the familiar four-headed Move pointer. Click and drag the callout to the desired location.

> **Tip: Why can't I get the callout to point exactly where I want it?** When you move a callout in the manner described in the preceding steps, it may seem impossible to get the callout's *lead* (the tail or pointer of the bubble or box) where you want it in addition to proper placement of the callout itself. You can easily rectify this problem by placing the main part of the callout where you want it, as described earlier, and then clicking the lead until a tiny yellow box appears at the end of it. When you see the yellow box, click it and drag the lead to the desired position. The callout itself stays in the location you put it, thus giving you the best of both worlds with regards to callout placement.

Turning Words into Art with WordArt

WordArt attempts to do exactly as its name implies: turn words into art (see Figure 5.10). Although WordArt may not be the perfect substitute for a corporate logo, it can be a great way to perk up a Web page or PowerPoint presentation.

FIGURE 5.10
WordArt lets you go far beyond basic text manipulation.

And there's much more to WordArt than meets the eye. After you select an initial WordArt style, you can tweak its shape, its font style, and its size; you also can rotate it and align it. Playing with all the settings can get downright addictive when you're searching for that perfect look.

> **Caution: Too big for their britches...** You should be aware that some of the bigger, bolder WordArt text shapes can spill out of their boundaries, thus requiring you to reposition the box of the object in question.

To design your own work of WordArt, do the following:

1. Double-click to set the insertion point in the document in which you want to place your WordArt.

2. Click Insert|Picture|WordArt from within an Office 2000 application. The WordArt Gallery shown in Figure 5.11 appears.

FIGURE 5.11
Use this gallery to select your initial WordArt style.

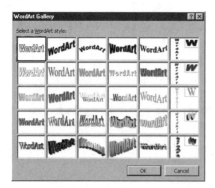

3. Select a WordArt style from the gallery by clicking it. Think of this selection as a starting point more than anything else, because you can alter the object in so many ways. Click OK after you've made your selection.

4. The Edit WordArt Text dialog box appears, prompting you to type in the desired text. Note that you can also select a font style and size at this time as well as specify that it appear in bold or italics. Click OK to save your selections. The piece of WordArt then appears in the location you specified. Note that a special WordArt toolbar (see Figure 5.12) also appears.

Tip: What's the point? If you have a hard time envisioning the size of your WordArt in terms of point size, consider resizing it (as shown previously) as opposed to selecting a font size at this stage. That way, you can save the time spent trying to guess the proper size out of thin air and put it to better use when you can actually see the WordArt in its final location.

FIGURE 5.12
You have all the powerful WordArt features at your fingertips with the WordArt toolbar.

1. Insert a new WordArt object.
2. Edit the text of the current WordArt object.
3. Revisit the WordArt Gallery.
4. Format your WordArt.
5. Change the shape of your WordArt.
6. Rotate WordArt text.
7. Define WordArt text wrapping attributes.
8. Vertically orient your WordArt.
9. Make all letters the same height.
10. Choose the alignment of WordArt text.
11. Specify the spacing between letters.

To resize the new WordArt object, click inside its boundaries, and then click and drag the white sizing handles in the desired direction. The text automatically resizes to fit the newly defined boundaries.

Repositioning the object is just as easy. Click it so the sizing handles appear, and then move your mouse pointer to the edge of the object until it turns into the four-headed Move pointer. Click and drag the object into position.

To change the WordArt text, simply click the Edit Text button on the WordArt toolbar. The familiar Edit WordArt Text dialog box appears, giving you the opportunity to not only change the text itself, but also to alter its font style. Remember to click OK to apply your changes.

Adding Dazzling Effects to Your WordArt

With a little bit of experimentation, you can turn standard WordArt text into something truly customized. Just take a look at what you can do with some of the advanced WordArt toolbar buttons:

- The WordArt Shape button—Click here to change the overall shape of your object. Make your selection by clicking one of the shapes on the resulting menu shown in Figure 5.13.

FIGURE 5.13
Click a shape to select it from the WordArt Shape menu.

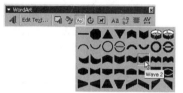

- The Free Rotate button—When you click this button, four green handles appear on the corners of the object's border. To rotate the object, click and drag one of the handles in the desired direction.

Tip: Don't like the change you just made? Remember, you can easily undo it one step at a time by pressing Ctrl+Z (or by clicking the Undo button on the application's Standard toolbar).

- The Text Wrapping button—Use this button to specify how you want the WordArt to interact with the text in the document. Text can form a box around the object, run through the object, and appear on the top and bottom of the object only, among other choices.

- The WordArt Same Letter Heights button—Clicking this button gives all the letters in the WordArt object a uniform height whether they're uppercase or lowercase. See Figure 5.14 for an example of how this object might look.

FIGURE 5.14
A before and after example of how the Same Letter Heights option affects text appearance.

- The WordArt Vertical Text button—Run your text down the side of a document using this button. Although this effect might seem neat at first, it's likely to cause some trouble from a readability standpoint.
- The WordArt Alignment button—Use the menu generated from this button to define the object's alignment. It works similarly to the text alignment found on the Standard toolbars of all Office 2000 applications.
- The WordArt Character Spacing button—This button lets you define how closely spaced WordArt characters are. Your choices range from Very Tight to Very Loose on a five-point continuum. In addition, you can tell WordArt whether you want the letters kerned.

Note: Kerning explained. If you're not familiar with the term *kerning*, don't worry; you're not alone. An oversimplification is that kerning enables the letters to fit together more precisely like puzzle pieces. The difference is very subtle in some instances but can add that extra touch of professionalism when it counts most.

Adding a Chart to Your Document

Whether you're writing a report in Word 2000, producing a newsletter in Publisher 2000, or creating a PowerPoint presentation, sometimes you can definitely communicate your point more effectively with a chart.

The Chart applet takes the rich functionality of Excel 2000 and brings it to just about any other Office 2000 application with minimal effort.

To insert a chart into your non-Excel document, just follow these simple steps:

1. Open the document into which you want to place the chart, and then click Insert|Picture|Chart. A work area like the one shown in Figure 5.15 appears.

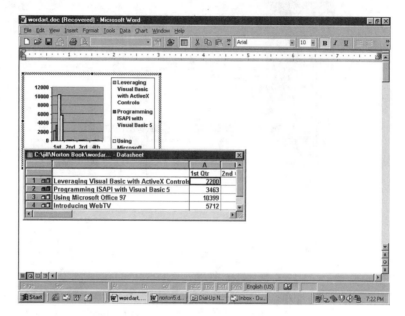

FIGURE 5.15

Work with an Excel-like environment, known as a datasheet, to create your chart no matter what Office 2000 application you're using.

2. To enter the names of the items you plan to track, double-click the cells immediately to the right of the row labels down the left side of the datasheet box. This action sets the insertion point in place so that you can begin typing the necessary text.

3. After you've entered the names of the items you want to measure, you need to label the columns to reflect the unit of measurement. The label may be a span of time such as a month or a quarter, or it may be something more specific such as a particular event. Double-click the cell that contains the words 1st Qtr so that you can type in your own label. Do so for as many columns as you need for your chart.

4. Fill in the data in the appropriate cell. As you do so, the chart that appears onscreen changes dynamically to reflect the information you've entered.

Tip: So big! If part of the text you typed is hidden beneath the column next to it, double-click the line between the column headers in the gray area at the top of the datasheet. The column automatically expands to fit the largest entry in the column to the left of the line you double-clicked. See the following illustration for clarification.

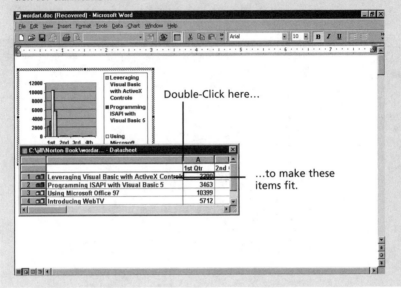

5. After you've filled in the datasheet, click the Close button at the top-right corner. You then see a full view of your newly created chart. From here, you can make a number of useful enhancements to the chart, including the following:

   - Changing the chart type
   - Repositioning the legend
   - Giving the chart a 3D view
   - Adding titles to your chart

Changing the Chart Type

If column charts don't appeal to you, or they simply fail to communicate the information in the best manner possible, you might want to consider changing the chart to a pie chart or another more appropriate type. To change the chart, you need to perform the following steps:

1. Right-click inside the Chart Area, and then select Chart Type from the shortcut menu. The Standard Types tab of the Chart Type dialog box shown in Figure 5.16 opens.

Caution: Chart Type isn't on my shortcut menu. Charts are kind of finicky objects. Rather than being made up of a single element like WordArt, they are made up of a number of elements layered upon one another. If you run your mouse pointer over a part of the chart and wait for the ScreenTip to appear, you see labels such as Legend, Walls, and Plot Area. To alter the chart type, you need to right-click inside the Plot or Chart Areas. The best way to ensure that you access one of these areas of the chart is to right-click near the chart's border. If all else fails, rest your mouse pointer over the various areas until you see the words Plot Area or Chart Area. After a couple of tries, you'll be an expert at finding the area on first sight.

FIGURE 5.16

Preview your data in the new chart type you select by clicking the Click and Hold to View Sample button.

Click here to preview.

2. Select a general chart type from the Chart Type list by clicking its name. A number of chart subtypes then appear in the right half of the window.

3. Click a chart subtype, if desired, and then preview it with the data you provided by clicking the Click and Hold to View Sample button.

4. If you want to turn the selected chart type into the default chart type, just click the Set as Default Chart button on the lower-left side of the screen.

5. When you're satisfied with the type of chart you chose, click OK to exit the dialog box.

Repositioning the Chart's Legend

Depending on where you place the chart in your document, you might need to relocate the legend to complement the layout. To reposition it, you need to do the following:

1. Right-click the Plot or Chart Area of the chart, and select Chart Options from the shortcut menu.

2. Open the Legend tab. Notice that a list of possible legend locations appears down the left side of the tab, and a preview of the selected orientation appears in the right half of the display. To choose an orientation, click its option button.

3. When you're satisfied with the legend's location, click OK to save your change. The Chart Options dialog box closes so that you can continue working.

Giving the Chart a 3D View

With the increased ease of publishing Office 2000 documents to the Web, creating documents with a strong visual impact has become more important than ever before. One way to achieve such an effect is to make use of less commonly used formatting options. If used sparingly and tastefully, they can give your work that extra finishing touch.

To apply the 3D effect to your chart, you first need to click inside the chart in the Plot or Chart Area, and select 3-D Effects from the shortcut menu. The dialog box shown in Figure 5.17 opens. Click the buttons as directed in the figure's callouts to achieve the desired effect.

FIGURE 5.17

You can easily preview your 3D effects before you apply them by checking out the dialog box's preview window.

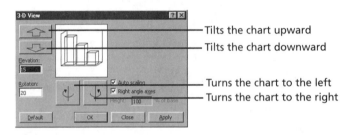

Tilts the chart upward
Tilts the chart downward

Turns the chart to the left
Turns the chart to the right

You can achieve the same effect by simply clicking a corner of the chart and dragging it, though many people find the exactness of a single mouse click (as described earlier) comforting.

When the chart looks exactly the way you want it to in the preview window, click Apply to save your selections, and then click OK to close the dialog box and continue working with the chart.

Placing Titles on Your Chart

If you really want to achieve the best in professionalism and clarity, you should label all the parts of your chart. Nothing's worse than looking at a chart without knowing what in the world you're looking at. Make it perfectly clear to your readers.

To label your charts, you need to access the Chart Options dialog box again via the shortcut menu and then open the Titles tab. There you are provided with a set of text boxes into which you can type the titles. As you enter each title, it appears in the preview window, so you can be certain of its placement. Click OK to save your titles with the chart.

Inserting an Organization Chart

Whether you have a plan to reorganize your corporation or a phone tree for your daughter's nursery school class, you'll find incredible value in having the Organization Chart applet around. And for smaller startup companies or nonprofit organizations with limited financial resources, it represents a fiscally responsible alternative to more pricey specialty charting applications. What's more, it's simple to use.

> **Note: Isn't using this Organization Chart tool similar to drawing a flowchart with AutoShapes?** In some respects it is, but they each have their place. The AutoShapes option lets you incorporate a variety or shapes (even computer networking shapes) in any imaginable configuration, but you have to do all the connections by hand. The Organization Chart tool, on the other hand, comes prepackaged with simple square boxes and automatic connectors (lines between the boxes), depending on the buttons you click. The flowchart is much more versatile, but the professionalism and speed of the organization chart can't be beat if your needs are simple.

To add an organization chart to your document, do the following:

1. Open the document into which you want to place the organization chart.
2. Click Insert|Picture|Organization Chart. The Organization Chart work screen shown in Figure 5.18 opens.

FIGURE 5.18

The Organization Chart workspace gives you a basic structure from which to start. Just click inside a box to begin inserting text.

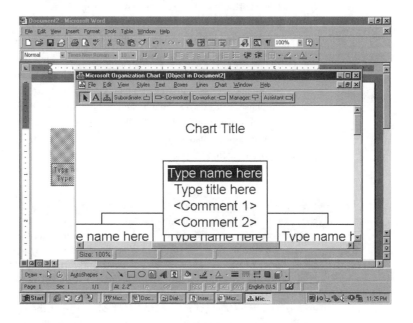

Note: Do it differently in Word 2000. For some odd reason, Microsoft made it a bit more difficult to find Organization Chart in Word 2000. Instead of using the menu commands presented in these steps, you need to click Insert|Object and then use the scrollbars to locate MS Organization Chart 2.0 on the list of possible objects. Double-click its name to close the dialog box and open the Organization Chart applet.

3. To begin inserting text into the structure provided, simply click inside one of the boxes and begin typing. Each box gives you up to four lines of text: one for the person's name, another for the person's title, and two for relevant comments about the person or position. Although the tool suggests content for each line, you needn't follow these suggestions to the letter. Insert as much or as little text as you need.

Tip: It's just not like that. If the default organizational structure does not meet your needs, open the applet's Style menu and choose one that's more suitable for your needs.

4. Add another member to the chart by clicking the applicable button on the Organization Chart toolbar. Notice that after you click the button, the mouse pointer takes the shape of the button you chose. To place the element on the organization chart, click the box to which you want the new element attached. The applet automatically draws the new element in its proper place and shifts the chart as necessary to maintain its readability.

5. Organization charts are unusual objects in that they have a lot more attributes you can change than other objects. Table 5.2 shows a list of changes you can make to the organization chart and how you can accomplish them while you're in the chart design phase. Before you make a change, however, you need to select a portion of the chart to change by clicking Edit|Select and then choosing the appropriate item. To make the change, you need to follow the steps in Table 5.2. Where you see a pop-up menu, all you have to do is make your selection. If you encounter a dialog box, you need to click OK each time to save your selections.

Tip: Go the extra mile; it'll show. Anybody can create a default organization chart, but if you really want to make the chart speak to your audience, consider using colors or borders to communicate additional information. For example, if you have a retail store that hires extra help for the holidays, you might want to show names of permanent staff in one color and temporary staff in another. That's just one idea; depending on your organization's structure, you might be able to think of even more valuable ways to boost the amount of information an organization chart communicates. And, of course, if the charts are used on the Web or in a PowerPoint presentation, these minor tweaks add visual appeal as well.

6. When you're happy with the chart, click the Close button to close the Organization Chart applet. The chart then appears in your document as defined. To edit these attributes later, just double-click the object, and the Organization Chart work screen reappears.

Table 5.2   A Busy Person's Guide to What's Hidden in All Those Organization Chart Menus

To Do This	Do This
Change text font/size	Click Text|Font, and then select the font, font style, and size using the lists provided.
Color text	Click Text|Color, and then click the desired color swatch.
Align chart text	Click Text, and then choose Left, Right, or Center.
Alter box appearance	Click the Boxes menu, and choose the item you want to change. You can define the box's color, its shadow effect, the color of its border, even whether the border is solid or dashed.
Change line attributes	Use the Line menu to thicken or narrow, color, or make dotted or dashed the lines that connect all the boxes.
Define chart's background color	Click Chart|Background Color, and then click the desired color box. Note that the organization chart is basically transparent, so any background you select for your document will serve as the chart's background as well unless you specifically choose a background color for the chart as described here. If you're using a theme or textured background, you might want to change the chart's background to a complementary solid color to make the object more readable.

Placing an Image on Your Computer in the Document

Perhaps you have an image of your corporate logo on your machine or server. Or maybe someone sent you a picture to include in your monthly newsletter. Whatever the case, you need to use the procedure to insert a picture from a file.

Before you have to decide how to insert the image into your document, you should also know that you can insert an image in multiple ways. You can embed it, link it, or paste it and link to the source file.

Although embedding (or *inserting* as Microsoft refers to the function) the file has the benefit of keeping the image file attached to the primary document, it has some drawbacks, too. For starters, the second copy of the image takes up extra space on your hard drive. And while that may not be a huge inconvenience to you, the fact that the original image could change and your document's image wouldn't, could be a problem, especially if that image came from a centralized logo file on your server.

If the original image may change, or if you need to conserve disk space, you might want to consider the other two options: You can define a link to the image, or you can insert it as well as link to it. Linking to the image means the image itself does not reside in the document's file, just a link to it does. You can still see the image in the document, and it prints normally as if the image were part of the file. Best of all, if the original image is ever changed, your document's image is current as well. The bad news is that if the image's file location is ever changed without your knowledge, or if the source file is being modified by someone when your document goes to access it, you're out of luck.

With the insert and link option, you can have the best of both worlds: Everything is stored in one place, but should the file change, the new version will appear in place of the old one in your document.

Now that you understand the pros and cons of each of these options, you can follow these steps to place an image in your document:

1. Set the insertion point in the location you want to place the picture.

2. Click Insert|Picture|From File to open the Insert Picture dialog box. This dialog box closely resembles a typical Open or Save As dialog box, except that it has a preview window on the right side of the box so that you can see the image before you insert it.

3. Browse your way to the desired file as you would to open a document. Click a file's name to see a preview of it.

4. When you've located the image you want to use, click the Insert drop-down button, and then choose Insert (also known as embedding), Link to File, or Insert and Link, as desired. An exact copy of the image is embedded into the document.

5. After you've selected your preference for inserting the picture (Insert, Link to Image, or Insert and Link to Image), the dialog box closes, and the image appears in the location you specified. You can size it and move it as explained in the last few sections of this chapter.

Inserting Pictures from Your Scanner or Digital Camera

You should also be aware that you can easily insert pictures you take with your digital camera or scan with your scanner the instant you produce them. Because all scanners and digital cameras are attached and configured differently, you need to consult the directions included with your device. But no matter what the instructions say, you need to click Insert|Picture|From Scanner or Camera to start the process from within the desired Office 2000 application.

Working with Objects

Throughout this chapter, you've learned dozens of ways to create and/or insert an object. But when these elements are in place, you can still can do a lot with them. You need to know how to move them, resize them, color them, and turn them into hyperlinks for a Web page.

The last few sections of this chapter are dedicated to manipulating objects so that you can get the kind of output you want.

Moving an Object

You should also be aware that not all objects used in Office 2000 behave in the same manner. Some, like WordArt, can be moved with a simple drag-and-drop procedure. You can identify drag-and-drop objects by the presence of eight little white handles around the object's perimeter.

Others, like Clip Gallery, Organization Chart, and Chart rely on the presence of text (or even simply a text alignment definition) in order to be positioned. These objects, called *inline objects*, display little black boxes in place of the white ones. You can position inline objects in one of two ways:

- If the object resides on its own line in a document, you can click it and align it just as you would text. In other words, you click the object and then click one of the text alignment buttons—Align Left, Center, or Align Right—in the Standard toolbar.

- If you want the object to work around text, you need to right-click it and then select Format Object from the shortcut menu. From there, you open the Layout tab. Notice that the In Line with Text option has been selected. If you select and apply an alternate selection, the chosen object can be dragged and dropped into place.

Caution: It's not moving! For a recently converted drag-and-drop object to move, it needs to have text in the document around it. It uses this text as a basis for its location; that's why the layout options are all expressed in terms of how the object interacts with text.

Resizing an Object

After you've inserted an object into the desired location, you might discover that it's larger or smaller than you had intended it to be. Don't panic; getting it just the right size is a snap.

Peter's Principle: It's the size that counts.

Objects can add tremendous value to your documents, both printed and electronic. Pay close attention to how the object will be used before you play with its size too much, though. Large objects can take an eternity to download when you're viewing them on the Web. On the other hand, if the object's content is meant to be read and comprehended (as in the case of an organization chart or a bar graph), then you should be certain the readers don't have to squint to see it.

The same holds true for printed documents. A huge, gaudy bar chart may cheapen an otherwise classy document when inserted amongst its text. When tastefully set off by a light border on its own, however, it can have an impact that's second to none.

To resize an object, click it to select it. Eight white handles surround the object. Move the mouse pointer over the handle you want to move until it turns into a double-headed Resize pointer, as shown in Figure 5.19. Click the handle, and drag it in toward the center of the object to shrink it or out toward the edge of the page to enlarge it. Remember to adjust the width as well as the height of the object so that it remains in proportion.

If the object is still a black-handled inline object, you need to resize it in a different manner. Right-click the inline object, and select Format Object from the shortcut menu. On the Size tab, you either can use the arrow buttons to tweak the size as expressed in actual measurements, or you can scale the object down proportionally from the default 100 percent value using those arrow buttons.

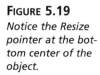

FIGURE 5.19
Notice the Resize pointer at the bottom center of the object.

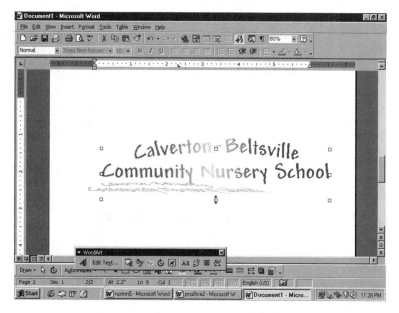

Coloring an Object

You can color the background of any object and its lines by using the Colors and Lines tab of the Format Objects dialog box. Just use the arrows, and select the desired color from the menu.

Looking Ahead

To learn more about all the rich fill effects you can apply as well, take a look at Chapter 9, "Creating Professional-Looking Documents with Word 2000."

Deleting an Object

Occasionally, you might even need to remove an object altogether to make room for more text or to make the document's layout more visually appealing. To delete an object, all you have to do is click it to select it, and then press the Delete key.

Turning an Object into a Hyperlink

Turning an object into a hyperlink is a neat trick worth considering. With this capability, you can enable readers to click a piece of WordArt, clip art, or other object, and be transported using any of the following options:

- Existing File or Web Page—This option leads the readers to a relevant Web site or to another document they can access on your company's intranet.

- Place in This Document—This option lets you take the readers to a specific section of the document you define. Again, the document must be made available to the readers either as a resident of a public folder or as a part of a Web site.

- Create New Document—When you're attempting to design a full-blown Web site, using this option is a quick and easy way to establish the links from the start.

- E-Mail Address—This option lets users click the specially defined object to launch their email program with the recipient's address already inserted in the To: line.

To turn an object into a hyperlink, follow these steps:

1. Right-click an object, and select Hyperlink from the shortcut menu. A dialog box like the one shown in Figure 5.20 appears.

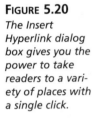

FIGURE 5.20

The Insert Hyperlink dialog box gives you the power to take readers to a variety of places with a single click.

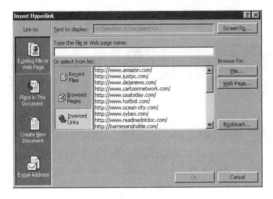

2. Click any of the four buttons described earlier. Depending on which one you choose, you are asked to provide various bits of information.

Looking Ahead

In Chapter 7, "Maximizing Word 2000," you'll get thoroughly acquainted with hyperlinking and all its related concepts.

---

3. Before clicking OK, click the ScreenTip button. A dialog box then prompts you to enter the desired text. ScreenTips give readers valuable clues about a hyperlink's content before they even click it. By running the mouse pointer over the link, the readers can tell whether it's a link to an email address, a Web page, or another document on your intranet.

4. Click OK after you define the ScreenTip. The dialog box then closes, and the hyperlink will be functional as long as the specified resource is available.

On Your Own

When you're preoccupied with work, various projects, and family commitments, keeping up with all the hidden treasures found in Office 2000 is impossible. Although some of the features were present in previous versions of Office, they've taken on a whole new meaning and level of importance now that the suite is so Web friendly. Combine that with the ever-shrinking cost of color printers, and you can finally see a purpose for using all that color and texture Microsoft has buried deep within the applications.

Think about the various projects you're working on. How can some of the attention-grabbing objects presented in this chapter be incorporated? Which tool or tools would help you most? Keeping these points in mind, select just one instance that could benefit from a well-placed object. After you've opened the best tool to produce that object, challenge yourself to communicate as much information as possible in that single object. Consider color-coding material, emphasizing certain aspects with differing borders, whatever seems appropriate given the situation. You might be surprised just how much information can be conveyed in so little space.

Internet Explorer 5.0 Quick Course

If you followed any of the press pertaining to this latest release of Internet Explorer, you may have heard it referred to as "a release geared primarily to the developer." Although it indeed has a lot of hidden improvements (at least from the user's standpoint), it also has some terrific new features that will make using it a pleasure. If you want to make the most out of Office 2000's new Web capabilities, Internet Explorer is a must-have as well.

In this chapter, you'll get a rundown of all the best new Internet Explorer 5 features and will learn how to use them.

Seeing the Sites

Internet Explorer 5 offers more ways to jump to a Web site than ever before (see Figure 6.1). The methods include any of the following:

- Type the URL into the Address Bar, and then press Enter (or click the Go button at the right end of the Address Bar).
- Click the Favorites menu item, and select a site from the pull-down menu of previously saved Favorites.
- Use the Favorites button to open a Favorites window on the left side of the browsing area. That way, you can hop from Favorite to Favorite without having to reopen menus.
- The drop-down arrow button to the right of the Address Bar opens a list of recently visited URLs. Just double-click one to pay a visit.
- The History button takes you back in time to sites you've visited over the past 20 days. I'll give you more details on how to work with this feature later in the chapter.
- After you've browsed several pages in the current Internet Explorer 5 session, you can click the drop-down arrow next to the Back button to jump back to one of the nine most recently visited sites.

- Click the Back button to browse back through recently visited Web pages one at a time.
- If you've used the Back button to return to other pages, you can use the drop-down arrow next to the Forward button to skip ahead to any of up to nine pages you visited in the current session.

Figure 6.1

Move to a Web page by using menu items, buttons, drop-down arrows, or the Address Bar.

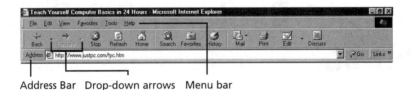

Address Bar   Drop-down arrows   Menu bar

Revisiting History with the History Button

Have you ever read something that you wanted to go back and find at a later date only to discover you couldn't remember where you read it? It happens more frequently than you might think. Maybe you're searching for a supporting statistic for your latest report. You see something that kind of works, but you continue to look for something better. A couple of days later, you decide to settle for the statistic you found earlier, but you didn't save the Web page as a Favorite. What do you do now?

Thanks to the History button, you're not out of luck. If you can remember the approximate date you visited the site, you stand a fair shot of finding it again. Just click the History button on the Standard toolbar, click the link that best corresponds to the suspected date (see Figure 6.2), and then glance through the list of sites until you locate a URL that looks familiar. This procedure may take a couple of tries, but you'll find that site eventually.

If you don't have time for a leisurely stroll down memory lane, then you'll love the View drop-down arrow in the upper-left corner of the History pane. Just click it and point to any of the following special views to help find that mystery page:

- By Date
- By Site
- By Most Visited
- By Order Visited Today

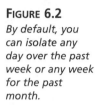

FIGURE 6.2
By default, you can isolate any day over the past week or any week for the past month.

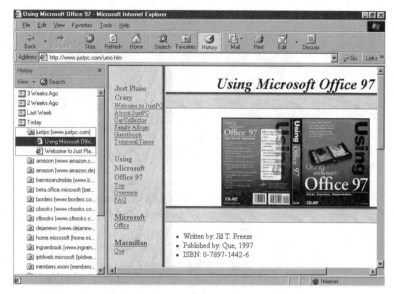

You can also search the History links by clicking the History pane's Search button or by selecting Search from the bottom of the View drop-down menu. Just type a word or words, and Internet Explorer 5 goes back in time to try to retrieve what you're looking for.

Getting out of History mode is a snap: Just click the History button on the Standard toolbar a second time, or click the X in the upper-right corner of the History frame. Your Internet Explorer 5 viewing area returns to its full size.

An Improved Way of Organizing Favorite Web Sites

When you've found a Web page worth revisiting, you'll want to file it in an easy-to-find location by right-clicking the page while it's onscreen and selecting Save As Favorite from the shortcut menu. These favorite Web sites are then stored in their own menu, the Favorites menu, located on the Internet Explorer menu bar.

The latest version of Internet Explorer gives you increased Favorites management capabilities. You can even exchange your Favorites lists with others.

Multiple steps are involved in organizing your Favorites, as you can see here:

1. With Internet Explorer up and running, click Favorites|Organize Favorites. The Organize Favorites dialog box pictured in Figure 6.3 opens.

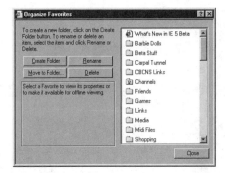

FIGURE 6.3

Using the Organize Favorites dialog box, you can quickly and easily keep your favorite Web sites in order.

2. The first thing you need to do is create some folders in which to store your favorite Web sites. Try to place your Favorites into specific categories such as Office 2000, Visual Basic, Project Research, Job Hunting, or whatever. Also keep in mind that you can nest folders. So underneath the Office 2000 folder, you might have subfolders for Word 2000 or Excel 2000, for example. When you have some good folder names in mind, click the Create Folder button. To create a nested sub-folder, just click the folder under which you want to place the new folder, and then click Create Folder.

> **Note: What is stored in these folders anyway?** Although it's true that you can save entire Web pages for viewing offline, they are not what's kept in the folders described here. These folders merely contain shortcuts—or simply URLs—to the various Web pages. Therefore, the sizes of your Favorites files are kept to a minimum.

3. A new folder appears at the bottom of the screen (or in the location you specified if it's a nested folder). Its blue highlights prompt you to enter a name for it. Type the chosen name, and then click Enter. The folder is then created.

4. Repeat the process until all your favorite Web pages have logical homes to move into.

5. Now comes the fun part—moving the pages to their new homes. Click the first link in your list of Favorites.

6. Click the Move to Folder button to bring up the Browse for Folder dialog box, as shown in Figure 6.4.

7. Click the folder to which you want to move the selected page, and then click OK.

8. The selected item appears in its new folder. Repeat the process of selecting a link and moving it until all the links have a home.

Figure 6.4

This dialog box displays each of the new folders you created.

9. To see which pages are located within a folder, click the folder name once. The page titles appear underneath their defined folder. Click the folder again to "hide" the pages.

10. From now on, you'll be able to access your favorite Web sites by looking in the appropriate folder off the Favorites menu.

Now you have a neat and tidy list of Favorites that's easy to navigate and easy to share with others, as you'll see a little later.

Browsing Web Pages Offline

Not every business has a full-time, high-speed connection to the Internet. In fact, most don't. But just because you don't have access to the Internet anytime you want and need it doesn't mean you have to do without the wealth of resources on the Net. Thanks to Internet Explorer 5's sophisticated offline browsing capabilities, you can schedule your favorite Web pages for downloading in the middle of the night (or during your lunch hour for that matter). That way, you don't have to tie up your small business's phone line during the day or arm wrestle a coworker for a single link to the Internet.

> **Caution: Look before you leap!** These offline features can be amazingly valuable, but you should know up front that they can suck up disk space faster than you can possibly imagine. Remember, the majority of Web pages out there today are very graphic intensive, so even a handful of offline sites could potentially cause a hardship on system resources. Before you begin the process of making pages available offline, take the time to find out how much disk space you have available, and then proceed with caution.

Before you get too far into the world of offline browsing, you should have a firm understanding of the methods of synchronization. When it comes to synchronizing items for viewing offline, you essentially have two options: manual synchronization and automatic—or scheduled—synchronization.

Manual synchronization basically means you download all the specified pages at once on demand with a single click of the mouse. It's also the best way to pick and choose the sites you want to synchronize from your list of offline Favorites. This solution works best for those who don't have full-time access to a phone line.

Automatic synchronizations are great when your computer is always attached to a phone line because it can autodial a connection to the Internet and perform the synchronization without human intervention.

In the next few sections of the chapter, you'll learn how to ready a Web page for offline browsing as well as schedule an automatic synchronization of your chosen offline pages.

Saving a New Favorite and Making It Available Offline

For Web pages not currently saved as Favorites on your system, you need to follow these steps to make them available offline:

1. With the desired Web page onscreen, right-click inside the page's viewing area to open the shortcut menu, and then select Add to Favorites to open the Add Favorite dialog box.

2. Place a check mark in the Make Available Offline box, as shown in Figure 6.5.

FIGURE 6.5
One click is all it takes to make a page available offline.

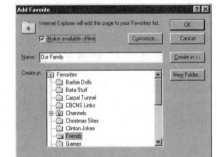

3. If you want the page to have scheduled automatic updates, click the Customize button to launch the Offline Favorite Wizard. Using the wizard is the easiest way to schedule an automatic synchronization, so it's worth considering. Even if you need to perform manual synchronizations, the wizard can be immensely helpful in working with multiple password-protected sites. (Refer to the Peter's Principle later in this section for a detailed explanation.)

4. On the welcome screen, you can place a check mark in the check box to keep the wizard from displaying its introduction screen each time you use it. Click Next to continue.

5. The next screen reiterates the page you've selected to make available offline and asks whether you want to save any of the pages that may be linked to the selected page. Unless you have disk space to burn, you may want to say No. Click Next to move to the next step.

6. You must now decide how and when you want the page synchronized. Choose the first option when you want to synchronize on demand only (manual synchronization). The second option lets you totally control the times of your automatic synchronization. Click Next to proceed.

> **Note: Your options increase.** If you've used this procedure to make a schedule before, you see three options instead of two in the dialog box because Internet Explorer 5 lets you lump the current site's schedule in with one defined at an earlier date. That way, your computer isn't constantly trying to perform synchronizations at various times.

7. If you opt to create your own schedule, you are led through the screen shown in Figure 6.6. Use the drop-down arrows to select the frequency and time for the synchronization, and then type a name for the schedule before clicking Next.

FIGURE 6.6

Define the frequency and time for your schedule, and give it a name.

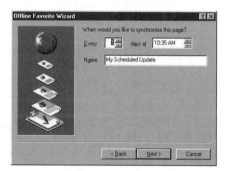

> **Note: Deja vu.** This wizard's primary function is to make a Web page available offline and save any necessary passwords that might be needed to access it. Although you can make a schedule for an automatic synchronization from here, the computer has to be connected to the Internet at the time of synchronization. In the "Surfing While You Sleep" section later in the chapter, you'll not only learn how to tell your computer to dial up for the synchronization, but you'll also discover how to set a lot of powerful options as well how to suppress a synchronization while you're working.

8. If you've created a schedule, you are taken directly to a screen that asks whether a username and password are required to retrieve the site. After you enter the user ID and password, click Finish.

9. Click the folder in which you want to store the Favorite, and then click OK to complete the request. Internet Explorer 5 performs its first synchronization on the spot, so you have a fresh version of the chosen page on your local machine. The Synchronization box appears to keep you apprised of the status of the synchronization.

Peter's Principle: Why work through the Offline Favorite Wizard if you want to do manual synchronizations?

It's true that you can select a page to be manually synchronized by simply checking its Make Available Offline check box, but if that page is password-protected, the Offline Favorite Wizard can remember it for you so that you don't have to manually enter it after each manual synchronization.

If you work with a lot of secure sites, the wizard will save you time in the long run and will be a lot less distracting, too, because each site won't have to prompt you for a user ID and password. A potential security risk does exist here, however. When that secure page is on your machine, anyone who has access to your machine can browse to it. Only you know how much of a security threat really exists in your particular work environment.

And remember, not all sites that request user ID and password information present a potential security hazard. Some sites request this information to generate customized sites based on preferences you expressed previously. News sites and last-minute travel sites immediately come to mind.

Making an Old Favorite Available Offline

For sites you've already saved to your Favorites list, follow these steps to prepare them for offline viewing:

1. From Internet Explorer's File menu, select Organize Favorites. The Organize Favorites dialog box appears.

2. Click the title of the Web site you want to make available offline.

3. Click the Make Available Offline check box, and then click Close to complete the transaction.

Clicking the Close button prompts Internet Explorer to synchronize your offline Web sites so that you have the most current version available. This first time, synchronization takes place to store a copy of the page on your system. Internet Explorer later uses this information when a synchronization is attempted to determine whether it needs to download a fresh copy of the page.

Manually Synchronizing Your Offline Favorites

If you don't have a full-time connection to the Internet or are unwilling to spend lots of time configuring update schedules, you might find that manually synchronizing your chosen Web pages works best for you.

To get the most up-to-date copies of your selected Favorites, click the Internet Explorer Tools menu item, and select Synchronize. A window like the one shown in Figure 6.7 opens, enabling you to place a check mark next to the items you want to have synchronized. Select Synchronize or Close as desired. Be forewarned, however, that the synchronization process may take a bit longer than you anticipate. It doesn't interfere with your work, but you might notice a decrease in system performance if you happen to be using several applications at once. A status bar keeps you apprised of the situation and alerts you to any problems it encounters.

> **Tip: You get out of it what you put into it.** This statement may be another tired cliché, but it's applicable in this case. Manually synchronizing your files is useful in some ways because you can pick and choose what you want updated with minimal hassle, but for the ultimate in offline convenience, you should schedule regular updates to the selected pages.

When the job is done, the Synchronization window closes automatically if no changes are detected in the pages. If changes in one or more pages are detected in a group synchronization, a Synchronization Complete status window appears. A click of the Details button tells you whether any problems occurred with the download. And, if you look in the Results tab, you can see which pages are updated with new content.

Viewing Your Favorite Pages Offline

Okay, you know how to mark a page for offline viewing and how to synchronize it, but how in the world do you view it? Just follow these quick steps:

1. Without connecting to the Internet, launch Internet Explorer.
2. The dialog box shown in Figure 6.8 appears, asking whether you want to work offline. Click Work Offline.

FIGURE 6.7

*Check the items
you want to syn-
chronize.*

FIGURE 6.8

*Click Work Offline
to keep the
phone line free
while browsing
your offline
favorites.*

3. Click the Favorites menu item, and drag the mouse cursor down until you find the page you want to view. Sites made available offline appear in normal type, whereas others are displayed in grayed-out type. If you choose a site that is available offline, it loads as usual.

If you inadvertently choose a site that you've not configured to view offline, Internet Explorer displays the dialog box shown in Figure 6.9.

FIGURE 6.9

*Choose Connect
to have Internet
Explorer 5 down-
load the most cur-
rent content from
the site, or click
Stay Offline to
retry your request.*

Should you decide that you want to make the content that wasn't available offline available after all, establish a connection to the Internet, and then click Internet Explorer's File menu item and deselect the Work Offline option. You need to take steps to make the site available offline as described earlier in the chapter.

If you're certain you made the content available offline, then link up to the Internet, click Tools, and point to Synchronize. If the item in question appears on the resulting list, try accessing it again offline. If it doesn't, redefine its offline availability as described earlier.

Surfing While You Sleep (or Go Out to Lunch): The Ultimate in Offline Functionality

If you ever wished you could read your favorite Web pages without being tied down to an Internet connection, you'll love the following section. Just think, you can finally browse your offline favorites from your laptop no matter where you are! One small caveat, however. The procedure for getting the automatic retrievals set up initially may seem a bit overwhelming at first glance, but don't let it get the best of you; I'll take you step-by-step through the whole thing.

As long as your computer is running and its modem is physically linked to a phone line, you can tell Internet Explorer to fetch your offline pages anytime you want to.

Think about that for a minute. Just before you wake for a long day at the office, your computer can link up, download the latest news from *USA Today*, *The Wall Street Journal*, *NASCAR Online*, or wherever, and make it available to you the instant your feet hit the floor. And best of all, you don't need to keep the phone line busy or wait for the pages to download because the job's already been done.

Setting Up Automatic Page Updates

The following steps assume that you've already configured your connection to the Internet in Windows 98, and that at the time of the scheduled download, the computer is turned on with physical access to a phone line.

1. With Internet Explorer up and running, click the Favorites menu and select Organize Favorites. The familiar Organize Favorites dialog box appears. If the page hasn't been saved as a Favorite, you need to do so before proceeding with these steps.

2. Click the page you want to schedule for automatic download, and verify that the Make Available Offline check box is marked.

3. Click the Properties button to open the Web Document section of the Properties dialog box.

4. Click the Schedule tab to begin the setup.

5. Click the Using the Following Schedule(s) option button, as shown in Figure 6.10. If you want Internet Explorer to use a schedule you defined earlier using the Offline Favorite Wizard, just check that schedule's check box, and then click Apply and then OK. The selected site is updated according to the chosen schedule.

FIGURE 6.10
Define how you want to update your offline pages in the Schedule tab.

6. To create a new schedule, click the Add button. A tiny dialog box appears, prompting you to enter the desired frequency and time of the synchronization. You are also encouraged to name the schedule, though if you don't, it'll read something like My Scheduled Update 1, My Scheduled Update 2, and so on. Choose a frequency for downloading the page based on how often it's updated by its Webmaster. Every day would be the choice for news sites, but every 7 days or even every 31 days may be more than enough for some specialized collectibles site, for instance.

Caution: Single site synchronization. If your synchronization needs are fairly simple, meaning you have only one site you want to make available offline, you can work up through step 6, and then click Apply and OK and be done with it. If, however, you want to tell the computer to dial up a connection, keep it from performing a synchronization while you're working, or some other advanced option, you should define the new schedule and then go on to edit it.

7. To make changes to any of these schedules or fine-tune some of the settings, click the Edit button to open the chosen schedule's dialog box.

8. Enter a new name for the schedule, if you want, in the General tab, and then click the Synchronization Items tab.

9. The Synchronization Items tab (see Figure 6.11) is the place where you tell Internet Explorer what you want downloaded and how you want it done. The Choose a Network Connection text box displays the name of your primary dial-up connection. If you have more than one way to establish a connection to the Internet, use the drop-down arrow to select the one you want to perform the scheduled updates.

FIGURE 6.11

Using the Synchronization Items tab, you can get specific about what you want downloaded and how.

10. In a large window in the middle of the same dialog box is a list of sites you've requested to be made available offline. Check those you want to have updated according to the schedule you're defining.

11. At the bottom of the Synchronization Items tab is a single check box that asks whether you want the computer to connect to the Internet to perform the downloads even if you aren't already linked. Make sure this box is checked because this is the very thing that makes scheduled downloads so valuable—the fact that you don't have to be there to do them. Click the Schedule tab to continue.

12. The Schedule tab is the place where you specify the frequency and time of the updates. Using the Schedule Task box, you can tell Internet Explorer how often you want the updates to occur. You can choose any of the following frequencies:

    • Daily—This option is great for news-based sites such as CNN, local newspapers, and the like.

    • Weekly—Many television sites publish weekly spoilers/scoops, and some merchants post weekly specials.

- Monthly—This option is terrific for capturing those monthly online magazines.

- Once—What a great way to capture "a day in history" data on your child's birthday for his or her time capsule! Or if your corporation is making a major announcement, you might want to capture all the sites that you expect will publish articles about it.

Caution: Watch your step! If you decide to capture data this way each year on your child's birthday, be sure to open the update while you're offline; otherwise, the very data you want to preserve will be lost as Internet Explorer refreshes the page. When you open the page offline, be sure to save the entire Web page with a descriptive title so that you can find it when you want to.

- At System Startup—Boot your system and go grab a cup of coffee while Internet Explorer pulls all the pages you need to prepare for the meetings of the day.

- At Logon—This option is really only applicable to those working on a computer network. When you log on to the company's network, the pages are fetched for your review at a later time.

- When Idle—Why not download your list of Web sites while you're reading another Web site?

13. In the Start Time box, you can schedule the update during your lunch hour or in the middle of the night, whichever is most convenient. Just enter the time followed by AM or PM in the Start Time box. You can also click a section of the time (that is, the hour or the minutes) and use the arrow buttons to specify the desired time.

14. In the Schedule Task Daily box, tell Internet Explorer 5 how often you want the update to run. This information is most applicable for the last three options described in step 12. Click the Settings tab to continue tweaking the setup.

15. The Settings tab shown in Figure 6.12 is of more use to power users because it lets you define how much time your computer must be idle before the update begins, whether the update should be allowed to begin if your laptop is running on batteries, and so on.

Tip: Play it safe. One option you may very well want to adjust is the Stop the Scheduled Task after ___ Hours box. By default, Internet Explorer gives itself 72 hours to complete the task. If an error occurs somewhere along the way, your phone line could be unnecessarily tied up for hours until you go to your computer next. Give the download a more reasonable limit, say an hour or two depending on the amount of material you've scheduled to be downloaded.

FIGURE 6.12

Using the Settings tab isn't critical for the majority of scheduled downloads.

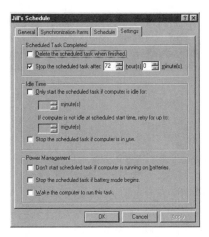

16. If you would rather not have your pages synchronized while you're using your computer, make sure the Stop the Scheduled Task If Computer Is in Use check box is checked. This option resides on the Settings tab as well. Although performing the synchronization doesn't hurt anything directly, it may slow down system performance. Depending on your work habits (and the speed of your machine), this reduced performance may or may not be noticeable.

17. Click OK after you've finished making your way through each of the tabs to return to the Schedule tab of the Properties dialog box.

18. Now for some finishing touches, click OK and then select the Download tab. This tab (see Figure 6.13) is the home of some pretty neat settings.

FIGURE 6.13

Have Internet Explorer 5 send you a note when an update to a page has been detected.

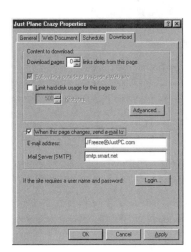

19. In the Content to Download Section of the tab, you can tell Internet Explorer how many links deep you want it to update. You can even include or exclude links that go to other sites. The default value is zero, which means only the page you saved as a Favorite is downloaded. You might want to increase that number depending on the site's design. Just do it with caution because such an update could easily take over your entire system.

> **Tip: Want the meat without the fat?** Click the Advanced button, and tell Internet Explorer to skip images, sound files, or other large Java or ActiveX controls. This way, you can speed up the download time while freeing up disk space.

20. If you're running tight on disk space, feel free to limit the amount of space these offline features can take up. Check the Limit Hard Disk Usage for This Page box on the Download tab, and then use the arrow buttons to tweak the amount of space allowed.

21. You can also request that Internet Explorer notify you by email when a downloaded page has changed. All you need to do is check the box saying you want such a message, and supply your email address and mail server name. When the page changes, you receive a note like the one in Figure 6.14 from Internet Explorer 5's Information Delivery Agent.

FIGURE 6.14
Internet Explorer 5's Information Delivery Agent can alert you to changes in a page.

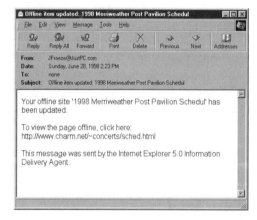

22. If the Web site requires a username and password, click the Login button at the bottom right of the Download tab, and type the username and password. Click OK when you're done.

23. Click Apply to save your settings, and then click OK to close the dialog box. Internet Explorer then performs the scheduled update at the time you specified.

Repeat the sequence of steps as needed until all your updated pages are scheduled to your liking.

Sharing Your Favorite Sites with Others

The capability to share Web sites and Favorites lists with others in a variety of ways is one of the most useful enhancements to the latest version of Internet Explorer. For the first time, you can effortlessly swap links with Netscape users and email Favorites folders of links to others sharing your interests. This capability even makes toting favorite links from work to home or vice versa a breeze.

With Internet Explorer, you can share your favorite Web sites with family, friends, and associates in the following ways:

- Emailing the link to the Web page
- Sending the entire Web page
- Exporting your entire Favorites list
- Exporting a single folder full of goodies
- Sending the page as an HTML file attachment
- Importing Favorites sent to you by others (or transferring your Favorites from work to your home machine)

We will cover each of these operations in detail in the sections that follow.

Emailing a Link to a Web Page

Follow these steps to send someone a link to one of your favorite sites:

1. While you're browsing the page you want to share, click File|Send|Link by E-mail. Internet Explorer launches Outlook 2000 or Outlook Express (depending on how your machine is configured) to assist with the task. The subject line is filled in with the Web page's title, and the link is already printed as part of the message.

Tip: Spell it out. Although Internet Explorer fills in the subject line of your message with the Web page's title, that bit of information can often be cryptic, especially if the Web page's author never defined a title. So unless you want the recipient to receive a message titled Default or something equally cryptic, you might want to manually change the Subject line.

2. Type the desired email address (or use the Address Book as described in Chapter 18, "Personal Information Management with Outlook 2000"), and then click Send. The recipient will receive a message similar to the one shown in Figure 6.15 (assuming he or she is using Outlook 2000).

FIGURE 6.15

The person receiving the link will see a message similar to this one in the mailbox.

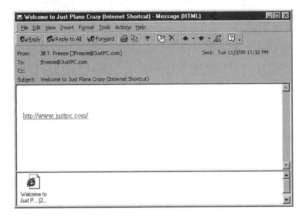

Emailing the Entire Web Page

Use the following steps to send the whole Web page to a recipient. Of course, before going to all the trouble, you should make sure the recipient can read HTML-formatted mail.

> **Caution: HTML or bust.** You should also note that for this feature to work, you must have your mail program set up to send messages in HTML as well. In Outlook 2000, you do so by clicking Tools|Options and then opening the Mail Format tab. Confirm that the Send Messages in This Format option is listed as HTML.

To send the Web page on, all you need to do is follow these steps:

1. Browse to the Web page you want to send.
2. Click File|Send|Page by E-Mail.

> **Caution: Why can't I send that?** Just because books, artwork, music, and so on are available free online doesn't mean they are copyright-free, therefore free for the taking. If you try to send a page of material that's password-protected or protected by some other measure, you might see a message that says you are unable to send the material. There is no workaround here; the prospective recipient either has to access the site himself or herself and register for a password, or settle for a summary of the information from you.

3. Internet Explorer launches Outlook 2000 or Outlook Express and gives you an opportunity to fill in the recipient's email address.

4. When everything's ready to go, click Send. Output similar to Figure 6.16 will be sent to the recipient's email account. Note that the recipient might need to maximize his or her email screen to see the page in its full glory.

FIGURE 6.16

Sending the entire Web page is one way to be sure the recipient checks out the page.

Exporting Your Favorites List

What if you change jobs and want to take your list of favorite professional-related Web sites with you? Or say you're getting a new computer and are handing your old one down to the kids. Wouldn't it be great if you could take your Favorites list with you? Follow these quick steps to get the job done:

1. From within Internet Explorer 5, click File|Import and Export. The Import/Export Wizard in Figure 6.17 appears. Click Next to begin.

FIGURE 6.17

The Import/Export Wizard is your starting point for exchanging Favorites.

> **Tip: Take it easy.** Maybe you don't want to share your entire Favorites list, but just a special folder or subfolder of interest to the recipient. You can do that by clicking the Choose Folder button and then double-clicking the name of the folder you want to export or share. Only that folder will be passed along.

2. Choose Export Favorites from the list of possible actions, and then click Next.

3. Choose the folder you want to export. Just click it, and then click Next. Note that you can export only one folder at a time.

4. The Export Favorites Destination screen gives you two options: to export your Internet Explorer 5 Favorites to another Web browser on your system (such as Netscape) or to save it to a file location by clicking the Browse button. When you've located the spot, give the file a descriptive, easy-to-remember name like Shopping or Cat Favs. Internet Explorer automatically saves it as an HTML file with an .htm file extension. After you've made your selection, click Next.

> **Tip: Where should I put this file?** If you plan to take the file to work, you might want to cut a disk containing the file, which means using the A: drive. If you're connected to a LAN or similar network, consider saving the file to one of the shared directories for easy retrieval. If you plan to email the file to yourself or somebody else, just tuck it away in an easy-to-remember spot on your C: drive.

5. The wizard displays a message saying that you've successfully completed the Import/Export Wizard. All you need to do is click Finish to complete the process. A small dialog box appears saying that the export is successful. Click OK to close the wizard.

To send your favorite sites via email, you need to launch Outlook 2000 or Outlook Express, begin composing a new message, and then click the paper clip icon and browse to the desired HTML file to attach it to the message.

Importing Those Favorite Links

If you're on the receiving end of a Favorites list passed on by email, you have to save the file attachment somewhere on your computer before you can perform the import.

Now it's time to get those imported Favorites where they belong—back on a computer. Follow these steps to import Favorites into another copy of Internet Explorer:

1. From Internet Explorer's File menu, select Import and Export. The Import/Export Wizard launches. Click Next to begin the process.

2. Select Import Favorites from the list of actions provided, and then click Next.

3. Browse to the location in which the Favorites list was saved. It may be your A: drive if you transported the list via disk or a location you specified when you retrieved the list from your mail server.

4. When you find the file, double-click its name, and then click the Next button.

5. At this point, you can specify a folder under which to nest the imported favorites by clicking it; otherwise, its own folder is created. Click Next to proceed.

6. A message appears saying you're about to complete the wizard. Click Finish to make it official. A small dialog box appears saying the import is executed. Click OK to acknowledge the dialog box and dismiss the wizard.

Note: But what about Netscape? As I mentioned, these HTML files can be imported into Netscape as well, but you need to consult the procedures in the help files of the target version of Netscape for the most up-to-date, step-by-step directions.

Searching the Web Using Internet Explorer 5's New Search Assistant

Searching for material on the Internet can be a really frustrating experience, especially when your boss needs to know the answer to a question fast, and you have no idea where to begin your search for the answer. If you've spent any time at all working with search engines, you've undoubtedly noticed how different they are. The same search string entered into multiple engines can produce wildly unpredictable results.

Although the folks at Microsoft can't decide which search engine is best for you, they can make it easier to call your preferred search engine into action. Follow these steps to try working with the new Search Assistant:

1. With Internet Explorer running and an active connection to the Internet, click the Search button on the Standard toolbar. The Search Assistant pane appears on the left side of the screen, as shown in Figure 6.18.

2. Click one of the five option buttons shown to specify the kind of search you want to perform.

3. Don't like the search engine you see listed underneath the Search text box? Click the Customize button. The page shown in Figure 6.19 appears, giving you a large selection from which to choose.

FIGURE 6.18
*The Search
Assistant pane
lets you search
while you surf.*

FIGURE 6.19
*Place a check
mark next to the
provider(s) you
want to use.
Don't forget to
scroll down the
page; you have a
lot of choices to
make for each
category.*

The Customize
button

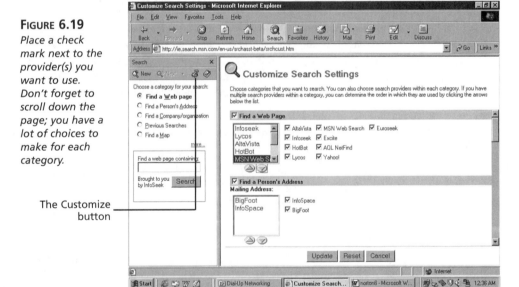

4. Place a check mark next to the search providers you want to use, and then click the Update button at the bottom of the screen.

Tip: Did you pick more than one provider? If you choose more than one provider in a given category, you can rank them in order by clicking a provider's name, and then using the up and down arrows underneath the list. That way, you can determine which provider is used first.

5. Enter your word or phrase in the text box, and click the Search button to perform the search as normal. The results appear in the Search Assistant pane, as shown in Figure 6.20.

FIGURE 6.20
Just click a link to view it in the main viewing window.

Search Assistant pane

6. To view a link, simply click it. The page is displayed in the main viewing window, as you can see in Figure 6.20.

7. When you want to switch to a new link, just click it. No more clicking the Back button 20 times in a single search to return to the search results page!

8. To try the next search provider in the order you've selected them, click the Next button at the top center of the Search Assistant pane. If you want to try the search in any of the other providers on your list, use the drop-down arrow from which you can select a search engine by name.

9. When you're finished with the search, simply click the Search button on the Standard toolbar again, or click the X in the upper-right corner of the Search Assistant pane. The Search Assistant pane then disappears, and your Internet Explorer screen returns to normal.

Express Searching: When Only the Fastest Will Do

Internet Explorer 5's new AutoSearch feature enables you to perform a search quickly from Internet Explorer's Address Bar. Say, for instance, you want to search on *Calico Cat*. In the Address Bar, you can type any of the following:

- ? calico cat
- go calico cat
- find calico cat

The links from which you can choose appear in the main viewing area of Internet Explorer.

> **Caution: There's always a downside.** Unfortunately, the new AutoSearch feature supports only one information provider—Yahoo!. Although Yahoo! is a great site, it doesn't have the breadth and depth of a traditional search engine. But then again, it doesn't have all the clutter either because humans, as opposed to machines, categorize each site.

Finding Things on a Web Page

Some Web documents can ramble on forever, which is why you should know how to perform a search within a specified Web page. Just follow these steps:

1. With the page you want to search displayed in Internet Explorer, click Edit/Find (on this page). The dialog box shown in Figure 6.21 appears.

> **Tip: A shortcut.** Instead of using the menu commands, you can press Ctrl+F to bring up the Find dialog box.

FIGURE 6.21

The Find dialog box helps you get where you want to go quickly.

2. Type the word or phrase you want to find on the current page.
3. Tell Internet Explorer whether you want it to look for a whole word match and whether you want it to match the case of the text you entered. Just place a check mark in the appropriate box(es).

4. Click the Find Next button to send Internet Explorer after the next occurrence of the word or phrase. You can even select the Up or Down button to tell Internet Explorer which way to go. (By the way, Down is the default search direction.)

5. When you're finished with the search, click the Close button at the top-right side of the Find dialog box, or click Cancel. Either action removes the box from the screen.

Adding a News Server to Outlook Express

For years, I've turned to newsgroups to discuss technical topics with other computer professionals, but now with tens of thousands of newsgroups out there on every conceivable topic (and some not so conceivable), everyone has the opportunity to discuss his or her passion. These text-based bulletin-board-style discussion forums may seem a bit out-of-date when you compare them to the glitz of the Web, but it's hard to top the dialogue!

For some odd reason, Microsoft decided to keep Outlook Express as its sole newsreader as opposed to making Outlook 2000 capable of browsing newsgroups. Luckily, the application comes tightly integrated with the Internet Explorer 5 suite of applications, so you don't have to go out of your way to find it. But not being able to read newsgroups and mail simultaneously is a real inconvenience, so much so that declaring Outlook Express as your primary email client may be worthwhile.

At any rate, if you plan to monitor or participate in newsgroups, you need to configure Outlook Express in such a way that it can find your news server. To do so, follow these steps:

1. Click the Outlook Express Tools menu, and select Accounts. The Internet Accounts dialog box appears (see Figure 6.22).

FIGURE 6.22
You can begin configuring your news server here.

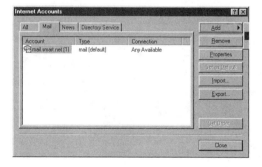

2. Click the Add button, and select News from the list. The Internet Connection Wizard launches.

3. The first screen asks you to enter your name as you want it to appear in the From field of your outgoing newsgroup posts. Type your name, and then click Next.

4. Providing your email address is the next step in the process. Click Next to continue.

5. You are asked to supply the name of your news server. Enter it, and then click Finish to complete the setup.

Tip: How do I find the name of my news server? Most Internet service providers have a standard naming scheme. Consider an ISP named Smart.net. The mail server is mail.smart.net, and the news server is news.smart.net. Try entering the word news followed by a period ahead of all the text after the @ sign in your email address. That should be a pretty darn good guess. If that trick doesn't work, consult your company's network administrator or your Internet service provider directly.

Subscribing to a Newsgroup

Before you can subscribe to a newsgroup, you need to see a list of your options. To do so, close the Internet Accounts dialog box if you haven't already done so, and then double-click the name of the news server you just configured. A list of all the newsgroups appears, as shown in Figure 6.23.

FIGURE 6.23
Literally, tens of thousands of newsgroups are out there.

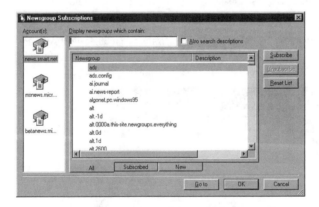

While viewing the names of the newsgroups in the Newsgroup Subscriptions dialog box, you can subscribe to a group using one of two methods. You can either double-click its name, or click it to select it, and then click the Subscribe button. From that moment on, the groups you subscribed to will have a special icon next to their names (as shown in Figure 6.24), and they will all appear in a separate window when you click the Subscribed tab at the bottom of the window. They will also appear on the File List in alphabetical order under the name of the news server.

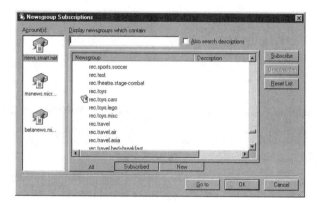

FIGURE 6.24
Newsgroups with the icon to the left of their names are the ones you've sub-scribed to.

If you're not certain you want to subscribe to a group, click its name and then click the Go To button at the bottom-right part of the window. When you attempt to leave the newsgroup, Outlook Express asks whether you want to subscribe.

In the case of newsgroups, a subscription simply means that only the newsgroups you choose are downloaded from the server, unless you specify otherwise. Unlike magazine subscriptions, newsgroup subscriptions are free. You should also know that unless you actively participate in a newsgroup, no one will ever know you're there. This passive monitoring of a newsgroup is often referred to as *lurking*.

> **Tip: Who's got time to browse?** If you're in a rush or simply don't feel like wading through such massive volumes of newsgroup titles, consider narrowing the field a bit. Simply type the desired term in the Display Newsgroups Which Contain text box. Outlook Express then tries to sift out all the newsgroups that meet your criteria.

Reading a Newsgroup

You needn't be subscribed to a newsgroup to be able to read it as I demonstrated earlier. However, typically you are subscribed to a newsgroup when you go to read it. Either way, the basic principles are the same.

Follow these steps to begin reading your favorite newsgroups:

1. Launch Outlook Express with a live connection to the Internet.

2. Scroll down your File List until you see the name of the newsgroup you want to read. If you cannot see the group on the list, and a plus sign appears next to the name of your news server, you need to click the plus sign to expand the folders underneath the news server. If the desired newsgroup still doesn't appear, double-click the news server's name, and then click the Newsgroup button if needed.

3. Click the newsgroup's name, and then click the Go To button to begin reading. By default, messages are presented in the order they were posted, with the freshest being shown first. A plus sign next to the message means the message is part of a *thread* (ongoing topic of discussion); you can see responses to it by clicking the plus sign. See Figure 6.25 for a look at how complex these threads can get.

FIGURE 6.25
An example of a multilayered thread.

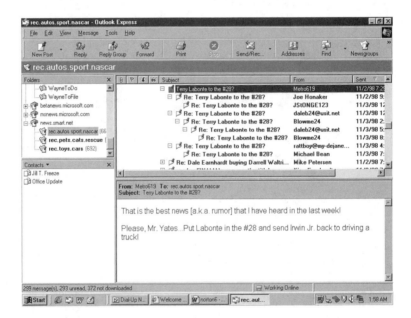

4. To begin reading a message, all you have to do is double-click it. The article appears in a window similar to the one shown in Figure 6.26. Remember, if a plus sign appears next to a message, additional messages appear underneath it.

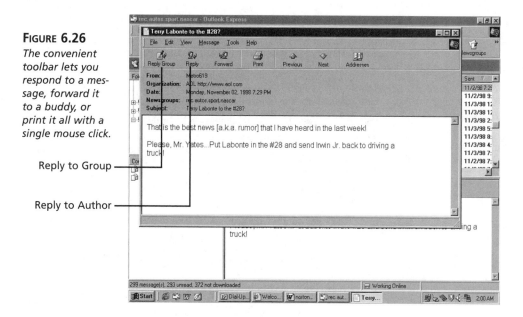

FIGURE 6.26

The convenient toolbar lets you respond to a message, forward it to a buddy, or print it all with a single mouse click.

Reply to Group

Reply to Author

5. From within a message, you can take multiple actions on an article, as shown here:

- Reply to Group—This button launches a Reply message window. Note that messages composed in this manner will be posted to the newsgroup for the entire world to see, as evidenced by the presence of the Newsgroup line item as opposed to the To line. You continue composing the message just as you would a regular email message, clicking Send when you're finished.

Peter's Principle: Netiquette reminders.

Before you respond to the group as a whole, make sure what you have to say has value or interest to more people than just the original poster of the message you're responding to. Posting simple "me too" or "I agree" messages is generally frowned upon unless you are a noted expert on the subject. If the primary purpose of your note is to show the author your support, then opt for Replying to Author instead.

Also, be sure to include enough of the message you're responding to to give readers a context for your remarks. Otherwise, if the text is not relevant, edit it in the interest of saving bandwidth. Saving bandwidth basically decreases the amount of time needed to download a message and conserves the amount of space it takes up on mail servers.

- Reply to Author—Clicking this button routes your message directly to the author of the post to which you're responding. In fact, Outlook Express even inserts the author's email address and the subject line he or she used prefixed with an RE: for you. Replying directly to the author is the best way to relate a relevant personal experience, show your support, or share an off-the-wall fact that may not be of general interest.

- Forward—If you want to send a newsgroup article to a friend or colleague via email, click this button, type the person's email address (or double-click the To: icon to use an entry from your Address Book), add any notes you want to include, and then click Send.

- Print—Click this button to send the message to your default printer. Outlook Express uses its default settings, which should be fine in the majority of cases, but should you want to have more control over your output, you can click File and choose Print to access the Print dialog box.

- Previous—Click this button to view the message that came before the one currently being displayed.

- Next—To move to the next message in the list, click this button.

- Addresses—Click this button to go in and work directly with your Address Book entries.

Marking Messages as Read and Viewing Only New Posts

One of the more basic ways to trim down the message list for a newsgroup involves marking messages as read and then changing the current view to reflect only new messages. This procedure makes skimming the messages much more efficient and undoubtedly frees up disk space on your machine. After you've gone through these steps for each newsgroup, you'll be set for the long run because you'll always have fewer messages to deal with.

To mark messages as read and change the current view, follow these steps:

1. Connect to the Internet, and launch Outlook Express as you would if you were going to read the newsgroups online.

2. Click the name of the first group you want to browse.

3. Begin reading the messages of interest. Note that Outlook Express automatically marks messages previewed for five seconds or longer as read.

> **Tip: Tweaking the number.** If you feel the five-second speed doesn't quite work for you, you can adjust it by opening the Tools menu, selecting Options, and then choosing the Read tab. In the Message Is Read After Previewing for ___ Seconds line, use the arrow buttons to nudge the amount of time up or down as desired.

4. After you've finished going through the entire group, open the Edit menu, and select Mark All as Read.

> **Tip: KISS.** Keep it simple—save. If you have messages you think you'll want to see again, save them. That way, you don't have to return to All Messages view and wind your way through thousands of messages.

5. Change your current view so that Outlook Express displays only unread messages. Click View, and then select Current View|Unread Messages. A lot fewer messages appear, huh? In fact, the display may remain empty until you refresh it by pressing F5.
6. When you leave Outlook Express and return at a later time, you'll see only new messages in the message list display.

> **Tip: Restoring the view.** If you want to see all current messages again whether they've been read or not, open the View menu, and then select Current View|All Messages.

Removing Old News Messages

Outlook Express currently stores news messages up to five days old on your machine for quick retrieval. If you feel newsgroup articles are taking up far too much space on your system, you might want to reduce the number of days' worth of messages that are stored locally.

To do so, click Tools|Options, and then click the Advanced tab.

In the Delete Messages ___ Days After Being Downloaded line, use the arrow buttons to reduce the number of days allowed.

Posting Your Own Message to a Newsgroup

If, after much observation and research, you decide to go ahead and post your own original question or comments to a newsgroup, follow these simple steps:

1. Click the name of the newsgroup to which you want to post your message.
2. Click the New Message button on the Outlook Express toolbar. A standard New Message box opens, with the name of the selected newsgroup already filled in.

3. Type the text of your message as you would do with an email message. And don't forget to check your spelling!

4. When the message meets with your approval, click the Post button. Outlook Express sends you a message like the one pictured in Figure 6.27 saying your message is about to be sent to the newsgroup server and that it may not show up immediately in your display.

FIGURE 6.27
Click OK to confirm that you've read the message.

5. Click OK to close the message box and continue working in Outlook Express.

The World of Offline Newsreading

If you subscribe to more than a couple of newsgroups, the time you spend online reading them can add up in a hurry. Outlook Express offers a way to read newsgroups offline at your leisure while freeing up the phone line for someone else.

You can read offline in essentially two ways. The first method involves having Outlook Express download all the messages for every newsgroup you subscribe to. The download can take some time, but at least you have all the articles at your fingertips.

The second method involves downloading message headers only, so you can get the gist of the current discussion and download only the messages you want. Although doing it this way adds a few steps to the process, it can also save you time in that maybe you'll scrutinize what you want to read a bit more carefully if you have to purposely mark it for download. This second method is great for groups prone to massive amounts of spamming, and those that routinely include only a small number of messages of interest to you. You'll be happy to know you can combine the approaches as needed.

Preparing Newsgroups for Offline Browsing

Before you can begin reaping the rewards of offline browsing, you have to do a little setup work. Use the following steps as a guide in getting prepared:

1. Double-click the name of your news server. A list of newsgroups you're currently subscribed to appears (see Figure 6.28).

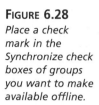

FIGURE 6.28
Place a check mark in the Synchronize check boxes of groups you want to make available offline.

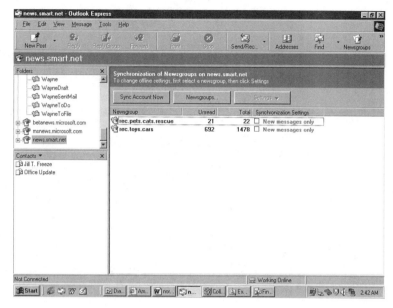

2. Place a check mark in the Synchronize check boxes of sites you want to view offline.

3. Click each newsgroup, one at a time, and click the Settings button. Here, you can define just how much or how little of the group's messages are downloaded upon synchronization. Your choices include All Messages, New Messages Only, or New Headers Only.

4. After you've tweaked all the settings for each group, click the Sync Account Now button. The first newsgroup synchronization is performed.

5. To download the specified information, click Tools|Synchronize. As long as you've got a live connection to the Internet, you can perform the operation.

6. Disconnect from the Internet, and begin browsing the newsgroups you've elected to have synchronized.

Downloading Certain Messages

If you opt to have Outlook Express download message headers only, then you need to complete the following steps in order to read the entire contents of selected messages. When you're connected to the Internet and ready to retrieve some of the messages, you need to follow these steps to complete the download:

1. In one of the newsgroups for which you downloaded header information only, click a message header you want to read the details of.

2. Click inside the Mark for Retrieval column (the downward-pointing arrow icon shown in Figure 6.29).

FIGURE 6.29
Click under this column to mark a message for retrieval.

Mark for Retrieval column

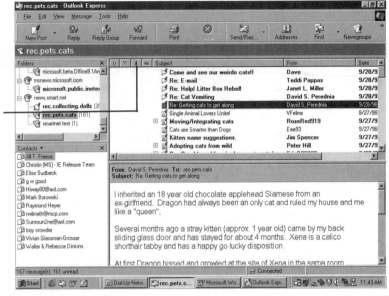

> **Tip: Know what you'll be getting.** If you mark a message that has a plus sign next to it (is not expanded), you get the whole thread in a single mouse click. To get a single message only, expand the thread by clicking the plus sign. Then choose the post you want to read, and follow the preceding steps for marking it.

3. Repeat these steps for each header whose message you want to read offline.

4. Click Tools|Synchronize.

5. Disconnect from the Internet to minimize time spent online.

6. To assist in viewing the messages you chose to read, click View|Current View|Downloaded Messages. Choosing this option tells Outlook Express to display only the messages you marked for retrieval.

On Your Own

This chapter gave you an awfully fast and furious look at Internet Explorer 5. Like the rest of this book, it focuses on the new features, some of the more obscure features previously available, and it draws attention to ways the application can help you work more efficiently. If you want a more in-depth look at Internet Explorer 5 and its supporting applications, consider reading *Sams Teach Yourself Internet Explorer 5 in 24 Hours* by Jill T. Freeze (Sams, 1999).

PART II

Using Word 2000

Maximizing Word 2000

We all wish we could add more hours to our days. It seems like we always have so much to do and so little time to do it in. Although Word 2000 may not be able to add those extra hours, it sure can do a lot to improve the speed with which you work.

In this chapter, you'll take a look at an assortment of features, settings, and techniques that can literally shave hours off your time at the keyboard. Not only will you have more time to do the things you enjoy, but you'll produce a more professional result as well.

Getting a Good View of Your Work

Whether you want to cram two Office 2000 documents onto your screen so that you can work on them at the same time, or you simply need to view a Word 2000 document in a larger type font to avoid eye strain, you should become familiar with the many options you have available to you. By merely changing your view of a document, you can see how it'll look printed on a piece of paper or as a Web page; you can even organize large chunks of a complex outline with a basic drag-and-drop procedure.

Maximizing the Amount of Screenspace Available

You can tweak several parameters if you want to fit more Office 2000 items onto your screen. For example, a click of the Restore button (see Figure 7.1) shrinks the size of the Word 2000 workspace. Just click its title bar, and drag it to a corner of your screen. Repeat the process with the second Office 2000 application or document window, dragging it into position in the opposite corner. Because the two windows will most likely still overlap one another, you can run the mouse pointer over the border of the active window until you see the double-headed Resize pointer. Click and drag the window's border in to make additional room for the other application or window. Click the second window, and attempt to resize it as well. With a little tweaking, you can soon have the majority of the content in both windows available to you.

The Zoom
drop-down
box

The Restore
button

FIGURE 7.1

*With a little work,
you can view two
applications or
documents at the
same time.*

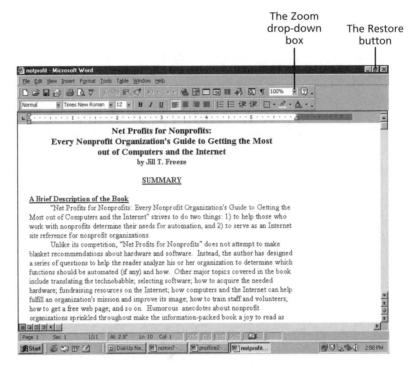

If parts of your document have spilled outside the application's border, consider adjusting the zoom of your document's view. For example, dropping the zoom level down one notch—say from 100 percent down to 75 percent—can make all the difference in the world in terms of how much you can see onscreen.

> **Tip: It's a small Word after all...**Of course depending on the size of the font you used in the document, changing the zoom down a level may result in text that's virtually unreadable. To remedy the problem, click inside the Zoom text box, and then type in a percentage that falls slightly below the number displayed. Keep nudging the numbers a hair until you're satisfied with the view. The window's size and position are saved for future use.

Making the View Fit the Function

As you'll see in the chapters to come, you can do everything in Word 2000 from creating stellar Web pages to building and reorganizing outlines for large documents. With such a wide variety of tasks, it's only fitting that special document views can assist you in these endeavors. You can switch to the special views described in Table 7.1 with a single mouse click, as shown in Figure 7.2.

Normal View   Outline View
button   button

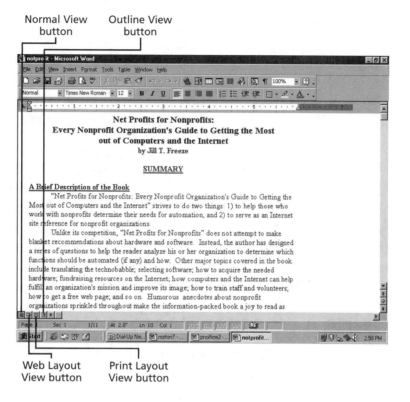

FIGURE 7.2

Change your view of a document by clicking any of these buttons.

Web Layout   Print Layout
View button   View button

Table 7.1 The Many Views of Word 2000

Use This View...	...In the Following Situations
Normal view	When you're working on a basic text-only document, this default view is just fine.
Web Layout view	If you're designing a Web page, you can look at your document in this view to make sure it meets with your approval for publication on the Web. You might choose to design the page in Normal view and then preview it in Web Layout view, or you might work with this view from the start.
Print Layout view	To save paper and a lot of hassle, you might want to consider viewing important documents using the Print Layout view before sending them to the printer. That way, you can adjust the margins, font size, page breaks, or other Word 2000 settings to get the output you want on the first printing. This is the best view to use for true WYSIWYG (what-you-see-is-what-you-get) performance because some elements, such as text boxes, don't show up in any other view.

continues

Table 7.1   Continued

Use This View...	...In the Following Situations
Outline view	Putting together a lengthy document can be a trying task at best. And what happens when you decide to reorganize parts of it? If cut-and-paste or drag-and-drop was your answer, you're partly correct. Provided you've used style codes for the headings in your document, you can click the Outline View button and drag parts of your document around. No more selecting huge blocks of text either! When you move a heading in the Outline view, the text under the heading automatically moves with it. For more details on working with outlines, see Chapter 8, "Going Beyond Basic Document Creation with Word 2000."

Jumping to the Location You Want

Many work projects require multiple days of work; some even require subsequent revisions or edits. How do you find the portion of the document you need? If you spend more than a few quick seconds skimming the document for the desired location, a better way might be possible. Consider the following:

- Moving to a specific page—Click the scroll box on the right edge of the screen, and drag it up or down as needed. The contents of the document appear onscreen, and a ScreenTip-like box displays the page number without disturbing the insertion point. You even see the heading you scrolled by most recently if you used Heading codes, which can be a tremendous navigational aid. When you see the page you want, just release the mouse button, and click the location you want to edit or resume working on. You can also double-click Word 2000's status bar or press F5, and enter the page number in the text box provided. Click the Go To button, and you're there.

- Jumping to a specific phrase—Perhaps you don't know the page number of the location you want to work with but simply remember writing about the $20,000 in grant money you were awarded in the previous year. Click Edit|Find or press Ctrl+F to reveal the Find and Replace dialog box shown in Figure 7.3. In the text box provided, enter the word, phrase, or number you want to locate. Then click the Find Next button. The first occurrence of the entered text appears highlighted onscreen. If it's not the instance you're looking for, simply click the Find Next button again. You can repeat this process as necessary.

FIGURE 7.3

In this case, the Find command was used to locate a specific table buried within a document.

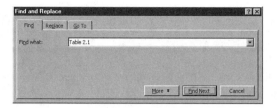

- Pulling out the map to find the right section—If you used style codes or even normally formatted headings in the document, clicking View|Document Map can take you to the desired location in a single mouse click. Just find the section you want on the document map (see Figure 7.4), click it, and Word 2000 takes you there.

FIGURE 7.4

The document map gives you a bird's-eye view of the content of your document.

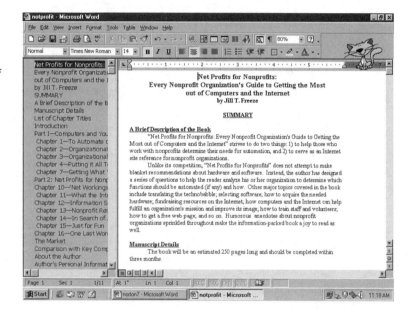

Note: How does it do that? Word 2000 is pretty smart when it comes to generating a document map. If it can't find obvious style-coded headings, it attempts to target nonformatted headings. It looks for text that stands on a line by itself or doesn't go completely to the end of a line with a solid block of text underneath. It takes all these clues and uses them to come up with the most accurate map possible.

Of course, all this guessing has its downside, too, especially when it occurs along with the traditional heading-style mapping. Word occasionally picks up figure captions or paragraph text and places it in the document map as well. If the document is short, you might be able to live with the distraction, but if you're collaborating on a huge planning document, for example, a clean document map can be tremendously helpful. To clean up stray document map text, select the text, and then click Format|Paragraph. Verify that the Indents and Spacing tab is open, and then use the Outline View drop-down box to change the text to Body Text. That way, it doesn't show up on the map, and it doesn't affect the document's appearance.

- Returning to the last location in which you worked—Say you're working on a lengthy report. You have to go back and fix a specific section, and then you want to return to the location in which you were previously working. Rather than burn up precious time trying to browse the document or using one of the more elaborate methods to track down the proper location, consider using this little shortcut. Word 2000 remembers the last three locations in which you worked. To revisit them, just press Shift+F5. Word takes you to the most recent site first and then works its way backward with each execution of Shift+F5. Best of all, it retains its memory even after you save the document.

- Getting to the end of the document—Arguably the most common scenario involves jumping to the end of a document to continue working on it. Although you can get there in any number of ways, the fastest is to press Ctrl+End.

Being Two Places at Once

Moving from one part of a document to another is great, but what if you need to see two parts of a document at the same time? No problem with the Split Screen feature. Just run your mouse pointer over the tiny button (the Split Bar) immediately above the up arrow on the horizontal scrollbar until the pointer turns into two horizontal lines with an up and a down arrow. When you see this pointer, click and drag the Split Bar down the screen. Your Word 2000 session should now have two viewing panes of the same document. Each pane has a separate set of scrollbars, so you can easily move to the parts of the document you want to work with.

Tip: Executive orders. Many lengthy professional documents are preceded by an executive summary, preparing the readers for what lies ahead. Although this summary is often written last, writing it can still be a daunting task, especially if the document is extra long. How can you be certain you've included all the salient points? By using the Split Screen feature, of course. Open your two windows, and then systematically work your way through the document, one section at a time. That way, you can rest assured that you've covered everything and in the proper sequence.

Editing Multiple Word 2000 Documents at One Time

With Word 2000's new single document interface (SDI), working with multiple Word 2000 documents is as easy as opening them all and clicking a document's name as needed on the Windows taskbar. No more multistep key commands or plowing through menus. Another subtle but phenomenally helpful improvement to Word 2000 is that the document's filename now appears before the application name on the Windows taskbar. It sure makes finding items on a cluttered taskbar easier!

Working with People Using Other Versions of Word

No matter how hard you try to avoid the situation, it's almost inevitable. Sooner or later, you'll find yourself exchanging documents with people using other versions of Word. Your strategy for dealing with the situation may vary depending on the nature of the exchange and the frequency with which data is passed back and forth. For instance, if you merely want to send a document to an old buddy to read for his own information only, then you needn't really worry about potential version incompatibilities. It's the content, not the formatting or presentation, that counts. If, on the other hand, you got Office 2000 with your newest PC at home, but your company has access only to Office 97, you might want to consider a more aggressive compatibility strategy to make sure none of your hard work done at home is lost when it's taken to the office. Your concerns about compatibility boil down to two points: whether the Word 2000 documents are to be edited by others and how frequently.

> **Caution: Save it for last.** If you plan to have someone who uses an earlier version of Word edit a document you created in Word 2000, do not waste your time making it look pretty on the front end. All your hard formatting work could be unintentionally lost as soon as that document is saved in that earlier format. Instead, incorporate all the suggested edits at the end as you go through and apply the finishing touches (special formatting, themes, and the like).

Getting Ready for Infrequent Document Sharing

If file exchanges with others using previous versions of Word are few and far between, the best strategy may very well be to save the specific document in a file format that corresponds to the version of Word the recipient uses. You can do so using the Save As dialog box. Just click the File as Type drop-down arrow, make your selection from the list, and click the Save button.

Caution: If the document is meant for Office 2000 use as well...If the document you're working with is to be used as an intranet Web document or is intended to take advantage of new Office 2000 features such as Discuss, be certain to save it in Office 2000 format under the preferred filename first. Click File|Save As, give the document a slightly different name (maybe just append a 97 to the end of the filename for Word 97 format, and so on), use the File As Type drop-down box to make your selection, and then click the Save button. That way, your document retains its Office 2000 functionality while being completely readable in another version of Word.

Preparing for Ongoing File Sharing

If document exchange between one file format and another is routine, then changing the default file format may be in order. This is especially true, for example, in cases in which you use one version of Word at home and another version at work. To reset the default file format in Word 2000, click Tools|Options and access the Save tab. Use the drop-down arrow next to the Save Word Files As text box to make your selection from a wide variety of choices (some of which, incidentally, include non-Microsoft applications such as WordPerfect).

This option enables you to easily collaborate on documents with others using various software products, yet it gives you instant access to Word 2000 features at the very end when you may be preparing the document for the Web, scaling the document to be printed on different sized paper, or printing multiple pages on a single sheet. Of course, you should save a version of the completed document before you apply the special Word 2000-specific features and formatting, save it in Word 2000 format, and then generate the output.

Tip: Word 2000 edits in a Word 97 world. If the document's destination file type is Word 97, and you occasionally work with it in Word 2000, you might want to consider disabling all features not supported in Word 97 for that document instead of going through the multiple saves in differing file types or changing your default file format. What does disabling these features do exactly? Well, Microsoft understands that remembering what was or wasn't supported in each version of Word can be hard. Given that, the folks at Microsoft give you a simple way to convert features in Word 2000 to features readable to Word 97 automatically. For example, the decorative underlines supported in Word 2000 automatically become basic underlines instead. To disable features not supported in Word 97, click Tools|Options and then open the Save tab. Place a check mark in the Disable Features Not Supported by Word 97 box, and then click the OK button.

No matter what the specifics of the situation are, a good rule of thumb is to try to maintain the document's integrity in the file format in which it is to be published to the Web, printed, or incorporated into other Office application documents. That way, no valuable work time is wasted making use of features that will go unseen in the end.

Changing the Default Font

In Word 97, the default font was 10-point Times New Roman. In Word 2000, it's changed to a much more readable 12-point font. Even so, you (or your company) might have reason to change it. Perhaps the font size is a design issue, or your organization serves a special population that could benefit from a larger font size. In any case, a new default font is a few quick mouse clicks away. Just click Format|Font, and make your selections from the extensive list of available fonts, font styles, font sizes, and font colors. When you're satisfied with your choices as displayed in the Preview window, click the Default button. You are asked to verify that you really want to make your selection the new default. Click OK if you agree, or click No to return to the Font dialog box and adjust your selection.

Note: From this point on... Just because you change the default font now doesn't mean all your old documents will be converted to the new defaults. Changes to the default document settings take place from the time you first set them, so anything created previously must be changed manually if consistency is desirable.

Getting Your Work Done Automatically

All those fancy "auto" features hidden in Office 2000 can really work to your advantage if you know how to handle them. Even if you don't intend to use them, you should be familiar with what they do because they can produce unexpected results on occasion. Consider the simple act of typing (c) as you might do for an outline. By default, Word 2000's AutoCorrect feature turns this key sequence into a copyright symbol—a fabulous thing if that's what you really want it to do, but potentially a frustrating quirk if you don't know how to stop it.

Note: So you aren't left hanging... Here's a workaround to the (c) problem described in the preceding paragraph. You can reject the AutoCorrected symbol (in this case, convert it back to the (c) instead of the copyright symbol) by pressing the Backspace key once immediately after the symbol appears.

In the sections that follow, I introduce you to all the Word 2000 auto features. You learn which feature to use when and how to leverage them to reduce your time at the keyboard while enhancing the professionalism of your documents. In the meantime, consult Table 7.2 for a look at auto features at a glance.

Table 7.2 Auto Features in Word 2000

This Auto Feature	Does This
AutoCaption	Helps you apply a numbering scheme to certain Word elements such as graphics or tables.
AutoComplete	Lets you insert dates and AutoText entries when you type a few identifying characters. Unlike AutoCorrect, AutoComplete prompts you with a ScreenTip box to accept or reject the change.
AutoCorrect	Automatically corrects many common typing, spelling, and grammatical errors as you type. It also can automatically insert text, graphics, and symbols.
AutoFormat	Automatically formats lists, numbers, and symbols as you type, when enabled.
AutoRecover	Helps you get back changes you made to a document before a power failure or other potential system glitch.
AutoSave	Allows you to automatically save your work at specified intervals.
AutoSummarize	Generates a summary of long documents to automatically be saved in a specific location. You can also choose summary attributes to make sure the summary contains the necessary elements.
AutoText	Stores defined text for future use. AutoText entries might include your return address, your company's name, or similar information.

Working with AutoCorrect

AutoCorrect is one of the most visible auto features in Word 2000. By default, it can turn a series of characters into copyright symbols or right-side-up smiley faces right before your very eyes. But it can also work behind the scenes, seamlessly correcting common typos. And if you think all that is impressive, wait until you hear what else this feature can do when appropriately set up:

- Correct TWo INitial CApitals
- Capitalize the first letter of a sentence

- Capitalize names of days
- Correct accidental usage of cAPS LOCK key

> **Note: It's not just for Word.** That's right, you can unleash the power of AutoCorrect from within Excel 2000 or PowerPoint 2000 as well as Word 2000.

Disabling AutoCorrect

If the loss of control over what exactly is happening in your document bothers you (or if you simply want to get rid of those copyright and trademark symbols that seem to appear out of nowhere), you might want to disable the AutoCorrect feature.

To do so, click Tools|AutoCorrect and verify that the AutoCorrect tab is in view, as shown in Figure 7.5. All you have to do to turn off AutoCorrect is uncheck the Replace Text as You Type check box by clicking it.

FIGURE 7.5

Make sure the Replace Text as You Type box is checked if you want to make use of AutoCorrect.

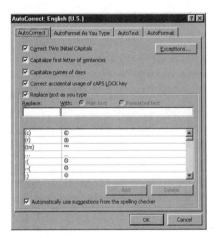

Because AutoCorrect offers many valuable common spelling error fixes, you might want to delete the copyright symbol AutoCorrect entry. To do so, visit the AutoCorrect tab as just described, click the entry you want to delete to select it, and then press the Delete key. Keep in mind, however, that deleting an AutoCorrect symbol entry means that you need to reprogram it to make use of it again. Reprogramming can be a complicated task, especially where symbols are concerned (see the following section for more information).

Programming AutoCorrect

Do you always seem to misspell certain words or names? Would you like to have bits of text inserted automatically without retyping them every time? If either of these scenarios rings true for you, you might consider investing a little time in some AutoCorrect programming.

> **Tip: AutoCorrect versus AutoText.** AutoCorrect is best used for typos or mis-spellings you commonly make. Or you can merely tell it to replace the words *myboss* with the proper spelling of his extra long name. If you want to have the option to insert longer bits of data (like that boss's biography) or even a graphic of your company logo, you should take advantage of Word 2000's AutoText feature.

AutoCorrect entries can be up to 255 characters long and can be retrieved with any set of keystrokes you specify. Be careful when you set these keystrokes because they are auto-matically replaced with the content you specify with no warning whatsoever. In other words, rule out using real words or words that AutoCorrect could mistake for a common typo.

To program AutoCorrect, you need to follow these simple steps:

1. You can program AutoCorrect one of two ways: by selecting the data you want to use for the replacement text from an existing document or by simply typing it into the appropriate box on the AutoCorrect tab. If you plan to enter the content direct-ly, you can proceed to step 2. To use text from another document, you obviously need to open that document and select the desired text as your first step.

2. Click Tools|AutoCorrect, and verify that the AutoCorrect tab is in front.

3. If you performed step 1, the selected text automatically appears in the With text box. If you started with step 2, you need to type in the desired data at this point.

4. Because Microsoft has preloaded so many common typos and misspellings into its database, you might want to scroll down the list of entries before filling out the Replace field.

5. After you've typed in the chosen Replace text, click Add and then click OK to save your entry and close the dialog box.

Editing AutoCorrect Entries

Editing AutoCorrect entries is equally simple. Just revisit the AutoCorrect tab as described in the preceding section, click the entry, make the necessary changes, and then click the Replace button. AutoComplete tells you that the entry already exists and asks you to confirm that you really want to change it.

Inserting AutoText Using AutoComplete

AutoComplete and AutoText are about as closely related as you can get. AutoComplete is responsible for retrieving AutoText entries to display as ScreenTips when you type the title of an AutoText entry. If you accept the ScreenTip by pressing the Enter key, AutoComplete replaces or completes what you typed using the predefined AutoText entry.

In addition to fetching AutoText entries, AutoComplete can also help you finish entering the current date, days of the week, or months of the year. Simply begin typing the desired information from the list, and within a few short keystrokes, you see a ScreenTip containing the whole month, day, or date. Unlike AutoCorrect, AutoComplete asks whether you want to make a change before it does anything.

Disabling AutoComplete

Although AutoComplete is turned on by default, many people find the ScreenTips distracting because they often pop into view unexpectedly, obstructing the workspace. You can disable AutoComplete by clicking Tools|AutoCorrect, selecting the AutoText tab, and then removing the check mark in the Show AutoComplete Tip for AutoText and Dates box, as shown in Figure 7.6.

FIGURE 7.6

You can turn AutoComplete on and off with a single mouse click.

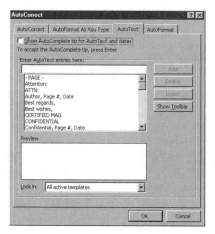

What Is AutoText?

To call these bits of material AutoText almost seems like a bit of a deception because an AutoText entry can store everything from clip art, to picture files, to WordArt, in addition to text. If you want to insert your company logo at a given point, keeping it as an AutoText entry is the fastest way to do it. Or for that wordsmithed mission statement or biography, you won't find a quicker way to include it in your current document. No more retrieving an old document and performing a tedious copy-and-paste operation!

Think of AutoText as the storage compartments for the items AutoComplete can retrieve. And again, Microsoft has preloaded a bunch of popular greetings, salutations, and other commonly used words and phrases, so you can take advantage of the feature even before you do any programming.

Defining AutoText Entries

To make your own AutoText entries, you need to execute a few steps to make sure everything's in place:

1. Before you can define an AutoText entry, you need to select the text or graphic you want to use for the entry. Either open a document that contains the information, or enter it anew in a Word 2000 document.

2. With the chosen text or graphic selected, click Insert|AutoText|New or press Alt+F3. A dialog box like the one shown in Figure 7.7 appears.

FIGURE 7.7
Use this dialog box to give the new AutoText entry a name.

Tip: AutoSimplify the process. Word 2000 may not have an AutoSimplify feature, but if you plan to define or insert multiple AutoText entries, you can speed up the process by displaying the AutoText toolbar. Do so by right-clicking any visible Word 2000 toolbar and then selecting AutoText from the shortcut menu. With this toolbar in view, you can create or insert AutoText entries with a single mouse click.

---

3. If the AutoText entry is to be created from text, Word 2000 proposes a name for it, though you may want to enter a descriptive name for the new entry—one that gives you a clear indication of the entry's content. You need to choose your own name for any graphic elements you want to define.

4. When you're happy with the entry's name, click OK to save it. You then see the entry's corresponding ScreenTip each time you type the characters you specified.

Inserting AutoText Entries in a Document

When it comes to using an AutoText entry in a document, you have several ways to do so. They include any of the following:

- Confirm that AutoComplete is enabled, type in the desired entry's title, and then press Enter when the ScreenTip appears. AutoComplete inserts the appropriate information.

- Click Insert|AutoText, and browse the drop-down menus for the desired entry's name. Click the name to insert the entry.

- Place the AutoText toolbar in view as described earlier, and then use the All Entries drop-down arrow to locate the name of the AutoText entry you want to insert.

Editing AutoText Entries

Should you later find an error in an AutoText entry or need to change it to reflect
changes in the information, you can do the following to rectify the problem:

1. Insert the AutoText entry you want to edit into a document, as described in the
   preceding section.

2. Make the necessary changes to the text or image, and then select the updated text
   or graphic.

3. Click Insert|AutoText|New, type in the original name of the entry, and then click
   OK. Word 2000 asks whether you really want to redefine the entry. Click Yes or
   No as appropriate.

Looking Ahead

Share your AutoText entries. In Chapter 8, "Going Beyond Basic Document
Creation with Word 2000," you'll discover how you can share those treasured
AutoText features with your coworkers.

Achieving Professional Results Using AutoFormat

In Word 2000, AutoFormat can mean a number of things. It can turn quotation marks
into more professional-looking smart quotes, it can automatically format numbered and
bulleted lists, and it can make fractions look more realistic. Best of all, you can either
format documents as you type, or you can format them at the very end and accept or
reject each formatting change as Word 2000 makes it.

Looking Ahead

The basic AutoFormat feature should not be confused with Word 2000's Table
AutoFormat feature, which we'll look at in greater detail in Chapter 9,
"Creating Professional-Looking Documents."

To begin tweaking your AutoFormat options, you need to click Tools|AutoCorrect and
then access either the AutoFormat as You Type tab (to define which changes Word makes
without asking) or the AutoFormat tab (which lets you specify which items you want
automatically formatted when you perform the AutoFormatting in a single pass) See
Figure 7.8 for a look at the AutoFormat as You Type tab. Word 2000 does a lot of formatting by default, so you should check the AutoFormat as You Type tab to make sure you
know what to expect. Keep in mind that each option's check box is essentially a toggle
switch; clicking it once changes the option's state and twice returns the option to its original state.

FIGURE 7.8

The AutoFormat as You Type tab gives you the power to have Word 2000 do as much (or as little) automatic formatting as you want it to.

Minimizing Data Loss Using AutoSave

Pressing that old Save button regularly as you work is always wise, but wouldn't it be great to have a backup? Thanks to Word 2000's AutoSave capability, you can tell Word to automatically save your work at specific intervals. That way, you can minimize the amount of work lost should you experience a power failure or system hiccup. And if you do encounter such a problem, Word's AutoRecover feature stands at the ready to help you find as much of the document as possible.

By default, Word 2000 AutoSaves your documents every 10 minutes. You can adjust this number up or down depending on the nature of your work by clicking Tools|Options and then opening the Save tab. Use the arrow buttons next to the Minutes text box to move the number in the desired direction (see Figure 7.9).

FIGURE 7.9

By clicking these arrow buttons, you can choose to save more frequently or less often.

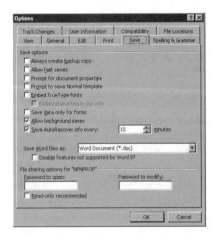

> **Tip: Working in slow motion...** While frequent saves may be desirable while you're working on a crucial project, you should be aware that these AutoSaves sap power from your system resources each time they are performed. When an AutoSave is in progress, your keyboard and/or mouse may become less responsive to commands, thus disrupting the flow of your work temporarily. The effect may be more pronounced the closer your machine is to the minimal specs for running Office 2000. On cutting-edge machines, you may barely notice any disruption.

When it's time to recover from a power failure or system lock-up, the first thing you should do is launch Word 2000. After a few moments, the documents you were working on should appear onscreen. After they've loaded, open the document with the original filename to verify which document has the most current information. If the AutoRecover document contains the most recent information, perform a Save As operation on it, and give it the name of the original document. When Word asks whether you really want to overwrite the file, click Yes. All the remaining AutoRecover files are purged when Word 2000 is shut down.

> **Tip: If the document doesn't open...**In the unlikely event that the document doesn't reload as expected, you might still be able to recover it. After you launch Word 2000, click File|Open, and then click your way to the Windows\Application Data\Microsoft\Word folder. In the Files of Type box, click All. AutoSaved files all have the name "AutoRecovery Save of *<filename>*" with an .asd file extension. Open the appropriate recovery file, compare it with the original document as described earlier, and save it as the original filename if it contains more recent data.

Dealing with Spelling and Grammar Errors

Nothing sticks out more in a critical document than a glaring typographical error that could have easily been avoided. The same goes for Web pages or PowerPoint presentations. Thanks to Word 2000's built-in spelling and grammar checker, you can minimize the odds of embarrassing yourself or your organization. When the application suspects a spelling error has been made, it underlines the word in question with a wavy red line. When it detects a possible grammatical error, a green wavy line underscores the offending text.

By default, Word 2000 marks these possible errors. In the sections that follow, not only will you learn how to handle these marked bits of text, but you'll see just how much you can customize the sensitivity of the spelling and grammar options.

Setting Spelling and Grammar Checking Options

If you click Tools|Options and select the Spelling & Grammar tab (see Figure 7.10), you can access a number of totally customizable options.

FIGURE 7.10

*On the Spelling &
Grammar tab, you
define just how
sensitive you want
the tools to be.*

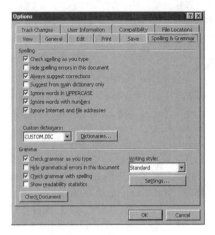

The preset defaults for spelling go a long way toward preventing false alarms. For example, the settings tell the spell checker to ignore words written entirely in uppercase (this eliminates tagging any acronyms you might use), to ignore Internet addresses (this way, the spell checker doesn't just think you crammed a few words together and mark it as an error), and to ignore words with numbers in the middle of them. If these options filter out more text than you would like them to, you can deselect any of them with a single mouse click. Every perceived error is marked automatically, and suggestions for the proper spelling are provided where possible.

Options for locating potential errors in grammar are a bit more complicated. Although the settings dedicated to grammar on the Spelling & Grammar tab are relatively few when compared to spelling, you should know that you can do a whole lot more besides turn grammar checking on and off and have it perform grammar checks the same time spell checks are done.

By simply clicking the Settings button, you can tell the grammar checker to be on the lookout for all kinds of errors (see Figure 7.11). Word 2000's grammar checker can review your text for such common errors as use of capitalization and punctuation, possessive and plural confusion, the use of passive voice, commonly misused words, and the detection of run-on sentences. You can see the whole list of possible errors it can tag by reviewing the Grammar options in the Grammar Settings dialog box, as shown in Figure 7.11. And remember, all possible grammar errors are marked with a green wavy line.

FIGURE 7.11

The Grammar Settings dialog box gives Word 2000 the power to detect just about every potential grammatical error.

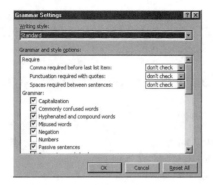

If you're impressed by Word 2000's grammar checking capabilities so far, just wait. In addition to monitoring your grammar, the grammar checker can be set to monitor punctuation usage that may differ depending on your circumstances. For instance, in grade school we were always taught to place two spaces between each sentence, yet to increase the readability of this book, we must include only one space. In the Required section (the top section) of the Grammar Settings dialog box, you can use the drop-down arrows to set your specific requirements for each element. The grammar checker can monitor these elements:

- Whether you require a comma before the last item in a list (not checked by default)

- Where punctuation should be placed with regard to quotation marks (not checked by default)

- How many spaces are required between each sentence (not checked by default)

Peter's Principle: You've got style!

Although enabling and configuring the two sections described in this section are more than enough to nip potential grammar usage problems in the bud, I can think of some real compelling reasons why you might want to enable some of Word 2000's Style options as well. In this day and age, being politically correct is vital to the success (or in some cases, even the survival) of a company or venture. Thanks to Word 2000's capability to mark the use of gender-specific words, you can rest assured that you won't inadvertently use words that might offend someone. Best of all, the grammar checker suggests alternatives to the word you used so that you don't have to waste valuable time trying to come up with an acceptable substitute yourself. You can enable this option by scrolling down the Grammar Settings list of options and selecting the desired check boxes in the Styles section toward the bottom of the dialog box. Take some time to browse these options; you might find others useful as well.

After you've selected all your options and have clicked OK to close the Grammar Settings dialog box, click OK a second time to close the Options dialog box. Now you're ready to begin working with your document.

Eliminating Content from Spelling and Grammar Checking

If you find yourself writing a lot of computer code or other technobabble that's bound to send the spell checker into a tailspin, let me share a trick you might want to use. Consider creating a special style code for this very purpose (see the section titled "Creating a Style" in Chapter 8).

After you've created this new style, you need to do the following to prevent it from being included in spelling and grammar checks:

1. From within any document based on the template containing the new style, click Format|Style to open the Style dialog box.

2. Select the special style in the Styles box, and then click the Modify button. The Modify Styles dialog box opens.

3. Click the Format button near the bottom of the dialog box, and then select Language from the pop-up menu.

4. In the Language dialog box, check the Do Not Check Spelling or Grammar option, and then click OK.

5. Close the Modify Styles box by clicking OK, and then click the Apply button to save your settings and exit the dialog box altogether.

Conducting a Spelling/Grammar Check

The last thing I do when I finish writing a document is skim through it to make sure I've addressed every error, be it a typo or a grammatical error. With Word 2000, you can process marked text in one of two ways. Assuming Word marks each potential error as it is found onscreen, you have the option to right-click the underlined text on the spot and respond according to the choices found on the resulting shortcut menu (see Figure 7.12). You can also choose to make your way through the marked errors in a single pass, as you'll see shortly.

If you right-click a spelling error to deal with it as you find it, you see a number of choices on the resulting shortcut menu:

• You see a list of words the spell checker thinks you may have intended to use. Just click one to have it replace the underlined word.

• You can select Ignore All for unique words used in the current document that you may never use again. Selecting this option unmarks the error and tells the spell checker not to mark it again should it reappear later in the document.

- The Add option is a wise selection for uncommon names or terms or jargon unique to your particular type of business. Selecting this option adds the word to your personal spell checker dictionary so it will be recognized in future spell checks.

- You also have the option to turn the misspelled word into an AutoCorrect entry so that Word 2000 will automatically correct it for you in the future. Of course, the AutoCorrect as You Type option needs to be enabled for it to help in this instance.

When you right-click a grammar error, the options are similar; however, the grammar checker seldom gives you more than one alternative solution. In that same shortcut menu, you also have the option to tell the grammar checker to ignore the sentence, or you can work your way into the grammar checker to reconfigure the options by clicking the Grammar button.

FIGURE 7.12

Right-click a marked spelling or grammar error to see a shortcut menu of possible actions, as shown here.

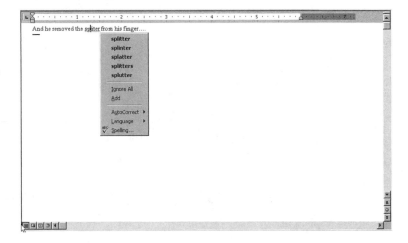

To make sure I deal with every potential problem in a document, I favor scrapping the on-the-fly approach to dealing with the errors and adopting a more systematic approach: clicking Tools|Spelling and Grammar, or pressing F7. This approach leads you through each marked item one at a time in the order that they appear. Instead of the shortcut menu shown in Figure 7.12, you see a more extravagant dialog box, like the one in Figure 7.13.

FIGURE 7.13

See the name of the rule the offending text broke, which, in this case, is Subject-Verb Agreement.

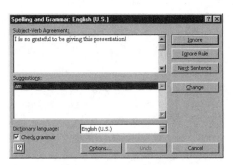

> **Peter's Principle: Always something there to remind you.**
>
> Many of my colleagues find the spelling and grammar markings distracting to them as they work, so they "hide" them by clicking Tools|Options, opening the Spelling & Grammar tab, and then deselecting the Check Spelling as You Type and Check Grammar as You Type options. Although I understand their reasoning, I find that keeping the marks turned on makes it a lot harder to forget to perform the spelling and grammar checks in the end. I'd rather put up with those squiggly lines than risk having a misspelled document leave my office.

From here, you perform a number of tasks based on the error. For the most part, these actions are pretty self-explanatory, but you might want to note a few points:

- You can always click the word or sentence in the top window and edit it as desired.

- The Ignore button unmarks the problem and moves the checker to the next incident.

- When you move away from the checker (that is, switch to another application) and revisit the checker, you see a Resume button. Click it to continue working with the checker.

- Remember the subtle difference between Change and Change All, for example. Although this difference seems obvious now, in the hurried frenzy of a project, you can easily select the wrong one.

Readying Office 2000 for Multilingual Use

Whether you work for a large multinational corporation that needs to publish documents in multiple languages, or you consistently create documents with bits of a foreign language, you can take advantage of Office 2000's multilingual features. Support for English, Spanish, and French comes with the English/U.S. version of Office 2000 and will be discussed here.

To work with other languages, you need to purchase and install the Microsoft Proofing Tools Kit or the Microsoft MultiLanguage Pack for Office 2000 from a certified retailer. In the case of Asian, right-to-left, or other idiomatic languages, you might also need to run a special language-specific version of your operating system. With Windows 2000, you can type in any language, but you first need to install support to do so.

> **Tip: What's on the menu?** With the Microsoft MultiLanguage Pack (which includes the Microsoft Proofing Tools, by the way), you can convert Office 2000's user interface to an alternative language as well. All the Office 2000 menus and help files appear in the new language. What a great way to ease someone who's new to speaking English and new to using computers into the job!

After multilingual support has been installed and configured, Word 2000 can AutoDetect what language you're working with and apply the corresponding spelling and grammar rules. It even makes the respective language's AutoCorrect and AutoSummarize information available.

Setting up Office 2000 to accommodate English, French, and Spanish is a snap; just do the following:

1. From the Windows Start menu, choose Programs|Office Tools|Microsoft Office Language Settings.

2. On the Enabled Languages tab of the resulting dialog box, select the check boxes next to the languages you want.

With this capability set in place, Word 2000 (and PowerPoint 2000) can detect what language you're working in and automatically apply the appropriate spelling and grammar rules.

On Your Own

This chapter covered a lot of ground, but many of the features are of immense value when it comes to cutting your time at the computer—whether at work or at play. Glance back through the chapter, and come up with at least five ways these features can save you time. Get specific here; being general is a waste of time. Instead of putting "Create AutoText entries" on your list of timesaving tricks gleaned from this chapter, go with something like this: "It seems like I'm always retyping our company's service mark. Maybe that would make a good AutoText entry."

If you come up with a list of specific actions, it's guaranteed you'll shave off some time for meeting with coworkers or even playing with the kids. And, hey, if you can come up with more than five, by all means do so. The more ideas you come up with now, the more time you'll save later.

Going Beyond Basic Document Creation with Word 2000

You've more than likely created dozens of documents with Word already, and odds are the vast majority of them were the basic "load a blank page and just start typing" variety. Even if you've ventured out to try one of the templates and wizards packaged with Office 2000, you've only begun to scratch the surface of what this powerful application can do for you, your work, and your professional image.

In this chapter, you'll discover a variety of ways Word 2000's often overlooked features can work to your benefit. In particular, you'll learn the following:

- How and why you'll want to deal with styles
- How templates can help your company maintain a uniform style in all its documents and Web pages
- How to build an outline and use it to quickly and effectively reorganize a long document
- When you might want to consider creating a master document

In addition, you'll learn how to define a document's properties and will become familiar with Word 2000's powerful new printing options so that you can get the output you want on the first try.

What Are Styles and What Do They Do?

Think about the last time you entered the title of a report into a Word document. After you typed in the text, did you select it, choose a new font, tweak its size, make it bold, and then click the Center alignment button? If you answered yes, then you'll be relieved to know that applying a style can save you vast amounts of time and numerous mouse clicks.

Basically, *styles* are sets of characteristics that define the appearance and formatting of the text to which they are applied. In Word 2000, you can choose from two types of styles: Character and Paragraph. Character styles are capable of taking the five steps outlined in the preceding paragraph and compressing them into two. Paragraph styles, on the other hand, dictate the alignment, line spacing, and tab stops of a given paragraph.

In addition to shaving off steps needed to format and define text attributes, styles make it a snap for you to change all the text assigned a certain code at once. Say, for example, you write a lengthy proposal for funding only to find that you exceeded your 10-page limit by 2 pages. You could spend several minutes marking each section of text and changing the font size to something smaller, or you could simply modify the style used in the body of the document to have Word 2000 do the work for you.

> **Tip: You might need styles down the road as well.** Many of Word 2000's more interesting features work better with styles in place. For instance, you get more accurate Document Map views when you apply styles; therefore, you can relocate sections of text by dragging and dropping their section titles in Outline view. Even tasks such as generating a table of contents become easier and more accurate thanks to styles.

To apply a style, just select the text you want to alter, and then click the Style List drop-down arrow on the Formatting toolbar. The currently available styles appear in the font and size in which they are defined (see Figure 8.1). Note that the point size and alignment of the type used for that style are displayed at the right end of the style's box.

FIGURE 8.1

In this drop-down list, you can see what a style will look like before you even apply it.

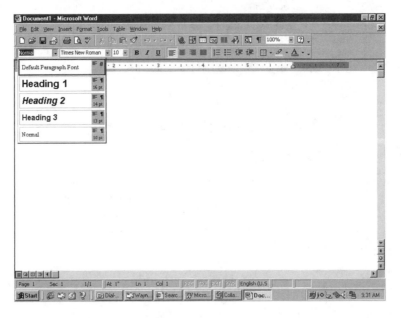

Tip: Don't see a style that fits the occasion? Click Format|Style to access the Style dialog box. Use the List drop-down arrow to select All Styles as the option (Styles in Use is the default display). Click any of the choices, and then see how it looks in the Preview window before clicking the Apply button.

Changing the style is as simple as selecting the text and making another selection from the list of available styles.

Caution: Don't be misled! Just because you change one section of text to a different style doesn't mean all other text carrying that same style will be changed automatically. To do that, you need to modify the style itself.

Modifying a Style

One of the most valuable benefits of using styles is that you can save yourself a lot of reformatting headaches should you (or your boss) not quite like the way a particular document looks. When you modify a style, all text assigned to that style is automatically modified.

To modify a style, follow these simple steps:

1. Open a Word 2000 document you want to modify, and click Format|Style. The Style dialog box shown in Figure 8.2 appears.

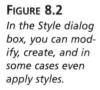

FIGURE 8.2

In the Style dialog box, you can modify, create, and in some cases even apply styles.

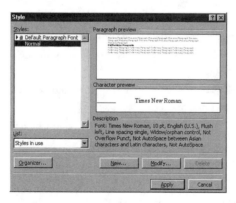

2. If you've used styles in the current document, the style in which the insertion point currently rests is pre-selected for you, thus simplifying the task of modifying the current text. If you want to modify another style used in the document, click it in the Styles box. If the style doesn't appear on the list, use the List drop-down arrow to select the All Styles option, and then click the style's name.

3. Click the Modify button to launch the Modify Style dialog box shown in Figure 8.3.

FIGURE 8.3

The Modify Style dialog box describes every aspect of the style in detail.

4. If you want any text entered after the Heading 1 line to appear in Normal style automatically, you can do so by clicking the Style for Following Paragraph drop-down arrow and making the applicable selection. That way, you can type in your Heading 1, press Enter, and then find yourself in Normal style without needing to do a thing. In cases in which you're simply changing the size or appearance of a font, the default is more than likely just fine.

5. Click the Format button, and then choose any of the following to modify:

   • Font—Changes the size and appearance of the style's text.

   • Paragraph—Defines text alignment, line spacing, indentations, and line and page break information for Paragraph styles.

   • Tabs—Lets you set the tab stops for the selected paragraph style.

   • Border—Defines special borders or shading for the style being defined. This feature works best for Paragraph as opposed to Character styles.

   • Language—Gives Word 2000's spelling and grammar checkers a heads up for text written in another language.

   • Frame—Turns the style into a frame around which text can be aligned.

   • Numbering—Specifies how numbered and bulleted lists are to appear.

6. If you want to save the modifications to the current template, check the Add to Template box. Keep in mind that all future documents created with the template will reflect your modifications. Given that fact, you should use caution when working with the Normal template because it acts as the application's default template.

7. If you want Word 2000 to automatically redefine a style based on any changes you make manually to text that carries that style, click the Automatically Update box. Note, however, that the Normal style cannot be updated in this manner.

8. When you're satisfied with the Preview and Description of the style, click OK. If you checked the Automatically Update box, the current document will reflect your changes almost instantly.

> **Tip: Heading modifications made easy.** When you're preparing a document for publication or distribution, making last-minute changes to the headings to achieve the appearance you want is not uncommon. If you applied a style to the heading and then subsequently modified the heading's appearance, just click the name of the heading's respective style in the Style drop-down box to open the Modify Style dialog box. Click Update the Style to have your changes reflected in all headings using the same style in the current document.

Assigning Shortcut Keys to Styles

After you get into the swing of using styles regularly, you'll find that you use some a lot more than others. If this is the case, you might want to consider assigning shortcut keys to those commonly used styles so that you can apply them without dealing with the numerous entries in the Style List.

> **Note: Some shortcuts already exist.** Word 2000 has predefined a few style shortcuts for your convenience. They include the following:
>
> Normal   Ctrl+Shift+N
>
> Heading 1   Ctrl+Alt+1
>
> Heading 2   Ctrl+Alt+2
>
> Heading 3   Ctrl+Alt+3

To assign a shortcut key to a style, follow the first three steps needed to modify a style presented in the preceding section. Then click the Shortcut Key button in the Modify Style dialog box to reveal the Customize Keyboard dialog box, as shown in Figure 8.4.

FIGURE 8.4
Word 2000 auto-matically converts the keystrokes to words for you.

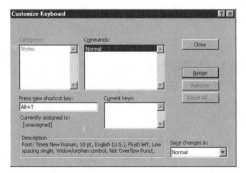

Click inside the Press New Shortcut Key text box, and then press the keys you want to use for the shortcut—for example, Alt+N. Word 2000 automatically enters the text for the keys you pressed in the box. And you needn't worry about inadvertently overwriting a shortcut key used in Windows or any Office 2000 application; Word tells you whether your selection is available.

By default, Word 2000 saves the shortcut key to the current template so that you can take advantage of it in all future documents. If, for some reason, you want to use the shortcut in the current document only, click the Save Changes In drop-down arrow, and select the name of the current document.

Peter's Principle: Make a note of it.

When I create new shortcut keys, I write them on a yellow sticky note and stick it to my monitor until I become familiar with them. After all, what good is a shortcut you can't remember?

After you've finished defining the shortcut and how you want it saved, click the Assign button to close the Customize Keyboard dialog box. You then need to click OK a couple of times to close all the dialog boxes related to modifying a style.

Creating a New Style

If you don't see a style you want to modify, or you simply want to create your own style, you can do so with ease.

You'll essentially discover just two differences between modifying a style and creating one. The first difference is that you need to click the New button instead of the Modify button in the Style dialog box (see Figure 8.2). Second, you should give the style a name that reflects its intended purpose. Try to keep that name relatively short because you'll want it to fit nicely on the Style List you access from the Formatting toolbar.

Of course, if you already have a paragraph or heading formatted just the way you like it, you can simply type the style's new name in the Style drop-down box on the Formatting toolbar and then press Enter. The newly created style will remain in the Style box for future use with any document based on the template in which the new style was created.

The Truth About Templates

In Word 2000, the word *template* can have a number of meanings. It can refer to one of the boilerplate resumes (or any other type of document or publication) included with the application; you just select the template on which you want to base your new document. A template can also be a predefined set of style and formatting rules that you can apply to an existing Word document to give it a polished look. Finally, a template can be something you or your company creates to give materials produced by a number of people a consistent appearance.

Note: Did you know...? In addition to specifying fonts, type sizes, formatting requirements, and themes for a template, you can include a number of customized elements designed to make working with the template easier. These elements might include customized toolbar buttons, AutoText entries, macros, or even entire toolbars that you've designed with the template's specific needs in mind. Furthermore, you can even define the template as the default in place of the Normal template so that you can be certain consistency will prevail. We'll take a closer look at building templates in a few short pages.

By far, templates are most frequently used when creating new documents. Seldom do people seem to apply a template to an existing document, even though the results can bring a whole new air of professionalism to the document. This may be due in part to the fear of what will happen to the original should they find the chosen template unacceptable.

One of the least used template capabilities—creating a custom template—is potentially one of the most valuable in the corporate or small business environment. If any of the following scenarios apply to your situation, you might want to consider investing the time into creating a template that can be easily used by all members of your organization:

- Do multiple people in your company or organization generate similar types of documents? For example, many staff members of small, nonprofit organizations handle their own correspondence. Wouldn't clients or supporters have a more positive reaction if all the documents were similar in appearance?

- Is your corporate Web site created and maintained by a number of people in a number of locations? If content is primarily created in Word 2000, using a custom template may very well be the way to achieve a uniform look throughout the entire Web site, no matter where the site's developers are.

- Are a number of your coworkers or employees new to using computers? If so, having a template in which you can simply click and type in the information has great appeal, especially if that template also comes with special toolbars that trim the fat in favor of fewer, more commonly used buttons.

- Do you serve a special constituency such as the visually impaired or senior citizens? If so, then you might want to use a template that sports easy-to-read fonts—nothing too small or over-embellished.

Of course, creating a good template is only half the battle. The other half involves educating the users about how to use the template and its related styles, macros, and such. If the people using the template don't know which styles should be used when, how can they possibly produce consistent-looking documents? Likewise, if they don't know the special shortcut keys you've created to speed up the process, then your efforts expended to create those shortcuts were in vain.

Should you decide to use templates within your organization with any degree of regularity, consider distributing a related user manual or at least a little "cheat sheet" that can be taped to the monitor for quick reference.

Creating a New Document Based on a Template

To build a template-based document from scratch, you need to click File|New (or press Ctrl+N) from within Word 2000.

> **Note: You can't just click a button.** Clicking the New button on the Standard toolbar just launches a blank Word document based on the default Normal template, so the best way to begin creating a document with a different template is to use one of the methods described in the preceding sections.

You then see a set of tabs as on the dialog box shown in Figure 8.5. Click the tab that most closely resembles the type of document you want to create. Within this tab, you then see the names of all the available templates and wizards. Double-click the name of the template you want to use, and then begin typing. It's as simple as that! Because Word 2000 wizards are even easier to deal with (they walk you every step of the way through creating a customized document), we won't be giving them coverage in this book.

FIGURE 8.5

Tabs in the New dialog box give you access to Word 2000 wizards as well as templates.

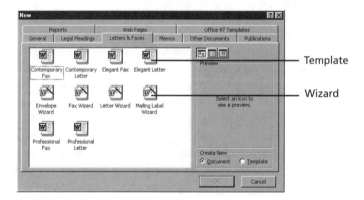

> **Note: A peek at what's hidden.** Although some of the tabs of the New dialog box are pretty self-explanatory, you should know that resume templates (and a Resume Wizard) can be found in the Other Documents tab. The new Calendar and Agenda Wizards also reside there. In the Publications tab, you can even find templates for building directories, brochures, and a thesis. And if you have some Word 97 templates you really found helpful, you'll be happy to know that you can still access them in the Office 97 Templates tab.

Attaching a Different Template to an Active Document

Say you created a resume using Word 2000's Contemporary Resume template, but you decide it's a bit too funky for the job you're applying for. You can always swap one template for another similar template in a few quick steps. To switch templates, just follow these simple steps:

1. Open the document for which you want to switch templates, and click Tools|Templates and Add-Ins.

2. To use all the styles in the new template in the current document, check the Automatically Update Document Styles check box, as shown in Figure 8.6.

FIGURE 8.6

Click the Automatically Update Document Styles check box to take full advantage of the new template's styles.

3. Click the Attach button, and then select the name of the template you want from the Attach Template dialog box. (It is identical to the standard Open dialog box, so all the navigational tools should be familiar.) Note that you might need to do some browsing to locate the templates you want.

4. After you've selected the desired template, click the Open button.

> **Note: Freshen up an old document.** You can also use these steps to apply a template to a document you created with the default Normal template. That's a quick and easy way to alter the appearance of an entire document. Because templates rely on styles to achieve their appearance, this technique works only if you've used styles throughout the document. What's more, the names of those styles have to correspond to those used in the new template. If you haven't made use of styles, try clicking Format|AutoFormat first. This approach may help you find the look you want without having to go back through all those styles.

Building Your Own Template

If you've decided that designing some custom templates may be the way to go for your business or company, then you'll be pleasantly surprised to see just how straightforward the process is. You can begin the process from scratch by verifying that the necessary styles are in place in an existing document, or you can base the template on an existing template to save a bit of time. In any case, you need to complete the following steps to accomplish the task at hand:

1. To base a new template on an existing document, click File|Open, and then open the document you want. If you want to base a new template on an existing template, click File|New. Click the name of a template that is similar to the one you want to create, click the Template option in the Create New section, and then click OK.

2. Click File|Save As, and then in the Save As Type box, click Document Template. This file type is already selected if you began creating your template with an existing template.

3. The default folder to which new templates are saved is the Templates folder (you can tell by looking in the Save In box). If you want to save the template in a tab other than the General tab, browse to the corresponding subfolder within the Templates folder.

Peter's Principle: Get your templates together.

It's not unthinkable that a company or small business would develop a number of its own templates for a variety of purposes. If that's the case, you might want to define your own company tab so that all your specialized templates appear in one easy-to-find location when you launch Word 2000. To do so, rather than browse to a new folder to complete step 3, create a new folder just as you would in any other directory. This action places your customized tab with all the other tabs you see on the application's startup or when you press Ctrl+N. Grouping your templates on one tab reinforces which templates should be used for corporate business, which in turn fosters a consistent, professional company image.

---

4. In the File Name box, type a name for the new template, and then click Save.

5. With this new template open, start adding the text and graphics you want to appear in all new documents that use the template, and delete any items you don't want to appear.

> **Tip: Make it worthwhile.** Small businesses operating on a shoestring budget might want to consider using a customized template as a virtual letterhead instead of having something professionally printed. And if you have people scattered everywhere who must develop Web pages for your company or organization, you might want to define a special Web template that includes a theme (if applicable), color schemes, and such

6. Make all the other changes you want to the template, including margin settings, page size and orientation, styles, and other formats. Remember, if you want to create special AutoText entries (say for a corporate mission statement), include special toolbars and/or buttons, or make certain macros available, you should do so now.

> **Note: Downsize your style selection choices.** Before saving the newly created template, delete any unwanted styles by clicking Format|Style, selecting the style you want to remove, and then clicking the Delete button. The fewer styles a user has available to him or her, the less likely he or she is to inadvertently misuse them.

7. When you're satisfied that the template looks and performs the way you want it to, click Save and then click File|Close.

Modifying a Template

Should you decide to make changes to a template at a later date, the process is almost trivial. Just open the template, make the desired changes, and then save the template. You can either overwrite the current version of the template by leaving the filename the same, or you can rename it to keep both versions intact. Should you decide to keep both versions around, however, give serious consideration to tucking the outdated version in another folder so that it isn't used inadvertently.

Working with Outlines and the Outline View

Outlines used to be little more than static road maps of where you planned to go with your document. Now, thanks to powerful word processing applications, outlines have become not only road maps, but dynamic organizational tools as well.

In the sections that follow, you'll learn how to build an outline with Word 2000. You'll also discover how to use the Outline view to organize your documents, whether or not they were created with an outline. Finally, you'll see just how the Document Map view can assist you in your work.

Looking Ahead

In Chapter 19, "Creating Basic PowerPoint Presentations," you'll learn how to use a Word 2000 outline as a basis for a PowerPoint presentation.

Building an Outline in Word 2000

If you have a lot of ground to cover in your document, you might want to take the time to outline what you have to say. Creating an outline also gives you the opportunity to later analyze the flow of what you wrote to make sure it has the maximum effect.

To begin creating an outline in Word 2000, follow these simple steps:

1. Start with a new blank document in Word 2000, and then switch to the Outline view, as shown in Figure 8.7.

FIGURE 8.7

Switching to Outline view is a single mouse click operation.

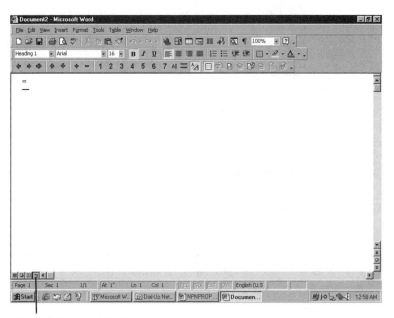

Click here to enter Outline view.

2. Enter each heading, pressing Enter after each item. Word 2000 automatically applies and formats the heading codes based on the Heading 1 style.

3. You can drag and drop a heading to a different level and apply the corresponding heading style. To promote a heading (make it more important), drag the heading's + or – symbol to the left. To demote a heading to a lower, less important level, drag the heading's symbol to the right. A gray vertical bar appears to let you know where to drop the text so that the level shift occurs.

4. To move a heading to a different location, drag the symbol up or down. A faint horizontal line tells you exactly where you are about to drop the text. Note that all the headings (and as you begin to draft the document, text as well) are relocated with the parent heading.

5. When you're satisfied with the organization of your outline, you can return to a standard document view—Normal view—to begin writing the body of the document. To return to Normal view, click the leftmost button immediately above the page number at the bottom of the screen.

> **Note: What you see is *not* what you get.** Should you decide to print your outline to give it more thought on the long train ride home, you'll be relieved to know that all those + and – signs will not appear on the printout. They exist primarily to serve as an online organizational tool, so you needn't worry about them distracting you.

Modifying the Outline

When the outline is finished, you can manipulate and view it in a number of ways. The tools described next work whether your outline is still being drafted, or you've finished writing the entire document and simply have some last-minute organizational changes. Just enter Outline view to begin modifying your outline.

Figure 8.8 shows the Outlining toolbar so that you can get acquainted with each of the button's locations onscreen. Table 8.1 lists each of the buttons by name and gives you a brief overview of what each one does.

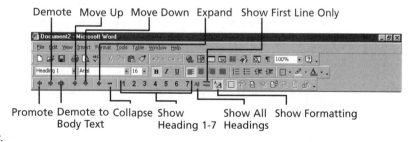

FIGURE 8.8
The Outlining toolbar gives you tremendous flexibility when you want to reorganize your outlines.

Table 8.1 Outlining Toolbar Buttons and Their Functions

Button Name	Function
Promote	Moves selected text up one level for each time clicked.
Demote	Moves selected text down one level of importance for each time clicked.
Demote to Body Text	Attributes a Normal text style instead of one of the many headings available to the text entered after the button is clicked.
Move Up	Moves the selected text above the preceding item with the same comparable heading number.
Move Down	Moves the selected text below the following item with the same comparable heading number.
Expand	Reveals more outline items, one level at a time, when a block of text is selected and the button is clicked.
Collapse	Takes away one level of selected outline material one level at a time (the reverse of Expand).
Heading 1-Heading 7	Shows outline headings carrying the corresponding heading number and higher (those with a lower number) when a number is clicked.
Show All Headings	Displays all levels of the outline.
Show First Line Only	Lets you see the first line of body copy only when viewing the outline.
Show Formatting	Toggles off and on the text formatting that corresponds to the heading levels. When this feature is turned on, items higher in priority carry a larger type font. When it is turned off, all items appear in an equal size.

Note: Printing the outline. When you want to print outlines, it's not an all-or-nothing proposition. In fact, by using the various techniques described previously in the outline sections, you can display as much or as little as you want. To print what you see onscreen, click the Print button. Note, however, if any body text is showing (even if it's just the first line), Word 2000 prints all the body text.

Remember, if styles are used for your document's headings—as is the case with documents created in Outline view—you can take advantage of the Document Map view described in the preceding chapter to see your document's layout as you write.

Using Master Documents to Manage Large Documents

Dealing with master documents falls somewhere in between advanced document creation and collaboration issues. If you happen to be writing a book, you can use a master document to keep everything together yet have Word 2000 generate a separate filename for each chapter. On the collaboration side, say you're a scientist for a major research foundation in the process of applying for a grant. Because you're applying for a hefty sum of money, you're required to turn in page after page of detailed analysis, information about your organization, and so on. In this scenario, using the master document may be the perfect way to divvy up the work among colleagues. In the end, the document is treated as one large document. In the meantime, though, you have maximum flexibility to delegate the various parts of the document to the people who are the most familiar with the topic at hand.

In the sections that follow, we'll explore the creation and use of master documents.

Creating a Master Document

If you think a project is large enough to warrant the creation of a master document, you should become familiar with the following steps needed to create such a document. Although any document can be converted to a master document, creating a master document from the ground up is easiest.

1. The first step in creating a master document involves creating an outline for the document. Whether you create the outline before you do anything else, or you look at your document in Outline view doesn't matter as long as the styles have a hierarchical structure. Master documents need these styles to generate their subdocuments.

> **Note: About this hierarchical structure...**A hierarchical structure results when you work with an outline and promote or demote its headings. If you've used Normal style for everything, headings promoted to the highest level take on the Heading 1 style along with its appearance.

2. To create the subdocuments, you need to select the text you want to be converted to subdocuments. Note that Word 2000 uses the outline level of the first item on your list to trigger additional subdocuments. Consider Figure 8.9 as an example. If you select the entire outline minus the title, as shown here, five subdocuments are created because level 2 is the first heading level selected, and this mock outline contains five heading 2's.

Caution: Watch where you click! Selecting text in Outline view can be tricky. To make sure text is selected and not moved by mistake, move the mouse pointer to the left side of the screen until it turns into a right-pointing arrow. Click and then drag down to select the desired text.

FIGURE **8.9**

Select this text to create five sub-documents.

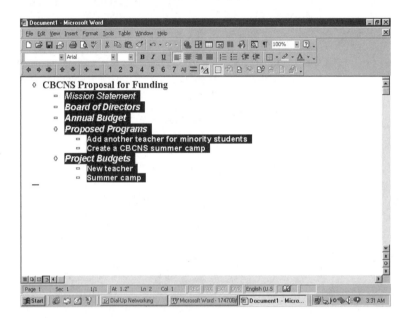

3. After you've selected the desired text, click the Create Subdocument button (refer to Figure 8.9). Word 2000 then draws a thin lined box around each subdocument to let you know where it divided things.

4. At this point, you might want to apply a template to the master document to make sure all the subdocuments have a consistent appearance.

5. If others are to be granted permission to work on the master document or subdocuments, you might want to set some security parameters in place. You'll learn more about security issues in Chapter 11, "Collaborating on Word 2000 Documents." Setting such parameters is important not just to protect the unauthorized editing of content, but also to guard against potential loss of work should a non-Office 2000 user attempt to work with the master document or subdocument.

6. Save your master document, and give it a name. Word 2000 has taken care of naming all the subdocuments for you. If the master document is to be worked on by a group of people, you also should move the document to a shared folder so that everyone who needs to can get to it.

Note: Naming subdocuments. When you create subdocuments, Word 2000 assigns a name to each one using the first few characters in the subdocument's heading. For example, if the subdocument's heading reads "Chapter 1: Word 2000 Survival Guide," the subdocument will most likely carry the name Chapter 1.doc. To see the filenames of all the subdocuments, open the master document in Outline view, and click the Collapse Subdocuments button. All the filenames of the subdocuments then appear as hyperlinks.

After you've created your subdocuments, you can take advantage of the special Master Documents buttons that reside on the right end of the Outlining toolbar. Table 8.2 introduces those buttons (from left to right) and tells you what clicking them will do.

Table 8.2   Buttons You Need to Know When Working with Master Documents

Button	Name	Function
	Master Document View	This view used to be the one you had to be in to create a master document, but in Word 2000, you use the Outline view. The two views have essentially been combined.
	Collapse/Expand Subdocuments	This button turns the subdocuments' names into hyperlinks on which you click to be taken to the desired subdocument. Collapsing subdocuments also frees them for use by others in your workgroup.
	Create Subdocument	After you've selected the portion of the outline you want to turn into subdocuments, click this button to have Word 2000 create the subdocuments.
	Remove Subdocument	This button is a bit deceiving. It doesn't remove a subdocument from the master document as you might think. Instead, it reverses the action to create the subdocument, thus stripping the subdocument attributes from the selected portion of the master document.

continues

Table 8.2   continued

Button	Name	Function
	Insert Subdocument	To use this button, first place the insertion point in a blank line between two existing subdocuments in the desired location. Click Insert Subdocument, and choose the file you want to include from the dialog box. When you find the file, click its filename, and then click Insert Subdocument. The specified document then becomes a subdocument of the current master document.
	Merge Subdocuments	Make sure that the subdocuments you want to merge are located next to one another in the expanded Outline view. Click the first icon you want to merge, hold down the Shift key, and then click each additional subdocument icon. When all the subdocuments you want to merge are selected, click the Merge Subdocuments button.
	Split Subdocument	Select the subdocument you want to divide. You also might need to create new headings or heading levels so that Word 2000 knows where to split the subdocument. When you have at least two heading levels at the same level as the current subdocument's highest level heading, click Split Subdocument to make the change.
	Lock Subdocument	This button serves as a toggle switch to lock and unlock subdocuments. If you see the padlock icon beneath a subdocument's icon when the subdocuments are expanded, then clicking the Lock Subdocument button grants you access to the subdocument most of the time.

Note: Before you start pressing buttons... All the buttons from Remove Subdocument on down (except where noted otherwise) require you to view the master document in Outline view and then expand the subdocuments before you can perform their respective operations.

> **Note: The subdocument I want to work with is locked; now what do I do?** Click the subdocument's icon, and click the Lock Document button on the Outlining toolbar. If that trick doesn't work, you might need to seek permission to access the file from the document's owner.

Working with a Single Subdocument

To work with a subdocument, whether it resides on your own machine for a book project or on a shared folder on your company's network for workgroup use, you need to open the master document in Outline view and then collapse the subdocuments. (By collapsing the subdocuments, you free documents you aren't working on for use by others.) With the list collapsed, you see a hyperlink that corresponds to each subdocument. Click the desired hyperlink to launch the subdocument in its own window. After you've finished working in the subdocument, save it as you would any other document, and then click File|Close to return to the master document.

> **Looking Ahead**
>
> In Chapter 9, "Creating Professional-Looking Documents," you'll learn how to maximize the benefits of using master documents to generate tables of contents, indices, and other professional elements.

Putting File Properties to Work for You

File properties are bits of information about a document that can better help you identify the document. The information might include the author's name, the date on which the document was created, or even how many lines of text are in the document.

These bits of information, which you can access by clicking File|Properties, come in three flavors: Automatically Updated, Preset, and Custom. Automatically Updated properties are items that Word 2000 keeps track of for you, such as dates, word counts, number of times edited, and so on. You needn't do anything to define this information; it's all handled automatically. Preset properties are properties that already exist—for example, Author or Title. You see a text box earmarked for the information on a Property tab, but you might have to enter the appropriate text. Some Preset properties, however, such as Author, are gathered from your computer's files to save you the keystrokes. Finally, you can label Custom properties yourself and apply values to them.

So why go to all the trouble to flesh out this information? For starters, file properties can give you more detailed search results when you're attempting to look for a file. The Author property can also be of great value in determining the owner or manager of a shared document. And if those reasons aren't compelling enough, consider the value of using file properties to draft notes about a particular version of a document or to notate the status of the project.

What File Properties Can Tell You

When you click File|Properties to begin working with or viewing the file properties, you see a dialog box with five tabs, like the one shown in Figure 8.10.

The Summary tab appears by default. From left to right, the Properties tabs are General, Summary, Statistics, Contents, and Custom.

The General tab contains many of the document's automatically generated properties, such as the type of document, its size and location, and dates for when it was last accessed and modified.

The Summary tab (refer to Figure 8.10) includes spaces for information such as the document's title (which Word 2000 generates from the first few words on the page), its author and the author's company (which it pulls from the personal profile data you entered during Office 2000's installation), and the name of the template on which the document is based. In addition, you can manually enter the document's subject, its manager, and even define some keywords for the document in the other fields.

The Statistics tab hosts some of the same data found on the General tab but delivers it in greater detail. For instance, here you can find the answers to any of the following questions:

- How many times has the document been revised?
- How much time was spent editing it?
- How many pages are in the document? paragraphs? lines? words?

Best of all, Word 2000 gathers all the answers for you!

In Word 2000, the Contents tab basically holds a map of all the headings you used in the document. To make sure this information appears in the Contents window, you can verify that the Save Preview Picture box in the Summary tab is checked.

On the Custom tab (see Figure 8.11), you can store any bits of data you want to track on a document that you can find elsewhere in the file properties tabs. For example, if you run a small consulting firm, you might want to keep track of which clients each document pertains to. Or if you anticipate generating a number of documents related to a certain project at work, consider assigning a Project property to each document so that you can quickly access all the files you need.

FIGURE 8.11
Word 2000 offers a bunch of predefined file property names from which you can choose.

Defining a Custom Document Property

You need to follow a number of steps to define a new file property, but they're quick and easy:

1. Launch Word 2000, click File|Properties, and then open the Custom tab.

2. In the Name box, either use the arrow buttons to choose a suggested file property name, or type in your own.

3. Select the type of data to be kept in the property from the Type drop-down box. Your options include Text, Date, Number, and Yes or No.

4. Fill in the Value box for the current document. Depending on the type of property you defined, the value could be the specific client's name, the name of the project, or something similar.

5. After you've entered all the information, click the Add button. The new property then appears in the listing at the bottom of the screen.

> **Tip: You've got to be committed.** The most complex set of file properties out there is utterly useless if you forget to fill in the information. To minimize the odds of facing tons of empty property fields, you can have Word 2000 prompt you for the information when you save the document for the first time. To do so, click Tools|Options, and then open the Save tab. Make sure the Prompt for Document Properties check box is marked.

Getting the Printed Output You Want

Printing your document might seem like a pretty straightforward task, but sometimes it can get a bit tricky, like when you want to print an outline or a master document. Throw in the fact that you can print documents to just about any size of paper imaginable and even print multiple pages on a single sheet of paper, and you end up with a staggering number of options.

In the final sections of this chapter, we'll take an in-depth look at various printing tips and tricks so that you can get the output you want when you want it. No more running back and forth to the network printer to retrieve unacceptable copies and wasting ream after ream of paper!

Printing Master Documents

Printing parts of a master document is a lot like printing an outline, as you can see in the following steps:

1. Display the master document in Outline view.
2. Expand all the subdocuments.
3. Expand or collapse the headings to display as much or as little of the document as you want to print.
4. Click File|Print, and then set all the printing options as described in the sections that follow.

To print the entire master document, expand the subdocuments while you're in Outline view, return to Normal view, and then print it as you would any other Word document.

Special Page Setup Considerations

Presumably, if you wanted anything other than the default margins for the current document, you've already visited the Page Setup dialog box. If your print job is pretty straightforward, you might not even need to visit this set of tabs. For your convenience, check out this set of questions to help you determine whether you need to enter Page Setup. If you answer yes to any of them, be sure to make the necessary adjustments before sending the document to the printer.

- Do you want your margins to take into account space taken away by the document's binding? If so, you can adjust the gutter size and location in the Margins tab of the Page Setup dialog box (see Figure 8.12). If you plan to print on both sides of the paper, make sure the Mirror Margins box is checked so that the gutter will appear in the proper place.

FIGURE 8.12

The Margins tab helps you factor in binding space.

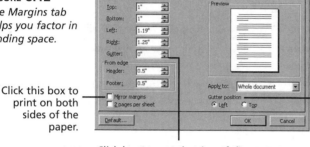

Click this box to print on both sides of the paper.

Click here to specify the gutter's location.

Click here to set the size of the gutter.

- Does your document require different-sized margins for various parts of it? If so, move the insertion point to the point at which you want to change margins, enter the Margins tab of the Page Setup dialog box, make your changes, choose From This Point Forward from the Apply To box, and then exit the dialog box. Repeat these steps with the insertion point in the location of the next desired change.

- Do you plan to print on a nontraditional paper size (anything other than letter, legal, executive, or a standard-sized envelope)? If the answer is yes, you need to define the paper or envelope size on the Paper Size tab of the Page Setup dialog box. Use the arrow buttons to define the needed width and height of the paper you plan to use. Depending on the size you define, Word 2000 changes the information in the Paper Size box for you. For example, if you change the width to 8 inches and the height to 10 inches, the words Custom Size appear in the Paper Size box.

- Do you want different headers and footers on odd and even pages? Do you want a different header or footer on the first page? If this is the case, you can alter some settings on the Layout tab of the Page Setup dialog box. For example, you can check the Different Odd and Even box or the Different First Page box.

Looking Ahead

In Chapter 9, "Creating Professional-Looking Documents with Word 2000," we'll explore working with headers and footers in detail.

Previewing Before You Print

Previewing a document before you print it is the best thing you can do to minimize the occurrence of unexpected printing surprises. Word 2000 gives you two methods for previewing a document: Print Preview (click File|Print Preview) and the Print Layout view (click the Print Layout View button above the Word 2000 status bar). Although the two views may look similar on the surface, they have a few subtle differences. Print Preview (see Figure 8.13) gives you access to a host of special tools that let you do any of the following:

- The Magnifier button lets you zoom in on text you need to edit at the last minute.
- A special Multiple Pages button lets you display as many as six document pages on the screen at one time.
- If you have one or two stray lines of text that spill over onto the final page of the document, the Shrink to Fit button compresses the material by tweaking the font size so that the last page is eliminated.

FIGURE 8.13
Print Preview gives you access to a lot of neat, useful tools.

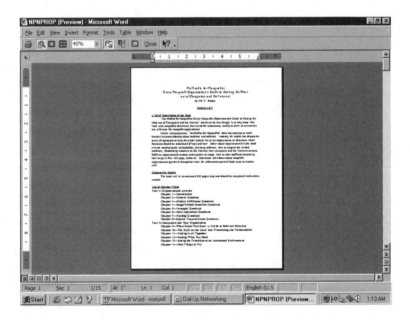

Exiting Print Preview is a snap: Just click the Close button, and you see the document in Normal view.

Last-Minute Text Editing in Print Preview

Say you're about to send your document to the printer and are taking one last look at it in Print Preview. Then it hits you; you think of an eloquent way to restate a paragraph you weren't really happy with from the get-go.

Rather than go back to Normal view, consider making the edits in Print Preview. Move the mouse pointer, which looks like a magnifying glass, over the paragraph you want to change, and then click it. Word 2000 zooms in on the paragraph. Click the Magnifier button to turn the mouse pointer into the traditional editing I-beam (you need to click the document to see the I-beam). Make all the changes you want. When you're finished, click the Magnifier button to turn the mouse pointer back to a magnifying glass. One click on the document brings the whole page into view.

> **Note: For simple jobs only.** The editing method described in the preceding paragraph works great for simple text changes, but if you need to make complex formatting changes as well, you might find the easy access to the usual formatting tools found in Print Layout view (or even Normal view for that matter) to be a tremendous help.

Seeing the Bigger Picture

In Print Preview, you can see as many as six pages at once onscreen (see Figure 8.14). To open all these pages, click the Multiple Pages button, and then drag the mouse pointer out until the desired number of pages is selected. Note that you can view two pages one on top of the other or view them side-by-side; the choice is yours.

> **Tip: Getting a clear view.** In general, the side-by-side display of pages produces clearer results than stacking them because Word 2000 can use a higher zoom percentage for pages shown next to each other.

FIGURE 8.14

View up to six pages at a time in Print Preview.

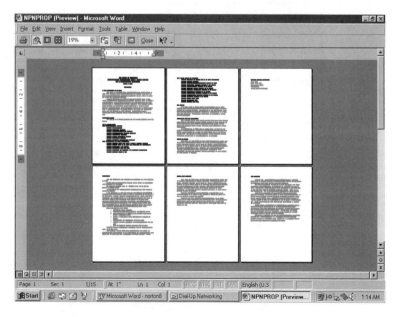

Using Shrink to Fit

Nothing's more frustrating than writing an important letter only to find one or two lines spill over onto a second page. The Shrink to Fit feature can be of tremendous use in shrinking short documents down to size. Word 2000 shrinks them by automatically selecting a new, smaller font size for each type used in the document. Although using this feature can be a terrific way to keep a document at one page and to save paper, it has its drawbacks.

Peter's Principle: Let me share the shrinking benefits of using Shrink to Fit.

Although you can easily undo a Shrink to Fit operation in the same editing session (click Edit|Undo Shrink to Fit), after you save and close the document, the only way to get your old font sizes back is to go back and set each one manually. Another potential downside is Shrink to Fit's effect on documents based on special corporate templates. If you tweak a font used in one of Word 2000's boilerplate templates, that's one thing, but if you attempt to do it with a customized template, the operation defeats the purpose of using a template to achieve a uniform look. Of course, if the document is to be printed as opposed to published on your company's intranet, it may not be a very big deal. Finally, readability should also be factored in. You don't want your readers to have to squint to see what you've sent them.

Nudging the Margins

Another, possibly more subtle way to fit more text onto a page is to nudge the margins out a hair. Even a tiny shift can make a world of difference. To nudge the margins in Print Preview, click the page you want to adjust to select it. The margin markers and rulers frame the active page on two sides. Click one of the margin markers (see Figure 8.15), and drag it toward the edge of the page. A dotted line helps you see just how much or little you've adjusted the margin you're working with. Note that margins nudged for the active page do not affect margin settings on other pages.

Tip: Don't squeeze the margin! If you're trying to work with a large number of pages, returning to Normal view and working with the margins in the Page Setup dialog box might be easier.

FIGURE 8.15
Push the margins out a tad to fit more on a page without changing font size.

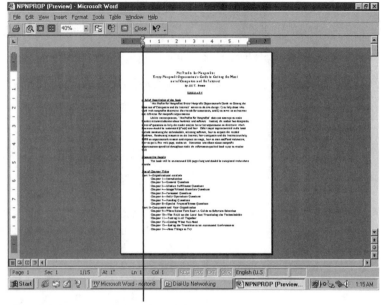

Click and drag toward the edge of the page.

Printing Efficiently

You already know that all you have to do to print a single copy of a document as you see it is to click the Print button. That way, you sidestep all the dialog boxes in favor of an express printing job. Should you want to make any changes (for example, print only a portion of a document or print multiple copies), however, you need to click File|Print or press Ctrl+P. That action calls up the Print dialog box shown in Figure 8.16.

FIGURE 8.16
The Print dialog box gives you dozens of printing options.

From within this dialog box (which, by the way, can vary in appearance, depending on the type of printer and print drivers you have installed), you can gain full control over what exactly is printed and how. The sections that follow will help you optimize your printed output both in terms of the output itself as well as system resources.

Printing a Portion of Your Document

In addition to printing the entire document, you can also print specified parts of it. See Table 8.3 for a description of how you can print various parts of a document.

Table 8.3 Ways to Print Various Parts of a Document

To Print This	Do This
The entire document as is	Click the Print button.
The current page only	Open the Print dialog box, and then choose Current Page in the Print Range section. Click OK to send the page to the printer.
A block of text you selected with a mouse	Select the desired text with the mouse as usual. Next, open the Print dialog box, click your selection in the Page Range section, and then click OK.
Certain page numbers	In the Pages text box of the Print dialog box, enter the range of pages (expressed as 1-5), the list of pages (each page number separated by a comma—1,2,5,8), or combine the two if needed (1,4,9-12). Click OK to send the pages to the printer.
All even or odd pages	In the Print drop-down list box at the bottom-left corner of the dialog box, click the arrow button and choose Odd or Even as desired.

Tip: Even/odd printing can you save time. Toner cartridges for a laser printer can get expensive; for that reason, most businesses choose to have their larger print jobs photocopied. What if the in-house photocopier isn't capable of duplex (front/back) copying? You have to copy the front sides and then feed the pages back through, right? With even/odd printing, you can let the copy machine run 50 copies of each front sheet (odd) unattended and then return to process the even sides, and you don't have to presort the paper output. Hey, this trick may not save you hours of time, but in the corporate world, every

How Many Copies Do You Want?

Although setting the number of copies you want is a simple task (just use the arrow buttons in the Number of Copies box), deciding whether to collate the copies may not be as cut-and-dried.

Collating the copies makes it easier and more efficient to grab a set of pages and staple them together hot off the press, but it can present some problems if you're talking about printing large numbers of copies.

When you choose to leave the copies uncollated, the print driver loads the first page into the printer's memory and then creates all the copies of page one before moving on to page two. When you tell Word 2000 to collate the copies, it has to load each page for every copy, thus sending more perceived output to the printer. Collating can occasionally bog down the printer and generate error messages in extreme cases.

Printing More Than One Page on a Sheet of Paper

Being able to print more than one page on a sheet of paper is the Word 2000 equivalent to those contact sheets you get from professional film developers, and it accomplishes many of the same things. It saves paper until you're ready to see the finished product, and it gives you a pretty good idea of the territory covered in the document (or film).

Word 2000 enables you to print 2, 4, 6, 8, or even 16 pages on a single sheet of paper. Just click the Pages Per Sheet drop-down arrow, and make your selection.

Peter's Principle: Get out the magnifying glass!

Of course, printing above two pages on the same sheet will most likely make all but the headings illegible, so you might as well print an outline instead and save even more paper.

Monitoring Your Memory Usage

The Device Options lever allows you to define how the print driver tracks printer memory usage. In other words, before a complex document is printed, the driver assesses how much memory is needed to do the job versus how much memory is available in your printer. The more conservative the setting, the less likely printer memory is to be over-committed. Using conservative settings could prevent many documents from being printed even if enough memory is available. An aggressive setting, however, may overcommit your printer and cause partial printout completions. For these reasons, the default value rests between the two extremes.

Fine-Tuning Your Print Job

Do you want to print your document in landscape rather than portrait orientation? Would you like to learn how to conserve toner when you're printing drafts for personal or in-house review? If so, then you should become familiar with the various settings you can adjust in the Print Properties tabs.

> **Caution: Not all print properties are the same.** What you find in the Print Properties tabs may vary greatly, depending on what type of printer you have (inkjet or laser), how old the printer is, and whether you're using the drivers that came with the printer or Microsoft's print drivers. In general, the newer and more expensive the printer, the more settings you can tweak. Commonly found settings include orientation, paper size, paper source, and graphics output. We'll explore these settings and a few others in the sections that follow.

To get there, click the Properties button on the upper-right corner of the Print dialog box.

Setting Paper Parameters

The Paper tab is one you'll encounter in just about every printer's print properties. If you want to print on a traditional but nondefault paper size, all you need to do is click its name icon in the Paper Size box, and you're all set. You can usually also select the orientation of the printout—portrait or landscape—on this tab as well as define the paper source for the document you're about to print. This last option is one you'll need to pay close attention to if your printer has multiple paper feeds or trays that can be used.

Getting the Full Picture

Most printers allow you to adjust the print quality of the output on something called the Graphics tab. One of the options you can adjust is the resolution. The lower the number, the fewer dots per inch in the image, thus the less toner you use. If reviewing the text is your primary concern, then high resolution isn't very important. If, on the other hand, your document contains a fair amount of line art, you should go with a higher resolution to help ensure the images' edges appear smooth and true to character as opposed to jagged from too few dots per inch being printed.

The next adjustment you may find is called *dithering,* which determines how color printouts are or are not handled. Finally, you can often use an Intensity lever to make images darker or lighter. Obviously, lighter saves toner, but darker gives you crisper photocopy reproduction.

Handling Fancy Fonts

Many laser printers offer you a Fonts tab. This tab lets you define how TrueType fonts are printed. By default, they are downloaded to your printer as soft fonts, which quickens the printing process. If, however, you are trying to achieve a special artistic effect, or if your document has lots of graphics and little text, the TrueType as graphic may be the way to go.

Printing's Not Just for Documents

Everyone knows you can print a document, but did you know you can print the comments associated with a document? Or how about the document's AutoText entries? You can also print styles, document properties, and key assignments. All this is fine and dandy, but why in the world would you want to print all this extra stuff? Printing the comments can be a great way to ponder your coworkers' input on a document during your daily commute or on a business trip without the bulk of your laptop. AutoText entries and key assignment printouts can serve as wonderful computer-side training aids to new staff members.

To print any of these elements, launch the Print dialog box, and then choose the desired element from the Print What drop-down list near the bottom-left side of the dialog box.

Scaling Documents to Size

If you've created a document in one paper size and want to print it on another, never fear; Word 2000 is prepared to handle the task. Its Scale to Size feature is just like the reduce/enlarge capability found on many photocopy machines.

In the Zoom section of the Print dialog box is a Scale to Size drop-down list box. Just click the drop-down arrow, and choose the size of paper you want to print the document on; Word 2000 does the rest.

On Your Own

Once again, we've managed to cover an enormous amount of territory in a single chapter. Perhaps the best way for you to absorb all this material is to think back to the most complex document you've ever created in Word. Could any of the document-creation techniques described here have made the document's development run more smoothly? Could any of the printing options have enhanced the presentation of the material?

What about any documents you might create in the future? Which techniques and options do you plan to explore firsthand?

With the basics of document creation and printing covered, we're ready to learn how to create more professional-looking documents. In Chapter 9, we'll look at many of Word 2000's new features and how to put some of our old favorites to good use.

Creating Professional-Looking Documents with Word 2000

Whatever you do, never underestimate the importance of creating a professional-looking document. If you think your time is misspent making documents look good, think again. Not only can sloppy presentation leave others with a bad impression, but it can cost you that dream job or your organization funding from that source you submitted a grant proposal to. Whether your text is accurate or not, people in critical decision-making positions may take documents laden with spelling errors and unclear formatting and presentation and translate that into a global lack of attention to detail. Don't let it happen to you!

This chapter will introduce you to all the Word 2000 features that can improve a document's presentation. From font selection tips to including a table, using borders, and generating a table of contents, it's all here.

Choosing Your Fonts

Although font selection may not seem like a complex topic, some good rules of thumb can help you achieve the desired effect. First, try to restrain yourself when choosing fonts. Use two to three different fonts at the most to maintain the document's readability, while preventing the readers from becoming distracted.

Several other factors have a bearing on which font(s) you use, how many different ones you select, and their size. These factors include the purpose of the document, the intended audience, and the format of the document. We'll examine each one in turn:

- Purpose—If the document is designed to be a handout or flyer, then larger, more flamboyant fonts may be in order. If, on the other hand, the document is a formal proposal or report, you should limit headings to a crisp, boldface font that doesn't overpower the text and keep body text in a closely related font (see Figures 9.1 and 9.2).

FIGURE 9.1

Tastefully applied fonts make your documents more legible and professional-looking.

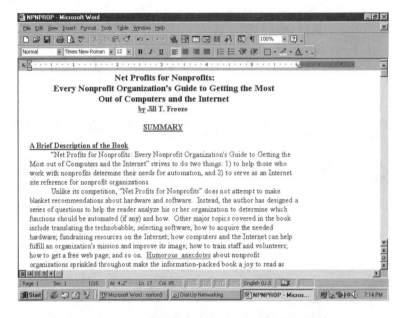

FIGURE 9.2

An overpowering heading like this one can potentially distract the readers and leave them with an unprofessional image of you and/or your organization.

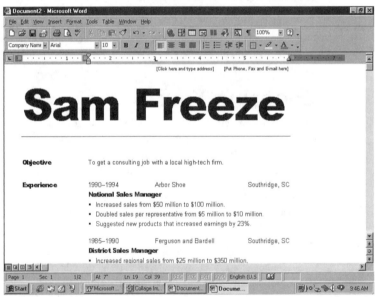

- Audience—The intended audience of the document should always be one of your foremost considerations. If the document is intended to entice people to come to your school's craft fair, then fun fonts are fine. But if the reader is a prospective employer, then you should shoot for something a bit more conservative.

- Delivery—How will your readers receive the document? If they'll get a hardcopy printout, then you can use any font on your computer. If, however, the document will be distributed electronically, you should make sure you use fonts typically installed on all Windows systems (Times New Roman or Arial are safe bets). If you use a special font, the entire effect may be lost at the other end because the readers don't have the font available.

- Format—Is the document a series of large blocks of text, or is the document full of short sections, giving the document an airy feel? Large blocks of text can handle larger, bolder text headings than their shorter counterparts.

Working with Tables

Tables are incredibly helpful in presenting statistical data or lists of numbers because they guarantee that the various items stay where you put them. With Word 2000, you can include tables in your documents in a number of ways. You can build simple and complex tables with Word, or you can paste, embed, or link Excel 2000 data in a Word document.

> **Tip: Tables are not just for numbers.** Consider using them to align text for a concert program or conference agenda. You can position the table anywhere you want on the page, and you can configure the cells' content in any way you deem appropriate.

In general, if the amount of data you want to include is minimal, doesn't already exist in another Office application, or includes primarily text, building a table in Word 2000 may be the easiest approach. If you need to perform calculations on the data, or it already resides in Excel, you have the option to paste, embed, or link the worksheet into Word 2000.

In the first few sections of this chapter, we'll devote some time to creating tables with Word 2000, and later we'll shift our attention to using Excel data in Word.

Building a Simple Table in Word 2000

If the data you want to include in your document is nowhere else on your computer, and the amount of material is minimal, creating a simple table is the easiest way to go. A simple table can be considered anything with fewer than five columns. Although the Insert Table grid shown in Figure 9.3 gives you only four rows, you can easily add more.

FIGURE 9.3
The Insert Table grid makes it easy to set up a basic table.

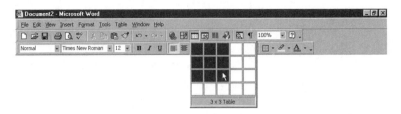

To begin setting up your table, you need to follow these steps:

1. Click the Word document in the location you want to place the table you're about to create.

2. On the Standard toolbar, click the Insert Table button to see the grid shown in Figure 9.3.

3. Drag the mouse pointer out and down until you've selected the desired number of columns and rows.

> **Tip: Need more rows?** As you're entering data into the table and you reach the last cell, you can quickly add another row of cells by pressing the Tab key. You can use this trick as many times as needed.

4. After you release the mouse button, the table appears in your document. You can begin entering text by clicking a cell and then typing the text as usual. If the text is too long for the cell, the text wraps to a second line within the cell to accommodate the excess.

5. To move to the next cell, press Tab; to move to the previous cell, press Shift+Tab.

Creating Complex Tables in Word 2000

Is the table you have in mind more than five columns wide? If so, Word 2000 gives you a simple way to build more complex tables, too. Just follow these steps, and you'll be on your way!

1. Open the Word 2000 document into which you want to place the new table, and then click the location you want the table to appear.

2. Click Table|Insert|Table. The Insert Table dialog box shown in Figure 9.4 appears.

Figure 9.4

You can define your new table parameters as the default table-creating format by checking the option at the bottom of the dialog box.

3. In the Number of Columns and Number of Rows boxes, either type the desired number, or use the arrow buttons to increase or decrease the default numbers.

Note: How big is big? Using this method to build your table, you can have up to 63 columns of information and an almost infinite number of rows. I say "almost infinite" because this number could potentially be restricted by your system's available memory or disk space. To reach that point, though, the table would be massive, and most likely would be something that you should manage in Excel anyway.

4. Define the AutoFit behavior for your table. By default, Word 2000 makes all columns across the page equal size, but you can also achieve any of the following effects (as shown in Figure 9.5):

   • Fixed Column Width—Instead of letting Word 2000 set the column size equally across the page, you can set it yourself using the arrow buttons in the text box next to the Fixed Column Width option. Of course, you might need to tweak the table alignment later to make it look nice.

   • AutoFit to Contents—Word 2000 gives you the specified number of columns that start out being very tiny. As you enter text or numbers, the columns automatically expand to fit the largest item. Each subsequent column remains the same small size until you add data. This option, too, may require some final touches to make it look better.

   • AutoFit to Window—This option starts out looking like the default in that the columns are equally spread across the page. Instead of being static in size, however, the columns change with the text you add. They never get smaller, but should they need to get bigger, they do. The remaining columns shrink to equal sizes until text is added to them. This method probably requires the least cleanup work because it already fills the page, thus making table alignment a non-issue. If you have special formatting in place surrounding the table, however, you might want to keep the table's width smaller than the entire page. In that situation, you should work with either the fixed column widths or AutoFit to Contents option to achieve the best results.

FIGURE 9.5
Getting to know the various AutoFit behaviors.

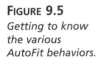

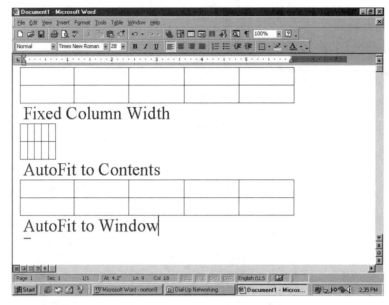

FIGURE 9.5
Getting to know the various AutoFit behaviors.

5. When you're familiar with using AutoFormat for tables (which you will be in a couple of sections), you can click the AutoFormat button to define how you want the table to look.

6. If you want to keep the settings you just defined as the default settings for creating a table using this method, just check the Set as Default for New Tables check box.

7. When you're satisfied with your settings, click OK. Word 2000 displays the table you defined as the dialog box closes.

Drawing a Table in Word 2000

Don't let the term *drawing* intimidate you; you needn't be a Claude Monet to draw a nice-looking table in Word 2000, but drawing tables does take some patience and practice.

> **Tip: If time is of the essence...** Need to get the document done in a hurry? I suggest you try to work with one of the other methods of table design in Word. They're much less finicky and produce quick, predictable results. If one of those methods doesn't work, you might want to consider using Excel. The Draw Table tool may be easy to use, but it takes longer to master and get all the pieces into place.

Follow these steps to begin drawing your own table in Word 2000:

1. Open the Word 2000 document into which you want to draw the table. Because you draw tables by hand, you need to make sure you have plenty of whitespace—or blank space—to work with. To produce the whitespace, just press Enter several times. Leftover space can easily be removed, so you might want to leave yourself a bit more room than you anticipate needing.

2. Click Table|Draw Table. Your mouse pointer turns into a pencil, and the Tables and Borders toolbar appears.

3. Click in the upper-left corner of your table, and then drag the mouse out and down until the table is the size you want (see Figure 9.6). As you move the mouse, the selected area is outlined, so you can easily see where the table's borders fall.

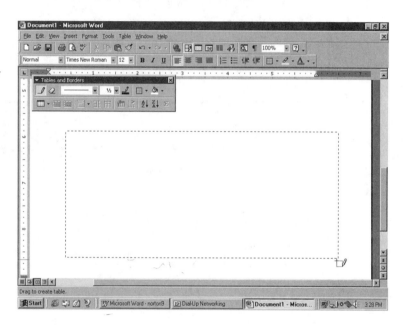

FIGURE 9.6

Drag and drop the pencil to draw each cell the way you want it.

4. Repeat the process until you've drawn all the cells you want in your table.

5. You can change cell and table attributes just as easily as you change fonts in Word itself. Just select the desired cell or block of cells, and then make your selection from the Tables and Borders toolbar.

6. To adjust the size of a cell, click the Draw Table button to restore the mouse pointer to an I-beam. Run the I-beam over the cell's border until it turns into the familiar double-headed Resize pointer, and then click and drag the border to the desired location. You'll learn more about formatting tables in the next few sections.

Converting Existing Text to a Table

If you've been using multiple tab stops to align columns of text, it's time to consider converting the text to a table for clarity. In fact, converting bits of text to a table is a necessity when you're planning to publish them to the Web because tab stops don't always translate well to HTML. In other words, those columns you try so painstakingly to line up with tab stops end up looking like they were never lined up in the first place.

Follow these steps to begin converting existing Word text to a table:

1. Word 2000 needs some kind of separator to tell it where to begin a new cell. That separator can be a tab, a comma, or even a period. Take a close look at the text you're about to convert to make sure only one separator follows each item. If you have more than one, the cells will be out of alignment.

2. Select the Word 2000 text you want to convert to a table.

3. Click Table|Convert|Text to Table to display the Convert Text to Table dialog box shown in Figure 9.7. Notice that Word has already entered the proper numbers to define the table size.

FIGURE 9.7

The jumbled text in the background is about to be converted to a professional-looking table.

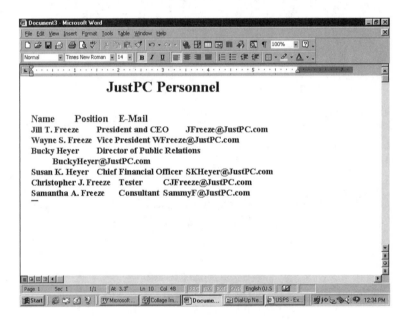

4. Specify the new table's AutoFit behavior. You can refer to Figure 9.5 for a reminder of what kind of results each option produces.

5. When you know how to use AutoFormat for tables, you can even define that formatting at this point by clicking the AutoFormat button.

6. Tell Word 2000 what kind of separator you used for the text by clicking the applicable option. If the separator you used isn't listed, click the Other option, and then enter the separator in the text box.

7. Click OK when you're done to have Word 2000 build the table.

Using AutoFormat for Instant, Professional Results

Word 2000 always gives you the option to format your tables and cells manually (in fact, we'll look at some of the more useful options in the next few sections), but when you need first-class results in a hurry, there's no substitute for AutoFormat for Tables (see Figure 9.8).

FIGURE 9.8

See what a few seconds in the AutoFormat dialog box did for the jumbled mess shown in the background of Figure 9.7?

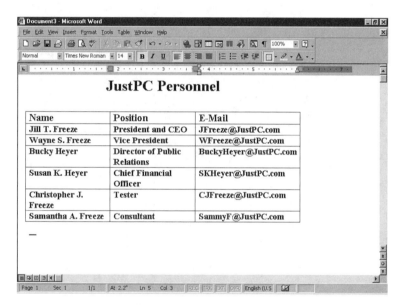

Although you'll see shortcuts to the AutoFormat for Tables dialog box everywhere (does this icon look familiar?), the following steps show you how to access it from within any table:

1. Click inside the Word 2000 table you want to format to set the insertion point in place. Although the exact placement of the insertion point isn't important, it does help Word detect that a table is the active element. This step frees the table-specific menu items for your use.

2. Click Table|Table AutoFormat to bring up the Table AutoFormat dialog box shown in Figure 9.9.

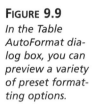

FIGURE 9.9

*In the Table
AutoFormat dia-
log box, you can
preview a variety
of preset format-
ting options.*

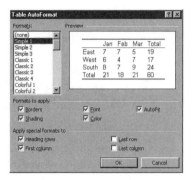

3. Click a format's name to see it in the preview window. Repeat the process until you see the one you want.

> **Tip: Will the table be made available on the Web or in a PowerPoint presentation?** When you're selecting the desired format, give some thought to how the table will be presented. If the table will be included as part of a printed grant application, then something simple in black and white with minimal shading is the best bet. If, however, the table is slated for use in a PowerPoint presentation, consider giving it some color for additional visual impact. Of course, you can colorize a table at any time, but the whole theme of this book involves producing the best results quickly, so why not do it now?

4. After you've selected the format you want, you can tell Word 2000 which parts of the format you want to keep or toss out. For instance, you can drop colorization or AutoFit by removing the check mark next to the given element. Logically, Word 2000 includes all parts of a displayed format by default.

5. You can instruct Word to apply special formatting to the first row of a table or not. Because Word assumes you have special column headers in place, you need to change options only if you don't have any special headers to which you want to apply special accented formatting.

6. Click OK to have Word begin formatting the table based on your selections.

Adding and Deleting Columns and Rows from Tables

No matter how you generate your table, you should be familiar with how to accomplish these tasks:

- Inserting a row—Word 97 users will be greatly relieved to see that you can now enter the rows above or below the selected row instead of just below the selected row. Click a row adjoining the area you want the new row to occupy, and then click Table|Insert|Rows Above (or Rows Below).

- Inserting multiple rows—Select the number of rows equal to the number you want to add, and then click Table|Insert|Rows Above (or Rows Below).

- Inserting a column—Click inside a cell that will border the new column, and then click Table|Insert|Column to the Left (or Column to the Right) as appropriate.

- Inserting multiple columns—This procedure is identical to inserting a single column, except that first you must select the same number of columns you want to add to your table. Then you click Table|Insert|Column to the Left (or Column to the Right).

When it comes to deleting parts of a table (or even the table itself), you need to be on your toes because the Delete function works a bit differently in Word 2000 than it did in previous versions of Word.

The only surefire way to see that only the cells you want deleted are, in fact, deleted is to select them with your mouse and then click Table|Delete|Cells. This way, you delete only the items you selected. If you choose any of the other options such as Table, Columns, or Rows, you might accidentally delete cells you intended to keep.

Caution: Whoops! If you delete the wrong thing by accident, remember the magic key sequence: Ctrl+Z. It's the quickest way to recover in a situation that could potentially cause panic.

On the positive side, options such as Table|Delete|Table, Table|Delete|Columns, or Table|Delete|Rows make deleting their respective elements a breeze. Just click inside a member cell of the group you want to delete, and then choose the appropriate option.

Note: Why can't I just press Delete? When you're working with tables, the Delete key erases only text inside the cells selected, not the cells themselves.

Adjusting Column Width

Unless you've made use of Word 2000's AutoFit feature, you may find yourself needing to adjust the width of your columns either for aesthetic purposes or simply to squeeze more information onto one line. The easiest way to adjust the width is to click inside the table you want to work with, and then click the column markers inside the ruler and drag them to the desired location. A dashed line running the length of the page helps you see exactly where the cell border would fall should you release the mouse button at a given point.

> **Caution: Make sure you know what you're asking for.** Before performing the operation, verify that you've selected the column marker(s), not just a single cell. If you choose a cell, only that cell's size changes, which produces some unpredictable results with regard to your table's appearance.

Merging Cells to Create Column Headings

Tables look a bit more formal and professional with a nice title. Unfortunately, those titles are often much longer than a single cell. So how do you add a title that fits in with the table? Easy. Merge the cells in the first row of your table to create a heading similar to the one pictured in Figure 9.10.

FIGURE 9.10
Merge cells to create an attention-grabbing title for your table.

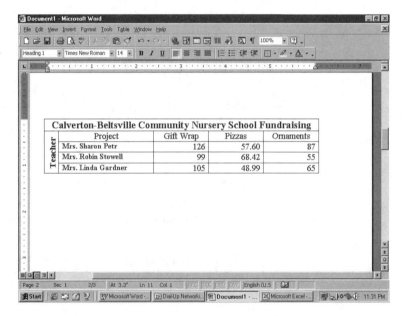

To merge cells, simply select the cells you want to merge to create the title, and then click Table|Merge Cells. That's literally all there is to this process. All the cells are now one big cell, ready for you to enter and format the appropriate title.

Changing the Direction of Text in Your Table

Using the technique for changing the direction of text in your table is a great way to accommodate long column labels or to accent row labels, as shown in Figure 9.10. Typically, you can begin by first merging a group of cells to make room for the altered text. Either that, or you could pull the edge of the cell wall out to make room. Type the desired text, select it, and then click Format|Text Direction. The Text Direction-Table Cell dialog box shown in Figure 9.11 opens. Choose the desired orientation for your text, and then click OK.

FIGURE 9.11

The large graphic buttons make it easy to see what you'll get before you make your selection.

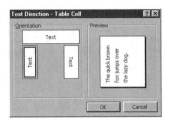

Performing Basic Calculations in Your Table

Although Excel 2000 is best for long lists of numbers or complicated formulas, Word 2000 is perfectly capable of performing some basic mathematical functions on its own.

For instance, if you want to add a column of numbers in a Word 2000 table, do the following:

1. After you enter all the data into the table, make sure an empty cell remains at the very bottom of the column of numbers you want to add. You might even need to add an entire row of cells.

2. Click inside that empty cell at the bottom of the column of numbers you want to add.

3. Click Table|Formula to reveal the Formula dialog box shown in Figure 9.12. Notice that Word 2000 has already "guessed" that you want to find the sum of all the numbers in the column above the cell. If you want a different calculation performed, erase the contents of the Formula box, and then use the Paste Function drop-down to select a new function. You need to put the word ABOVE inside the parentheses.

FIGURE 9.12

Word 2000 attempts to guess what calculation you want to perform.

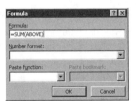

4. Click the Number Format drop-down box to tell Word how you want the final number displayed.

5. When you're finished, click OK. Word 2000 then enters the answer in the specified cell.

> **Tip: Totaling rows.** When you're defining the formula for adding a row of numbers (assuming the answer is to be displayed in a cell at the far right of the row), you need to substitute the word LEFT for ABOVE. In many cases, Word 2000 figures out that point on its own. You should also note that Word does not automatically update it numbers like Excel does. If you change any table items, you need to have Word recalculate (or update) the results. Do so by clicking the cell in which you display the calculated results and then pressing F9. The updated number then appears in the chosen cell.

Using Excel 2000 Worksheets in Word 2000

Earlier in the chapter, I alluded to Excel being a viable option for presenting more complex data or for reusing data that already resides in Excel. Essentially, you have three ways to do this: paste it, embed it, or link it.

The topic of *object linking and embedding (OLE)* can be a bit overwhelming if approached from a strictly theoretical standpoint. But if you look at it from a practical angle, which method you should use when gets a bit clearer. Before we get into the what and when of things, however, let's take a look at the characteristics of each operation:

- Pasting—This process moves your cells to the Word 2000 document, but you cannot alter the formula from within Word. Say, for example, you paste in a column of numbers that you performed AutoSum on in Excel. All the numbers appear, including the answer, but should you change one of the numbers inside Word, the result isn't updated because the Excel functionality is not imported along with the data. Pasting is the most static of all the options.

- Paste Special (or embedding)—When you embed an Excel object, you bring the functionality of Excel 2000 along with the data. By double-clicking an embedded object, you gain access to the familiar Excel 2000 grid and tools. That way, you can tweak the numbers in the document and see accurate results. Of course, changes made here affect the Word document only, not the Excel spreadsheet the data came from. Also, note that embedded worksheets make the Word file larger than either of the other options, but embedding may also be safer because the source document isn't changed along with the Word document. The embedded worksheet therefore has a static but flexible view because it's modifiable but doesn't change the source.

- Paste Link (or linking)—When a link to a worksheet is pasted into Word, that means the data can be viewed in Word, but it's actually stored in the Excel file from which it came. It also means if someone changes the worksheet in the Word document, the source file is altered as well. Linking keeps down the Word file size and is great for incorporating numbers that may be changed in Excel by someone else. It gives documents a dynamic, fresh feel.

Given all that information, which option should you use when? Table 9.1 provides some answers.

Table 9.1   When to Paste, Embed, or Link a Worksheet

Scenario	Paste	Embed	Link
You have a worksheet with numbers that won't change or need to be edited.	X		X
Your worksheet contains data that changes regularly, and you want the Word document to reflect those changes.			X
You want others to be able to play with the numbers in Word without affecting the source file.		X	
The document will use the worksheet to take a snapshot of your company at one point in time.	X		X
Disk space on your machine is tight, and you'll always have access to all your files.			X

Pasting an Excel 2000 Worksheet into Word 2000

If you have simple needs and decide that pasting the worksheet into the document is the way you want to go, you need to follow these steps to do the job:

1. Open both the Word 2000 document into which you want to include the worksheet and the Excel 2000 worksheet containing the data you want to paste into Word.

2. In Excel 2000, use your mouse to highlight the range of cells you want to include in Word.

3. Right-click the shaded area, and select Copy from the shortcut menu.

4. Click the button for the desired Word 2000 document on the Windows taskbar, and then click the location into which you want to paste the worksheet.

5. Click the Paste button on Word 2000's Standard toolbar to put the worksheet in its place.

> **Caution: Word 2000 can't add pasted cells!** Remember, if you change any of the cell numbers in a pasted worksheet while in Word, none of the changes you make are reflected in any formulas that may be included with the worksheet. Either make the necessary changes in Excel, or consider embedding the worksheet instead.

Embedding Excel Worksheets in Word 2000

In situations in which you can't quite make up your mind how you want to use worksheets in Word, embedding is a good, safe bet. You don't have to worry about having the source document available at all times, and the integrity of various calculations remains intact.

To embed a worksheet, follow these simple steps:

1. Again, you need to open both the Word 2000 and the Excel 2000 documents you want to work with.

2. Select the desired range of cells in Excel 2000, and then right-click and select Copy from the shortcut menu.

3. Move over to the Word 2000 document, and then set the insertion point where you want the worksheet to appear.

4. Click Edit|Paste Special. The Paste Special dialog box shown in Figure 9.13 appears.

FIGURE 9.13

In the Paste Special dialog box, you can specify what kind of object you want to paste into the document.

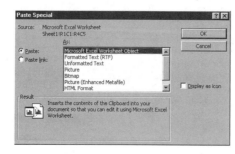

5. Select Microsoft Excel Worksheet Object from the As list, and then click the OK button. The worksheet appears in the document.

6. To edit the object using Excel 2000 tools, double-click it. The worksheet cells appear in their familiar Excel grid, and an Excel toolbar appears in place of Word's.

7. Click outside the worksheet's border to return to the traditional Word environment.

Linking an Excel Worksheet to a Word Document

When you want the closest thing to live data in a document (or when someone other than yourself may change the worksheet numbers), linking may be your best method of choice.

The method for linking a Word document to a worksheet mirrors the steps for embedding in the preceding section, except that in the Paste Special dialog box, you must select the Paste Link option immediately to the left of the As list.

Editing a linked worksheet is also a bit different. Rather than launch a tiny version of Excel when you double-click a linked worksheet, you are taken directly to the source document where you can make your changes.

Making Lists in Word 2000

Whether you have a list of your company's goals for the fourth quarter, the names of PTA volunteers, or a list of items needed for a local charity drive, they'll stand out a lot more (not to mention look a lot better) with a bit of formatting. What's more, you can even sort these lists or give them fancy picture bullets for use on the Web or in PowerPoint presentations.

Giving Lists Style

First, the basics—making those lists look good! Follow these steps to add style to your lists, no matter what their purpose:

1. Place each item or phrase to be included on a separate line, pressing Enter after each line.
2. Select the entire list to which you want to apply special formatting.
3. If a simple numbered or bulleted list is all you want, just click the respective button on Word 2000's Formatting toolbar, as shown in Figure 9.14.

FIGURE 9.14
Word 2000 gives you instant access to simple list formatting options.

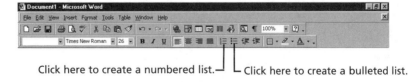

Click here to create a numbered list.┘ └Click here to create a bulleted list.

4. For something a bit fancier, you need to click Format|Bullets and Numbering. In the resulting dialog box, you will find two tabs and a button that will be of great help: the Bulleted and Numbered tabs and the Picture button. For simplicity's sake, we'll focus on the tabs for now.

5. Click the Bulleted or Numbered tab as desired. You then have eight options before you from which to choose.

6. When you've found the format of the bullets or numbers you want to use, click its button, and then click OK. Word 2000 then adds the specified formatting to your list.

If the list is slated to appear on the Web or in a PowerPoint presentation, give serious thought to using Word 2000's new picture bullets. They add color and personality to your lists in no time.

> **Tip: Get ready!** Before you get into selecting picture bullets, you might want to verify that your Office 2000 CDs are nearby. Chances are, you don't have all the picture bullets preinstalled on your machine, so why not save yourself some time and hassle up front?

Follow these steps to apply the new picture bullets to your list:

1. Make sure each list item appears on its own line followed by a hard return.

2. Select the items you want to be considered part of the list, and then click Format|Bullets and Numbering.

3. Verify that the Bulleted tab is open, and then click the Picture button. A Picture Bullet dialog box like the one shown in Figure 9.15 opens.

FIGURE 9.15

The Picture Bullet dialog box bears a striking resemblance to the Clip Gallery because it's actually part of that shared application.

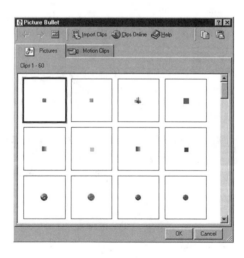

4. After you've found the picture bullet you want to use, click it, and then select Insert Clip from the resulting menu bar. Depending on your installation configuration, you may be asked to insert your Office 2000 CD so that the picture bullet can be loaded onto your machine.

Sorting Your Lists

Word 2000 makes it easy to sort your lists into numerical or alphabetical order no matter how they appear. To begin sorting your lists whether or not they've already been formatted, follow these steps:

1. Make sure the list members appear on their own lines.

2. Highlight the list members, and then click Table|Sort. The Sort Text dialog box shown in Figure 9.16 appears.

FIGURE 9.16

In the Sort Text dialog box, you can sort up to three items in each list.

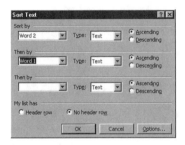

3. In the Sort By drop-down box, Word attempts to give a name to each part of a list member like Word 1, Field 1, or something similar. If the list is made up of one-word items, this box says Paragraphs by default. Use the Sort By drop-down box to select the list item you want Word 2000 to sort by first. If each list member contains a single word, you needn't make a selection; the default is fine.

4. Choose the type of sort you want to perform: Text, Number, or Date; then specify whether you want an ascending or descending sort by clicking the applicable option.

> **Tip: Last things first.** When you're sorting lists of names in which the first name precedes the surname, you should be sure Word 2000 sorts according to Word 2 first and then by Word 1.

5. If you're sorting a simple list, you can click OK to perform the sort. For sorts with multiple criteria (putting a list of names in alphabetical order, for example), move to the first Then By drop-down box, and select the appropriate options as you did for the first sort criteria. Click OK to sort the names.

> **Caution: Don't be deceived!** If your list contains members such as ice cream, hard drive, tennis ball, or macaroni and cheese—items that have multiple words but that should be treated as one—Word might trick you by listing multiple sort criteria in the Sort By or Then By drop-down lists. In these cases, just perform the simple default sort. That way, everything is kept in order. This point may seem obvious as you read this advice, but after you spend several hours at the keyboard putting the finishing touches on that big report, it may not be so clear.

6. If the situation warrants it, fill in the final Then By set of sort options, and then click OK. As the dialog box closes, Word 2000 presents you with the sorted list.

Working with Headers and Footers

By using headers and footers, you can print page numbers, document titles, and other repeating information at the top or the bottom of the page. Headers and footers make your documents look more professional, and page numbers can really help keep things in order in a frenzied work world.

To begin inserting headers and footers, move to the Print Layout view, and then click View|Header and Footer. A dash-lined box appears at the top of the page to define the header area, and the Header and Footer toolbar (see Figure 9.17) is launched as well.

FIGURE 9.17
The Header and Footer toolbar makes adding elements a snap!

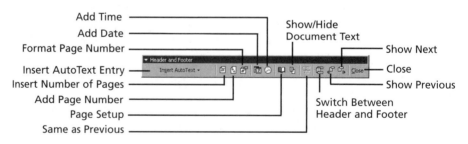

Add Time
Add Date
Format Page Number
Insert AutoText Entry
Insert Number of Pages
Add Page Number
Page Setup
Same as Previous

Show/Hide Document Text
Show Next
Close
Show Previous
Switch Between Header and Footer

Inserting an item is as simple as clicking a button. The callouts in Figure 9.17 will help you see at a glance which button does what. By default, the item you insert is left-aligned. To center it, press the Tab key. To right-align it, press Tab again.

You'll discover a lot of tips and tricks when you're working with headers and footers. Some of them give your documents that final touch of polish, whereas others save you numerous steps. Here are a few you might find useful:

- Choose a "canned" solution—Take a look at the Insert AutoText drop-down menu on the Header and Footer toolbar. Microsoft has predefined some of the more common sets of header/footer information so that you might not need to insert one element at a time.

- Use different headers and footers for odd/even pages—You'll definitely want to consider this option if the document is to be printed on both sides of the paper. That way, for example, the page number can appear on the outer-bottom corner of a page instead of the same spot no matter what. To set up the page number this way, define the header and/or footer for page 1 (what will become the odd pages) as described previously. Then click the Page Setup button on the Header and Footer toolbar, and check the Different Odd and Even option. Click OK to close the dialog box, and then move to the next even page's header by clicking the Show Next button. (You might need to click this button twice if you have footers defined as well.) Define the header or footer for the even pages, clicking Close when you're done.

- If you just want to include page numbers—Sometimes simple is best. If page numbers are the only header or footer information you are planning to define, consider using this less-complicated alternative. From within any view of your Word 2000 document, click Insert|Page Numbers. Choose the position and alignment of the page number using the drop-down lists provided. If you want, you can even prevent Word from printing a page number on the first page (a must if that first page is a cover or fancy title page) by deselecting the Show Number on First Page option.

- When working with documents divided into sections—Typically, either the document's header or footer stays the same throughout the document. In the case of a book, for example, the static item throughout the document may be the book's title and author's name, which appear in the footer. You may, however, want the header to reflect the current chapter title. You can set the footer in the first section and then set the Same as Previous option in subsequent footers. That way, you have to redo only the header for each section.

Inserting Footnotes and Endnotes

Whether you're writing a report on your latest scientific research findings or working on your graduate school thesis or dissertation, you'll find that footnotes and endnotes are must-haves.

> **Note: The difference between footnotes and endnotes.** For those who may not have worked extensively with them before, *footnotes* are bits of text at the bottom of the page that further explain or document resources used. *Endnotes* serve the same purpose but are all presented at the end of the document instead of on each page. You can tell an item has a corresponding footnote or endnote because it has a little raised number next to it. When you run your mouse pointer over the footnote or endnote number, you see the contents of the element in the usual yellow ScreenTip box.

Follow these steps to insert footnotes or endnotes into your document:

1. Set the insertion point in place after the last letter of the text the footnote or endnote will refer to.

2. Click Insert|Footnote to bring up the Footnote and Endnote dialog box.

3. By default, Word 2000 assumes you want a footnote. If you want an endnote instead, you need to click the Endnote option.

> **Tip: Replacing numbers with symbols.** By clicking the Symbol button in the Footnote and Endnote dialog box, you can replace the raised numbers with a symbol of your choice. Just click the symbol you want to use, click OK, and then click OK again to exit the Footnote and Endnote dialog box.

4. Click OK to close the dialog box. Word 2000 places a raised number in the location you specified, and a separate Footnotes/Endnotes panel appears at the bottom of the screen, as shown in Figure 9.18.

FIGURE 9.18

In the Footnotes panel, you can type your footnote content.

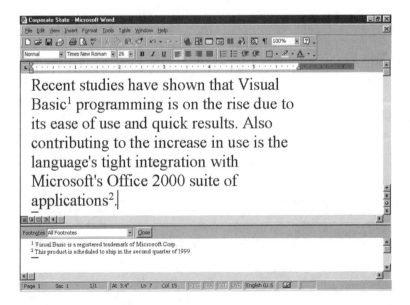

5. Type the comments or resource information into the Footnote panel next to the number that corresponds to the footnote that you just created. The insertion point should move to the proper position on its own.

6. When you're finished entering material, click inside the document to continue working.

Generating a Table of Contents

When you're skimming through a long document, the table of contents can be a real life-saver. It can tell you in an instant where to find what you're looking for. And best of all, generating one of these exceedingly professional-looking elements is easy.

Before I build a table of contents, I always make sure that my document is formatted with heading style codes or level styles generated when I create an outline in Word. Word depends on these style codes to build the table of contents.

With all the formatting and style codes in play, it's time to begin building that table of contents:

1. With the style-coded Word 2000 document open, set the insertion point in the place you want Word to put the table of contents.

> **Tip: Put the table of contents on its own page.** If you simply tell Word to put the table of contents at the front of your document, you'll spend valuable time repaginating the document. Instead, consider doing the following: Press Ctrl+Home to move to the top of the page, press Ctrl+Enter to insert a hard page break, and then press the Page Up button to move the insertion point to the new, blank page. This trick ensures that the table of contents occupies its own page or pages without spilling over to and affecting the formatting of your main document.

2. Click Insert|Index and Tables to launch the Index and Tables dialog box.

3. Open the Table of Contents tab to begin setting your table of contents preferences. By default, the table of contents goes three levels deep, and the numbers are shown right-aligned with periods between the entry and the page number.

4. If you want to select a new format for the table of contents, you can do so using the Format drop-down list. You can see how they look in the Print Preview and Web Preview screens at the top of the tab before you apply them.

5. Click OK to have Word 2000 generate a table of contents similar to the one pictured in Figure 9.19.

FIGURE 9.19

With little effort, you can produce a table of contents that rivals those found in professionally published books.

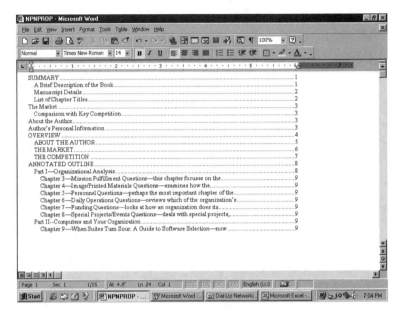

After the table of contents has been generated, you'll need to refresh it if you add new content later. To do so, click anywhere inside the table of contents' boundaries to select it, and then press F9.

> **Caution: There's something you should know before you update your table of contents...**If you applied any special formatting to the table of contents after you built it, it will be lost in the update. The format you specified in the Format drop-down list will remain, but that's it. The moral of the story is: Don't touch your table of contents until the document is completely finished.

Building an Index

For the ultimate in professional appearance and convenience in dealing with large documents, try building an index. Although building it takes a fair amount of time, the increased navigational capability will be worth it. And if you happen to be in the self-publishing business, indexing capabilities are a necessity.

Before you can generate an index, you need to mark the text you want to use for your index entries. To do so, follow these steps:

1. Open the document you want to index, and select the first word or phrase you want to create an index entry for.

2. Press Alt+Shift+X to launch the Mark Index Entry dialog box. Note that the text you highlighted automatically appears in the Main Entry text box.

3. Specify whether the main entry is the place where you want document page numbers reflected (the default), or if you would rather refer the readers to another index entry for the information.

4. Select Mark to mark the current occurrence of the word or phrase only. Mark All, which is available only when you select text before opening the Mark Index Entry dialog box, marks the first occurrence of the word in each paragraph in the document.

> **Caution: Staying on the case.** Unfortunately, the Mark All command is extremely case sensitive. Every letter must match for the entry to be included. After you've marked all occurrences of the word, you might want to go back and perform a search for the same term in its capitalized form. That way, you can mark each one found individually to tag it as part of the index listing you defined previously.

5. Close the Mark Index Entries dialog box to free some workspace.

With all the index entries marked, you're ready to do the easy part—build the index. Follow these steps to produce an index for your document:

1. Because the pagination of the document must be precise for the index to be accurate, you need to verify that the formatting marks that were visible when you marked index entries are hidden again. When done, the pages will fall into place as they should. Remove these elements from sight by clicking the Show/Hide All button on the Standard toolbar (see Figure 9.20).

FIGURE 9.20

Click this toggle switch to show or hide important formatting marks and invisible text.

Click here to hide the formatting marks.

2. Click the spot where you want Word 2000 to begin building your index. You might want to put a hard page break after the last page of your document to make the boundaries absolutely clear.

3. Click Insert|Index and Tables, and select the Index tab. In the Index tab, you can set all kinds of options, including the number of columns your index should occupy, and whether the page numbers immediately follow the text or are right-aligned. You can even use the Format drop-down list to choose the appropriate format for your index given the tone and purpose of your document.

4. After you've finished setting your options, click OK. Within a few seconds, Word 2000 will build the entire index.

> **Tip: Don't go changin'...**So you just finished building the table of contents and index for your document when the boss walks in. Sheepishly, she suggests some changes. Rather than get upset, you can rest easy knowing that you can update both the table of contents and the index with a mouse click and a keystroke. After you've made the changes and have applied any necessary style codes or have marked any new index entries, press Ctrl+A and then press F9. All the material will be updated within seconds. You should note, however, that any formatting changes you made to the elements after they were created will be lost.

Adding Pizzazz to Your Documents

Pizzazz and professionalism need not be mutually exclusive. In fact, with more and more work being done on the Web and in multimedia presentations, as you find in PowerPoint, elements that were once considered frills are now becoming expected.

The previous sections in this chapter focused on issues that improved a document's organization, readability, and professionalism. In the final sections, we'll devote a bit of time to aesthetic considerations.

Inserting Symbols into a Document

As you're scanning through the fonts available on your machine, you might notice a number of wingding or dingbat fonts—fonts that have pictures or symbols in place of traditional letters, numbers, and punctuation.

Rather than hunt and peck your way through the entire alphabet until you find the symbol you want to use, try clicking Insert|Symbol. When you select the Symbols tab, you see a grid of all the symbols available in Word 2000 (see Figure 9.21). From copyright symbols to arrows, they're all available. Use the Fonts drop-down list to select one of the other fonts of interest. A similar grid then appears. Just double-click the symbol you want to use to place it in your document where the insertion point rests. When you're done, just click the Close button.

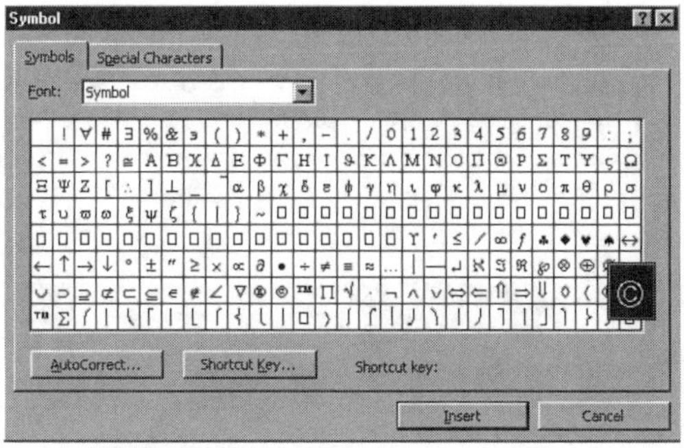

FIGURE 9.21
Click a symbol once as shown here to get a better look at it.

> **Tip: Everybody loves a shortcut!** Microsoft has predefined shortcut keys for a few of the most commonly used symbols in Word 2000. They are Alt+Ctrl+C for the copyright symbol, Alt+Ctrl+R for the registered symbol, and Alt+Ctrl+T for the trademark symbol.

Emphasizing Text with Shading and Borders

If used judiciously, borders and shading can be extremely effective at drawing attention to selected text. And with Word 2000's Web functionality, you can use colored shading to accent a custom background color or chosen theme.

To apply a border to a block of text, follow these steps:

1. Select the block of text you want to emphasize with the border.
2. Click Format|Borders and Shading to open the Borders and Shading dialog box.
3. In the Borders tab, choose the border effect you want from the Settings menu.
4. Select the Style, Color, and Width of your border. By default, any border you select is black.
5. Tell Word 2000 whether you want to apply the border to the current paragraph or text. If you've chosen a block of text, make sure Text is selected. Click OK to apply the border you defined.

With minimal hassle, you can also apply a border to an entire page or to the entire document. Follow steps 1 through 4 in the preceding steps, but this time, make sure you're working in the Page Border tab. In the Apply to drop-down list, specify which page or pages you want to apply the border to.

Shading is even easier to deal with. Just follow these simple steps to accent text in your Word 2000 documents:

1. Select the text you want to accent with shading.
2. Click Format|Borders and Shading, and choose the Shading tab.

Tip: Select the text you really want. Are you tired of having to take entire lines of text whether you want them or not? What are you supposed to do if you want only half of several lines? Try setting the insertion point in place, pressing the Alt key, and then clicking and dragging your mouse. The following figure shows you just how precisely you can select the text you want with this little trick.

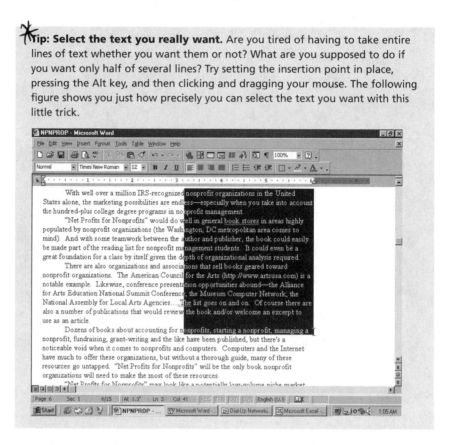

3. The first order of business is to choose a fill color for the shading. Word 2000 gives you several choices on the main tab, but should you feel adventurous and want to mix colors to get a very specific color, you can click the More Colors button and have some fun.

4. In the Pattern section, you can choose how to display the fill color. A style of clear shows only the fill color. A style of 100% shows only the pattern's color, not the fill color. Any other style blends the fill color and the pattern's color with the specified pattern style. Although these colors might look great in the swatches, keep in mind that they will have text over them, which could get more than a little busy.

5. Again, you need to tell Word 2000 whether to apply the border to the selected text or to the current paragraph. Click OK to apply the border.

Applying a Theme to Your Document

If you think a theme is little more than a fancy background design, then you might be shocked to see just how much a theme is carried through in Word 2000. When you apply a theme in Word 2000, not only is the background changed, but the following elements are customized as well to coordinate with the chosen theme:

- Body and heading style attributes
- Bullets
- Horizontal lines
- Hyperlink colors
- Table border colors

If you combine themes with custom templates, you have an almost infallible way to achieve a consistent look and feel to company Web pages designed by multiple people, especially because these themes are shared among all Office 2000 applications.

To apply a theme, all you need to do is click Format|Theme, pick the name of the theme you want, and then click OK to apply. You might want to have your Office 2000 disks close at hand in case the theme you want to use is not loaded on your machine.

On Your Own

Without question, Word 2000 is a feature-rich application. In every document you create, there are more ways to enhance it than you can possibly imagine. As long as you moderate your use of all the fancy features, you should be okay.

To tie up this chapter, think back to a major document you recently created. Did you find any tips and tricks in this chapter that could have helped save you some time? Did you find ways that could have made the document look even better? What things would you like to try next time you write a longer document?

Next stop, working with mail merge. In the meantime, remember that with regard to document creation, prudence is the key. If you use glitzy colors and fancy fonts with discretion, you can create documents with professional appeal that's second to none.

Working with Mail Merge

Everyone likes to feel important, and what better way to make people feel important than to call them by name? Whether you're producing hundreds of letters to tell clients about a new company offering or are sending a handful of thank you notes to a few of your organization's biggest supporters, you'll want to spend the extra time to make each recipient feel valued. And thanks to the power and flexibility of mail merge, you can customize a letter's content as well as its address information and salutation.

In this chapter, you'll learn how to put the power of mail merge to work for you. You'll find out how to generate batches of personalized email messages, discover the best place to store the data you'll use as the data source, and learn how to create a membership directory or similar type of document.

Anatomy of a Mail Merge

If you've never ventured into the wild world of mail merge, you should know a few facts to get up to speed. If you've worked with databases in the past, however, you'll recognize many of the terms even if they don't mean the exact same thing in the context of mail merge.

To generate a customized document, a set of mailing labels, or a large number of envelopes, you essentially need two parts: a main document and a data source. The main document (produced in Word 2000) contains the boilerplate text and formatting (the parts that are the same for every document). It also contains the directions (or field codes) for what customized text should go where in the document. In the case of mailing labels or envelopes, the main document may be nothing more than field codes and paper size property settings.

After you've created the main document, you need to create or attach the data source. It is the file that contains the definitions for each of the field codes included in the main document. This data source file can be a specially formatted Word 2000 document, your Outlook Address Book/Contact List information, or a database built using Excel or Access.

To break down this process even further, let's take a closer look at the parts of a data source. Each bit of data to be used to customize a letter, address label, or envelope is referred to as a *field*. Common fields might be named FirstName, LastName, ZIPCode, and so on. Each recipient or person listed in the data source has his or her own set of fields; this set of fields is called a *record*. As you'll see later in the chapter, you have tremendously powerful capabilities at your fingertips with mail merge: You can sort and filter these records so that your message gets to the right people with minimal waste of resources.

Planning Ahead

One of the best ways to maximize your use of time and resources is to plan your strategy ahead of time. With a bit of forethought, you can avoid having to reinvent the wheel—so to speak—a few projects later. Give some thought to the following:

- Is a data source (or potential data source) already in place? Before you shake your head no, check around. Has someone else in another office or division of your company already set up a data source? This question goes for small, nonprofit organizations as well. Perhaps an intern or volunteer set up something for a special project. Even if the data source needs editing and updating, using it may still be easier than starting from scratch.

- What types of output do you plan to generate? Do you plan to run mailing labels for a newsletter produced offsite? Create intricately customized letters? Build a membership directory? Your output doesn't affect what type of data source you choose, but it does affect what types of fields you should plan to collect for each record. You should also be aware that although you can always add fields to any data source, some sources (Excel, Outlook, and Access) make it easier to find (and fill in) the new information.

- Which applications are most familiar to those who will need to create or edit the data source in the future? Although all the Office 2000 applications are designed to work similarly, some people may just not feel comfortable working with applications they've never used before. If this is the case, you might want to use the most familiar application for the data source to keep the workflow moving smoothly.

- Do most of the records already reside in your Outlook Address Book? That's great if all you need are address labels, envelopes, and letters customized with the recipient's name only, but the information is very restrictive beyond that.

- Do you have a large number of records that you'll need to update regularly and want to have numbered? Excel and Access give you the most control over sizable data sources, and their capability to give you quick, accurate counts of the number of records can also be useful.

When you have a strategy in place, you're ready to begin designing your first mail merge document. And with the help of the Mail Merge Helper, you are guided every step of the way through the process.

Doing It All in Word 2000

Many books just cover the Word part of mail merge in a single chapter; creating a data source in other applications is relegated to the respective application-specific chapters. Because we believe that time is often of the essence when learning how to do something like this, we've included everything you need to know about mail merge right here.

In this section of the chapter, we look at the entire mail merge process in Word 2000. You see how everything fits together from start to finish. In subsequent sections, we deal with creating and attaching data sources from Excel, Outlook, and Access.

Choosing a Main Document Format

The first step in creating a customized document involves building a main document. To do so, you need to follow these steps:

1. Open a blank new document in Word 2000, and then click Tools|Mail Merge. The Mail Merge Helper dialog box shown in Figure 10.1 appears.

FIGURE 10.1

The Mail Merge Helper takes you through each step in the mail merge process.

2. In the Main Document section, click the Create button, and then choose Form Letters from the drop-down menu.

> **Tip: To build a catalog or membership directory-like document...**Choose Catalog instead of Form Letters from the Create drop-down menu. Just as a point of clarification, you should know that in the context of mail merge, a *catalog* is defined as a document in which all the merged output is placed in a single document instead of created in a special document for each merged record. An organization's membership directory is perhaps the best example in which one document contains information—or a listing—on all persons in the data source.

3. Word 2000 asks whether you want to create the main document in the active window or in a new window. Choose Active Window if have you followed the directions exactly as printed here. If you launched the Mail Merge Helper from within another open document, be sure to click New Main Document.

The Mail Merge Helper dialog box remains open. To continue setting up your mail merge, you need to create the data source, which we'll look at in the following section.

Building a Data Source in Word 2000

Your instincts might lead you to believe that editing the main document should be the next step in the mail merge process, but it isn't. Building the data source comes next because Word relies on the fields defined in this file to build the Insert Field drop-down menu in the main document. This menu enables you to format the customized part of your main document with a few simple mouse clicks.

To begin building your data source in Word 2000, you need to do the following:

1. From the Mail Merge Helper dialog box, click the Get Data button. The resulting drop-down menu lets you choose whether you want to create or open a data source. For the sake of these steps, choose Create Data Source. The Create Data Source dialog box shown in Figure 10.2 opens.

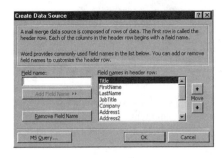

FIGURE 10.2

The Create Data Source dialog box comes with an assortment of predefined fields.

2. To add a field to the list, type its name in the Field Name box, and then click the Add Field Name button. The new field appears at the end of the list.

Peter's Principle: Save a stamp.

If you know that most of your prospective recipients have email accounts, give serious thought to collecting that data as well. That way, you have the immediacy of email at your disposal for hot news, and you can save some postage in the process.

---

3. Unwanted fields can be removed just as easily. Click the name of the field you want to remove in the Field Names in Header Row box, and then click the Remove Field Name button.

Note: Delete the wrong field? The name of the erased field appears back in the Field Name box until you exit the Create Data Source dialog box, delete another field, or add a new field to the list. That way, you have a second chance to verify your actions.

---

4. If you want to rearrange the order in which your fields appear in the data source, just click the name of the field you want to move, and then click the up or down arrow as desired. You can always place fields in any order within the main document.

5. When you're satisfied with the fields that appear on the list, click OK. The Save As dialog box appears.

6. Give the data source a recognizable name, and tuck it into a folder where you can easily find it when you need it. Then click the Save button.

7. Word 2000 displays a message saying that the data source contains no records. Click the Edit Data Source button to begin entering data for each record.

8. A Data Form like the one shown in Figure 10.3 appears. Work your way through each field, filling in all available information. Remember to use the scrollbar because not all fields are in plain sight. Click Add New after completing each record's entry to save the information and begin entering the next record. Clicking OK closes the Data Form.

FIGURE 10.3

Data Forms like this one make it easy to fill in the necessary information.

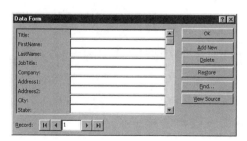

9. After you've finished entering your last record, click the View Source button. Word 2000 then displays all the records in a Word table, as shown in Figure 10.4.

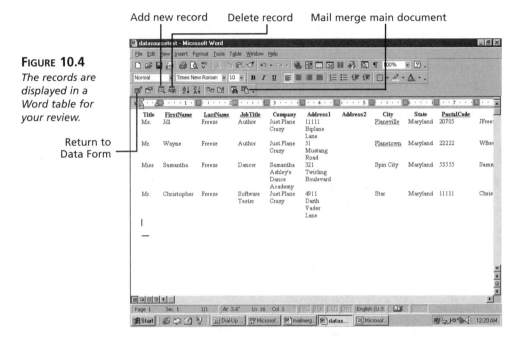

Add new record   Delete record   Mail merge main document

FIGURE 10.4
The records are displayed in a Word table for your review.

Return to Data Form

10. As you can see in Figure 10.4, you can actually perform some basic functions from within the Source view's Database toolbar; for example, you can add a field or delete a selected record. You can also return to the Data Form with a single mouse click should you feel more comfortable working that way.

> **Tip: Got more records than you can enter at one time?** Interns and volunteers, if you have access to these valuable assistants, can be a great help with this project because it doesn't take long to learn how to enter records, and having a complete data source could really benefit the organization or company in the long run.

11. Save the data source file, and then click the Mail Merge Main Document button to begin setting up that document.

Preparing the Main Document

With the data source all laid out, you're ready to begin working on the main document. The Mail Merge toolbar will be your biggest help in getting things in order because much of what you need is a single click away.

Follow these steps to begin setting up your main document:

1. Begin typing the document as you would any other document, adding various font sizes and effects. When you get to the point where you want to insert customized text, click the Insert Merge Field button on the Mail Merge toolbar, and select the desired field name from the drop-down menu, as shown in Figure 10.5.

FIGURE 10.5
Make your selection from the convenient drop-down menu.

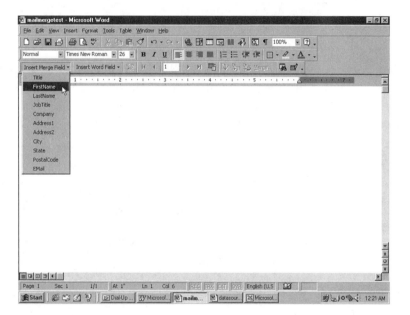

Tip: Consistency counts. If the merge is to be performed on a regular basis as part of a weekly email newsletter or as a way to produce monthly billing statements, you might want to consider creating a special template for the task at hand. That way, you can eliminate the rekeying of your company's address, staff member names, and such. You can also use this template to apply a stylish theme or other attention-grabbing elements.

To get started with this method, click Tools|Mail Merge, select the desired template as the basis for the main document, and then write the document as you want it. You should also verify that no changes have been made to the information in your data source before you perform the Get Data operation in the Data Source section of the Mail Merge Helper. From that point on, you can perform the mail merge as described earlier.

2. Repeat the process outlined in step 1 until the document is complete.

3. Save the document, and then click the View Merged Data button, as shown in Figure 10.6. That way, you can see whether your formatting is correct before performing the merge (see Figure 10.7). Think of this step as print preview for mail merge.

FIGURE 10.6
Turn these cryptic codes...

Click here to view merged data.

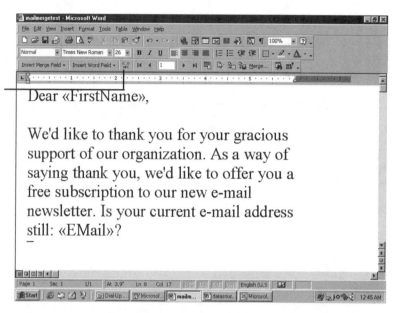

FIGURE 10.7
...into this polished document.

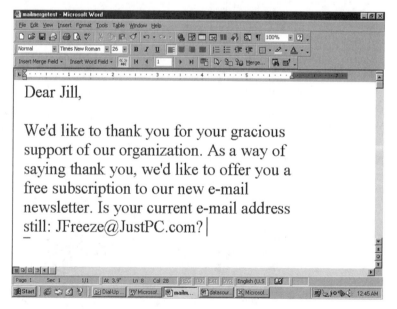

4. At this point, you can do one of three things: close the mail merge documents so that you can resume the job later, edit the data source, or merge the documents.

Editing the Data Source and Main Document at a Later Time

Because setting up the entire mail merge process can take a sizable chunk of time (especially if your data source contains a large number of records), chances are you'll need to go back and edit the data source before performing the mail merge. It's also possible one of your recipients might send in a change of address form; in that case, you'll need to go back in and change the information in the data source to make sure he or she receives your mailings.

Adding a Data Source Entry

To add a record to your data source, follow these simple steps:

1. From within Word 2000, open the data source file as you would any other file.

2. The data source will most likely open in Source view. To simplify matters, click the Return to Data Form button, as shown in Figure 10.4. The Data Form you saw in Figure 10.3 appears.

> **Tip: Where's my Return to Data Form button?** The data source might launch without the Database toolbar in view. If this happens, right-click any visible toolbar, and select Database from the shortcut menu.

3. Click the Add New button. The fields turn blank so that you can enter the new information.

4. After you've finished entering all the new records, click the View Source button, and then save the document as usual.

Locating and Editing an Existing Record

If you receive a change of address for someone or need to delete the name of a member from your data source, you first need to find the desired record and then perform the necessary functions.

Follow these steps to begin working with existing records:

1. Perform steps 1 and 2 from the preceding section to open the Data Form.

2. To locate the record you want to modify, click the Find button. The Find in Field dialog box shown in Figure 10.8 appears.

FIGURE 10.8

The Find in Field dialog box helps you locate the records you need to work with.

3. Enter the known item in the Find What box. Best bets are obviously things such as LastName or even FirstName because you could have large numbers of people residing in the same town, for example.

4. Click the drop-down arrow button next to the In Field box to tell Word 2000 which field contains the known item entered in the Find What box.

5. Set the search in motion by clicking Find First. If you were in the process of entering records when you decided to execute the search, Word 2000 returns a message saying it has reached the end of the database. It then gives you the option to begin your search at the beginning of the database by clicking Yes.

> **Caution: It's not returning any results!** The first matching record appears in the Data Form dialog box, which is usually hidden by the Find in Field dialog box. To rectify the problem, click the title bar of the Find in Field box, and drag it out of the way.

6. After the first matching record is found, the Find First button turns into a Find Next button. Just click it to move to the next matching record.

7. When you find the record you want to work with, click the Close button on the Find in Field dialog box. Closing this dialog box allows you to freely access the record.

8. To delete the record, simply click the Delete button.

> **Caution: Help! I deleted the wrong record!** Whenever you edit your data source, try to do so with Source view in the background even if you prefer to work with the Data Form. Why? Because should you inadvertently delete the wrong record, you can click the View Source button and then press Ctrl+Z in the table to retrieve the record. If the Data Form is the only part of the data source open, you're out of luck. The Restore button merely changes back fields edited in the current session; it does not restore deleted records.

9. To make changes to a field, just click inside its text box and edit as usual. Should you find you need to revert back to the original record you opened in the current session, just click the Restore button.

10. Make sure your additions and edits are properly saved by clicking the View Source button, and then save the data source just as you would save a normal document.

Editing the Main Document

Has any of the information in the main document changed since you first created it? If so, you'll be happy to know that editing a main document is no different than editing a regular document: Just open it and make the desired changes. You can erase a field by backspacing over it, or by selecting it and pressing the Delete key.

Performing the Merge

Now that the data source and main document have been prepared, it's time to merge the two for output. You have four distinct choices when it comes to the type of output you can generate with a Word 2000 mail merge. They include the following:

- New Document—This option generates a new document with a copy of each merged letter in it. Although it gives you an accurate record of the output, it can also be quite costly in terms of disk space should you be dealing with a large list.

- Printer—With this option, you can send your output directly to the printer so the documents can be prepared for mailing.

- Electronic Mail—With Word 2000, you can send merged documents to recipients via email. This option can save you tons of money in postage over the course of a year.

- Fax—Faxing output is another low-cost option for recipients who don't have access to email. You can either send the fax using your computer's fax software (assuming you have a fax/modem, that is), or you can format the documents with a special cover page for faxing from a standalone fax machine.

No matter which method of output you select, you need to first open the main document with its data source attached and then click the Merge button on the Database toolbar to launch the Merge dialog box shown in Figure 10.9. (Remember, you might need to right-click a toolbar and select Database from the shortcut menu if you don't see the toolbar when the document opens.)

FIGURE 10.9

The Merge dialog box is the place where it all begins.

Merging to a New Document

If your mail merge serves a critical purpose like notification of an overdue bill or something similar, you might want to first merge the main document and data source into a new document. That way, you have a record of exactly who received which notes. On the flip side, this solution can suck up system resources faster than you can blink. If you have tons of extra disk space, it might not be an issue to you.

In any event, you need to follow these steps to merge the documents into a new document:

1. From within the Merge dialog box, make sure the Merge To box says New Document.

2. In the Records to Be Merged section of the dialog box, you can choose to merge all the documents (the default) or specify a range of record numbers.

3. By default, Word 2000 does not print blank fields. But should you decide you need the blanks to create uniform blocks of text, you can do so by clicking the Print Blank Lines When Data Fields Are Empty option in the When Merging Records section of the dialog box.

4. When the options meet with your approval, click the Merge button. The results of the mail merge are stored in their own new document for processing later.

Looking Ahead

Later in the chapter, we'll take a closer look at more advanced mail merge options, including error checking and setting data query options.

Merging to Your Printer

If the documents are to be sent out via the United States Postal Service and keeping track of who received what when is not of concern, then merging to the printer is the way to go.

To send merged output directly to the printer, you need to do the following:

1. In the Merge dialog box, choose Printer from the Merge In drop-down list.

2. If all the records in the data source are to be merged, you can skip to step 3. Otherwise, select a record number range in the From and To text boxes provided. Remember, these fields reflect the record numbers, not the page numbers of the document.

3. By default, Word 2000 does not print blank fields. But should you decide you need the blanks to create uniform blocks of text, you can do so by clicking the Print Blank Lines When Data Fields Are Empty option in the When Merging Records section of the dialog box.

4. When the options are set, click the Merge button. A single copy of each merged document is printed on the printer you designated as the default for your machine.

Merging to Electronic Mail

One of the most cost- and time-effective ways to get your message across is to send an email message. However, just because you're sending an email message to multiple recipients doesn't mean you have to sacrifice individuality. In fact, mail-merged email messages make it look like the message was sent to the individual in the salutation only, not to a whole sea of people in an endless To: line or a suppressed mailing list. Those are telltale signs of a mass mailing.

With Word 2000, you can easily send the message as a Word attachment, so the integrity of the message's formatting, theme, font selection, and such remain intact.

To create and send your customized email messages, just do the following:

1. With the main document open, click the Merge button on the Database toolbar.
2. Use the Merge To drop-down arrow button to select Electronic Mail.
3. Click the Setup button. The Merge To Setup dialog box shown in Figure 10.10 appears.

FIGURE 10.10

In this dialog box, you define all the critical email settings.

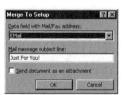

4. The first thing you need to do in this dialog box is tell Word 2000 which data field houses the email address. Use the Data field with Mail/Fax Address drop-down list to select the appropriate field given the way you defined your data source.
5. The next order of business involves entering the mail message subject line. Make it good because it is the first thing your recipients will see.
6. If maintaining the message's formatting is important, you can tell Word 2000 to send the message as a Word attachment by clicking the Send Document as an Attachment check box. If you leave the option unchecked, the message looks like a typical email message.
7. Click OK to return to the Merge dialog box.
8. Tell Word 2000 whether you want all records merged or just those within a certain number range, and specify whether you want blank lines to appear where you have blank fields. You would be wise to stick with the default here because blank lines could be a dead giveaway that a computer, not a human, generated the message.

9. Before you do anything else, make sure you have a live connection to the Internet.

10. Click the Merge button to set the process in motion. Word 2000 then calls your default email program into action to do the job.

> **Tip: Need to change your default email program?** Launch Internet Explorer 5.0, and then click Tools|Internet Options. Open the Programs tab, and then click the E-mail drop-down arrow to make the desired selection. Click Apply to save your change, and then click OK to close the dialog box.

Faxing Merged Output

If you have a fax/modem and some faxing software installed on your machine, you can fax mail-merged documents just as easily as you can email them. Even if you don't have the necessary hardware and/or software, you can easily prepare the documents for faxing from a standalone fax machine.

To do so, follow these steps:

1. After you've created the data source and main document, keep the main document open, and then click File|New. In the Letters and Faxes tab, double-click the Fax Wizard. The Fax Wizard launches with a description of what it does. Click the Next button to begin working your way through the wizard.

2. In the first screen, the Fax Wizard asks you to specify which document you want to send (see Figure 10.11). The Fax Wizard displays the name of the most recently opened document in the The Following Document text box. If the filename is incorrect, use the drop-down list in the same field to make the desired selection. You are then asked whether you want the fax to have a cover sheet (one is included by default). Click Next to continue.

FIGURE 10.11
The Fax Wizard helps you make the right decisions in the right order.

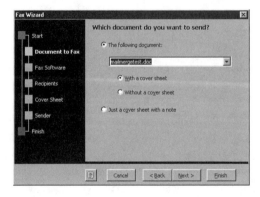

3. Specify how your fax will be sent. If you have the proper hardware and software available on your PC, you need to use the Which of the Following Is Your Fax Program drop-down list to tell Word 2000 which program you want to use. Chances are, its name already appears in the window. If you plan to send the fax from a standalone fax machine, click the I Want to Print My Document So I Can Send It from a Separate Fax Machine option. Then click Next.

4. Because you are faxing a merged document, the wizard screen in Figure 10.12 appears, asking you to help define where various bits of information are stored in the data source. Use the two text boxes at the top of the screen to tell the wizard which data source fields contain the recipients' names. You also need to specify which field holds the fax number and whether all recipients are to receive the fax (the default). Click Next to continue.

> **Note: On being selective...**If you choose to have the fax go to certain recipients only, you need to fill in the Data Query screen, which we'll cover in detail later in this chapter.

FIGURE 10.12

Use the convenient drop-down lists to help the wizard find the information it needs.

5. Choose from three available styles for the cover sheet of your fax. Obviously, this screen may not appear if you've suppressed the cover page in an earlier screen. Click Next.

6. You are then asked to fill in information about who is sending the fax. Your name and company/organization appear by default because this information can be found in your computer's user profile. After you've filled in the fields you want included, click Next.

7. The Fax Wizard tells you that you're ready to go and offers suggestions for resolving errors should any occur. Click Finish to send the faxes on their way.

Using If...Then...Else Fields for Extra Customization

If your Word 2000 data source contains only basic information about each record such as name, membership status, and the like, how can you produce customized messages without adding new fields to each record? The If...Then...Else field! If you can tie a special message to an existing data field, you're in business.

For example, you might want a letter from a member of your organization to read "We hope you will continue to help us help others in the new year." You might want a non-member's letter to say something like "We hope you will consider lending your support in the coming year." As long as your data source indicates who is and isn't a member, you can easily achieve these targeted results by using the If...Then...Else field.

Think of the possibilities. You could tell people with a certain postal code that you're opening a new store in their area. You could tell customers in a certain city that a famous author is appearing at their local store. You could inform residents of a given state about new legislation that may affect them....The possibilities go on and on.

Basically, the If...Then...Else field lets you look for certain criteria and apply a special message if they are met. If the criteria are not met, you can instruct Word 2000 to enter a different message or to simply not do anything.

To make use of this powerful feature, just follow these steps:

1. With the main document to which you've already attached a data source open, set the insertion point in the location you want the customized text to appear.

2. Click the Insert Word Field button on the Mail Merge toolbar, and then select If...Then...Else from the drop-down menu. The Insert Word Field: IF dialog box shown in Figure 10.13 opens.

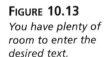

FIGURE 10.13
You have plenty of room to enter the desired text.

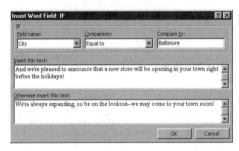

3. The first order of business involves setting the condition that the two options are weighed against. You need to select the field on which the criteria is based from the Field Name drop-down list. This information customizes Word 2000's action.

4. You need to specify the Comparison that will be performed against the field. Must the record's field match the item you're about to compare it to exactly? Should Word respond only if the field is left blank? If you're using a number, does Word react if the number is higher or lower? Make the appropriate choice from the Comparison drop-down list.

5. In the Compare To text box, enter the field text that you want Word to search for exactly as it would appear in the data source. For example, don't enter MD here if Maryland was used consistently in your data source.

6. Enter the text you want Word to include in your letter should the criteria be met in the Insert This Text box.

7. In the Otherwise Insert This Text box, enter the text you want Word to include should the condition not be met. Note that you don't have to enter anything here.

8. Click OK to apply the customization. When you're back in the main document, you'll see that the customized text has been printed in the location of the insertion point. Note that the text that appears in the main document is the text that is appropriate for the first record in the data source. If you're still not convinced things went as planned, you can use the Next Record button (the right-pointing arrow) on the Mail Merge toolbar to flip your way through each record.

> **Caution: But it doesn't match!** Most likely, the IF field will produce text in the Word 2000 default font and font size. Don't panic; a fix is just a few mouse clicks away. Select the customized text, and apply the font, font style, and font size used in text surrounding the IF field. The change is then made to the entire merged document whether it's the Insert This Text copy or the Otherwise Insert This Text copy.

Setting Filter and Sort Options for Your Word Data Source

Whether you want to process selected merged documents only, or you simply want to sort them in postal code order to take advantage of cheaper bulk mailing rates, you should learn how to work with Data Query options.

The two operations Data Query can perform are known as *filtering* and *sorting*. When records are filtered, only some of them are processed. When they're sorted, they are processed in alphabetical or numerical order (or reverse alphabetical or numeric order if needed).

Filtering the records processed can be a very economical way to engage in highly target-ed direct mail campaigns, and it can help you save bundles in postage when using email is an option.

To select records for processing, you need to follow these steps:

1. When you're filling out Merge options in the Merge dialog box, click the Query Options button. The Query Options dialog box shown in Figure 10.14 opens. You can also access this dialog box if you choose Selected Recipients in the Fax Wizard.

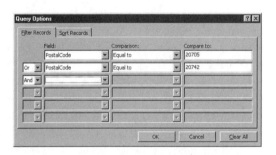

2. To set up the filter, you need to define a field to be used as the filter. Most commonly, you use the City, State, or PostalCode field, but you can choose any of them from the Field drop-down list.

Peter's Principle: Getting the information you need.

Unless you've lived in an area your entire life, chances are you won't know what other cities (let alone postal codes) should be targeted in your mailing. Here's a prime example. I searched for postal codes within 5 miles of my house using ZipFind and found nearly 20 matches. Think of all the people I might have missed when sending out new store announcements. This concentrated marketing information is especially important in densely populated areas where a single city might have well over a dozen postal codes.

So how do you learn which zip codes are closest to the destination? If you work for a small, nonprofit organization that seldom does this type of targeted mailing, you can get all you need from ZipFind's Web site at `http://www.link-usa.com/zipcode/`. Just perform the desired search over the Web, and manually key all the postal codes into separate Compare To fields in the Query Options dialog box.

If you work for a major corporation and use this type of information regularly, you might want to consider purchasing a disk containing similar information. And if you have a team of in-house programmers, you might even want to invest in application development tools that can make these complex filtering jobs a snap.

3. You need to set the comparison value. Must a record's entry in the same field match the one you're about to define exactly, or can it be larger or smaller? And what if the field is left blank? Again, you have a convenient drop-down list to help you make a valid selection.

4. In the Compare To box, you type in the text as it should appear in the field. In Figure 10.14, you can see that I'm trying to filter the records so that only those containing one of the two postal codes listed are returned.

5. To the left of each set of fields (except for the first one) is a tiny drop-down list box in which you need to choose And or Or. By default, the Query Options are set to And, meaning that both criteria defined must be true for the record to be returned. In the postal code example illustrated in Figure 10.14, notice that Or was selected because I wanted records with either zip code returned.

6. Click OK to filter the records, or select the Sort Records tab to have the filtered records display in a certain order as well.

Sorting Records with the Query Options

With Word 2000, you can sort the records in place of or along with data filtering. Because bulk mailing often requires items to be sorted in zip code order, this feature can be a great time (and money) saver. Of course, you should make sure the letters and their respective labels or envelopes are processed in the same manner to simplify merging the two when you're ready to prepare them for mailing.

To sort your merged documents, just do the following:

1. When you're ready to merge the document with its data source, open the main document, and click Merge on the Mail Merge toolbar. When the Merge dialog box opens, click the Query Options button. From there, select the Sort Records tab (shown in Figure 10.15).

FIGURE 10.15

The typical sort is by postal code order, as shown here.

2. Most sorts are either by postal code order, as shown in Figure 10.15, or alphabetical by surname, though you can sort any field (and as many as three in a single pass) in ascending or descending order. The first thing you need to do is specify which field you want your data source sorted by first.

3. Choose between ascending or descending order. If you forget to set this option, Word 2000 assumes ascending order.

4. Would you like to sort by a second field as well? Define the field name and sort preference as you did in the preceding two steps.

5. If you have a third sort preference, go ahead and define it as well.

6. When all your sorting options are in order, click OK to have Word 2000 perform the sort.

Merging from Your Outlook Address Book

If you use Outlook 2000 to manage your contacts and have defined Outlook 2000 as your default email client, you can use your Outlook 2000 information as a data source.

> **Note: But what about my Outlook Express Address Book information?**
> Unfortunately, it has to be imported into Outlook 2000 to be of any use in mail merge. From within Outlook 2000, click File|Import and Export to begin importing the information with the help of a wizard.

To use your Outlook Address Book as a data source in a mail merge, follow these steps:

1. Use the Mail Merge Helper to begin working your way through the project, as described earlier in the chapter.

2. When you get to the point where you're ready to select your data source, click the Get Data button, and select Use Address Book from the drop-down menu. The Use Address Book dialog box shown in Figure 10.16 appears.

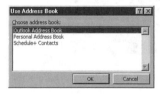

FIGURE 10.16

This dialog box lists all possible Address Books on your machine. If you don't see the one you want listed here, you have to import it into Outlook 2000 before you can use it.

3. Select Outlook Address Book from the list, and then click OK.

> **Caution: Nothing changes.** Because using Outlook 2000 information really only generates a Word data source for the current information in your Address Book, you might want to dispose of the document after using it. That way, it won't inadvertently get used again and contain out-of-date information.

If you want to put the power of Outlook 2000's filtering capabilities to work for you (you'll learn more details in Chapter 18, "Personal Information Management with Outlook 2000"), you might want to consider initiating a mail merge from within Outlook 2000. To do so, follow these steps:

1. Using Outlook 2000's capability to create customized views, get the contacts you want to merge into a document onscreen. Begin by clicking the Contacts button on the Outlook Bar, and then use the Views menu (or the sort and filter functions you'll learn about in Chapter 18) to get the contacts you want to use onscreen.

2. From within that Outlook 2000 view, click Tools|Mail Merge. The Mail Merge Contacts dialog box shown in Figure 10.17 appears.

FIGURE 10.17

The Mail Merge Contacts dialog box makes getting what you want from your contact list a piece of cake.

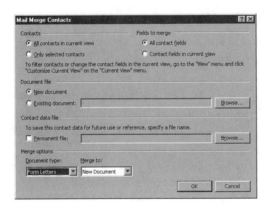

3. The first thing you need to do is tell Outlook 2000 which contacts you want included in the merge. By default, it includes all the contacts in the current view. If you've singled some out, you should click the Only Selected Contacts option.

4. As you know, the fields made available by the data source define the fields available for use in the main document. Given that fact, you might want to keep the default All Contact Fields option intact. If not, you can tell Outlook to make only the fields in the current view available for the mail merge.

5. The Document file section of the dialog box asks you to specify whether this information is to be merged to a new document or to be applied to an existing one. Click the Browse button to find the desired document if necessary.

6. By default, data sources created with Outlook 2000 are stored as temporary files in your machine and are deleted three days later. They are deleted to prevent you from merging documents with outdated data because the contact list and data source are not linked. Should you decide to keep the data source you create around for a while, you can create a permanent file with a single mouse click. And don't forget to give the file a recognizable name.

7. You need to set a couple of merge options. Using the Document type drop-down list, you need to select a document type (Form Letters is the default). You also need to define whether the results are to be merged to a new document, to the printer, to email, or to a fax using the Merge To drop-down list.

8. Click OK. If you are using an existing main document, the merge is performed. If a new main document is needed, Word 2000 launches with the Mail Merge toolbar ready for service.

Using Excel 2000 as the Data Source

Using an Excel 2000 worksheet as a data source is also pretty straightforward, assuming that each column is labeled with a meaningful header. These headers become the fields available in the main document, so having short, meaningful column labels is an asset.

To begin using an Excel 2000 worksheet as your data source, follow these steps:

1. Start using the Mail Merge Helper, as described in "Choosing a Main Document Format" near the beginning of this chapter.

2. When you reach the step in which you need to specify a data source, click Get Data, and then choose Open Data Source from the drop-down list.

3. A traditional Open dialog box appears, enabling you to click your way to the desired file. Note that you might need to change the View Files of Type option to find an Excel worksheet.

4. When you've found the file you want, double-click it. A Microsoft Excel dialog box opens and asks whether you want to use the whole worksheet or a specified range. Click OK when you've made your selection.

5. If you try to attach the worksheet to an existing main document, Word 2000 may find some discrepancies, as shown in Figure 10.18. Word gives you the option to remove the invalid field code by clicking a button, or you can use the drop-down list to replace it with a similar field found in the data source. Click OK when you've made the desired choice. Word then goes through this process as many times as necessary to make sure the field codes all work properly.

FIGURE 10.18

The Invalid Merge Field dialog box helps you recover gracefully from potential problems.

6. When all the field codes are reconciled, you can go about performing the merge as usual.

Using Access 2000 as a Data Source

Merging documents using data from Access is identical to using data from Excel. I don't devote additional space to the topic here; you can just follow the procedure for merging using Excel data (except select Access for all your application-related options), and then consult the Access part of this book for tips on building and working with an Access 2000 database.

Checking and Reporting Mail Merge Errors

Nothing is worse than setting a mail merge to run while you go out to lunch, only to return and find the whole thing stalled. Mistakes and/or problems can occur, which is why you might want to have Word check for and report any errors found during the merge. By clicking the Check Errors button in the Merge dialog box, you launch a Checking and Reporting Errors dialog box like the one shown in Figure 10.19.

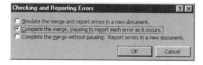

FIGURE 10.19

Word 2000 gives you multiple ways to handle mail merge errors.

From this dialog box, you have three options for how Word should handle and report errors it finds:

- Simulate the merge and report errors in a new document.
- Complete the merge, pausing to report each error as it occurs (the default).
- Complete the merge without pausing. Report errors in a new document.

The good thing about the first option is that it's an all-or-nothing proposition, so you don't need to worry about some people getting their letters, while others do not. This timing issue is especially critical for emailed and faxed transmissions. Its drawback, however, is that you're forced to sit through the merge twice even if there are no errors to report.

The default option is fine if you're right at your machine to deal with errors, but should you run the job over your lunch hour, everything's put on hold until you get back.

Finally, the last option pushes everything through and then reports the errors at the end in a new document. The report contains an error message along with the number of the record involved so that you can easily go in and make fixes.

The option you choose should be the one that meshes best with your personal work style.

Printing Labels from Your Data Source

You've gotten through all that merging; now it's time to create the mailing labels for all those documents. To begin the process, just do the following:

1. Launch Word 2000, and then click File|New. Click the Letters and Faxes tab, and then double-click the Mailing Label Wizard icon to launch the Word 2000 Mailing Label Wizard shown in Figure 10.20.

FIGURE 10.20

Welcome to the Mailing Label Wizard.

> **Note: My wizard look different.** If you have your Office Assistant set to show dialog box messages, the wizard dialog box will appear as an Office Assistant word balloon.

2. The first thing the wizard asks you is whether you want to create a single mailing label (or a page of labels from the same address) or a bunch of labels from a mailing list. Because this chapter covers working with mail merge, select the second option, and then click OK.

3. You are taken to the familiar Mail Merge Helper dialog box, where you're asked to select the data source. Click Get Data, select Open Data Source from the drop-down list, and then double-click the data source's filename when you find it.

4. Word 2000 returns a message saying you now have to set up the main document. Click the button presented to reveal the Label Options dialog box shown in Figure 10.21.

FIGURE 10.21
This dialog box helps you set up the labels just right.

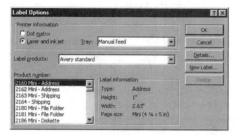

5. You are first asked to provide information about your printer and how the labels will be fed to the printer.

6. Pick the brand of the label product you intend to use from the Label products drop-down list, and then use the scrollbars in the Product Number text box to select a match for your labels.

7. After you've selected the proper label product, click OK. A Create Labels dialog box appears.

8. Use the Insert Merge field button to place the desired fields on the label. Make sure to include spaces and punctuation marks between items where appropriate.

9. Because using a postal bar code can help speed up the delivery of your letters, click the Insert Postal Bar Code button. The resulting dialog box asks you to specify which data source fields hold the zip code and street address. The drop-down lists make these choices quick and easy. Click OK when you're done.

10. Click OK to close the Create Labels dialog box as well.

11. Click Merge in the Mail Merge Helper dialog box, and set the merge options as usual.

Printing Envelopes

Don't be shocked, but printing envelopes is a whole lot like printing labels. A friendly wizard guides you through this task as well.

> **Tip: Printing envelopes is even easier!** If you enter a default return address that can be included automatically, this is a simple task. To do so, click Tools|Options from within Word 2000, and then select the User Information tab. Enter the address as you want it to appear in the Mailing Address text box, and then click OK. It's as simple as that!

To begin printing your envelopes, follow these basic steps:

1. From within Word 2000, click File|New, and select the Letters and Faxes tab. Double-click the Envelopes Wizard icon to launch it.

2. You are first asked to specify whether you want to print one envelope or several envelopes for a mailing list. Select the second option, and then click OK.

3. You then return to the Mail Merge Helper dialog box from which you need to open the data source. When you find it, Word instructs you to go back and set up the main document. To do so, click the button it displays along with this message. An Envelope Options dialog box like the one shown in Figure 10.22 opens.

FIGURE 10.22

In this dialog box, you start setting up the format of your envelopes.

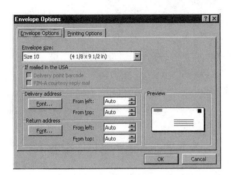

4. Use the drop-down list box provided to select the size of the envelopes you want to print.

5. The address is printed in a 12-point Ariel font, whereas the return address is printed in a 10-point Ariel font. You can change these settings by clicking the respective Font button.

6. In the Printing Options tab, you need to specify how the envelopes will be fed to the printer. After you're finished, click OK. The Envelope Address dialog box opens.

7. Use the Insert Merge field button to place the desired fields on the envelope. Make sure to include spaces and punctuation marks between items where appropriate.

8. Because using a postal bar code can help speed up the delivery of your letters, click the Insert Postal Bar Code button. The resulting dialog box asks you to specify which data source fields hold the zip code and street address. The drop-down lists make these choices quick and easy. Click OK when you're done.

9. Click OK to close the Envelope Address dialog box as well.

10. Click Merge in the Mail Merge Helper dialog box, and set the merge options as usual.

On Your Own

What amazing power mail merge gives you! And best of all, it has become easier to use than ever before, thanks to the help of assorted wizards and drop-down list boxes.

Many people dread using mail merge because, on the surface, it seems so complicated. Main documents…data sources…records…fields…They can all be intimidating until you actually sit down and play with them a bit. When you do, I'm sure you'll find that the potential value, saved time, and improved corporate image offered by using mail merge far outweigh any downsides.

To make sure you fully appreciate the scope of mail merge, I'd like you to take a few minutes and think about the types of documents your workplace produces. Could the company benefit from sending out more personalized correspondence? Do generic letters that leave the office really deserve personalization?

Sit back and make a list of five ways mail merge could enhance the image and productivity of your company or organization. This number may seem like a lot now, but when you get started, you'll probably run out of numbers before you run out of ideas.

Collaborating on Word 2000 Documents

Working on a document as a group can pose all kinds of interesting dilemmas. How do you gather and document comments from members of the workgroup? What's the best way to synthesize all the information you've gathered to come up with the best document possible? And is it really worth saving versions of a document as opposed to simply over-writing the file?

Word 97 had a lot of useful collaboration features, but Word 2000 has taken collaboration to a whole new level. Now you can engage in threaded discussions within a document or Web page on your intranet or local area network (LAN). You can even subscribe to a document so that you'll be notified by email when it has been edited. And perhaps the neatest new collaboration feature is the capability to use NetMeeting to work on documents together in real-time whether you're across the street, across the continent, or across the world.

In this chapter, we'll not only learn how to use the various collaboration tools, but we'll explore related security issues as well.

Tracking Changes in Your Documents

By tracking changes to a document, you can quickly see what's been changed by whom. You can then go through and accept or reject each change one at a time or even accept all of them at once. Using this feature is a great way to synthesize input by multiple authors when you consider the alternatives.

And here's a pleasant surprise: The Track Changes feature works in Excel 2000 and PowerPoint 2000 as well.

Enabling and Disabling the Track Changes Feature

To enable the Track Changes feature, open the document you want to edit, and then click Tools|Track Changes|Highlight Changes. The Highlight Changes dialog box shown in

Figure 11.1 appears. In this dialog box, you can choose to highlight changes onscreen only, in printed documents only, or in both. Just click the Track Changes While Editing option, and then check one or both boxes below it. To turn off the feature, just remove the check mark next to the Track Changes While Editing option. You can also access this dialog box by right-clicking the TRK button at the bottom of the Word screen and choosing Highlight Changes from the pop-up menu.

FIGURE 11.1

Place a check mark in the Track Changes While Editing box to mark changes made to the current document.

Note: Once turned on, always turned on. Generally, if Track Changes is turned on, the setting is saved with the document, so the feature will automatically be enabled when the document is opened the next time. Of course, you might find exceptions to this rule, depending on the version of Word used by others working with the document or the configuration of their Office setup. You can verify that the feature is turned on as indicated by the darkened TRK in Word 2000's status bar, as shown here.

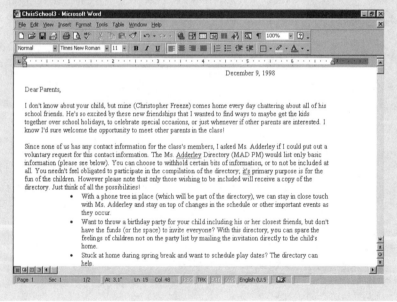

Setting Track Changes Options

By default, Office 2000 marks changes in the following manner:

- Inserted text—Each author's text appears underlined and in a different color than the default. Each of the authors (up to eight) has his or her own unique color, so you can easily see who's made what changes.

- Deleted text—Text that has been deleted from the document is displayed in strikethrough text in different colors for each author, as described in the preceding bullet.

- Changed formatting—Changes made to a document's formatting are invisible by default.

- Changed lines—Word 2000 includes a thin, black vertical line in the outside border of a document so that you can see where changes have been made.

With a few clicks of the mouse, you can change each of these settings to meet your personal needs. Because each of the four types of changes listed here has a Mark and a Color option, the possible combinations are almost endless. The Mark option is pretty straightforward (just pick one from the drop-down list, and the corresponding changed text will appear as directed); the Color option, however, can be a bit confusing.

With regard to the Color option, you essentially have three choices: By Author, Auto, or By Color. You've already seen how the default By Author setting works, but what about the others? Auto simply means that all changes made appear in the document's default text color (usually black). You can see them only if you apply a special mark to them, or you make use of the Changed Lines feature. The third option involves clicking one of the color swatches in the Color drop-down list. By choosing a color, you can make certain the changed text stands out from that which has not been changed. Keep in mind, however, that when you select a specific color for the changes, all changes appear in the exact same color no matter who made them. If you're working with one other person, using the same color isn't a big deal; if you're working with a group of six, however, things could get a bit confusing.

To set these options, access the Highlight Changes dialog box as described earlier, and then click the Options button. The screen in Figure 11.2 appears.

When you're satisfied with all the settings, click OK to save them.

> **Tip: Who did it?** Sure, each author typically has a different color of text assigned to his or her changes, but how do you tell whose changes are whose? Just run the mouse pointer over the text in question, and a tiny ScreenTip box appears with the name of the author and the date and time of the change.

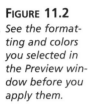

FIGURE 11.2
*See the format-
ting and colors
you selected in
the Preview win-
dow before you
apply them.*

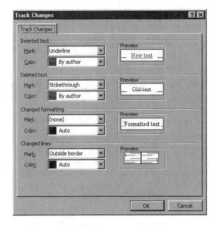

Accepting or Rejecting Changes

After changes have been made to a document, you can deal with the various changes one
at a time. To begin working with these changes, open the document containing the
changes, and then click Tools|Track Changes|Accept or Reject Changes. The Accept or
Reject Changes dialog box appears, telling you that no changes were selected. You can
click the Find button with the right-pointing arrow to move to the first change after the
insertion point (in the case of a newly opened document, it is the first change in the document). You can also click any change in the document to move to it directly; the choice
is yours.

> **Tip: Take things slowly...**To make sure you don't miss any of the changes you
> intend to address, you would be wise to simply open the document and then
> click the Find button with the right-pointing arrow. That way, you hit each and
> every change in turn, so you're less likely to miss one.

By default, when you select a change, it appears highlighted onscreen. In the Changes
section of the Accept or Reject Changes dialog box, you see a bunch of information
about the change, including who made it, on what date, and at what time of day (see
Figure 11.3).

FIGURE 11.3

The change you selected is highlighted and details about it are provided in the Changes section of the dialog box.

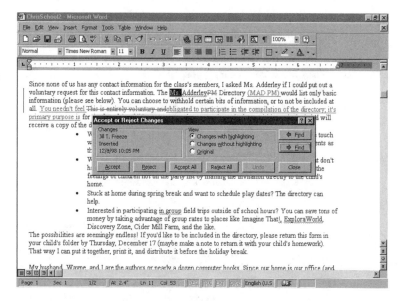

FIGURE 11.3

The change you selected is highlighted and details about it are provided in the Changes section of the dialog box.

Peter's Principle: Don't think you need that kind of information?

Consider this scenario: You've been working with your workgroup on a document over a span of a week or more. You finally schedule a meeting to discuss the document in detail and then decide to go back into the document to make some changes as a result of the meeting. Knowing when various changes were made to the document would be immensely helpful. That way, you don't undo what's been mutually agreed upon, and you lessen the likelihood of misunderstandings because you know exactly when the person made the changes in question.

The Accept or Reject Changes dialog box gives you two additional ways to view the document. You can view the document's changes without highlighting, which lets you see just what the document would look like should you accept all the changes. This view is especially useful for determining if formatting changes actually helped or hurt the appearance of a document. To enter this view, just click the Changes Without Highlighting button in the View section of the Accept or Reject Changes dialog box. And remember, even though you can no longer see the changes, Word 2000 remembers them just fine. When you click the Find button in either direction, Word highlights the change it finds (if any) so that you can process it as usual.

If you want to see the original document without any of the changes or resulting Track Changes marks, click the Original option in the View section of the Accept or Reject Changes dialog box. The original document appears onscreen. After you've skimmed over it to refresh your memory about how things were in that document, you can return to the edited document with its marked changes by clicking the Changes With Highlighting option in the Accept or Reject Changes dialog box.

When you select a change, you can either skip over it by clicking one of the Find buttons, or you can take any of the following actions on it by clicking the respective button:

- Accept—When you click this button, you accept the changes for the currently selected text only. Clicking this button is the safest, most conservative way to deal with multiple changes—one at a time so that you can verify whether you really want the change.

- Reject—Click this button to restore the selected text to its original state.

> **Tip: When what you get is what you only thought you wanted...**If you either accept or reject a change you didn't intend to, you can always click the Undo button to restore the text to its changed state so that you can select the desired option. Because you can use this trick only for the most recently invoked accept or reject operation, you should check your work carefully before making the next change. And yes, clicking Undo works to reverse Accept All or Reject All accidents as well.

- Accept All—If you want to accept every change made to the document without reviewing them one at a time, click this button. Although it's the quickest way to turn the document into a clean copy based on all the changes, it brings with it some potential dangers, too.

> **Caution: Before you select the Accept All option...**Depending on how many people worked with the document, some vitally important changes could slip through the cracks, maybe even putting you in a situation in which inaccurate or just plain false information leaves your organization. Because the Accept All option is such a radical one, Word 2000 makes you verify whether you really want to accept all the changes before it performs the operation. As I mentioned earlier, you can undo an Accept All (or Reject All), but only immediately after you choose the option. And after you do perform an Accept All, you might want to flip through the document to make sure all its formatting is intact. If a reviewer were to accidentally delete a paragraph symbol, for example, two paragraphs might inadvertently get merged.

- Reject All—Just as Accept All implements every change without individual consideration, Reject All throws them away without consideration. Choosing this option, too, can end up costing you in the long run because valuable information passed along in the changes can get inadvertently discarded.

Editing Documents in Track Changes Mode

Although Word 2000 gives you access to the usual editing tools in Track Changes mode, a few things are noticeably different. For example, when you backspace over an item using the default Track Changes options, rather than disappearing, it appears printed with strikethrough marks. So how do you reverse your actions? The simplest way to take care of small errors like getting overzealous with the Backspace key is to press Ctrl+Z. This key sequence removes the marks one character at a time. For larger blocks of changes, just right-click it, and select Reject Change from the shortcut menu. The selected text is then restored to its normal state.

> **Tip: Don't bite off more than you can handle.** Sometimes undoing changes one at a time may take longer than you've got. At other times, undoing a large change isn't an option either because you might want to retain parts of the change. You'll be happy to know that, yes, there is a happy medium. Just select the portion of text you want to restore to its original state, right-click it, and select Reject Change from the shortcut menu.

Another Track Changes mode oddity is the way line spacing is handled. If you have a blank line between lines of text in an original document and try to remove that empty line with Track Changes turned on, the text doesn't automatically shift up as it would in a traditional editing environment. In fact, the only indication you have that the deletion actually took hold is the presence of the thin black vertical line down the left margin of the change's location.

Other than these small oddities, you should find working in Track Changes mode nearly identical to working with a standard Word document.

Comparing Two Copies of a Document

What happens if someone makes extensive changes to a document but forgets to turn on Track Changes? Provided a copy of the original document also exists (either on your machine because someone edited it remotely or as an original copy on your company's server), the Compare Documents feature can be a real lifesaver. Unfortunately, this feature is not supported by Excel 2000 or PowerPoint 2000.

> **Tip: Comparing versions of a document.** If the documents are merely versions of one another as opposed to separate files, you need to save the newly edited version (the one you want to analyze against its original or predecessor) under a new name first. That's the only way Word 2000 can perform the comparison properly.

To perform the comparison, just follow these steps:

1. Open the newly edited document in Word 2000. If it's a version of the document you want to compare it to, now is the time to save it with its own filename.

2. Click Tools|Track Changes|Compare Documents. The Select File to Compare To Current Document dialog box opens; this dialog box is nearly identical to the traditional Open dialog box.

3. Click your way to the desired document, and then double-click its name.

4. If neither document contains revision marks, the newly edited document appears marked with tracked changes. If one of the documents contains revision marks already, Word displays a message to this effect, saying that not all changes may be detected. You can compare the two anyway by clicking Yes in the message box.

5. When the edited document appears with revision marks, you can work your way through the document and process the detected changes one at a time.

Working with the Version Saving Option

When you want to save drafts of a document at various stages of its development, you basically have two options: You can save each draft with its own filename, or you can save a version of the document.

So what's the difference? When you save each document separately, you obviously have to give each one a unique and meaningful name. Then, if you're wise, you create a special folder to house them so that you don't have to weed through so many files to find what you're looking for. This method can quickly start to gobble up system resources, namely disk space, because multiple copies of the complete document are stored.

When you save versions of a document, however, all the versions are stored in a single file. What's more, only the changes of each version are stored, so significantly less disk space is required to save the same amount of information.

Saving a Version of a Document

To save a new version of the current document, you need to do the following:

1. From within the document you want to save as a version, click File|Versions. The Versions in *[Document Name]* dialog box appears (you'll see this box a bit later in Figure 11.4).

2. If you want to save a new version of the document every time you close it, check the Automatically Save a Version on Close check box in the upper-right corner of the dialog box. Word 2000 inserts the Date and Time and Saved By fields so that you can quickly reference the version you want.

3. Click the Save Now button. A Save Version dialog box appears, offering you the opportunity to enter comments about the version you're about to save. Notice that the date, time, and saved by information appears automatically at the top of the dialog box.

4. After you enter your comments, click OK. The version is then saved, and you can continue working in the document as usual.

Opening a Specific Version of a Document

When you open a file that contains multiple versions of a document, the most current version always appears by default. To open a different version of the document, just open the file, and then click File|Versions. The dialog box shown in Figure 11.4 appears.

FIGURE 11.4
All the information you need to locate the desired version is displayed here.

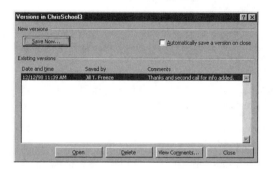

To open the desired version, double-click its entry in the dialog box. The specified version is then launched.

Inserting Comments into a Document

Sometimes you might want to ask a coworker to verify information in a document, but altering the text might not be necessary or desirable. Inserting comments is a great alternative. Each comment is noted with the reviewer's initials followed by a comment number.

In addition to adding comments to Word 2000 documents, you can add them to Excel 2000 worksheets or PowerPoint 2000 presentations.

Tip: Want a (Screen) Tip? With ScreenTips enabled, commented text appears highlighted in yellow. To view the related comments, run your mouse pointer over the text to see the comments as a ScreenTip. To turn on the use of ScreenTips, click Tools|Options, and then make sure the Screen Tips option in the Show section of the View tab is checked. When this option is enabled, commented text looks like this when you run the mouse pointer over it.

school friends. He's so excited by these new friendships that I wanted to find ways to maybe get the kids together over school holidays, to celebrate special occasions, or just whenever if other parents are interested. I know I'd sure welcome the opportunity to meet **Jill T. Freeze:**
Check with Ms. Adderley to see if
this title is okay with her.

Since none of us has any contact information f[   ]Ms. Adderley if I could put out a voluntary request for this contact information. The Adderley PM Directory[jtf1] would list only basic information (please see below). You can choose to withhold certain bits of information or to not be included at all. This is entirely voluntary and for the fun of the children. However please note that only those wishing to be included will receive a copy of the directory. Just think of all the possibilities!

- With a phone tree in place (which will be part of the directory), we can stay in close touch with Ms. Adderley and stay on top of changes in the schedule or other important events as they occur.
- Want to throw a birthday party for your child including his or her closest friends, but don't have the funds (or the space) to invite everyone? With this directory, you can spare the feelings of children not on the party list by mailing the invitation directly to the child's home.

To begin inserting comments into a document, you obviously need to open the document first, but then you need to do the following:

1. Select the text you want to comment on. This text will be highlighted in yellow if you have ScreenTips turned on.

2. Click Insert|Comments. Your initials and a comment number appear next to the selected text. If you have ScreenTips enabled, the text now appears highlighted in yellow.

Tip: Got lots to say? If you plan to insert a large number of comments, you might find it easier to do so using the Reviewing toolbar instead of executing the menu commands each time. Just right-click a toolbar onscreen, and then select Reviewing from the shortcut menu. You'll learn more details on the Reviewing toolbar shortly.

3. In the Comments pane at the bottom of the screen (see Figure 11.5), enter the desired comments just as you would normally type in text.

FIGURE 11.5

Not only can you enter text comments, but you also can enter voice comments.

FIGURE 11.5

Not only can you enter text comments, but you also can enter voice comments.

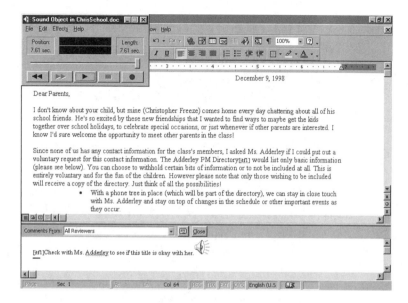

Note: Be heard, not seen. Whether you're a better speaker than you are a writer, or you're trying to convey a thought that hasn't quite gelled in your mind, voice comments may be the way to go. To add a voice comment, you must have a sound card and microphone attached to your PC. To insert such a comment, click the Insert Sound Object button immediately to the left of the Close button on the Comments pane toolbar. A recorder like the one shown in Figure 11.5 appears. To record the comment, click the Record button at the far right end of the recorder's row of buttons. Click the button immediately to the left to end the recording. You can play the comments with ease by double-clicking the Speaker icon next to the comment in question.

4. Use the standard Word 2000 scrollbars to work your way to the next bit of text you want to comment on, and repeat steps 1 through 3.

5. Click the Close button after you've entered the final comment to close the Comment pane.

Note: View comments. If the comments related to a version of the document spill off the edge of the page, you can still read them by clicking the desired version in the Versions dialog box and then clicking the View Comments button. You then see the entire contents of the Comments field in a separate dialog box.

Using the Reviewing Toolbar to Simplify Document Editing

When you're asked to collaborate on or review a document, chances are you'll want to make use of both the Track Changes feature and the Comments feature. The most efficient way to do so is to use the Reviewing toolbar (see Figure 11.6).

FIGURE 11.6

Meet all your document reviewing needs with a single toolbar!

Previous Change — Next Change
Track Changes — Accept Change
Delete Comment — Reject Change
Next Comment — Highlight
Previous Comment — Create Microsoft Outlook Task
Edit Comment — Save Version
Insert Comment — Send to Mail Recipient (as Attachment)

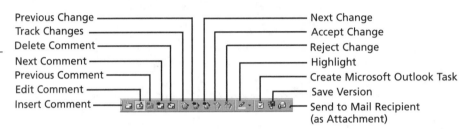

Although many of these buttons may seem self-explanatory, a few of them deserve further elaboration. Take a look at Table 11.1 for a quick reference of what the Reviewing toolbar buttons do.

Table 11.1   Powerful Collaboration Tools on the Reviewing Toolbar

Button	Function
Insert Comment	After you've highlighted the text you want to comment on, click this button to begin entering the comment text.
Edit Comment	This button brings up the Comment pane if it's not already open. Either double-click the highlighted text in the document to move to the desired comment, or just click inside the comment's text in the Comments pane to begin editing.
Previous Comment	When the insertion point is set inside the highlighted text of a comment, you can use this button to move back to the previous commented text in the document.
Next Comment	With the insertion point set inside commented text, use this button to move to the next bit of commented text.
Delete Comment	To remove a comment, click inside the commented text, and then click the Delete Comments button. Alternatively, you can click a comment inside the Comments pane and then click the Delete Comment button.

Button	Function
Track Changes	Click this button to toggle in and out of Track Changes mode.
Previous Change	Click this button to move to the preceding change or the one that appears right before the currently selected change.
Next Change	Click this button to move to the next change in the document.
Accept Change	To accept the currently selected change, click this button.
Reject Change	Reject the currently selected change by clicking this button.
Highlight	Select text and then click this button to highlight it. If you want to choose a different color for the highlighting (either to differentiate purposes for highlighting or to set one author apart from another), click the drop-down arrow immediately to the right of the Highlight button and make a new selection.
Create Microsoft Outlook Task	Clicking this button launches the Microsoft Outlook Task Scheduler. (You'll find more information about scheduling tasks in Chapter 18,"Personal Information Management with Outlook 2000.") With tool, you can schedule the review of the current document for completion by a certain date.
Save Version	Use this button to save newly made changes as a new version of the current document.
Send to Mail Recipient (as Attachment)	Clicking this button launches Outlook 2000 so that you can send the current document to a colleague via email.

Merging Comments and Changes from Multiple Reviewers into One Document

When you have a number of people making changes and comments to a document, things can get a bit chaotic, especially when you try to save some time and have everyone review the document simultaneously instead of routing it. So how can you synthesize this collective wisdom? By merging each of the edited documents into the original, that's how!

To begin merging all these documents, you need to follow these steps:

1. Open the document into which you want to merge all the newly reviewed documents. It would most likely be the original document you distributed for review.

2. Click Tools|Merge Documents. The Select File to Merge into Current Document dialog box appears. It, too, looks like a typical Open dialog box. Just click your way to the desired file, and then double-click its name to open it and merge it into the original.

Note: If you get a document without Track Changes enabled... Remember, if a document does not contain revision marks because the author forgot to turn on Track Changes, you can always compare the two documents as described previously. After they've been through the Compare process, you can then merge the result with the original as directed.

3. Repeat the first two steps. With each subsequent merge, notice that each author's contributions appear in a different color.

4. After all the recently reviewed documents have been merged together, work your way through all the changes and comments with the help of the Reviewing toolbar as described previously.

Discussing a Word 2000 Document

Time is always a critical factor in today's business world. And what do you do if you want to discuss or debate a certain aspect of a document if you don't have time to route it over and over again? This question goes for Excel worksheets or for PowerPoint presentations as well.

Making use of Office 2000's new Discussion feature may be just the ticket if your company or organization is serviced by a local area network or intranet. If your company does not use a local network of any sort, you might want to check out the "Low-Tech

Solutions for High-Tech Results" section near the end of this chapter. As long as your network administrator has the new Office Server Extensions (or a Web server at bare minimum) installed on the server, you're all set!

> **Note: So where do I get all this fancy stuff, and how much does it cost?**
> Office Server Extensions and Web servers may sound like esoteric pieces of software, but in actuality, they come with Office 2000. So even the tiniest of organizations with a LAN can maximize these powerful new Office 2000 features.

Although discussions behave a bit like comments, you'll notice some significant differences. For starters, discussions are threaded much like newsgroup posts. That means you can actually debate an important issue and have the responses nested underneath one another in the order that they were posted. No more sifting through random comments placed here and there in a document! Also of note is the fact that multiple threaded discussions can take place at one time. This way, thoughts and dialog are kept much more organized. And you needn't worry about the dialog getting old; discussion entries are immediately saved to the server so that others can access them the instant they open and/or refresh the Discussion pane of the document.

Configuring the Discussion Server

Before you can do much of anything with the Discussion feature, you need to set up your discussion server. To do so, follow these steps:

1. Open the document you want to add a discussion to, and then click Tools|Online Collaboration|Web Discussions.

2. The Discussions toolbar appears at the bottom of the screen, and the Add or Edit Discussion Servers dialog box shown in Figure 11.7 opens.

FIGURE 11.7

When you see this dialog box, be ready to provide the name of your local discussion server.

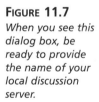
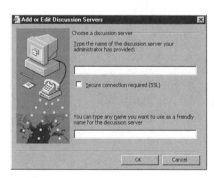

3. In the Type the Name of the Discussion Server Your Administrator Has Provided box, enter the Web address of your discussion server. Because this feature is so new, you might need to call your network administrator to confirm the information.

4. Does the security of this server depend on the use of the Secure Sockets Layer (SSL) message protocol? If so, select the Secure Connection Required (SSL) check box.

5. You need to give the server a name you'll want to know it by. In the You Can Type Any Name You Want to Use as a Friendly Name for the Discussion Server box, type the name you want to use for the server.

6. Click OK twice to complete the configuration.

Adding an Inline Discussion to a Document

Using inline discussions—or discussions that physically appear in close proximity to the text, table, or image they refer to—can be a great way to make perfectly clear what the subject of the discussion is.

You need to follow these steps to insert an inline discussion in the current document:

1. Click Tools|Online Collaboration|Web Discussions.

2. To select the element you want the inline discussion to apply to, click anywhere in the paragraph or table, or select the desired graphic.

3. On the Discussions toolbar, click Insert Discussion in the Document.

4. Give the discussion a descriptive name. Type it in under Discussion Subject.

5. Under Discussion Text, type your comments, and then click OK. The Discussion pane appears, and a Discussion icon appears at the end of the paragraph, table, or graphic to which you added the discussion.

6. Repeat these steps as needed until you're finished with the document.

> **Tip: Freshen up!** If you've been working with the document for quite some time, and others can access it because it's on a public folder, you might want to refresh the discussions periodically. That way, you don't miss anything. To refresh the discussions, click the Discussions button at the left end of the Discussions toolbar, and then select Refresh Discussions.

Inserting a General Discussion About a Document

Some people find inline discussions annoying or distracting at best because of their position right in the middle of everything. If this is the case for you (or any of the members of your workgroup), you might want to consider using general discussions instead. This way, all the information is placed into a separate Discussion pane.

To add a general discussion to the current document, do the following:

1. From within the document, click Tools|Online Collaboration|Web Discussions.

2. Click the Insert Discussion About the Document button on the Discussions toolbar.

3. Enter the discussion and text just as you would for an inline discussion.

Controlling What You See

You view the discussions either within the document (inline comments) or in a separate Discussion pane at the bottom of the screen (general discussions) just as you would view document comments. To toggle the Discussion pane on or off, click the Show/Hide Discussion Pane button on the Discussions toolbar. To view a specific discussion, either click its icon next to the text or picture it refers to (inline discussions), or click the respective icon in the Discussion pane.

By default, Word 2000 displays the following header information about a discussion entry: the display name of the contributor, subject, text, and time. You change which items appear by clicking the Discussions button on the Discussions toolbar and then selecting Discussion Options. The Discussion Options dialog box shown in Figure 11.8 appears. Just check or uncheck the options you want to display in the Discussion Fields to Display section of the dialog box, and then click OK to save your settings and close the dialog box.

FIGURE 11.8
See what fields you can include or remove from the discussion headers.

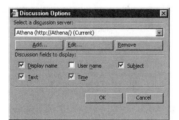

Editing Discussions

Unless your network administrator defined it otherwise, you have permission to alter or delete only your own discussion entries. Most commonly, however, you'll find yourself wanting to respond to a discussion item already posted. To perform any action on an existing discussion item, you first need to follow these steps:

1. Open the document that contains the discussion you want to work with.

2. Click Tools|Online Collaboration|Web Discussions. If you don't see the Discussion pane right away, click the Show/Hide Discussion Pane button on the Discussions toolbar.

3. Select the specific discussion you want to work with. To work with an inline discussion, click the Discussion icon next to the applicable text, table, or graphic, and then click the Show a Menu of Actions button in the Discussions toolbar. To select a general discussion, click Show General Discussions on the Discussions toolbar, and then click the Show a Menu of Actions button next to the discussion you want to work with.

4. From this menu, you can perform any of the following actions on the selected discussion:

   • Reply—Under discussion text, type your reply, and then click OK. Your reply appears nested under the remark you replied to.

   • Edit—Enter the desired changes, and then click OK. Remember, you can work only with your own discussion items unless your network administrator defined it otherwise.

   • Delete—This action removes the desired discussion remark; however, you can typically remove only your own remarks.

Filtering the Discussions You See

If you just read through all the discussions and remarks two days ago, you might not want to waste the time weeding through everything to get to the new entries. Or say you're about to go into a meeting with your boss. You might want to skim his or her contributions to the discussion beforehand to make sure you address all major concerns during the meeting. With Office 2000's capability to filter discussion content, you can see only what you want—or need—to see.

To filter discussion content, you need to follow these steps:

1. Open the document that contains the discussion remarks you want to filter, and then click Tools|Online Collaboration|Web Discussions.

2. On the Discussions toolbar, click Discussions|Filter Discussions. A special dialog box appears.

3. In the Created By box, select the name of the person whose remarks you want to view. This is the option you set to hone in on your boss's remarks.

4. In the Creation Time box, select the timeframe you want. Selecting times is the best way to eliminate content you've seen before. You can use these two fields separately or in combination with one another.

5. Click OK to close the dialog box. The discussion remarks that met your filtering criteria then appear in the Discussion pane.

Subscribing to Documents

With a seemingly endless stream of meetings and phone calls to make, who has time to stay on top of every change made to a document? Sure, you can periodically open the document and filter its discussions to track down new content or use the Reviewing toolbar to browse for new changes, but that takes time. Wouldn't it be neat if you could subscribe to a document just as you can a Web site in Internet Explorer 5.0? That way, you could be informed of changes if and when they occur so that you don't revisit the document unless you need to.

Well, your dreams have come true! By following these steps, you can be informed by email when a change is made or a discussion remark is added. And best of all, this procedure works in Excel 2000 and PowerPoint 2000, too.

1. Open the document or folder you want to subscribe to. Click Tools|Online Collaboration|Web Discussions as usual.

2. On the Discussions toolbar, click Subscribe. The Subscribe To dialog box appears.

3. Under the Subscribe To section, do any of the following:

   - To subscribe to the currently open file, click File.
   - To subscribe to all files in a Web folder, click Folder, and then choose the options you want.

4. In the When box, specify the conditions you want to have trigger the notification.

5. Enter your email address into the Address box.

6. Tell Office 2000 how often you want to be notified of changes by making a selection from the Time box.

7. Click OK to save the subscription information and close the dialog box.

Canceling these notifications is a piece of cake when you compare the process to trying to cancel a magazine subscription. All you have to do in this case is launch Outlook 2000 and open one of the messages you received notifying you of a change in the document or folder you want to cancel the subscription to. Click the specified hyperlink at the bottom of the note, and the notifications stop coming for good.

Scheduling an Online Meeting

Does your workgroup consist of telecommuters or employees who work offsite in another office? Or perhaps you've been asked to help draft a critical document for your parent company, which happens to be across the country. Whatever the case, you'll grow to appreciate the real-time online collaboration opportunities offered by NetMeeting 2.1 or higher.

Note: Don't worry, you have it (or at least have access to it). If you have Office 2000, then you have the Internet Explorer 5.0 suite of applications as well. This suite of applications includes NetMeeting 2.1, the most recent version of this powerful collaboration tool.

To schedule an online meeting, just follow these steps:

1. Launch NetMeeting by clicking Start on the Windows taskbar, and then selecting Programs|Internet Explorer|NetMeeting. Depending on how or when you installed NetMeeting, it might be elsewhere on your Start menu.

2. If the person you want to call is listed with the directory server you've defined to launch upon the application's start, just use the scrollbars to find his or her entry in the Directory List. If it's not the same server, use the Server drop-down box to change the server you're logged on to.

Peter's Principle: Always have a contingency plan.

As we all know, servers are not infallible. Things happen, but even when they do happen, business should be able to go on as normal. For this reason, having a company or organizational preferred server and a backup is a good idea just in case. That way, everyone in your organization knows what to do should the server go down.

Another precaution you might want to take right before an important online meeting is to increase the frequency with which your email program refreshes itself. That way, you quickly know when someone encounters a problem reaching you on a directory server, rather then refreshing email manually or waiting 15 minutes for the next automatic refresh.

3. When the person's name is in view, double-click it to place the call. The person then has the option to accept or ignore your call.

Caution: Think before you fret. Keep in mind that NetMeeting delivers the same message to you whether the person you called specifically ignored your call or was simply away from the computer. You would be wise not to react harshly until you know the complete story.

4. If the recipient accepts your call, you are connected within seconds (see Figure 11.9).

FIGURE 11.9
*NetMeeting's
Current Call view
shows who is
connected.*

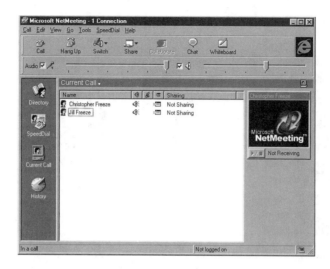

5. If the recipient doesn't accept the call, you have the option of leaving him or her a message. Click Yes to launch Outlook 2000 (or Outlook Express if that's your default email program) with a pre-addressed New Message window to the person you attempted to call.

6. After you set up your meeting (or you've called—or been called by—someone), launch the application containing the document you want to share with the rest of the people in the meeting.

> **Note: Is everybody ready?** To collaborate on a Word 2000 document, all the meeting's participants should have Word 2000, or at least some version of Word. The same holds true for Excel or PowerPoint. To participate, attendees need to have the applicable application available on their local machines.

7. While you're in the Current Call view, click the Share button, and then click the name of the application and/or document you want to show others in the meeting (see Figure 11.10). Others can see what you do but cannot modify the document in any way.

8. If you decide to let others edit the document as well, click the Collaborate button on the toolbar in the Current Call pane. To participate, others must click their Collaborate buttons as well.

FIGURE **11.10**
Click the Share button, and select the desired application from the pop-up list.

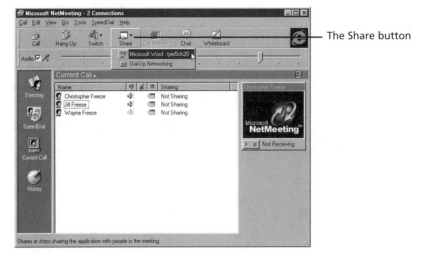

— The Share button

Caution: Give it some thought. Remember, when you collaborate, others can make changes to your master document. Although you can see everything that they do, sharing a document is not a decision you should make lightly, especially without making a backup copy of the document first. You should also be sure that you stay at your computer while collaboration is taking place. That way, you can monitor any input as it comes.

9. Other users can gain control of the document one at a time by clicking inside its window. Note that while the document is being edited by another person (his or her initials appear next to your mouse pointer), everyone else's mouse devices are essentially rendered useless. Not only is the mouse unavailable in NetMeeting, but you are kept from working anywhere else on your PC as well.

10. Should you decide to stop others from making changes to the document, just press the Esc key when you can regain control of the document.

11. You can end the collaboration for good by clicking the Collaboration button and then telling NetMeeting you want to stop sharing as well.

12. To end the meeting, click Hang Up to end the call.

If you're a meeting attendee versus the host, you receive a message when you are called asking whether you'll accept the call. The message box displays the caller's name as well, so you know who's at the other end of the connection before you make your decision to accept or reject the call.

Keeping Your Documents Secure

All the new file sharing options are pretty amazing, but there's a downside to using them: document security. When a document is stored in a public folder, it can become vulnerable to unauthorized tampering. For some documents, tampering may not be a huge concern, but for others—such as a formal long-range plan for your company—the results could be devastating.

A good rule of thumb is that before a document is saved to a public folder, it should be saved on someone's local machine and backed up on disk or tape as well. In addition, you can set a few document-specific options to protect the material. The options form a three-point continuum from least strict to most secure. The options include opening as read only, requiring a password to open, and requiring a password to modify.

Setting Security Options

To set the security options, follow these steps:

1. Open the document you want to protect, click Tools|Options, and then select the Save tab (see Figure 11.11).

FIGURE 11.11

All three security options can be set on this tab.

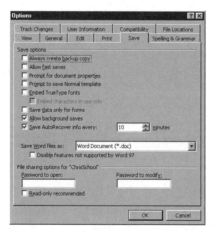

> **Tip: There's more than one way to get here.** You can also access this tab from the Save As dialog box by clicking Tools|General Options and then following the rest of the steps.

2. Depending on which security measure you want to use, do the following:

   - Open as read only—Check the Read-Only Recommended box at the bottom-left corner of the tab.

- Password required to open—In the Password to Open box, type in the desired password.

- Password to modify—Enter the password you want to use in the Password to Modify box at the bottom-right side of the tab.

> **Caution: Write it down!** A password can be up to 15 characters long and can be produced from a variety of letters, numerals, spaces, and symbols. It is also case sensitive. No matter what type of password you choose, be sure to write it down and keep it in a safe place; you cannot open or modify the document without it.

3. Click OK to save the settings and close the dialog box.

Changing or Removing a Password

If you find that you want to change or remove the password, you should be familiar with the following steps:

1. Open the document containing the password.

2. Click Tools|Options, and then select the Save tab.

3. Select the asterisks in the text box of the password you want to change, and then press the Delete key to remove the password, or type in the new password.

4. If you change the password, you are prompted to enter it again.

5. Click OK to save your settings and dismiss the dialog box.

Low-Tech Solutions for High-Tech Results

If you skimmed through this chapter and found yourself saying, "Gee, all this stuff is pretty cool, but it does me no good. My organization's not linked to the Internet, nor are our computers attached via a LAN," you're not alone.

Office 2000 does offer some powerful—and just plain nifty— collaboration tools, but not everyone has access to the hardware and networking to really make it shine. Rather than write off making use of some of these features, consider some of the following low-tech alternatives:

- Want others in your office to contribute to an important proposal for funding? Consider turning on Track Changes, and then save the document to disk. That way, everyone in your office can pass the disk around and make changes, and you can still benefit from the Track Changes feature.

- Are the people you want to work with offsite? Couriers, the post office, and overnight couriers can all transport the disk a variety of distances within 24 hours or less.

- Comments within a document can be handled in the same manner. Remember those old routing envelopes? They may still be of some use.

So maybe the alternatives leave a bit to be desired when you compare them to the connected solutions, but for a small, nonprofit, inner-city dance company, these solutions may be all they've got!

On Your Own

The tight integration between NetMeeting and Office 2000 presents some wonderful opportunities to work in real-time across great distances. If you don't already use NetMeeting on a regular basis, find a buddy and give it a try. Explore some of the capabilities that go beyond basic document sharing and collaboration such as using the white board or chatting. When you do, you can begin saving your company or organization huge amounts of money on long distance phone charges, and you can benefit from the expertise of colleagues across the globe.

Peter Norton

Building Web Pages with Word 2000

When you want to build Web pages with Word 2000, you'll find basically three scenarios:

- You want to prepare an existing Word document for publication on the Web.
- You need to use Word as an editor for adding text and formatting to Web component-based pages.
- You want to use a familiar application to design your whole Web site.

No matter what your situation, Word 2000 is ready to tackle the task. For the first time ever, the application offers total roundtrip editing, which means you can view and edit a Word document from your Web browser. You can also design more sophisticated Web sites thanks to Word 2000's capability to apply a single theme to the entire site and to support the design of frame pages. Finally, a powerful Web page design wizard makes it a snap to achieve professional results with a minimal time investment.

Hyperlinking Basics

Before delving into the finer points of Web page development with Word 2000, I need to address the basics of hyperlinking. By definition, a *Web* is a series of sites and/or pages that are linked to one another. These hyperlinks can be bits of text or a graphic that, when clicked, takes you to an alternate location. That location can be anything from another Web site on the Internet to a different location in the current document or page to an email link that automatically fires off your default email program.

Hyperlinked text often appears underlined and in a different color from the default Web page text. When you run the mouse pointer over it, the arrow turns into a pointing finger, signifying that you can click the spot to be taken to a new location. With graphics, it's a bit different. You often can't tell that a graphic is a hyperlink unless you run the mouse pointer over it and see the tell-tale pointing finger.

You should keep in mind that hyperlinks aren't just for Web pages any more. They also can be extremely helpful in connecting a series of related documents on your intranet or local area network (LAN).

Creating a Basic Text Hyperlink

You need to follow these steps to create a basic text hyperlink:

1. If you want to convert existing text into a hyperlink, select the text you would like to turn into a hyperlink.

2. Press Ctrl+K to launch the Insert Hyperlink dialog box shown in Figure 12.1.

FIGURE 12.1

Possibilities abound on the Insert Hyperlink dialog box.

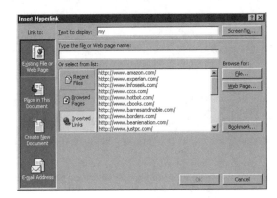

3. In the Text to Display box, you see the text you highlighted in the current document. If you haven't selected any text, you can type some here. Just remember that everything displayed in this text box is converted to a hyperlink.

4. The next thing you need to do is to make a selection from the Link To bar down the left side of the screen. You essentially have four choices: Existing File or Web Page, Place in This Document, Create New Document, and E-Mail Address. Just click the one you want. The contents of the main part of the dialog box change radically with your selection.

5. If you choose Existing File or Web Page (refer to Figure 12.1), you can define the link in one of three ways. You can type the complete file path or Web page address if you know it off the top of your head, you can use one of the three buttons down the left side of the list displayed to browse commonly visited sites and recently used documents, or you can click the File or Web Page button to browse for the desired source that may be buried a bit deeper on your system. After you've made your selection, skip ahead to step 9.

6. If you choose Place in This Document, you see a window from which you can select a specific heading or bookmark within the document. Just click the name of the desired element, and then move on to step 9.

> **Tip: How do I set a bookmark?** Open the document you want to create a bookmark in, click the location you want to place the bookmark, and then click Insert|Bookmark. Type a name for the bookmark in the Bookmark name box, and then click Add.

7. If Create New Document is your choice, then you are given the opportunity to name the document, specify its file path, and tell Word 2000 whether you want to edit it now or later. After you fill in all the information, you can move on to step 9.

8. If E-Mail Address is your choice, then you need to insert an email address and subject line that will be entered into the reader's default mail program automatically when it launches.

9. When you're satisfied that all your options are properly defined, click OK to save the settings and dismiss the dialog box. The text then appears in the document with its hyperlink characteristics.

Turning Graphics into Hyperlinks

Turning a graphic into a hyperlink requires steps similar to the ones outlined in the preceding section; however, you will notice a few subtle differences.

For starters, you select the graphic object instead of text. But beyond the obvious are a couple of additional points. Because a graphic may tell you less about where a link is taking you than its text counterpart, you might want to consider defining a ScreenTip for graphic hyperlinks. To do so, click the ScreenTip button at the top right of the Insert Hyperlink dialog box. The Set Hyperlink ScreenTip dialog box shown in Figure 12.2 opens.

FIGURE 12.2
This ScreenTip example could be used to clarify a link embedded in a picture of a racecar.

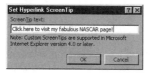

Type the desired text for the ScreenTip, and then click OK. From that moment on, the text you just entered will appear as a ScreenTip whenever the mouse pointer is passed over the selected graphic. In addition, the mouse pointer will turn into the pointing finger, letting the reader know that the image is, in fact, a hyperlink.

Caution: The invisible ScreenTips. Unless the visitor to your Web page is using Internet Explorer 4.0 or higher, he or she cannot see these customized ScreenTips.

Working with the New Web Folders

Creating Web pages may be a lot simpler with Office 2000, but how about publishing them to the Web? That task, too, has become significantly easier thanks to the new Web folders. If your LAN or Internet service provider runs a Web server capable of supporting Web folders, then you're well on your way to seeing the easiest Web publishing and editing ever!

Has your company's Web page become stale because uploading new information is a pain in the neck? Wouldn't it be nice—and a whole lot easier to keep Web content fresh—if editing Web documents were as simple as editing any old Word document? It is now, thanks to Office 2000.

Building Your New Web Folder

After you've checked with your network administrator and/or Internet service provider to make sure the Web server in use supports the new Web folders, you need to follow these steps to create your first Web folder:

1. If you're a Windows 98 user, click the Show Desktop button on the Quick Launch bar to reveal the entire desktop. If you're a Windows 95 user, you have to minimize each application one at a time.

2. Double-click My Computer, and then double-click Web Folders.

3. Double-click Add Web Folder, and then work your way through the Add Web Folder Wizard.

4. To save files to the Web server, drag them and any supporting folders to the newly created Web folder. Either that, or save them there directly from within Word 2000's Save As dialog box.

Note: What goes in must come out. Any file can be dragged into a Web folder, not just those saved as Web pages. Although virtually anyone using any type of computer can access a Web page with a standard Web browser, other file types stored there can be viewed only if the reader has the application that created the file (or one capable of reading the file's format) on his or her local machine.

Preparing a Word 2000 Document for the Web

The simplest of the three scenarios presented at the beginning of the chapter involves making an existing Word document ready for publication to the Web. That way, you can take advantage of many of Word 2000's powerful editing and formatting tools while making the document viewable with a Web browser. And should you decide to edit the document you're viewing, one click of the Edit button on the Internet Explorer 5 toolbar, and you're ready to begin working in Word. It's that easy!

For the most part, your Word document stays intact when you save it as a Web page, but I can think of some noteworthy exceptions. For example, if you have an informal table you built with a series of tab stops, you might want to first convert that text to a legitimate table, as described in Chapter 9, "Creating Professional-Looking Documents with Word 2000." This conversion helps ensure that your material stays lined up as you intended.

To save the current Word 2000 document as a Web page, you need to do the following:

1. Open the document you want to save as a Web page, and click File|Save as Web Page. The traditional Save As dialog box appears with a few Web-specific fields and options.

2. Click to the location in which you want to store the Web page. You might choose one of your Web folders if the document is ready to be published, or in the case of a work in progress, you might choose a standard working folder on your machine.

3. Enter a name for the file in the File Name box.

4. Click the Change Title button near the bottom right of the Save As dialog box. The Set Page Title dialog box shown in Figure 12.3 opens.

FIGURE 12.3

In the Set Page Title dialog box, you can tell Word 2000 exactly what you want the reader to see.

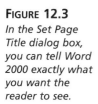

5. Type the words you want the reader to see in the title bar of his or her browser when viewing the current page. Click OK when you're happy with the text.

6. Click the Save button to preserve all your settings and dismiss the dialog box.

Your document is now ready for the Web. If, however, you want to remain true to the nature of the Web, you should add some hyperlinks to other resources before you actually publish the document.

Using Word 2000 as an Editor for Office 2000 Web Component Pages

In the chapters to come, you'll learn about some phenomenal new interactive Web components that let readers manipulate data live on a Web page. Although the functionality is truly remarkable (at least it is if you have Internet Explorer 5 and Office 2000 on your system), it's of little use without a bit of explanation. Without such an explanation, the readers might never know that they are looking at anything other than a plain old Excel worksheet pasted into a Web page (see Figure 12.4).

FIGURE 12.4

Get professional, understandable results by adding explanations to any Web components you may use.

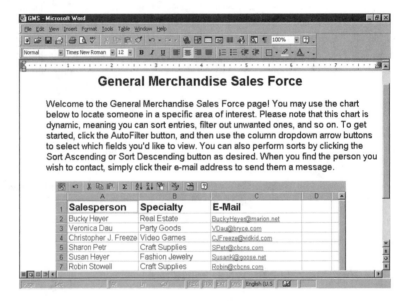

Including this explanation is hard if you've used any of these new Web components because Excel and Access aren't particularly adept at placing text where you want it on a page in relation to other objects. The solution is to use Word 2000 as your HTML editor. Sure, you could use FrontPage Express or FrontPage 2000 (if you have Office 2000 Premium Edition or better) to do the job, but why learn a new application if you don't have to?

To use Word 2000 as the HTML editor for your Web component-based pages, just follow these steps:

1. Make sure the Web component you want to edit has been properly saved as a Web page in its native application.

Looking Ahead

To learn more about Web components based in Excel 2000, turn to Chapter 16, "Excel 2000 on the Web."

---

2. Launch Word 2000, and then click File|Open.

3. Click your way to the Web page's directory, and then change the Files of Type setting to Web Pages. When you see the desired filename, click it to select it.

4. Click the drop-down arrow next to the Open button, and then select Open in Microsoft Word. Within a few seconds, the Web component appears in the Word 2000 window.

5. Edit the document as you would any other Word document. You might even want to add callouts to your page to help walk the reader through this new interactive experience. (For additional information on callouts, return to Chapter 5, "Shared Applets and Tools Available in Office 2000," and read the section "Creating Flowcharts and Callouts with AutoShapes."

6. When you try to save your work for the first time, Word 2000 displays a message saying that the page was created in another application. It warns that if you save the current file with Word elements under the same old filename, you won't have the source Web page to fall back on. This represents little problem if you kept a copy of the worksheet, chart, or whatever in the application's non-Web native format as well.

7. After you've finished adding the final touches to the page, it's ready to be published to the Web.

For Big Jobs, Consider Using the Web Page Wizard

Designing a Web site (or even a single Web page) can be an overwhelming undertaking for the novice computer user, which is why Microsoft invests so much time and money in developing wizards to assist with the task. As you'll see when we explore Publisher 2000 in depth, wizards are at the core of making complex tasks simpler, nonthreatening, and less time-consuming. They eliminate a lot of the grunge work so that you can focus your energy on content and design considerations rather than on making the Web page work, so to speak. If you need top-notch results in a hurry, you can seldom go wrong with a wizard.

To begin working your way through the Word 2000 Web Page Wizard, do the following:

1. Launch Word 2000, and then click File|New. On the Web Pages tab, double-click the Web Page Wizard icon.

> **Note: Have those disks close at hand!** Unless you installed every Office 2000 component out there, you may be prompted to install the Web Page Wizard from the Office 2000 installation disk.

2. The first screen of the Web Page Wizard presents the purpose of the wizard's existence. Click the Next button to get to work.

3. The first thing you need to do is enter the Web site's name and determine the location to which the pages you are about to create will be saved. For simplicity's sake, you might want to click the Browse button and create a new folder especially for the task at hand. Click Next to continue.

4. The next feature you need to consider is site navigation, or the way people make their way around your Web site. The most commonly employed navigational aid today is frames. In this wizard screen, you can opt to have the static links appear on the left side of the page or at the top. You can also use a separate page technique if you suspect the majority of your visitors aren't equipped to deal with frames. Click the desired option button, and then click Next. Note that a left-side-oriented frame is the default here.

> **Note: Frames explained...**Think for a moment of the picture frame that holds your child or spouse's photo on your desk. As the child grows, the picture is often replaced, but that finely carved frame always remains the same. That's exactly the way it is with Web page frames. The links that are stored on a Web page's frame remain there no matter what flows through the content section of the page. Frames help visitors keep their bearings while winding their way through a complex Web site. You'll explore creating your own frames later in the chapter.

5. Think you'll be needing more than three Web pages? The Add Pages screen is the place to add those pages. From here, you can perform these four basic operations:

   - Add New Blank Page—Click this button to insert another page without any special attributes or formatting.

   - Add Template Page—Click this button to add a page with predefined formatting such as an FAQ page, a Table of Contents, and the like (see Figure 12.5).

FIGURE 12.5

Choose from several predefined formats.

Caution: Not that kind of template... If you want to build a Web page based on a customized company template, take a look at the next section; you can't do that from within this wizard.

- Add Existing File—If you've prepared documents for the Web previously, you can use this button to add them to your new site one-by-one.

- Remove Page—Click a page to select it, and then click this button to remove it from the site.

6. After you click Next to move to the next screen, you get the chance to name and organize your pages. To name them, click a page to select it, click the Rename button, type the desired title, and then click OK. Repeat as needed. You can also change the order in which a page appears by selecting it, and then clicking the Move Up or Move Down button until the page appears in the desired location. When every page is named and in order, click Next to continue.

7. You are asked to select a visual theme for your site. Your selection dictates the page's background, how bullets look, and the default text color, among other attributes. Click the Browse Themes button to see the choices available, though keep in mind you might need access to the Office 2000 disks to install a selected theme and its preview graphic. When you find a theme you like, click its name, and then click the OK button. Click Next to move to the final screen.

8. The Web Page Wizard tells you it has everything it needs to build your Web site. Click the Finish button, and within a few moments, your brand new Web site appears onscreen, ready for you to fill it with content.

Building a Web Page Based on a Custom Template

If you've gone to all the trouble to create a special template for all your company's correspondence, why not carry that uniform, professional appearance over to your Web page as well?

To begin designing a Web page based on a custom template, launch Word 2000, and then click File|New. In the General tab, double-click Web Page. Choosing this option opens a new, blank Web page from which you can apply that custom template, as described in Chapter 8, "Going Beyond Basic Document Creation with Word 2000."

Web Page Design Considerations

The beauty of using Word to design a Web page is that you're already intimately acquainted with many of the techniques you will employ. But that doesn't mean you have nothing left to learn!

Countless design considerations come into play when you're trying to create a professional, readable, easy-to-navigate Web page. Some of them include the following:

- Finding easy ways to get where you're going—Whether the tactic involves the liberal use of hyperlinks, a series of frames, or some cleverly designed navigational buttons, you'll want to be sure readers can find what they're looking for on your Web site.

- Toning it down a bit—Bright fuchsia text on a turquoise background may make a powerful statement when you have fewer words in a bigger font size on the page, but when the page is loaded with text, you should keep things simple. Use this tip as a guide: If the page is more like a brochure, you can be a bit more playful with color usage. If it's more of a document or newsletter type of thing, stick with the basics that don't clash.

- Reducing eyestrain—Although you might be tempted to cram as much onto a page as possible, be sure to stay away from miniscule fonts. Smaller fonts make Web content extremely hard to read, especially in the case of alternate surfing devices like WebTV where the lower resolution can make text appear a bit fuzzier.

- Going easy on the images—If you're thinking about putting all sorts of graphics on your Web page, think again. These graphics may look nice, but they can often take the better part of a lunch hour to download. If you must include graphics, consider using smaller, thumbnail prints, or giving the readers a text hyperlink to the graphic.

- Breaking up the information   In addition to having navigational aids like frames or buttons, you should give serious thought to breaking up information into tinier, more manageable chunks. People want to jump in, get what they need, and get out. With both strategies in place, navigating your site will be a breeze.

- Not overstimulating your visitors—Animated GIFs and background music may seem like they add an extra touch of class, but they can have their drawbacks, too. Animated GIFs can pull your readers' attention away from important text, and music can take an eternity to download. However, if you use these elements sparingly, they can go a long way toward making a big impression.

Settings You'll Want to Explore

When you design a Web page, you might want to take advantage of several features—ones that you wouldn't have bothered with if the output was via printer only. For example, why bother with specially colored fonts, text animation, or fancy backgrounds when they would just be wasted on a black-and-white printout?

In the next few sections, I'll explain the features you may not have had the opportunity to explore fully. Give serious consideration to putting them to work for your Web page.

Selecting a Background for Your Web Page

Your choices for a Web page background run the gamut from a basic solid color to patterns based on two colors to rich textures like marble and wood. When you're selecting the background for your page, remember that the text color and special effects you choose will need to complement this background.

Peter's Principle: Consider the purpose and audience before you choose.

Whatever you do, don't overlook the fact that your Web page background has the power to set the readers' moods and expectations with regard to the content of your site. A subdued marble background with fancily scripted headings may be just the ticket for a four-star restaurant's Web page, but the small town candy store may do extremely well with Word 2000's preset Sweets theme. The presentation (background, fonts, and/or presence of special effects) also gives readers a clue as to whom the Web page was designed for. If you see lots of bright colors and cute teddy bear clip art, you can expect a page containing information about babies or at least content that's geared toward the youngest surfers.

Before you settle on a background, you might want to take a few minutes to walk through this quick tour of Word 2000's Web page background features. Even if you don't end up choosing one of the backgrounds you see here for your current project, at least you'll know the full extent of what you can do within Word in the future.

To begin exploring the various background options, you need to do the following:

1. Open or create the Word 2000 document to which you want to apply a special background.

2. Click Format|Background. The drop-down menu of sorts shown in Figure 12.6 appears.

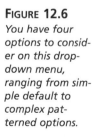

FIGURE 12.6

You have four options to consider on this drop-down menu, ranging from simple default to complex patterned options.

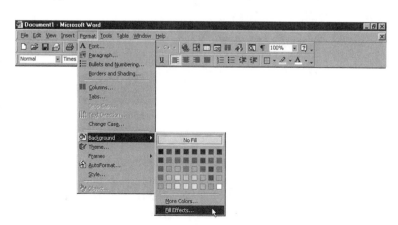

3. To have your Web page appear with the reader's default browser background, click No Fill Effect.

4. If the color you want to use appears on the menu's color swatches, just click it to select it.

5. Want more color choices at your fingertips? Click the More Colors button. On the Colors dialog box (see Figure 12.7), you can click any color you want and then click the OK button to apply it. If you're comfortable tweaking the appearance of a color by setting the saturation, the hue, or the amount of red it contains (among other settings), then the Custom tab of the Colors dialog box (see Figure 12.8) is for you. Just click inside an options text box to enter a value, or use the arrow buttons to nudge it a bit in the desired direction. When you're satisfied with the color that appears in the New box, click OK to apply it.

FIGURE 12.7
The Colors dialog box gives you a much larger selection of colors to choose from than the original swatches.

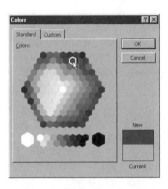

FIGURE 12.8
For the adventurous, the Custom tab can help you find the exact color you're looking for.

6. To apply special patterns or textures, click the Fill Effects button, and then read the following sections to learn how to achieve the results you want from each of the tabs.

Applying a Gradient Effect

You've seen neat gradient effects before, where one color gradually blends into another, or when vibrant rainbows fill the screen. With Word 2000, you can create these stunning effects yourself. Just follow these steps:

1. With the desired Word 2000 document open, click Format|Background|Fill Effects. The Gradient tab shown in Figure 12.9 appears by default.

FIGURE 12.9

On the Gradient tab, you can choose the colors you want to blend or choose from several preset selections, including a rainbow.

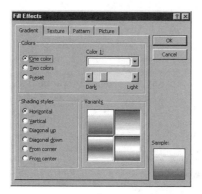

2. The first thing you need to do is define the colors you want to use. In this section, you have to set several options, including the following:

   • The number of colors—Down the left side of the screen in the Colors section are three option buttons. Choose One Color, Two Colors, or Preset. Your choice dictates the rest of the fields that appear in the Colors section.

   • The color(s)—If you choose One Color or Two Colors, you then find an equal number of drop-down boxes in which to make your choices. If you choose Preset, you see only one drop-down box containing a list of special effect names.

   • The Light/Dark lever—If you choose the One Color option, you then see a lever that enables you to tweak the lightness and darkness of the blending that takes place. Remember to keep an eye on the Sample box at the bottom right of the tab to see your results.

3. Selecting a shading style is the next order of business. By clicking the desired option button, you can tell Word 2000 how you want the shading to appear.

> **Tip: You can adjust the shading style of preset color schemes as well.**
> Just because a color scheme is preset in Word 2000 doesn't mean you can't adjust its shading style. You can do some pretty funky things with the Rainbow setting.

4. You can choose from among four available variants (in special circumstances, only two are available). Just click the one you want.

5. When you're happy with your selections, click OK to apply them. Within seconds, the entire screen is "painted" with the parameters you defined.

Using Textures to Bring Your Page to Life

From the casual feel of wood grain to the richness of marble, background textures can do a great deal to enhance the mood or feel of a Web page.

Although textures are powerful in their impact, they're significantly easier to deal with than the gradient effects described in the preceding section. Just follow these steps to apply a texture to your page:

1. Open or create the Word 2000 document you want to apply the texture to.
2. Click Format|Background|Fill Effects, and then select the Texture tab, as shown in Figure 12.10.

FIGURE 12.10

The Texture tab gives you a number of effects to choose from.

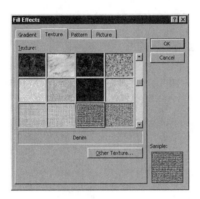

3. Use the scrollbars to view the textures included with Word 2000. When you find one you like, click it, and then click the OK button to apply it.
4. If you don't see one you like but think one may be stored elsewhere on your machine, click the Other Texture button, and then click your way to the desired file. When you see it, double-click its name.

Tip: Don't know the file by name? You can click a filename you think is correct to view it in the preview window before selecting it.

5. After you've made your selection, click the OK button to apply it.

Tip: Don't see what you're looking for? Turn to the Web to uncover tens of thousands of new textures and backgrounds using your favorite search engine or subject index. Just because these textures are on the Web doesn't mean they're free for the taking. Some sites request that you publish a link back to their site when you use their material on your personal home page. In a majority of cases, commercial sites are asked to seek permission to use the material, and in some cases are even asked to remit a fee. Before using any material you find on the Web, be sure to consult the specific site's requirements for use of the material.

Calling Patterns into Action

You'll be amazed at what patterns can do to perk up a Web page. Take two colors, assign a pattern, and achieve a result that can run the range from sophisticated to playful.

Caution: You can't judge a pattern by its looks. That pattern you spent so much time choosing may look great on its own, but try adding text. Many of the patterns make the page so busy that it becomes hard to read what's been written. Even when you do find a text color that shows up well, the pattern may be hard on the readers' eyes after an extended period of time. In general, use patterns when you have a small amount of largely formatted text, and avoid them in text-intensive situations.

To create a background pattern of your own, do the following:

1. With the desired document open, click Format|Background|Fill Effects, and then select the Pattern tab, as shown in Figure 12.11.

FIGURE 12.11
Just select a pattern, pick two colors, and you're ready to go.

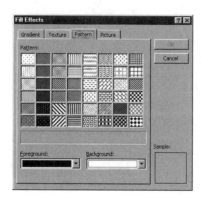

2. Select a pattern you like in the Pattern section of the tab by clicking it.

3. Select the Foreground and Background colors using the drop-down boxes at the bottom of the tab. You can view your selections in real-time by keeping an eye on the Sample box at the lower-right corner of the tab.

4. After you've made your selection, click OK to apply it, and then continue working in Word.

Using a Picture as a Background

If you want, you can even use that photo of your new golden retriever puppy as a background for a Web page. Beware, however, that a photo background may make the text excruciatingly hard to read. You might be better off just including the picture on the page. But should you decide to use it as a background anyway, click Format|Background|Fill Effects, and then select the Picture tab. Click the Select Picture button to browse your machine for the desired image. When you find the one you want to use, click its filename to select it, and then click OK. Within moments, your picture will be turned into a vibrant Web page background.

Tip: Lighten up! If you have a good graphics program at your disposal, you might want to doctor the photo a bit. With a little lightening up, a busy photo can turn into a wonderfully unique background. Just keep in mind that using images increases the page's download time, so use them sparingly, or at least make sure they complement the message you're trying to convey.

Enhancing the Appearance of Your Text

You've probably used italics and underlining in your Word documents before, but have you ever put special effects like embossing or outlining (see Figure 12.12) to the task? If not, Web pages are the perfect place to give them a try.

FIGURE 12.12
Even a plain old Times New Roman font can take on a whole new appearance when enlarged and outlined.

To alter the appearance of your text, highlight it, and then click Format|Font. The Font tab (see Figure 12.13) should open as the default. Simply check off the effects that you want to use, view them in the preview window, and when you're happy with the result, click OK.

FIGURE 12.13

You can change every attribute imaginable about a font in this one dialog box.

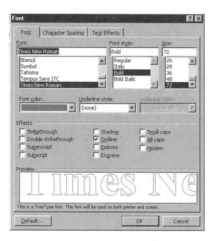

> **Tip: Bigger may be better.** When you apply some of the more subtle special effects, you might find that they show up better when the text appears in a larger size. Certain text and background color combinations are also more conducive to these special effects, but there are no hard and fast rules. The best advice is to take plenty of time to look at the text before publishing it. Maybe even have a friend or co-worker eyeball it because you may be too familiar with the text to be totally objective.

If you want to animate your text to draw attention to it, just click the Text Effects tab in the Font dialog box. Although the number of choices is somewhat limiting (only six are available), you never know when Microsoft will make more available.

Peter's Principle: Are the animations up to the task?

Although the special effects provided could be a fun addition to a personal home page, they may not quite be up to high-quality professional standards. That's no fault of Word 2000's; it's more a function of the impression made by most text animations. Unless they're truly spectacular, professionally created animations, they tend to produce the opposite reaction: They can make an otherwise classy site potentially look tacky. When it comes to your personal home page, use them to your heart's content. As for commercial use, proceed with caution.

To use one of these special effects, click its name, see how it looks in the preview window, and then click OK to apply it.

Adding Scrolling Text to Your Page

A neat way to grab your readers' attention without resorting to the potential gimmicks of text animations is to incorporate scrolling text into your Web site. To do so, you need to complete a number of steps:

1. Open the document you want to work with, and then click in the location you would like to place the scrolling text.

2. Right-click one of Word 2000's toolbars, and then select Web Tools from the shortcut menu. Choosing this option launches the Web Tools toolbar.

3. Click the Scrolling Text button, as shown in Figure 12.14.

FIGURE 12.14

Click the Scrolling Text button to begin defining the attributes of the text you want to put in motion.

The Scrolling Text button

4. The first thing you need to do in the Scrolling Text box that appears (see Figure 12.15) is define the desired behavior of the text. You have three choices:

   • Scroll—Feeds the text in from the right side of the screen and lets it run off the left side only to re-enter on the right and repeat the cycle.

   • Slide—Feeds the text in from the right side of the screen until it hits the left edge of the page, where it freezes in place.

   • Alternate—Brings the text in from the right and then bounces it back and forth inside the boundaries of the page.

Selecting the best text behavior given the situation is much more than a simple aesthetic judgment. Scroll works well no matter what size and amount of text you want to put in motion. Slide works only for text that fits within the boundaries of the Web page. If it's any longer, the readers will never see it because it will stop moving as soon as the beginning reaches the left edge of the page. For Alternate to work, the block of text needs to be small enough to give the illusion of bouncing back and forth. Hunks of text that push the boundaries of the page take on an almost spastic appearance because they have no freedom of movement. Of course, you can counteract some of these problems by tweaking the font size.

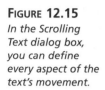

FIGURE 12.15
In the Scrolling Text dialog box, you can define every aspect of the text's movement.

5. By default, the background of the scrolling text is invisible; that is, it takes on the appearance of the background you selected for the page. You can change it for emphasis by using the Background Color drop-down box.

6. If, for whatever reason, you want the text to scroll to the right instead of to the left, you can make it do so by using the Direction drop-down box. Note that the direction you choose is the destination direction, not the originating direction.

7. You can specify how many times the motion is repeated using the Loop drop-down box. You can pick any number between one and five, or you can leave the text motion in the default infinite loop.

8. Is the text moving too quickly or too slowly? Use the Speed lever to make the necessary adjustment.

9. About halfway down the dialog box is a large text box ready for you to enter the text you want to have moved across the screen. Remember that you can adjust the text's font attributes after the element is placed on the Web page.

10. Take a look in the Preview window. If you're happy with what you see, click the OK button.

> **Note: When moving text is not supported...**The text appears in a fixed position if the reader's Web browser does not support moving text for whatever reason. This could, however, present a problem in cases in which you want large amounts of text to scroll across the screen.

Working with Frames

Using Web page frames can be a terrific way to simplify navigation throughout the site or to achieve a uniform appearance no matter what page in a site you're viewing, but building them can also be a major headache. If a single frame is really all you need, then using the Web Page Wizard is the quickest way to get the job done. If, however, you want two or more frames, you need to do the job manually.

Before you jump into the creation of frames, you need to understand that frames basically let you see multiple Web pages at a time. Each separate section of a page makes up a frame. The Web page that acts as a container for all these pages is called the *frames page*. To see all the pages at once, you view the frames page. This information will make a bit more sense as you go about designing the frames for your own Web site.

Building the Frames

The first step you need to take in designing a frames-based page is to map out the frames themselves. To begin doing so, follow these simple steps:

1. Create a new blank Word 2000 document.

2. Click Format|Frames|New Frames Page to launch the Frames toolbar shown in Figure 12.16.

FIGURE 12.16

The Frames toolbar is one of the most clearly labeled, self-explanatory toolbars available.

3. If you want to create a frame across the top (header) or the bottom (footer) of a page, you need to create it first so that it extends the entire width of the page. Click the New Frame Above or New Frame Below button as desired.

> **Tip: Before you decide you don't need them...**Header and footer frames can be extremely useful on your Web site. The header frame typically holds a nice-looking title for the site, and the footer frame can contain information such as copyright data, the last revision date, and so on.

4. To resize a frame, move your mouse pointer over its border until you see the pointer turn into a four-headed arrow. When the Resize ScreenTip appears onscreen, click the frame's border, and drag it in the desired direction.

5. When you're satisfied with the layout of your frames, be sure to save the frame page as usual.

Setting Up the Frames

After you've saved the frames page, you're ready to set up the frames. This task entails designing an attractive header frame (if you used one), preparing the hyperlinks in your navigation frame, and defining the default Web page for the primary viewing frame.

The following sections will guide you through the entire process of preparing your frames page for publication to the Web.

Preparing the Header or Footer Frames

Use traditional Word 2000 editing techniques to whip these frames into shape. Consider using a font that reflects the mood and purpose of the site, and choose a background that seems suitable for the site's message.

Preparing the Navigation Frame

Typically, the navigation frame appears down the left side of the screen. Type the text you intend to use for hyperlinks, and then follow these steps to prepare them for use in a frames environment:

1. Select the text you want to define as the first hyperlink.

2. Right-click it, and select Hyperlink from the shortcut menu.

3. Follow the directions for hyperlinking provided earlier in the chapter.

4. Before you click OK, take a close look at the bottom of the dialog box. There, you see a diagram of your frames page. Click the frame that you want the source document to appear in (see Figure 12.17).

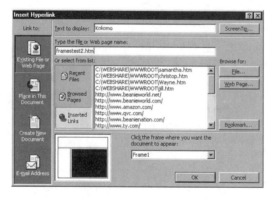

5. Click OK. When you click the hyperlink in the navigation frame, the defined hyperlink source appears just where you told it to.

6. Repeat the steps as necessary until all the hyperlinks in your navigation frame are defined.

7. Click Save to protect your work.

Defining the Main Viewing Area's Initial Page

With the header and/or footer frames and navigation frame all set to go, you're left with one final decision: What should the main viewing frame display when you first launch the frames page?

To set this information, right-click inside the frame, and choose Frame Properties from the shortcut menu. You then see an Initial Page text box in the Frames tab. Click the Browse button immediately to the right of it to locate the desired resource. Double-click it when you find it to automatically insert its file path into the Initial Page text box.

More Useful Frame Properties

You'll find several neat settings tucked away in the Borders tab of the Frame Properties dialog box. You can toggle the frames borders on and off, adjust their thickness, and pick a border color (see Figure 12.18). You can even click inside a particular frame and define whether it's displayed with scrollbars or can be resized from within a browser.

FIGURE 12.18

The Borders tab can help you make frame borders invisible, among other things.

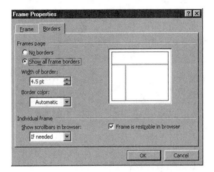

When you have the frames all configured to your liking, save them in regular .doc format, and then save them a second time as a Web page. When Word 2000 does the conversion, it alerts you to any potential conflicts between what you currently see versus what can be displayed in a Web page. You always have options for reacting to the conflict, so you needn't feel like there's no turning back. Within a surprisingly short amount of time, you can produce your own frames-based Web site like the one shown in Figure 12.19.

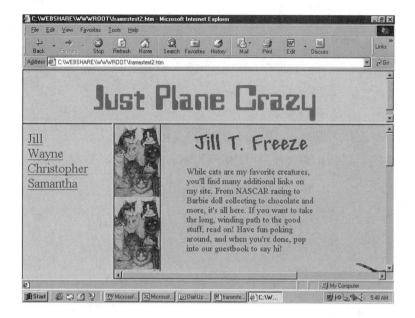

On Your Own

Do you have a copy of your resume on your machine? If not, spend a couple of minutes entering your contact information and a couple of your most recently held jobs. Don't worry about fancy formatting here; the purpose of this exercise is to go through a resume-like document and create hyperlinks to everything you can think of.

- Create a hyperlink to your email address.
- Link to your alma mater's home page.
- Link to an important report you drafted for one of the jobs listed.

What you link to isn't as important as the fact that you attempted to define various kinds of hyperlinks. Hyperlinks are such a fundamental concept in understanding how Web pages are created that it's vitally important you feel comfortable working with them at a variety of levels.

PART III

Using Excel 2000

13

Creating Excel Spreadsheets

If Word 2000 is the word warrior, then Excel 2000 is the supreme defense against unorganized data. Whether you need a simple database to keep track of your home audio CD collection, or you're a corporate executive who could benefit from the flexibility of data analysis with PivotTables, Excel 2000 is the way to go.

If you just upgraded to Excel 2000, you won't see a whole lot of difference between this version and its predecessors, at least on the surface. The biggest changes involve Excel's use on the Web. For the first time, you can publish Excel data to the Web and let your readers manipulate the data in any way they see fit. Although this capability may not excite the casual home user, the corporate user can do some amazing things. You could publish data about your sales force on your intranet so that the various teams can see how they're doing in relation to one another. Or, if you're putting up a small e-commerce site, you could use Excel as a front end to your inventory database so that the customers can see what is and isn't in stock.

In this chapter, I'm going to review some basic concepts about how Excel works. Even if you already know the concepts inside and out, seeing them before you all at once may help you see the application in a new light.

And if you were always primarily a Word user who never quite found the courage to venture into the world of spreadsheets, you'll need a firm grounding in these concepts before you can fully exploit the powers of Excel.

After I've discussed each of the concepts, I'll go through many of the functions available in Excel that you can use to create your own formulas. After all, what good is a spreadsheet without formulas? You can use Word if you just need a static list of items!

The Anatomy of Excel 2000

Many people use Excel on a regular basis, but how many know the proper terms for each element? For example, while everyone else in the world uses the term *spreadsheet*, Microsoft uses the name *worksheet* to describe a grid containing rows and columns of numbers and formulas. And although it's also true that some of the concepts such as *cell* are universal among spreadsheet applications, here too you'll find some disparity between typical terms and what Microsoft chooses to call them.

Figure 13.1 illustrates some of the key items you'll see while using Microsoft Excel.

FIGURE 13.1
An Excel work-book contains many different components.

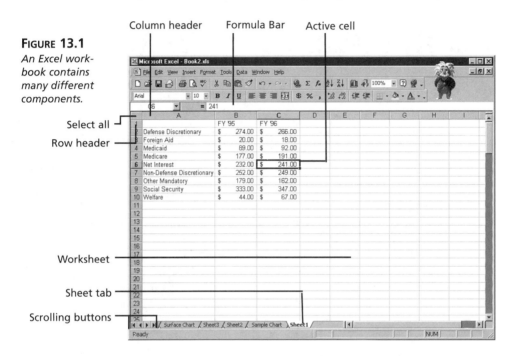

Now that you've got a good feel for where things fall on the Excel workspace, let's take a closer look at each of the elements.

Much like Word documents are referred to as, well, *documents*, Excel documents are referred to as *workbooks*. Within each of these workbooks, you might find a series of *sheets* and *worksheets*. Think of these sheets and worksheets as Excel's counterpart to *pages* in a Word document.

> **Note: Sheets versus worksheets—what's the difference?** Here again, Microsoft makes a subtle distinction between the two terms. The word *work-sheet* can be used interchangeably with *spreadsheet* because it contains the grid full of rows and columns of data. *Sheet,* on the other hand, can refer to a worksheet, a chart, a PivotTable, or a PivotChart. So, in the case of Excel, *sheet* is the general term for parts of a workbook, whereas *worksheet* means some-thing more specific.

In Excel, unlike Word, however, Microsoft makes switching from one sheet to another a breeze. Simply click the desired sheet tab, and you're there; none of this scrolling through a document or using the Find command.

And those who've used Excel in the past will be thrilled to learn that one of the more annoying Excel problems has been fixed in this release. Remember how you would select a range of cells, and they would be so darkly highlighted that you couldn't make any major formatting changes without repeatedly selecting and deselecting the block of cells? Well, thanks to the new See-Through view, you can see the effects of these changes as you make them. The old inverse video highlighting method has been replaced with something much lighter, which in the end will reduce the amount of time you spend at the keyboard reformatting worksheets.

Just above the column headers, you'll notice a long text box preceded by an equal sign. Technically known as the Formula Bar, this text box displays the exact content of the currently selected cell without any formatting. So, if the selected cell actually contains a formula rather than a simple number, you see the syntax of the formula in the Formula Bar. This formula appears in the Formula Bar—for example, =SUM(A1:A4)—while the number that the formula generates remains displayed in the active cell.

As you browse the toolbars above the Formula Bar, you'll notice a number of Excel-specific buttons, including special formatting buttons (such as Currency Style or Percentage Style), formula buttons (such as AutoSum or Paste Function), and database-like buttons (such as Sort Ascending or Sort Descending).

Peter's Principle: Think of Excel as a database.

Sure, Excel 2000 is technically a spreadsheet application, but I use it just as often as a mini database application. When my needs are simple, dealing with Excel as a database is far easier than working my way through an Access wizard. Using Access may be overkill for many situations. In fact, I liken using Access for a simple database task to shelling out $1000 for a fancy desktop publishing package when Publisher 2000 (which comes free with Office 2000) fits the bill.

So when should you consider using Excel as your database? If you don't want to waste the disk space loading Access for a single task, use Excel. If your database will have fewer than 256 fields each for 65,536 records, use Excel (but don't expect it to run too quickly if you max out the size).

Managing Sheets

Each sheet in the workbook has a tab containing its name. Just click the name of the sheet you want to view, and you're there! If you've arranged your sheets in a nice, logical order, you can even do a simple presentation from within Excel by starting with the first sheet and clicking through each of the sheets in the workbook. When time is of the essence, using this trick beats exporting everything to PowerPoint and formatting it there!

Naming the Sheets

Picture a file cabinet full of unlabeled manila folders, and that's what you have when you look at a workbook containing only the default names Sheet 1, Sheet 2, and so on. Why not save yourself unnecessary aggravation by giving the parts of your workbook meaningful names?

Sheet names can have as many as 31 characters and can contain any character (including spaces) except for these: /, \, ?, *, [, or]. The size of the sheet tab is automatically adjusted so that the full sheet name is shown. That way, the name you choose will never be hidden.

Inserting and Deleting Worksheets

As you're working on a project, you might find it beneficial to create additional sheets for elements such as graphs, charts, or PivotTables. That way, items are not only kept separate, but they're also easy to find!

To insert a new sheet in your workbook, click Insert|Worksheet. This action adds a blank worksheet to your workbook before the currently selected sheet; you can format it as desired. If you're fond of shortcut menus like I am, you can also right-click a sheet tab and select Insert from the pop-up menu. Choosing this option displays a dialog box (see Figure 13.2) from which you can choose either a chart or a worksheet, or you can choose from any of the available spreadsheet solutions such as invoices, purchase orders, or expense statements. Using one of these worksheet templates can save you a great deal of time because it may already contain a structure that you find useful.

FIGURE 13.2

Using worksheet templates can save you time by allowing you to use a previously created worksheet.

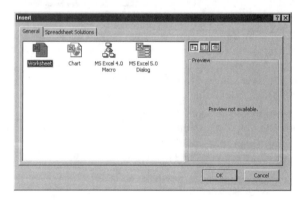

Deleting a worksheet is even easier. To do so, simply click Edit|Delete Sheet, or right-click the sheet tab you want to delete and select Delete from the shortcut menu.

Renaming a Sheet

After you've spent great amounts of time working on your workbook, the day might come when you need to share it with others either via the Web or by emailing them the Excel file. In either case, you can save yourself (and the recipients of your workbook) a great deal of time by giving the workbook's tabs clear, concise names. Using appropriate names keeps you from having to go into a lengthy explanation of what's located where in the workbook, and it dramatically reduces the number of questions your readers are likely to have. Unfortunately, you might have to rename some of the tabs.

You can rename a sheet by double-clicking its tab and then making the necessary edits right on the tab itself.

Changing the Order of the Sheets

After you've completed your workbook, you might need to rearrange the order of the sheets. The order in which I create the sheets is seldom the order in which they should logically appear, so I'm forever doing this myself. Click Edit|Move or Copy Sheet to move the current sheet to a different position on the set of tabs (see Figure 13.3). Just click the name of the sheet before which you want to place the selected sheet, and then click OK to dismiss the dialog box.

If you select the Create a Copy check box, then a copy of the worksheet is placed in the selected position. This function is extremely useful when you want to create a second worksheet that's heavily based on the current worksheet.

FIGURE 13.3

Rearrange worksheets to present them in the order that you feel is most important.

Moving or copying worksheets from one workbook to another may also be in order, but should you decide to do so, use extreme caution. If a formula in the sheet you're about to move or copy is dependent on information found elsewhere in its native workbook, the results may be way off.

Having said all that, here are the steps you need to follow to move or copy worksheets from one workbook to another:

1. Open the workbook that will receive the worksheet(s).
2. Open the workbook containing the worksheet(s) to be moved or copied.

3. Click the sheet tab of the worksheet you want to copy or move. If you want more than one worksheet, click the first one, press Shift, and then click the last one (for adjacent worksheets), or click each one while holding down the Ctrl key.

4. Right-click the sheet tab(s), and choose Move or Copy from the shortcut menu. The Move or Copy dialog box appears.

5. The To Book box lists the destination workbook. Use the drop-down arrow button if needed to select a different workbook or to build a new one from the worksheet(s).

6. Tell Excel where to place the sheet(s). You can place it before any of the worksheets in the destination document, or you can append it to the end by clicking the desired option.

7. By default, Excel moves the worksheets. If you want them copied instead, check the Create a Copy option.

8. Click OK to process your request.

Using Excel's Data Recognition to Your Benefit

As you may already know, a cell contains a single piece of information. It can contain a number (such as an inventory number or the cost of an item in the inventory,), a text value (such as the description of an inventory item or the name of its supplier), or a formula that returns a value that is then displayed in the cell.

To enter a value into a cell, select the cell and then simply type the value. In most cases, Excel automatically recognizes the type of the data and displays it in the appropriate format. For instance, entering 10% into a cell actually enters the value .1 and formats the cell as a percentage.

> **Caution: What you see is not always what you get!** Use extreme caution when you're performing calculations on Excel data. Double-check—even triple-check—your cell formatting to make absolutely sure you know what's being included in a calculation. If you don't, you may end up with some very unexpected results.

Likewise, entering $45.00 places the value 45 into the cell, formats the cell as a currency value, and shows the first two decimal places. Entering the number 44 into the same cell preserves the formatting information; it is displayed as $44.00. If you type $45 into a different cell, the same value and format are entered into the spreadsheet, but no decimal places are displayed.

The same holds true for date formatting. If you enter something like 7/27/65, Excel recognizes it as 7/27/1965.

Entering a text value into a cell is no different from entering a number; you simply type in the value. Excel then analyzes it. If Excel determines the value is not a number, it treats that number as text just as you intended.

Tip: Forcing cell content to be treated as text. You can also force Excel to treat your value as text, even if it's a number, by entering an apostrophe (') as the cell's first character. This trick is especially useful to know when you're entering street address numbers and the like. The leading apostrophe is not displayed in the cell, so if you actually want your cell's text value to begin with an apostrophe, you have to type it twice.

Selecting Cells

Whether you're trying to print a certain part of your worksheet, or you're merely trying to align the cells' contents, selecting the cells is the first step. The method that works best for you depends on which part of the worksheet and how much of it you want to select.

Naturally, the active cell is always selected. To select a range of cells, click the left mouse button, and hold it while dragging the mouse. The selected cells are highlighted in a light blue (the new See-Through view), and are outlined with a bold border.

You can also select a row of cells by clicking on the desired row header, or a column of cells by clicking on the column header. Select multiple columns or rows by pressing and holding the left mouse button while moving the mouse pointer over the headers you want to select. Finally, pressing the Select All button allows you to select all the cells on the spreadsheet in a single operation.

Tip: Power typing. If you need to enter a series of values into your spreadsheet, simply select the range of cells you want to enter, and begin typing the value into the first cell. Pressing the Enter key takes you to the next selected cell below the current cell. This process continues until you reach the last cell in the selected area of the first column. At that point, the insertion point is moved to the first cell in the next column. When you've reached the last selected cell in the last column, pressing Enter returns you to the first cell. Pressing Enter without typing a value preserves the current contents of the cell; otherwise, whatever you type replaces the contents of the active cell.

Editing a Cell

As the saying goes, The only thing constant is change. The same holds true for computing. Any number of circumstances may require you to change the content of your worksheet. Perhaps the cost of goods went up, or maybe your sales projections changed based on action taken by your competitors. Whatever the case, you'll most definitely find yourself editing your worksheets time and time again.

You can edit a cell in many different ways. If you double-click the cell (or press F2 to edit the active cell), the raw contents of the cell are displayed with an edit cursor. You can use the left or right arrow keys to move the cursor from one character to another, or you can use the mouse to position the cursor anywhere in the cell. Changes are then made just as they are in any other Office program. To apply the edit, select another cell or press Enter.

You can also edit the contents of the cell in the Formula Bar. With the cell you want to edit selected, simply click the Formula Bar and begin editing as necessary.

Clearing the Contents of a Cell

To clear the contents of the active cell, either press the Delete key, or right-click the cell and select Clear Contents from the pop-up menu. You can also select a range of cells and clear their contents the same way.

> **Note: It's Clearly not Deleted.** Clearing a cell is not the same thing as deleting a cell. Clearing a cell merely removes the cell's value and leaves all its formatting information intact. Deleting a cell physically removes the cell from the spreadsheet and shifts other cells to replace it.

Moving Cells

Just like you can drag words from one place in a Word document to another, Excel lets you drag ranges of cells. Simply select the cells, and move the mouse pointer toward the cells' border until it changes into an arrow. Then click the right mouse button, and drag the cells to their new destination while holding the button. Releasing the button drops the cells into place.

If any of the destination cells have data or formulas in them, Excel asks whether you want to replace the contents of the destination cells with the material you just moved. If you click Cancel, the move is canceled; otherwise, clicking OK causes the old cells to be replaced with the moved cells.

Of course, you don't always have to use drag and drop to move cell data. After you've selected one or more cells, you can use the standard Windows Cut command to move cell contents to the Clipboard. Select another location on the worksheet, and select Paste to move them.

These commands are available under the Edit menu, on a pop-up menu that you can display by right-clicking a range of cells, or by pressing Ctrl+X for Cut and Ctrl+V for Paste.

Peter's Principle: Drag and drop versus cut and paste—which is better?

Perhaps the real question is not which is better, but which method you should use when. If I'm working on a single sheet, I use drag and drop. It's the fastest way to move cells when both the selected cells and the destination cells are in plain view. When I'm working with multiple sheets or even multiple workbooks, I have no choice but to use cut and paste. After all, you can't drag cells to a location you can't see!

How many bits of text you plan to gather also comes into play here. If you're gathering data from multiple files to consolidate into a single file, then the new Clipboard is without a doubt the way to go with its easy collect-and-paste capabilities.

Inserting and Deleting Cells

To insert an empty cell or range of empty cells into your spreadsheet, simply select the range of cells adjacent to the location where you want the new cells to be inserted, and click Insert|Cells,Rows, or Columns as desired. You can also right-click the cell and choose Insert from the pop-up menu. If Excel can't determine what to do with the rest of the cells, it prompts you to choose whether to move the cells down or to the right. It also lets you choose to insert new rows or columns.

Deleting a range of cells works the same way, though the cells are moved in the opposite direction. You can move the cells to the left or up, or you can delete the affected rows or columns. If you select one or more rows or columns before selecting the insert or delete command, then Excel does not prompt you for additional information. It just goes ahead and performs the requested operation.

Letting Excel Type for You Using AutoComplete

To make your life easier, Excel attempts to guess any text value you enter based on values in your spreadsheet. Say, for example, you're entering a list of audio CDs for a small, used CD store. In your database, you have the CD title and the artist, among other fields. As you type each character in the artist field, Excel searches for a cell in the same field that has the same leading characters. If it finds exactly one match, it displays the rest of the value using white text on a black background rather than the normal black text on a white background. So following through on the example, if I type in a B, and Bach is the only artist beginning with the letter *B* in the database, Excel shows Bach in highlighted text. If multiple artists in that field have names beginning with the same letter, I have to enter enough letters so that Excel recognizes that there's only one match. Pressing Enter accepts the suggested value, whereas typing a nonmatching value clears the suggestion and enters a new one in Excel's "memory" for future use.

> **Note: It worked that way before.** In Excel 97, when multiple values matched the characters you entered, the first matching value was displayed. In Excel 2000, nothing is displayed until only one value matches.

AutoFilling Your Worksheet

One of the most useful features in Excel is its capability to complete a series automatically. A *series* can be a set of numbers such as 1, 2, 3 or 2, 4, 6, or letters such as A, B, C. It can also be a set of dates such as Jan-99, Feb-99, Mar-99, or the days of the week. You can even define your own series that Excel will automatically extend.

To use AutoFill on your spreadsheet, follow these steps:

1. Enter the first few values of the series into your spreadsheet.
2. Select the values by dragging the mouse pointer over them while holding down the left mouse button.
3. Move the mouse pointer to the lower-right corner of the selected area, and wait for it to change into a fill handle.
4. Drag the mouse pointer over the range of cells you want to fill while holding down the left mouse button.
5. Releasing the left mouse button fills the selected range of cells with the series you highlighted.

You can create your own series by clicking Tools|Options and then choosing the Custom Lists tab (see Figure 13.4). To create your own list entry, select NEW LIST in the Custom Lists box, and begin typing your list in the List Entries pane. Enter one list item at a time, pressing the Enter key to move to the next line. When you're finished, click the Add button to make your list available, and then click OK to dismiss the dialog box.

Peter's Principle: Save yourself some work!

Do you have a block of data that you always seem to be typing? Perhaps it's a list of sales force members or a list of Boy Scouts for whom you track fund-raising data. Whatever the case, Excel can save you the hassle of typing data over and over again by creating a custom AutoFill list. Although this feature works a little differently, think of it as Excel's counterpart to Word's AutoText. If the list you want to create already appears in a worksheet, open it, click Tools|Options, and then open the Custom Lists tab. Click the button at the right end of the Import List from Cells box. The dialog box shrinks, giving you ample room to highlight the cells you want included in the list. After you've made your selection, click the button at the right end of the Import List from Cells box, and then click the Import button. You then have the list at your disposal each time you work with Excel.

To edit a list, simply select the list you want to change in the Custom Lists window, click on the List Entries box, and then make the necessary changes. When you're finished making your changes, click the Add button to save the changes to your list, and then click OK to close the dialog box.

FIGURE 13.4
Add your own custom list that you can use with AutoFill.

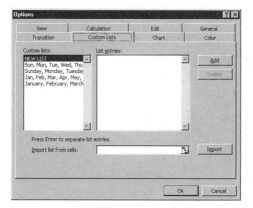

Tip: Keying quickly. Press Ctr+D to fill the active cell with the value from the cell above it, and press Ctrl+R to fill the active cell with the value from the cell on its left.

Checking Your Spelling

Let's face it, an Excel spreadsheet often has more text than numbers on it, especially when it's turned into a database. While you're likely to double-check the numbers, do you remember to double-check the text in an Excel workbook? If you're like me, probably not. However, now that Excel has access to the same tools that Word uses (including AutoCorrect and the spell checker), you're less likely to be caught off-guard by embarrassing spelling errors.

AutoCorrecting Common Errors

AutoCorrect analyzes the words you type and automatically corrects them right before your eyes by using its dictionary of commonly misspelled words. AutoCorrect also changes values like (c) to © automatically.

Of course, these automatic corrections may annoy some people who aren't expecting it or who simply want to have full control over what's going on in their documents. You can easily disable AutoCorrect or edit the list of misspelled words by clicking Tools|AutoCorrect (see Figure 13.5). Uncheck the Replace Text as You Type option to disable the automatic replacements.

You can edit the list of words that AutoCorrect will fix by clicking Tools|AutoCorrect (refer to Figure 13.5). To enter a new pair, simply type the incorrectly spelled word in the Replace field, its proper spelling in the With field, and then click the Add button. If you want to remove a correction from the list, scroll through the list, select the pair, and click the Delete button.

FIGURE 13.5

Edit the list of words that AutoCorrect will replace on-the-fly by using the AutoCorrect dialog box.

> **Tip: How do you spell that again?** Do you have a boss or business associate with a hard-to-spell name? If so, you might want to consider adding a special AutoCorrect entry for him or her. That way, you'll never have to worry about misspelling it again, no matter what Office 2000 application you're working with.

Performing a Spell Check

Although AutoCorrect can catch some commonly misspelled words, you still need a spell checker to verify that the rest are spelled correctly. Excel uses the same spell checker used by Word and the other Office 2000 applications, including the same dictionaries. Simply select the range of cells you want to check (or select any single cell to check the entire spreadsheet), and then click Tools|Spelling. Then process the words marked as misspelled using the dialog box shown in Figure 13.6.

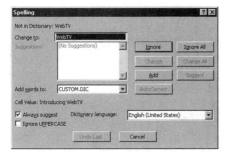

> **Tip: You don't have to fix it twice.** If you have a commonly misspelled word, you can easily add it to the AutoCorrect list of words to replace as you type by clicking the AutoCorrect button on the Spelling dialog box. Likewise, you can add the word to your custom dictionary by clicking the Add button.

Using Formulas to Perform a Variety of Calculations

As you've seen throughout this book, you can create basic tables natively in just about any Office 2000 application now. Although these tables look nice, they're sorely lacking in functionality when compared to Excel. With Excel, you can add, multiply, divide, and perform a host of other less common mathematical operations on a set of numbers. This is all possible because of Excel's capability to embed formulas into cells.

Anyone who is familiar with algebra will be right at home creating formulas in Excel. It's literally as easy as 1+1!

You enter a formula into a cell by typing an equal sign (=) followed by an expression. For example, if you enter =1+1 into a cell, Excel displays the value 2. Of course, the real benefit to using the Formula Bar comes in referencing other cells. You can build extremely complex formulas in Excel using operators, functions, and references to other cells.

Referencing Other Cells

Every cell in a worksheet has a unique address referenced by column and row headers. For instance, the first cell in the worksheet is known as A1.

A range of cells is known by the addresses of the cells at the upper-left corner and the lower-right corner of the range. Thus, if you select the first two rows and first five columns of a worksheet, the range would be known as A1:E2.

You can address a cell from another worksheet in the current workbook by including the worksheet name followed by an exclamation point and the cell address. That means the first cell in the worksheet named Sheet1 is called Sheet1!A1. You can also use sheet names in a range such as Sheet1!A1:E2, which would be identical to the previous range if those cells were located on Sheet1.

The concept of referencing cells forms the foundation of Excel. For instance, I've used it in the past to create a simple spreadsheet that mimics the 1040 Tax Form. I entered the line numbers down one column and the values down the second. Where the tax form instructed me to add two numbers together, I simply entered a formula that used cell references to add the two cells together.

Using Relative Cell References in the Formula Bar

If you enter the formula =A1 into cell A2, whatever you type in cell A1 automatically appears in A2. Likewise, if you enter =Sheet1!A1 into cell A1 of Sheet2, whatever value you enter in cell A1 of Sheet1 automatically appears in cell A1 of Sheet2. The format used to reference cell A1 is known as a *relative address*. Excel recognizes a relative address as your intent to base the formula not upon a specific cell, but rather on a specific spatial relationship. For example, if cell A2 contains the formula =A1, Excel recognizes that you want the value of A2 based on the value of the cell to its immediate left. Moving (or copying) the cell to A3 automatically updates the formula to be =A2.

Keeping the Cell Reference Absolute

Sometimes you don't want Excel to adjust the cell addresses when you copy a range of cells. For instance, assume that you want to create a spreadsheet to compare the various financing options for your new home. At the top of your worksheet, you enter information such as the purchase price of the house, the estimated taxes, and homeowner's insurance. Then, in a series of lines below this information, you enter the data for each lender's financing package. For example, in each line, you enter information about the term of the loan, the interest rate, and the required percent down. Then, elsewhere on that same line, you enter a formula that computes your monthly mortgage payment based on the information from the lender, plus the general information about your house.

To add another vendor along with the pertinent data about their financing options, it would be nice if you could just copy the cells for the last lender's information. That way, you needn't re-enter the formulas, just the new data. Although the references to cells in the same line are copied correctly, the references to the cells at the top of the form are one line off because these cell addresses are automatically adjusted. In that instance, the results could be skewed because the formulas may be factoring in the estimated taxes as opposed to the cost of the house as you intended.

To prevent this situation from happening, you need to use a technique called *absolute addressing*. This technique uses dollar signs to fix the location of the column or row or both. For example, the formula =A1 always references cell A1, no matter where the formula is moved or copied. However, when you copy cell A2 containing the formula =$A1 to cell B3, Excel recognizes the absolute reference to column A and the relative reference to row 1. The cell reference is updated to read =$A2. Likewise, copying the formula =A$1 from A2 to B2 translates the formula to read =B$1.

A Refresher on Cell Values, Names, and Ranges

A cell is either empty, or it has a value. If the cell has a value, then the value can be numeric, a string of characters (usually referred to as simply a string), a logical (True or False) value, or an error condition.

Unless you've studied computers (or math) in depth, you may not fully understand the differences between these types of values. Because these values form the basis of Excel, let me take a little time to explain them in a bit more detail.

A numeric value, for example, can simply be a number you entered into a cell, or it can be the result of a formula.

A string, on the other hand, can be any combination of letters, numbers, or punctuation marks. Mailing addresses with their street numbers and names are the perfect example of a string.

When you compare two values together, you get a result of either True or False. This is a logical value. For instance, the formula =A1=A2 returns True if A1 and A2 both contain the same value; otherwise, it returns False. You can use this information elsewhere in your worksheet to apply conditional formatting or other more advanced Excel options.

The final value is an error condition. An error condition happens when a value is too large for a cell or when a formula returns an unpredictable result. Table 13.1 presents these error conditions and their respective causes so that you'll be prepared to handle them.

Table 13.1 Error Values

Error Value	Description
#####	The number is too large to be displayed in the space available.
#DIV/0!	You attempted to divide by zero.
#N/A	The value is not available.
#NAME?	The text in a formula is invalid.
#NULL	You specified an intersection between multiple ranges, but they had no cells in common.
#NUM!	An invalid number appeared in a formula.
#REF!	You used a bad cell reference.
#VALUE!	An invalid value was used with a function or operator.

Creating Basic Formulas with Simple Expressions

The technical name for characters such as plus (+), minus (-), multiply (*), and divide (/) is an operator. Excel has a wide range of operators that perform different functions. Using them, you can perform a calculation on a group of cells, or express some kind of relationship between them and have Excel respond accordingly.

These operators fall into several different categories. Although the category in which each operator belongs may seem unimportant, it does shed some light on how the operators in the group can be used to your advantage. I've listed the most useful operators in Table 13.2. They're grouped together by the type of result they return. To help you understand what the operator is capable of, I've included a simple example of how the operator works with the result shown in parentheses.

Whether you want to add a range of cells or simply want to add several numbers and have the result displayed in a cell, you should be familiar with the Addition arithmetic operators. Everyone knows what a plus sign does, but the fact that an asterisk means multiplication in Excel may be somewhat of a mystery.

So when might you want to use a arithmetic operator? Consider your monthly household budget for a moment. Instead of entering separate line items for gas, electric, phone, and such, you can add them all together using the Formula Bar (for example =35+122.48+94.75) and place the return value ($252.23) into a single Utilities line item.

To learn the various operations you can perform on a range of cells or a group of numbers within a cell, you should get to know the arithmetic operators listed in Table 13.2. They use one or two numeric values (or cell ranges), and return a single numeric value.

Table 13.2 Numeric Operators

Operator	Description
+	Addition: 1 + 1 (2)
-	Subtraction: 2 - 1 (1)
	Negation: -1 (-1)
*	Multiplication: 2 * 2 (4)
/	Division: 4 / 2 (2)
%	Percent: 20% (.2)
^	Exponentiation: 2^3 (8)

Saving Time and Effort by Using Functions

A *function* is a predefined formula that performs a calculation on specific values that must appear in a certain order or format. As such, functions can save you a great deal of time and effort over entering each value followed by the appropriate operator. For example, adding the values in cells A1 through A5 with a function would look like this: =SUM(A1:A5). Using the standard arithmetic operator, you have the following: =A1+A2+A3+A4+A5. Obviously, the more cells involved, the more effort you save.

In addition to performing mathematical operations, a function can also do some basic conversions. For instance, the function Roman(1999) returns the string value "MCMXCIX". Other functions such as Int(3.1) return the value 3. The input values are known as *arguments*, and the value the function returns is known as the *return value*.

Usually, you enter a function directly into a cell by typing a formula. Thus, if you enter "=Max(1,2,3)" into a cell, Excel processes the function and displays the result 3.

Perhaps the easiest way to enter a function is to use the Paste Function feature. Clicking the Paste Function button displays a dialog box (see Figure 13.7) in which you can choose a function from Excel's rich collection. Functions are listed by categories such as Financial, Date and Time, and Math and Trig. As you scroll through the functions, you'll see a brief description of what the function does and its parameters.

FIGURE 13.7

The Paste Function Wizard helps you add any function available in Excel to your formula.

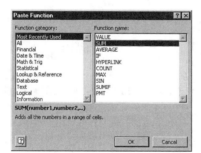

After you choose a function, click OK to see the dialog box shown in Figure 13.8. Each of the parameters for the function is listed next to a text box where you can enter a value, a cell reference, or an expression. After you have entered all the required parameters, the value of the formula is displayed. This value can help you verify that you're using the formula properly.

FIGURE 13.8
*After you choose
a function, the
Paste Function
Wizard prompts
you for the
parameters.*

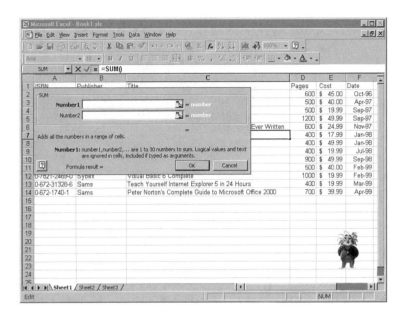

Discovering Functions That Increase Productivity

Because Excel includes functions too numerous to mention, let alone elaborate on, I'm going to present the ones I've found most useful over time. I'm not saying that the rest of the functions aren't useful. However, they are somewhat specialized and are probably of more value to statisticians, engineers, and financial specialists than to the average Excel user.

Calculating Loans and Depreciation Using the Financial Functions

Probably the most common use of spreadsheets is to analyze financial information. Excel has a rich set of functions that perform every normal financial function and many specialized functions as well (see Table 13.3). For example, you can use the Pmt function to compute the monthly payment based on interest rate per period, the number of periods, the present value of the loan, the future value of the loan, and whether the loan is paid back at the beginning or end of the period.

Assume you want to buy a Porsche. After your down payment, you still owe $50,000, which you want to finance. The dealer has offered you 8 percent annual interest on a 60-month loan. Thanks to Excel's financial functions, you quickly use the formula =Pmt(8%/12, 60, 50000, 0) to find out that the car of your dreams will cost you only $1,013.82 per month for the next five years!

In addition to standard loan functions, accountants and other business professionals may find use in some of the more unique depreciation functions shown in Table 13.3.

Table 13.3   Common Financial Functions

Function Name	Description
DB	Returns the fixed-declining balance depreciation of an asset
DDB	Returns the double-declining balance depreciation of an asset
FV	Returns the future value of an asset based on a series of equal periodic payments and a constant interest rate
NPV	Computes the net present value of investment based on a discount rate and a series of payments (negative values) and income (positive values)
Pmt	Returns the payment for a loan based on a series of equal periodic payments and a constant interest rate
PV	Returns the present value of an asset based on a series of equal periodic payments and a constant interest rate
Rate	Returns the interest rate for a period on a loan or annuity
SLN	Returns the straight-line depreciation of an asset

Producing Statistics Like the Pros

Even though the word *statistics* may scare some people, it shouldn't. Many statistical functions in Excel, such as Sum and Count, make this group of functions the most frequently used group of functions in Excel. Table 13.4 lists some of the most common functions.

One of the most commonly used statistical functions in Excel is the Sum function. In fact, it's so commonly used that it has its own icon on the toolbar. As its name implies, this function totals a range of values on your worksheet. My favorite use of this function is when I have to add up a series of numbers; it might be a list of my monthly bills or even a list of Christmas gifts I plan to order from a catalog. More than likely, you have such a list already saved in an Excel sheet. Use the Sum function to get a total. Then you can verify the value's accuracy by merely checking to see whether you entered the numbers properly. No more rekeying reams of data into a calculator to double-check your work!

Table 13.4   Common Statistical Functions

Function Name	Description
Average	Computes the average of the numeric cells in the range
Count	Returns the number of the numeric cells in the range
CountA	Returns the number of nonempty cells in the range
Max	Returns the largest value in the range
Min	Returns the smallest value in the range
Sum	Computes the sum of the values in the range
StdDev	Computes the standard deviation of the values in the range
Var	Computes the variance of the values in the range

Putting the Comparison Function to Work for You

Comparison functions either return values of True or False, or evaluate a logical value to determine which of two other values should be returned.

The If function, for example, is far more useful than it may appear at first glance. Consider a worksheet that you would use to prepare a contracting estimate. If the customer spends over $2,000, he or she would receive a special 10 percent discount. Assume that the subtotal for the estimate is stored in cell D18. Then the formula If(D18<2000,0,20%) could be used to compute the proper discount automatically.

Other comparison functions you might want to explore can be found in Table 13.5.

Table 13.5   Common Logical Functions

Function Name	Description
And	Returns True if all if the specified values are true.
If	Returns the second value if the first value is true; otherwise, the third value is returned.
Not	Returns True if the specified value is false and returns False if the value is true.
Or	Returns True if at least one parameter is true.

Preparing Yourself for the Year 2000 Using the Date and Time Functions

The date and time functions allow you to manipulate date and time values (see Table 13.6). Date values are stored in Excel as a number representing the number of days from 1 January 1900. If you enter a two-digit value for the year in the range of 00 to 29, Excel assumes that you want years in the range 2000 to 2029. Otherwise, Excel assumes you want a year in the range of 1930 to 1999. Time values are stored as a fractional value, where .000 represents midnight, and .500 represents noon. Thus, 6:00 a.m. is .25 and .420 is 10:04:48 a.m.

You can use these functions to perform a number of different date and time calculations. For instance, you can extract the day of the week from a Datetime value by using the Weekday function. Then sort your worksheet to group the rows by the day of the week.

Note: 1900, 1901, 1902, 1903, 1904. Excel 98 for Macintosh stores its dates as the number of days since 1 January 1904. Because this is different than what was used in Excel 97, Microsoft added a setting to Excel 2000 to let you choose between either base year by setting the 1904 Date System on the Calculation tab of the Options dialog box. Choosing this option prevents the wrong date from appearing in Excel 2000 when you're loading a worksheet created on a Macintosh or when you're saving a worksheet that will be read by a Macintosh.

Table 13.6   Common Date and Time Functions

Function Name	Description
Date	Converts year, month, and day parameters into a date value
DateValue	Converts a string containing a formatted date into a date value
Day	Returns the current day of the month from a date value
Hour	Returns the current hour from a time value
Minute	Returns the current minute from a time value
Now	Returns the current date and time
Second	Returns the current second from a time value
Time	Converts the hour, minute, and second parameters into a time value
TimeValue	Converts a string containing a formatted time into a time value
Today	Returns the current date
Weekday	Returns a number in the range of 1 to 7 corresponding to the current day of the week
Year	Returns the current four-digit year from a date and time value

Verifying a Cell Type Before Performing a Calculation

Many times when dealing with values in a worksheet, you need to determine a cell's type before performing a calculation (see Table 13.7). When using these functions combined with the If function described in the comparison functions section, you can make sure that you don't try to do arithmetic with a text string or an empty cell.

Table 13.7   Common Information Functions

Function Name	Description
IsBlank	Returns True if an empty cell was passed to the function
IsError	Returns True if the value passed to the function is an error value (#N/A, #VALUE!, #REF!, #DIV/0!, #NUM!, #NAME?, #NULL)
IsLogical	Returns True if a logical value was passed to the function
IsNumber	Returns True if a number was passed to the function
IsText	Returns True if a text value was passed to the function
Type	Returns 1 if the specified value is a number, 2 for text, 4 for logical, 8 for a formula, 16 for an error value, and 64 for an array

Functions of Interest to Specialists

In addition to the more commonly used functions presented in the preceding sections, Excel offers a host of possibilities for specialists in the fields of mathematics, engineering, and statistics. In fact, the names of some of these functions are so obscure that most normal people wouldn't even recognize them.

If you happen to make your living by working extensively with numbers, you should take the time to browse through the Paste Function lists; you might be amazed at what you'll find there!

On Your Own

When you're using a tool like Excel, simply knowing that a function exists means that it may be worth the time searching for it and giving it a try. After all, who has the luxury of infinite amounts of time to go browsing through menus and dialog boxes in search of nifty functions or tools?

Try creating your own spreadsheet to do the following tasks. Add up a list of numbers; then find the average, min, and max values of the same list. Next, display today's year, month, day, hour, minute, and second values in separate cells using the Now function only once. (**Hint:** Use the If function six times.) Now try computing the house payment for a loan of $100,000 at 6 percent over 30 years.

Finally, build a simple spreadsheet for an order form with room for ordering one item. Include columns for item number, quantity, description, unit price, and total price. Total price is computed as the product of list price and quantity. Then copy the single detail line to create a total of 10 lines in the order form.

After that big workout, you should be ready to venture into the next chapter with ease!

Peter Norton

Charting Your Results

When you're attending a presentation, which has a greater impact on you—a table listing the amount of federal spending in a variety of categories or a colorful pie chart depicting what percentage of the federal budget is allocated to each category? If you're like most people, the chart will grab you almost instantly, whereas the table will leave you skimming the list over and over again to see how each category ranks in comparison to one another.

Displaying information in a tabular form can often be confusing, especially to people who are not as familiar with what the numbers actually mean. For instance, in 1996 the federal government spent $266 billion on defense and $538 billion on Social Security and Medicare. Showing these statistics as part of a pie chart clearly illustrates that together the federal government spends more than twice as much money on Social Security and Medicare as any other single category (see Figure 14.1).

FIGURE 14.1
Charts often convey information more clearly than a set of numbers.

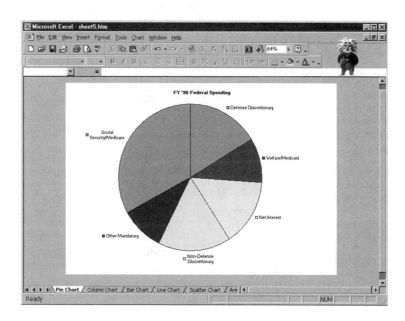

In an age in which time is money, who wouldn't benefit from getting their message across in a more succinct, universally understood manner? I often used charts when writing grant proposals for small nonprofit organizations I worked with because I found the proposal's reviewers appreciated the speed with which they could gather information from them. It was also apparent that the charts left reviewers with a sense of the organization's professionalism, which they in turn translated into an impression that the organization was well run. And that, more often than not, meant a favorable review.

And if that example doesn't speak to you, think back to some of the seminars you've attended. What do you remember about the visual aids? Do you remember tables with numbers, or does a certain chart stand out in your mind? Unless you're a mathematician or an accountant, chances are it's the chart you recall.

In this chapter, I'll introduce you to the concepts you need to know to be able to produce great-looking charts. But even more important than that, you'll learn which type of chart to use when, because the type of chart you choose can have a radical effect on the message you convey. That's right—much like statistics can be massaged to your advantage, so too can charts!

Fundamentals of Charting

To create a chart in Excel, you first must create data values that you want to place on the chart. Usually, these values are arranged into one or more series of values in which each series of data contains a set of related data. Associated with the data values is a series name.

Table 14.1 contains two series of data, FY '95 and FY '96. Each series of data contains a set of data points—such as Defense Discretionary and Social Security and Medicare—that enable you to compare data points within or across a series.

Table 14.1   Federal Government Spending (in Billions of Dollars)

Federal Spending	FY '95	FY '96
Defense Discretionary	$274	$266
Net Interest	$232	$241
Non-Defense Discretionary	$272	$267
Other Mandatory	$179	$162
Social Security/Medicare	$510	$538
Welfare/Medicaid	$133	$159

Figure 14.2 contains a chart based on the data found in Table 14.1. This simple column chart uses the FY '95 and FY '96 data series. I've added a title called Federal Government Spending to the chart and a title on the y-axis to indicate that the spending

levels are in billions of dollars. In addition, I've included a data table at the bottom of the chart to show the details to anyone interested in the exact numbers. Finally, I've included a legend at the right side of the chart, though in this instance the data table duplicates this information.

Chart title

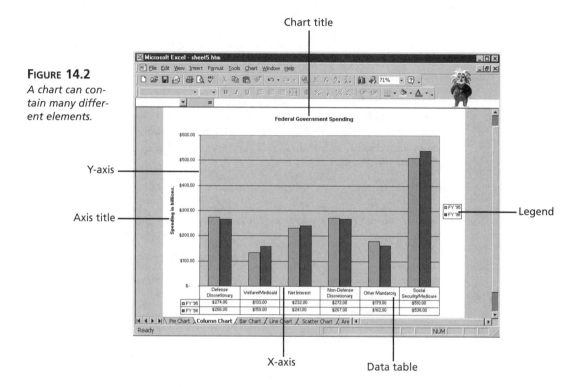

FIGURE 14.2
A chart can contain many different elements.

Y-axis

Axis title

Legend

X-axis

Data table

The *x-axis* is displayed along the bottom of the chart, and the *y-axis* is displayed along the left edge of the chart. The *z-axis*, not shown in Figure 14.2, is used to add depth to the chart. *Legends* tell you how to find the different series of data plotted on the chart. The *chart title* should describe what appears on the chart. An *axis title* can be used to provide additional information about the values. A *data table* can provide additional information about the data that generated the chart.

Choosing a Chart Type

The first thing you need to decide when you begin to create a chart is what type of chart you want to create. You can choose from a large set of standard chart and custom chart types.

The chart type you choose depends on the type of data you want to present and how you want to present it. Not all chart types are appropriate for all types of data. Some are useful for showing how things change over time, whereas others are better for showing how a set of values contributes to the whole. Most of the chart types come in both two- and three-dimensional variations, which gives you additional ways to present your information.

In the sections that follow, I'll introduce you to each type of chart you'll encounter in Excel and will demonstrate how they might best be used.

Line Charts

The most basic chart form is a line chart. A line chart is often used to plot the growth of a single value over time. It might reflect a small nonprofit organization's expanding budget, or it might show the exodus of local children from the public schools to the private schools over a five-year period.

A line chart simply draws a line constructed from each series of data supplied on an XY chart. Each series should share the same data points in order for the chart to be effective. Typically, the data points are a value of time or some other periodic measure. For the chart to be meaningful, each value should be similar in size; otherwise, you cannot see the difference between individual data points.

Column Charts

If you want to compare one item to another, a column chart may do the trick. You can create a column chart that shows the participation of each division of your company in the current United Way campaign, or you could show a funding committee just how many minorities your nonprofit serves each year as a testimony to its recent growth.

Column charts are similar to line charts in that each data point is plotted on an XY chart. However, instead of connecting each data point in a series with a single line, a rectangle is drawn from the x-axis to the data point. With column charts, unlike line charts, you can use nearly anything as a data point. Region, product, and organization are all good data points, for example.

A special type of column chart is known as a *stacked column chart*. In this case, data points from multiple series are displayed in a single column. This type of chart is useful when you want to show how data from multiple series adds up to a single value, like the profit from a series of divisions adds up to make the total corporate profit.

Pie Charts

If you remember early elementary school math, then you probably recall how these friendly pie charts helped you learn the basics of fractions.

Pie charts are popular when you want to break down a value into smaller chunks and compare each chunk to the whole. A pie chart is constructed by creating a single series of data with up to seven data points. Although Excel can handle more data points, too many slices will make your pie chart difficult to read because each slice will be too small to be significant.

You also might want to display the percent of the pie associated with each slice to emphasize how large (or small) each slice of the pie is relative to the whole.

> **Tip: Make the most of it!** Fine-tuning the craft of charting takes some time. The process involves much more than simply knowing what kind of chart to use when; you have to be shrewd enough to know how to make your numbers appear in the most favorable light possible. Consider the following data as an example. In 1997, your dance company gave only one performance in a public school, but in 1998 the number was two, and you have four slated for this year. A simple column chart can communicate the steady increase in performances, but a pie chart considering the three-year period as a whole with half of it allocated to 1999 performances makes a far more dramatic statement of how the number increased. Take some time to play with your data using a variety of chart types. You might be surprised at what you discover!

Scatter Charts

Scatter charts are also similar to line charts, except that they tend to be used to chart clusters of data. One or more series of y values are plotted against a set of x values. For example, you could plot predicted sales figures in one color and actual sales in another so that you can see how the two compare to one another.

In a scatter chart, unlike a line chart, however, the set of x values does not represent a distinct set of points, but rather a continuous range of values. This type of chart will be most useful when you're charting measurements when analyzing scientific data.

> **Tip: Thinking unconventionally.** Instead of thinking in terms of values over time, you might want to consider plotting value against value. For instance, plotting price versus performance of a car, a stock, or whatever clearly shows what the bargain performer would be.

Bar, Cone, Cylinder, and Pyramid Charts

A bar chart is simply a variation of the column chart where the columns have been moved from the x-axis to the y-axis. Think of this type of chart as a column chart in landscape orientation. It can be useful when you have more horizontal space for the chart than you do vertical space.

Cone, cylinder, and pyramid charts are just variations of the column and bar charts. The only significant difference is their shapes.

Peter's Principle: Keeping your chart simple can pay off.

Using unusually shaped charts may hold some appeal if you're trying to make a stylistic statement, but I tend to shy away from them. Over the years, I've found them to be harder to read and occasionally even distracting to the reader. In professional documents, basic column or pie charts will always rise to the occasion.

Radar Charts

Believe it or not, radar charts are actually a variant of line charts. The only real difference is that the data points are plotted relative to a center point rather than against an axis. This means that a horizontal line on a line chart would look like a perfect circle on a radar chart.

You might want to consider using a radar chart, for example, when you want to examine how a group of products compares in several categories. A well-balanced product will be shown on the chart as a circle. If two products are well balanced, the larger circle indicates the better product. Products that are not well balanced will be displayed as irregular shapes, usually with one or two protruding points that disfigure what could have been a circle. The more unbalanced the product is, the more irregular the shape.

Doughnut Charts

If you need to display two or more pie charts using the same data labels but with different data points, consider using doughnut charts. A simple doughnut chart is identical to a pie chart with the center removed. You can stack multiple doughnuts inside each other by selecting more than one data series. This way, you can easily see the relationship among multiple series of data.

Bubble Charts

Like scatter charts, bubble charts plot data against continuous ranges of x and y values. With bubble charts, unlike scatter charts, you can include another piece of information for each point you plot. This value controls the size of the bubble drawn at each point. The larger this value, the larger the bubble is drawn.

You might want to use this type of chart when you want to indicate the accuracy of the value. The smaller the bubble, the more accurate the value plotted. Likewise, a larger bubble shows that the correct value for that point might be located anywhere in the bubble.

Another possible use would be to add a third piece of information to two pieces of information normally shown in a scatter chart. For instance, you might want to chart the price and performance of some new computer systems and change the bubble size to reflect the reliability.

Stock Charts

Stock charts present multiple data elements in a single graphical element. At a minimum, the stock's high value, low value, and closing value are displayed. You can also display opening value and volume in the same graphical element. To do so, you must format your raw data properly. For high-low-close charts, the first series must correspond to the stock's high price, the next series must correspond to the low price, and the last series must correspond to the closing price.

Building Complex Charts Quickly Using the Chart Wizard

The easiest way to create a chart is to use the Chart Wizard. This four-step process asks for the basic information needed to create a chart. However, before you begin creating your chart, you need some sample data that can be used to create the chart.

Follow these steps to begin getting acquainted with the Chart Wizard:

1. Create (or open) a worksheet that contains the data you want to chart. Then select the cells you want to use as input to the Chart Wizard.

2. Start the Chart Wizard by clicking Insert|Chart, or simply click the Chart Wizard button on the toolbar.

3. On the Standard Types tab, choose the chart type you want to create based on the preceding discussion. Figure 14.3 shows you how the wizard will ask you to make the selection. Click Next to move to the next step.

Tip: Know what you're getting ahead of time. Picking the right chart type can be challenging enough as it is, so why not save yourself an extra step or two by previewing the chart type you selected before proceeding to the next step in the wizard? Do so by clicking and holding down the Press and Hold to View Sample button. When you release the button, the tab returns to its normal state.

FIGURE 14.3

You can choose from many differ-ent types of charts in Excel.

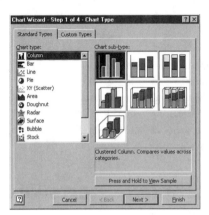

4. The wizard then prompts you to select the data you want to chart on the Data Range tab, which opens by default. If you selected some cells before you started the Chart Wizard, a sample chart will be displayed, as shown in Figure 14.4. Skip ahead to the next step in the wizard by pressing Next. Otherwise, you can click in the Data Range text box and then enter the cell range of the data you want to chart.

You can also click the button at the end of the Data Range text box. Clicking this button hides the wizard and shows the Data Range dialog box, as you can see in Figure 14.5. Then you can select the range of cells you want to chart. This infor-mation will be displayed in the dialog box. Pressing Enter or clicking the button at the end of the Data Range text box returns you to the Chart Wizard dialog box where you left off.

In addition to choosing the cells, you need to let the wizard know whether the data series are arranged in rows or columns. In many cases, your data may be organized either way. I usually try to choose the way that results in the fewest series.

FIGURE **14.4**

After you select the cells for your chart, a sample chart is displayed.

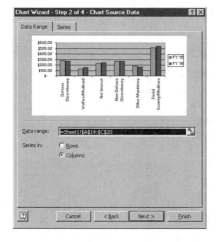

FIGURE **14.5**

Select cells the easy way with the Chart Wizard dialog box.

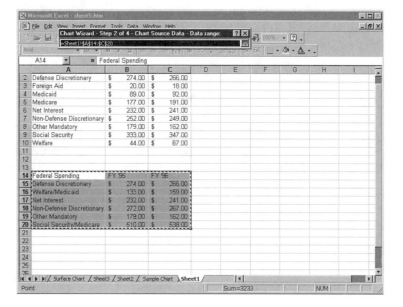

5. You can also add the data you want to chart one series at a time by clicking the Series tab and then selecting the cells using the same technique I just discussed (see Figure 14.6). This method also allows you to change the data you selected or remove a series from the chart altogether.

FIGURE 14.6
*You can also add
a single series to
your chart.*

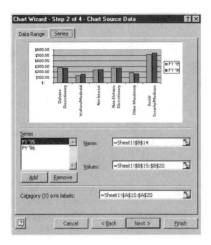

6. After you've selected the data, you can set the chart's options. You can skip to step 13 by clicking Next if you are willing to live with the default values, but taking a minute or two to set the options will leave you less cleanup work to do after the wizard is done. You can also choose the same dialog box after you create the chart by right-clicking the chart and selecting Chart Options or clicking Chart|Chart Options from the main menu.

> **Caution: I can't find it.** Excel displays only the information you can change for a particular type of chart. Not all chart types support all the tabs, and sometimes information on a tab may be grayed out so that you can't change those values. For example, because a pie chart has no axes, you don't see the Axes or Gridlines tabs on the Chart Options dialog box.

7. On the Titles tab, you can add a title to the chart by simply typing the text into the Chart Title text box (see Figure 14.7). Likewise, you can also enter text that will be displayed along the x- and y-axes, assuming that the chart type you selected can display these values, of course.

8. On the Axes tab, you can choose to display either the x-, y-, or z-axis. The actual axes displayed depend on the chart type. You can also let Excel decide whether the axis contains the category names or time-scale values.

FIGURE 14.7

Fill in the titles you want added to your chart.

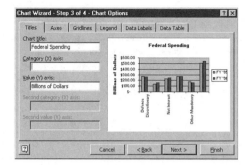

> **Note: The XYZs of charting.** Normally, the x-axis is displayed along the bottom of a 2D chart; however, on a bar chart, the x- and y-axes are reversed, so the x-axis appears on the left side of the chart. On a 3D chart, the z-axis, not the y-axis, holds the value information.

9. On the Gridlines tab, Excel gives you the option to display major and minor gridlines on each axis. Gridlines are useful when you want to make it easier for someone to trace a value back to one of the axes. You can choose to display major or minor gridlines for each axis as well. You can easily use too many gridlines, however, so providing a gridline that clearly marks the various values on the chart is all that you really need. Any more than that and you could start to compromise the legibility of the chart.

10. Using the Legend tab, you can place a legend nearly anywhere on your chart. After you have displayed the legend, you can also drag it around on your chart and resize it. Dragging makes it easy for you to position the legend so that you can put it in the best spot. And be sure not to make it too small; your readers may be counting on this information to understand what exactly the chart is trying to tell them.

11. On the Data Labels tab, you can choose to display some information about each data point, near where the data point is displayed. Depending on the chart type you selected, you can display the data point's value, the percent of the total, the label, or the size of the bubble. You can also include the legend key next to the data point to make reading the chart easier for your audience. This feature is useful when you're creating pie charts with small slices where multiple labels are close together.

Tip: This chart is too small to see. Often, when you're viewing charts in the pre-view area of the wizard, the chart appears to be distorted. Don't worry about this distortion. It occurs because the character fonts are shown larger than what would be used in the final chart. If the text is still too large when the wizard finishes building the chart, you can either remove it or make the font size sm aller.

12. On the Data Table tab, you choose whether to show a data table and also whether to show legend keys. A data table shows the raw information used to create the chart. Although this tool is not available for all chart types, it is useful for elimi-nating the need for a separate table containing the data in a presentation. (The worksheet containing the data is obviously still needed to create the chart, however.)

13. In the final step of the Chart Wizard, you're asked where you want to place the chart (see Figure 14.8). You can include the chart as an object on any of the exist-ing sheets in your workbook, or you can create a separate sheet containing only the chart. The separate sheet is inserted before the sheet you extracted the data from.

FIGURE 14.8
Put your chart into your work-book.

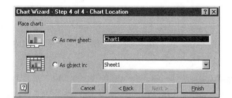

Tip: Store your chart on its own. Where you put your chart depends mostly on how you plan to use it. In situations in which you're going to include the chart as part of a Word document or in a PowerPoint presentation, where you store it really doesn't matter. I generally prefer to store it on its own sheet. Placing it there makes the chart easy to find and to edit. This way, I also can easily flip through a series of charts to choose the one I want to copy.

Tweaking the Chart for Best Results

Earlier in the book, I discussed the importance of an object's size in relation to the infor-mation around it. The same holds true for charts. If the chart will take up a solo position on a PowerPoint slide, bigger may be better (at least from the visibility standpoint). But if the chart is to be used as part of a Word document's narrative, then judicious sizing may be everything.

After creating a chart with the Chart Wizard, you might decide it doesn't quite meet your needs. Maybe the title is too small, or the labels along the y-axis aren't formatted properly. Or perhaps it's too large to fit in with the Word document you planned to import it into. You can easily change these factors by using the proper dialog boxes. Simply right-click one of the chart objects in the following list, and then select the Format from the shortcut menu for that object.

- Axis borders the plot area and provides a scale for the values drawn in the chart.
- Chart Area refers to the entire chart.
- Chart Title is a text field that is displayed at the top of the chart.
- Data Labels is a text field that displays the value associated with a data marker.
- Data Marker can be a bar, column, point, slice, bubble, or other graphical object corresponding to a single data value.
- Data Series is the collection of data markers corresponding to a set of data.
- Data Table contains the data used to create the chart.
- Error Bars are used to indicate the potential degree of error for a series.
- Floor is the bottom part of the plot area in a 3D chart.
- Gridlines are lines drawn on the chart to make it easier to match a data marker with information displayed along the axes.
- Legend is a box that associates the name of a data series with its graphical representation.
- Plot Area is the area in the chart containing the data series and bounded by the axes.
- Trendlines are lines that are derived from a data series that attempt to project where the data series is headed.
- Wall is a vertical part of the plot area in a 3D chart.

Although each of these objects is different, most of the formatting options are the same. You can use the familiar font, number, and alignment dialog boxes to make changes in how your text information is displayed. However, a number of dialog boxes you might not be familiar with can make a big difference in your chart.

You can choose the color or set the pattern used to display many of the objects. These dialog boxes come in two flavors: line oriented and area oriented. You can change the scale used on each axis, which may be helpful when you don't like the scale chosen by Excel.

> **Tip: Tipping the scales to your advantage.** Adjusting the scale up or down can do a lot to amplify your findings. If the scale is small and the values are close in size, the smaller scale will more effectively help the reader detect subtle differences. If, on the other hand, you want your data to appear more even than it may actually be, nudging the scale up will give the chart a more level appearance. The way data is presented can have intangible effects all of their own.

Most of the options are associated with a data series. For example, you can choose the shape of the columns or bars in a bar chart. This way, you can turn an ordinary column chart into a pyramid chart. You can also change the order of the series and tweak how the data series is presented on the chart. Also, on 3D charts, you can adjust your viewing angle. You can even add error bars on some charts, showing the degree of confidence you have in the value.

Making Chart Lines More Visible

When it comes to charts (or anything for that matter), one size does not fit all. Because line charts, scatter charts, and radar charts make extensive use of lines, they can be harder for readers to see if they're used as a slide or scaled down to fit multiple pages on a sheet of paper. Luckily, Microsoft thought of this potential dilemma and offered a solution.

Clicking Format|Data Series from the main menu or double-clicking the data series on the chart displays the Format Data Series dialog box, as shown in Figure 15.9. The Patterns tab (available on line charts, scatter charts, and radar charts) controls how the data series will be drawn. Typically, both the line and marker are set to automatic. However, sometimes you might want different values. For instance, you can make the line weight heavier so that it will show up better on a projection screen. You may also want to choose a color to correspond to each source of data so that a viewer can instantly see which line belongs where.

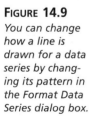

Figure 14.9

You can change how a line is drawn for a data series by changing its pattern in the Format Data Series dialog box.

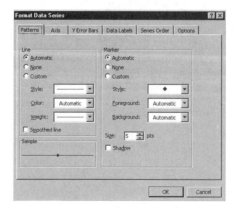

In addition to choosing the color, style, and weight of the line, you can also smooth the line. This capability can be very useful when you're plotting data from a series of points in a scatter chart.

And did you know that you can select the marker you want to display on each data point in the series? For the marker, like the lines, you can choose from a set of standard styles such as diamonds, squares, and triangles. You can even choose one color for the foreground (outside edge) of the marker or the background (interior) of the marker. Even the size of the marker can be controlled and displayed with a shadow for a 3D effect.

You can also change how a single data point in the series is displayed. Clicking the data point selects the entire series, and the cursor changes into a up/down arrow. Then double-clicking the same data point displays the Format Data Point dialog box. You can change the pattern used to display the point, change the data labels that are associated with the point, and set various other options.

Adding Color to Your Charts

When you're attending a slide presentation in an auditorium full of people, being able to see where one slice of a pie chart begins and the other ends may be impossible. Color variance can be the answer presenters and audience members alike have been waiting for.

Using a host of options tucked away in Excel, you can change how areas such as the plot area and pie slices are displayed by using techniques similar to those found when you're using line patterns (see Figure 14.10). Simply double-click the pie slice, or choose Format|Data Series from the main menu. Although you can choose both the color of the area and how the border will be displayed around the area, the most powerful tool is setting how the area is filled.

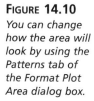

FIGURE 14.10

You can change how the area will look by using the Patterns tab of the Format Plot Area dialog box.

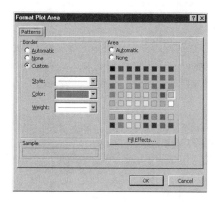

> **Tip: Back and Foreground.** When you're designing your chart, you must keep in mind how your chart will be used. In general, it's better to use light and soft colors in the background, and bright or dark colors in the foreground. Using colors this way makes your chart much easier to read because it emphasizes the lines and columns on the chart rather than the stuff behind them. Of course, if the chart's primary purpose is to be printed in black and white, you can focus your attention on pattern fills as opposed to color.

Achieving a Dramatic Effect

We've all seen the fancy PowerPoint slides in which one rich color flows gently into another, creating an effect that exudes professionalism. Well, you can add more than basic colors and patterns to your charts, too.

Of course, gradient fills work only on chart elements such as a bar in a bar chart, a slice of a pie, or the plot area that has a 2D or 3D representation. To add a gradient fill, double-click the desired chart element, and select the Patterns tab. Then click the Fill Effects button to display the Fill Effects dialog box shown in Figure 14.11. On the Gradient tab, you can choose to create an effect in which one color is changed into another color. You can choose from three basic options: One Color, Two Colors, and Preset.

Figure 14.11
You can specify a gradient fill for the area.

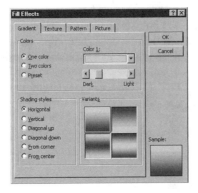

By using One Color, you can gradually change your chosen color into another color that is either lighter or darker than itself. You can choose how light or dark the second color is by moving a slide bar from light to dark. Moving the slider to either end results in the second color being either white or black.

In Two Color mode, you can explicitly choose the two colors used. In Preset mode, you can choose from a set of already-defined gradients. Here, you will find bold rainbow effects, stunning sunrise color schemes, and the like. In many cases, you can't duplicate the preset pattern because more than two colors are used.

> **Tip: A color for every mood.** Although this advice may sound corny on the sur-
> face, don't underestimate the power of suggestion. Everyone knows that colors
> such as red, orange, and yellow project a warm image, whereas blues and
> greens project a cooler image. The same goes for textures, which I'll introduce
> in the next section. A wood grain background would be great for presenting
> construction statistics, and water would be clever for surfing vacation destina-
> tion numbers. By using the right colors and textures in the background, you can
> communicate a whole mood along with the data itself.

After you have chosen the desired gradient colors, you need to choose which style you
want to use. The styles determine how the color change will be made. You can choose
from a variety of styles, each of which results in a different effect. Choose the one that
best fits your chart without making it look too cluttered.

Texture Fill: More Than Just Color

Imagine a fancy marble texture for a classy company chart or a denim effect for a blue
jeans manufacturer. Whether your chart is destined for the Web or a live presentation,
texture fills can add depth and character.

Peter's Principle: Taste versus tact.

If you apply texture tastefully to your chart, the reader can be left with a very
favorable impression. Adding texture somehow communicates to the reader
that you cared enough to go the extra mile in making a nice presentation. But
again, the line between class and clutter can be a blurry one, so you might
want to seek a second opinion or two before committing yourself to a texture.

When you select the Texture tab on the Fill Effects dialog box, you can choose from an
assortment of predefined textures. Simply click the texture you want to use, and then
click OK to return to the Format Data Series dialog box.

FIGURE 14.12

*You can choose a
predefined tex-
ture to fill the
area.*

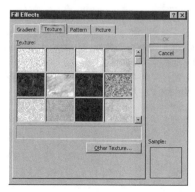

Combining Color and Patterns to Achieve a Unique Effect

If you want to design a series of charts in your school colors or simply just have a preferred color scheme for your company, you can use the Pattern tab of the Fill Effects dialog box to combine them in dozens of ways, ranging from polka dots to stripes in any conceivable direction to zigzags. Remember, to get to the Fill Effects dialog box, double-click the chart element you want to change to open the Format dialog box. Then select the Patterns tab, and click the Fill Effects button. Just like gradient fills, pattern fills require 2D or 3D chart elements. They do not work on lines.

Using the Pattern tab, shown in Figure 14.13, you can specify two colors and a pattern that will be used to fill the area you selected. I usually choose my colors in the drop-down boxes at the bottom of the tab first, and then I pick a pattern. That way, I can tell which patterns work best because all the pattern swatches change to reflect the colors chosen.

FIGURE 14.13

You can choose a two-color pattern to fill an area on your chart.

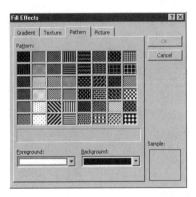

Picture Fill: For an Extra Personalized Effect

One of the most powerful features in Excel charts is the capability to use a graphic image to fill an area (see Figure 14.14). You can stretch a picture so that one picture fills the entire area, or you can stack as many pictures as you want to fill the area. Just double-click the chart element you want to change to open its Format dialog box. Then select the Patterns tab, and click the Fill Effects button to display the Fill Effects dialog box. You can choose the picture you want to use on the Picture tab.

> **Note: It's a matter of size.** If you choose to stack pictures, the last picture may not be complete, depending on the data value. You can also specify a scale factor so that each picture represents a certain number of units on the value axis.

FIGURE 14.14
You can specify an image that will be displayed in the area.

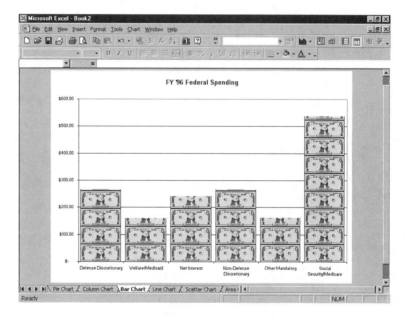

Imagine the possibilities! Your corporate logo or maybe even your star product could be an integral part of your charts. You can also use picture fill on a 3D chart using standard columns or bars. It, however, does not work with 3D shapes such as pyramids or cylinders. You have the option to apply the pictures to all sides of the chart or just the sides you select. When you're choosing pictures, just be careful that they add value to your chart rather than make it more difficult to read.

> **Tip: You're surrounded!** If you don't display the picture on all sides, then the color that was displayed on the chart object before using picture fill will continue to be used. To change this color, simply use the Pattern tab of the regular Format dialog box. Then use the Picture Fill dialog box to reselect the picture.

> **Tip: A picture is worth a billion dollars.** Although you can use picture fill to create interesting background images, you can also use it to fill in the bars in a bar chart. By selecting the Format option Stack and Scale To and specifying the Units/Picture on the Picture tab, you can use graphics such as dollar bills to represent money, cars to represent auto production, and insects to represent software bugs.

Livening Up Charts with 3D Shapes

Tired of the same old columns and bars? If you want something a little out of the ordinary, you might want to explore your options when it comes to changing the shape of your chart elements. Of course, to choose a new 3D shape, you need to have a 3D chart. (See the section titled "Choosing a Chart Type" for more information about the various 3D charts available.)

Choosing a new shape in a 3D column or bar chart involves nothing more than clicking Format|Selected Data Series and choosing the Shape tab (see Figure 14.15).

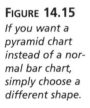

Figure 14.15

If you want a pyramid chart instead of a normal bar chart, simply choose a different shape.

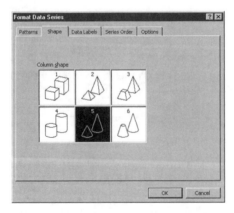

Putting Data Series in Order

Excel allows you to change the order of the series being displayed in a chart. You might do so because the data is displayed in the wrong order or some data is hidden in a 3D chart. (In 3D charts, some data values might be hidden by other values that are in front of them, so you might want to make sure that the smallest values are displayed first.) In any event, using the Series Order tab in the Format Data Series dialog box is easier than returning to the worksheet where the chart's data is kept. Click Format|Selected Data Series and choose the Series Order tab.

To change the order of the data series, simply click the series you want to move, and then click the Move Up or Move Down buttons to adjust its relative location (see Figure 14.16). As you make the changes, you can see the immediate effect on the chart by looking at the chart preview.

FIGURE 14.16
You can change the order series are displayed in your chart without returning to the worksheet with the data that is being charted.

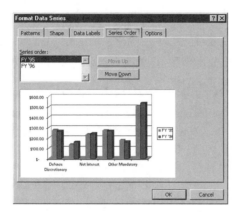

Setting Data Series Options

Just when you thought you had seen all the flexibility and versatility Excel has to offer, there's even more! Using bar and column charts, you can configure how the bars and columns are displayed. On the Options tab of the Format Data Series dialog box (see Figure 14.17), you can adjust the gap between the bars. On 3D charts, you can also adjust the chart's depth; on 2D charts, you can adjust how much the bars overlap.

FIGURE 14.17
You can adjust how the data series appear on the chart.

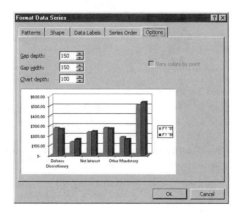

> **Tip: A great space saver, bar none!** If you're trying to cram a lot of data onto a chart and it doesn't quite fit on the page, you can take two steps to rectify the situation without modifying the data. You can adjust the size of the chart object itself by clicking its border and dragging it in, or you can remove the gap between bars on a chart (where applicable, of course).

Other chart types have their own set of options that can be set. For example, with pie charts, you can specify where the first pie slice starts; this capability is useful when you want to rotate the pie to show the most important slice first. With doughnut charts, you can specify the size of the hole in the center. Setting the size of the hole helps to size the chart so that it can be used to hold multiple types of data in a single chart.

Changing the Viewpoint in a 3D Chart

For years, psychologists have tried to get people to change their perspectives on life. Although Excel may not be able to change the way you look at your life, it does give you options when you're looking at your data.

By right-clicking a 3D chart, you can choose the 3-D View from the pop-up menu (see Figure 14.18) when you click the walls or floor of a chart. This feature doesn't work when you click a data series. Choosing the view allows you to position the viewers so that they can best see the chart. You can rotate the viewers around the chart (also known as *rotation*), you can raise and lower them as long as the distance to the object remains constant (also known as *elevation*), and you can also adjust how close the viewers are to the chart (*perspective*).

FIGURE 14.18

You can adjust the point of view of the chart in three dimensions.

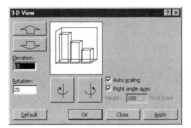

> **Caution: What's your perspective on this chart?** I've found that I can easily distort a chart while playing with the 3D view. Although you often can improve the presentation of the data, you can just as often mess it up. When this happens, simply click the Default button to return to the standard values and begin tweaking your viewpoint again.

Scaling the Chart

You can easily tweak the scales on your chart to reflect the values you want it to show. You do so by right-clicking an axis and choosing Format Axis. Then you can select the Scale tab of the Format Axis dialog box (see Figure 14.19) to change the minimum and maximum values displayed on the axis, and the places where the major and minor ticks will be displayed.

Figure 14.19

You can adjust the point of view of the chart in three dimensions.

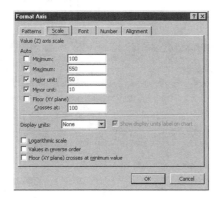

By checking the Logarithmic Scale box, you can create a log chart that compresses large values together at the top of the chart. This type of chart is often useful in the sciences, and you might want to use it if you're analyzing data on a scatter chart.

> **Tip: Don't waste the space.** By default, Excel always starts your chart at zero. However, sometimes this setting results in a chart in which none of the values occupy the bottom half of the chart (such as a chart of the Dow Jones Industrial Average), which can make it hard to see differences in the data values. To make better use of the space in your chart, adjust the chart so that the smallest data value is near the bottom and the largest data value is near the top.

Accentuating Data by Drawing on the Chart

Pivotal data can easily blend in with a chart, especially if the reader's not sure what to look for. It's often desirable to add comments or other information to your chart that doesn't come directly from the data. This might take the form of comments about a particular data value or a highlight on a particular range of values (see Figure 14.20). You draw on the chart by using some of the shared Office applets discussed in Chapter 5, "Shared Applets and Tools Available in Office 2000."

- Using AutoShapes, you can draw a large number of shapes quickly and easily. You might use this tool to draw arrows to point to various parts of your chart or even create a callout.

- Using the Clip Gallery, you can insert clip art images into your chart. Adding company logos or other artwork might add value to your chart.

- Using WordArt, you can take ordinary text strings and transform them into graphical text. This capability is useful when you want to add more interesting chart titles.

FIGURE 14.20
You can add comments to your charts using the AutoShapes.

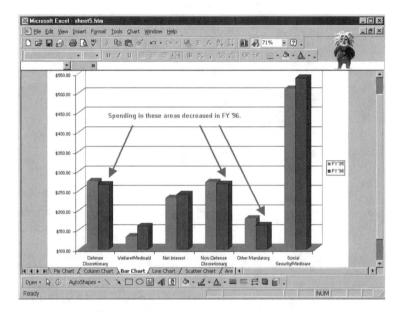

Mapping Your Data Geographically

The last charting feature I want to talk about is called Microsoft Map. This feature allows you to take a worksheet filled with values that are associated with geographic areas and chart them. Thus, you can easily create a chart that shows the total sales for each state in the U.S., or the relative population level of each country in the world.

Tip: Check out MapPoint 2000. Although Microsoft Map is a part of Excel 2000, it is essentially unchanged since Excel 97. However, with Office 2000, Microsoft has released a new, more capable standalone product called MapPoint 2000. If you are serious about charting your data with maps and demographic information, you should check out this product.

> **Tip: Microsoft map is not installed.** By default, Microsoft Map is not installed on your system. If it doesn't work, you have to use the setup program to install it.

Creating Your Map Data

As you do with all the other charting techniques discussed in this book, you need to create your data before you create your chart. In this case, you need to organize your data into a series of columns. The first column should contain the name of the geographic locations, and the remaining columns should contain the data values associated with the geographic location. You also need to include column headers at the top of each column. This information will be used to determine which data is included in the chart. Figure 14.21 shows a sample worksheet containing some geographic data.

FIGURE 14.21
Geographic data can include text and numeric values.

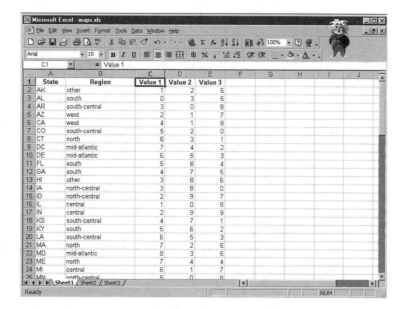

> **Tip: Demographically speaking...**Microsoft Map includes a workbook located in \Program Files\Common Files\Microsoft Shared\Datamap\mapstats.xls that contains demographic data for the United States and the other countries of the world. You might find it useful to compare this information to your own data.

Creating Your Map

After you enter your data, follow these steps to create your customized map:

1. Select the data you want to include in your map.

2. Click the Map icon on the toolbar, or click Insert|Object and then choose Microsoft Map from the Object dialog box.

3. Mark the area on the worksheet where you want the map to appear by clicking the top-left corner and dragging the cursor to the opposite corner while holding down the left mouse button.

4. Microsoft Map then automatically draws the map. If it can't determine which map you want to use based on your data values, it prompts you to choose a map. Simply select the map you want to use (see Figure 14.22).

FIGURE 14.22
Choose the map you want to use.

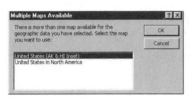

5. A map is then created using your data. Don't worry if the map doesn't show your data exactly as you expected it to. You can always change how the map looks later.

Adjusting Your Map

After you've created your map, you can change how the data is plotted. Double-clicking the map places you into the Edit Map mode (or you can right-click the map and choose Edit Map from the shortcut menu if you prefer).

When you are in the Edit Map mode, you can use the Microsoft Map Control to change how the information is plotted on your map (see Figure 14.23). If the control isn't visible, click the Show/Hide Microsoft Map Control icon on the Map toolbar.

Notice that the columns you have created are displayed in the column heading area. To plot something on the map, simply drag a format and a column heading into the plotting box. Your map is then updated with your changes. To remove something from the map, simply drag the format off the plotting box.

Grouping Similar Values Using Value Shading

Value Shading places your data into different groups based on the value for a location. Each value is mapped into a particular range. By default, value shading is organized so that an equal number of items appears in each range. However, by clicking Map|Value Shading Options, you can open the Format Properties dialog box. Using this dialog box, you can define ranges that are an equal spread of values. In the same dialog box, you can also choose the number of ranges and the color used to display the information.

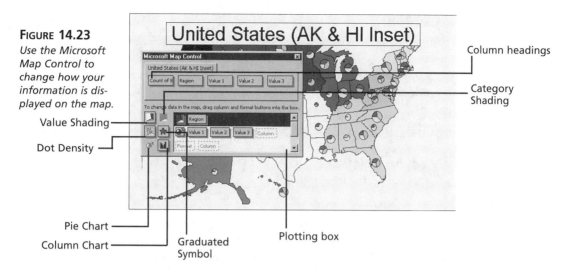

FIGURE 14.23
Use the Microsoft Map Control to change how your information is displayed on the map.

Column headings

Category Shading

Value Shading

Dot Density

Pie Chart

Column Chart

Graduated Symbol

Plotting box

Defining a Relationship Using Category Shading

Category Shading displays the same color for all the geographic locations with the same value. This capability is especially useful for charting sales force data because sales personnel often have territories that encompass more than one state, for example. Unlike the rest of the formats, category shading can work with non-numeric data.

> **Tip: Color coding the country.** You might want to group states into larger territories within the United States. Simply include a column in your data where each state has a value that indicates a particular territory like Midwest, Mid-Atlantic, and so on. Then, using category shading, you can identify the various territories on the map.

To change the colors associated with each category, click Map|Category Shading Options to display the dialog box. Each of the categories is listed. Simply select the category along with its new color. Click OK when you're finished to accept the new colors.

Charting the Density with Dots

Dot Density draws a set of dots in each area based on the value associated with each location. By clicking Map|Dot Density Options, you can change the size of each dot and the number of dots per unit of value.

Graduated Symbol

Graduated Symbol shows in each location a single symbol whose size changes as the relative value changes. By clicking Map|Graduated Symbol Options, you can choose the font (including color) whose value will be displayed at each location.

Pie Chart

The pie chart option draws a pie chart in each location based on your data. Each column of data is represented on your map as a pie slice. However, if the corresponding cell in the worksheet is blank, the slice is omitted. If all the cells are blank for a location, the pie chart is not drawn.

> **Tip: Categorically speaking...**You can combine category shading with pie charts to show the territories with their data. Simply include data for only one location within the territory, and then use pie chart formatting options to make the pie larger. This way, you see only one pie chart per territory.

Clicking Map|Pie Chart Options opens the Format Properties dialog box. In this dialog box, you can choose the color used for each pie slice. You can also choose the size of the pie chart. By default, the size of each pie is based on the total of each of the slices. However, if you uncheck the Graduated Sizing Method, all pies are displayed at the same size.

Column Chart

Column Chart draws a column chart in each location based on your data. You can drag as many columns with numeric values beside the column chart icon as you want. Each column you drag represents one column in the column chart. If the corresponding cell is empty on the worksheet, the column is omitted from the chart.

Choosing Map|Column Chart Options opens the Format Properties dialog box. Like pie charts, column charts vary in size based on the sum of the column values. You can easily change this size by choosing Independent Scale for Sizing Method. You can also specify the size of the column chart and the colors used for each column.

Defining Your Map Using a Legend

Each format you can display on the map has its own legend. You can choose the title and subtitle for each legend and edit the legend entries by using the Legend Options dialog box associated with each of the format options. You can also display a compact legend and select an option to display numeric values as currency values. If you don't want to display a legend, simply uncheck the Show Legend box on the Format Properties dialog box, or select the legend on the map and press the Delete key.

Adding Features to Your Map

Double-clicking a map displays the Map Features dialog box. This dialog box allows you to include other maps (such as adding Canada's map to the United States map) or add other useful information such as major cities, major highways, and airports to your map.

Getting Down to the Details with Pin Maps

A pin map can be wonderfully fascinating to look at. Corporate executives can see at a glance how many people in how many locations purchased their product by simply looking at the density of pins on the map. It's also a wonderful tool to help marketing professionals discover where their efforts are working as well as where more work might be needed.

With Excel, you can place custom markers on your map. Each marker consists of a character and a label at a specific location on your map. This information is stored in a separate file called a Custom Pin Map file.

> **Tip: Locating Offices.** Consider using Custom Pin Maps to show the location of various key places related to your organization, such as your organization's headquarters, the location of various field offices, franchises, and so on.

To create a pin map, you need to follow these steps:

1. Click Map|Open Custom Pin Map.

2. To create a new custom pin map file, enter the filename in the Type a Name for the New Custom Pin Map You Want to Create box. Otherwise, select the name of an existing pin map file from the drop-down box. After you make your choice, click OK.

3. Click the Custom Pin Map icon on the Map toolbar. Clicking this icon turns the cursor into a pushpin. Then, when you click anywhere on your map, Excel places a symbol for the location and allows you to enter a legend for the symbol. Press Enter after you finish entering the legend, or click elsewhere to place your next pin map symbol.

4. When you are finished, click the arrow button on the Map toolbar to return the cursor to normal.

5. You can change the symbol or its legend by simply double-clicking the symbol or legend. Or you can delete it by clicking the symbol and pressing the Delete key. Editing the symbol displays the Symbol dialog box. You can choose any of the displayed symbols, or you can click the Font button to display the normal Font dialog box from which you can choose a different font or change the symbol's properties.

6. After you have finished with the custom pin map, you can close it by clicking Map|Close Custom Pin Map. Note that closing the map removes all the custom pin map symbols from your map. Obviously, the pushpins are safely stored until you open the custom pushpin map again.

Adding Labels

You can also add labels to your map. Labels can come either from your data or from the labels associated with the map itself. To add a label to the map, do the following:

1. Click Tools|Labeler, or click the Map Labels icon on the map toolbar. This action displays the Map Labels dialog box.

2. Choose the map feature you want to label, and tell Excel where the labels will be extracted from. Choose Map Feature Names to get the information from the map feature you selected, or choose Values From to choose the data column that contains the values you want to use. Click OK when you're finished.

3. Double-click the map where you want the label to appear.

4. When you're finished, click the arrow icon on the Map toolbar.

5. To change any of the labels on the map, double-click the label and simply enter your changes. To change how the label is displayed, right-click the label and choose Format Font. You can then change any of the label's font properties.

6. To delete a label, select the label and press the Delete key, or right-click the label and choose Clear.

On Your Own

Creating charts is one of the most popular activities in Excel. Charts allow you to convey a complex set of information quickly and often give you a better feel for how the data is related to each other.

I didn't show you what every different chart type looks like in this chapter. To make sure you're at least somewhat familiar with them, you should enter the data from Table 14.1 into a worksheet and then create (or at least preview) each of the different chart types. This data doesn't work for stock charts, so you can copy some data from the stock market and create a stock chart for that portion of the exercise. Finally, pick your favorite type of chart, and create it if you don't already have one on a worksheet. Use the Drawing toolbar to identify at least one point on the chart with an arrow, and then add a comment about the data point.

Analyzing Your Data in Excel

The primary reason people use Excel is to analyze data. Perhaps you're a high-level executive who wants to use PivotTables to analyze company sales by a variety of factors, including by region, by model, by marketing campaign, or whatever other data you might have at your disposal. Or maybe you're the volunteer grant writer for a local nonprofit organization, and you need to generate a nice-looking budget for an application for funding. With Excel, you can tweak the numbers as you go to make sure the budget meets the foundation's guidelines. (No, I'm not advocating padding your budget; I'm merely suggesting that you'll want to be aware of how the money is spent because most organizations grant funds for a very specific purpose.)

Understanding how to perform calculations is important, but there's more to analyzing data than simply performing calculations. In this chapter, I'll introduce you to a number of techniques and features that can help you make more sense of random bits of data. You'll learn how to gather the data, import it from various formats, and perform various sorts and analysis on it.

Gathering Data to Analyze

To analyze data within Excel, you have to get the data into Excel first. The most obvious way to do so is to enter the data directly into a worksheet. But what if the data comes from another application, such as Access, Word, a Web page, or even your company's SQL Server?

Importing Data from Other Applications

Excel can extract information from many different file types automatically. Whether you have an old Lotus 1-2-3 spreadsheet or an ancient Quattro Pro DOS file, you can pull it into Excel 2000.

Note: So who needs it? DOS? Who in the world would even have access to old files for DOS programs? You might be surprised. According to the IRS, well over a million nonprofit organizations are registered in the United States, many of which rely on volunteers and donated goods to survive. It's this very type of organization that may have had an old intern build a database way back when the organization had access only to an 8086 PC running DOS. Although data that old may no longer be relevant, it could have some value showing historic trends if analyzed properly in Excel with corresponding current data.

To open another file type in Excel, follow these steps:

1. Launch Excel 2000, and then click the Open button.

2. Use the Look In drop-down arrow to move to the location of the file you want to import.

3. Select the type of file you want to import from the Files of Type drop-down box.

Tip: Don't see what you're looking for? If the file type you need isn't listed, perhaps you need to install some additional file converters. Many are included on the Office 2000 disks, and others can be found on Microsoft's Office on the Web site (click Help|Office on the Web). If that's too much of a hassle and you have the data's native application on your machine as well, open the file in that application, and then try to save it there in a format recognizable to Excel (such as a .txt file).

4. To open the file in Excel, you need to do one of two things, depending on where the data last resided:

   • If the file was last saved in another Office application, click the Open drop-down button, and choose Open in Microsoft Excel.

   • If it's a non-Office file, simply double-click it.

5. The imported data isn't an Excel document yet. You have to perform a Save As first by clicking File|Save As. Then give the file a name, choose Microsoft Excel Workbook (*.xls) from the Files of Type list, and then click Save.

If that approach doesn't work, you could open the file in the other application and copy its data to the Clipboard. Then you could just paste the data into an Excel worksheet. This approach isn't always practical, however. The next few sections cover additional data-gathering strategies you might be interested in.

Importing Comma Separated Value Files

Many companies' needs are so extensive that they store and process data on a large mainframe computer. Not everyone has access to (or even knows how to use) common mainframe data analysis tools, but wouldn't it be great if you could pull that data onto your PC to analyze it in a familiar tool, or build fancy graphs or charts from it? In many cases, you can do just that by converting the material to a Comma Separated Value file.

> **Caution: Save yourself some work.** If you're working with a newer database that speaks ODBC (see the upcoming section titled "Importing Database Data by Using Microsoft Query"), using Microsoft Query to perform the task may save you significant time and effort. After all, why go through an extra step if you don't need to, right?

Comma Separated Value (CSV) files consist of a number of lines of text, where each line contains a set of fields separated by commas. Each line of the file corresponds to a single row in a worksheet, and each field in the line corresponds to a cell in the worksheet. If the data stored in the field contains a comma, then the field must be enclosed in quotation marks. Excel automatically treats this field as a text string. If the field is numeric, Excel treats the field as a numeric field.

> **Tip: A great backup plan.** Converting a file to CSV is also a good option if the proper converter doesn't already exist, or if locating it to install it would take more time than you have to give the task. This is especially true for database or spreadsheet applications that can effortlessly generate files in this format.

This approach does not let you import formulas into a cell because the syntax between programs may differ, but when you get the data, you can always redefine the formulas in Excel using the proper format.

> **Caution: Cut the commas!** Be aware that converting files that use a comma for the thousands separator within numbers to CSV will cause some serious problems. This is due primarily to the fact that a CSV file relies on commas to know where to separate parts of the file. If commas are used within large numbers, the numbers are automatically subdivided. For example, the number 10,862 would be perceived as two separate values, 10 and 862—a huge difference! Stripping the commas from the original data source may take some time, but doing so is mandatory for accurate results. If you can't cut the commas, consider using a different character as a delimiter, such as a tab or semicolon.

To open a CSV file in Excel, click the Open icon, and then browse to the CSV file you want to import. Double-click its name to open the file. Excel is smart enough to realize it's a CSV and will respond accordingly.

> **Tip: Separate but equal.** Because a CSV file doesn't have any binary information—even numeric values are stored as a string of characters—a CSV file can easily be translated from an IBM mainframe, which uses EBCDIC characters, to your PC, where you use ASCII characters. The mere process of copying the file using FTP or other transfer mechanism converts the data from one character set to the other so that it can be properly read on the destination computer.

Excel also can save a worksheet as a CSV file. Of course, any formulas and formatting information are lost, but the output file can be used as an input file to many other applications. Basically, you have the freedom to move Excel data back to the mainframe or any other application supporting CSV format. However, because the Excel workbook format is very popular, many other applications such as Quicken and Microsoft Money have filters that allow them to read this data. At last, you can convert that simple check register worksheet to a more user-friendly application that can then be imported from there to a tax program and so on.

Importing Data the Easy Way Using the Text Import Wizard

In general, if you can create a normal text file containing your data, you can load it into Excel using the Text Import Wizard. Although, technically, a CSV file is a text file as well, Excel is smart enough to verify that a file with a CSV file type is really a CSV file. Excel then loads it properly without using the wizard. (You saw how this process works in the preceding section.) Other text files, however, need the wizard's help to be successfully converted.

Each line of a text file corresponds to one row in a worksheet. The trick behind the Text Import Wizard is to examine one line of the file and attempt to break it into the fields that correspond to the cells in a row.

> **Tip: Make a mistake? Don't despair.** If you discover you made an error when you imported your text file, you can select any of the cells you just imported and choose DataIEdit Text Import to rerun the Text Import Wizard to load the same data again.

To convert a text file to an Excel spreadsheet using the Text Import Wizard, you need to do the following:

1. Launch Excel 2000, and then click Data|Get External Data|Import Text File. The Import Text File dialog box, which resembles a standard Open dialog box, appears. You should always import your file into an empty worksheet.

> **Note: Automatically importing.** If you open a file using the File|Open dialog box, and Excel doesn't recognize the file type, it automatically starts the Text Import Wizard to help you define how the file should be loaded.

2. Browse to the text file you want to import, click the filename you want, and then click the Import button. Step 1 of the Text Import Wizard opens (see Figure 15.1).

FIGURE 15.1

The Text Import Wizard tries to determine how your data is structured.

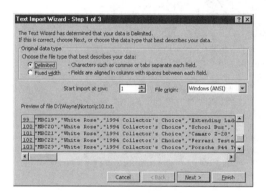

3. You must then tell the wizard whether the data you want to import is Delimited (has commas or other characters separating the fields) or Fixed Width (where the data is aligned in columns or within a certain amount of space) by clicking the appropriate option. You can then preview the file's contents so that you can select which line the import should begin on. Click Next to move to Step 2 of the wizard.

4. Step 2 varies depending on whether the file is delimited or fixed width. If it's delimited, you need to tell the wizard what type of character separates each field by clicking the applicable option. For example, the name Freeze, Christopher J. would actually be split apart because of the comma, but if you specified quotation marks as the text indicator, then "Freeze, Christopher J." would be considered a single field. You can see the option's effect on the data in the Preview window. Fixed-width files can be edited in the Preview window as described by the wizard. Click Next to proceed to the final step.

> **Tip: And checking it twice...**You can see the effect of specifying how the fields are defined by looking in the Data Preview window. You should skim through the data shown here to make sure that the fields are separated properly. If they aren't, you can change your definitions and see the effect immediately. Checking your data first can prevent problems before the data is loaded.

5. Step 3 of the wizard is the same no matter which type of file you're working with. Here, you get to assign a data format to each field in the file (see Figure 15.2). By default, General is used (which is great for numeric values); however you can also specify that the field contains only text or only dates. You can also choose to ignore this column by selecting Do Not Import Column. Click Finish to perform the import.

FIGURE 15.2

You can easily choose how the information on your spreadsheet is displayed.

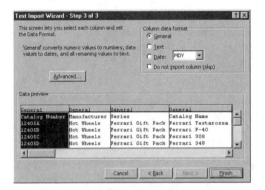

> **Caution: Tip-type shape.** Take the time to assign a type to your fields when you import the file rather than do it later. Otherwise, Excel tries to determine the type based on the field's value, which could lead to some fields being treated as numeric, whereas others will be treated as text in the same column.

Importing Data from the Web by Using Web Query

On the Internet, you can find a lot of information that you might want to analyze. For example, several different Web sites provide stock market quotations or sales statistics. Imagine being able to pull down data related to your stock portfolio and produce performance statistics or graphs! You could even design a Web query that enables your daughter to place a value on her Beanie Baby collection using data from a Web site.

To begin defining a new Web Query, follow these simple steps:

1. From within Excel, choose Data|Get External Data|New Web Query from the main menu to launch the New Web Query dialog box (see Figure 15.3).

FIGURE 15.3

You can use Web Query to get information from the Internet.

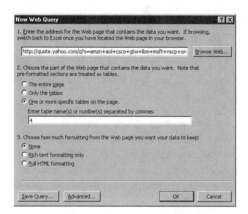

2. In item 1 of the New Web Query dialog box, you need to provide the address of the Web site you want to retrieve information from. If you don't know it offhand, you can click the Browse Web button to surf to the desired site. When you locate it, Excel will fill in the address for you.

3. Specify which information you want to retrieve from the Web site—the entire page, all the tables, or only the listed tables. Click the option that best meets your needs.

4. The New Web Query dialog box also prompts you to choose how much formatting should be kept. You can keep the full HTML formatting, limit yourself to the formatting available for a rich text document, or drop all the formatting.

5. If the query is one you think you'll use again, click the Save Query button, and give the query a descriptive name. You can run it again at a later date by clicking Data|Get External Data|Run Saved Query and then double-clicking the query name.

> **Tip: Simply the best option.** When the purpose of grabbing the data is simply to analyze it, choose None as the desired formatting option. Choosing this option greatly reduces the potential formatting problems when you begin to manipulate the data.

6. When you return to the main New Web Query dialog box, click OK to run the query. When the query finishes, it prompts you to enter where in Excel you want to place the data, and then it adds the data to your workbook.

> **Tip: Having it all.** Although Web Query is optimized to retrieve the information from an HTML table, it doesn't mean you can't run it on a Web page without tables. When faced with this situation, I often find it useful to retrieve an entire Web page onto a separate worksheet. Then I can create a second worksheet and reference the appropriate cells on the first worksheet created by the Web Query Wizard.

Importing Database Data by Using Microsoft Query

Sometimes the data you want to analyze is stored in a database somewhere. The database could be a simple Access database that you use to collect information about your home art collection, or it may be an SQL Server database containing information about your corporation. In any case, if the data is in a database and you want to look at it using Excel, you need a tool such as Microsoft Query to fetch it and begin working with it.

Microsoft Query allows you to access a number of different databases such as the Microsoft Jet database (often used in Access, Visual Basic, and Visual FoxPro applications), Microsoft SQL Server, and any other database that supports ODBC access, such as Oracle, Sybase, and IBM DB2. It even allows you to access things that aren't strictly databases such as Excel files and text files, though in those instances, you can use other methods, as you saw earlier.

> **Note: ODBC, OLE DB, ETC.** To access a database, you need to speak the proper language. Nearly all databases on the market today speak ODBC, which is one of the languages spoken by Microsoft Query. Excel can also speak a more advanced language called OLE DB that is supported by many Microsoft products, including Access and SQL Server. The main advantage of OLE DB is that anything can be a database if someone is willing to supply the right drivers. Microsoft Query employs this technique to access Excel files and flat files using Microsoft Query.

To begin importing data from a database using Microsoft Query, follow these simple steps:

1. From within Excel, click the cell into which you want to place the first chunk of imported data.

2. Click Data|Get External Data|New Database Query to begin working with Microsoft Query.

3. On the Databases tab, which should be open by default, double-click the database you want to extract data from.

> **Note: You might need a bit more information.** Note that you need a user ID and password to access most databases, and you also need to know where in the database to find your information. If you're not familiar with the database you want to use, you should contact your friendly database administrator for more assistance.

4. You then are led through a series of self-explanatory wizard steps that may vary slightly, depending on the type of database you're working with. Follow each step until you reach the Finish screen.

5. On this screen, you might want to save your query for future use by clicking Save Query and giving it a name.

6. Click Return Data to Microsoft Excel, and then click Properties to go in and set up the data's formatting.

7. Click the Finish button to place the data in the desired location within Excel.

Realizing the Power of Data Analysis

Now that you know how to get just about any kind of data into Excel, it's time to learn how to get something out of it. All the numbers in the world don't mean a thing unless there's some rhyme or reason to them.

For instance, a spreadsheet containing a list of all your mail order customers and the amount of money they spent with you for each order is little more than a big list. But if you can massage that data to discover that your new color catalogs have really upped sales, well, that's certainly getting something out of the data. Likewise, if sales are pretty much level, you might decide to scrap the fancy catalogs because it's obviously the merchandise and/or the prices that are attracting sales, not the glitzy catalog. You can leverage this information to make more powerful, educated business decisions. And thanks to Excel 2000's ease of use, the average user can tap into this valuable resource as well. I'll show you how in the following sections.

Organizing Your Worksheet

Before you can perform a thorough data analysis, you need to organize the information in your spreadsheet. To maximize your ability to use some of the tools in Excel, you should try to organize your data so that each row contains information about a single item (for example, a person's name), and each column contains information about a specific aspect of each item (the person's address, membership status, or other key information).

At the top of each column, you should include a column header in the first row of your worksheet that describes the column's contents (again, something like Address, City, or Member would work). Excel will use this value later when you want to perform various operations against the data in the column. For example, it can sort in alphabetical order by state, count the number of members, and so on. These column headers also serve to remind you what information is contained in each column. Microsoft refers to this type of organization as using Excel as a *list*.

The classic example of this situation is the order invoice. Each line of the invoice contains information about an item in the order. Each column contains a specific attribute of the item, such as its number, description, or price. Headers are included at the top so that anyone reading the list of items can understand the information in each column (see Figure 15.4).

FIGURE 15.4

Your raw data should be organized as a list of rows, where each row contains information about a specific item.

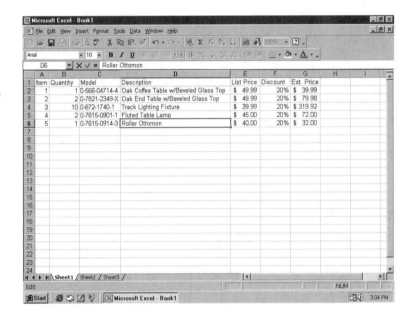

Performing Calculations on the Data

When you have your data organized properly, you can use it to start performing calculations. These calculations enable you to take an organized list and deduce additional information from it, such as the average customer order size, the number of people from the company's home state who ordered, and the like. That way, you can make decisions based on the data—for example, whether to open a retail outlet in a specific area.

Although you can technically put formulas anywhere on your spreadsheet, I usually restrict myself to just two types of calculations: row-oriented and column-oriented calculations. Using just these two types makes it easier to maintain the information in my worksheet and helps me verify that my numbers and formulas are correct.

Performing Row-Oriented Calculations

In a row-oriented calculation, only those cells in the current row can be used in a formula. For example, by multiplying the discount times the list price, you can compute a discounted price. Or by multiplying discounted prices times the quantity, you can arrive at an extended price.

The advantage of using row-oriented calculations is that the row becomes a self-contained unit. That way, it doesn't matter if you insert or delete a row because only the row that you are working with is affected, not other parts of the worksheet or even the workbook. If the row you deleted accessed other rows, this wouldn't be true. When you delete a row that is referenced by a formula in another row, that second formula will most likely return an incorrect value. That incorrect value could then cascade throughout your worksheet, giving you a host of inaccurate information on which you might potentially base major decisions.

Peter's Principle: Accurate results in an instant!

Typically, my personal worksheets aren't overly complex. In fact, the majority of the time, I'm simply adding a group of numbers. Given that, I tend to use AutoSum on a regular basis. You can tell that Excel is used to performing row- and column-oriented calculations as well because of the way it behaves. For example, if you click a cell to the right of a row of filled cells (and no numbers appear immediately above the cell), clicking AutoSum results in Excel "guessing" that you want to add all the numbers to the left of the selected cell (row oriented). Likewise, if you click a cell at the bottom of a column of filled cells, AutoSum guesses that you want to add the entire column. Using AutoSum is the best way to perform simple addition in my book because you needn't worry about formula syntax and the like. And if you don't want to capture the whole column or row, just click inside the selected AutoSum area, and drag the border in the desired direction.

Another advantage of restricting your calculations to a self-contained row is that when you copy that row, all the formulas are copied properly. This capability can be useful when you want to insert a new row into your list. Simply insert the blank row as usual, and then copy the cells from another row containing the formula you want to use. Then all you have to do is enter the new values, and your formulas (along with their results) will be correct.

Performing Column-Oriented Calculations

Performing operations on specific columns in the list also helps you maintain control over the results you get. For instance, you might want to compute the number of rows in the list using the Count function, or you might want to add the particular values in another column using the Sum function.

> **Tip: The Sum also rises.** Computing the value of a column of data is so common in Excel that Microsoft added a shortcut to compute a sum. Simply select the cell beneath the list of values you want to add, and click the AutoSum icon. Excel scans upward looking for the first blank or non-numeric cell to determine the range for the sum. It then displays the range with a flashing dashed line. You can press Enter to complete the formula, or you can use the cursor to select a different range.

Sorting Your Data to Put Things in Order

Believe it or not, sorting data in Excel can make it look completely different. Imagine that you have a list of your customers and how much they have purchased over time. You can sort the list by total purchase to find your biggest customers (so that maybe you can send them a special holiday discount offer). Or you could sort the list by the most recent purchase date to determine those customers who haven't purchased from you recently. (Why keep customers on your mailing list who haven't ordered in a few years, right? That's a big waste of money!)

You can sort rows in two ways in Excel 2000. First, you can click a cell and click either the Sort Ascending button (to sort A to Z, 1 to 100, and so on) or the Sort Descending button (to sort Z to A, 100 to 1, and so on) on the Standard toolbar. Excel automatically selects all the cells containing data that are adjacent to the cell you selected and then sorts them based on the values in the column you selected.

The other way to sort data is to select the list you want to sort, and then click Data|Sort to display the Sort dialog box (see Figure 15.5). If you include column headers in the first row, Excel lets you choose the columns that you want to sort by the names that you gave them. If the columns haven't been named, you need to specify the column name (Column A, Column B, and so on) you want to use.

Clicking the Options button displays a pop-up window from which you can select several different options. You can choose to sort the data normally or according to a custom list (for example, days of the week or months of the year). You can also make the sort case sensitive (that is, uppercase Z sorts before lowercase a), and you can choose to sort by rows instead of by columns.

FIGURE 15.5
Using the Sort dialog box, you can sort up to three columns at one time.

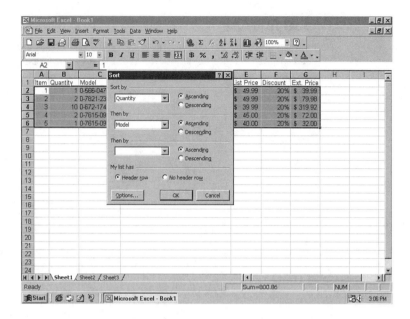

Caution: I thought I selected everything! Use caution when selecting cells to be sorted. If you have three columns in your spreadsheet but select only two of them before sorting your data, the cells in the remaining column will *not* be sorted. This could cause serious problems if the unselected cells are associated with specific row values. If you don't think it's a big deal, consider this: a list of names, addresses, and phone numbers where only the names and addresses are selected for the sort. In that instance, you would have the wrong phone numbers associated with each person. Luckily, the undo facility (either the Undo button or Ctrl+Z) works wonders in this type of situation.

Filtering Rows to Eliminate Unwanted Data

Perhaps you want to build a list containing only names of members of your organization. Or maybe you want to extract records from a certain state only. Filtering data enables you to do so. When you filter a list, the other rows are still there; however, they aren't visible. The cells are also still there, so any formulas that reference them will continue to return the correct results. Although some more advanced filtering tools are tucked away in Excel, AutoFilter will rise to the occasion in the majority of cases.

Select a cell from the list of cells you want to filter, and then click Data|AutoFilter. Excel adds an arrow at the end of each header cell in the list. Clicking the arrow displays a list of filter criteria from which you can choose (see Table 15.1). To apply a filter, click the arrow in the desired column, and then select the option that best meets your needs. Here again, Table 15.1 can help you make the proper selection.

Looking Ahead

In Chapter 16, "Excel 2000 on the Web," you'll learn how you can use Excel 2000 to take this interactivity to the Web. That's right; people can manipulate your data in any way they desire without damaging the source data!

Table 15.1   Filtering Rows

Filter Criteria	Description
All	Displays all the rows in the list. This option restores the list to its unfiltered state.
Top 10	Filters for the Top 1 to 500, the Bottom 1 to 500, or a percent such as the Top 10 Percent or Bottom 3 Percent. (As you can see, the name is misleading.)
Custom	Allows you to specify up to two conditional expressions, which when true means that the row will be displayed.
Value	Lists each of the distinct values in the column. Selecting one displays only those rows with that value.
Non-blanks	Displays just the rows where the cell is not blank. (Available only when at least one blank cell is in your list.)
Blanks	Displays just the rows where the cell is blank. (Available only when at least one blank cell is in your list.)

By using multiple arrows, you can hone in on the exact bits of data you need, which you can then use to assess a given situation more accurately.

Getting Organized by Using the Outline Mode

If you thought outlines were only used in Word, are you in for a big surprise! It's very easy for a worksheet to get so large that finding information on it becomes difficult. One technique that I find helpful in managing unwieldy worksheets is to use Excel 2000's Outline feature. The Outline feature allows you to organize your worksheet like a Word outline, where you can display or hide various levels of detail as you desire. Outline mode enables you to see the subtotals of a large spreadsheet, for example, without the clutter of each line item. Although an outline is usually organized by rows, it can also be organized by columns or by rows and columns.

Viewing Your Outline

I realize it may be difficult to grasp the concept of using an outline for a spreadsheet, so let's take a quick look at how you might manipulate one to see the information you want.

You can manipulate the outline by using the buttons supplied to hide entire levels or individual groups (see Figure 15.6). Clicking the 1 button displays only the highest level of the outline. Clicking the 2 button collapses the outline so that only Levels 1 and 2 are visible. If only Level 1 was shown before you clicked the button, then Level 2 is displayed. If levels beyond 2 are visible, they are collapsed. Sounding familiar? I thought so!

Clicking a plus button on the left side of the spreadsheet expands only those cells associated with the button. Likewise, clicking the minus button collapses the cells associated with that button. Only those cells are visible, thus eliminating the clutter of unwanted data without physically altering the spreadsheet itself.

FIGURE 15.6
Outlines give you a lot of flexibility on the amount of detail you display in your work-sheet.

Level buttons ——

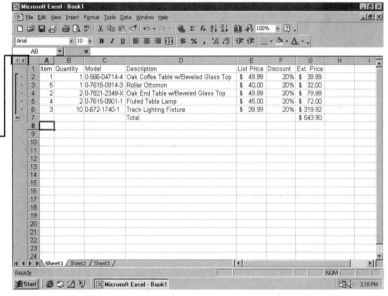

Defining Your Outline

Now that you feel a bit more at ease with the concept of using outlines in spreadsheets, I'm going to show you how to create one on your own. To create an outline, you need to follow these steps:

1. Open the spreadsheet you want to generate an outline from. Select the rows you want to move to the next lower level—Level 2—of the outline.

Note: You get out of it what you put into it. Because everything is considered as Level 1 unless you specify otherwise, you need to choose some items to demote to Level 2 for the outline to be of any use.

2. Click Data|Group and Outline|Group to turn the selected text into Level 2 content. Repeat this step to move content down even more levels, one level at a time.

Note: Keep a level head! You should know that the selected cells' physical position does not change, only their relative position in the outline. It's also worth noting that if the level doesn't already exist, it is automatically created for you. If other cells are adjacent to the recently moved cells, they are merged together so that they can be treated as one outline unit. Again, no change is made to the spreadsheet or the cells themselves; it's all in how they appear in Outline mode.

3. After you've defined what data is to be considered Level 1, Level 2, and so on, you can begin expanding and collapsing your outline as needed.

You can promote (or move to a higher level) a block of text's outline attributes by clicking Data|Group and Outline|Ungroup. Of course, you can't move the cells higher than Level 1. And if you move all the cells to the top level, the outline is turned off.

Tip: Clearing the air. If you want to restore a spreadsheet to its normal state, click Data|Group and Outline|Clear Outline.

Creating Subtotals

If you have a spreadsheet containing sales information, you might want to have Excel generate subtotals for each type of item and then produce a grand total at the bottom of the page. No formula programming needed!

Using the Subtotals dialog box, you can easily add totals and subtotals to your worksheet. It examines your list of data looking for when the value in the specified column changes. It then inserts a new row containing a subtotal for the selected columns. At the end of the list of data, it also inserts a grand total (see Figure 15.7). At the same time, it organizes your list of data into an outline with the original data stored at Level 3, the subtotals stored at Level 2, and the grand total stored at Level 1. That way, you can cut-to-the-chase, so to speak, in an instant and get the answers you need.

To begin generating these automatic subtotals and grand totals, follow these steps:

1. Select a cell in the area in which you want to create the subtotals.

2. Click Data|Subtotals Group to display the Subtotals dialog box.

3. Specify a column for each change using the drop-down arrow button.

4. Click the OK button to have Excel compute the answers. Subtotals will be inserted into your worksheet for the rest of the columns each time this value changes.

FIGURE 15.7

The Subtotals function converts your worksheet into an outline with totals and subtotals added.

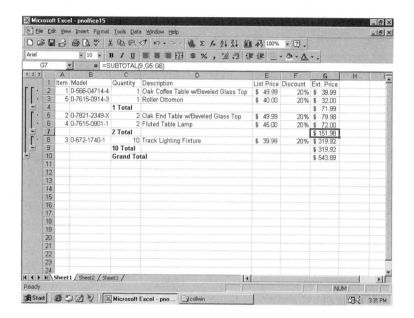

In addition to choosing which column to take breaks on, you can choose the column where you want to place the subtotals, place a page break between the subtotals, place the summary information below the data or beside the data, and replace the current subtotals. You can do all this by simply clicking the corresponding option on the Subtotals dialog box.

In addition, you can create the subtotals and grand total from such functions as Sum, Count, Average, Min, Max, and Product, plus several other statistical functions. These capabilities make this tool extraordinarily valuable to general business people as well as specialists in fields such as science, math, engineering, and statistics.

> **Tip: I didn't mean to push that button.** If you decide that you don't like how the subtotals look, simply select a cell in the range where grouping has been applied, display the Subtotals dialog box, and choose Remove All. All levels above the bottom level of the outline are then removed.

Advanced Data Analysis

In addition to performing basic statistical analysis against a list of data, you can use various features in Excel to help you answer different types of questions.

Many of these tools come in the form of special add-ons, either provided on the Office 2000 disks or downloaded from Microsoft's Web site. These special tools are of immense value to the busy professional because results are virtually foolproof and speedy to achieve without the hassle of complex programming.

You may have heard of some of these tools but haven't had the time to explore them, let alone consider what they may be able to do for you. In the next couple of sections, I'll introduce you to two of the more valuable tools: Goal Seeker and Solver.

Achieving a Goal by Using Goal Seek

At one time or another, we all play what-if games. A growing business owner may aspire to earn a certain amount of money a month but wants to know how much he needs to sell to do that. Or a young couple may ponder how nice a home they could afford if their salaries were just a bit higher. Goal Seek is a super tool for this very type of task.

Goal Seek needs three pieces of information to do its thing: the cell containing a formula that generates a result (known as the Set Cell); the target value that the formula should return (known as the To Value); and the cell containing a constant it can change to generate different results (known as the By Changing Cell).

The best way to illustrate how this tool works is by using a common example (see Figure 15.8). Let's assume you want to buy a new house and finance $125,000. However, the largest payment you can afford is $750 per month. The worksheet shown in Figure 15.8 shows how to compute a mortgage payment based on a principle of $125,000, an 8 percent annual interest rate, and a 30-year mortgage (360 payments).

Figure 15.8

Goal Seek needs information about your problem before it can find a solution.

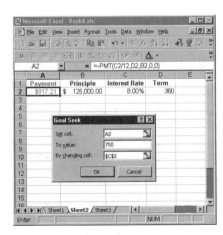

To use Goal Seek, follow these steps:

1. Enter your problem into a worksheet, such as the loan example provided here.

2. Click Tools|Goal Seek to display the Goal Seek dialog box.

3. Select a cell location for Set Cell, and specify a value for the To Value.

4. Click OK to run Goal Seek.

Let me follow through with the preceding mortgage example to help clarify just how Goal Seek works. In the Goal Seek dialog box, I chose cell A2 (Payment) as the Set Cell because that's the cell I want to change to $750. I entered 750 as the To Value. Then I selected cell C2 (Interest Rate) as the By Changing Cell because I want to find what interest rate will give me a payment of $750. Clicking OK runs Goal Seek on the information provided. When Goal Seek is finished, the information on the worksheet is adjusted, and the dialog box in Figure 15.9 is shown.

FIGURE 15.9
Using Goal Seek, you can quickly find the answers to your questions.

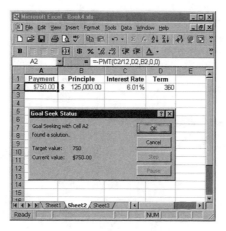

Using Solver for More Complex Situations

If your problem is more complex than you can solve with Goal Seek, then consider using Solver. Unlike Goal Seek, Solver can vary multiple values at the same time. It can also impose constraints on those values to prevent Solver from choosing new values that would be unacceptable. You can easily create a problem that can be solved by Solver.

> **Note: Now for the math stuff...**The Solver add-in uses the Generalized Reduced Gradient (GRG2) nonlinear optimization algorithm and the simplex method with bounds on the variables and the branch-and-bound method to find optimal solutions to your problem. If you understand these terms, then you are definitely a candidate for using Solver.

You use Solver primarily to solve Min/Max problems in which you want to adjust a series of values subject to certain constraints to produce the largest or smallest target value. For instance, assume that you make cat food from three different compounds. Each compound has a complex discount schedule based on how much you buy. You also have a formula that specifies that a minimum percentage of the first two compounds will be used to create the cat food, while a maximum of the third compound will be used. Although setting up this type of problem in Excel is time consuming, it is typical of the entire class of Min/Max problems in which you are looking for an optimal solution to a problem that may have many possible solutions.

To run the Solver add-in, choose Tools|Solver from the main menu to display the Solver dialog box (see Figure 15.10). The Set Cell you used in Goal Seek corresponds to the Target Cell in Solver. You can instruct Solver to find the maximum value for the cell, to find the minimum value for the cell, or to find a specific value. Using the same example I used for Goal Seek, I chose the formula to compute a loan payment as the Target Cell and instructed Solver to look for the minimum payment.

FIGURE 15.10

With Solver, you might be able to answer questions that Goal Seek couldn't.

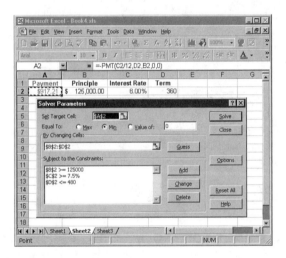

Clicking the Guess button displays the list of cells that directly or indirectly affect the value displayed in the Target Cell. You can use these values or remove those that you don't want. In Figure 15.10, I decided to let Solver vary the principle (B2), the annual interest rate (C2), and the term of the loan (D2).

Finally, you can add a series of constraints. A constraint limits the acceptable values of a cell. In Figure 15.10, I made sure that the interest rate in cell C2 had to be at least 7.5 percent, and the term of the loan could be no longer than 480 months. I also added a constraint to ensure that the minimum loan amount was $125,000. If I didn't want to include this constraint, I could have dropped cell B2 from the list of cells that Solver can change.

When you're finished setting up your problem, clicking the Solve button runs the Solver. After the Solver is finished, it generates a report indicating whether it was successful. It can also generate a set of reports, if you want, containing information about how the solution was reached.

> **Note: I can't solve my problem if I can't find it.** Solver is an Excel add-in. If you can't find it on the Tools menu, click Tools|Add-Ins, and check the Solver Add-in check box. You might need to provide your Office disks at this point for the installation. When it's successfully added, Excel then makes Solver permanently available under the Tools menu.

Using PivotTables to View Data from Different Points of View

When you're trying to understand the relationships among various elements of data, a PivotTable comes in very handy. A PivotTable provides a three-dimensional view of your data. Data elements are arranged along three different axes, and you can drag them around on the worksheet from one axis to another to see different views of the data.

Building a PivotTable with Internal Data

To begin defining a PivotTable on data already residing in Excel, follow these steps:

1. Click Data|PivotTable and PivotChart Report to display the PivotTable and PivotChart Wizard. You then see the dialog box shown in Figure 15.11.

2. You are prompted to enter two pieces of information: the source of the data, and whether you want to build a PivotTable only, or a PivotChart and a PivotTable. The data used for the table can be taken from either an external data source or a source within Excel, such as a data list or another PivotTable.

> **Tip: Sometimes it just doesn't matter.** To have a PivotChart, you must first have a PivotTable, so you'll end up building the PivotTable either way. Note that you can always create a PivotChart from the PivotTable, so in the end, it doesn't really matter which option you choose.

3. Clicking Next displays a dialog box that helps you choose the cells you want to load into the PivotTable. By default, Excel tries to use the cells selected prior to starting the wizard. Click Next to continue.

4. The wizard then asks you where the PivotTable should be placed. I suggest that you put it on a separate sheet to prevent confusion later.

5. Click Finish to display the initial PivotTable.

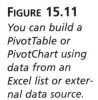

Figure 15.11
You can build a PivotTable or PivotChart using data from an Excel list or external data source.

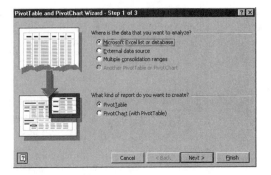

Building a PivotTable with External Data

If you want to use external data in your PivotTable, you follow the same process you used with internal data, except that when the wizard prompts you for the range of cells you want to use, you need to specify the source of the external data. The same Microsoft Query Wizard (see Figure 15.12) that is used to retrieve data from an external data source is used to identify the source of the data.

Figure 15.12
Choose a data source for your PivotTable data.

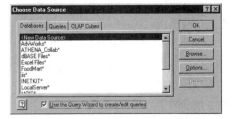

You can access any database table, database query, or an OLAP cube. Information from database tables and queries is imported into Excel and manipulated independently of the database, whereas data from an OLAP server is primarily kept on the OLAP server. Only the OLAP summary information is sent to Excel. This way, you can analyze larger volumes of data faster than you could by importing all the data into Excel.

> **Note: OLAP is YACCTTIMTNG.** OLAP is Yet Another Cryptic Computer Term That Is Meaningless To Non-Geeks. It stands for On Line Analytical Processing. This fancy term means that you can look at your data interactively. It often refers to the process of translating data from a data warehouse database into a three-dimensional data object like a PivotTable.

Understanding the Parts of a PivotTable

Understanding the parts of a PivotTable and how they work is key to learning how to use them. Consider a list of data with four columns: Salesperson, Product, Quarter, and Total Sales. This list of data can be represented as a cube in which each axis of the cube represents a particular column in the list. For example, Salesperson could be placed along one dimension, Product along the second, and Quarter along the third. In each of the smaller cubes within the big cube would be stored the Total Sales value associated with the specific values for Salesperson, Product, and Quarter.

A PivotTable is a two-dimensional representation of this cube. Think of it as a slice of the cube. For any specific value of Salesperson, Product, or Quarter, you would see a two-dimensional table containing all possible values for the other two variables and the data corresponding to those values (see Figure 15.13). The constant value field is known as the *Page field*. The other two fields are known as the *Row* and *Column fields*. The individual cells are known as the *Data items*, and the source of the values is known as the *Data field*.

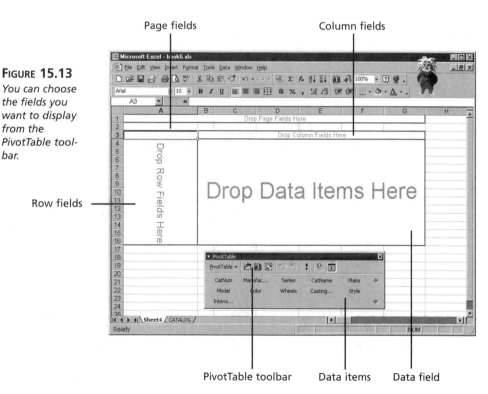

Figure 15.13
You can choose the fields you want to display from the PivotTable toolbar.

Also associated with the PivotTable is a toolbar containing the icons to help you format the chart, draw PivotCharts, refresh the data in the chart, and perform other useful functions. Below the icons is a series of buttons containing the fields from the original data list. You populate the PivotTable by dragging the fields onto the desired areas on the worksheet. I created the PivotTable shown in Figure 15.14 by dragging Quarter to the Page field, Salesperson to the Column field, Product to the Row, and Total Sales to the Data items area.

FIGURE 15.14

By dragging fields from the toolbar to th worksheet, you can easily create a PivotTable.

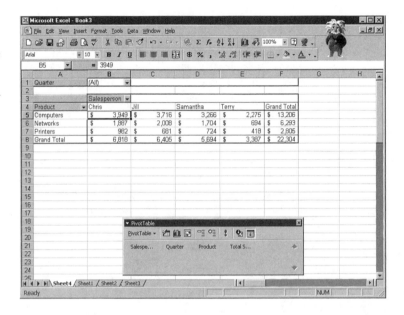

Note: Free totals. Because PivotTables automatically generate totals for all your cells, you don't have to worry about including them in your data list.

Customizing the Way You View Your Data with PivotTables

You can work with PivotTables by dragging and dropping data around on your worksheet. You can drag fields from the toolbar to the worksheet, and you can drag fields from one place on the worksheet to another. You use this flexibility to change how the data is presented without making any actual changes to the data itself.

The Page, Column, and Row fields all have drop-down boxes containing the values that are found in the field. You can select all the different values or just those that you want to display on the table.

You can also display two or more fields in each of the three chart areas. So if you move the Salesperson field from the Column field area to the Row field area, you get a display like the one shown in Figure 15.15.

FIGURE 15.15
You can place multiple fields in a single area of the PivotTable.

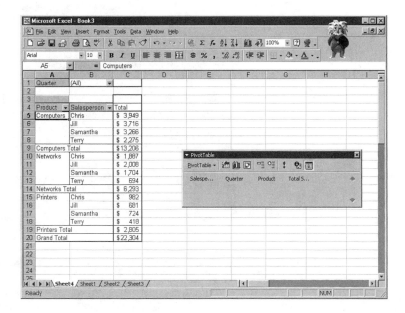

Tip: Just do it. PivotTables are not magical; they simply make it easy to look at your data in many different ways. Many years ago, I used to write statistical analysis programs. Each year, I produced a standard report that was printed on a few dozen boxes of paper. This report was used to anticipate requests for information. I also had to create many one-time programs to produce special reports. None of this would have been necessary if Excel, PivotTables, and OLAP data sources were available back then. I could have done a few months' worth of work in an afternoon with these tools.

Representing Your Data Graphically with PivotCharts

PivotCharts are a natural extension of PivotTables. They display the data created in a PivotTable in a graphical format (see Figure 15.16). Unlike regular charts, PivotCharts can be manipulated in the same fashion as PivotTables. You can drag around fields from the toolbar to the Page, Row, and Column fields and among the various fields themselves. You can also select which information is displayed, much like you can on a PivotTable by clicking the drop-down button on the field and selecting the specific items.

FIGURE 15.16
PivotCharts present a graphical view of a PivotTable.

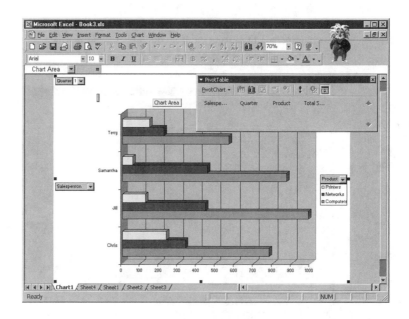

Sharing Workbooks with Others

Shared workbooks can be useful in a networked environment where you want to let more than one person access the same workbook at the same time. Although shared workbooks are great for collaborating on a project, sometimes the data should be protected from unauthorized tampering or inadvertent modifications.

In the sections that follow, I'll show you how to ready your spreadsheets for shared use.

Marking a Workbook Read-Only

The simplest way to share a workbook is for you to create a master copy and place it in a shared folder where others can access it. To ensure that only you can modify the document, you can select some special options when you save your document.

To protect your document from unauthorized modifications, display the Save As dialog box by clicking File|Save As. Then on the Save As dialog box, select Tools|General Options to display the Save Options dialog box (see Figure 15.17). You should check the Read-Only Recommended box and then enter a password in the Password to Modify text box. Another dialog box appears prompting you to re-enter your password. Entering your password again simply verifies that the first word you typed is really the password you want or intended. After entering the password and clicking OK, you can save the document normally.

Figure 15.17

Protect your document before you save it so that others can't change it.

When other users try to open your workbook, they will see a message prompting them for the password (if they want to modify the workbook) or to simply open the workbook in Read-only mode (see Figure 15.18). If they do open the file with the proper password, a reminder is displayed recommending that they should open the file with the password only if they intend to update the file and save the changes.

Figure 15.18

Opening a protected workbook requires a valid password if you want to modify it.

You can remove a password from your workbook by simply clicking Tools|General Options from the Save As dialog box and clearing the Password field. Also, remember to clear the Read Only Recommended check box.

> **Caution: I forgot.** If you lose your password, you're out of luck. You can't open your document without it. If you're like me, you have way too many passwords to memorize. In cases like that, you might want to write down the password and hide it somewhere. But no matter what you do, don't pick an obvious password like your nickname or the name of your family pet. Passwords like that can easily be cracked by someone intent on doing harm.

Sharing Workbooks with Your Workgroup

Before you can share a workbook with others, you must enable the workbook for sharing. To do so, click Tools|Share Workbook, and check the box that says Allow Changes by More Than One User at the Same Time (see Figure 15.19) on the Editing tab of the dialog box. Of course, enabling a shared workbook isn't going to accomplish much unless you place the workbook in a shared location, such as on your file server where everyone can have read and write access to the file.

FIGURE 15.19
You can let multiple people update your workbook at the same time.

> **Note: Shared aren't real.** Shared workbooks aren't updated in real-time, so don't expect to see changes that others enter into their copy of the book quickly. You need to save your copy of the workbook to see the changes that others have made. Note that the other users have to save their workbook also for you to be able to see their changes.

Before you enable your workbook for sharing, you might want to review the options on the Advanced tab (see Figure 15.20). Although keeping a change history is important, you might want to think about how may days' worth of changes you really need to keep. The default of 30 days is probably good for most situations, but it could easily be too small if you need to be able to identify every change in the document since the workbook was created.

FIGURE 15.20
Choose your sharing options carefully.

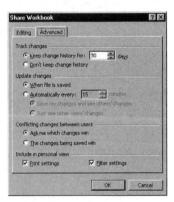

Because you don't see the changes others make to the workbook immediately, you can choose how frequently the workbook is updated. By default, the workbook is updated with the information entered and saved by others each time you save it. However, you can also request that your copy of the workbook be updated every 15 minutes (or any other value you choose).

One problem with shared workbooks is that more than one person can change the value of a cell. You can opt to review these changes to choose which one is correct, or you can let Excel automatically save the most recent changes.

Tracking Changes in Your Workbook

As with most documents that have multiple people working on them, it is desirable to flag which changes were made by which individuals. To flag these changes in Excel, click Tools|Track Changes to display the Highlight Changes dialog box, as shown in Figure 15.21.

FIGURE 15.21
Highlighting any changes made to your workbook is easy.

To track changes, check the box labeled Track Changes While Editing. Then you can decide whether you want to track all the changes made along with everyone who made them. Although you can choose to just track changes by others and flag only the changes since the last save or those that haven't been reviewed, tracking all changes by everyone ensures that nothing gets lost.

> **Tip: The difference that makes no difference...**Because the Track Changes features work similarly for Excel and Word, you might want to flip back to Chapter 11, "Collaborating on Word 2000 Documents," to learn more about the versatility of this tool.

Consolidating Multiple Workbooks

When you're using shared workbooks, you can let others make their changes in a local copy of the workbook and then merge the changes back into your master copy. Clicking Tools|Merge Workbooks displays the typical Open dialog box from which you can choose the file you want to merge with the current workbook. After you select the file and click OK, the two documents are processed, and the cells that were changed in the new document are merged back into the original. If you choose to let Excel do the work, the most recent change is saved.

> **Note: It was my name originally.** The name of the file you want to merge must be different from the name of the master document for the merge to work properly. Also, the file to be merged must be derived from the current master document.

On Your Own

If you use powerful tools like the ones presented here, your job can be made much quicker and easier. And because using Excel to perform basic list management is so easy, try entering a list of the computer books you own for this exercise.

In this list, include columns for the title, author, publisher, page count, cost, and software discussed by the book. Next, sort the list by author and publisher, and compute the total page count and the total cost of all books. Remember, the AutoSum feature can help with some of this exercise, too.

Using the Subtotal feature, you should then try to compute the values by publisher for all the books in your list. Then apply an AutoFilter to see all the books published by Sams.

To understand PivotTables, you really need to build a set of data that contains at least four columns with one strictly numeric value. You can duplicate the example I built in this book by entering 48 rows of information for four different people, three different products, and four quarters' worth of data. Don't forget to insert a row at the beginning with the proper header information.

Take this data and import it into another worksheet as a PivotTable. Try pushing around a few of the fields to see how the resulting table will look. Then create a PivotChart, and push a few fields around the chart. See how radically different the data can look?

Finally, explore the set of commands under the Data menu. Although I've discussed most of these commands, you might want to explore others, such as the Validation and Consolidate features. You might find these features useful as you analyze even more data with Excel.

Displaying Your Results

One day earlier this year, my son came home from school with a sheet of statistics on how his school performed on standardized tests in relation to other schools in the country. Some state data was mixed in there as well. The more I looked at the sheet, the more clear it became that the figures someone worked so hard to gather were virtually useless.

Calculating values in a spreadsheet isn't sufficient. Displaying the information in a meaningful fashion is equally important so that your readers can take something away from the material you've presented. As you saw in the preceding chapter, using charts is one way to represent a body of information, but there are many other ways as well.

In this chapter, you'll see just how much of a difference a few formatting changes, the addition of a border, and countless other tweaks can make. You'll also discover ways to get the exact printed output you want the first time around.

Adding Style to Your Worksheets by Formatting Cells

Think about the last nice-looking Word document you created. Were the section titles done in the same size font as the body text? How were words or bits of text formatted for emphasis?

Just because a worksheet typically contains more numbers than words doesn't mean you should ignore formatting issues. In fact, it could be argued that these elements are even more important in a spreadsheet where items stand a better chance of blending in with one another.

You can easily format a cell or range of cells. Simply right-click the selected cell or cells, and choose Format Cells from the shortcut menu. When the dialog box shown in Figure 16.1 appears, you can choose a tab dedicated to any of the formatting options shown in Table 16.1. I'll go into the specifics of each tab in subsequent sections of this chapter.

Table 16.1 Formatting Cells

Format Option	Description
Number	Allows you to display a number as a currency value, a date or time value, a scientific value, or many other pre-defined and custom formats
Alignment	Allows you to specify how the value is positioned within the cell, including its orientation
Font	Allows you to choose a different character font, and its size, style, color, and effects
Border	Allows you to choose which lines are drawn around the cells you select on your spreadsheet
Patterns	Allows you to specify which color or pattern is displayed in the background of the selected cells
Protection	Allows you to lock the selected cells (which prevents others from changing their contents) or hide formulas in the selected cells (which prevents others from seeing the underlying formula that generated the displayed value)

FIGURE 16.1

You can easily choose how the information on your spreadsheet is displayed.

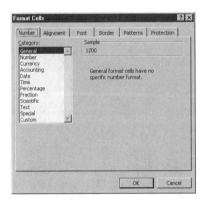

Caution: What happened to my settings? When you're changing format settings on multiple cells, you often see your selections blank or grayed out. This happens when a particular setting has more than one value in the selected cells. Although you can't change the grayed-out settings, you can change the blank ones. Choosing a new setting forces all the selected cells to be changed to the new setting. If you leave the setting alone, the cells remain unchanged.

It's obvious how some of the formatting changes can make a difference in your worksheets. For example, changing the font size of the column headers and making them bold makes it crystal clear what's a heading versus what's part of the spreadsheet. Or centering a cell's contents to make the columns look less crowded is a logical improvement. But Excel's formatting can also benefit your audience in determining what they won't see. Why in the world would you want to hide a formula, for example?

Let's say you sell a commodity whose price fluctuates on a regular basis—perhaps gold or sterling silver jewelry. Rather than disclose your cost and customer markup to your employees, you can hide the formula that calculates the price and the markup so that all the employees need to do to get the price for the item is weigh it.

Conveying the Proper Information by Formatting Numeric Values

Have you ever looked at a block of information and been totally baffled about what exactly it's measuring? I can't tell you how many times I've encountered a table of data and have been left guessing whether the numbers are expressed in real terms, in percentages, in thousands, or in some other term I may not have thought of. By using specific numeric formatting, however, you can avoid a lot of the ambiguity.

Excel comes with several predefined formats for numeric values. With most of these formats, you can specify the number of decimal places displayed or insert the default thousands separator for your system (see Table 16.2).

Table 16.2 Formatting Numeric Values

Number Format	Description
General	Displays values as a string of digits without any specific formatting rules.
Number	Displays values as a string of digits. You can optionally display a thousands separator (usually a comma) and choose how negative values are displayed (in black or red and with a leading minus sign or inside parentheses).
Currency	Displays values with a selectable currency symbol ($). You can also choose whether negative values are displayed with a minus sign or enclosed in parentheses, or whether they are displayed in the default font color or in red.
Accounting	Is similar to Currency, but the currency symbols and decimal points are lined up in a column.
Date	Displays a date value in the specified format.

continues

Table 16.2 Continued.

Number Format	Description
Time	Displays time values in a variety of formats, some of which also include the date.
Percentage	Displays numbers with a percent sign. This option automatically multiplies the number by 100 for display (for example, .25 = 25.00%).
Fraction	Displays a value as a whole number followed by the closest fraction (for example, 5.48 is displayed as 5 1/2, 5.89 is displayed as 5 8/9, and 5.92 is displayed as 6 when you select Up to One Digit).
Scientific	Displays values in scientific format (for example, 1234.56 is displayed as 1.23E+03).
Text	Displays values as they were originally entered. Note that if you format a formula as text, Excel displays it as text, not the value it computes.
Special	Displays values using special formatting rules such as Social Security number and phone number.
Custom	Displays values formatted with a user-supplied format string.

When You Don't See What You Want, Try Custom Formats

Does your company use a special date format you can't easily reproduce with one of Excel's standard formats? If so, custom formatting may be for you.

Excel 2000 lets you create your own formats using its Custom Format feature. To begin working with this feature, access the Number tab of the Format Cells dialog box, and then choose the Custom option.

A custom format is a string of characters that provides instructions Excel uses to display the value of a cell just the way you want it.

A custom format has four sections: the format for positive numbers, the format for negative numbers, the format for zeros, and the format for text. Semicolons are used to separate each of these sections. If you specify only one section, that format is used for all values. If you specify only the first two sections, zero values are displayed using the same format as it used for positive numbers. If you omit the negative numbers section but include the zero numbers section, the cell is left blank.

> **Tip: Try before you buy.** Custom formats can get rather complicated, so you
> might want to try them on some test data before you incorporate it into an
> important worksheet.

Each section in a format contains a sequence of characters. Some characters have a special meaning, as shown in Tables 16.3, 16.4, and 16.5. The global formatting characters
apply to all types of data, whereas the date and time help you format date and time values. The text and numeric formats are used to format text and numeric values.

You can arrange these characters to get the format you want. Some sample formats are
shown in Figure 16.2. As you type characters into the format box, the value of the currently selected cell is formatted and displayed in the dialog box. If you enter an invalid
format, Excel displays an error message asking you to correct the error. Just delete the
bad character and try it again.

Table 16.3   Global Common Custom Format Characters

Number Format	Description
"text"	Displays the text inside the quotation marks without change as part of the value. The following characters need not be enclosed in quotation marks: space, $, -, +, (,), and :. A backslash (\) must precede any of the following characters: !, ^, &, `, ', {, }, =, <, or >.
[color]	Displays the value as one of the following colors: black, blue, cyan, green, magenta, red, white, or yellow. Must be the start of the format section.
[condition]	Displays the value using the specified format only if the condition is true; otherwise, the next section of the format is used. Must be present at the start of a format section, and you are limited to two conditions.

Table 16.4   Date and Time Common Custom Format Characters

Date or Time Format	Description
[h]	Displays the value as elapsed time in hours.
[m]	Displays the value as elapsed time in minutes.
[s]	Displays the value as elapsed time in seconds.
AM/PM	Displays AM or PM when used with a time value. Also modifies an h or hh format to display hours in the range of 0–12 or 00–12, respectively.)

continues

Table 16.4 Continued.

Date or Time Format	Description
am/pm	Same as AM/PM except that the letters are displayed in lowercase.
a/p	Same as AM/PM except that a or p is displayed in place of AM or PM.
d	Displays days as 1–31.
dd	Displays days as 01–31.
ddd	Displays days as Sun–Sat.
dddd	Displays days as Sunday–Saturday.
E+	Displays the number in scientific notation (for example, 0.000E+0 displays 0.00012345 as 1.235E-4).
h	Displays hours as 0–23.
hh	Displays hours as 00–23.
m	Displays months as the numbers 1–12. (Also displays the minutes as 0–59 if immediately preceded by an h or hh or followed by an s or ss.)
mm	Displays months as the numbers 01–12. (Also displays the minutes as 00–59 if immediately preceded by an h or hh or followed by an s or ss.)
mmm	Displays months as Jan–Dec.
mmmm	Displays months as January–December.
mmmmm	Displays months as the first letter of the month.
yy	Displays years as 00–99.
yyyy	Displays years as 1900–9999.

Table 16.5 Numeric and Text Common Custom Format Characters

Number or Text Format	Description
0	Displays the specified digit in the number or a zero.
@	Displays a text value exactly as entered. When it is used by itself, this is the equivalent of the Text format.
*	Fills the cell with the character preceding the *. (For example, -* fills the cell with dashes.)
_	Displays a space that is exactly the width of the following character. (For example, the format 0.00_-;0.00- lines up the decimal points for positive and negative numbers.)

Number or Text Format	*Description*
#	Displays the specified digit in the number or nothing.
?	Displays spaces for leading zeros so that decimal points line up properly.
/	Displays values as a fraction. (For example, #/# displays 1/5 if the number is 0.2.)
,	Displays a thousands separator or displays a number in units of thousands if the comma is specified at the end of the format string. (For example, 0.0,, displays 123456789 as 123.5.)
$	Displays a dollar sign as part of the number. You also can use other currency symbols by directly entering them into the format section.
%	Displays a number as a percentage of 1. (For example, a value of 0.05 is displayed as 5%, whereas 1.23 is displayed as 123%.)

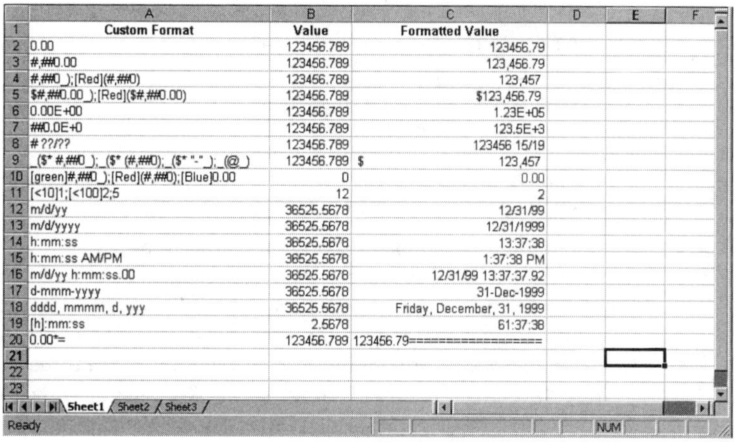

Custom Format	Value	Formatted Value
0.00	123456.789	123456.79
#,##0.00	123456.789	123,456.79
#,##0_);[Red](#,##0)	123456.789	123,457
$#,##0.00_);[Red]($#,##0.00)	123456.789	$123,456.79
0.00E+00	123456.789	1.23E+05
##0.0E+0	123456.789	123.5E+3
# ??/??	123456.789	123456 15/19
_($* #,##0_);_($* (#,##0);_($* "-"_);_(@_)	123456.789	$ 123,457
[green]#,##0_);[Red](#,##0);[Blue]0.00	0	0.00
[<10]1;[<100]2;5	12	2
m/d/yy	36525.5678	12/31/99
m/d/yyyy	36525.5678	12/31/1999
h:mm:ss	36525.5678	13:37:38
h:mm:ss AM/PM	36525.5678	1:37:38 PM
m/d/yy h:mm:ss.00	36525.5678	12/31/99 13:37:37.92
d-mmm-yyyy	36525.5678	31-Dec-1999
dddd, mmmm, d, yyy	36525.5678	Friday, December, 31, 1999
[h]:mm:ss	2.5678	61:37:38
0.00*=	123456.789	123456.79=================

FIGURE 16.2
You can create many different custom formats.

Putting Data in Its Proper Place by Aligning Values

This one tab—the Alignment tab of the Format Cells dialog box—can do more for the readability of your worksheet than almost any other. We've all seen worksheets with verbose, single-line column headings filled with a series of two- or three-digit values. The numbers almost get lost in the huge expanse of whitespace! And if a worksheet has multiple large column headers, you might not even be able to print the whole worksheet on a single sheet of paper. By using this tab, you can even center the cell's values to make it doubly clear which values belong where. This capability is especially helpful to those who might be skimming the worksheet for information in a hurry.

Using the Alignment tab of the Format Cells dialog box, you can adjust how the cell's value is displayed relative to the cell's borders. You can align the value both horizontally and vertically. If the value is too wide to be displayed in the cell, you can wrap the value so that the cell contains as many lines as necessary to display the value. All you have to do is click the Wrap Text option. You can also shrink the size of the font until the value fits in the cell by clicking the Shrink to Fit option. Each of these options helps the readers clarify which data belongs in which column.

Another interesting alignment option is Orientation. This option lets you slant the text along any angle; by doing so, you can easily add a title to a column that is relatively narrow (see Figure 16.3).

FIGURE 16.3

Orient a column title so that it will fit in a limited amount of space.

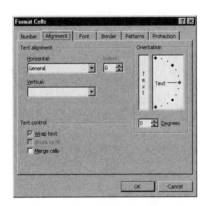

Peter's Principle: Get in align.

Although text alignment is often a matter of personal preference, I'd like to share some of my personal rules of thumb. For column headers, I usually avoid the Shrink to Fit option because I want to have full control over the appearance of these headings, and I want them to be consistent across the spreadsheet. If my spreadsheet contains only a few columns (maybe three to four), I typically use the Wrap Text option. That way, my worksheet fills the page without using any unnecessary whitespace. If I have a large worksheet (five columns or more), I make use of the angled Orientation option. This way, I can fit a tremendously large number of columns on a single sheet of paper while maintaining the worksheet's readability. Again, these are just my personal guides. Your desired action will vary depending on the length of the column titles and other aesthetic factors, including whether you're printing the worksheet in portrait or landscape mode.

Choosing Fonts for Your Spreadsheet

Give your spreadsheets a finished look by choosing fonts that draw attention to critical parts of the document. For example, use a font that's bigger and bolder than the body text for column headers, subtotals, grand totals, and any other information you might want to draw the readers' attention to.

> **Tip: Font changes quick and easy.** Sure, you can set these options via the Font tab of the Format Cells dialog box, but it may be simpler to select the cell or range of cells you want to format and then use the Font drop-down boxes and other buttons on the Formatting toolbar to make the desired changes.

You can display a cell's value using any font on your system and with any size (see Figure 16.4). The height of the row is automatically adjusted if the font is too tall to be displayed in the cell.

FIGURE 16.4
Choose any font on your system to format cells in your worksheet.

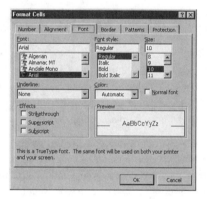

Giving Your Worksheet That Finished Look by Drawing Borders Around a Cell

Even though you see lines on your spreadsheet onscreen, they aren't really there. No, you aren't seeing things; it's just that these lines can be compared to the page break lines you see in Word. The lines aren't printed, but rather they serve as a guide for where one page ends and another begins. In Excel, the lines are called *gridlines,* and they can easily be turned on and off. Their role is merely to help you see the cells in the worksheet.

Borders, on the other hand, are lines that you can selectively turn on and off at the cell level. You can choose from a bunch of different line styles and even draw the lines in color (see Figure 16.5). Using borders is a great way to draw attention to parts of your worksheet as well as give it that finished look.

FIGURE 16.5
*Use borders to
make the impor-
tant parts of your
spreadsheet stand
out.*

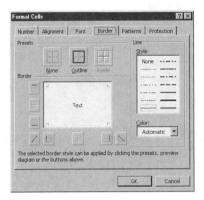

> **Tip: Borders only.** Turning off gridlines lets you see the real effect of the bor-
> ders you apply. To turn them off, simply click Tools|Options, open the View tab,
> and then uncheck the Gridlines check box in the Window Options section.

Livening Up the Background of Your Cells by Using Patterns

With Excel 2000's tremendous Web capabilities, you might find it desirable to add some
color to your worksheets. The same holds true if you plan to export the worksheet to
PowerPoint 2000 as part of a presentation. Even something as simple as coloring every
other row of your worksheet can liven it up as well as enhance its readability.

Consider this: Changing the properties of the fonts used in your worksheet affects only
the foreground part of the cells, whereas applying a pattern changes the background of
the cell. You can choose from an assortment of colors and patterns to be displayed in the
background of a cell. Just right-click the cell or cells you want to apply the pattern to,
and then access the Patterns tab to see your choices (see Figure 16.6).

FIGURE 16.6
*Select fonts to
change how the
foreground looks,
or select patterns
to change how
the background
looks.*

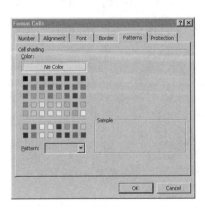

Tip: Dark gray plus white equals 3D. You can create your own 3D effects through the use of borders and patterns. First, select a light gray pattern that's the same color as the background of the dialog box. On the Border tab, select dark gray as the line color (hint: two color boxes above the light gray color box), and add top and left border lines. Change the color to white, and add the bottom and right border lines.

Protecting Your Worksheet from Unauthorized Modifications

When you think of protecting a worksheet, one thing instantly comes to mind—protecting the data from unauthorized changes. But you also should consider another type of protection, and that's the protection of potentially valuable information. If a worksheet containing pricing formulas for your company's products were to get in the wrong hands (namely a competitor), valuable trade secrets could be lost.

If you plan to let others access your worksheet, you might want to consider locking the cells so that others cannot change their values. Any attempt to change a locked cell results in an error message. Likewise, you can hide a formula used in a worksheet so that others can't see how you arrived at the displayed value.

By default, every cell in a worksheet is locked but not hidden. You can easily change this attribute by clicking the Select All button, right-clicking the worksheet, and selecting Format Cells from the shortcut menu. Open the Protection tab, and then check or uncheck the Locked and Hidden check boxes to apply the respective options to all the cells on your current worksheet.

Tip: Be selective. If you want colleagues to be able to play what-if games with the formulas you provide, consider locking only the cells containing the formulas. That way, you protect the sheet and maintain the interactivity. Just select the cell or range of cells you want to lock and/or hide, and then proceed with setting the options.

Tip: Don't lock the door and leave the key. Locking cells and hiding formulas are only the first steps in protecting your spreadsheet. The next step is to enable the worksheet's protection by clicking Tools|Protection|Protect Sheet from the main menu. You might optionally supply a password, which would be required if you later want to unprotect your worksheet.

Before and After: A Spreadsheet Makeover

In the highly competitive business world, you always need to put your best foot forward. Everything that you do and produce—the clothes you wear, the things you say, and the documents you produce—leaves people with a strong impression of you and your company.

Sometimes improving a spreadsheet's appearance doesn't take much time or effort. For example, in Figure 16.7, you can see how an unformatted spreadsheet looks using Print Preview. To create the spreadsheet in Figure 16.8, I made all the characters bold. Then I increased the font size to 12 point for the header at the top of each column. I used borders to draw a heavy line around my data, a double line between the headers, and the detail lines and normal border lines between each of the columns. Adding a gray pattern to every other line in the worksheet concluded my finishing touches. Which one would you rather show to your boss or your customer?

FIGURE 16.7
Before a little formatting magic...

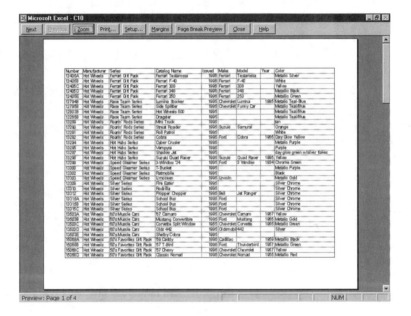

FIGURE 16.8
...after tweaking the alignment, font, border, and patterns format options.

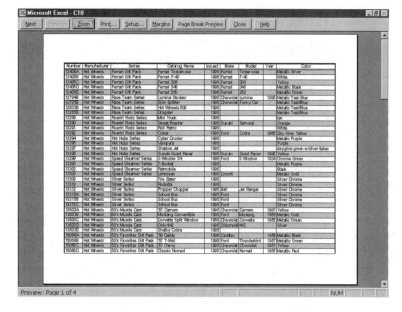

Using AutoFormat to Achieve Professional Results Quickly

In a perfect world, we would all have the time to leisurely peruse our spreadsheets and make them look just right. In reality, however, we are often forced to compromise quality for the sake of speed. With AutoFormat, your work needn't look like it fell victim to time constraints.

If you're not already familiar with AutoFormat, you should know that using this tool is an easy way to apply a set of standardized formats to a worksheet (see Figure 16.9). To do so, select a cell on the worksheet in the area you want to format, and click Format|AutoFormat. AutoFormat searches outward from that cell looking for empty cells to determine which cells you want it to format. Then it applies the format you selected from the list provided (see Figure 16.10). Note that this worksheet looks similar to the one in Figure 16.9, but took a lot less work to produce.

Figure 16.9
Choose a stan-dardized format to apply to your table.

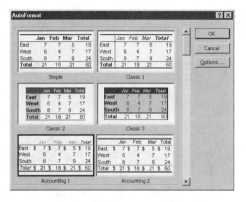

Figure 16.10
A professional-looking format-ting job is only a mouse click away.

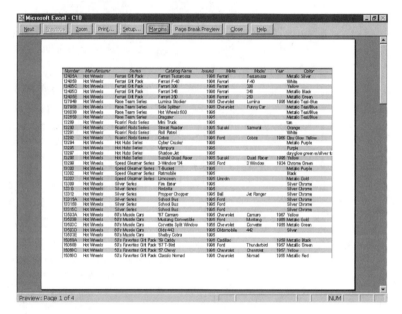

If you click the Options button on the AutoFormat dialog box, you can control which for-mats are applied. By default, AutoFormat adjusts the following properties: Number, Font, Alignment, Border, Patterns, and Width/Height. You can uncheck any of these properties before applying the AutoFormat.

Making Selected Data Stand Out Using Conditional Formatting

If your company maintains its inventory in Excel, wouldn't it be neat if you could have an item's entry turned yellow as stock starts to get low, or red when the values get critically low? Or how about having Excel flag values that dip below a certain percentage? All this is possible with *conditional formatting.*

Using conditional formatting, you can set borders, patterns, and selected font properties based on the value of a cell or a formula. To use conditional formatting, click Format|Conditional Formatting. A dialog box then appears with the fields to enter the first condition.

> **Note: How many conditions can I have anyway?** You are allowed to specify up to three different conditions for each cell. The formatting associated with the first condition that is true is used even if more than one condition is true.

To add a subsequent condition, click the Add button. The next condition you define then appears below the first one. To remove a condition, click the Delete button. A small dialog box appears asking which condition(s) you want to delete.

To set the formatting for a condition, click the Format button to display the normal Format Cells dialog box with tabs for Font, Border, and Patterns. You can select any combination of these formatting options, and the resulting format is displayed in a small window next to the Format button.

Formatting Based on Cell Value

As the examples I provided earlier would indicate, formatting a cell based on its value is perhaps the most common use of conditional formatting. To apply it, click Format|Conditional Formatting to display the dialog box shown in Figure 16.11. In the first drop-down box, choose Cell Value Is. In the second drop-down box, choose a relationship.

If you choose Between or Not Between as an operator, spaces for two values are displayed next to this box because you need to provide a range of values for the condition to be considered met. Choosing Equal To, Not Equal To, Greater Than, Less Than, Greater Than or Equal To, or Less Than or Equal To displays only a single value field. Enter the value or values into the field or fields, and then select the formats you want to use. Click OK to close the dialog box.

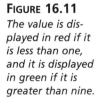

Figure 16.11

The value is displayed in red if it is less than one, and it is displayed in green if it is greater than nine.

Formatting Based on a Formula

So when would you want to format based on a formula? Let's revisit the inventory example I provided earlier. If you base formatting on a cell's value, you have to enter a separate condition and value for each inventory item because you obviously stock different amounts of each item. If, however, you base the formatting on a formula (for example, if the amount available is less than 25 percent, flag for reorder), then you needn't set each value separately. Why not let Excel do the work for you?

So if you need to choose formatting based on something more complicated than the cell's value, you should choose Formula Is from the first text box in the Conditional Formatting dialog box (see Figure 16.12). Then you can enter a formula that returns either True or False. If the formula returns True, its associated format is used. Just enter the formula as you would any other Excel formula.

Copying Conditional Formats

To copy a conditional format, select the cell with the format you want to copy, and then click the Format Painter icon. Next, you need to select the area where you want to use the same format. As soon as you release the mouse button, the conditional formats are applied. This is the perfect way to implement the inventory by the formula conditional formatting described in the preceding section.

Adjusting Rows and Columns to Achieve the Desired Effect

When you're formatting an important document, you often have requirements with regard to space or the desired visual effect. As you already know, Excel makes it easy to change the appearance of text, but it also makes it easy to adjust the height and width of the rows and columns in a worksheet. You can simply click the line following the column header or row header you want to resize, and drag the line in the desired direction to adjust the column width or row height. A small ToolTip appears while you are dragging the line, telling you the size of the cell(s) in points and pixels.

Tip: Automatic resizing. The most common reason for adjusting a column's width is to allow the complete value in a cell to be displayed. This is especially true when you're dealing with a column full of text values such as a column header, a person's name, a mailing address, or something similar. Although you can makes these adjustments manually as I showed you in the preceding paragraph, you can also have Excel do it for you by selecting the column or columns you want to adjust, and then clicking Format|Column|AutoFit Selection. Excel determines the width of the largest value in each column and adjusts the width of the column(s) accordingly. Choosing Format|Row|AutoFit Selection does the same thing for setting row height.

If uniform column size is a priority for whatever reason, you can set a standard column width for the current worksheet by clicking Format|Column|Standard Width. This new column size is used any time you insert a new column into the worksheet. Any existing columns are automatically adjusted to the new standard column width as well.

Tip: One leads but many follow. If you want to set the column width or row height for multiple columns or rows, select multiple headers and then drag the dividing line following any of the selected headers. This action automatically sets all the selected columns or rows to the new value size.

Hiding Critical Worksheet Information

Earlier in the chapter, you learned how to hide a cell's formula, but what if you want to hide entire columns or rows of your spreadsheet? Hiding information might be desirable if you want to enter actual costs of materials on the worksheet instead of in the formula itself.

Peter's Principle: Nipping potential problems in the bud.

Many people, myself included, find it easier to edit values in a cell instead of in a formula, as would be the case if you simply hid the formula. That way, complex formulas don't inadvertently get modified. All it takes is an accidental key press or an incorrect piece of data, and you could find yourself spending hours trying to figure out where the problem started. Did you enter an incorrect value into a cell? Which formula contains the problem? I find having everything in front of me makes it easier to spot problems. That way, I'm not browsing every single cell trying to uncover subtle formula errors.

You can hide columns in Excel by selecting one or more columns and then clicking Format|Column|Hide from the menu bar. When your worksheet is displayed, those columns are simply no longer displayed. They are present on the spreadsheet and can be included in any calculations, but the users can't see them.

To redisplay the columns, select a range of columns that include the hidden cells, and then click Format|Column|Unhide. The cells then become visible once again. Note that you can also hide rows using the same technique. The main difference is that you choose Format|Row rather than Format|Column.

> **Tip: Hide and don't seek.** Suppose you are a salesperson visiting a customer's site, and you have your list of products stored in an Excel worksheet. You might want to use the hide feature of Excel to conceal your cost for a product or any other confidential information, for example.

Printing Excel Output

If you've used spreadsheet programs for several years, you're undoubtedly familiar with the various printing headaches you can encounter. Will the whole spreadsheet fit on the paper? Will your column data line up? Can you put a border where you want it?

Printing a worksheet can be as easy as clicking the Print button, but what you get might not be what you really want. Investing a few minutes of effort setting a few options will generate a large return in how your document looks.

Selecting Cells for Printing

Just because your worksheet has 89 rows of data doesn't mean you want to print all 89 rows of data. Printing a summary of cells that recap the essence of the entire worksheet is often desirable, especially if that worksheet is to serve as a handout for a presentation. People want—and need—their information fast, so saying what you want quickly and succinctly is more important than ever before.

By default, Excel prints all the nonempty cells on your worksheet. If you want to print only some of the cells, select the cells you want to print, and then click File|Print Area|Set Print Area. This action sets the print area, which you can confirm by using Excel's Print Preview feature. Your selection is saved for use down the road as well, so you needn't reselect the desired range of cells unless you want to print a different range.

Tip: Why can't I just select the cells I want to print, and then choose Print Selection on the regular Print dialog box? Although it's true that you can print selected cells that way as well, your selection is not saved for future use, as is the case with the method just described. If you're printing the data one time only, the most efficient method is to select the cells and go directly into the Print dialog box, but for repeated use, you should go through the steps to set the print area. That approach will save you tons of time in the future.

If you want to undo your selection, simply click File|Print Area|Clear Print Area to reset Excel's default to printing all nonempty cells instead of the set print area.

Setting Page Breaks

If your spreadsheet doesn't fit on a single page, Murphy's Law says that the page break will always occur in the wrong place, usually cutting off something critical like a grand total. Using manual page breaks, however, overrules Murphy's Law by letting you place the page breaks where you want them to occur, not where Excel decides they should go.

To set a page break, select the row header that you want to start the new page with, and then click Insert|Page Break from the menu bar. A dashed line then appears between the row you selected and the row above it. This line indicates where the page break now actually occurs.

Tip: Suck it in! If all of a worksheet but one or two lines fits onto a single sheet of paper, I usually try to tweak the top and bottom margins until it all fits. The easiest way to adjust the margins is to click the Print Preview button and follow the detailed directions given in the "Graphically Setting Margins" section later in the chapter.

You can also set vertical page breaks by selecting the column header before the desired page breakpoint and clicking Insert|Page Break.

Tip: Breaking pages. If the rows in your worksheet span more columns than you can fit on a single page, consider inserting vertical page breaks and repeating some information at the start of each row to make it easy for people to follow the row across multiple sheets of paper. This information might simply be the row headers or names you've given the rows.

See What You're Getting Ahead of Time by Using Print Preview

Spreadsheets can be finicky beasts to print, so why not do what you can to make sure you get what you want before sending the output to the printer? Not only will you save time and paper, but you might save a trip across the office to the network printer for unacceptable output.

Short of printing your worksheet, the best way to know what it will look like when it is printed is to use Excel's Print Preview feature (see Figure 16.13). In addition to viewing the page, you can use Print Preview to change many of the parameters such as page orientation, page headers and footers, and margins. You can access the tools needed to change these parameters by using the buttons described here. I'll go into greater detail on some of the more complex selections in the following sections.

- Next—Takes you to the next page in your document. If you are at the last page in the document, this button is disabled.
- Previous—Moves you to the previous page. This button is disabled when you are on the first page of your document.
- Zoom—Switches the preview display from full page to full-size text.
- Print—Displays the Print dialog box.
- Setup—Brings up the Page Setup dialog box.
- Margins—Allows you to define the page margins graphically.
- Page Break Preview—Returns you to the normal worksheet view, but shrinks the worksheet and displays bright blue lines that you can move to adjust the page boundaries.
- Close—Returns you to the normal worksheet view.

Setting Up Your Pages to Get the Output You Want

The first Print Preview tool that requires further explanation is the Setup tool. When you click the Setup button from within Print Preview (or click File|Page Setup from the menu bar while working in Excel), the Page Setup dialog box opens. This dialog box has four tabs—Page, Margins, Header/Footer, and Sheet—that you can use to adjust how the worksheet will be printed.

FIGURE 16.13

Print Preview shows what your worksheet will look like before you print it.

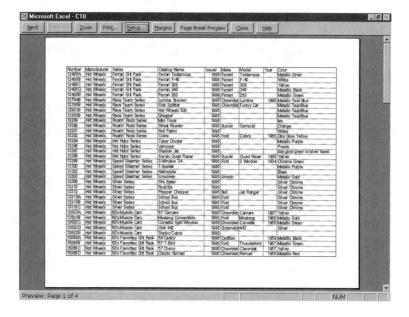

Getting Data to Fit by Tweaking Page Tab Settings

If you have a wide spreadsheet, the printed output's going to look a whole lot better if you print it in landscape mode, even if it means rolling over to a second sheet of paper. Of course, if uniform font size isn't a big issue, you could try Excel's page scaling feature. You can find all these options on the Page tab of the Page Setup dialog box. I won't get into the nitty-gritty of how to set these various options because you already know how to do that. I'm here to point out the value of some of the unique features you may not have had the time to discover and to show you how you can use them to your advantage.

On the Page tab (see Figure 16.14), you also can set various printer options such as paper size and print quality and even access the printer driver details by clicking the Options button.

FIGURE 16.14

On the Page tab, you can define the physical characteristics of the printer page.

One of the most interesting options that you can set on this tab is scaling. You can tell Excel to increase or decrease the size of your worksheet by specifying the percent of normal size. You can also instruct Excel to shrink the worksheet so that it fits within the specified number of horizontal pages and vertical pages.

> **Tip: Less is more.** Try to structure your worksheet so that it is no more than one page wide. If you can't fit the page in portrait mode, try landscape. Reduce any column widths you can and, if necessary, shrink the worksheet to fit. Reading a worksheet that is two or three pages wide and one, two, or even three pages tall is more difficult.

Setting Margin Values Manually

If you've ever had to squeeze an enormous amount of information into a tiny space, then you've undoubtedly already used the old margin trick. You know the one I'm talking about—the one in which you reduce the size of a page's margins so that you can fit as much data on there as humanly possible. I've seen it employed on the grant applications of many small nonprofit organizations. Of course, there's an art to this tactic, too. You must make enough of an adjustment so that everything fits, but it should be subtle enough so as not to draw immediate attention.

Using the Margins tab on the Page Setup dialog box, you can specify the size of each margin and the placement of any headers and footers (see Figure 16.15). You can also choose to center the worksheet on the page horizontally or vertically.

> **Tip: It depends on the effect you're after.** If you have plenty of room on the page for your data, adding headers and footers can give your document that polished look. If you're cramped for space, however, why not omit them? That way, you can leave more room for what's really important!

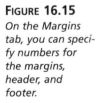

FIGURE 16.15

On the Margins tab, you can specify numbers for the margins, header, and footer.

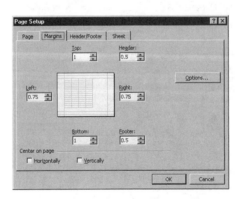

> **Tip: We control the horizontal.** Unless you specifically tell Excel to center your worksheet horizontally and vertically by clicking the applicable options on the Margins tab, the worksheet might look somewhat unbalanced. Why? Because, by default, Excel pushes the worksheet to the top of the page against the left margin. Centering it, however, gives you a much more professional-looking result.

Giving Your Worksheets Professional Appeal with Headers and Footers

One good way to help readers define the purpose and intent of your spreadsheet is to include headers and footers. Not only do these elements communicate information above and beyond that which can be expressed in worksheet titles and/or column headers, but they give a document a finished, professional look. Headers and footers can also help identify stray documents because the elements might contain a name, organization, or other identifiable information.

Excel allows you to specify a standard header and a standard footer to be displayed on each printed page. You can choose from a series of predefined values or create your own by clicking Custom Header or Custom Footer (see Figure 16.16).

FIGURE 16.16
Creating custom headers and footers is easy.

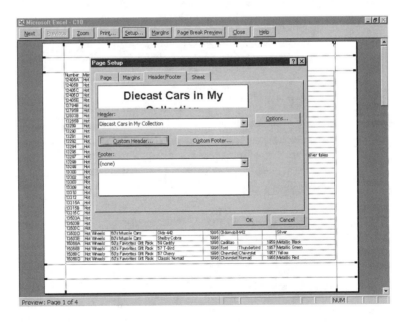

The three sections in the Custom Header or Footer dialog box allow you to specify text to be printed against the left margin, centered on the page, or justified against the right margin. You can also insert special variables that can display the current page number, page count, date, time, filename, and worksheet name. You can do so easily by using the buttons located immediately above the section windows.

You can also change the character font used in your headers or footers. Just select the text you want to modify, and then click the Font (A) button. The standard Font dialog box appears, ready for you to make your selections as you normally would. Just remember that you need to repeat this step for each section of the header and/or footer you want to modify.

Polishing the Document by Using Sheet Tab Options

If you want to know where to go to have the gridlines printed on your worksheet, the Sheet tab of the Page Setup dialog box is the place. Or if your worksheet spans multiple pages and you want the column headers to appear on every page for the sake of readability, you should become familiar with this tab.

> **Tip: Make it easy on yourself.** If you're going to select column or row headers to be repeated on every page, click the button at the far right of the option's text box you want to set. The dialog box disappears but leaves the text box ready to receive the data. Click the text box's title bar, and drag it out of the way if needed. Next, select the column(s) or row(s) you want to have repeated based on the option you chose, and then click the button inside the text box again to reopen the entire dialog box. You'll notice that the cell range of the repeating cells is entered for you using the proper syntax, so you needn't worry about a thing.

The Sheet tab provides some additional options you might want to set (see Figure 16.17). In addition to the options I just pointed out, you can choose to convert the document to black and white before printing and print it using draft quality to conserve toner when printing drafts. And if your worksheet doesn't fit on a single sheet of paper, you can specify whether multiple pages are printed and then numbered left to right first, or up and down first.

FIGURE 16.17
Find more ways to tweak your worksheet on the Sheet tab.

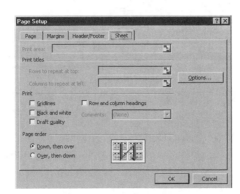

Tip: The starting grid. Disabling gridlines when you're printing a worksheet makes any borders you may have applied really stand out. However, if your worksheet doesn't use borders, make sure that the Gridlines box is checked to improve its readability. The gridlines make it significantly easier for readers' eyes to follow the data.

Graphically Setting Margins

The easiest way to tweak your worksheet so that everything fits on one piece of paper is to adjust the margins graphically. Sure, you can set new values for the margin size, but that's little more than making a stab in the dark. By adjusting the margins graphically, you can actually see what you're getting while you work, which will save you time in the long run.

Clicking the Margins button on the Print Preview toolbar (see Figure 16.18) displays the current margin settings. To adjust them, run the mouse pointer over the line until the pointer turns into a double-headed arrow, and then click and drag the lines around on the worksheet preview until you achieve the desired result.

FIGURE 16.18

By changing margins graphically, you know immediately how the worksheet will be affected.

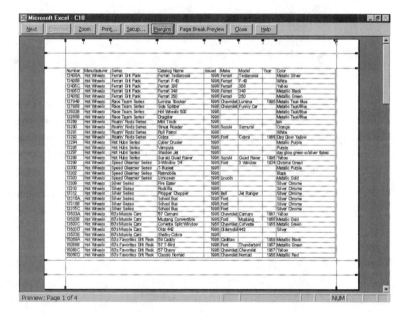

Getting Page Breaks to Fall Where You Want Them

Choosing the right place to put a page break is often confusing because you're never quite sure how the pages will look until you go into Print Preview and scroll through the various pages of your workbook. However, Print Preview enables you to display a large view of your worksheet so that you can see where the page breaks occur. Just click the Page Break Preview button on the Print Preview toolbar to see the view shown in Figure 16.19.

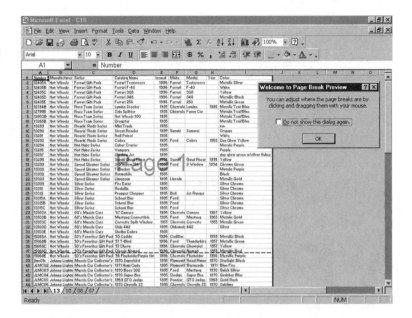

Each page is clearly marked with the page number and a bright blue border, which you can move to adjust where the page break occurs. Just run your mouse pointer over the line until the double-headed arrow appears, and then click and drag the line into position. You can also use the Insert|Page Break and the Insert|Remove Page Break menu commands to change the page breaks while in this mode.

When you're finished, click the Print Preview button. The button that was labeled Page Break Preview is now labeled Normal View. Clicking Normal View returns you to the worksheet in Normal view.

> **Note: You might not get what you're expecting.** Note that if you click the Close button at this point, you return to your worksheet in Page Break Preview mode instead of the Normal view.

Excel and the Web

Although Excel 97 could save documents in HTML format and publish them to the Web, it often had many limitations that prevented this feature from being truly useful. For example, readers could not interact with the document in any way; the result was a static Web page much like a typical text-based page.

Excel 2000 removes these limitations. Not only can you save workbooks as HTML documents, but you can now allow people to manipulate them using their Web browser! They can sort and filter data over the Web and turn static information into meaningful data right before their very eyes. What a wonderful decision-making tool for corporate executives!

Publishing Pages with Ease Using Web Folders

Web folders are a new feature of Office 2000; they allow you to access files on a Web server just like they were found on your local hard disk. They make publishing an Excel document to the Web a trivial matter. Of course, you need the proper information (server names, passwords, directory names, and such) from your network administrator or Webmaster to access the Web server and get your Web folders properly mapped.

After you finish all the setup work, publishing to the Web is as easy as saving a document.

Saving Excel Documents in HTML Format

Before you can place a spreadsheet on the Web, you need to make sure it's in a format that can be read by Web browsers as opposed to requiring the reader to download the file and view it using Excel 2000. This universal format is known as HTML. To save an Excel document in HTML format, simply click File|Save As Web Page from the menu bar.

When you save your Excel document in HTML format, you have a number of decisions to make. First, you can save a static version of a single worksheet or the entire workbook. The static versions of these documents can't be manipulated by using a Web browser. But saving static versions may be just fine for publishing documents where the object is to communicate information as opposed to provide data for analysis by others. You simply select either the entire workbook or the current selection, and then click Save to save the document or click Publish to display the dialog box shown in Figure 16.20.

If you select an individual object such as a chart or worksheet, you can also check the Add Interactivity With box to allow people with Web browsers to interactively work with your worksheet or chart.

Caution: Stalled interactions. Of course, if you want to incorporate this inter-activity into your document, you need to make sure that the Excel Web Components and Office Server Extensions are installed on your Web server.

Figure 16.20
Publish your Excel document as a Web page.

On the Publish as Web Page dialog box, you can choose the level of functionality for interactive documents. Otherwise, it does the same basic job that the Save As dialog box does. Note that if you want to view PivotTables interactively over the Web, you must publish the document and select PivotTable functionality.

Tip: Gee, that's obvious. If all the users who will access your workbook have Excel available on their computers, you can also make your workbook available in .XLS format on your Web site. Users with Internet Explorer 4.0 or greater can automatically start Excel inside the browser when they reference the workbook.

HTML Formatting Issues for Interactive Documents

In Excel 2000, you can save workbooks in HTML format and load them back into Excel again without any loss of data. However, this doesn't mean that your HTML version of the document will look identical to the native version of the document. They might look different because Excel allows you to perform some tasks that are impossible in HTML. For instance, because you can't display rotated text in HTML, any cells containing rotat-ed text are displayed as horizontal text. Table 16.6 lists some of the key differences between HTML documents and regular documents. You should take all these points into consideration when designing your document for the Web.

Table 16.6   Key HTML Limitations

Feature	Description
Rotated text	Is displayed horizontally
Dotted or dashed borders	Are displayed as a single solid line
Conditional formatting	Is not used; the default format is used instead
A single cell with multiple fonts	Is displayed using the default font
Graphics	Are lost if you publish the entire worksheet
Drawing objects	Are lost
Cell comments	Are lost
Outlining information	Is lost
3D charts	Are converted to 2D charts
Surface charts	Are converted to column charts
Custom positioning and sizing of chart objects	Are lost; defaults are used instead
References to other worksheets	Are converted to a value

Accessing Workbooks via the Web

Accessing workbooks on the Web is easy; just fire up your Web browser and open the document. There are, however, some major differences in the way the various static and interactive documents work.

Viewing Static Documents on the Web

To view a static document, simply enter the URL into your browser's address bar. If you're viewing a workbook, you might see a display like the one shown in Figure 16.21. You see the base Web page and a list of worksheets and charts available at the bottom of the document, similar to the way the tabs for the worksheets and charts are displayed at the bottom of the workbook in Excel. Clicking the name of a worksheet displays the worksheet or chart in the area above.

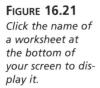

FIGURE 16.21
*Click the name of
a worksheet at
the bottom of
your screen to dis-
play it.*

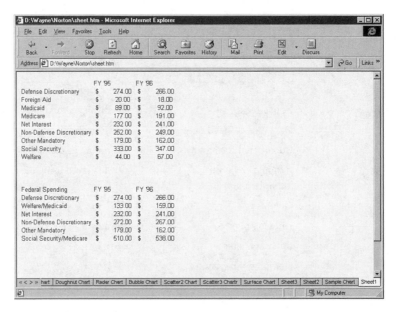

Whereas a single Web page can hold one worksheet or chart, an entire work-book needs to generate multiple Web pages, one for each sheet. Given that, sav-ing the workbook in HTML format results in more information than you might expect. Excel automatically creates a base Web page with the name you specify for the workbook. Then it creates a directory with the name of your workbook followed by files to hold the individual Web pages corresponding to each of the worksheets and charts in your workbook.

> **Caution: I've been framed.** Viewing an HTML-formatted workbook requires a browser that supports frames; therefore, many older browsers and most light-weight browsers may have a problem viewing your workbook.

Letting Users See Data Their Way Using the Spreadsheet Component

The Office Web Components allow you to access your worksheet and make changes to it while using a Web browser (see Figure 16.22). Although this facility is not nearly as powerful as Excel itself, it is useful when you want to create some worksheets that others might use. For example, this function could be used to let people enter data and calculate information for an employee expense report, and then send the Web page to someone else for processing. Take a look at Table 16.7 to get an idea of just how powerful these interactive Web features are.

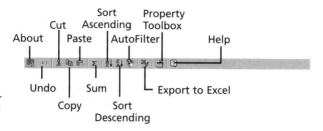

FIGURE 16.22
Viewing an interactive worksheet over the Web.

Table 16.7   Interactive Spreadsheet Buttons

Button	Function
About	Displays an About menu for the Office Web Components
Undo	Reverses the previous change
Cut	Copies the data to the Clipboard and deletes it from the worksheet
Copy	Copies the data to the Clipboard
Paste	Copies data from the Clipboard to the worksheet
Sum	Adds a series of values
Sort Ascending/Sort Descending	Allows you to sort the data in a worksheet in ascending or descending order
AutoFilter	Allows you to hide rows in your worksheet based on the information you provide
Export to Excel	Starts an Excel session using the data from the Web site
Property Toolbox	Displays this dialog box
Help	Accesses the help subsystem

> **Caution: I've lost all my work!** One disadvantage of using a Web page to distribute a worksheet is that the users can't save the results of their data manipulation. Although they can send the Web page to someone or export the page into Excel, the original Web page itself remains untouched. Of course, many people would also look at this as a big advantage if the data is sensitive in nature.

As you saw in Table 16.7, the typical Undo, Cut, Copy, Paste, Sum, and Sort buttons are available in the Web-based worksheets also. The AutoFilter function allows you to choose which rows are displayed in a table. This capability is useful when you have large tables and you want to see only a subset of the values. For example, an online Olympic spreadsheet would let you view only gymnasts, only United States athletes, and so on. As long as the fields exist, you can sort and filter by them.

> **Note: Somewhere out there.** Even though some filtered rows aren't displayed, their values are still available for calculations.

Achieving Advanced Functionality via the Properties Toolbox

One of the buttons mentioned in Table 16.7 that merits further investigation is the Properties Toolbox button. Using the Property Toolbox (see Figure 16.23), you can perform a lot of the more advanced functions that exist in Excel but that are difficult to work with using just a Web browser. Normally, you could access these functions by right-clicking and selecting from a shortcut menu in Excel, or by accessing one of Excel's many toolbars. Table 16.8 gives you a quick glance at the settings available on the Property Toolbox.

FIGURE 16.23

Using the Property Toolbox, you can change many of the elements on the worksheet.

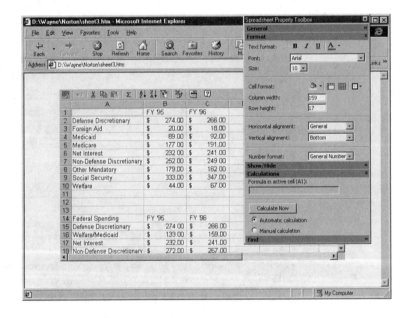

Table 16.8 Property Toolbox Options

Option	Function
General section	Supplies an Undo button and a button to access the help facility
Format section	Allows you to change the characteristics of a cell and its data
Show/Hide section	Allows you to change how the worksheet is displayed in your browser
Calculations section	Displays the current value or formula in a cell and recalculates the values in the worksheet
Find section	Displays a simple Find command that can find a text string in the worksheet

Probably the two must useful sections of the Property Toolbox are the Format and Calculations sections. Using the Format section, you can make basic changes in the selected cells' format, including changing the font (including color, size and font name); merging cells and setting borders; setting the row height and column width for a cell; specifying alignment; and specifying the number format used to display numeric information.

The Calculations section shows the name of the current cell and its contents. You can also click the Calculate Now button to force the spreadsheet to recalculate the results on the spot, or choose to let the Office Web Component recalculate the values in the worksheet automatically or upon demand.

Getting Live Visual Results with the Chart Component

If you thought being able to manipulate data on the Web was neat, you'll be thrilled to see that you can incorporate the same level of interactivity into online charts.

An interactive chart uses the Office Web Components to display a chart and a worksheet containing the data used to create the chart (see Figure 16.24). All the functions of the interactive worksheet are available for you to change the data in the chart. Any changes to any of the cell values charted are immediately reflected in the chart.

FIGURE 16.24
*You can change
the data in an
interactive chart
on the Web.*

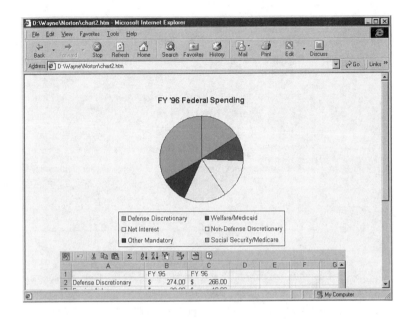

> **Caution: For your eyes only.** Any changes you (or anyone else) make to the
> Web page are not saved. As soon as you leave the site, the data is restored to its
> original state.

Although you can't change the chart type or any of the chart's characteristics, you can
change the number of data points displayed in the chart. For example, inserting a new
row adds a new set of values to the chart. Of course, the new row must be added after the
first row and before the last row in the chart because you can't change the range of cells
included in the chart.

You can also use the AutoFilter feature of the worksheet to select or hide rows. Any hidden rows are not displayed in the chart. You can build one large chart containing a lot of
information and then use this feature to focus on smaller subsets of the information
rather than build several smaller charts. For example, a company might publish a chart
about the productivity of its sales force, and you can further break it down to discover
who sold the most units of a particular item or which sales team had the biggest percentage of sales for the month.

Flexible Data Analysis Using the PivotTable Component

The ultimate Web-based data analysis tool is Excel's PivotTable Component (see Figure
16.25). Using this tool, you can manipulate the PivotTable just as if you were using

Excel. You can drag and drop fields into different positions on the PivotTable, and it is automatically updated to display information just as you want to see it. You can also select which values you want to see in a particular field by clicking the drop-down arrow button at the end of each field.

FIGURE **16.25**

View an interactive PivotTable over the Web.

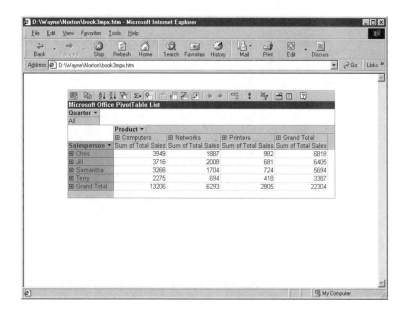

The only drawback to using PivotTables over the Web is that you cannot create a new PivotTable; you can only manipulate one that has been published to the Web with PivotTable functionality. Of course, PivotTables are still powerful and dynamic analytical tools for managers and just about anyone else who might want to put a different spin on the data that's available.

Peter's Principle: Make sure it says what you want it to.

Anyone who's been in business for a period of time knows the power of statistics. The way you present the information can make all the difference in the world as to how the data is perceived and received. Consider annual sales statistics as an example. Total sales of $125,000 for the past year might not seem like a lot to the onlooker unless you point out that this number is more than double what it was the previous year. Whenever I contemplate publishing an interactive worksheet, I spend a fair amount of time playing with the data first to make sure that the information I've made available can't be used against me, so to speak. If the data looks worse one way than another, either consider publishing a static worksheet, or remove the problem fields from the worksheet so that they can't be used.

In addition to PivotTables, the PivotTable Component allows you to manipulate PivotCharts (see Figure 16.26). The PivotTable Component displays the PivotChart with the PivotTable beneath it. Unlike Excel, in which you can manipulate the values directly on the chart, on the Web you have to manipulate the PivotTable below the PivotChart to change the information on the PivotChart.

Figure 16.26
On the Web, you manipulate a PivotTable to change the PivotChart.

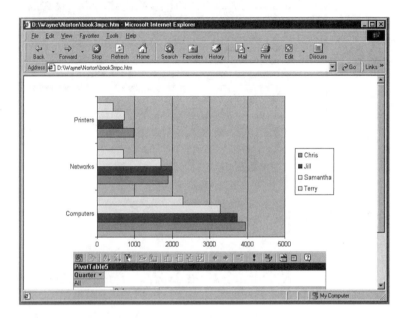

On Your Own

This chapter concludes my coverage of Excel, but you still have a lot more to learn. And the best way to learn it is to practice, so just for practice, enter some data into a worksheet. Have some fun with it. Use your coworkers' names and some mock statistics making you out to be the top salesperson of the year. Or plug in the names of your family members (including pets), and insert fantasy incomes for the next five years. What you put in the worksheet doesn't matter as long as you have data to work with. Be sure to include column headers for each column and row headers for each row. Add row totals at the end of each row and column totals at the bottom of each column.

Then change the worksheet's format so that it becomes more readable. Try shading every other row in the worksheet to make it easier to associate a specific cell with its row headers. Use borders to highlight and separate header information from the body of the table. Also, separate the totals from the main body of numbers. Don't display any gridlines for the main body of numbers, but add a title to the worksheet that spans more than one column.

Next, take the formatted worksheet, make a few adjustments, and send it to the printer. Delete the header, and add a header and footer using page setup. Adjust the margins so that the worksheet's information is centered horizontally but is at the top of the page vertically.

Finally, create a chart or two using the techniques found in Chapter 15, "Analyzing Your Data in Excel," and save the complete workbook as a static Web document. Save one of the charts to the Web also with interactive support enabled. Then load the chart in your Web browser (you can do so locally—you needn't actually publish it to the Web), change some of the data, and verify that the chart reflects your new changes.

Did it work? It's amazing how much you can do with Excel, and we've only scratched the surface! As a cool-down after all this work, think about your workplace or an organization you may volunteer for. How could they tap into the power and flexibility of these new Web Components?

PART IV

Using Outlook 2000

Using Outlook 2000 for Email

When you want to email with Office 2000, you have numerous options. If you have extensive personal information management needs as well, you can use Outlook 2000 as your messaging and collaboration client. Combine it with the use of Exchange Server on your company's network, and you'll have unsurpassed power and functionality for meeting, planning, and scheduling, as well as offline folder synchronization.

If you want to send richly formatted messages to others with HTML-enabled email clients, you can opt to send Office 2000 documents saved as HTML via Outlook 2000. That way, others (even WebTV users) can view your Word 2000 and Excel 2000 documents without even having the application installed on their machines.

Finally, if your needs are simply emailing and managing a contact list, Outlook Express may be more than enough for the task at hand. Outlook Express has the added advantage in that its resident newsreader eliminates the need for you to learn a separate application for both functions.

> **Note: Looking back...**Chapter 6 included an Internet Explorer 5 quick course that also addressed news reading in Outlook Express. Note that although emailing with Outlook Express is not covered specifically in this book, doing it is nearly identical to the process used for reading the newsgroups.

In this chapter, I'll introduce you to the concept of emailing with Outlook 2000. We'll look at everything from managing multiple signature files to designing stationery to filtering and organizing messages.

Getting Started

When you launch Outlook 2000 for the very first time, you see a wizard that asks whether you want to migrate your current email program settings and files to Outlook 2000. If you're sure you want to make the leap, work your way through the next few wizard screens. They're pretty self-explanatory, so you needn't worry about completing them on your own. I have bigger plans for you in the pages that make up this chapter.

If you're upgrading from an earlier version of Outlook, the settings and files are imported into the new Outlook automatically. If you're like me and have decided to take a peek at Outlook 2000 before moving everything over, you'll need to learn how to add your email accounts and import messages and address information. We'll pick up with that discussion in a moment.

IMAP4 and POP3: Do You Know the Difference?

Internet Mail Access Protocol (IMAP) and Post Office Protocol (POP) are the two most commonly used types of email accounts in existence today, but they behave very differently.

When you view email residing on an IMAP server, the messages stay on the server until you specifically move them to a local folder or mark them for deletion and then purge them from the Inbox. As a result, you can view mail from a variety of locations, making IMAP the superior choice for business people on the go or for users who need to access mail on different computers (as might be the case in a multicomputer family). IMAP folders can also store drafts of notes so that you can work on them from the office or from home without having to copy the drafts onto a disk or email them to yourself. And because you can select which messages to download for viewing, you can save valuable long distance connection time while on the road by grabbing the important messages only and then logging off.

Peter's Principle: Got IMAP?

IMAP is an undiscovered treasure. In fact, many Internet service providers (ISPs) still don't support it because few people have discovered that they really want—or need—it. Investigating the option may be worth your time if you find yourself checking mail from multiple locations. Just think—no more cutting disks to work on something at home; no more missed messages because someone accessing the POP account from another machine forgot to tell you about the message; and no more sending yourself email just to get the job done. If your Internet service provider does not currently support IMAP, nor does the provider have any intention of doing so in the near future, now may be the time to look for another ISP. IMAP support typically does not cost any more than POP, and it really can save you a lot of time and headaches.

POP3 is a whole different matter. When you attempt to read messages from a POP3 server, the messages are immediately downloaded to your computer unless you've explicitly set your options to the contrary. Having the files downloaded could spell trouble when accounts are shared or accessed from more than one location if you're not careful.

With all of IMAP's good points, I can think of one potentially annoying side effect to using it. (Isn't there always?) Just keep in mind, however, that it ultimately may affect only a minute percentage of users. Some major companies might route local mail and scheduling differently than they route Internet mail, which may mean you have two separate Inboxes to keep an eye on. I'll provide more details on this issue shortly.

Adding a New Email Account

Whether you need to set up your Outlook 2000 email server for the first time or simply need to add a second email account, you need to follow these steps to get the account up and running:

1. Launch Outlook 2000, and then click Tools|Accounts.

2. Click the Add button on the Internet Accounts dialog box, and then select Mail from the drop-down menu. The first screen of the Internet Connection Wizard appears.

3. The first bit of information you are asked to provide is your Display Name, or the name that appears in the From line of all your outgoing email messages. Enter it as you would like it to appear, and then click Next.

4. Entering your email address is the next order of business. Type it in, and then click Next.

5. You then are asked to supply information about your email servers, including the type of server (IMAP or POP) and the names of both the incoming and outgoing mail servers. Note that server names are often made up of the following components: `type.domain.extension` as in `pop.smart.net`. That's not always the case, however, so you might need to verify the information with your Internet service provider. Click Next to proceed.

6. Internet mail logon information comes next. This information includes your username, password, and whether you are required to log on with Secure Password Authentication (SPA). Click Next.

Caution: It's not the same. The Internet Connection Wizard assumes that the first part of your email address (the user ID or anything before the @ sign) is also the Account Name in step 6. This may not be the case at all, especially if you have multiple email addresses sharing the account or need special information to log on to your company's server. Be sure to verify that this field is correct before moving to the next screen. Doing so will save you endless amounts of time and frustration from aborted logon attempts.

7. Choose your connection type by clicking the respective option button, and then click Next.

8. Outlook 2000 congratulates you on successfully configuring your connection. Click Finish to save your settings.

Importing Mail Data from Other Email Clients

If you used another email client in the past, you might decide to import your email settings, addresses, and messages themselves to Outlook 2000. You can do so using the Import and Export Wizard, as described here:

1. Launch Outlook 2000, and then click File|Import and Export. The Import and Export Wizard shown in Figure 17.1 appears.

FIGURE 17.1
The Import and Export Wizard makes it easy to import exactly what you want.

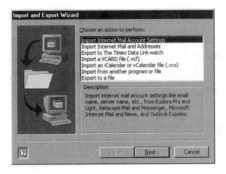

2. Click the action you want to perform, verify it is the correct action by reading Microsoft's description, and then click Next to continue.

3. In the next screen, select the name of the email application from which you want to import files, and then check the boxes that apply. For example, you can import the mail but not the addresses, or vice versa. Click Next after you've verified your selections.

4. Select a destination for the items within Outlook 2000. After you've done that, you need to tell Outlook 2000 what to do with duplicate information. By default, Outlook 2000 creates the duplicate entries. To save disk space, you can opt to replace duplicate Outlook 2000 entries with the ones to be imported, or you can tell Outlook 2000 not to import the duplicates at all.

5. Click Finish to set the import in motion.

> **Caution: Good things come to those who wait.** And wait is what you may be doing if you plan to import large numbers of messages and Address Book entries. Although you can continue to work on your computer during the import (and that does include working in Outlook 2000), you should still be aware that this is not a simple one-minute operation. You might even want to run the Import and Export Wizard over a mid-morning break or while you're away at a meeting so that your machine can dedicate all its resources to the task without hindering your work.

IMAP and POP Appear Differently in Outlook 2000

The default view when you launch Outlook 2000 is something called Outlook Today (see Figure 17.2). The view displays all your upcoming meetings, tasks, and email.

FIGURE 17.2

Use the Outlook Today view to see what lies ahead for today and beyond.

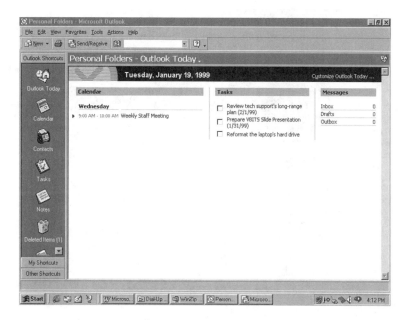

Notice that if you created an IMAP account, the Messages section of Outlook Today does not accurately reflect the contents of your IMAP folders because the IMAP folders are stored on the mail server as opposed to being stored locally. For this reason, Outlook has no real way to display the number of items in these locations. Instead, it creates a separate button for the IMAP account on the Outlook Bar. Click it while you're connected to the Internet, and you are taken directly to your IMAP account's folders.

When you actually try to open your Inbox, the way you do it and the way the messages appear when opened vary slightly between POP and IMAP as well.

To open your POP3 Inbox, click the Inbox hyperlink in the Messages section of Outlook Today.

> **Note: Local email may appear in this section as well.** If you work with a large company and/or make extensive use of Microsoft Exchange Server for in-house messaging and scheduling, your system administrator may have configured the network in such a way that local mail from coworkers appears in the Outlook Inbox instead of in an IMAP folder. Check with the administrator if you have not already been briefed as to how all this will work for you. Keep in mind, however, that only people making use of IMAP mail servers are affected by the possibility of mail appearing in two different locations. POP3 users gather everything in one convenient spot.

Your POP3 Inbox (shown in Figure 17.3) appears with a split window; one pane contains the message list, and the other contains a preview of the selected message.

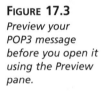

FIGURE 17.3

Preview your POP3 message before you open it using the Preview pane.

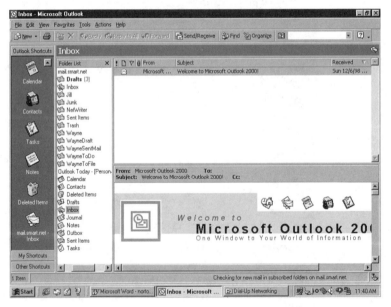

To access your IMAP Inbox, make sure Outlook 2000 recognizes your connection to the Internet (click File|Connect to [*Server Name*] on the Outlook 2000 menu bar to be certain), and then click your IMAP server's button on the Outlook Bar. The Inbox appears by default, as shown in Figure 17.4.

FIGURE 17.4
Notice that IMAP messages have a fifth column of information displayed immediately before the basic message information: the Download state.

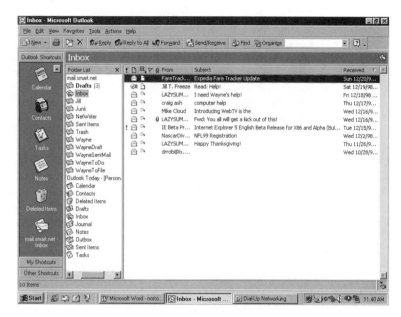

Taking Action on a Message

Whether you use POP or IMAP, you need to double-click a message's header to read it and then take action on it. As you can see in Figure 17.5, you always have the standard email options available to you: Reply, Reply to All, Forward, and Print. But you can make use of some other unique and powerful features , too.

FIGURE 17.5
Both POP and IMAP messages give you access to the same set of tools.

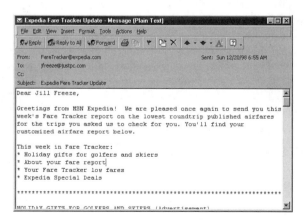

Replying To or Forwarding a Message

When you receive an Outlook 2000 email message, you can basically take three actions on it: you can reply to its author, reply to all the people it was sent to, or forward it to someone entirely different. In the first two cases, email address information is filled in for you. All you need to do is type in your response and then click the Send button.

> **Caution: Watch what button you click!** Before sending a message you're replying to, you would be wise to always check and double-check the To: and CC: fields to make sure only the people you intended to receive the message actually see it. I can't tell you how many stories I've heard about people clicking Reply to Group by mistake only to find themselves extremely embarrassed because their notes got into the wrong hands. In this one instance, you can never do too much double-checking!

In the case of forwarding a mesage to someone not on the message's original mailing list, you need to click the Forward button, enter the email address manually in the To: line (or click the To button to select an entry from your Address Book), fill in your message, and then click Send.

Opening a File Attachment

When a file is sent along with the email message, you see a paper clip icon to the left of the message's subject line. Double-click the message to open it. You then see a special Attachment line that lists all the attached files along with their respective program icons (refer to the file type icon chart in Chapter 4, "Office 2000 File Management Issues," if you don't recognize what you see).

> **Caution: Know the sender!** We've all seen the virus scares that are circulated in a frenzy of activity. "Don't open messages with a Subject Line: 'Good Times' or it'll blow your hard drive away!" Sometimes it's hard to sift out which are legitimate concerns and which have entered the realm of urban folklore.
>
> Generally speaking, you cannot get a computer virus from simply opening an email message. Viruses need some kind of executable file to be able to propagate. It might be a mysterious .exe file someone sends you saying that it's a game when it's really a debilitating virus, or it could be a Word document containing a potentially harmful macro.
>
> The best way to protect yourself is to know the sender of the message before you open any executable files or Office documents that may contain damaging macros.

To open an attachment, double-click its filename in the Attachment line. If you have the application that generated the file on your computer, it launches with the selected file preloaded. If you don't have the application, Outlook 2000 attempts to find a helper application from which you can view the file.

The file is held in a temporary Windows folder until you specifically save the attachment to a location on your machine.

Sending an attachment of your own is pretty simple, too. Just open a New Message window, click the paper clip icon, browse to the file you want to attach, and then double-click its name. The filename then appears in its own Attachment line, so you can instantly verify that the proper files have been attached.

Copying to a Folder

If you want to file a copy of a message away in a Windows folder while retaining a copy in the Inbox for future action, you'll find this function extremely useful. Just click the Copy button on the opened message's toolbar, and then move to the folder in which you want to place the copy using the File List. Click the folder to select it, and then click File|Paste to place the copy in the specified folder. That way, all material related to a certain project or client can be stored together even if you must deal with outstanding issues.

Flagging for Follow-Up

Have you ever received an email message that reads something like: "We're thinking of planning a staff retreat for some time in October. Can you please check your availability and tell us what looks best for you?" The message is not definite enough to store in your calendar, and creating a task may seem to be a bit overkill for what's really needed. Flagging the message for follow-up may be the perfect solution, especially if the sender of the note needs a response by a certain date.

To flag a message for follow-up, follow these steps:

1. From within the desired message's window, click the Flag for Follow Up button. The Flag for Follow Up dialog box shown in Figure 17.6 opens.

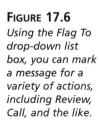

FIGURE 17.6

Using the Flag To drop-down list box, you can mark a message for a variety of actions, including Review, Call, and the like.

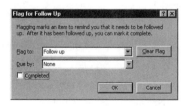

2. By default, the Flag To box is set to Follow Up. You can change it to something else using the drop-down arrow button.

3. Supply a date for the Due By box. Click the drop-down arrow to reveal a calendar from which you can select a date with a single mouse click. You can also click the Today button if appropriate; 5:00 p.m. is specified as the time due. You can change the time by clicking inside the text box and entering the new information.

4. Click OK to save the flag settings. Notice that a red flag now appears next to the message to remind you that it needs your attention. A yellow banner (or InfoBar) containing the follow-up information is displayed immediately under the message's header information, so you'll notice it right away.

After you've completed the task, you might want to mark the flag as complete by right-clicking the message and selecting Flag Complete from the shortcut menu. A checkered flag appears next to the message. If you want to remove the flag altogether, choose Clear Flag from the same shortcut menu.

Moving the Message to Another Folder

After you've read a message and have decided to file it, you can do so from within the message by clicking the Move to Folder button and then selecting the Move to Folder option. This action launches the Move to Folder dialog box, which holds a list of all the mail folders available on your machine. Double-click the name of the folder into which you want to place the message.

Looking Ahead

For more details on organizing your messages and folders, see the section titled "Using Outlook 2000's New Organize Tool to Automate Filing" later in this chapter.

If you can't see the Folder List, open your Inbox, click the Inbox drop-down arrow, and then click the pushpin to anchor the Folder List in place. The contents of your Inbox are shifted to the left so that none of the Inbox is covered by the File List.

To create a new mail folder in which to store messages, just follow these steps from within your Inbox:

1. Click the New arrow drop-down button, and then select Folder from the list.

2. Enter a title for the folder in the Name text box. Try to make the name as short yet descriptive as possible so you'll have little question in your mind what fits into it.

3. Specify the folder's contents using the Folder Contains drop-down list. In this case, choose the Mail Items option.

4. Click to the location you want to place the new folder (see Figure 17.7). At this point, the process potentially gets a little tricky. Consider the folders shown in Figure 17.7 as an example. If you click Drafts, you might expect Outlook 2000 to create the new folder at the same hierarchical level. Instead, that folder becomes a subfolder of the folder you selected. To create a folder at the same level as the Drafts folder, you need to scroll down the File List and click Personal Folders.

FIGURE 17.7

The Create New Folder dialog box enables you to put the folder exactly where you want it.

5. Click OK to create the folder and dismiss the dialog box.

Using Stationery

There aren't many ways to individualize your email messages, but Outlook 2000 gives you some of the best tools available to do just that: stationery and signature files. Stationery does exactly what its paper counterpart does—brings color and style to your messages. You can use the stationery included with Outlook 2000, design your own, even tell Outlook which stationery to use when using the Stationery Picker.

Before you can work with stationery at any level, though, you have to make sure your mail settings are configured properly. To get started, launch Outlook 2000, and then click Tools|Options. Select the Mail Format tab, and verify that the Send Message in This Format option is set to HTML as opposed to the default Plain Text. Click Apply, and then OK.

You have to pay a price for the richness of HTML, however. When Outlook 2000 is configured to send email in HTML format, it takes longer to fire off the new message screen. Although the momentary delay may be barely noticeable on the faster systems out there, you will notice it on a Pentium 233 or slower. For the casual user, the availability of stationery and Web page sending may outweigh any lack of speed. For the power user who needs to get messages out in a hurry, the delay may not only be annoying, but it may also actually disrupt your train of thought as you wait for the new message window to open. You have to try both ways for a while to get a good feel for what does or does not work for you.

> **Note: What you see is what they'll get.** Note that when you reply to a message sent to you, Outlook uses the same type (HTML, plain text, or rich text) used by the message's author. That way, you can be certain the person at the other end will be able to see what you send in its full glory.

Composing a New Message Using Existing Stationery

To compose a new message using one of the pieces of stationery provided with Outlook 2000, launch Outlook, and then click Actions|New Message Using|More Stationery. Click the desired selection, and then click OK to apply it.

> **Tip: Save a step or two.** If you recently used a certain piece of stationery, its name will appear on the drop-down menu above More Stationery. Just select the stationery's name from the drop-down menu, and bypass the Select a Stationery dialog box altogether.

Setting Your Default Stationery

When you've settled on a look you would like to use all the time, you can set it as your default stationery so that you needn't select it manually each time. To do so, follow these steps:

1. With Outlook 2000 open, click Tools|Options, and then select the Mail Format tab.

2. In the Message Format section, verify that HTML is selected as the Send Message in This Format option. Stationery is disabled unless this option is selected.

3. In the Stationery and Fonts section, you can get down to the nitty-gritty. To use one of Outlook 2000's pieces of stationery, simply click its name in the Use This Stationery by Default drop-down box.

4. The stationery you selected has certain font attributes associated with it. If they are acceptable, you needn't do a thing except skip ahead to step 6.

5. To change the fonts, you need to click the Fonts button underneath the Use This Stationery by Default option, and then click Choose Fonts next to the HTML option near the top of the page. This action takes you to a standard Fonts dialog box from which you can do just about anything to the default font.

6. Click Apply, and then click OK to save your settings and dismiss the dialog box.

Saving Neat Stationery You Receive for Future Use

If you receive an email message that's truly exceptional, you might want to consider saving the stationery so that you can use it later. Of course, you should be cautious about any potential copyright infringements, but should you get the green light, all you have to do to save the message is follow these steps:

1. Open the message containing the stationery you want to save.

2. Click File|Save Stationery. The Create New Stationery dialog box shown in Figure 17.8 appears.

FIGURE 17.8

Give the stationery you're about to create a descriptive name so that you can easily find it in the Stationery Picker.

3. After you've finished entering its name, click OK. The dialog box closes, and the new piece of stationery you just created becomes available in the Stationery Picker or in the menus used to create a new message based on a piece of stationery.

Creating Stationery from Scratch

If you're feeling particularly inspired and want to create your very own stationery, Outlook 2000 guides you every step of the way. You can incorporate company logos, favorite colors, and expressive fonts to name a few options. You name it, you can add it to produce a personalized effect (see Figure 17.9).

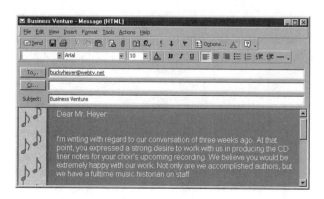

FIGURE 17.9

Express yourself with stationery that speaks volumes about your personality or profession.

Follow these simple steps to get started creating your very own stationery:

1. From within Outlook 2000, click Tools|Options, and then choose the Mail Format tab.

2. Verify that the Send Message in This Format option is set to HTML.

3. Click the Stationery Picker button in the Stationery and Fonts section of the Mail Format tab. The Stationery Picker dialog box opens.

4. Click the New button to launch the Create New Stationery dialog box. (Refer to Figure 17.8 to see what this dialog box looks like.)

5. Give your stationery a descriptive name in section 1 of the dialog box, and then verify that the Start with a Blank Stationery option is selected. Click Next to move on.

Tip: Carry the image through. If you built your own corporate template and/or letterhead for printed correspondence, consider using the same design here to maintain the uniform look you tried so hard to achieve. To base stationery on an existing template or file, make sure the Use This File as a Template option is selected as opposed to the Start with a Blank Stationery option. You also need to browse to the desired file before clicking Next to move on with the

6. You first need to define the attributes of the message font for this stationery. Click the Change font button near the top-right corner of the screen, and set your options as you would in a standard Fonts dialog box.

7. When you're ready to choose a background, you can opt to use a picture, a solid colored background, or no background at all. Just click the desired option button, and then in the case of the Picture option, browse to the desired file and double-click it to select it. You then see the results of your selection in the Preview screen near the bottom of the dialog box.

Caution: Stationery that moves you... Yes, the stationery feature does allow you to use animations typically supported in HTML, but because the images are tiled to produce the background, the screen tends to become incredibly busy and, in many cases, just plain illegible. If you must incorporate animation, go for something pale in color and subdued in its motions, and pay very close attention to the size and color of font you select to make sure the messages can be

8. Click OK to add the stationery you just created to the Stationery Picker.

Downloading More Stationery from the Web

Don't see anything that strikes your fancy included with Outlook 2000? Then consider venturing out to Microsoft's Web site to take a peek at what's there. With a connection to the Internet, launch Outlook, click Tools|Options, select the Mail Format tab, click Stationery Picker, and then click the Get More Stationery button on the bottom-left corner of the tab. Microsoft's Web site will appear within moments.

Because these Web sites are frequently redesigned, your best bet is to follow the onscreen prompts on the Web page for downloading the stationery that interests you.

Personalizing Your Messages with Signature Files

Whether you simply want a signature file that eliminates the need to type your name and contact information at the end of every note, or you want something a bit more stylish that contains a favorite quote, link to your Web site, or something similar, you can do it all in Outlook 2000.

Creating a Signature File

Unlike stationery, no preset default signature files are available for you to simply plug in to your messages on-the-fly. Given that, you need to create at least one signature file before you can start using the feature. To do so, follow these simple steps:

1. With Outlook 2000 open, click Tools|Options, and then open the Mail Format tab.
2. Click the Signature Picker button in the bottom-right corner of the tab to launch a blank Signature Picker dialog box.
3. Click the New button to open the Create New Signature dialog box.
4. In the first section, enter a recognizable name for the signature file you're about to create.
5. Verify that the Start with Blank Signature option is selected, and then click Next.
6. The Edit Signature screen shown in Figure 17.10 opens, giving you a sizable text box into which to type the desired text for the signature file.

Note: No-effort hyperlinks. That's right, if your options are set up to generate messages in HTML, Outlook 2000 automatically creates mailto and Web links as you type them. No HTML coding needed whatsoever!

FIGURE 17.10
Enter the signature text, and then format it as necessary.

7. To change the font of the signature, select the text you want to change, click the Font button, and make the necessary selections. If you want your name to appear in a stylish font while keeping your contact information legible, you might want to repeat the process.

8. If you want to center your text or turn it into bullets, select the text you want to format, and then click the Paragraph button to make the appropriate selection.

9. When everything appears to be in order, click the Finish button. The newly created signature file now has an entry in the Signature Picker screen.

Setting the Default Signature

If you've created a basic signature that you would like to have Outlook 2000 automatically apply to your outgoing messages, doing so is simple. Just launch Outlook, click Tools|Options, select the Mail Format tab, and then use the drop-down list provided to select the name of the signature you want to use as your default. Click Apply and then OK, and you're set.

Applying a Signature on a Per-Message Basis

Do you use your email account for a combination of work and play? If so, you might not feel comfortable specifying a default signature. No problem; just apply one as you write the message. To do so, compose the message as you normally would, click Insert|Signature, and then choose the signature's name from the list. If the desired signature doesn't appear, choose More to go to the Signature Picker, and then select the one you want.

Tracking Messages

In the business world today, time is of the essence. Major decisions need to be made quickly, so you often need a prompt response to an email message. In instances in which you send critical messages via email, it's nice to know if and when the message is actually read.

Outlook 2000's Read Receipt option can assist with your tracking; however, it's not a bullet-proof system. Think of it as the Internet counterpart to your local telephone company. Your telephone company offers caller ID service for a fee; it also offers caller ID blocking services for a fee to keep your number private; then it offers services to unblock the blocked ID...You get the picture. Read receipts are much the same. You can request one, but the recipient can suppress the return of the receipt with a single mouse click. Combine that with the fact that some email clients don't even support receipt generation. I'm not trying to be cynical here; I'm just trying to tell it like it is. It's a neat feature, but not one without loopholes.

Setting Message Tracking Options

To begin configuring your message tracking options, follow these steps:

1. From within Outlook 2000, click Tools|Options, and then select the Preferences tab.

2. Click the E-mail Options button, and then click the Tracking Options button on the resulting dialog box. The Tracking Options dialog box shown in Figure 17.11 appears.

FIGURE 17.11

In the Tracking Options dialog box, you can tell Outlook when to request read receipts and specify how you want to handle requests for read receipts.

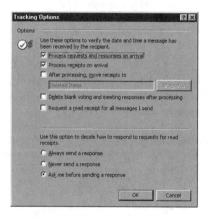

3. Notice that you can request read receipts for every message you send by checking the option at the bottom of the first section of the dialog box.

4. In the bottom section of the dialog box are three options for handling requests for read receipts you receive from others. By default, Outlook asks you what you want to do before responding in any way; however, you also have the option to automatically send the receipts every time they are requested or to never send them.

5. When you're satisfied with the settings, click OK. You need to click OK several times before all layers of the dialog box are dismissed.

Requesting a Read Receipt on a Per-Message Basis

Although Outlook 2000 gives you the option to request read receipts on everything you send, requesting them only when it's truly important is probably wisest. To request one on a message you're about to send, click the Options button on the message's toolbar to reveal the Message Options dialog box, as shown in Figure 17.12.

FIGURE 17.12

Check the Request a Read Receipt for This Message box to be notified by email when the recipient reads the message.

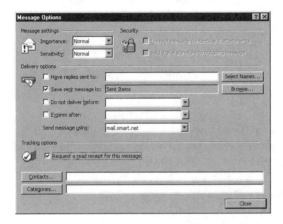

Place a check mark in the Request a Read Receipt for This Message check box to request the receipt. When the recipient reads the message and authorizes the return of a read receipt, you'll receive a message like the one in Figure 17.13 in your Inbox telling you exactly who read the message when.

FIGURE 17.13

The read receipt discloses all the details of who read the message when.

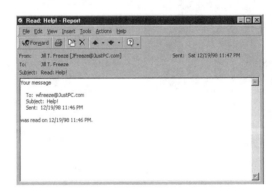

Automating Tasks Using Message Rules

The Outlook 2000 Rules Wizard makes it a breeze to filter and process your messages according to a wide variety of criteria you define. If you don't think message rules can be of use to you, consider these situations:

- Have outgoing messages to known recipients automatically filed in designated local folders.
- Play a special sound when a critical message arrives.
- When you're out of the office for an extended period of time, have Outlook automatically send a note to people who've sent you mail telling them of your absence and anticipated return date.

> **Caution: If you subscribe to any mailing lists...**Of course, if you subscribe to any Internet mailing lists, you'll either want to unsubscribe to the list while you're out or have list messages postponed until further notice. If you don't, Outlook 2000 does its thing each time a message is posted to the mailing list and tells everyone on the list that you're gone. This happens for *every* message sent to the group. Talk about a quick way to get run off the Internet!

- Automatically delete junk mail or mail with adult content.
- Forward certain messages to other staff members in your absence.
- Mark messages about a certain subject as highly important.
- IMAP users can apply a set of rules to messages hanging out in the Sent Mail folder to file them automatically.

The list could go on and on. The fact of the matter is well-defined message rules can save you hours of work each week by automating many of the tasks once done by hand.

Are you convinced of their value? I thought so. Read on to learn how to make use of this powerful wizard.

Defining the Rules

Follow these steps to begin defining message rules:

1. From within Outlook 2000, click Tools|Rules Wizard. The Rules Wizard dialog box opens, displaying the names of any previously defined rules.
2. Click the New button to move to the first screen.
3. Specify which type of rule you're trying to create. Click the options that most accurately describe the purpose of the rule, and then click Next.

4. Tell Outlook which condition(s) you want it to check by placing a mark in the respective check box(es).

5. If any of the checked conditions are underlined, as shown in Figure 17.14, click the underlined text and enter the requested information.

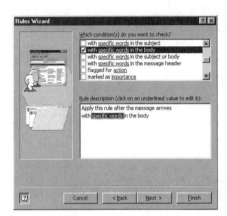

6. Click Next after each condition has been appropriately defined.

7. On the next screen, you tell Outlook 2000 what to do with the message. It can bounce a reply back to the sender, route the message, file it, or play a special sound. Select the necessary option by clicking its check box. Just remember that you need to clarify any underlined items here as well. Click Next when you're ready to move on.

8. If you think of any exceptions to the rule, enter them on this screen, remembering that some underlined items might need further elaboration. Click Next when ready.

9. In the final screen, you are asked to give the rule a name and then tell Outlook whether you want to run the rule now on messages already in your Inbox. You're also asked whether you want to turn on the rule. Just click the buttons next to the options you want to enable.

10. Click Finish to save your settings.

Setting the Rules in Motion Manually

To apply a rule to items currently in your Inbox or in a local folder, you need to set them off by hand. To do so, follow these steps:

1. With Outlook 2000 up and running, click Tools|Rules Wizard.

2. Click the Run Now button at the bottom of the Rules Wizard dialog box.

3. In the box at the top of the screen, you're asked to check off the boxes of the rules you want to run.

4. By default, the rules will be run against your Inbox. If you want them run against any other folder, you need to click the Browse button, and then click the desired folder.

5. If you want the rules applied to messages in the folder's subfolders as well, be sure to check the Include Subfolders check box.

6. Tell Outlook to run the rules against all messages, all read messages only, or all unread messages only by using the drop-down arrow.

7. Click the Run Now button to run the rules through the specified messages.

Using Outlook 2000's New Organize Tool to Automate Filing

If you typically store copies of messages you send in the Sent Items folder, then you know how overwhelming it can be to file everything at one time. Wouldn't it be so much nicer if Outlook could do the job for you?

Earlier in the chapter when I showed you how to create message rules, you got a glimpse of just how easily you could automate message filing. With Outlook 2000's new Organize tool, you can accomplish this feat by following these steps:

1. Open your Outlook 2000 Inbox, and then click the Organize button on the Standard toolbar. By default, the Using Folders tab of the Organize tool is opened (see Figure 17.15).

FIGURE 17.15
The Organize tool gives you five ways to organize your mail folders.

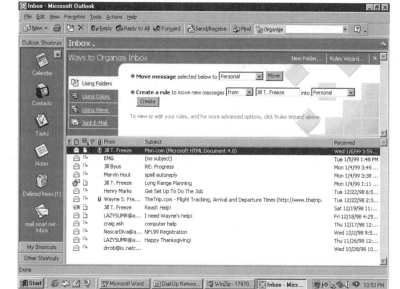

2. If you have just a few messages to move, select them, and then use the Move Message drop-down button to choose a destination folder. After you've marked all the messages you want to move, click the Move button to move them to the new folder.

3. Got a huge list of messages to wade through? Consider creating a rule to file them. From this tab, all you have to do is use the drop-down box to select From or Sent To, click a message to have the specified person's name entered into the second text box, and then use the final drop-down box to choose a destination folder. Click the Create button to run the rule on the spot.

Note: Get connected. If you plan to apply the rule toward messages stored on your mail server, you need to be connected to the Internet first to perform the task.

4. Keep moving batches of messages or defining rules until all the messages you want to move have been successfully relocated.

Using Color to Help Messages Stand Out

Have you ever wished you had an easier way to spot the messages you're looking for? Perhaps color-coding them is the answer you've been looking for.

When I have a folder containing hundreds of email messages, I find it a lot easier on the eyes to spot messages of a different color rather than skim through the entire list trying to find a certain name.

Choosing a color for certain messages is a lot like creating message rules, as described in the preceding section. To do so, open the Organize tool from within the folder you want to work with. Choose the Using Colors tab (see Figure 17.16), and then select From or Sent To in the first drop-down box. Next, click a message to help fill in the second text box, and then use the last drop-down box to choose a color for the messages you just defined. Click the Apply Color button to change the color of the defined messages. See? Isn't finding red messages amidst black ones a whole lot easier than scanning for Sharon Peters messages amidst Karen Peters messages?

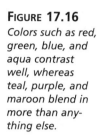

FIGURE 17.16
Colors such as red, green, blue, and aqua contrast well, whereas teal, purple, and maroon blend in more than anything else.

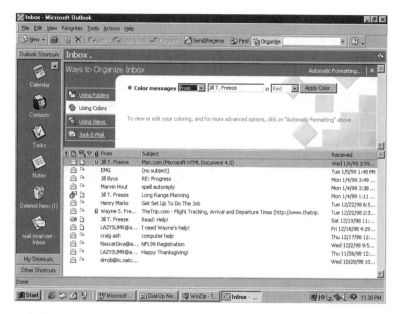

Changing Your View of the Mail Items

Altering views can give you immense versatility when you want to look at blocks of information in different ways. For example, did you know that by clicking the Received column header on your Inbox list, you can sort the messages from oldest to newest? A second click reverses the order. You can perform this sort on any of the column headers.

The Outlook 2000 Organize tool adds a whole new dimension to this capability, however. By clicking the Using Views tab, you can access a large list of predefined sorts, such as grouping messages marked for deletion, sorting flagged messages based on the type of action needed, grouping unread messages, and so on. Just make your selection, and the screen changes before your eyes (see Figure 17.17).

No matter which options you try, keep in mind that this feature changes only the appearance of your data, not the data itself.

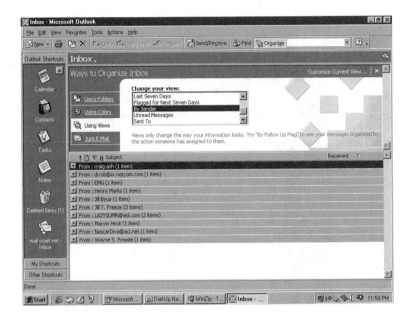

Processing Virtual Junk Mail Automatically

If you've been surfing the Net and emailing since the Information Superhighway was a winding dirt road like I have, then you've undoubtedly found yourself on more junk mail lists than you can shake a stick at. In fact, you needn't have been online long at all for the virtual junk mail to start trickling in.

Outlook 2000 comes with some preprogrammed junk mail and adult content filters that you can apply to keep your Inbox as clutter free as possible. To use these filters, open the Junk E-Mail tab of the Organize tool. Once there, you can use the drop-down boxes to have junk mail or adult content messages color-coded, routed to a different folder, or flat out deleted. Click the Turn On button to enable this feature.

Although I think the concept of a junk mail filter is a great one, I'm a bit conservative when it comes to passing judgment on its effectiveness. A part of me still wonders if a funny joke from an old college buddy would get inadvertently deleted. So until I'm total-ly comfortable with the filters, I plan to take less drastic measures such as coloring the messages or moving them into the Junk Mail folder instead of having them automatically deleted.

On Your Own

This chapter assumed you had a certain degree of familiarity with basic email functions and concepts, but one thing you might not have been totally aware of is the massive power of message rules. With a little planning and work up front, you can save yourself mounds of work by letting Outlook perform some of the more mundane tasks for you.

Think about your email work habits for a moment. What do you spend the most time doing? Can the task be automated using the powerful Outlook 2000 Rules Wizard?

Before you read another word, take the time to put at least two message rules to work for you. Sure, coming up with these rules might take some time now, but I'm betting that time will be made up several times over within the first month you use the rules.

Personal Information Management with Outlook 2000

Personal information management (PIM) means a lot of different things to many people. For some, it means collecting all those phone numbers and email addresses scrawled on the back of matchbook covers and putting them into the computer so that they can be found again. For the corporate executive, it can mean the ability to schedule staff meetings when everyone is available. It can even mean maintaining a list of all tasks that need to be accomplished in a given timeframe. No matter what you need to get organized, Outlook 2000 can help with its variety of functions.

A quick glance at the Outlook Shortcuts section of the Outlook Bar (see Table 18.1) gives you a good feel for the breadth of functions you can perform from within Outlook 2000.

Table 18.1 Functions Accessible from the Outlook Bar

Button	Gives You the Following Capability
Outlook Today	Gives you a view of the day's calendar and list of tasks as well as quick access to your POP3 email account Inbox. (IMAP accounts have their own special button on the bottom of the Outlook Bar.)
Calendar	Lets you schedule meetings as well as view your schedule and task list.
Contacts	Lets you view names and other pertinent information about personal contacts or add new entries.
Tasks	Allows you to see what tasks you need to accomplish in the near future or enter new items on your list.
Notes	Allows you to view and/or create notes to yourself.
Deleted Items	Lets you take one last look at information you've deleted from folders before it's gone for good.

In this chapter, you'll look at each of these functions and learn how to use them to your advantage.

Managing Contacts in Outlook 2000

Even if you don't plan to schedule meetings with a contact, you might want to keep contact information close at hand for a number of compelling reasons. Using your contact list, you can do the following:

- Dial a contact's phone number with your computer
- Send an email message or fax without needing to dig for additional information (provided the email address and fax number are in the contact's listing, of course)
- Print a telephone or address list to take with you on the road
- Insert the contact's name and address into a Word document with just a few mouse clicks
- Generate form letters, email messages, or faxes with Word 2000 using contact information fields for personalization
- Schedule meetings with others over the Internet using the new iCalendar standard for information exchange

Automatically Adding Entries to Your Contact List

One option you might want to take a closer look at is Outlook 2000's capability to automatically add information to your contact list. With a single mouse click, you can have Outlook add to your contact list the names and email addresses of those whose email messages you replied to. Of course, if you want or need more information than that, you need to enter it manually. Even having just the basic information available in your contact list can save you a fair amount of time, however.

To verify that this option is enabled, click Tools|Options from within Outlook 2000, and then select the Preferences tab. Click the E-mail Options button in the first section of the tab, and then look for the Automatically Put People I Reply To In option at the very bottom of the tab. If the item is checked, Outlook 2000 automatically saves the names and email addresses in your contact list.

Building a Contact List from Scratch

Unless you imported your contacts or Address Book from another application or have spent a great deal of time responding to email messages that are automatically added to your contact list, you might need to create a number of entries from scratch. Because you can do so much with the contact list, I'll include all the tips and tricks you might want to use while defining a contact in this list of steps. Although it may make the action of defining a contact appear to be an overwhelming task, I believe seeing the steps all together the first time around will help you plan ahead for what you may or may not need to include in a contact's entry.

Keep the following in mind as you define your contacts and decide what information to capture:

- In general, if you already have information on a contact, enter it all in that person's contact entry. That way, you'll always have it close at hand, and you won't have to ask for it again when you eventually do need it.

- Just because a contact may not have Internet access doesn't mean you should exclude that person from your list. Sure, many of the most powerful capabilities of the contact list rely on Internet access and/or a connection to the contact via LAN or intranet, but don't underestimate the value of having all names, addresses, and phone numbers in a single location. You can also easily generate personalized letters or faxes to nonconnected contacts.

> **Caution: Single doesn't mean only.** Sure, having your contact information centralized is great, but what if the server goes down, and you've stored your contact list there? Or what if your hard drive dies a horrible death? Call me conservative, but I keep a backup copy of this information on paper as well. Whether it's in a rolodex or a daytimer is beside the point. The fact of the matter is it's always wise to have a backup of vital information, and contact lists are certainly no exception, especially when the contacts may have taken decades to acquire.

- Categorizing contacts can be a valuable tool for grouping contacts or tagging them for future action (such as your company's holiday card list). Think of categorizing as the broad grouping such as clients, prospective clients, colleagues, donors, members, and the like, and linking contacts as the lower level grouping for specifying who's tied to whom in the larger group.

- Don't overlook filling in the Details tab with as much information as you have available. This information can help you remember important dates and facts about a contact, which, in turn, can leave the contact with a very favorable impression of you and your company.

Although you don't need to complete each and every one of these steps, doing so will give you the most thorough listings and the most potential to grow into using all of Outlook 2000 with minimal hassle.

To produce a complete contact listing, follow these steps:

1. From within anywhere in Outlook 2000, press Ctrl+Shift+C. The Untitled Contact dialog box shown in Figure 18.1 appears.

FIGURE 18.1

The enormous amount of information you can maintain on a contact will amaze you.

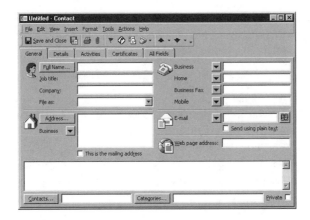

2. Simply type the contact's name into the Full Name field, and have Outlook break it into fields for you. If you want to ensure consistency in collecting titles and suffix information (like Jr., III, and such), you might want to consider capturing the data via the Check Full Name dialog box, as shown in Figure 18.2. Doing so helps ensure that each of the fields is filled in in a uniform manner. Note that after a name has been entered, the dialog box's title reflects the contact's name.

FIGURE 18.2

Use the Title and Suffix drop-down lists to make sure contact information is as uniform as can be.

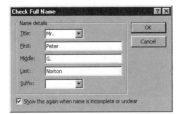

3. In the Untitled Contact dialog box, enter the address in the box provided. Outlook 2000 is very reliable when it comes to breaking address parts into the appropriate fields such as City, State, and so on, but if you deal with a number of foreign addresses or simply want to verify the way an address was processed, click the Address button. Use the drop-down arrow button to label the type of address (Business, Home, or Other), and then with the preferred mailing address in view, place a check mark in the This Is the Mailing Address box.

4. Continue filling in the General tab as much as you can. Keep in mind that you can use the arrow drop-down buttons to select the field labels you want and/or need.

> **Tip: Know what you're getting into.** Believe it or not, a host of mail readers still simply cannot deal with HTML messages. Instead of the glitzy output we see in Outlook 2000, they see a bunch of gobbledygook (known as raw HTML code to you and me). If you know a person is incapable of dealing with HTML messages, do him or her a favor and mark the Send Using Plain Text box in that person's contact entry.

5. If you want to link the current contact to other contacts in your list, click the Contacts button. That way, you can see the names of a contact's associates in the Contact box at the bottom of the contact's General tab.

> **Note: Linked contacts are not the same as a distribution list.** Although linking contacts as described in step 5 establishes a connection among contacts, it does not enable you to email a group of them with a single mouse click. You need to create a distribution list to do that, and you'll learn how to do so later in this chapter in a section titled "Creating a Distribution List."
>
> So why link? It lets you see at a glance who may know whom or that the names listed are in some way tied to one another. Just double-click the desired associate's name to launch his or her contact file from which you can send email, assign a task, invite him or her to a meeting, visit his or her Web page, and the like.

6. Click the Categories button to choose a category (or categories) for the contact. Outlook 2000 offers predefined categories such as Competition, Hot Contact, and Personal, but you can create your own categories by clicking the Master Category List button, typing the category title in the box provided, and then clicking the Add button. Repeat as necessary, clicking OK after you've finished adding categories. Place a check mark next to the applicable categories for the current listing, and then click OK to dismiss the Categories dialog box.

> **Peter's Principle: What's the use?**
>
> The Categories field isn't just another potentially useless piece of data. In fact, if you do some careful planning, it can go a long way toward helping you nurture the loyalty of clients. How? A simple act like grouping clients into a Holiday Cards category can leave the clients with a lasting impression of your style and class as a company. Just perform a mail merge based on the Holiday Cards category to create the labels (or preferably envelopes) for the cards, sign them by hand if possible, and then mail them out. You can even take this idea a step further for highly valued clients. Put them into a Gifts category, and remember them during the holidays with the gift of a fruit basket or fine chocolates. Your actions won't soon be forgotten.

Of course, categories can have a more tangible purpose, too, in that you can periodically pull out lists of prospective clients to call and follow up with them. You also can tag some preferred contacts who may receive advanced notice of special promotions, or you can group suppliers for your business needs so that you can find them all in a hurry. The possibilities are almost endless.

7. If you want to keep the contact's information from being shared with others, click the Private option in the bottom-right corner of the tab. Of course, this option is useful only when your contact information is stored on your company's server and/or in a shared folder. Checking it as Private doesn't make it visible on your PC should someone decide to sneak a peek.

8. Move to the Details tab, and enter as much information as you can provide. Among the information you can collect here is Spouse's Name (great for sending invitations to a company social event), Birthday (useful to make a client feel appreciated with a card or even discount for services or merchandise), or Profession (so you can target conversations to the contact's potential interests). If the contact is not connected to the Internet (or at least to your local network), you can leave the Online NetMeeting Settings and Internet Free-Busy sections blank.

9. Click the Save and Close button to save your settings and dismiss the dialog box.

The information you can keep on a contact is far from static. If you've decided to maintain journal entries on a contact, you can find tons of goodies in this tab, including email sent to and received from the contact and where it's stored, Office documents on your machine authored by the contact, tasks and meetings related to the contact, and the like.

The Certificate tab stores the digital IDs you use to send verifiable mail to the contact. These digital IDs can be obtained from sanctioned issuers such as VeriSign. Or, to send encrypted messages over a LAN only, your network administrator might be able to generate this ID or certificate for you. If you intend to send encrypted messages to the recipient, you need to have a copy of his or her certificate on file, too. It gives you the "key" to unscrambling the messages that person sends.

On the All Fields tab, you can create a table of contact information in any order you want to see it. You can even define custom fields not already included in the contact's card by clicking the New button, giving the field a name, and using the drop-down arrows to define the type of content to be contained in the new field.

Viewing Your Contact List

By default, Outlook 2000 displays your contact list in Address Cards view (see Figure 18.3) when you click the Contacts button on the Outlook Bar. As you can see, the view contains the contacts' names and email addresses only. If you have a sizable list of contacts, you can use the thumb tabs to the right of the screen to navigate your way to a desired entry.

FIGURE 18.3

Double-click an item to access its set of Contact tabs.

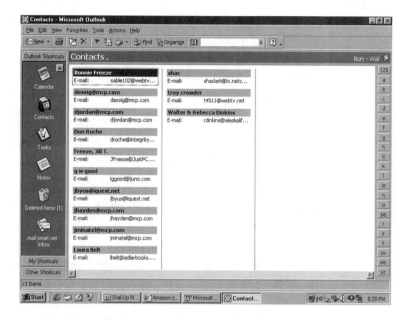

> **Caution: Take a long, hard look.** If you've instructed Outlook to automatically add items to your contact list, you might be in for a big surprise when you see the Address Cards view for the first time. Because Outlook 2000 uses information from a person's email From header to fill in the Full Name fields, you might find just about anything there. It could be the person's email address alone, or it could be his or her name in a different order than you've selected as the default for new contact list entries. Whatever the case, this mish-mash of output is bound to make finding contacts a nightmare. To fix this problem, you might have to manually go into the contact's tabs and edit the entry. You'll learn how to do so later in the chapter in a section titled "Editing and Deleting Contact List Entries."

You can easily change your view of the contact list from the Address Cards view by clicking View|Current View and then selecting the desired view from the drop-down menu. Some of the more useful views include By Company, By Category, and By Location.

Customizing Your Contact List View

If none of the preset views fully meet your needs, then you can customize the current view to produce the results you want. This capability is particularly important because you might want to pull together a very specific list of contacts from which to generate a mail-merged letter, fax, or email, as you learned about in Chapter 10, "Working with

Mail Merge." I use this feature a lot when I'm headed out of town for a conference because it helps me pinpoint contacts I might want to get in touch with in the local area of the event.

You can customize your view in essentially two ways: sort the contacts or filter them. Obviously, sorting the contact list puts contacts in the order you define, whereas filtering them returns only the contacts you want. To follow through with my conference example, I would use the Filter feature to find any contacts who live in Baltimore. That way, I see only contacts from Baltimore, not my entire contact list in alphabetical order by city.

Sorting Your Contact List

As you learned in Chapter 10, sorting letters by zip code can potentially save you a lot of money on bulk mailings. To put your contact list in zip code order (or into any other order for that matter), just follow these steps:

1. Launch Outlook 2000, and click the Contacts button on the Outlook Bar.
2. Click View|Current View|Customize Current View to open the View Summary dialog box.
3. Click the Sort button to launch the Sort dialog box shown in Figure 18.4.

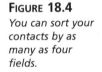

FIGURE 18.4

You can sort your contacts by as many as four fields.

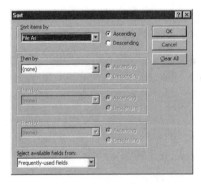

4. Click the Sort Items By drop-down arrow at the top of the box to see whether the field you're looking for is listed. Don't panic if you don't see what you need. The fields displayed come from a list referred to as the Frequently Used Fields list. By changing the Select Available Fields From option at the bottom of the page, you can quickly find the set of fields you need. For example, to sort by zip code, you select Address Fields at the bottom of the box and then move back to the top, where you now can select Zip/Postal Code from the list of options.
5. Specify whether you want the items sorted in ascending or descending order. Ascending (in alphabetical or numerical order) is the default value.
6. Repeat steps 4 and 5 to fill in the Then By fields as necessary.

7. When you're finished, click OK to close the Sort dialog box, and then click OK again to dismiss the View Summary box. Your contact list then appears sorted in the order you defined.

Filtering Your Contact List

If you need to single out certain contacts for whatever reason, you can filter them using these steps as a guide:

1. Launch Outlook 2000, and click the Contacts button on the Outlook Bar.

2. Click View|Current View|Customize Current View to open the View Summary dialog box.

3. Click the Filter button to launch the Filter dialog box shown in Figure 18.5.

FIGURE 18.5

Using the Contacts tab of the Filter dialog box, you can extract the contacts you want with ease.

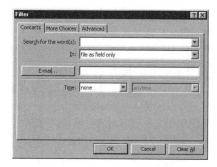

4. Verify that the Contacts tab is open, and then enter the word or words you want Outlook to search for in the Search for the Word(s) text box. This tool is great if you can recall only bits of information about the contact. Maybe you search by a birth date because that person has the same birthday as your daughter. Or perhaps you remember the phone number because it's similar to yours in some way. Who knows what you'll remember most about a contact. It's nice to know that no matter how obscure the detail is, you can track it down with this tool (provided you actually entered the information into the contact's listing, of course).

5. Tell Outlook 2000 where to look for this information. Do so by selecting the appropriate set of fields in the In box.

6. Click OK to close the Filter dialog box, and then click OK again to dismiss the View Summary box. The items you filtered down to appear onscreen.

7. To remove a filter and restore your contact list to the normal Address Cards view, click View|Current View|Customize Current View, and then click the Filter button to launch the Filter dialog box. Once there, click the Clear All button. All your contacts then appear back on the desktop.

Editing and Deleting Contact List Entries

People are always moving, changing jobs, or something similar, so you need to know how to modify a contact list entry or even delete it altogether.

To edit an entry, find the entry you need to modify, and then double-click it. You are taken directly to the set of Contact tabs described earlier. Just click inside the text box you need to edit, make the necessary changes, and then click Save and Close.

Deleting a contact is even simpler. Just click the item to select it, and then press the Delete key. Use this method with caution, however, because Outlook does not ask you to confirm the removal of the entry.

Building a Distribution List

Whether you edit a weekly electronic newsletter that's distributed by email, or you simply want to have the capability to email your entire staff at once without manually selecting each address, you can get a great deal of use out of creating a distribution list.

To create a distribution list, you need to do the following:

1. From within Outlook 2000's Contact tool, click Actions|New Distribution List. The Untitled—Distribution List dialog box appears.

2. In the Name box, type in a short, descriptive name for the distribution list you're about to create. Make it a name that's easy to remember and type—for example, techs for your technical support team or friends for people you exchange jokes with over your lunch hour.

3. To begin adding members to the list, verify that the Members tab is open, and then click the Select Members button near the top-left edge of the tab. The Select Members dialog box shown in Figure 18.6 appears.

FIGURE 18.6

You can also type the name of a contact in the Find box to find it more quickly.

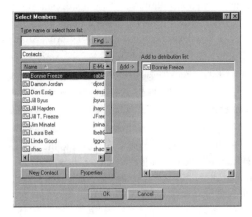

4. Each member of your contact list appears in the left window of the Select Members dialog box. Double-click each contact's name you want to add to the new distribution list. The contact name then appears in the Add to Distribution List window on the right as well.

5. After you've finished adding all the contacts to the distribution list, click OK, and then click the Save and Close button. The distribution list is now ready to be used just as a single contact would be.

Taking Action on a Contact or Distribution List

After you've defined a contact or distribution list, taking action on it is a breeze. Just select the desired item from the Address Cards view in Contacts, perform a sort, or apply a filter, and then click Actions followed by any of the commands presented in Table 18.2. You can find the details of executing each of these commands throughout this book, most of them right in this chapter.

Table 18.2 Actions You Can Take on a Contact or Distribution List

Menu Command	Pertinent Information
New Message to Contact	Launches a new message screen with the contact's email address already filled in.
New Letter to Contact	Launches Word 2000's Letter Wizard with the contact's primary mailing address already printed on the page.
New Meeting Request to Contact	Produces a pre-addressed meeting request form like the one you'll see later in this chapter.
New Appointment with Contact	Produces a pre-addressed form similar to the meeting request, except that the recipient need not respond.
New Task for Contact	Assigns a task to the selected contact with a single mouse click.
New Journal Entry for Contact	Keeps a timed running log of phone calls, conversations, and other interactions with a contact.
Call Contact	Dials the contact's phone number.
Call Using NetMeeting	Logs you into the contact's preferred NetMeeting Directory Server and places a call to that person.
Flag for Follow Up	Marks a contact to remind you to call, schedule a meeting, or send email to that person by a specified date.

Printing Phone Number or Address Lists

Believe it or not, I still have some friends and associates who don't own a computer. When I'm faced with that situation, the only way I can share information with them is to print a hard copy.

Follow these simple steps to print an address or telephone list to share or take on the road:

1. Click the Contacts button on the Outlook Bar.

2. If you want to print only the information for certain contacts, use the Filter feature as described earlier to get the desired contacts in view.

3. To access the Print dialog box, click File|Print.

4. Select the desired print style from the Print Style box. This style defines how your contacts are printed.

5. Select the items you want printed in the Print Range section. By default, all contact information is printed. You can also select contacts for inclusion by clicking and, while holding down the Ctrl key, choosing the Only Selected Items option. If you want to print the results of a filter you may have applied, click the Only Selected Items option.

6. Specify how many copies of the list you want printed. To do so, enter the desired number in the Number of Copies text box.

7. Click OK to send the output to the printer.

Getting Organized with the Outlook 2000 Calendar

Getting everyone together for a meeting can be a major hassle, especially if you need to call each potential attendee to verify his or her schedule. Wouldn't it be nice if you could check this information anytime you want without ever having to make a single phone call? With Outlook 2000, not only can you have Outlook AutoPick a meeting time that meets everyone's needs, but you also can schedule online meetings with associates across the country using NetMeeting and can even have the calendar remind you of the meetings as the time approaches.

Learning the Definitions to Make Calendar Work for You

Because the Outlook 2000 calendar is so powerful, you need to understand some subtle differences in terms to be able to get the most out of the tool. For example, meetings, appointments, and events may sound similar in the general scheme of things, but in Outlook 2000, the difference is significant. *Appointments* are activities you schedule on your calendar that don't involve inviting other people or reserving resources. *Meetings*, on the other hand, are simply appointments that include other people or resources. And if you need to schedule something that spans more than a 24-hour period of time (such as your association's annual conference or the family vacation), you consider it an *event* for the sake of Outlook 2000.

Tailoring Calendar's Options to Meet Your Needs

Before you jump into using Calendar, you might want to tweak some options to get the most out of this powerful tool. To begin working with the Calendar options, click Tools|Options. The Preferences tab shown in Figure 18.7 appears.

Figure 18.7

Use this tab to tell Calendar how far in advance you want to be reminded of your meetings.

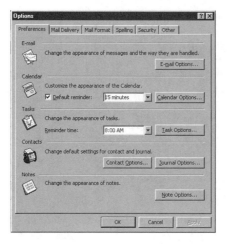

In the Calendar section of this tab, notice that Outlook 2000 reminds you of an appointment 15 minutes in advance by default. You can turn off the automatic reminders by removing the check mark or use the drop-down list to adjust the time as needed.

Peter's Principle: Keep an eye on the time.

Although knowing you'll always be reminded of an upcoming meeting or appointment may be comforting, it's unrealistic to believe that a single amount of time for the reminders will work. Consider my schedule as an example. I may want a five-minute reminder to get to my weekly staff meeting down the hall, but I need an hour reminder to get out of my office in time for my monthly computer group meeting across town. You basically have two options in this situation. You can disable the default reminders and trust that you'll remember to set the appropriate reminder time each time you book a meeting or appointment, or you can leave the default in place and change the amount of reminder time only when it's necessary. Of the two, I believe the second option to be the best because you'll never have to worry about missing a meeting entirely. You might be late if you didn't set the needed amount of reminder time, but you'll never forget the meeting was on your calendar!

Microsoft realizes that not everyone has the same work week or hours. A doctor may work long shifts Thursday through Sunday, whereas a community college professor might start the day at 1:00 p.m. and end it at 10:00 p.m.

By clicking the Calendar Options button on the Preferences tab of the Options dialog box, you can take full control over which days and times are actually part of your work week. In the Calendar Work Week section of the Calendar Options box (see Figure 18.8), place a check mark next to each day in your work week. Monday through Friday are chosen by default.

FIGURE 18.8
You can even choose a new background color for your calendar using the drop-down box provided.

If your work hours stray much from the 8:00 a.m. to 5:00 p.m. default, you can use the Start Time and End Time drop-down boxes to adjust the time accordingly.

To add holidays to your calendar, click the Add Holidays button. The Add Holidays to Calendar dialog box opens with a list of countries from which you can choose. By default, the country reflected in your Windows installation is used. Click OK to have the holidays imported to your calendar. This process takes only a couple of seconds.

The final option you need to consider is the Free/Busy option. If you're connected to a server that can store your free/busy information, you need to click the Free/Busy Options button at the bottom-right corner of the dialog box. Clicking this button launches a separate Free/Busy Options dialog box like the one shown in Figure 18.9.

First, you need to specify how much of your calendar is available to others. If the default of two months is not acceptable, just type in a new number. You can also tell Outlook how often to upload your free/busy information to the specified server. If the Publish My Free/Busy Information option is enabled, Outlook 2000 updates it on the server every 15 minutes unless you tell it otherwise. To share your free/busy information, place a check next to the Publish My Free/Busy Information option, and then enter the URL to which the information is published in the box provided. In the case of free/busy information being stored on the Internet, that URL takes the usual http:// form. If the schedule is to be stored on your local Microsoft Exchange server, you simply need to enter the name of the server.

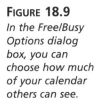

FIGURE 18.9

In the Free/Busy Options dialog box, you can choose how much of your calendar others can see.

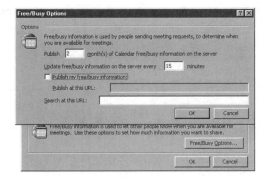

> **Note: For all this to work...**To take full advantage of Outlook 2000's powerful meeting planning tools, you and the rest of your colleagues at the office need to be using Outlook 2000 along with Microsoft Exchange Server. You can send meeting requests without Exchange Server, provided everyone is connected to the Internet as well as to your intranet, but Exchange Server is what powers the Outlook 2000 meeting planner and its AutoPick feature for scheduling the best meeting times. Even if you don't have Exchange Server, all hope is not lost. Outlook 2000 is one of the leading supporters of the new iCalendar standard, which enables Outlook 2000 (or other iCalendar-compliant software) users to swap free/busy information over the Internet.

Scheduling an Appointment Using Calendar

Keep in mind that for the sake of Outlook, an appointment is an activity to which no one else is invited. This could mean anything from a doctor's appointment to the chunk of time you routinely spend at the gym to a job interview.

Follow these steps to block out an appointment on your calendar:

1. Launch Outlook 2000, and then click the Calendar button on the Outlook Bar. The Outlook Calendar view opens.

2. Click the New button in the upper-left corner of the Calendar toolbar to launch the Untitled—Appointment dialog box, as shown in Figure 18.10.

3. Enter a name for the appointment in the Subject box, and then type in the location of the appointment in the Location box. Outlook "remembers" the location and keeps it stored in the Location drop-down box for future use.

FIGURE **18.10**
*Hide confidential
appointments
from others by
clicking the
Private option in
the lower-right
corner of the
Appointment tab.*

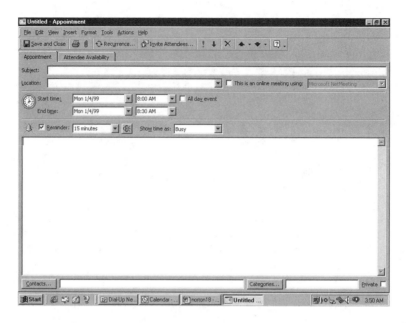

4. Specify a start and end time for the appointment using the drop-down list boxes provided. After you've set these times, use caution in changing them. Say you've set a meeting to go from 9:00 to 11:00 but decide that 9:30 to 11:00 should give you enough time. If you simply change the first box, Outlook—for some quirky reason—assumes you just want to move the meeting rather than increase or decrease its duration, so it moves the second box to 11:30. Just be sure to confirm the selection in both time boxes before moving on with the scheduling or sending the meeting requests.

> **Tip: Short and sweet.** Outlook 2000 automatically assumes that each appointment is a half-hour long. If that's really the case for the appointment you're blocking out, you need to define only the start time.

5. To be reminded of the appointment before it starts, make sure the Reminder option is checked. Depending on the meeting's location, you might need to tweak the amount of time Outlook reminds you in advance.

> **Tip: Appointment reminders are music to your ears.** By clicking the speaker icon to the immediate right of the Reminder time box, you can change the sound that plays when a meeting reminder is issued. Just click the Browse button to navigate to the sound file you would like to use, and then click OK.

6. Using the Show Time As drop-down box, you can have the appointment's time reflected as free, tentative, busy, or out of the office. Others see this appointment this way when they view your calendar.

7. If you want to keep the nature of the meeting hidden from others who may have access to your schedule, just click the Private check box at the bottom-right corner of the Appointment tab.

8. When you're satisfied with the settings for the appointment, click the Save and Close button. The appointment you scheduled then shows up on your calendar, as shown in Figure 18.11.

FIGURE 18.11
With Outlook 2000's calendar, you can easily see when meetings begin and end.

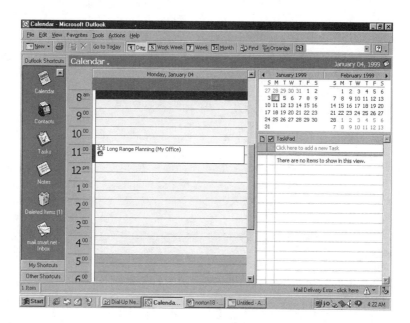

Planning a Meeting

Planning a meeting with a group of people can be tricky business, especially if you need to reserve resources and pick a time that meets everyone's needs. The Outlook Meeting Planner can help with all those details, but it does have some limitations that you should be aware of.

If you just need to schedule meetings with people connected to your company's network, you can make full use of the meeting planner as long as everyone is using Outlook 2000 and Microsoft Exchange Server is installed on the company server. Without Exchange Server, you can't view free/busy schedules or have Outlook pick the best time for everyone's schedule. And without Outlook, meeting request messages appear blank unless you've typed the details in the large text box provided.

To schedule meetings with others over the Internet, you all need to publish your schedules in iCalendar format as described previously and need to be using iCalendar-compliant software as an email and scheduling client. Obviously, Outlook 2000 gives you the most seamless performance because you don't have any compatibility issues to contend with.

Sending a Meeting Request

When you're requesting a meeting with one or two people in your office, sending a simple meeting request may suffice because you don't need any specific resources, and you may already know the individuals' schedules.

You can approach this task from a couple of different angles. You can either click a contact in Contact view and click Actions|New Meeting with Contact to launch the Meeting Request form, or you can move to Calendar view and click Actions|New Meeting Request.

When the Meeting Request form is in view, you need to do the following to fill out and send the meeting request:

1. To invite people to the meeting (or to add names of people to the list if you started the process by selecting a contact), click the To button to open the Select Attendees and Resources dialog box shown in Figure 18.12. If you opened the Meeting Request form by selecting a contact and do not need to invite anyone else, you can skip to step 3.

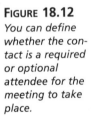

FIGURE 18.12
You can define whether the contact is a required or optional attendee for the meeting to take place.

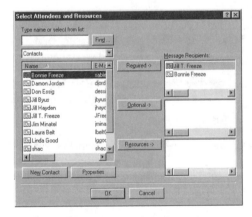

2. Invite a contact by clicking his or her name and then clicking the Required or Optional button as desired. The chosen contacts' names appear in the Required or Optional Message Recipient box as you specified. After all the names of the attendees have been placed on the appropriate list, click the OK button.

3. Type in the subject of the message, and specify the location. If the location has been used before, you can select it from the Location drop-down list.

4. If you're planning an online meeting using NetMeeting or NetShow, check the This is an Online Meeting Using option, and then choose the appropriate tool from the drop-down list.

5. The Start Time and End Time drop-down boxes make setting the length of the meeting a snap. You can even place a check mark in the All Day Event check box if applicable. If the attendees have made their schedules available over the Internet or intranet, you can take a glimpse at the Attendee Availability tab to make sure the chosen time works for everyone.

6. To be reminded of the meeting so that you won't be late, place a check in the Reminder box, and then use the drop-down box to tell Outlook how much time in advance you want to be reminded of the meeting.

7. Use the Show Time As drop-down box to mark the meeting as tentative, out of office, or busy. This information is what others see when they go to look at your calendar.

8. Although all the preceding information helps you manage your schedule, it appears as nothing but a blank message to a non-Outlook user. Given that, you can include a text message reiterating all the pertinent information for non-Outlook users. You do so by typing the information into the large text box on the bottom half of the Appointment tab.

Caution: Outlook Express doesn't count either. Outlook Express (which is considered part of the Internet Explorer 5 suite of applications) is admittedly a powerful email and newsreading client, but when it comes to meeting planning, it doesn't make the grade. Outlook Express was never intended to be a meeting planning tool. So even if your contacts use Outlook Express, you still need to include the text clarification of the meeting logistics.

9. Double-check the information one last time to verify that everything is correct.

Tip: Attaching files to the meeting request. Outlook 2000 makes it easy to include a meeting agenda or other document to be discussed at the meeting with the meeting request. To do so, click the Insert File button (the paper clip icon on the Meeting Request toolbar), browse to the file you want to include, click the filename to select it, and then click the Insert drop-down arrow button. From there, you have the option to include the file as email text, to attach it to the message request for processing like any other mail attachment, or to create a shortcut, or link, to the message if it's stored on a server accessible to the recipient(s).

10. When all the information meets with your approval, click the Send button. The meeting requests are then routed to their destination.

Using the Outlook 2000 Meeting Planner

The more elaborate the meeting, the more complicated the arrangements. The moment you raise the number of attendees to the point where you have to move the meeting to a conference room instead of an office, you add a whole new level of complexity.

As long as your associates all publish their free/busy information, and the resources (such as conference rooms, VCRs and the like) are managed using Microsoft Exchange Server, you can take full advantage of Outlook 2000's meeting planning capabilities.

To organize a meeting using this meeting planning tool, follow these steps:

1. From within Calendar, click Actions|Plan a Meeting. The Plan a Meeting dialog box shown in Figure 18.13 appears.

FIGURE 18.13

Notice that your schedule appears onscreen the instant the Plan a Meeting box dialog opens.

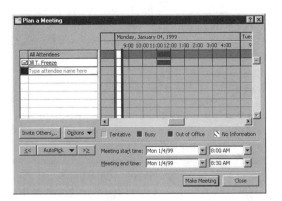

2. You need to invite others to the meeting by clicking the Invite Others button. This action launches the familiar Select Attendees and Resources dialog box shown in Figure 18.12. Choose the desired attendees by clicking their names and then clicking the Required or Optional button as appropriate. To select the needed resources, click a resource to select it, and then click the Resources button to move it into the Resources box. Click OK to return to the meeting planner. Note that each attendee's schedule now appears onscreen with yours.

Note: Tell them where to go automatically. If you select a conference room and choose Required instead of Resources, the chosen conference room does not automatically appear in the meeting's Location box. In this case, simply clicking the right button can save you a bit of work.

3. You can select the time for the meeting in one of three ways:

- Click the AutoPick button to have Outlook 2000 choose the first commonly available free meeting time. It looks for half-hour chunks of time, though the tentative time band it returns can easily be clicked and dragged in one direction or the other to accommodate longer meeting lengths.

- If your eyes instantly fall on a block of free time, click inside the time slot to make the time band appear. Again, you can drag out either side if more than a half hour is needed.

- You can also enter the exact times using the Meeting Start Time and Meeting End Time drop-down boxes.

4. After you've chosen a time and attendees, click the Make Meeting button. Clicking this button takes you to the standard Meeting Request form, which you can fill out and process as described in the preceding section.

Scheduling a Recurring Activity

Whether it's a weekly staff meeting, a daily workout, or an annual vacation at a time-share property, you might need to schedule recurring activities. You do so by clicking the Recurrence button from within any Meeting, Meeting Request, or Appointment dialog box. The Appointment Recurrence dialog box shown in Figure 18.14 then appears. You should note that this function is used in lieu of the Start Time and End Time drop-down lists.

FIGURE 18.14

Define the activity's recurrence pattern using numerous easy-to-use drop-down lists.

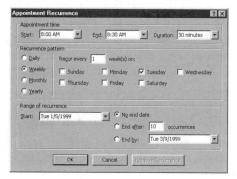

When you want to schedule a recurring activity, click the Recurrence button, and then do the following:

1. In the Appointment Time section, specify the activity's start and end time using the drop-down boxes provided. Alternatively, you can set the start time and then pick a duration for the meeting or appointment.

2. In the Recurrence Pattern section, specify whether the given activity occurs daily, weekly, monthly, or yearly. You can also set weekly, biweekly, and such appointments to occur on a certain day of the week; this way, even if you don't know the dates, you're covered.

Peter's Principle: A healthy worker is a productive worker.

This saying may be trite, but it's true nonetheless. Time flies by quickly, making it easy to forget the things that are truly important, such as an annual physical or biannual dental visit. Consider using these tools to remind yourself that you need to make an appointment.

---

3. In the Range of Recurrence section at the bottom of the dialog box, define when the recurring appointments should begin and when they should end. You can express these appointments in terms of concrete dates (don't worry, there's an easy-to-use drop-down calendar), you can specify that the appointments remain ongoing, or you can tell them to stop after they've occurred a certain number of times.

4. After you've accurately defined the recurrence of the activity, click the OK button. You are returned to the Meeting, Meeting Request, or Appointment dialog box to continue defining the activity's details.

Processing a Request for a Meeting

When you receive a request for a meeting and open it in your Inbox, it looks like a traditional email message. Click the Accept, Tentative, or Decline button as applicable to launch a new message window pre-addressed to the meeting requester. Type in a message if you want, and then click Send to route the response back to the requester of the meeting.

Printing Your Outlook 2000 Calendar

Laptop computers may have gotten smaller over time, but they can still be a nuisance to lug around at a conference, for example. At times like that, I usually print my calendar so that I can keep it with me throughout the entire event.

You may also want to print your calendar to assist you in creating time reports for your boss. That way, your meetings and appointments are already noted, so all you need to do is jot down the tasks and activities that filled in the time in between meetings.

To print your calendar, follow these simple steps:

1. Enter the Calendar mode of Outlook by clicking the Calendar button on the Outlook Bar.

2. Click File|Print to open the Print dialog box shown in Figure 18.15.

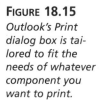

FIGURE 18.15
Outlook's Print dialog box is tailored to fit the needs of whatever component you want to print.

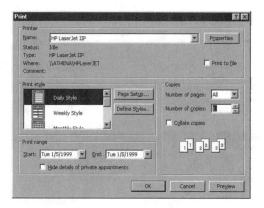

3. Choose the style of calendar you would like to print by clicking one of five options in the Print Style box.

4. Use the Start and End drop-down lists in the Print Range section of the Print dialog box to tell Outlook which dates you want included in the printout.

5. If you have private meetings on your calendar, and you don't want them to be printed, be sure to check the Hide Details of Private Appointments option in the bottom-left corner of the dialog box.

6. Tell Outlook how many copies of the calendar to print in the Number of Copies box in the Copies section of the dialog box.

7. Click the OK button to send the output to the printer.

> **Tip: Make sure you're getting what you want.** If you're just starting to experiment with printing in Outlook 2000, you might want to consider previewing the output before you send it to the printer. To do so, click the Preview button instead of the OK button at the bottom of the Print dialog box. Click the Print button at the top of the Print Preview screen to return to the Print dialog box, where you can either make changes or send the output to the printer.

Managing Your To-Do List with Outlook 2000's Task Component

Outlook 2000 gives you an easy way to maintain a personal to-do list, track progress of projects, and even assign tasks to others.

After they're entered onto your task list, items needing attention appear on your Outlook Today desktop. And should they stay there without being completed, they even turn red to underscore the urgency of the matter.

Creating a New Task

Follow these steps to begin adding items to your personal task list:

1. Enter Task mode by clicking the Task button on the Outlook Bar.

2. Click the New button at the far-left end of the Task toolbar to open the dialog box shown in Figure 18.16.

FIGURE 18.16

Track all kinds of details about a project's progress using the Task tool.

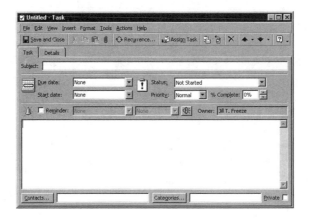

3. Give the task a descriptive name in the Subject field.

4. Specify the start and due dates using the drop-down boxes provided.

> **Tip: Staying on top of things...**After you enter a due date, the yellow InfoBar appears across the top of the task's screen, telling you exactly how many days you have left to complete the task.

5. If you want to be reminded of an upcoming deadline, check the Reminder option, and then use the drop-down boxes to specify a date and time for the reminder.

6. Make any notes to yourself in the large text box covering the bottom half of the Task dialog box, and then click Save and Close.

> **Tip: Do it again!** You can make a task recur on your list by entering the Task dialog box and following the steps presented in the "Scheduling a Recurring Activity" section earlier in the chapter.

That's the minimum you'll want to do to create a task entry. If the task involves working with a document in some way, you can attach the document, just its text, or even a link to the file on the server to the task. Just click the paper clip icon, browse to the file, click the filename to select it, and then use the Insert drop-down arrow button to specify how you want the file to be associated with the task.

Assigning the Task to Someone Else

Although Microsoft's naming of the Assign Task option makes it sound like it's a tool for managers to assign tasks to their staff members, don't let it limit your thinking about the feature. Be creative! In fact, I use the Assign function a lot to route a document for review by others whom I consider to be my peers, not my staff.

To assign a task to someone else, either create the new task as described in the preceding section, or open the task by double-clicking its entry on your task list. Note that both you and the recipient need to be using Outlook 2000 to take full advantage of the task tracking capabilities.

Follow these steps from the Task dialog box to make the assignment:

1. From the open Task dialog box, click the Assign Task button near the center of the dialog box's Task toolbar. The dialog box in Figure 18.17 then appears.

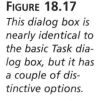

FIGURE 18.17

This dialog box is nearly identical to the basic Task dialog box, but it has a couple of distinctive options.

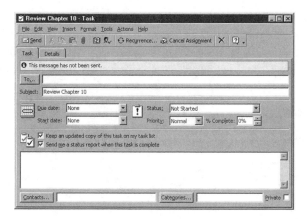

2. Click the To button to choose the task recipient from your list of contacts.

3. Specify a due date for the task. You can specify a start date as well if it's a long task and you want to mark when progress should start being made toward the completion of the task.

4. Give the task a priority level using the drop-down box provided so that the recipient knows how to proceed in relation to his or her other tasks.

5. By default, Outlook stores an updated copy of the task's progress on your task list, and it requests that you be notified upon the project's completion. You can remove either of these requirements simply by deleting the check mark next to its respective option.

6. Add any special notes to the text box provided, and then click the Send button to make the assignment.

Monitoring the Progress of a Task

To track the progress of a task, just open it and use the drop-down boxes to reflect what portion of it has been completed. If you need to track exact amounts of time spent on the task, click the Details tab, and use the drop-down boxes to enter the amount of time spent on the project, the percentage that's been completed, and so on. If the task was assigned by someone else, you can send that person a quick status report by clicking the Send Status Report button near the right end of the task's toolbar.

Specifying Which Items to Log in Your Journal

Outlook 2000 makes it easy to keep track of interactions with selected contacts. Not only does this include email exchanged and meetings attended with the contact, but it can include Office documents sent to you by those contacts as well. You can even add entries manually for items that don't fall into any of Outlook's predefined tracking categories. To set up your Journal options, follow these steps:

1. From within Outlook 2000, click Tools|Options, and then verify that the Preferences tab is in view.

2. Click the Journal Options button, which you find in the Contacts section of the tab. Clicking this button launches the Journal Options dialog box shown in Figure 18.18.

FIGURE 18.18
Click the elements you want to track for each contact you specify.

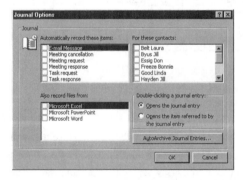

3. Check the items you want to monitor in the Automatically Record These Items box. You can also log the receipt of Excel, PowerPoint, and Word files by checking them in the box at the bottom left of the dialog box.

4. In the For These Contacts box, you can check off the contacts you want to keep journal entries for.

5. Click the OK button to save your settings and dismiss the dialog box.

Outlook 2000 automatically stores journal entries for a contact in the Activities tab of his or her set of Contact tabs. Just double-click the item to open it.

Getting to Know the Outlook 2000 Notes Tool

Outlook 2000 contains a tool that's the electronic counterpart to those little yellow sticky notes. The Notes component helps you keep track of things that aren't quite tasks, but you want to be reminded of them just the same.

To create a new note, follow these steps:

1. Click the Notes button on the Outlook Bar to enter Notes mode.

2. To create a new note, click the New button at the far-left end of the Notes toolbar. A little yellow box like the one shown in Figure 18.19 appears.

FIGURE 18.19

Notice that the date and time the note was written are printed on the bottom of the note box.

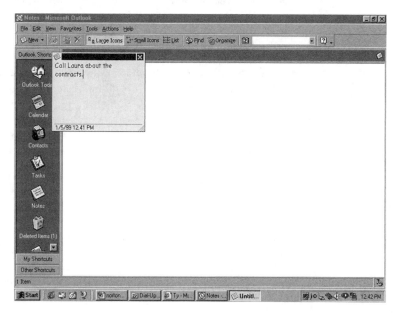

3. Type in the desired text, and then click the Close button to place it in the Notes desktop.

To see the full content of the note again, double-click its icon on the Notes desktop. You should also know that the content of these notes will work with the Clipboard, so you can transfer the text to another application if needed. Although that's not real likely with a typical note that serves as a reminder, it's great to know you have this capability if you're keeping notes for a magazine article idea or some other creative tidbit.

On Your Own

Outlook 2000 is so full of features that it could take you weeks just to get set up to use them all. Take a few minutes to think about how you use your computer. Do you have a staff that you need to assign tasks to? Would it be possible for you and your colleagues to take advantage of some of the scheduling aids Outlook 2000 offers? Do some checking around to find out what software you and your associates have available. Maybe even give your company network administrator a call to see whether you have access to Exchange Server.

If you find many company resources are going untapped, consider mentioning the tools to your supervisor. Making use of them could potentially make all your lives easier in the long run.

If you're not involved in the corporate scene, I'm betting you can still find countless ways to help yourself get better organized. Use the task scheduler to stay on top of graduate school assignments, remind yourself to pay the bills, or send a greeting card. See? You needn't be a corporate maverick to benefit from some of Outlook 2000's tools.

PART V

PowerPoint Essentials

Creating Basic PowerPoint 2000 Presentations

If there's one Office application that tends to go unexplored by the average person, it would have be PowerPoint. Sure, many people never use Access either, but that's mostly because their database needs aren't overly complicated or because the complexity of the application itself intimidates them. With PowerPoint, the problem is often simply that people just aren't sure what the application does.

Historically, PowerPoint has been used to create slide show presentations, overhead transparencies, and paper handouts. With PowerPoint 2000's integration with the Internet Explorer 5 suite of applications, presentations can be made to remote locations in the same office complex or to branch offices across the globe. With a little work and planning, you can even put these new interactive features to good use as a rudimentary computer-based training tool for distance learning via the Web.

In this chapter, I'll discuss the basics of generating a PowerPoint presentation by taking advantage of several new ease-of-use features and explore how and when to use multimedia effects.

Introducing the New and Improved PowerPoint Workspace

If you've used PowerPoint in the past, you'll recall that you often had to switch slide views to complete various tasks. With PowerPoint 2000's revolutionary new Tri-Pane view (see Figure 19.1), you can now see the outline of your presentation, any notes you may have added, and the current slide all at once.

FIGURE 19.1

PowerPoint 2000's new Tri-Pane view gives you a bird's-eye view of your entire presentation.

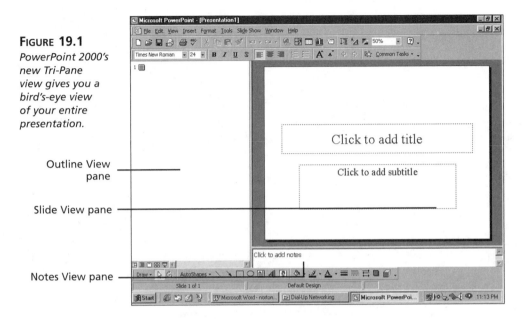

Outline View pane

Slide View pane

Notes View pane

This new three-way view makes adding slides, reorganizing your presentation, and entering notes a single mouse click away.

Creating Presentations in PowerPoint 2000

When you launch PowerPoint, you are greeted by a dialog box that gives you four potential plans of action. From here, you can do any of the following:

- Create a new presentation using the AutoContent Wizard
- Create a new presentation using a Design Template
- Create a new blank presentation
- Open an existing presentation

Although the last two options are fairly self-explanatory, the first two could use a bit more explaining.

When you create a presentation with AutoContent, you go through a series of questions that are used to generate a sample presentation complete with content that you can modify as needed. With the Design Template, you have the option to create a presentation based on any of the shared Office 2000 themes, but the content and its format are totally up to you.

Using the AutoContent Wizard to Create a Presentation

Because you may not be familiar with how these PowerPoint tools work, let's take a closer look at each of them along with the presentations they produce.

To begin building a presentation using the AutoContent Wizard, follow these steps:

1. When you launch PowerPoint 2000, you are prompted to tell the program how you want to create the presentation. Select the AutoContent Wizard option, and then click the OK button.

> **Tip: Coming at it from another direction...**To find the AutoContent Wizard when you already have PowerPoint open, click File|New, verify that the General tab is open, and then double-click the AutoContent Wizard item.

2. The AutoContent Wizard launches and gives you a brief explanation of what it is about to do. Click the Next button to begin working with the wizard.

3. In the following screen, click the button that best describes the type of presentation you want to create, and then select the most applicable item from the window on the right side of the screen. Click Next when you're satisfied with your selection.

> **Tip: I know it's here somewhere...**If you're not sure where the type of presentation you want to create is stored, click the All button rather than waste time skimming each of the categories. The list of default items isn't outrageously long, so it shouldn't hold you back.

4. In the next screen, specify how the presentation will be given. Your choices include onscreen presentation, Web presentation, black-and-white overheads, color overheads, and 35mm slides. Make your selection, and then click Next.

5. In the next screen, you are asked to give the presentation a title. You also have the opportunity to type in material you would like to appear on each slide (for example, your company name or the name of the presenter). Finally, you can check whether you want the modification date and the slide number to be printed at the top of each slide. Click Finish to have PowerPoint 2000 build the presentation as you defined it (see Figure 19.2).

Note: But shouldn't I click Next instead of Finish? After you've completed step 5, you've given PowerPoint all the information it needs to do its job. Clicking Next merely takes you to one last screen that does little more than say, "Hey, congratulations; you're finished!" You've got better things to do with your time.

FIGURE 19.2
Content for each slide is suggested, and PowerPoint 2000 even picks the presentation's theme for you.

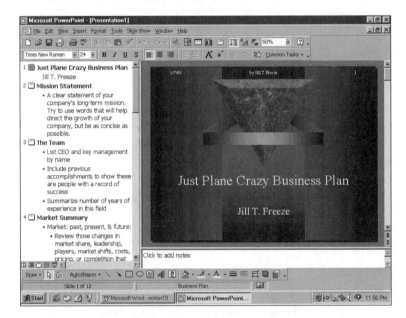

With AutoContent Wizard-generated presentations, you're given advice on what kind of information to include in each slide. Although a theme is automatically chosen for you, you can quickly change it by clicking Format|Apply Design Template. Click a name of a Design Template to preview it on the right half of the resulting dialog box. When you find one you want to use, click the Apply button. Your presentation instantly appears sporting the Design Template you just applied.

Building a Presentation from a Design Template

If you've already adopted a shared Office 2000 theme for your organization's Web site, why not maintain the continuity by using the same theme for your PowerPoint presentation as well? Building a presentation with a Design Template essentially lets you choose the theme and color scheme for the presentation from the onset; that way, you don't have to go through and define each element individually. It's also a good option if you already have specific content and a layout in mind.

To start creating a presentation from a Design Template, you need to do the following:

1. If you're launching PowerPoint, select Design Template from the initial dialog box and then click OK. If PowerPoint is already running, click File|New, choose the template you want from the Design Templates tab, and then click OK.

2. The New Slide dialog box shown in Figure 19.3 appears. Click your chosen layout for the first slide, and then click OK. Now you're on your own to begin exploring all the neat options and settings tucked away in PowerPoint 2000.

FIGURE 19.3
PowerPoint 2000 lets you choose from just about any imaginable slide configuration.

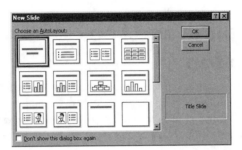

Starting with a Blank Presentation

For a totally customized approach to designing a presentation, start by choosing the Blank Presentation option on the opening dialog box (or if PowerPoint is already running, click File|New, and then double-click Blank Presentation in the General tab). This action launches the New Slide dialog box (refer to Figure 19.3) from which you can select the slide layout of your choice.

Because no content, themes, or templates are offered, you can build the exact presentation you want from the ground up.

Creating a Presentation from a Word 2000 Document or Outline

If you already have a Word 2000 outline or document you would like to use as the basis of a presentation, PowerPoint 2000 makes the job almost trivial. Why not benefit from the hours of organization you put into that big report for the boss?

To begin creating a presentation based on a Word 2000 file, just create a blank presentation, and then dismiss the New Slide dialog box by clicking the Cancel button. Then click Insert|Slides from Outline. A dialog box that closely resembles a standard Open or Save As dialog box appears. Browse to and then double-click the name of the file you want to generate the presentation from.

Caution: But wait, there's a slight catch. For the slides to be generated, the Word document or outline must make use of the hierarchical Heading 1 style, Heading 2 style, and so on.

PowerPoint 2000 creates a slide for each Heading 1 that appears in the chosen outline or document (assuming you used style codes). All Heading 2 material is treated as first-level text for each Heading 1 slide and so on.

Coordinating the Look of Your Presentation

Many people enter the contents of their entire presentation before they get around to setting a background or color scheme. They believe these finishing touches should be added only when the presentation meets with their approval. I, on the other hand, tend to approach this process from the opposite direction.

Because the background you choose and the color scheme you select can have a direct effect on the fonts you choose as well as the size of the text, your decision can definitely have an impact on the presentation's content. You might want to adjust the amount of text on each slide, depending on how visible the words are with your selected background and color scheme. Why force yourself to go through the entire presentation twice (or more) when you can nip many of the potential problems in the bud with the first go-round?

When you're dealing with PowerPoint presentations, nice-looking output is not a luxury; it's a necessity.

Choosing a Simple Background for Your Presentation

Simple but elegant is often in order, and when it is, you can follow these steps to choose a basic, single-color background for your presentation:

1. Open the presentation to which you want to apply a background.

2. Click Format|Background to launch the Background dialog box.

3. Use the drop-down list box, as shown in Figure 19.4, to make your selection from a small number of colors based on the presentation's default color scheme.

FIGURE **19.4**

Use the drop-down list box as shown here to choose a background color.

4. If you don't see something that catches your eye, click the More Colors option, and then click the color swatch you want on the palette. If you're really adventurous and into mixing colors, open the Custom tab and tweak the settings until you see the desired result in the New window. Clicking OK returns you to the Background dialog box.

> **Tip: Lighten up!** If you're creating the presentation to be used as transparencies on an overhead projector or are planning to generate printed handouts from it, lighter backgrounds will serve you best. If, on the other hand, you're creating a slide show or online content, darker colors can give you richness and depth that are second to none.

5. Click the Apply to All button to apply the new background to the entire presentation, or simply click Apply to use it on the current slide only. This command also dismisses the Background dialog box so that you can continue working with your presentation.

Creating Rich Background Effects

The background you choose (or create for that matter) literally sets the mood for the entire presentation. Whether you want a serene blue gradient or an eye-popping rainbow blanket of color, these rich elements are must-haves for today's presentations. These special effects can run the gamut from classy to playful, too, so don't be afraid to explore.

To begin building that special background, you need to do the following:

1. Open or create the presentation you want to work with, and then click Format|Background to open the familiar Background dialog box.

2. Select Fill Effects from the drop-down box at the bottom of the dialog box. This action launches the Fill Effects set of tabs from which you can choose to work with any of the following effects:

    • Gradient—Blend one or two colors into one another in a variety of ways. Choose your own color scheme by selecting the One- or Two- Color option, or opt for one of the preset schemes that include some colorful rainbow blends. Use the Shading Styles and Variants options to achieve the effect you're looking for.

- Texture—Whether you want marble, wood grain, or water, you can find a texture to meet your needs in the Texture tab. Click the Other Textures button near the bottom of the dialog box to import textures residing on your PC.

- Pattern—Check out this tab for eye-popping combinations of lines, dots, and other patterns based on two colors you choose. Although the effects look great on their own, you should be aware that very few of them work well with normal-sized text.

- Picture—Perhaps you want to use a faded version of your corporate logo for the presentation's background. You can do so by visiting this tab, browsing to the appropriate image file, and then double-clicking it to apply it.

3. Click OK to see your chosen fill effect previewed with the current color scheme.

4. Click Apply to All or Apply as desired.

Defining the Presentation's Color Scheme

After you've chosen a suitable background for the presentation, you can make sure the presentation's color scheme complements as opposed to detracts from the effect you're trying to achieve. A color scheme basically defines how text, bullets, and objects appear.

To begin selecting a color scheme, click Format|Slide Color Scheme. The Color Scheme dialog box shown in Figure 19.5 appears. The Standard tab gives you seven predefined color schemes from which to choose.

FIGURE 19.5

If none of these color schemes work with your background, consult the Custom tab.

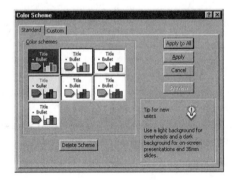

Don't see anything you like? Open the Custom tab, where you can define the exact color of each element. Just double-click its color swatch to choose a color from the large palette, click OK, and then see the modification instantly in the preview window in the lower-right corner of the dialog box. When everything looks to be in order, click Apply to All or Apply as needed.

> **Tip: Some things are just worth saving.** If you come up with a color scheme that really seems to work for you, click the Add as Standard Scheme button. That way, all your hard work is saved in the current Design Template on the Standard tab for future use.

Manipulating Slide Text

When you have a framework and a color scheme for your presentation, you can start adding text. If you've built the presentation from an outline, the AutoContent Wizard, or a Word 2000 document, some of the text will already be present. Simply click inside the text's placeholder to activate the chosen block of text, and then delete, edit, or add text as you would do in any other text box. You can even use traditional Microsoft Word text selection methods to choose a block of text and make it bold, turn it into a bulleted list, center it, or any other common task.

Using PowerPoint 2000's New AutoFit Feature

If the text is close to fitting in the defined placeholder but doesn't quite make it, PowerPoint 2000's new AutoFit feature first tweaks the line spacing and then the font size to try to make it work. This feature is enabled by default, but if you want to disable it to maintain a consistent feel throughout the entire presentation, you can do so by clicking Tools|Options, opening the Edit tab, and then deselecting the Auto-Fit Text to Text Placeholder option. Click the OK button to save your setting and exit the dialog box.

> **Tip: When AutoFit doesn't cut it...**Of course, if you have too much text for AutoFit to do its thing, you can always enlarge the text's placeholder. Just run your mouse pointer over the border of the placeholder until you see the double-headed resizing arrows. Click and drag the frame up or down as needed.

Introducing the New AutoNumbered Bullets

In its ongoing attempt to make the Office suite of applications truly integrated, Microsoft has introduced a number of Word functions into the newest version of PowerPoint. One of these features is the capability to generate automatically numbered lists. When you select an item, click Format|Bullets and Numbering, open the Numbered tab, choose the desired format, and then click the OK button, your list automatically numbers itself each time you enter an item and press Enter. You can even choose a color for the bullets using the Color drop-down box if a default color scheme isn't in place. No more manual numbering! Even if you enter an item in the middle of a list, PowerPoint renumbers the list's members automatically as necessary.

Making an Impression with the New Graphical Bullets

One of the new enhancements to Office 2000 as a whole is its capability to apply picture bullets. This enhancement comes as a direct result of the suite's expanded Web publishing capabilities because graphical bullets are now Web page staples. Although many possibilities come prepackaged with the suite of applications, you can use just about any image that suits your purpose.

To use one of the new graphical bullets in your presentation, follow these simple steps:

1. Make sure the slide you want to apply the graphical bullets to is in view.

2. If bulleted text already exists, select it and then click Format|Bullets and Numbering. If you still need to enter the text, just click Format|Bullets and Numbering to launch the Bullets and Numbering dialog box.

3. With the Bulleted tab open, click the Picture button near the bottom-right corner of the dialog box. Clicking this button takes you to the Pictures tab of the Picture Bullet dialog box, as shown in Figure 19.6.

FIGURE 19.6

Your choices range from simple colored square bullets to textured button-like bullets.

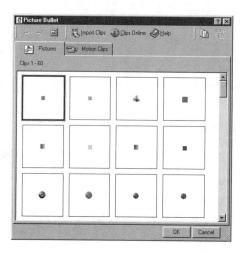

4. Browse through the selection until you find one you want to use. Click it to select it, and then click OK. A new graphical bullet appears each time you enter text and then press Enter.

If you don't see an image you want to use, click the Keep Looking icon at the bottom of each group of Picture Bullet images. Repeat as necessary until you get to the end of the list.

Still don't see the perfect bullet? If the desired graphic resides on your machine, click the Import Clips button, browse to the desired file (this action may require you to change the Files of Type setting), and then double-click the filename. A copy of the image's file is placed in the Clip Gallery picture bullets tool for future use as well.

If you still come up empty after exhausting all these options, you might want to click the Clips Online button to continue your search for the perfect bullet there. If you need a refresher on how to use Clip Gallery Live over the Internet, turn back to Chapter 5, "Shared Applets and Tools Available in Office 2000."

Adding a Unique Touch with Character Bullets

Remember those funny themed wingdings or dingbat fonts you see in the Font drop-down box? Now you can finally put them to good use—as graphical bullets. What better way to capture the essence of a presentation than to incorporate simple images that reflect the nature of the presentation?

> **Tip: Make your choices count.** Whatever you do, choose your wingdings care-fully. Some are so busy that they can be downright distracting, whereas others (like the box—or square—bullet) can go a long way toward enhancing your message. Consider those box bullets as an example. When used for a checklist, they prompt the viewer to add a check mark after the bullet item is complete.

Using one of these characters as a bullet involves completing these simple steps:

1. Verify that the slide you want to work with is in view.

2. If all the text for the bullets already exists, select it and then click Format|Bullets and Numbering. If you still need to enter the text, just click Format|Bullets and Numbering to launch the Bullets and Numbering dialog box.

3. With the Bulleted tab open, click the Character button to launch the Bullet dialog box, as shown in Figure 19.7.

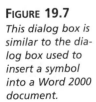

FIGURE 19.7

This dialog box is similar to the dialog box used to insert a symbol into a Word 2000 document.

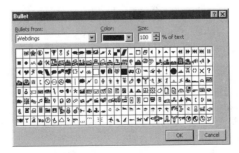

4. Choose a set of characters using the Bullets From drop-down box. You see a preview of each of the symbols in the large window below.

5. If a color scheme is not already in place to define the color of the bullets, use the Color drop-down box to choose one.

6. Click the character you want to use to see a slightly larger version of it. Note that the symbol is shown in reverse color. That is, a black computer silhouette on a white background appears as a white computer silhouette on a black background.

7. After you've found a symbol you want to use as a bullet, click it and then click the OK button.

AutoFormatting as You Type

It's a subtle difference, but one that can set an amateur presentation apart from a professional one. In PowerPoint 2000, the application now has the Word-like capability to recognize ordinals, fractions, smart quotes, and AutoCorrect entries and format them accordingly. This option is also turned on by default, but you can disable it by clicking Tools|AutoCorrect, and then deselecting the Replace Text as You Type option from the middle of the dialog box. For a quick review of how this option works and can be configured, turn back to Chapter 7, "Maximizing Word 2000."

Adding and Deleting Presentation Slides

If you build your presentation using the Design Template or Blank Presentation option, you start with only one slide in your presentation. Because you'll undoubtedly want to add more slides, you'll be grateful to see just how easily you can do that with PowerPoint 2000's new Tri-Pane view.

To insert a new slide, simply click the slide in the Outline pane after which you want to place the new slide. Click the New Slide button on the Standard toolbar to launch the New Slide dialog box (see Figure 19.3). Choose the desired layout for the slide, and then click OK. The new slide then appears in order after the slide you chose.

Should you ever need to delete a slide, all you have to do is click its numbered icon in the Outline pane and then press the Delete key.

> **Tip: Just a friendly reminder...**If you put in late nights at the keyboard like I do, you'll be comforted to know that the old faithful Ctrl+Z command (also known as the Undo command) works to bring back slides you hadn't intended to delete. Of course, you need to notice your mistake before you complete too many additional tasks.

Inserting a Duplicate Slide

Perhaps you have a slide in the current presentation that you would like to base another slide on. Rather than rekey everything, why not just duplicate the slide and insert it into the presentation?

To do so, just click the numbered icon of the slide you want to duplicate in the Outline pane, and then click Insert|Duplicate Slide. The new copy of the slide appears immediately after the one you duplicated.

Including a Slide from Another Presentation

If you give presentations regularly, you'll find that you'll want to keep using some slides again and again. And just because a slide resides in another presentation doesn't mean that including it in the current one is impossible.

To include a slide from another presentation, you need to do the following:

1. Click the numbered icon of the slide that will precede the one you want to import.
2. Click Insert|Slides from Files to launch the Slide Finder dialog box.
3. Browse to the file containing the slide you want to use, and then double-click its name. When you return to the Find Presentation tab of the dialog box, notice that the chosen file's name now appears in the File text box.
4. Click the Display button to pull up small thumbnail images of each slide in the presentation (see Figure 19.8).

FIGURE 19.8
Preview all the slides available in the chosen presentation file.

5. All you need to do to import the slide is click it (its border turns blue instead of gray) and then click the Insert button. If you want to import more than one slide, you can do so by clicking each slide you want to include in the current presentation before clicking the Insert button. You can even import the whole presentation by clicking Insert All.

The new slide or slides appear immediately after the slide you chose in the current presentation.

Moving Slides Around Within a Presentation

Thanks to the new Tri-Pane view's ease of use, moving slides around inside a presentation is almost a trivial task. To move a slide, all you need to do is click its numbered icon and drag it into position. A floating horizontal line lets you know exactly where things stand before you drop the slide into position.

Changing a Slide's Layout

As you enter a slide's text, you might decide that the layout you chose originally doesn't fully meet your needs. To change the current layout of a slide, just click its numbered icon in the Outline pane, and then click Format|Slide Layout. The Slide Layout dialog box then opens; it is identical to the New Slide dialog box. Simply make your selection with the click of a mouse, and then click OK. The slide and its contents then reappear sporting the new layout you just applied.

Peter's Principle: You can take it with you!

As you work with PowerPoint more and more, you'll find that you perform some tasks or commands more regularly than others. These commands—New Slide, Slide Layout, and Apply Design Template—can be found on the PowerPoint Common Tasks tear-off menu at the far-right end of PowerPoint 2000's Formatting toolbar. Just click the Common Tasks button, place your mouse pointer on the bar across the top of the drop-down menu, and then click and drag it into the desired location onscreen. That way, all your most commonly used commands are right at your fingertips. You can even dock it into toolbar space where it can serve as its own toolbar.

Adding Tables to Your PowerPoint Presentation

Using tables is one of the best ways to achieve consistent text alignment, especially when the text might be presented in a variety of formats including slide shows, online content, and printed handouts.

In the past, you had to import tables from other applications to be able to use them in PowerPoint. Not so with PowerPoint 2000's new native table building support!

To begin building a table in PowerPoint, use these steps as a guide:

1. Click the existing slide after which you want to place the new table, and then create a new blank slide in which to place the table.

2. From within this new slide, click Insert|Table. The Insert Table dialog box shown in Figure 19.9 appears.

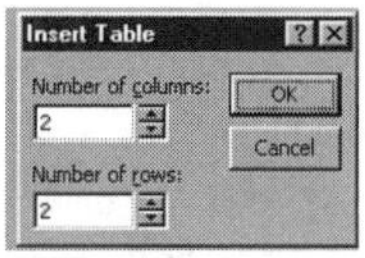

FIGURE 19.9

Use the arrow buttons to select the exact number of rows and columns needed.

Tip: Watch the numbers. Keep in mind that a slide is not nearly as large as a regular piece of paper and that the fonts used are generally bigger for the sake of increased visibility during a presentation. As a result, you might not be able to fit as many rows and columns onto a slide as you might hope. Finding the optimal mix of table size, font size, and content takes a little experimenting, but it will be worthwhile in the long run.

3. Use the arrow buttons to choose the number of rows and columns you need.

4. When the numbers meet with your approval, click the OK button to have the table drawn on the blank slide.

5. Enter table content by clicking inside a cell, typing in the desired information, and then tabbing to the next cell.

When the table is created, notice that the Tables and Borders toolbar automatically appears. To refresh your memory on how to use each of these options, turn back to Chapter 9, "Creating Professional-Looking Documents."

Making Global Changes to Your Presentation Using Slide Master

As you've learned throughout this chapter, you can change bullet colors, fonts, and text color—among other attributes—to your heart's content. However, changing them in every presentation slide can be a major pain. With PowerPoint's Slide Master view, you can make global changes to the presentation in one convenient location. And best of all, you can rest assured that if you made any changes manually (such as colored a block of text for effect), these changes override any settings you change in Slide Master.

To enter Slide Master mode, click View|Master|Slide Master. When you're in Slide Master mode, you see a screen much like the one shown in Figure 19.10.

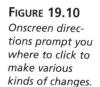

FIGURE 19.10
Onscreen directions prompt you where to click to make various kinds of changes.

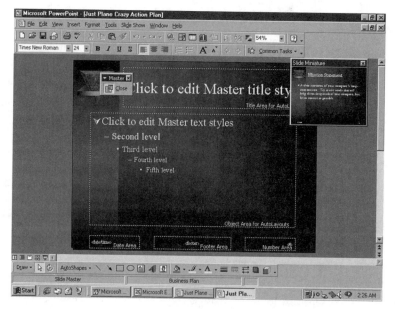

Basically, all you need to do to make a global change is click inside a marked area or select an element and make the desired change to font style, size, color, or effect. In some cases, you might need to apply the effect outright, as is the case with bullets. An onscreen slide miniature lets you see the changes as you make them before you apply them. In any event, whatever changes you make in this view are applied to the current presentation as a whole (except where any manual formatting has been entered) and to any new slides you add to the presentation. Simply click the Close button on the floating Master toolbar to return to the default Tri-Pane view.

Including Speaker Notes with Your Presentation

Another task that's been trivialized by the new Tri-Pane view is the addition of speaker notes to a presentation. In PowerPoint 2000, all you need to do to add speaker notes is to click inside the Notes pane at the bottom of the screen and begin typing. That's literally all there is to it!

In the next chapter, I'll show you how to call on these notes during a live presentation.

Navigating Your Presentation Using Action Buttons

With PowerPoint 2000's effortless adaptability to the Web, navigational aids are even more important than ever. Obviously, you won't need navigational buttons for your slide show for the board of directors, but you will need them should you decide to put the entire presentation on the Web or on the Internet.

To place Action Buttons in your presentation, follow these simple steps:

1. Open the slide in which you want to place the navigational aid.

2. Click Slide Show|Action Buttons, and then grab the tear-off menu and move it into place onscreen.

3. After you've located the type of button you want to add, click it, and then click the location on the slide in which you want to place the button. The Mouse Click tab of the Action Settings dialog box opens, as shown in Figure 19.11.

FIGURE 19.11

The Hyperlink To drop-down list box makes jumping to the desired slide a snap.

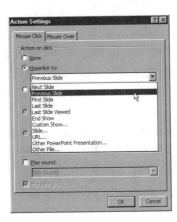

4. To jump to another slide in the presentation, click the Hyperlink To option, and then use the drop-down box to make your selection. Note that if you opted to insert a Previous Slide button, PowerPoint intelligently assumes that you want the button to take you to the previous slide in the presentation. It does so for each of the specific location Action Buttons.

> **Note: Where do you want to go today?** PowerPoint Action Buttons need not link only to other slides. In fact, if you carefully study the Hyperlink To drop-down list, you'll notice that you can link to a variety of locations, including Web sites, other PowerPoint presentations, non-PowerPoint Office documents stored on your company's intranet, and so on.

5. After you've defined the link, click the OK button. You are then taken back to the Tri-Pane view in which you see the new Action Button.

6. You might need to move and/or resize the button to make it fit in with the presentation. Make these adjustments by clicking and dragging the borders of the object (or the whole object itself) into position.

7. To change the look of the button, right-click it and choose Format AutoShape from the shortcut menu. Make the desired changes, and then click OK to save your settings and apply the changes.

Enhancing Your Presentation with Multimedia Effects

When you consider the value of multimedia effects in a presentation, a fine line exists between what is attention grabbing versus what is plain distracting. And to make matters even more complicated, throw in the Web-related performance issues in the case of online presentations. In general, multimedia effects should be used sparingly.

Animating one bullet point for emphasis may drive the point home, but having all six bullets on the slide screech into place can conjure up images of an eight-car pileup on the local beltway.

If your presentation is designed specifically for the Web, consider giving the readers the option to experience some of the multimedia aspects of the presentation. An Action Button (or plain old hyperlink for that matter) with the words "Click here for an important message from our president" accomplishes several things. It gives the readers the option of listening to it, it doesn't make the visitors endure download times if they don't want to hear the greeting, and it keeps the basic presentation uncluttered.

Adding an Image to Your Presentation

Whether you have a scanned photograph of your corporate headquarters, a fancy logo created by a graphic design artist, or an animated GIF designed to lighten up your presentation, you can place it in a PowerPoint slide with ease.

> **Tip: Mirror image.** If you want a particular image such as your corporate logo to appear on every slide, you need to insert it in Slide Master mode.

Follow these steps to insert an image into your presentation:

1. Open the slide into which you want to insert the image.

2. Click Insert|Picture|From File to launch the Insert Picture dialog box, which is shown in Figure 19.12.

FIGURE 19.12

Preview the picture on the right side of the dialog box before you select it.

3. Browse to the image you want, keeping in mind that a single click lets you preview the image on the right side of the dialog box.

4. When you locate the image you want to use, double-click it to insert it into the presentation in the location you specified.

Animating Text and Objects to Grab Attention

Animating text can be a unique way to give your presentation a powerful impact. For instance, with a little work, you could time the appearance of each bullet point so that it appears just as you're ready to discuss it.

You can put just about anything on a PowerPoint slide into motion by following these steps:

1. Open the slide you want to work with, and then select the item you want to animate, be it a block of text or an object.

2. Click Slide Show|Custom Animation to start setting your options.

3. In the Order & Timing tab, specify whether the animation will be set off by a mouse click or whether it will happen automatically after a certain amount of time. Use the arrow buttons to tweak the amount of time before the animation occurs.

4. The Effects tab is the place where things really start to get interesting. In the Entry Animation and Sound section of the tab, you have a host of drop-down list boxes from which to make your selections.

5. Feel free to experiment with the various options, and then preview your work before applying it by clicking the Preview button.

6. When you're happy with the result, click the OK button to save the settings for the chosen object or block of text. The dialog box closes, and you return to the default Tri-Pane view.

Inserting Sounds and Movies into Your Presentation

With all the multimedia goodies available in the Microsoft Clip Gallery, you can introduce sound and video into your presentation with minimal hassle. To do so, just do the following:

1. Move to the slide in which you want to place the sound or movie file.

2. Click Insert|Movies and Sounds, and then choose either of the movie or sound options on the pop-up menu.

3. If you choose a From Gallery option, the Microsoft Clip Gallery launches, presenting you with some options from which to choose. If you chose From File, you need to browse to the specific file on your machine.

4. When you double-click the desired selection, movie clips are automatically inserted on the slide. In the case of sound clips, a dialog box like the one shown in Figure 19.13 appears asking if you want the sound played automatically when the slide is launched or only when the sound icon is clicked. Choose Yes or No as appropriate.

FIGURE **19.13**
*Tell PowerPoint
how you want the
sound triggered.*

You can double-click a speaker icon from anywhere in PowerPoint to hear the associated sound file, but you need to enter Slide Show or Web Page Preview view to see the movie clips in action.

Using Audio CD Tracks for Background Music

Using the right mood music—so to speak—can make all the difference in the world when you want to get a response from your audience. Driving percussion beats can rev up the audience and get them excited, whereas soothing harmonies can ease tension. Although you may not always be able to find a suitable sound file on your machine or even on the Internet, odds are you can think of a CD that evokes the desired effect.

If that's the case, then you might want to consider using your CD for background music by following these steps:

1. Open the presentation you want to add the CD track to, and then move to the slide in which you want to trigger the music you're about to define.

> **Tip: For the long haul...**If you want to use the same track or CD through the whole presentation, consider setting up the CD audio track options from Slide Master mode.

2. Click Insert|Movies and Sounds|Play CD Audio Track. The Movie and Sound Options dialog box shown in Figure 19.14 opens.

FIGURE **19.14**
*Convenient arrow
buttons let you
choose the exact
start and end
times.*

3. Use the arrow buttons to select the track you want to start on and/or the exact moment in that track you want to begin playing. Do the same for the ending options.

4. If desired, you can instruct the CD to loop until the presentation is exited by checking the Loop Until Stopped option at the top of the dialog box.

5. When the options meet with your approval, click the OK button.

Recording a Sound Slide-by-Slide

In the next chapter, I'll show you how to rehearse and record a narrative for your entire presentation. For the sake of this chapter, though, we'll take a look at how to record a sound on a slide-by slide basis.

To begin recording a sound for a slide, you need to do the following from within the slide you want to include the recording:

1. Verify that your computer not only has a working sound card, but also that a microphone is attached in the proper location.

2. Click Insert|Movies and Sounds|Record Sound. The tiny Record Sound dialog box shown in Figure 19.15 appears.

Stop playing or recording the sound

FIGURE 19.15
Use your virtual tape recorder to record short sound clips.

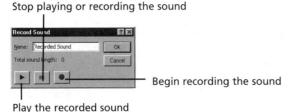

Begin recording the sound

Play the recorded sound

3. Use the buttons as shown in the callouts for Figure 19.15 to record the sound.

4. After you finish recording, click inside the Name text box to assign a name to the sound. Make it a descriptive name because the sound will appear on the list of sounds available in the Effects tab of the Custom Animations dialog box. The sound will also remain embedded in the slide to which you attached it.

> **Caution: If you want to record speech...**Although this tool can record speech, it's best suited for sound effects and single word recordings. For speeches, you'll get far better results out of the Record Narrative feature, which we'll discuss in the next chapter.

On Your Own

If you were intimidated by PowerPoint in the past, now is the time to give it another shot. The new Tri-Pane view has made the PowerPoint environment significantly more inviting, and it has cut down the number of steps needed to perform a task many times over.

To encourage you to explore the world of PowerPoint on your own, here's an interesting exercise. Think about how you feel at this very moment. Now go over to your computer, launch a blank PowerPoint presentation, and make a slide based on the following:

- What kind of background fits your mood best? Is it a bright, cheerful rainbow gradient effect, or is it a basic gray?

- Take a look at the Font drop-down box to see what's available. Are you having a Courier kind of day, or is Lucida more appropriate? Type in the first few words that come to mind.

- If you could overlay a CD track onto your mood slide, would it be playing The Backstreet Boys, Madonna, Yanni, or Bach?

The exercise may seem irrelevant on the surface, but its purpose is primarily to underscore the importance of color choice, font selection, and background music in the creation of a well-targeted, situation-specific presentation.

Preparing for (and Making) Your PowerPoint 2000 Presentation

Now that you have all the presentation's slides in place, it's time to shift your focus to making the presentation. With PowerPoint 2000, you have the power and flexibility to do any of the following:

- Save your presentation to a server so that it can be reviewed again by attendees.
- Put company benefit information on archived presentations that employees can access on demand.
- Rather than pitch an idea via an unstructured conference call or by a static Word document, make a live presentation complete with PowerPoint's multimedia effects.
- Don't waste time on an airplane traveling around the country to make your presentation; give it over the Internet with the help of NetMeeting.
- Leverage the work you did for your presentation with custom slides to produce custom shows for separate, targeted audiences.
- Distribute easy-to-read handouts from your presentation so that the audience will be less bogged down by note taking.
- Have only a certain amount of time to speak? Let PowerPoint help you budget the time you spend on each slide by setting the time spent on each one in advance.

In this chapter, you'll discover just how easily you can put all this power to work for you.

Putting Slides in Order Using the Slide Sorter View

One of the last things you should do to your presentation is verify that the slides are in the order that you want them to appear. The best way to check their order is to enter the Slide Sorter view by clicking the Slide Sorter View button (see Figure 20.1). The Slide

Sorter view gives you a bird's-eye view of every slide in your presentation, and it gives you an easy way to reposition slides as well. To relocate a slide, all you have to do is click it and drag it into its new position.

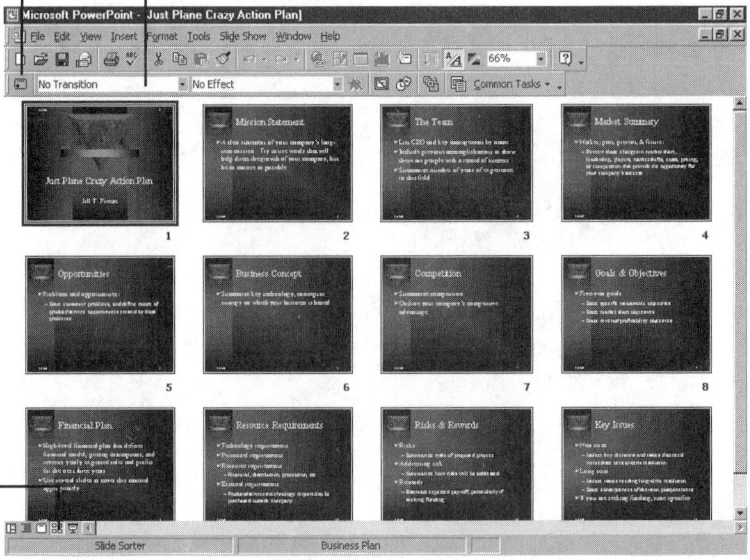

Slide Transition button   Slide Transition Effects

FIGURE 20.1
PowerPoint 2000's Slide Sorter view makes it easy for you to place your slides exactly where you want them.

Slide Sorter View button

Applying Impressive Slide Transitions

Effectively applied slide transitions can go a long way toward impressing your audience. They can literally take a presentation that looks no different than a standard overhead projector presentation and turn it into a full multimedia event.

In the preceding chapter, you learned how to include images, sounds, video, and animation in your presentations. The final touch you might want to place on your presentation is the inclusion of slide transitions. Here again, the basic rules of multimedia effects apply. Use these transitions sparingly so as not to dilute their effect or distract the audience, and try to match the effect to the mood or impression you're trying to leave the viewers with.

Peter's Principle: Learn how to control the "wow factor."

Sure, the slide show can contribute greatly to how your presentation is perceived and even received, but you want your audience "wowing" about what you've said, not about the latest and greatest new PowerPoint slide transitions. Choose one or two transitions that fit the mood of your presentation. Consider even omitting transitions altogether except in the case of two or three of the most powerful slides in the show. That way, the viewers' attention is focused where you want it and when you want it.

To include transitions in your presentation, follow these steps:

1. Open the presentation you want to work with, and then enter Slide Sorter view as described previously.

2. Click the slide to which you want to apply the transition. If you want to apply the effect to more than one slide, hold down the Ctrl key as you click each slide to select it.

3. Click the Slide Transition button at the far-left end of the Slide Sorter toolbar (refer to Figure 20.1) to see the dialog box shown in Figure 20.2.

> **Tip: Quick and easy slide transitions.** If the default speed of the slide transition is acceptable, you can bypass the Slide Transition dialog box and simply click the Slide Transition Effects drop-down box on the Slide Sorter toolbar to choose a transition for the selected slides.

FIGURE 20.2

The Slide Transition dialog box also gives you control over the speed of the transition.

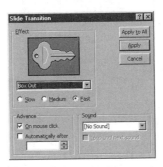

4. Underneath the picture in the Effect section of the dialog box is a drop-down box from which you can select the desired transition.

5. You can tweak the speed of the transition from Slow to Medium to Fast by clicking the corresponding option button.

6. Control how the transition is triggered in the Advance section in the lower-left corner of the Slide Transition dialog box. Your choices include triggering the transition via mouse click or automatically after a certain amount of time. Check the option you prefer. In the case of the timed option, use the arrow buttons to select the amount of time that must elapse before the next transition.

7. You can preview the effect before you apply it by clicking the sample slide in the dialog box.

8. Click the Apply button to apply the chosen effect to the selected slide(s) only or Apply All to use the same transition throughout the presentation.

Responsiveness Is the Key to Effective Presentations

The best presentations are the ones that thoroughly engage the audience—the ones that make people think, "Hey, this person is really talking to me!" or "Wow, this person's ready for just about any question we can throw at her!" PowerPoint 2000 gives you two techniques to make your presentation appear to be responsive to the audience's concerns and/or questions: the capability to build Custom Shows and the capability to hide slides, which you can pull out only if the need arises.

Building a Custom Show

Custom Shows are essentially specialized presentations within a presentation. Say, for example, you need to give a presentation about your latest software product to a group of managers and a group of trainers at two different times. Rather than design two nearly identical presentations, you can create Custom Shows that cater to each group's specific needs while making use of a core of common slides.

Among the advantages of building Custom Shows are the following points:

- Because all the slides for related Custom Shows are stored in a single presentation file, taking them on the road is a snap. The amount of disk space needed is also smaller because many slides are shared between presentations.

- Custom Shows eliminate the need for moving and copying slides from one show to another.

- Custom Shows make your presentations look finely targeted even if a fair quantity of the material is shared among various presentations. The inclusion of even just a couple of group-specific slides makes the entire presentation appear geared toward the audience in question.

Before you begin setting up your Custom Shows, make sure that all the slides for each Custom Show have been created and that they reside in one parent presentation.

After you get through all that work, you can begin building Custom Shows from an existing presentation by doing the following:

1. Open the presentation on which you want to base the new Custom Shows, and then click Slide Show|Custom Shows.

2. Click the New button in the Custom Shows dialog box. A Define Custom Show dialog box like the one pictured in Figure 20.3 appears.

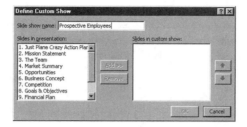

Figure 20.3

Give the slide show a descriptive name, as I've done here, so that you can quickly find the show you want.

3. Enter a name for the slide show in the Slide Show Name box. Make sure that name adequately captures the purpose and/or intended audience of the Custom Show you're about to define.

4. In the Slides in Presentation box on the left side of the dialog box is a list of all the slides residing in the current presentation. To add a slide to the Custom Show, click its title, and then click the Add button. The slide then is moved to the Slides in Custom Show box on the right side of the dialog box.

> **Tip: The more, the merrier.** To select multiple slides for the Custom Show, hold down the Ctrl key as you click each slide's title, and then click the Add button to include them all in the Custom Show. To select a range of contiguous slides, click the top slide on the list, hold down the Shift key, and then click the bottom slide. All the slides are highlighted. Include them in the Custom Show by simply clicking the Add button.

5. To change the order in which a slide appears in the Custom Show, click its name in the Slides in Custom Show box, and then use the arrow buttons to move the slide up or down in order as desired.

6. When all the slides appear in the proper order in the Slides in Custom Show box, click the OK button to save the newly created Custom Show.

7. You then return to the Custom Shows dialog box. There, you can click the Show button to preview the chosen Custom Show or the Close button to dismiss the dialog box and continue working in PowerPoint.

Later in the chapter, I'll show you how to launch the Custom Show as its own presentation or as the finale to a primary presentation.

Hiding a Slide So You'll Be Ready for Anything

We've all heard the Boy Scout motto: "Always be prepared." Well, the same kind of saying holds true for live presentations. Although we would all like to believe that our audience will accept what we have to say unconditionally, that's not always the case. Instead of crossing our fingers and blindly going into the presentation thinking we'll land on our feet no matter what, wouldn't it be far better to be armed with the information and statistics to support our case?

That's where the hidden slides come in. You can gather all the data to support your position, put it on a compelling PowerPoint slide or two, and then hide them in the presentation. That way, you don't appear to be needlessly defensive should your audience be agreeable to your viewpoint, yet you aren't caught off guard should they question you.

Hiding a slide is simpler than ever before thanks to PowerPoint 2000's new Slide Sorter toolbar. Just launch the presentation you want to work with, enter Slide Sorter view, click the slide you want to hide, and then click the Hide Slide button on the Slide Sorter toolbar. It's that easy! The hidden slide's number is crossed out, as shown in Figure 20.4, so you can quickly tell which slides are hidden and which are not.

FIGURE 20.4

Note that the Hide Slide button on the Slide Sorter toolbar also appears pressed when the hidden slide is selected.

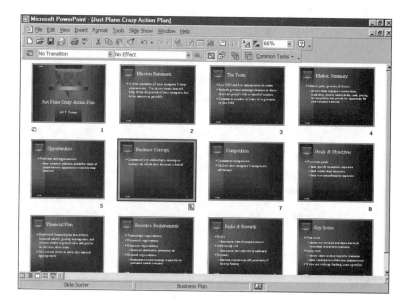

To retrieve a hidden slide during a presentation, you can do one of two things:

- Right-click the slide that precedes the hidden slide, choose Go, and then choose Hidden Slide from the shortcut menu. Note that this option appears only if the next slide is actually hidden.

- To retrieve the hidden slide from within anywhere in the presentation, right-click any slide, choose Go, and then choose Slide Navigator from the shortcut menu. The Slide Navigator dialog box opens. Just double-click the slide you want to open. Note that the numbers of hidden slides appear in parentheses.

Setting the Timer to Advance Slides Automatically

If you plan to run your presentation continuously in kiosk mode at a trade show or similar event, you can set the timer to advance your slides automatically. To do so, you need to follow these steps:

1. Open the presentation you want to set the timer for, and then enter Slide Sorter view.

> **Tip: All slides are not created equal.** If you want some slides to display longer than others, you have to set their timers separately. Select all the slides you want to appear the longest, and then set their timers. Do the same for the slides you want to skim past and then for those that fall somewhere in the middle. The point is you need to set their timers in batches.

2. Click the Slide Transition button at the far-left end of the Slide Sorter toolbar to launch the Slide Transition dialog box shown in Figure 20.2.
3. In the Advance section of the dialog box, click the Automatically After option, and then use the arrow buttons to set the amount of time you want each slide to appear onscreen.
4. Click Apply to All to have the chosen time apply to every slide in the presentation. If you intend to have a variety of slide timings, click Apply, and then define the rest of the slides in the presentation.

Customizing the Timer to Match Your Speech Requirements

I admit it; I can't tell how much time I want to spend on a slide until I do a dry run-through of the presentation. Given that, this method of customizing the timer tends to be the one I use most when making PowerPoint presentations.

To begin rehearsing the slide show, make sure you have your speaker notes in close proximity, and then do the following:

1. Open the presentation you want to rehearse, and then click Slide Show|Rehearse Timings. The presentation begins in Slide Show view, and the Rehearsal dialog box shown in Figure 20.5 appears in the upper-left corner of the first slide. Notice that the timer starts the instant the slide show appears.

Tip: Take two! Because the slide timer starts instantly, I often find myself lost for words the first second or so. It's as if my brain isn't quite ready to launch into the presentation without notice. Given that, I tend to use the Repeat button a lot to start rehearsing my presentation again when I'm more composed.

FIGURE 20.5

The Rehearsal dialog box gives you full control over how much time you spend on each slide.

Time spent on the current slide ———————————— ———— Repeat the current slide's rehearsal
Pause the rehearsal ——————
Move to the next slide ——————

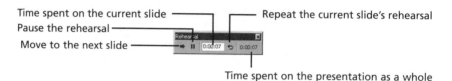

Time spent on the presentation as a whole

2. Click the right-arrow (Next) button to move to the next slide in the presentation.

Tip: Watch what you're doing! Keep a constant eye on the Slide Time window to monitor how much time you spend on the current slide and on the Presentation Time display to make sure you're falling within the amount of time allotted.

3. After you've finished rehearsing, click the Close button in the upper-right corner of the Rehearsal dialog box.

4. PowerPoint 2000 then displays a message like the one shown in Figure 20.6. It tells you how long the presentation lasted as you rehearsed it. You are asked whether you want to save the timings created by the rehearsal (click Yes), or if you would rather keep your old settings or move the slides manually (click No).

FIGURE 20.6

Click Yes if you want to have PowerPoint change your settings based on the rehearsal times.

Recording a Narrative for Your Presentation

No one can be in two places at once, so just because your company's CEO can't attend the presentation doesn't mean you have to do it without him or her. Consider recording special voice narratives for the high points of your presentation. Imagine having the CEO welcome your audience as a slide with a photo of corporate headquarters displayed. Or maybe include that celebrity testimony you received from a famous athlete who benefited from your services on a slide with his or her picture. The possibilities are endless, but with PowerPoint 2000, the process is a simple one. With a little planning (and a computer with a sound card and microphone), you can start recording your narrative by following these steps:

1. Verify that the microphone is properly connected to your computer.

2. Open the presentation for which you want to record the narrative, and then click Slide Show|Set Up Show. Make sure the slides are set to be advanced manually by clicking the Manually option in the bottom-right corner of the Set Up Show dialog box. Then click OK to dismiss the dialog box.

3. Click Slide Show|Record Narration. The Record Narration dialog box shown in Figure 20.7 opens.

Caution: I can see it, but I can't get to it! If the Record Narration menu item is disabled, you might want to double-check your sound card configuration and microphone installation. The option is automatically grayed out if these components are not properly in place.

FIGURE 20.7
This dialog box tells you how much sound you can record based on the amount of disk space you have available.

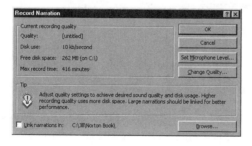

4. If this is the first time you've recorded a narration, click the Set Microphone Level button. A Microphone Check box opens. You are requested to read a paragraph so that the microphone recording levels can be set for the best results possible. Click OK to start the test, and click Cancel to close this dialog box.

5. To set the sound quality of the recording, click the Change Quality button. In the resulting Sound Selection dialog box, click the Name drop-down box to select the type of sound quality you want to record. In the Attributes drop-down box, you can tweak the quality further by specifying whether the recording should be mono or stereo, and so on. After you've made your selections, click OK to close the dialog box.

Tip: The better, the bigger. No, I don't mean the bigger, the better. When it comes to recording sound files, the better the sound quality, the more disk space the sound files take up. To achieve the best compromise, I try to bump up the sound quality on a particularly important slide and then omit narration altogether in some of the less important slides. So in the examples mentioned earlier, I would maximize the sound quality for the CEO welcome message and the celebrity endorsement and then give the remainder of the presentation live. That way, the little bits of sound that were prerecorded actually sound good instead of coming across like a staticky cell phone about to go out of range.

6. By default, the sound files are stored in the presentation itself. If you want to conserve disk space on your machine, you can link to your server and store the sound files there by checking the Link Narrations In option.

Caution: Logistically speaking... If you plan to take the presentation on the road, embedding the sound files may be wisest because the whole presentation can be stored safely on a single laptop, floppy disk, or whatever. If you link to the files, they might inadvertently get left behind when you leave for the big presentation. You should be aware, however, that PowerPoint 2000 automatically links to sound files greater than 100KB. Although this is a great way to prevent two copies of huge sound files from being stored on your machine (one in its original location and the other with the presentation), it could cause a problem when you take the presentation on the road in that the sound file might accidentally be left behind. To reset this option, click Tools|Options, and then open the General tab. Use the arrow buttons in the Links Sounds with File Size Greater Than box to adjust the file size up (if you want fewer files linked) or down (if you want more files linked). Of course, you can avoid many of the hassles of potentially forgetting part of a presentation if you use PowerPoint's Pack and Go Wizard to package everything together.

7. Click OK to begin making your way through the slide show. As each slide appears, record the applicable narration, or simply click the slide to advance to the next slide without commenting.

> **Note: The sounds of silence.** If you've included any other sound effects in the presentation, you should be aware that you won't hear them while recording the narration. You won't hear them because sounds cannot be played and recorded simultaneously.

8. When you've finished the presentation, PowerPoint tells you the narration files have been saved with their corresponding slides. You are then asked whether you want to save the new slide timings as well. If you've recorded narration for every slide, click Yes. If you skipped some slides, click No.

9. By default, the narrations play along with the slides when you give the presentation. To suppress the recordings, open the presentation, click Slide Show|Set Up Show, and then check the Show Without Narration option near the bottom of the Show Type column.

Some Final Preparations

Before you head off to the presentation site, you can still do a few things to maximize the odds of the presentation running smoothly. For starters, I always run a spell check on my presentations by clicking the Spelling button on the Standard toolbar.

> **Peter's Principle: For once, it's good to procrastinate!**
> Few things are as embarrassing as standing up in front of a room of hundreds of people with a glaring typo on a slide. Perform this check right before you pack up the presentation to go; that way, you don't have to worry about whether any edits were made after you performed the last spell check.

Another setting I visit is the Set Up Show dialog box shown in Figure 20.8. To get there, open the presentation you're about to make, and then click Slide Show|Set Up Show.

Figure 20.8

Save some time onsite by verifying your settings before you leave.

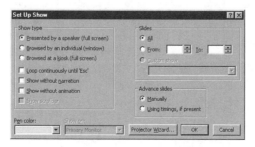

By visiting this dialog box beforehand, you can ensure that the presentation is set to go in the format you want, as well as with the desired options in place. You can even specify a range of slides to be shown. Just use the following questions to guide you as you make your way through the dialog box:

- How will the presentation be viewed? In the top half of the Show Type section, you are given three choices for how the presentation is to be given: Presented by a Speaker, where the presentation is made in full screen mode and will most likely have speaker input or control over the slides; Browsed by an Individual, where one person on a computer will view the presentation; and Browsed at a Kiosk, where the presentation is given on autopilot.

- What characteristics should the presentation have? In the bottom half of the Show Types section, you can specify that the presentation keep running until the Esc key is pressed, that it play without the prerecorded narrations, and that it be shown without the animations.

- Which slides do you want shown? In the Slide section of the dialog box, you can choose which of the slides in the presentation you want shown the next time you run the presentation. By default, all slides will be shown. You can also click the From option and use the arrow buttons in the boxes provided to specify a range of contiguous slides, or you can cue up a Custom Show you built from the presentation by clicking the Custom Show option and making the desired selection from the drop-down box.

Tip: But what if I want to show a random assortment of slides? If none of the Slides options meet your needs, consider doing either of the following to get the desired results. Use the Slide Sorter view to position the slides you want up front, and then abort the presentation after you've displayed the last slide you want to show. Or use the Slide Navigator to pull up the desired slide from within the presentation (you'll find more details on Slide Navigator later in the chapter). The option that works best for you depends on how likely you are to use the same configuration of slides again and how comfortable you are dealing with PowerPoint while presenting.

- How will the slides be advanced? If you've recorded a narration for the entire presentation and/or are working under tight time constraints, then you'll want to use the timings you rehearsed. If, on the other hand, you're anticipating questions from the audience, you might want to advance the slides manually so that you can linger where you need to and then breeze through the sections that need little clarification. Set this option in the Advance Slides section in the lower-right corner of the Set Up Show dialog box.

- What color of electronic pen do you want to use? If you plan to draw on your slides for emphasis during the presentation, you can set the color of your electronic pen in advance using the Pen Color drop-down box at the bottom-left corner of the dialog box. Note that the colors readily available are offered based on the design template and/or theme you used for the presentation, though other colors are available if you click the More Colors item on the Pen Colors drop-down menu.

> **Note: You can set the color, but you can't ready the pen!** Note that although you can set the electronic pen's color in advance, you need to actually turn on the pen in the presentation at the time you make it. I'll tell you more about using an electronic pen later in the chapter.

Getting Ready to Go with the Pack and Go Wizard

Few things in life are foolproof, but the Pack and Go Wizard is pretty close when it comes to pulling together things you need for the presentation. With this wizard, you can be certain that you have everything you need to pull off the presentation. You can even pack a lightweight PowerPoint viewer just in case the machine at your destination doesn't have the latest and greatest version of PowerPoint on it.

To use the Pack and Go Wizard, just follow these steps:

1. Launch PowerPoint 2000, and then open the presentation you want to pack up.
2. Click File|Pack and Go to launch the Pack and Go Wizard. Click the Next button at the bottom of the welcome screen to begin working with the wizard.
3. The first order of business is to choose which files to pack. For now, this just refers to the presentations themselves, none of the linked files. Because you already have open the presentation you want to pack up, click Next.

> **Tip: Need more than one?** Although Custom Shows within the presentation are included automatically, you need to manually select any other presentations you need. To do so, keep the Active Presentation option checked, and then check the Other Presentation(s) Option as well. Use the Browse button to make your file selections as you would in any typical Open or Save As dialog box, and then click the Select button to include the presentation(s) in your package.

4. Choose a destination for the package of files. By default, PowerPoint assumes your A: drive (floppy disk drive) is the destination, though you can choose a B: drive (which you may have configured as a Zip or Jaz drive or CD writer) or browse to another destination, which might include your network server. After you've chosen the destination, click Next to move on.

5. By default, PowerPoint includes any files linked to the presentation in the Pack and Go package. You can also have PowerPoint take along any unusual TrueType fonts you may have used by checking the Embed TrueType fonts option. Choosing this option helps ensure that you maintain the style and appearance you intended for the presentation. Click Next to continue.

6. The next screen asks whether you want to take a PowerPoint viewer along with you. Unless you are 100 percent certain that your destination has PowerPoint 2000 available, you might want to pack the viewer to avoid any unexpected surprises at the other end.

7. Click Finish to compress all presentation-related files onto the destination device or media, and you're set to go.

Caution: Don't make any changes without revisiting the Pack and Go Wizard! If you make any changes to the presentation after running the Pack and Go Wizard, you need to run the wizard again to make sure you have the most current version of the presentation.

Of course, when you get to your destination, you need to know how to unpack your presentation. To unpack it, follow these steps:

1. Insert the disk in the destination machine, or connect to the network location in which you packed the presentation.

2. Using Windows Explorer (click the Start button on the Windows taskbar, and then select Programs|Windows Explorer), browse to the location in which you stored the presentation.

3. Double-click the Pngsetup item, and then enter the location to which you want to copy the presentation.

4. To run the presentation, right-click its filename in the new location, and then choose Show from the shortcut menu.

Caution: No show. If the Show option doesn't appear when you right-click the unpacked presentation, that means neither PowerPoint nor the PowerPoint viewer is available on the destination system. You either have to install PowerPoint on the system (only if the software is licensed in such a way that it can be placed on the machine, of course) or repack the presentation with the special PowerPoint viewer included in the Pack and Go Wizard.

Printing PowerPoint Handouts

Have you ever attended a presentation where you're so busy taking notes that you lose track of what the speaker is saying? I have, and I can't tell you how much critical information I've missed as a result. Do your audience a favor, and consider distributing printouts of the slides. That way, they can focus on the subtle nuances of your presentation rather than on capturing the data on the slides.

> **Tip: Last-minute preparations.** I recommend printing the handouts after you've completed the final Pack and Go on the presentation. That way, you're far less likely to make last-minute changes that could result in frenzied reprinting and photocopying.

Before you jump into the Print dialog box, you might consider looking at one particular setting. From within the PowerPoint presentation you plan to print, click Tools|Options, and then open the Print tab. To continue working in PowerPoint while you print, you might want to deselect the Background Printing option. That way, your work needn't stop while your computer is generating output.

To produce handouts from your presentation, you need to do the following:

1. Open the presentation from which you want to generate printed output.

> **Tip: Hand-pick the slides from which you want to generate printed output.** Before opening the Print dialog box, select an assortment of slides either in the Outline or Slide Sorter view, and then choose the Selection option in the Print dialog box to include only those slides in your handouts. These methods enable you to choose printed output using the name of the slide or the way it looks as opposed to using generic slide numbers, which may or may not mean anything to you.

2. Click File|Print to launch the Print dialog box shown in Figure 20.9.

3. Use the Name drop-down arrow to select the printer you want to use. Because printing handouts produces smaller versions of the slides, you should pick the best quality printer you have available to make sure each slide is legible.

4. In the Print Range section of the dialog box, you have these five distinct options for printing slides, including:

   - All—Check this option to have all the slides in your presentation printed as a handout.

   - Current Slide—If you want to print only the currently selected or displayed slide, click this option.

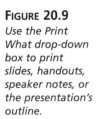

FIGURE 20.9

Use the Print What drop-down box to print slides, handouts, speaker notes, or the presentation's outline.

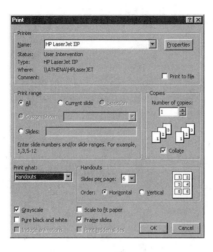

- Custom Show—If the active presentation contains one or more Custom Shows, you can use this drop-down box to select the show(s) you want to print handouts from.

- Slides—To print an assortment of slides by number, you can enter slide numbers or ranges into this box using commas as separators and dashes to communicate ranges. For example, to print slides 1, 3, 6, 8, 9, 10, and 11, you enter 1,3,6,8-11 into the box.

5. In the Copies section, you tell PowerPoint how many copies you want as well as whether you want the output collated (or printed in numerical order). By default, PowerPoint sends one collated copy to the specified printer.

6. In the Print What section of the dialog box, use the drop-down arrow to select Handouts.

7. Immediately to the right of the Print What box is a special Handouts section. Here, you tell PowerPoint how many slides to print on a page (the default is six). You also specify the order of the slides. If you choose Horizontal, the second slide appears next to the first. If you choose Vertical, the second slide appears underneath the first.

8. At the bottom of the dialog box are some handout attributes. Your slides are framed by default, so readers can easily see where one begins and the other ends. Also note the Scale to Fit Paper option, which comes in handy should you want or need to use a paper size other than the standard 8 1/2 by 11.

9. When you're satisfied with all the options, click OK to send the output to the printer.

> **Tip: Encore, encore!** If your job entails giving the same presentation over and over again with a few minor updates here and there, then you'll be happy to know that a new set of handouts is literally a mouse click away. That's right, PowerPoint 2000 "remembers" your most recently used set of Print options, so you can generate a fresh set of handouts by simply clicking the Print button on the Standard toolbar. No need to walk your way through the entire Print dialog box again.

Displaying a Presentation on One Device While Controlling It from Another

When I give a presentation, I typically take the presentation with me on my laptop and use either a large monitor or projection screen at the meeting. Not only does this method give me the security of knowing that the presentation is all ready to go, but it keeps setup time to a minimum as well. If you use this solution, you can control the presentation with confidence and sneak a peek at your speaker notes for each slide if necessary.

To conduct a presentation in this manner, you need to do the following:

1. Connect the external display port on your laptop to the monitor or projector you plan to use for the presentation. Make sure the destination device is turned off before you attempt to connect the two.

2. Turn on the projector or monitor, launch PowerPoint 2000, and then open the presentation you will be using.

3. Click Slide Show|Set Up Show, and then click the Projector Wizard button to launch the In Focus Projector Wizard shown in Figure 20.10.

FIGURE 20.10

Within a few seconds of turning on the second device, you see this image onscreen.

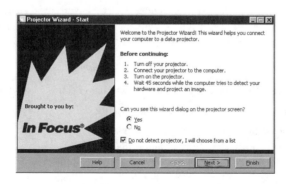

4. If you see the Projector Wizard onscreen, click Yes and then click the Next button.

Note: When the answer is no... If the image doesn't appear onscreen after a few minutes, you should click No and then the Next button. You then are given directions on how to activate your laptop's external video port. In the majority of cases, following these directions fixes the problem.

5. You are asked to use the drop-down box to specify the name of the projector you are using. You also are told to make sure the screen resolution of your laptop matches that of the projector or monitor. Click Next to continue.

6. If the projector supports sound, you might have to attach a separate sound cable between the two. After you've connected the cable, you can click the Test Sound button on the Projector Wizard to test the volume and quality of the output. When everything meets with your approval, click Next.

7. The final screen tells you your computer's settings are about to be changed to work with the chosen projector. Click Finish to set the change in motion.

With this setup, the audience sees the presentation in full screen mode, and you have the freedom to view speaker notes, take meeting minutes, or assign tasks based on the presentation.

Setting Up the Presentation to Run Unattended

Why not let PowerPoint communicate the more mundane information about your company at your next trade show while you take the time to interact with prospective clients? By setting the presentation to run in kiosk mode, passersby can learn about your company and its offerings without interruption. Because the presentation automatically starts over again when it finishes, it's basically maintenance free, so you can spend your time where it's needed most—with the people.

To run a presentation in kiosk mode, do the following:

1. Launch PowerPoint and open the presentation you want to set up.

2. Click Slide Show|Set Up Show to open the Set Up Show dialog box.

3. Choose the Browsed at a Kiosk (full screen) option. Note that the Loop Continuously Until 'Esc' option is then checked and grayed out so that it cannot be deselected. It works this way because one of the primary benefits to kiosk presentations is that they keep running unattended unless they are deliberately stopped.

4. Move to the Slides section, and specify which part of the presentation you want to run.

5. Choose whether the presentation is to be run manually or by preset timings.

Note: Take it from the top! If a presentation slated to advance manually is left idle for more than five minutes, the presentation moves back to the beginning so that the next viewer can begin checking it out from the start.

6. Click OK to save your settings, and then press F5 to start the show.

Publishing Your Presentation to the Web

Making your presentations available on the Web is one way to archive them for future viewing so that those who missed a presentation can see it at a later date. It also maximizes the time you spend building the presentation by letting it do double duty on the Web as well.

To publish a presentation on the Web, you need to follow these steps:

1. Open the PowerPoint 2000 presentation you want to publish to the Web.

2. Click File|Save as Web Page to open the Save as Web Page dialog box.

3. Use the folder list to browse to the server location in which you plan to publish the presentation. (If you're not certain where you should publish the files, check with your network administrator.)

4. Click the Change Title button, and type a more appropriate title for the presentation. Visitors to your presentation see this title in their Web browser's title bar. Click OK to return to the Save as Web Page dialog box.

5. Click the Publish button to open the Publish as Web Page dialog box shown in Figure 20.11.

6. In the Publish What? section of the dialog box, you can choose what parts of your presentation get published. Your choices are similar to the ones found in the Print dialog box.

Caution: Don't look! By default, PowerPoint publishes a presentation's related speaker notes. To suppress this feature, deselect the Display Speaker Notes option at the bottom of the Publish What? section.

7. Selecting the presentation's browser support is the next order of business. By default, Microsoft Internet Explorer 4.0 or later is chosen. Although this option produces smaller file sizes and better graphics display, its results may be less desirable on some of the older generation browsers where the viewers have no special frames-based navigational aids and such, unless you include separate hyperlinks to each possible destination within the presentation. So which option is best? Obviously, if your presentation is meant for your company's intranet where everyone runs Internet Explorer 5.0, then go for the Internet Explorer 4.0 or later option. If you're after universal readability, then choose the second option. Choosing this option may ultimately be the best solution for making presentations available to everyone on the Web, even if it does mean a bit of extra work to build all the hyperlinks.

Note: Get coordinated. By clicking the Web Options button, you can change the color of the automatically generated slide navigator bar in the General tab. The buttons appear as white text on black by default, but you can choose other options to coordinate with your presentation's theme and/or color scheme.

8. Click the Publish button to save the presentation to the Web. The result, when viewed in a Web browser such as Internet Explorer 5.0, is a presentation that looks similar to the one shown in Figure 20.12.

FIGURE 20.12
PowerPoint 2000 builds a frames-based presenta-tion navigator for you automatically.

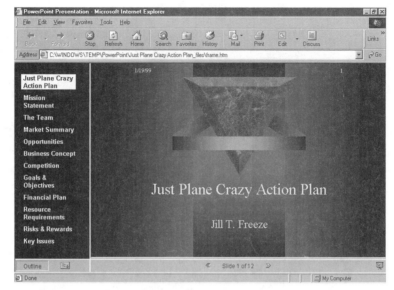

Broadcasting a Presentation over the Web

One of the biggest leaps forward in PowerPoint 2000 is the capability to schedule and present live presentations over the Web. With this capability, you can meet with project teams across the globe without ever leaving your office. Of course, sometimes there is no substitute for face-to-face contact, but there is a place for presentation broadcasting. Say your national company is launching a new benefits program. Rather than go to each place and announce it, you can broadcast a live presentation about the matter and archive it on the server or publish it to the Web for viewing by those who may have missed it or who simply want to look at it again.

You should note that a NetShow Server is needed for audio and video streaming to 16 or more viewers.

Basically, a presentation broadcast has three parts: scheduling it and setting it up, giving the broadcast, and watching the broadcast.

Scheduling the Presentation's Broadcast

To prepare for the live broadcast, you need to follow these steps:

1. Open the presentation you plan to give live.
2. Click Slide Show|Online Broadcast|Set up and Schedule. Choosing this option launches the Broadcast Schedule dialog box in which you can start to set options for the presentation's broadcast.

3. Select the Set Up and Schedule a New Broadcast option, and then click OK.

4. The Description tab of the Schedule a New Broadcast dialog box appears with the presentation's Title, Speaker, and Contact information already filled in. Type a description for the presentation to be published to the presentation's automatically generated lobby page (see Figure 20.13 later in the chapter). You can click the Preview Lobby Page button at the bottom-left corner of the tab to see what it will look like on the Web.

5. Move to the Broadcast Settings tab. In the Audio and Video section of the tab, you can define which of the two you intend to support. Note that video support requires a NetShow Server and an extremely fast machine (300MHz or better). Audio requires that NetMeeting be available at both ends of the broadcast.

6. If you want the audience to email you questions during the broadcast, check the Viewers Can E-mail option, and then verify that a valid email address has been entered.

7. To record the broadcast and archive it for later viewing, check the Record the Broadcast and Save It in This Location option, and then browse to the location in which you want to store the presentation.

8. You can also grant viewers access to your speaker notes if you want by checking the Viewers Can Access Speaker Notes option.

9. Click the Server Options button, and then specify a shared file location in Step 1 of the resulting dialog box. Choose a location on a company server rather than on your own machine so as not to bog down the presentation's performance.

> **Note: You really need to share.** A shared location is simply a directory on your server that others have permission to access. Because PowerPoint 2000 does not save the presentation scheduled for broadcast to an unshared directory, you might want to contact your network administrator to see which directory (or directories) he or she has configured to be shared.

10. Define your NetShow server if one is to be used.

11. Click OK after you've defined the servers and shared locations. You then go back to the Broadcast Settings tab.

12. To begin scheduling the broadcast, click the Schedule Broadcast button. Outlook 2000 launches with a meeting scheduling window. Set all the scheduling options as described in Chapter 18, "Personal Information Management with Outlook 2000."

Starting the Broadcast

Because most of the presentation's setup occurred long before the actual presentation (when the event was scheduled), starting the broadcast is relatively easy. Just follow these simple steps:

1. Open the presentation to be broadcast.

2. Click Slide Show|Online Broadcast|Begin Broadcast. At that point, your presentation is saved to the specified location in HTML format. PowerPoint 2000 then runs a quick audio and video check to make sure everything's working properly.

3. Have any last-minute messages or instructions for your attendees? Click Audience Message, type the information, and then click Update. Your message then is displayed on the presentation's lobby page.

4. When you're ready to begin the broadcast, click the Start button, and you're on your way.

Viewing a Presentation Broadcast

As high-tech as all this presentation information seems, all you really need to have to view the broadcast is Internet Explorer 4.0 or newer. If this is the first broadcast you've ever attended, try to get there a few minutes early in case you need to download any special add-ins for the presentation.

> **Tip: Running late? Don't despair!** If the presentation has already begun when you move to the lobby page, you can click the View Previous Slides link to see what you may have missed.

You can go to the presentation in one of two ways. If you're using Outlook 2000, click the View This NetShow button when the broadcast's reminder appears onscreen. If you use another email client, find the broadcast's invitation message, and point your Web browser to the URL included in the message.

No matter which method you use, you are taken to a presentation lobby page like the one shown in Figure 20.13. Here, you see any last-minute messages from the presenter as well as a countdown to the presentation's start time.

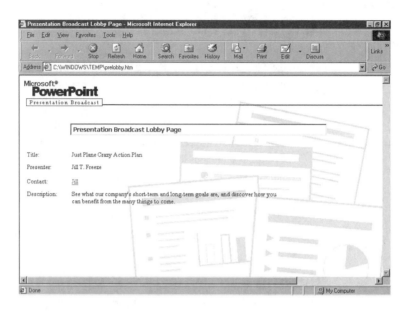

Beyond Presentation Basics

Now that you're familiar with just about every way imaginable to give a PowerPoint presentation, let's wind down the chapter with a look at a few items of interest to presenters. Among them are using the electronic pen, jumping to a slide using Slide Navigator, viewing speaker notes during a presentation, and keeping track of the presentation using Meeting Minder.

Using an Electronic Pen for Emphasis

When I want to draw the viewers' attention to part of a slide, I use the electronic pen to circle, underline, or otherwise mark the item I want them to notice. Earlier in the chapter, you learned how to choose the pen's color via the Set Up Show dialog box.

To turn on the pen, you need to start the presentation, right-click the first slide, and then choose Pointer Options|Pen. The mouse pointer turns into a miniature pen. To write on a slide, move the pen into position, and then click and drag the mouse in the desired direction. The best part of all is that the marks aren't permanent, so you can draw all you want to.

Jumping to Another Slide Using Slide Navigator

Whether you want to reveal a hidden slide or simply want to skip over part of the presentation, you can do so with ease using the Slide Navigator.

> **Peter's Principle: When you need to build presentations, make an educated choice.**
>
> In the vast majority of cases, creating a Custom Show is the optimal solution for getting the desired slides in a particular order because it doesn't alter the primary presentation, and you don't have to do any cleanup work as a result of temporarily moved slides. Although the Slide Navigator is a viable option, too, it can be a bit distracting while you're presenting unless you have someone to run the slides for you.

From within any slide, right-click and choose Go|Slide Navigator. The Slide Navigator dialog box shown in Figure 20.14 opens.

FIGURE 20.14

Each of the slides in the active presentation is listed by name.

Click the name of the slide you want to appear next, and then click the Go To button. The presentation jumps to the chosen slide.

Viewing Speaker Notes as You Present

If you're controlling the presentation from one machine while the audience views it on another device, you can easily sneak a peek at your speaker notes as you present. From within any slide, simply right-click and choose Speaker Notes. A dialog box like the one shown in Figure 20.15 appears. You can move the notes anywhere on the page by clicking and dragging the blue title bar. You can even add additional notes as you think of them.

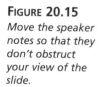

FIGURE 20.15
Move the speaker notes so that they don't obstruct your view of the slide.

Taking Notes and Tagging Action Items During a Presentation

As you give or attend a presentation, you might think of some tasks you may need to perform or delegate to others. You may also find yourself wanting to take notes of what transpired during the presentation. PowerPoint 2000's Meeting Minder is just the tool for the job.

From within a slide show, right-click and choose Meeting Minder from the shortcut menu. You can also click Tools|Meeting Minder from within any PowerPoint view.

Use the Meeting Minutes tab to jot down relevant notes about the presentation. When you're done, you can export them to Word by clicking the Export button. Both meeting minutes and action items are then sent to Word 2000.

To log an action item, click the Action Items tab (see Figure 20.16).

FIGURE 20.16
You can easily export action items to your Outlook 2000 task list by clicking the Export button.

On the Action Items tab, you can describe the task, enter the name of the person to whom it is assigned, and specify a due date. To enter the task on the list, click Add. All the tasks generated from the current meeting then appear on the list. You can edit or delete a task by selecting it and clicking the button that corresponds to the action you want to take on the task. After tasks have been officially added to the action items list, you can export them to your Outlook 2000 task list. From that list, you can assign them to others or simply track your progress toward getting them done.

Finally, if the presentation spawns the need for a meeting of some sort, just click the Schedule button. Up pops Outlook 2000's scheduling window, from which you can invite people, check availability, and so on.

On Your Own

So there you have it—your whirlwind tour of PowerPoint 2000! Although the application has made great strides forward with its new broadcasting and collaboration features, it has also undergone a fair amount of fine-tuning as well. The new Tri-Pane view is a prime example of just how much better things have gotten with PowerPoint.

Another noticeable improvement is the ease with which you can rehearse and set timings for a presentation. In previous versions of PowerPoint, rehearsing and timing were awkwardly coupled. Now you can perform a run-through almost effortlessly and tweak your timings accordingly. Why don't you give it a shot and see for yourself. Either open an existing presentation, or generate one using the AutoContent Wizard. Whether or not you have a microphone, begin rehearsing the presentation as discussed near the beginning of the chapter. Just read the slide content if you can't think of anything to say. The point here is not to craft the perfect presentation, but rather to see just how easily you can practice and fine-tune your presentation timings. That way, when you are crafting the perfect presentation, you can do it with style (not to mention within any time constraints you might have).

PART VI

Publisher Essentials

Producing Publisher 2000 Documents

Have you ever found yourself sitting in front of a word processing application trying to design a nonstandard document like a tri-fold brochure, a business card, a certificate of appreciation, or even a newsletter?

Although Word 2000's powerful features make all these things possible (and certainly easier to pull off than it was in the past), you'll find Publisher 2000 dramatically reduces your work time while helping you achieve higher quality results.

To help you understand how you can achieve these results, let's take a closer look at who already uses Publisher. According to Microsoft, more than three-quarters of Publisher's users work with a small business or volunteer-run organization of fewer than 10 people. Given that, Microsoft has enhanced Publisher 2000 with these users' needs for economical professional output and ease of use. But make no mistake about it, that doesn't mean Publisher won't scale up to meet the needs of even larger companies and organizations. With Publisher's capability to generate output that's ready for commercial color printing, a host of templates and wizards to design everything from menus to programs to invitations, and a tool to quickly convert Publisher-generated documents to Web sites, you can easily see how this application could rise to the occasion in just about any environment.

Ways to Create a Publication in Publisher 2000

When you want to design publications in Publisher 2000, you have several options. They include the following:

- On the Publication by Wizard tab that opens by default, you can click a type of wizard you want to use in the Wizards pane, select a design style from the Quick Publications pane, and then click the Start Wizard button. Note that if a design style is not specifically chosen, the first one on the list is automatically applied. See the section titled "Reducing Your Work by Using the Quick Publication Wizard" later in the chapter for additional details.

- Click the Existing Document button to create a new document based on an existing document. Open the document you want to pattern the new document after, and then click File|Save As to give the document its new name.

Peter's Principle: Why not create a template instead?

Although Publisher 2000 lets you turn a document into a template much like Word does, you don't have as many compelling reasons to do so. In Word, styles are key to generating a consistent appearance, but in Publisher, the best you can do is include text with the desired attribute that says "Enter your headline here" or something similar. You click inside the text frame, type the desired material, and it appears in the specified format—not much different from basing a document on an existing publication. Why spend your time creating a template with generic text if you can convert something that already exists?

- The Templates button gives you quick access to any templates you may have created or added to your Publisher 2000 setup. Just click the button, and then browse to the desired template where you can double-click its filename.

- Using the Publication by Design tab, you can create themed sets for general business purposes (business cards, invoices, and the like), special events, and fundraisers among others. Just click a Design Set in the left pane, choose a type of document in the right pane, and then click the Start Wizard button. The publication appears in Publisher's workspace with much of the information such as your name and company already filled in. In many cases, you'll have minimal work to do to complete the publication.

- On the Blank Publications tab, you can start building your project from the ground up, but even then, you can enlist the guidance of the Quick Publication Wizard to get the job done.

Tip: Blank pages quick and easy! If you simply need one basic blank 8 1/2- by 11-inch page, you can jump to it from within anywhere in the Microsoft Publisher Catalog by clicking the Close button in the upper-right corner of the catalog screen or by clicking the Exit Catalog button in the lower-right corner of the catalog.

You can access each of these options from the Microsoft Publisher Catalog (see Figure 21.1), which launches automatically when you start Publisher 2000 (or choose File|New).

FIGURE 21.1

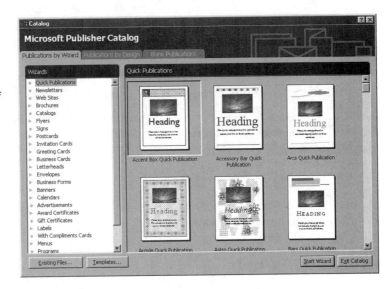

*The Microsoft
Publisher Catalog
helps you create
dozens of types of
publications with
as much (or as lit-
tle) help as you
need.*

In the sections that follow, I'll walk you through each option so that you have a better idea of which ones will serve you best.

Creating Professional-Looking Newsletters Quickly Using a Wizard

Using newsletters is an outstanding way to stay in touch with your clients or employees. My cable TV company publishes one, as do the electric and natural gas companies that provide service to my home. These newsletters not only showcase the company's good will toward the community by including articles about their charity work, but they also provide a number of money-saving tips, introduce me to new programs they may be offering, and keep me informed as to what lies ahead in terms of potential fee changes or service enhancements. All these things are invaluable when it comes to keeping customers happy and informed. Chances are, your business or organization could benefit from this image-enhancer as well. And with Publisher 2000, producing a great-looking newsletter is a snap. Furthermore, you can quickly and easily modify it to work on the Web, too.

Looking Ahead

I will present details on how to convert Publisher documents to Web pages or sites in Chapter 22, "Publisher 2000 Prduction Issues," a chapter that focuses on getting your Publisher material ready for publication and distribution.

Although you can use wizards to generate an enormous variety of publications, Publisher 2000's Newsletter Wizard demonstrates just how powerful and versatile these wizards can be. And if building something complex like a newsletter is easy, then imagine how easily you can generate other publications!

Just follow these steps to begin creating a newsletter in Publisher 2000:

1. Open the Microsoft Publisher Catalog shown in Figure 21.1 either by launching Publisher 2000, or if Publisher is already open, clicking File|New.

2. Click Newsletters in the Wizards pane, and then scroll through the Newsletters pane until you see the style you want to base your newsletter on. If you don't choose one, the first one is used by default.

3. Click the picture of the newsletter style you want to use to select it, and then click the Start Wizard button.

4. The Newsletter Introduction screen opens in the left side of the screen, and the corresponding newsletter displays its first page on the right (see Figure 21.2). Click the Next button at the bottom of the Newsletter Wizard pane to begin customizing your publication.

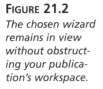

FIGURE 21.2

The chosen wizard remains in view without obstructing your publication's workspace.

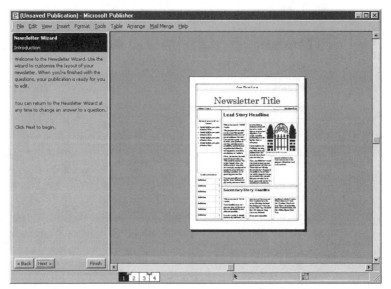

Note: What happened to the menus? The new ability to see the wizard while being able to view a complete Publisher page is great from a practicality standpoint, especially because you can immediately see the effect of your answers to the wizard questions. But it does throw you a curve ball in some respects. Because I could see a complete page of the newsletter, I found myself going for the menus to make some slight changes or to seek additional information about a given element. But guess what—the menus were disabled just as they are with any other wizard. I couldn't even crack into the Help menu! I can understand why it works that way, but it'll definitely take some getting used to. In the meantime, if you need help, you can always use the old F1 key.

5. Picking a color scheme is the first order of business. When you've found one you like, click it to select it, and then click Next.

6. You then are asked how many columns you want your newsletter to have. Three columns—the most common format—is used by default. Just click the desired option to select it. Publisher takes a few moments to rebuild the display so that you can approve your selection before clicking Next to move on to the following question. To change the number of columns, just click another option. Again, Publisher adjusts the page's display.

7. If you plan to mail the newsletter, you might want to instruct Publisher to leave a placeholder for the recipient's address by clicking the Yes option. That way, you can mail merge the names and addresses directly onto the newsletter or at least have room for a mailing label without covering up content. Unless you specifically tell it to do so, Publisher 2000 does not automatically leave room for an address. Click Next to continue.

Note: You might need to check the address placeholder. If you opt to have Publisher save room for the recipient's address, you may be asked to move to the page containing the placeholder to verify that its placement is correct. You can move to the specified page by clicking the page number button at the bottom-left corner of the page.

Looking Ahead

In Chapter 22, I'll show you how to mail merge to a Publisher publication.

8. You need to tell the wizard whether you plan to print the newsletter on two sides of the paper or just one by clicking the appropriate option. Click Next to move on.

Caution: The whole truth about double-sided printing. Please understand that you don't need a fancy laser printer capable of duplex printing in order to select the Double-sided option (which, incidentally, is the default). Double-sided in this case just means that the newsletter's headings are printed in such a way that the publication can be photocopied on both sides of the page and look the way it should look with symmetric headings. Use the Single-sided option only if you are using a nonduplex-capable printer for final output and have no intention of photocopying the newsletter onto two sides of the paper.

9. Finally, you are asked which Personal Information set you want to use for the current publication. By default, the Primary Business profile is used. It automatically extracts your name and organization name from your machine's settings. Click the Update button to confirm your selection or define another Personal Information set, and then click Finish. The wizard then begins building your newsletter to your specifications.

Looking Ahead

For more information on working with Publisher's Personal Information sets, see the section titled "Editing Your Personal Information Profile" later in this chapter.

Patterning Your Publication After an Existing Document or Template

With Publisher 2000, you can maximize the design time spent on one document by basing future documents on the same document. Whether you spent tons of hours tweaking the masthead and format of your corporate newsletter and want to continue using it, or you sat down and took the time to build a special template before you even needed it, the techniques for both methods are nearly identical.

To base a new publication on either an existing document or template, click the Existing Files or Templates button at the bottom-left corner of the Publications by Wizards tab. You then see a dialog box that looks nearly identical to the standard Open dialog box. Simply browse to the desired file (be it a document or template), and then double-click the appropriate item.

The publication or template opens, ready for you to enter the new text. Before you do anything else, however, you should choose Save As to give the document a new name (or, in the case of a template, just name it and save it). To begin inserting the new text, triple-click a headline or paragraph to select it, and then simply begin typing. The existing text is replaced with the new text.

Tip: Take no chances. If you intend to base countless future documents on an existing document (or are simply afraid you'll inadvertently damage the original by forgetting to choose Save As instead of Save), you might want to turn the original document into a template. This trick accomplishes two things: It keeps you from changing the original by accident, and it places the file you may need in an easy-access location—the Templates folder. That way, you won't waste valuable time browsing your file directories for an item you may use only occasionally.

Creating a Publication by Design

Want to create a set of matching documents for your business? Perhaps your dance company is holding a fund-raising recital to generate funds for its international tour to Scotland. Why not build a whole set of coordinating materials—a brochure describing the dance company and how the funds are to be used, an invitation to the event, a matching Web page, and a flyer about the event to hand out or hang on merchants' bulletin boards?

With Publisher 2000, you can choose from a variety of predefined sets, so you can achieve a consistent appearance with minimal effort. Clicking the Master Sets option in the Design Sets pane of the Publications by Design tab lets you see which of the design templates are supported throughout Publisher 2000. This means you can create any part of your promotional materials with confidence and know that you'll be able to design others that match later.

> **Note: Special circumstances call for special designs.** As you click some of the more specialized design sets like Restaurant Sets, Holiday Sets, or We're Moving Sets, you see some new design set names. They're included to reflect the nature of their purpose more than to serve as your company's master design set. Consider the Holiday Set as an example. The Holiday Set is great for promoting that special winter sale or concert but may not serve you well for promoting your business in general in the middle of summer. Although coordinating your marketing and promotion materials does much to convey a sense of professionalism, you shouldn't be so fixated on achieving consistency that you overlook the power of specialized materials for the proper occasion. Look back at the holiday set example for a moment. By having a flurry of snowflakes (or other holiday theme) on your brochures, the readers can assume a certain sense of timeliness. In other words, they will know that what the brochure has to say has to do with a certain time of the year as opposed to being the usual material they receive from you.

When you want to use one of these specialized design sets, you'll find little difference between using them or the items in the Publications by Wizards pane. Just click a type of design set in the Design Sets pane, and then scroll through the window on the right to click your chosen publication. Click the Start Wizard button to begin building the new document.

You then enter a special wizard that helps you design the document just the way you want it. The number of steps available in the wizard varies depending on the complexity of the publication. Notice that the wizard has already incorporated all the information it can from your primary Personal Information set. After you've completed all the steps in the wizard, you can continue entering text into the document as usual.

> **Tip: Are you finished yet?** There's no rule that says you must complete every single step of a wizard. If you've worked with a wizard a lot in the past and know that the defaults are fine, you can simply click Finish right at the start. That way, you can instantly free up your menus to begin working with the publication.

Starting with a Blank Publication

If you don't see a design set you like, or if you just want to start with a clean slate, the Blank Publications tab may be for you. It gives you the complete freedom to choose your color scheme, formatting, and layout while taking care of the toughest part for you. When you start with a blank publication, you don't just have to see an empty 8 1/2- by 11-inch page; you are given the opportunity to specify the size of the pages and how they are to be oriented (see Figure 21.3). That way, if you want to produce a French fold (or side fold) card, you needn't worry which panels must appear right side up versus upside down. Publisher 2000 takes care of that for you.

FIGURE 21.3
Let Publisher do the tricky page orientation stuff for you.

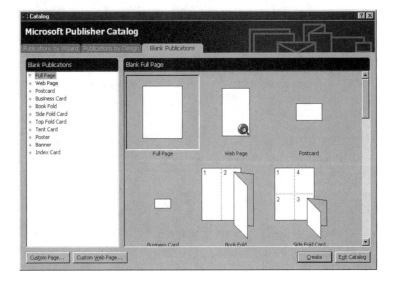

To set up your blank publication, choose an option from either pane. You don't have to select one option for each pane in this case because one pane is just a text-based list, and the other is graphical. After you've made your selection, simply click Create. Your new publication will appear, ready for you to begin work. Note, however, that the Quick Publication Wizard appears on the left side of the screen to guide you through the process of creating the publication if needed.

Reducing Your Work by Using the Quick Publication Wizard

When the Quick Publication Wizard first launches, you see an Introduction screen that tells you to revisit the wizard at any time to change your answers to the wizard questions. This capability makes it incredibly easy to make radical changes to your publication. For example, if you create a black-and-white flyer to photocopy and hand out to people, but you want to turn it into something more colorful for the Web, you can do so with a couple of clicks of the mouse. Likewise, you can have the wizard lay out your page at the very start, so you needn't draw the text and/or image frames manually.

Here's a quick run-through of what each of the wizard's steps do. Keep in mind that you can revisit each of these steps at any point to change your selection. That may, however, require you to do a bit of fix-up work in the case of special folds and such.

1. Launch Publisher 2000, or click File|New to open the Microsoft Publisher Catalog.

2. Create a blank publication using any of the methods presented earlier. After you create the publication, you'll notice that the Quick Publication Wizard appears on the left side of the Publisher workspace.

3. Click the Design wizard item. In the lower wizard box, which becomes the Design box, you'll see a lengthy list of design possibilities. You might recognize some of their names from other Publisher wizards. As you click a name to select it, Publisher takes a few seconds to apply the design to the blank page.

4. Next is the Color Scheme item. When you click it, the Color Scheme pane appears with a large selection of choices, ranging from plain old black and white to sunrise color hues. Make a selection that fulfills your needs, and then click it to watch Publisher apply it to your document.

Peter's Principle: Simple but elegant.

Many smaller businesses may have a color printer, but they don't have the funds and/or the equipment to produce color output in quantity. If this situation describes your business, then you have essentially two choices: go with a grayscale color scheme that photocopies well, or use some of the fancy designer paper available through mail order or at office supply stores. The first option is probably best for those limited by funds, whereas the second option works well in place of color printers and such. Organizations on a tight budget should note, however, that these colorful papers can get quite expensive, too, so they may not be a viable option. And even if your organization does hand out a black-and-white flyer, you can quickly adapt it to the Web by opening the document, clicking the Color Scheme wizard item, and then choosing the scheme that best fits your Web site's color scheme. Best of all, because moving from one color scheme to another is such a simple process, you needn't even bother saving two versions of the same document.

5. If you want, you can adjust the page orientation and size by clicking the Page Size wizard option. The most basic option you can tweak is the orientation of the page, which, by default, is portrait. For additional options, click the Page Setup button. (You'll find more details on the Page Setup dialog box later in the chapter.)

6. By clicking the Layout wizard option, you can choose from a sizable list of common predefined page layouts. The element frames will be drawn and aligned for you, so all you have to do is insert the images and type the text. Here again, Publisher takes a few seconds to apply your selection so that you can see what you'll be getting before you get too far into things.

7. The final Quick Publication Wizard item to consider is which Personal Information set you want to use for the current project. The Primary Business set is always used unless you click another option. You'll learn more about working with Personal Information sets later in the chapter in the section titled "Editing Your Personal Information Profile."

> **Tip: The only thing constant is change.** You can change the information found in any of the Personal Information sets by selecting the set you want to edit and then clicking the Update button. You can add a new Personal Information set in the same manner: just click the name of an undefined set, and then click Update. For more information on the value and use of these information sets, read on.

8. When you've finished using the Quick Publication Wizard, you can hide it by clicking the Hide Wizard button, or you can leave it open in case you want to make any quick modifications. Of course, you can close it and then reopen it almost instantly using the Show Wizard button.

The Quick Publication Wizard can really be considered a happy medium between stepping through some of the more elaborate wizards and designing a publication freehand. It gives you basic guidance, while giving you the freedom to produce the document you need. Later in the chapter, you'll learn everything you need to know to design the publication entirely on your own. But first, you need to understand just how Publisher 2000 works.

The Theory Behind Publisher 2000 Document Design

One of the things you'll first notice about Publisher is that you can't just arbitrarily click anywhere on a page and begin typing in text as you can with Word 2000. If you're working with an existing document or a template, or if you've used one of the wizards to get started, you may not notice this at first because you can just click text and swap it out with new text as needed. If you started with a blank publication, though, it'll hit you immediately.

It may even frustrate you for a few moments as you try to figure out why in the world you can't type on a perfectly clean page.

So what exactly is responsible for this seemingly unusual behavior? In a word, frames. Every element in Publisher, be it a column of text, a headline, or a piece of clip art, must occupy its own space or frame. These frames make it easier to align parts of a document and move them around if necessary. Using frames also adds significantly to the professional appearance of the document because you can control exactly how much or how little space each element takes up. Think back to previous discussions about working with the new Clip Gallery, and you'll see that frames aren't by any means a new concept. The fact that Publisher uses frames for text too, however, does make it somewhat unusual. You'll get used to it in time though.

Another characteristic makes Publisher documents different from, say, Word documents. It's the fact that Publisher documents can be layered, which means one framed component can overlap another. Publisher even has special toggle buttons that let you bring an object to the front or push it to the rear with a single mouse click. In other applications, a frame allocates space that cannot be used by another frame. Not only do these differences affect the way a publication is designed, but they affect how you work with the documents as well, as you'll see in the sections that follow.

Publisher's New Status as a Fully Integrated Office Application

Whether you're brand new to Publisher or have worked with earlier versions of the product, you'll notice some striking similarities between it and the other Office applications. Although Publisher was included with certain flavors of the Microsoft Office suite in the past, it's now more than just a neat application that's been tacked on to the package. Now that Publisher is finally considered a fully integrated Office application, you'll find that it supports the following features commonly found in other Office applications:

- Uniform menus—Publisher not only shares many standard Office menu commands, but it also can use the new Personalized menus.

- Standard toolbars—Every application has some specialized buttons, but, at last, even Publisher's standard buttons match those used by other Office applications. This familiarity makes learning Publisher a lot easier and less intimidating to new users.

- Common auto features—Publisher now makes use of AutoFormat and AutoFit Text to generate bulleted and numbered lists automatically, for example.

- Shared spelling tools—Whether you add the spelling of a new term to your dictionary in Word or in Publisher, it is shared with all other Office applications. This shared spelling and dictionary tool helps ensure that all your documents go out error-free whether they were designed in Word, PowerPoint, or Publisher.

- Familiar Open and Save As dialog boxes—Use these familiar Office dialog boxes to locate and organize your Office files quickly and efficiently. Now you won't waste time getting acclimated to unfamiliar filing environments!

- New Office Assistants extended to Publisher—Now these animated assistants can help you get context-sensitive help in Publisher as well. Of course, you can opt for the new standard text-based HTML help files as well.

- Common designs—Throughout this book, I've emphasized the importance of achieving a professional and consistent image for your company, be it a small home-based craft business or a multinational corporation. In Office 2000, you can use a core group of designs from within Word, PowerPoint, or Publisher. Using these designs makes achieving a consistent look a snap.

Presenting the Publisher 2000 Workspace

Before you can do much with an application, you need to familiarize yourself with its workspace (see Figure 21.4). As you look at it, you'll be able to spot many of the features consistent to all Office applications.

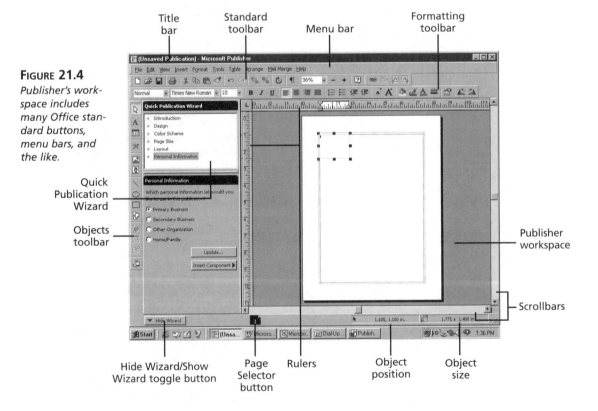

FIGURE 21.4
Publisher's work-space includes many Office stan-dard buttons, menu bars, and the like.

A lengthy explanation of how each of these items works isn't really needed because many them are self-explanatory; however, Table 21.1 quickly describes what each of these elements does so that you won't have any lingering doubts or questions.

Table 21.1 Parts of the Publisher Workspace and Their Specific Functions

Item	Purpose
Title bar	As is the case in any Windows application, this bar carries the title of the application as well as the current document if applicable.
Menu bar	You can access many of Publisher's features through standardized, text-based menus. Note that you can personalize them to show the most frequently used commands first, just as other Office applications can.
Standard toolbar	You can use familiar Office buttons to save a document; perform cut, copy, or paste functions; and execute multi-level undo commands.
Formatting toolbar	Editing Publisher text is no different than editing Word text, thanks to these familiar buttons and drop-down boxes.
Rulers	These rulers help you measure the absolute position of an object on a page for more exact placement.
Objects toolbar	On this Publisher-specific toolbar, you can find the tools to build text and picture frames, draw shapes, insert Design Gallery objects such as pull quotes, or even start adding forms to an online document. To learn more about this integral Publisher toolbar, read the section titled "Building the Framework of Your Publication" later in the chapter.
Quick Publications Wizard	You already have a good understanding of how this wizard works as a compromise between the more structured wizards and the process of building a document from the ground up.
Publisher workspace	This part of the screen displays your document so that you can format it and adjust its layout in an aesthetically appealing manner.
Hide Wizard/Show Wizard toggle button	Clicking this button hides and shows the Quick Publications Wizard, respectively.
Scrollbars	You can use these familiar objects to get the necessary part of the page in view so that you can work with it or simply read it.

continues

Table 21.1 Continued.

Item	Purpose
Page Selector button	To move to a specific page, just click the appropriate page number. Note that you may see two pages face-to-face when you have a multipage document configured to print on both sides of the page.
Object position	This indicator displays the distance the current object is from the left side and top of the page, respectively.
Object size	The Object Size display tells you just how large the currently selected object is.

With a firm grounding in the parts of the Publisher workspace, you're ready to learn the basics of freestyle document design using Publisher 2000.

Editing Your Personal Information Profile

As you saw in the wizard descriptions earlier in this chapter, Publisher is smart enough to pull in key information from your Personal Information profile. Although some of this information, such as your name and company /organization name, is extracted from other files on your computer, other information, such as your address and phone number, must be supplied by you.

To begin working with the Personal Information profiles, click Edit|Personal Information. In the resulting Personal Information dialog box, you can define up to four separate profiles. By default, the Primary Business profile is defined first. Each of the self-explanatory fields asks you to provide additional information about yourself and/or your company. Publisher even provides a sample format for this data so that you know how to enter everything.

Perhaps the most noteworthy option on this dialog box is the option to specify a color scheme for print publications and Web documents. If you check the Include Color Scheme in This Set option, all documents created with the current Personal Information profile adhere to the scheme you selected. Note that using this option is a tremendous way to ensure consistent-looking publications.

As I pointed out earlier, you can create up to four profiles. Just click the profile's name, and begin editing. You have plenty of options to define custom profiles for your work, your family, your part-time business selling collectibles, and your daughter's gymnastics team.

Building the Framework of Your Publication

Because everything you do in Publisher requires having an applicable frame in place, you should become well acquainted with the Objects toolbar; it's the place where frame construction begins. Table 21.2 introduces you to each frame-building tool on the Objects toolbar.

Table 21.2   Frame-Building Tools Found on the Objects Toolbar

Tool	Tool Name	Function
	Pointer tool	Click this tool, and then click an object to select it.
	Text Frame tool	Click this tool to begin building a text frame.
	Table Frame tool	Click this tool to start building a table from within Publisher.
	WordArt Frame tool	Click this tool to incorporate fancy WordArt objects into your publication.
	Picture Frame tool	Click this tool to draw a frame for a file residing on your computer or input from your camcorder, digital camera, or scanner.
	Clip Gallery tool	Click this tool to draw a frame for images from the shared Clip Gallery. As soon as you draw the frame, the Clip Gallery launches.

To begin building a frame, click the appropriate tool, and then move your mouse pointer to the spot you want as the top-left corner of the object you're about to create. Click and then drag the mouse pointer down and to the right until the frame is the desired size. When you're ready to start working with the frame, just double-click it (in the case of a text frame, you need to click only once), and the applicable dialog box or applet launches. With text frames, the insertion point simply becomes active at the top of the frame, ready to receive text.

Filling in a Text Frame

Perhaps the most common way a text frame is filled in is by someone manually entering the information, but with Publisher 2000, you have a number of additional options. You can use a standard cut-and-paste operation from within any Windows-based application, or you can import an entire file by clicking inside the text frame, clicking Insert|Text File, browsing to the file's name, and then double-clicking it. The text appears in the text frame you created.

> **Tip: Import your text with style.** If the material you're about to import has special formatting you want to keep in the Publisher document, right-click inside the text frame you want to use, and choose Paste Special. The Paste Special command preserves the formatting from the other document.

Publisher 2000 accepts text from any previous version of Word or Publisher, many versions of WordPerfect, text (.txt) files, rich text format (.rtf) files, and Excel and Lotus 1-2-3 files, among others.

When the Text Runneth Over...

Nobody's perfect. No matter how hard you try to guess the exact size of the frame you'll need, it seldom happens. Often, text that's imported ends up in an overflow area. When this happens, Publisher asks whether you want the text to AutoFlow to the next available frame. Depending on how the frames are laid out, this option may or may not be the best one for you. You have to pay close attention to which frame Publisher wants to use when it asks whether you want to AutoFlow the text.

When you experience this dilemma, you can do any of the following to remedy the situation if AutoFlow isn't an appropriate option:

- Cut the fat—Perhaps the most obvious solution is to edit the text down so that it fits the frame.
- Manually adjust the text size—Select all the text within the frame, and then choose a new font size using the Size drop-down box.
- Adjust the margins—Click the Text Frame Properties button (see Figure 21.5) near the right end of the Formatting toolbar to open the Text Frame Properties dialog box. Type smaller numbers into the Left and Right margin boxes, and then click OK. This way, you can fit a bit more text into the frame.
- Consider that bigger may be better—When you click inside a text frame, eight dark resizing handles appear around its perimeter. Click any of the handles, and drag the edge of the frame in the desired direction. The mouse pointer changes into one of the shapes shown in Figure 21.6 to serve as a guide as to which direction you should move the mouse.
- Get connected—If you have room on the page to create another text frame (or if a text frame that meets your needs already exists), consider creating the frame and then connecting the two to accommodate the overflow. To connect two text frames, click the one containing the text, click the Connect Text Frames button (see Figure 21.7), and then move the pitcher-shaped mouse pointer to the second frame and click inside it. The two frames then can accommodate the overflow.

FIGURE 21.5

The Text Frame Properties button makes it easy to access the frame's settings.

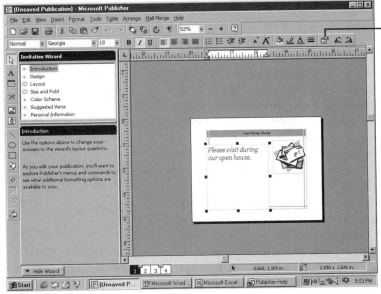

Text Frame Properties button

FIGURE 21.6

The resize mouse pointer changes depending on which handle you click.

FIGURE 21.7

The pitcher-shaped mouse pointer lets you "pour" the over-flow text into the destination frame.

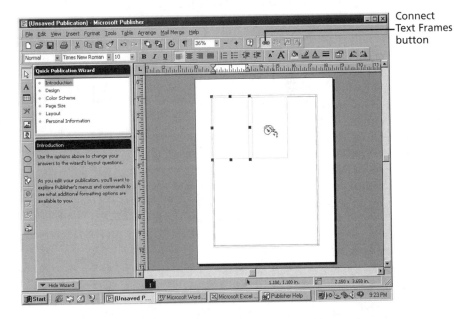

Connect Text Frames button

- Consider copyfitting—There are two variations of copyfitting. The first, called Best Fit, works best for headlines because it takes the text and sizes it so that it fits within the text frame. It shrinks or expands the text as needed, even if you resize the frame. Just click Format|AutoFit Text|Best Fit to turn on the feature for the active frame. The other copyfitting feature, Shrink Text On Overflow Only, lets Publisher take into account text caught in the overflow area. If you click Format|AutoFit Text|Shrink Text On Overflow inside a frame, Publisher factors in overflow text and continues to reduce the font's point size until no more overflow text exists.

> **Note: Putting a stop to the ever-changing text.** Should you ever find the need to disable copyfitting in any of your text frames, you can click inside the applicable text frame to select it and then click Format|AutoFit Text|None. From that point on, the text will stay the size you make it.

So which option is best? Obviously, the answer depends on your situation. Some choices are cut and dry. For example, if the author of an article is particularly verbose, you might be able to trim some of the embellishment without anyone even noticing. And if you're working with a text frame with overflow text, using the Best Fit copyfitting technique does you no good. Even tweaking column margins may be a futile effort when the overflow is significant. Naturally, you have more to consider than simply whether the text all fits into the text frame. You have to factor in readability, consistency, aesthetics, and other intangible issues. In the end, what you do will always be a judgment call.

Putting Your Best Foot Forward with Text Styles

When you have to format the text itself, there's little new you need to know here. Virtually anything you can do in Word can now be done in Publisher. That includes modifications such as spell checking, text alignment, font selection, and text color.

One element, however, serves the same purpose as Word's styles, but it's designed and configured in a slightly different manner. Text Styles, as Publisher calls them, are applied in the same way styles are—through a drop-down box on the Formatting toolbar. They can be extremely useful when you're formatting a publication's paragraphs because they leave no doubt whether paragraphs are indented, whether a blank line appears between paragraphs, and so on.

To begin defining a new Publisher Text Style, just follow these steps:

1. From within Publisher 2000, click Format|Text Style to open the Text Style dialog box shown in Figure 21.8.

FIGURE 21.8

Here, you can see the specifications along with a sample of the Normal Publisher text style.

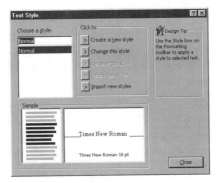

Tip: But I already have the perfect block of text... If the document already contains a block of text that fits the bill, select it, and then click inside the Style drop-down box. Type a special name for the style, and then press Enter. The Create Style By Example dialog box appears, as shown here. Confirm that the new style's name is spelled properly, and then click OK. The new style then becomes available in the Style drop-down box.

2. Click the Create a New Style button to launch the Create New Style dialog box shown in Figure 21.9.

FIGURE 21.9

The Create New Style box gives you five general options you can change with the click of a mouse.

3. You need to give the style a name. Make it something short and descriptive so that it fits in the Style drop-down box yet adequately describes the style's intended purpose.

4. Click the Character Type and Size button to set the all-important font parameters. The parameters include the font and its size, along with any applicable style or color. Click OK to return to the Create New Style box.

5. You click the Indents and Lists button to define specialized styles such as numbered or bulleted lists. You can also tell Publisher how you want the first line of the new style's paragraph to appear. Again, clicking OK returns you to the Create New Style dialog box.

6. If you want to compress or expand the amount of space between lines, the Line Spacing button is the place to begin. You can nudge the numbers up or down and see your changes instantly reflected in the sample. Click OK.

7. The Character Spacing button takes you to a dialog box in which you can fine-tune the amount of space between characters. It is probably one of the least visited settings for a new style because many changes could potentially have a negative effect on the style's readability.

8. Using the Tabs button, you can set the style's tab stops as well as specify whether the tab is led by any special characters such as dots, dashes, bullets, or lines.

9. When the sample meets with your approval, click OK. You then need to click OK to exit the Create New Style dialog box.

Building a Table in Publisher

Although you can import a Word or Excel table with relative ease, what do you do if the data doesn't exist anywhere else? Do you launch another application and build the table there? With the Table Frame tool, you can easily generate a professional-looking table from within Publisher in no time. To do so, just follow these simple steps:

1. Open or create the Publisher 2000 document you want to work with.

2. Click the Table Frame tool, and then draw the frame as you normally would. As you release the mouse button, the Create Table dialog box shown in Figure 21.10 appears.

FIGURE 21.10

Publisher lets you create tables ranging from simplistic to complex.

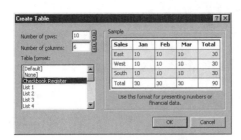

3. Type the number of rows and columns in the respective boxes, or use the arrow buttons to bump the numbers up or down, little-by-little.

4. Choose a table format by clicking its name and previewing it in the Sample window.

5. When the settings look all right, click OK to have Publisher build the table. Then just enter your data as you would into any other type of table.

Adding Images to Your Publication

In Chapter 5, "Shared Applets and Tools Available in Office 2000," you learned how to work with WordArt and the Clip Gallery. These tools work the same in Publisher with one small difference: You start the process by clicking the desired tool on the Objects toolbar and then draw the frame for the object. This way, you get much more control over the object's size from the start. After you've applied an image, going in and changing it is as easy as double-clicking the frame and making a new selection.

The Picture Frame tool works the same way, except that you must browse your system for the desired file through the new Office 2000 image dialog box, which gives you the opportunity to preview an item before you select it. Just double-click an image's name to select it and have it placed in the frame you drew.

For the artistically inclined, you'll notice a few AutoShape-like tools on the Objects toolbar. For a review of how they work, skim back through Chapter 5.

Manipulating Frames

Because frames are at the heart of Publisher, you need to know how to manage them. Table 21.3 shows you how to execute some of the more basic frame tasks.

Table 21.3 Manipulating Frames in Publisher

To Do This	Do This
Copy a frame	Right-click the desired frame, and then choose Copy from the shortcut menu. Right-click the location in which you want to place the frame, and then select Paste from the shortcut menu. The frame then appears, ready for you to move or resize as needed.
Resize a frame	Click the frame to select it, and then click and drag one of the eight resizing handles in the desired direction.
Delete a frame	Right-click the frame, and then choose Delete Object to delete the whole frame or Delete Text to remove the contents only.
Move a frame	Click inside the frame you want to move, and then place the mouse pointer inside it until it becomes a moving van (see Figure 21.11). Click and drag the frame to the desired location.

Applying Borders to Publisher Objects

Adding a border to a Publisher frame has never been easier. Just click the frame to select it, and then click the Line/Border Style button near the right end of the Formatting toolbar. A drop-down menu appears with a few of the most common choices. For something a bit more extravagant, choose More Styles. The Border Styles dialog box opens. In the Line Border tab, you can define the border's thickness as well as color. If that's still not fancy enough, try the BorderArt tab (see Figure 21.12). There, you can find a number of artsy borders, including elegant abstract designs, seasonal selections, and dashed coupon-like borders.

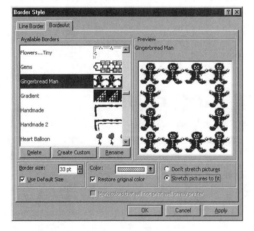

Peter's Principle: When it comes to business, keep it simple.

Hairline borders are almost always acceptable because they do the job in a simple but elegant way. Some of the more flamboyant border art should probably be reserved for casual occasions as opposed to business matters. Or if you must use them, use them on full-page flyers where the border art doesn't take up even more room than the text.

On Your Own

Publisher 2000 is amazingly versatile. In fact, the more you plow through the wizards, the more new publications you'll discover.

Because I couldn't possibly take the time to discuss every single wizard in detail, here's an interesting exercise for you. Browse through the Microsoft Publisher Catalog and its accompanying wizards, and tell me which of the publications listed below is *not* generated automatically by a Publisher wizard or template:

Paper airplane	Religious service program
Wallet size calendar	Audio cassette case liner
Marry Me banner	Origami parrot
Lemonade for sale sign	Congrats on your tax refund card

Okay, did you figure out which one could not be found in Publisher 2000? It's the tax refund greeting card, of course. But just because Publisher doesn't have a wizard for it doesn't mean that you couldn't make it on your own!

Publisher 2000 Production Issues

When it comes to publications, the term *production* means a whole lot more than simply printing or photocopying the document. Production considerations can run the gamut from preparing a publication for the Web to incorporating last-minute design elements like pull quotes.

In this chapter, you'll learn about many of these production-related issues and will explore the rich Publisher features that make getting your publication ready for commercial printing a breeze.

Adding Style to Your Publication with Fancy First Letters

When you turn to the first page in a chapter of a book, what usually grabs your attention? The chapter number and title are the most obvious answers, but what about those fancy letters that lead you into the body text? In a book without pictures, these fancy first letters may be the only visual cue you have as to the mood of the story. For example, a book of Victorian poetry might have intricately detailed leading letters, whereas a murder mystery might boast meatier letters dripping with blood.

Setting the mood is not the only purpose of these fancy first letters, however. Many publications (including magazines and newsletters) use them as a style element in much the same way a special headline font would be used. Not only do these letters add visual appeal to your publication, but they give the document a personality of its own as well.

So why is a formatting issue like this included in a production chapter? Simple; because few people consider these details until they get to the production stage. Perhaps you print a copy of the publication and find it looks a bit too blase for your liking. Or maybe while browsing the document in print preview, you discover you need a fancy first letter to balance the image on the opposite side of the page. Whatever the case, you can consider fancy first letters a finishing touch as you go into production.

In Publisher 2000, these fancy first letters are referred to as *drop caps*. To add these finishing touches to your document, just follow these simple steps:

1. Open the Publisher document you want to work with, and then click inside the text frame to which you'd like to apply the drop cap.

> **Caution: Fill 'er up first!** You cannot set up drop caps until you've entered at least some text into the frame you intend to work with. This restriction actually works to your advantage in another way as well, in that the drop cap previews are built from your specific sample of text.

2. Click Format|Drop Cap to open the Drop Cap dialog box shown in Figure 22.1.

FIGURE 22.1

The Drop Cap tab gives you a number of predefined drop caps from which to choose.

3. If you see a drop cap sample you like, click it, click OK to apply it, and you're done. If none of the samples strike your fancy, click the Custom Drop Cap tab.

4. The first thing you need to do in the Custom Drop Cap tab (see Figure 22.2) is define the letter's position and size in the Choose Letter Position and Size section of the tab. Two positions are preset, and a third can be tweaked with arrow buttons as desired. As for the letter's size, you can use the arrow buttons provided to tell Publisher just how large (or small) to make the letter. The final option in this area gives you the power to specify how many letters should be treated as drop caps. Rarely would you stray from the default value of one, but the option is available should you decide to venture into a more contemporary style.

FIGURE 22.2

*In the Preview
window, you can
see the drop cap
as it would
appear with your
text.*

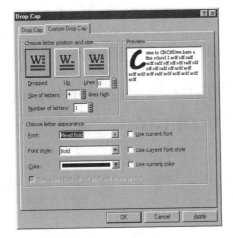

5. In the bottom half of the tab, you can define the letter's appearance. You can use the check boxes to the right of each option to maintain the text frame's font, style, and color in the drop cap as well, or you can use the drop-down boxes to select an entirely new look.

6. When you're happy with the image in the Preview window, click OK and the drop cap you defined is applied to the current text frame.

Peter's Principle: To drop cap or not to drop cap...

Fancy first letters walk the fine line between being distracting and making a publication look polished. When used sparingly, these letters can add a touch of class to your newsletter or other publication. They can, however, quickly detract from the content if used too frequently or with stories or blocks of text that are too short. When I format a newsletter, I tend to use drop caps only on a page's leading story, and even then only if the story is long enough to warrant it. If the story is little more than a blurb, the drop cap has an overpowering, distracting effect. Use your judgment because a lot of factors come into play here (such as the drop cap's font, the letter's boldness and level of detail, its size, and its color). Just keep in mind that, in the case of drop caps, fewer may be better.

Of course, when you apply one of these fancy first letters, you might decide that it really is too overpowering for the document. At that point, you can either remove the drop cap altogether, or you can change it in such a way that makes it fit in better.

To remove a drop cap, click inside the text frame that contains the drop cap you want to remove. Next, click Format|Change Drop Cap. The familiar Drop Cap dialog box opens. Simply click the Remove button, and then click OK. The text then returns to its pre-drop cap state.

If you want to change the drop cap's appearance in any way, just repeat the steps for removing a drop cap, except this time make the necessary changes instead of clicking the Remove button. Click OK to dismiss the dialog box.

Using Pull Quotes to Draw Attention to Key Information

At one time or another, everyone has read a news magazine such as *Time* or *Parade* (which you find in many Sunday papers). Their articles often feature in-depth interviews with celebrities or high-ranking officials who have something insightful to say regarding a pivotal event in their lives. Many times, snippets from these insights are showcased in something called a *pull quote* (see Figure 22.3).

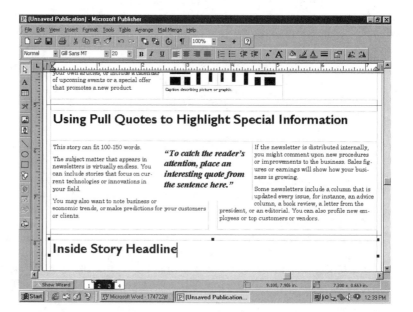

Using pull quotes can be an extremely effective way to pull readers into an article, but these quotes work only if they fulfill their role of drawing readers in as opposed to making the page look too cluttered. They're also useful when you want to add visual appeal to an article that doesn't lend itself well to clip art.

Peter's Principle: The Design Gallery...more than just pull quotes.

Although the use of pull quotes can go a long way toward creating a polished look for your publications, several other valuable objects are tucked away in the Design Gallery. When I design a newsletter from the ground up, I rely on the Design Gallery Masthead objects to create a sharp-looking title and the Table of Contents objects to format a nice table of contents. The Advertisement and Coupon objects also come in handy. Once I even used the Phone Tear-Off object to design a poster for a buddy advertising his basement apartment for rent.

With Publisher 2000's Design Gallery, professional results are a few simple mouse clicks away. And best of all, each of these smart objects behaves in the same manner, so you can use them with confidence. So go ahead and explore; you'll see that the Design Gallery has a lot more to offer than just pull quotes.

I lump pull quotes into the same category as fancy first letters—elements a publication's designer may decide to add at the last minute when the publication doesn't look quite right.

To add pull quotes to your publication, you need to do the following:

1. Open the Publisher document into which you want to place the pull quote.

2. At the bottom of the Objects toolbar, click the Design Gallery Object button. Clicking this button launches the Microsoft Publisher Design Gallery with the Objects by Category tab open.

3. Click the Pull Quotes item in the Categories pane. A number of selections then appear on the right side of the screen (see Figure 22.4).

4. Browse through the pull quotes presented until you find a design that fits in with the publication you created. Click it to select it.

5. Click the Insert Object button at the bottom-right corner of the Design Gallery window. The pull quote's frame appears on the current document page, ready for you to drag it into place.

6. When the pull quote frame is in place and you've resized it as needed, click inside the frame and begin typing in the desired text. Note that you might need to resize the frame a second time to accommodate the text you entered.

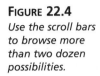

FIGURE 22.4

Use the scroll bars to browse more than two dozen possibilities.

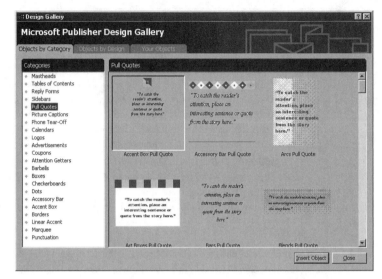

> **Note: What's that button hanging off the lower-right corner of my pull quote box?** The button you see is a special wizard associated with smart objects; it enables you to change the appearance of the smart object with a single click, much like the Quick Publication Wizard helps you make instant changes to your document. That way, you can change your block colored pull quote to something more subdued in an instant. Of course, all this begs the question: What is a smart object? A *smart object* is simply an object with a wizard attached to it.

7. Does the pull quote fit in well with your document, or is it too distracting? Or does it blend in a bit too well with its surroundings? No matter what the situation, you can click the smart object's wizard button, and then try a new design by simply clicking its name (see Figure 22.5). You can exit the Pull Quote Creation Wizard by clicking the Close button in the upper-right corner of the wizard's box.

When the pull quote is in place, you can manipulate it just as you would any other object—by clicking and dragging it. Furthermore, you can access the associated smart object wizard at any time by clicking the wizard button.

Changing the Color Scheme of Your Pull Quotes

Although the exact color of a publication's elements might not matter if it's destined for black-and-white print distribution, it becomes a major issue when the Web is involved. And depending on how you created the publication, the pull quote's color scheme might not adequately meet your needs.

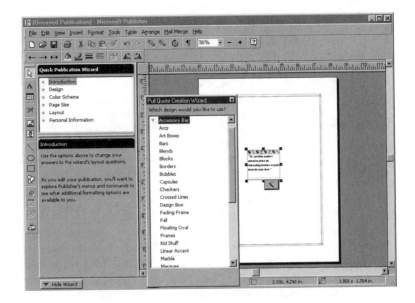

FIGURE 22.5
*Changing the
appearance of a
pull quote is a
breeze thanks to
the Pull Quote
Creation Wizard.*

Luckily, Publisher 2000 gives you a variety of ways to address the situation depending on your needs. If you have a preferred color scheme you use for all your publications, the solution is as simple as clicking Format|Color Scheme, choosing the desired item from the Available Schemes list, and then clicking OK. All colored objects on the page are modified to reflect the new selection.

Customizing Pull Quote Colors to Meet Your Needs

If an appropriate choice doesn't exist, you can build a custom color scheme by clicking Format|Color Scheme and then opening the Custom tab. Use the six drop-down boxes to choose your colors and/or fill effects. Some of the choices make very subtle differences, so you might have to look extra hard to see how the changes look. When the image in the Preview window meets with your approval, click the Save Scheme button, enter a name for the scheme, and then click OK. You need to click OK again to dismiss the Color Scheme dialog box itself. From this point on, you'll be able to use this custom color scheme in any document you create.

Tip: Shave off a few steps. Perhaps you see a preset color scheme you kind of like, but you want the text to appear in some color other than its default color of black. In this situation, creating a custom color scheme based on an existing color scheme is easiest. From within the document you're working with, click Format|Color Scheme. Choose the color scheme you want to base the new color scheme on in the Available Schemes pane, and then open the Custom tab. The colors of the scheme you selected appear in the New drop-down boxes. In the case of changing the text color only, all you have to do is select the desired color in the Main drop-down box, click Save Scheme, name the scheme, click OK to save the scheme, and then click OK again to dismiss the dialog box.

Creating the Desired Effect Manually

The final option requires a bit more of a hands-on approach. With Publisher 2000, you can zoom in on an object such as a pull quote, click a design element (which may be something as minute as an oval in a repeating pattern), and then change the color of that particular element. To change the element's color, all you have to do is right-click it, select Change Oval|Fill Color (or whatever the selected object's shape is), and choose the desired option. You can change the color to another color in the current scheme by clicking the appropriate color swatch, or you can visit the More Colors or Fill Effects dialog boxes you learned about earlier in the book.

Tip: Change the appearance of other objects with a single mouse click. If the object on which you changed the color is part of a design series (for example, one oval out of a pattern of six), you can change the color of the other objects in the pattern by merely clicking them. Say you have a design row that contains a square, a circle, a square, a circle, and so on. If you recolor one of the squares, you can click any of the other squares to recolor all the squares in the series. Think of the squares as linked objects—where changing one can change them all.

Because these alterations affect the selected object only, you might want to save the redesigned object to the Design Gallery for future use. To do so, click the object to select it, and then click Insert|Add Selection to Design Gallery. The screen in Figure 22.6 appears. Enter a name for the object in the text box provided, and then enter the name of the object's category. The new object is then stored in the Your Objects tab of the Publisher 2000 Design Gallery.

FIGURE 22.6

You can even create different categories for each type of object so that the objects you create are just as organized as the Design Gallery's native objects.

Converting a Publisher 2000 Document to a Web Site

The economy and exposure of publishing to the Web make it a natural extension to producing print publications. Although not everyone has access to the Internet, tens of millions of people do, so why not maximize your company's advertising dollars by making your publications available on the Web? It's also an unbeatable way for nonprofit organizations to fulfill their educational missions on international levels with minimal expense.

> **Caution: For maximum flexibility...**The Convert to Web Site Wizard works best for publications created using the Publication by Wizard tab or the Publication by Design tab. You can, however, save other Publisher documents as Web pages by clicking FilelSave as Web Page. The big difference is that you have to do all your own hyperlinking.

No more blind mass mailing—save your postage and printing costs by letting those who are interested come to you! And the beauty of it all is that you can convert your existing Publisher documents to a Web site with ease with the help of a friendly wizard. You can choose to have Publisher generate all the hyperlinks for you for a self-contained Web site, or you can plug in your own series of hyperlinks.

Just follow these steps to convert a Publisher document to a Web site:

1. Open the Publisher 2000 document you want to convert to a Web site.

2. Click the Convert to Web Site item at the bottom of the wizard window. The wizard asks whether you want to reuse the content in the current publication for the Web site. Click the Create button to do so.

3. The wizard then asks whether you want it to create a complete Web site with hyperlinks, or whether you want to do your own layout and hyperlinks. For the quickest results, choose the top option—which does everything for you—and then click OK.

4. Publisher displays a message box asking whether you want to save the document before converting it to a Web site. Click Yes to save the changes in print before running the conversion; click No to go ahead with the conversion without saving the changes in the standard .pub file; or click Cancel to abort the mission. Publisher takes a few moments to convert the document.

5. The new Web site is ready for all your changes, colorizations, and such.

Setting the Web Site's Properties

By setting properties for your new Web site, you can specify keywords for search engines (after all, what good is a Web site that nobody can find?), define the text that appears on a reader's Web browser title bar and Favorites list, and even attach a file for background music.

To begin setting Web site properties, click File|Web Properties. The Site tab shown in Figure 22.7 opens by default.

FIGURE 22.7

The Keywords and Description boxes give you ample room to describe your site to search engines.

Here, you can enter keywords for search engines, and you even get to write a description of your Web site. Some search engines use this description in place of the standard summary made up of the first few characters on the page.

And finally, you can specify whether your targeted audience uses Internet Explorer/Netscape Navigator 3 or later, or Internet Explorer/Netscape Navigator 4 or later. Generally, unless your Web site is destined for an intranet where everyone uses the latest and greatest Web browser, you should go with the older option. What you might lose in terms of flashy features and saved disk space, you gain many times over in universal readability because everyone will be able to view your site. Once set, the Web Properties Site tab items are saved for the entire Web site.

On the second Web Properties tab, the Page tab, you enter the filename, extension, and title of the current Web page. You can also assign background music to the page on this tab; however, you should note that doing so takes up more disk space on your Web server and increases download time for the readers.

> **Tip: The site is alive with the sound of music.** First, remember that you have to set the background music option for each page on your site that you want to have play music. Here again, you have a wonderful opportunity to set the mood of the Web site. I've seen psychologists' Web sites stream relaxing classical melodies and high-tech consulting firms use a bouncy synthesized techno-music. You're the best judge of whether the tunes will detract or add value given the purpose of your site.

If you want a hyperlink to the current page to appear on the automatically generated navigation bar, click the Add Hyperlink to Navigation Bar option. After you've set all the options, click OK to apply and save them to your Web site.

Previewing the Web Site Before You Publish It

Before I publish anything to the Web, I always test my page or site first. Testing accomplishes two things: it ensures that the finished product will look the way I want it to, and it helps me verify that all the links work properly.

To preview a Web page or site, click File|Web Page Preview (or Web Site Preview if desired). Your default Web browser (most likely Internet Explorer 5 if you plan to use the interactive and collaboration features of Office 2000) launches, displaying your Web page or site. Does it look right to you? Now click each link. Do they all take you to the desired location?

> **Note: My links don't work!** Naturally, if you choose to preview only the current Web page, none of the links work properly; therefore, you must use the File|Web Site Preview command for anything more complex than a single page without links.

If you see something you don't like in the preview, you must return to Publisher to change it. Note, however, that the changes you make in Publisher do not automatically show up on your Web browser. You must execute the File|Web Page (or Site) Preview command each time you make an edit to see the changes in the browser.

Publishing Your Web Site to Your Intranet

One of the great things about Office 2000 is its simplified Web publishing capabilities. For corporations that want to leverage the benefits of Web technology for communication and collaboration, it can't be beat.

After your network administrator has helped you set up some Web folders, getting the site published is a breeze. Just follow these steps to publish a Web site to one of the predefined Web folders:

1. After you've finished designing your Web site and have set all the options you want, click File|Save as Web Page. The Save As Web Page dialog box appears.

2. On the Places Bar, click Web Folders, and then click the name of the folder to which you want to publish the site.

3. Click OK and you're done. The steps are really that simple if the Web folders are in place.

Publishing Your Web Page to the Internet

Of course, the most typical situation is one in which a consumer or small business simply wants to publish a Web page to an Internet service provider's (ISP's) server.

Although Microsoft guides you through the process with a special Web Publishing Wizard, you can get some information from your Internet service provider up front to speed the process along. That information includes the following:

- The address (URL) of your Web site. You need this information to tell the wizard where to upload the files.

- The preferred name of your home page—the main opening page of your Web site. Publisher uses Index.html by default, so if your ISP wants something different, you need to open your Web site in Publisher and change the Page Web Properties options accordingly.

- Whether the ISP prefers you to upload Web sites via File Transport Protocol (FTP). If that's the case, you need to get the name of the FTP server along with the default directory you should publish to.

With all that information in your hands, you are now ready to publish your site. The way you access the Web Publishing Wizard depends on whether you installed it with a previous version of Publisher. If you used Publisher in the past, you click the Start button on the Windows taskbar and then choose Programs|Microsoft Web Publishing|Web Publishing Wizard. If you're new to Publisher, you click the Start button and then point to Programs|Internet Explorer|Web Publishing Wizard. And on Windows NT systems, the wizard has been known to show up when you click Start and then select Programs|Accessories|Internet Tools|Web Publishing Wizard.

Note: My wizard is hiding. The Web Publishing Wizard is installed by default when you install Internet Explorer 5 with Office 2000. If you chose not to install IE5, then you need to do so to be able to use the Web Publishing Wizard. You should also be aware that the exact location of the wizard may differ depending on how you installed IE5, whether it came installed on a new computer, and so forth.

When the wizard launches, you are guided each step of the way through the publishing process. The information you need to provide will vary slightly depending on your ISP's needs and preferences.

Printing Your Publications Locally

If you're printing just a handful of copies or plan to photocopy the publication in black and white, the Print options are pretty straightforward. Thanks to Publisher's sophisticated wizards, you seldom have much to do with respect to printing. All the page orientation issues are taken care of for you, which is especially great when things start to get tricky with special paper folds and all.

Peter's Principle: Create colorful publications without a color printer.

When I need to produce a professional-looking brochure in a hurry, I run out and get some of that preprinted fancy paper at the office supply store. It gives me the benefit of a colorful brochure without the cost and hassle of color printing. But beware: These papers can get expensive, too.

Even so, you'll want to know every little nook and cranny of the Print options available to you so that you can get the output you want the first time around. After all, improper output is costly in terms of time, paper, and toner. Getting the printed results you desire begins with the Print dialog box (see Figure 22.8).

FIGURE 22.8

In the Print dialog box, you can specify how much (or how little) of your document you want printed.

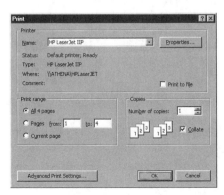

Note: Your mileage may vary. If you recall my discussion about printing in Word back in Chapter 8, "Going Beyond Basic Document Creation with Word 2000," you'll remember how I said Print dialog boxes don't all look the same. The options you have available depend on the Print drivers you use to power your printer as well as the kind of printer you have. The bottom line is that you shouldn't panic if the dialog box you see isn't identical to the one shown in Figure 22.8; you'll still have the most important options available to you.

Unless you're planning to take your document out for professional color printing (more on that later in the chapter), there's not much new about Publisher's Print dialog box. Basically, you need to click File|Print to select a printer from the drop-down box provided and specify the pages you want to print, the number of copies you want, and whether you want the pages collated.

Tip: Express printing. If you want a single copy of the current document as a whole, just click the Print button on the Standard toolbar.

Of those options, collating is the only one that really requires much thought. When you tell Publisher to collate as it prints, you save the valuable time required to collate pages by hand, but the option is not without its own set of drawbacks. If you print and collate 10 copies of a multipage newsletter, Publisher has to send 10 complete sets of the document to your printer, which tends to slow down the whole process. When it prints all the page ones, followed by all the page twos, and so on, each page is loaded into the printer only once, thus speeding up the print time but adding on time needed to collate the publication for distribution by hand.

In addition, you have access to the usual set of Properties tabs from which you choose the paper size, the resolution of the graphics, and so on.

After you've set all your options, you need to click OK to have the output sent to the specified printer. Also note that you might need to click an OK button for the Properties dialog box as well if you decided to adjust anything there.

Printing Addresses Right on the Publication

If you plan to print copies of the publication for recipients using your printer, Publisher can address them for you as long as you have a data source in place. This option is great for small businesses or organizations that want to keep all production in-house but that might not have access to a photocopy machine or to extra hands to address the mailings.

And by mailing the publication itself, you eliminate the cost of envelopes and the labor needed to stuff and seal those envelopes.

Peter's Principle: About your data source...

As you start working with mail merge in Publisher, you'll see references to Publisher Address Lists. Although using such lists is a valid way to create a data source for your publications, I prefer a more versatile solution. I store all my information in Outlook 2000's contact list so that I can use it to send email and schedule meetings, draft personalized letters or print labels in Word, or address Publisher publications. Of course, I have to import the contact list into Excel to analyze it, but seldom is that necessary with basic contact information. If emailing and scheduling meetings aren't needs you anticipate having, you might still want to go with something a bit more flexible in which to store your data—such as Excel. I recommend using Publisher Address Lists only if Publisher documents are the only thing you intend to use the addresses with. That way, your options for using the data are far greater. For example, if you work for a major corporation or have a large mailing list that requires you to photocopy the output, you'll be better served by maintaining your data source elsewhere so that you can import it into Word and print labels.

Publisher uses Office 2000's mail merge capabilities to perform the addressing, so you might recognize some of the steps you're about to see from Chapter 10, "Working With Mail Merge."

To have Publisher address each publication for you as it's printed, you need to do the following:

1. Make sure you have a data source that contains all the information you need to address the publication. For a quick review of how to create a data source, you might want to flip through Chapter 10 again.

2. Open or create the publication you want to have Publisher address for you.

3. Make space for the address. The easiest way to do so is to have Publisher make the space for you as you're creating the document. Most Publisher wizards ask whether you want this element created for you. Even if you said no the first time, you can usually go back to the Quick Publication Wizard and change your answer to yes. If you designed the publication yourself, a simple, well-placed text frame will do.

Tip: The big cover-up. Even if you plan to use mailing labels, you should create this address placeholder. That way, the label obstructs none of the publication's content.

4. Click inside the text frame that serves as a placeholder for the address to select it, and then click Mail Merge|Open Data Source. The Open Data Source dialog box appears.

5. In this dialog box, you are given three choices: Merge from an Outlook Contact List, Merge Information from Another Type of File, and Create an Address List in Publisher. Click the desired option's button.

Caution: But I can't find my data source! For some reason when you select the Merge Information from Another Type of File option, Publisher, by default, just displays Publisher Address List files. Seeing this list might cause you a brief instant of panic over your inability to find what you're looking for. To save yourself some aggravation, routinely check the File of Type drop-down box first any time you have to go browsing for files. That way, you don't waste time looking for something you'll never find—a Word data source in a list of Publisher Address Lists!

6. When you make your selection, a series of dialog boxes helps you find the data source you want to use. The steps you're walked through here vary depending on what type of data source you select and whether the application that houses the data is open.

7. After the data source has been successfully attached to your Publisher document, an Insert Fields dialog box like the one shown in Figure 22.9 appears. Click its title bar, and drag it out of the text box's way if necessary so that you can see to do your work.

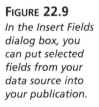

FIGURE 22.9

In the Insert Fields dialog box, you can put selected fields from your data source into your publication.

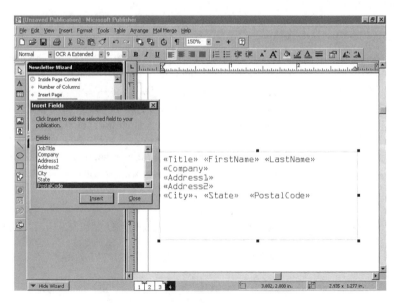

8. If you had Publisher create the address placeholder for you, click inside the text box to highlight all the text. That way, all the placeholder text will disappear as soon as you insert the first field. If you're working with an empty text box, just verify that the insertion point is set in the location you want the first field to appear.

9. To begin inserting fields, click the name of the field you want to insert, and then click the Insert button. Repeat as necessary until all the fields have been entered. And remember, you have to manually insert any punctuation marks, spaces, or returns you need to format the data fields.

Tip: A double-click'll do. When you're more familiar with mail merging in Publisher, you might find it quicker to simply double-click the field you want to insert instead of clicking it and then clicking the Insert button.

10. After all the fields have been inserted into the placeholder, click Close to dismiss the Insert Fields dialog box.

Tip: More than just an address. If your data source has the fields to accommodate it, you can use mail merge throughout your publication to make it more personalized. If you have a small veterinary practice, for example, you might want to incorporate the names of your customers' pets into a newsletter or something similar. The key here is that the information has to be available in the data source before you can use it in this fashion.

11. Click Mail Merge|Merge to merge the data source with your publication. A Preview Data dialog box opens (see Figure 22.10), and the first record's information appears in place of the field codes. You can use the arrow buttons to scroll through the addresses if you like. Click Close when you've finished previewing.

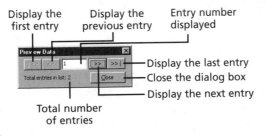

FIGURE 22.10

Use the Preview Data dialog box to ensure that all the address information is properly imported and formatted before you print the output.

12. If everything appears to be in order, you can start printing the publication. Click File|Print Merge to get started.

13. By default, Publisher prints a copy of the publication for every record in your data source and omits any blank fields so that no unexpected blank spaces appear in your addresses. If this is acceptable, click OK to send the publications to the printer. From there, you can prepare your publications for distribution as usual.

> **Tip: Testing, testing, 1-2-3.** If you have a large number of publications to print, you might want to click the Test button to have only one copy of the publication printed. That way, you can verify that the addresses are printed correctly before you inadvertently waste a bunch of paper, time, and toner.

Weighing Your Printing Options

No matter how large or small the job is, we would all like to get the best results possible. But what's best depends on the size and other specifics of the job. You won't find any clear-cut answers here. The three basic ways you can produce your publications are as follows:

- Desktop printing—Described earlier in this chapter, desktop printing involves printing a copy for each recipient from your in-house printer. This choice is generally best for small black-and-white jobs of 50 copies or fewer, for printing publications on demand, or for publications that have been personalized with mail merge.

- Copy shop—If you need 500 or fewer black-and-white copies of your publication, taking a printout to your local copy shop might be the most economical option. And you can even have the copies stapled!

- Commercial printing—When the job is enormous (500+ copies) and/or you need high-quality color output, commercial printing might be the only way to go. Because commercial processes and their output can become expensive, commercial printing might not be a viable option for small businesses or nonprofit organizations on a budget, but for the corporate environment, it might be the only way to achieve acceptable results.

At first glance, your choice might seem obvious, but a variety of factors can sway your decision. For example, if it's late at night and you're putting the finishing touches on a publication that's due the next day, you might have no other choice than to print it on your printer. Likewise, if you run a small startup company where you're trying to demonstrate your professional Web page design skills, you might want a full-color glossy brochure that does justice to your work. Brochures can be expensive to produce but may have numerous paybacks in the form of additional business.

The bottom line is that you really need to look at every aspect of the job before picking a printing method. Sending your publication to a copy shop to cut printing costs in half might seem like a good idea at first, but not if it means you have to close your one-person office for an hour to do it.

Commercial Printing: When Only the Best Will Do

Publisher supports two basic kinds of commercial printing: *process* and *spot color*. The differences between the two lie primarily in their color reproduction capabilities and the cost of printing. Process printing (also known as *four-color printing*) is generally used to reproduce photographs and multicolor graphics on a high-resolution offset press. Spot color, on the other hand, is best used for one- or two-color print jobs for which you want to highlight text or line art. Of the two, spot color is more economical because the process is less complicated. And in the end, its results can be just as dramatic and effective as those achieved by its more pricey counterpart.

Preparing Your Publication for Process Printing

Sometimes only photo-quality output will do. Maybe you're a water color artist wanting to create a brochure with samples of your work. Or perhaps you're launching a mail order business to sell jewelry; black-and-white images would hardly do it justice.

If your publication requires you to produce photo-quality output, you need to follow these steps to prepare it for commercial printing:

1. Open the publication you want to prepare for commercial printing.

2. Click Tools|Commercial Printing Tools|Color Printing. The Color Printing dialog box opens.

3. In the Print All Colors As section, click the Process Colors (CMYK) option. You'll notice that each color swatch now carries its own CMYK (cyan, magenta, yellow, and black—the four colors used to create the photographic effect) value.

4. Click the OK button to have Publisher convert all the colors into CMYK values, and then build four separate color plates for the commercial printer.

5. If your commercial printer can accept the material in Publisher format, run the Pack and Go Wizard, as described later in this chapter. If you need to convert the files to PostScript format to hand them off, consult your commercial printer to see how you should proceed because you need to know which PostScript driver(s) the printer supports.

Note: Revisit the colors you chose. Because CMYK values might not match your color choices exactly, you might want to look over your publication to make sure it's still acceptable. If it isn't, you can always change the colors manually until you achieve the desired result.

For a Touch of Color, Try Spot Color

Using spot color is an effective way to add a dab of color here and there. Maybe you want to colorize your headlines or line art. Or perhaps you have a snazzy two-color logo you want to reproduce. Spot coloring can be a cost-effective way to do it.

Tip: Watch what you're changing! In general, you should avoid coloring any fonts smaller than a 12-point serif font. Coloring such text can make your document hard for people to read.

With spot coloring, you can choose one or two colors in addition to black. When one color is chosen, all nonblack elements—no matter what their color—are converted to shades of the spot color you defined. If you choose two colors, only the elements that match the second color exactly are converted to that color. All other colors except black are converted to shades of the first spot color.

To ready your publication for spot coloring, you need to do the following:

1. Open or create the publication you want to print commercially using the spot-color process. Make sure color appears in the locations you want to apply spot coloring.

2. Click Tools|Commercial Printing Tools|Color Printing to open the dialog box.

3. Choose the Spot Color(s) option in the Print All Colors As section of the Color Printing dialog box. Notice that Publisher chooses a dominant spot color for you given the color scheme you specified in your Personal Information profile.

4. To select a new spot color, click the Change Spot Color button. The Choose Spot Color dialog box shown in Figure 22.11 opens.

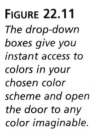

FIGURE 22.11

The drop-down boxes give you instant access to colors in your chosen color scheme and open the door to any color imaginable.

5. Click the Spot Color 1 drop-down arrow, and either select a color swatch from the publication's current color scheme or choose the More Colors option.

6. If you select a color, it appears in the Spot Color 1 box. You can also define a second spot color at this point by clicking the Spot Color 2 check box and then selecting a color from there. If you choose the More Colors option, a Colors dialog box like the one shown in Figure 22.12 appears. You can select a color swatch from one of the basic ones shown, or you can click the All Colors option at the top of the dialog box and tweak the color values on a palette like the one shown in Figure 22.13.

FIGURE 22.12
Click a swatch on the grid to use it as a spot color.

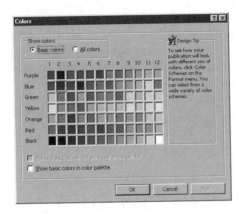

Click here to choose a color

Click and drag to fine-tune it

FIGURE 22.13
You can choose a color and adjust its values in several ways.

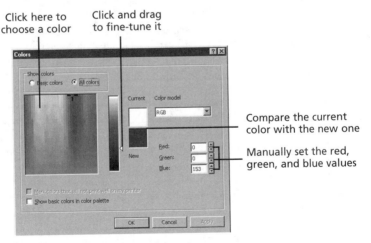

Compare the current color with the new one

Manually set the red, green, and blue values

7. Click OK until all the dialog boxes have been dismissed.

8. Skim through the publication to make sure it meets with your approval, make any necessary color changes, and then save it one last time in preparation for running the Pack and Go Wizard.

Helping Your Printer by Printing Color Separations

Think of color separations as the commercial printer's counterpart to photography proofs—they let the professional see exactly what he or she has before putting on the finishing touches. By taking separations to your commercial printer along with the document files, you can help him or her ensure that the results meet your expectations.

When you print color separations, interestingly, they appear in black and white whether you use a color printer or not. For every page in your publication, one page is printed for each color needed to reproduce the page. In other words, a newsletter with black text and red spot-colored line art produces two sheets for every page of the publication—one sheet for all the material to be printed in black and one for all of the material to be printed in red. Process color produces four pages for each document page—one in cyan, one in magenta, one in yellow, and a fourth in black. A professional can look at them and use them as a guide for monitoring output.

To print these color separations, you must first set up your document for commercial printing using one of the methods described previously. Then click File|Print and select the Print Separations option in the Separations section of the Print dialog box. Click OK to send the output to your printer.

Using the Pack and Go Wizard

If you read the PowerPoint 2000 chapters closely, you'll recall its Pack and Go Wizard, which was designed to take presentations on the road. Publisher's Pack and Go Wizard does something similar—it packages everything your printer needs to produce your publication in the way you intended it to be produced. This means all linked graphics are packaged, special fonts are included, and the like.

Peter's Principle: Who doesn't take work home anymore?

I find I never have enough time in the day to get everything done, so it seems I'm always in a state of lugging files back and forth between my work and home machines. With Publisher, moving files back and forth can be a tricky proposition, especially because my font and clip art selection are never the same on the two machines. Thanks to the Pack and Go Wizard, I can move files effortlessly from one machine to another without worrying about whether I'll have what I need. To use it, just run the Pack and Go Wizard, select the Take to Another Computer option instead of Take to a Commercial Printer, and then continue as usual.

Getting the Publication Ready to Go

After you've finished designing your publication and have set it up for commercial printing, you need to follow these steps to package it for your commercial printer:

Caution: Are you sure you're ready to pack 'er up? If you make any changes to the document after running the Pack and Go Wizard the first time, you need to run the wizard again to be sure it contains the most current copy of your document. The best policy is to run the Pack and Go Wizard at the very last minute so that you end up going through it only once.

1. Open the publication you want to pack up in its final form. Make sure it's already been formatted for commercial printing, too.

2. Click File|Pack and Go|Take to a Commercial Printing Service. The Pack and Go Wizard launches, explaining its many functions. Click Next to begin working with the wizard.

Note: Save me! If you attempt to use the Pack and Go Wizard before the document has been saved, you are prompted to save it before you can continue.

3. The wizard asks you where you want it to pack your files. If you want to package it on a disk to take to the printer (the most common use for the wizard), click the A:\ option. If you want to place it on another server in your network, click the Browse button to find the proper location. When you've settled on a location, click Next.

4. When you are asked whether you want to include graphics and fonts in your package, click all the options that apply, and then click Next.

5. The final screen recaps what the wizard will include in the package and tells you that Unpack.exe will be copied to the source you specified.

6. Click Finish to complete the package.

Note: Print and go. Depending on how you have Publisher installed, you might also be given an opportunity to print the publication as you pack it. Producing a printed copy for the commercial printer to use as a guide might not be such a bad idea, but it isn't absolutely necessary.

Unpacking Publisher Files

Unpacking the files is a simple process. All you have to do is follow these steps:

1. Insert the disk with the packed files into the appropriate drive on your computer.

2. Double-click My Computer on the Windows desktop.

3. Double-click the name of the drive that contains the packed Publisher files (usually A:\).

4. Look for a file named Unpack.exe, and then double-click it.

5. Click the Browse button to choose a directory and folder in which to unpack the files, and then click OK twice. Should the publication be stored on multiple disks, you will be prompted when to insert subsequent disks.

6. A message box appears, notifying you that the publication is unpacked. Click OK to dismiss the message box.

7. Switch to the folder into which you copied the files, and then double-click the file with PNG in the name and a .pub extension. The document's file is then opened in Publisher.

On Your Own

With Publisher 2000, converting a newsletter (or any other Publisher document) to a Web site is easier than you could ever imagine. It even creates all the hyperlinks for you, so you needn't worry about making everything fit together.

For this exercise, come up with an idea for a newsletter. Perhaps you have a redesigned corporate newsletter for your company, or maybe you want to start a newsletter on a special topic of interest. It can even be something totally fun like a holiday newsletter you send to family and friends.

Design the newsletter as you would any other Publisher document, and then convert it to a Web site. Open it in Internet Explorer 5 to see how the links work. Isn't it amazing? By creating just one document, you've managed to create a print and electronic publication all at once!

PART VII

Access Essentials

23

Creating Access 2000 Database Applications

How do you keep track of your business' contacts? Do you just keep a list on a piece of paper on your desk or in your wallet, or do you wish you were that organized? If you do keep them on a piece of paper somewhere, how often have you lost it and had to start over again? Or perhaps you're constantly finding business cards in odd places—as a bookmark in the latest Tom Clancy novel, for example.

If any of these descriptions fit the way you manage data, it might be time for you to consider using Microsoft Access 2000 to keep track of information. You can create your own database application that replaces the bits of paper and allows you to easily add new items as you acquire them. And best of all, you can easily create reports that reflect your changes.

And if you think Access is just for corporate moguls, think again. You can use Access to track anything from your organization's financial records to your child's beanbag toy collection to the list of volunteers for your neighborhood community center.

Given the complexity of what Access does, I've had to step up the pace a bit. You are bound to feel a bit overwhelmed by this chapter (and the next, for that matter) if you're new to databases. You have to wade through a whole lot of background information before you can jump into database design. Unlike Word or Excel, where the majority of the terms and concepts are familiar (after all, who doesn't know what a word or plus sign is, right?), database theory in Access is a whole different bag. Combine that with the fact that Access is probably the least commonly used Office application, and it makes for a lot of mundane reading. I promise I'll try to make the process as painless as I can.

I equate chapters like this to the freshman survey courses offered in colleges. In the Intro to Music History class, you spend the semester inundated with the name of every major composer and era of music. Not until the senior level History of Baroque Music do you get to the good stuff and learn about your favorite composer's secret insanity!

My mission is to give you what you need to get started with Access. Admittedly, two chapters on the subject aren't even close to comprehensive coverage, but when you're a busy professional, these chapters will provide the minimum you need to know to make the application work for you.

Introducing Access 2000

If you're reading this book, you obviously know what Access does in general, but do you really know how to put it to work for you? The sample applications Microsoft provides might be fine for some purposes, but they're by no means a one-size-fits-all solution. Given that, it's mandatory that you know all the parts of a database by name so that you can craft them into a viable application that gives you what you need when you need it. So let me start at the very beginning...

Access 2000 is a tool that creates database applications. You can create your own applications or customize any of the applications supplied with Access to meet your needs. Microsoft uses state-of-the-art relational database technology to ensure that your Access application is fast and reliable. The folks at Microsoft realize that time is money, so much emphasis has been placed on optimizing features and performance. Microsoft also uses drag and drop techniques to make it easy for you to create forms and reports, which in turn enable you to turn your raw data into valuable information. Basically, with an Access database application, you can turn those scraps of paper and stray business cards into something even more meaningful. For example, a programmer for a major university who's looking for a new job might suddenly discover that his mainframe background has given him a tremendous number of contacts at IBM, but he has yet to meet anyone from Microsoft, the very place he'd like to go to work!

> **Note: For more information...**Access 2000 is based on the relational database model and the Structured Query Language (SQL). Therefore, anyone using Access has a great deal of flexibility when building applications. If you're familiar with SQL, you can take advantage of some really advanced features that I don't have space to cover in this book. If you're interested in learning more about these advanced Access 2000 capabilities, Que publishes a number of good books (including Using Microsoft Access 2000 and Special Edition Microsoft Access 2000) that can help you maximize this powerful tool.

Choosing When to Use Access Instead of Excel

You can track data on your PC in three basic ways. You can keep a data list in Excel (see Chapter 15, "Analyzing Your Data in Excel"); you can create a custom database application using a database server such as SQL Server and a programming language such as Visual Basic; or you can create an Access application.

Each of these approaches has its strengths and weaknesses. Excel data lists become more difficult to manage as the number of rows (or records) grows. When you reach 50 or 100 rows, adding new rows in the right location becomes time consuming, and the lack of data editing may begin to show up as errors begin to creep into your data.

Likewise, a full-scale application development platform such as Visual Basic and SQL Server is overkill for many needs. These tools are designed for applications tracking data ranging in size from a few thousands of rows to those with a million or more rows.

An Access 2000 application fits into the gap between an Excel data list and an application developed using full-scale application development tools. Access is designed to manage anywhere from a few dozen rows of information to several thousand rows. And unlike a traditional application development platform, Access comes with a number of applications that can quickly and easily be tailored to meet the needs of busy users.

Parts of a Database Application

An Access 2000 database application is composed of two parts: an Access database and an Access application. The Access database contains a series of tables and indexes, which hold your data. In addition, Access also uses a set of tables in the database to hold information about your application.

A *database* is a collection of data about a particular subject (or data that is used for a particular purpose) for which the individual pieces of data can be located quickly and easily. Hence, a dictionary, encyclopedia, or even a rolodex could technically be considered a database. When we're talking about computers, however, the term *database* generally refers to a set of software that allows you to store and retrieve data on your computer in a structured fashion.

An *application* is a collection of one or more computer programs that are designed to perform a particular task. Microsoft Word and Excel are applications. So is Access. However, the primary job of Access, unlike Word and Excel, is to build other applications. It bears almost as much resemblance to a programming language like Visual Basic as it does to a typical application like Word 2000. Access applications tend to be similar to one another because they all store and retrieve data using a set of formatted windows, and they generate reports using some canned formats.

The Parts That Make Access Tick

So how is it possible that Access can help you make sense out of random bits of data? Let me turn to another analogy to explain. Although an Access database holds all the components of an Access application, traditionally the database is viewed as an object that holds one or more tables or indexes. Access merely adds its own tables to store the information it needs to support forms, reports, and other objects.

The most fundamental object in a database is a table. A *table* is an object that resembles an Excel data list and consists of a set of cells organized into a series of rows and columns. A *row* of the table (or data list to carry on the Excel analogy) contains information about a single object, such as a member of your organization or an inventory item in your small collectibles store. Where databases are concerned, each row is referred to as a *record*.

A column within the Access table contains a single piece of information about a single item (record), such as a person's surname or the date an inventory item was first placed into service. Given your experience with Excel, you'll immediately recognize these elements as *fields*.

Peter's Principle: Are you still awake?

I remember how boring I thought learning terms was, so if you find your attention very unfocused right now, I'm not surprised. I will say, however, that with database design in particular, a firm grasp of the proper terms for the elements is a must if you want to design an application that truly meets your needs. The wizards and prefab databases included with Access 2000 are great for learning. And thank goodness we have them, too, because there often isn't time in a frantic corporate world to design things in the manner they should be designed. The wizards and prefab Access applications give you a quick, workable solution, but when you have the luxury (and sadly that is the proper term) of time to really do it right, you'll be grateful to have the foundation you need to jump into the project with conviction.

A data type describes the type of data stored in the column (or field, if you prefer to think of it that way). Some typical data types include Integer for integer numbers (for numbers of items in your inventory), Text for strings of characters (such as a person's name or the color of a diecast car in your collection), Datetime for values containing date or time information (such as the date a collectible was retired or the time an auction expires), and Currency for values representing money (such as an item's price or cost).

> **Tip: The string thing.** Let me share some interesting things you need to know about strings. First of all, mailing addresses (both snail mail and email) should be stored as strings even though they might contain numbers. You store them this way because these items more than likely contain text as well, which must be contained in a string. Another item that should be held in a string is a phone number. Why not as an integer? Because you can store only 10-digit numbers with a 2 as the leading number. So if your phone number is (555) 555-5555, you're out of luck. Of course, a clever workaround might be to store the area code and the phone number in separate fields. Items with spaces must also be classified as strings.

In addition to specifying a field's type, you can also specify its size. As with nearly any rule, however, there is an exception. In this case, it's the 10-digit limit on the length of integer fields. By setting a field's size, you can minimize space taken up on hard drives and on printed output, be it on the screen or on paper.

A *key* is a set of one or more columns in a table that can be used to uniquely identify a row. The primary key uniquely identifies a particular row in the table. Examples of a primary key might be a book's ISBN number or a product's SKU number. An *index* is a database component associated with a table that helps you find a specific row in the table more quickly. Think of an index as a label that appears in front of a file cabinet's drawer that reads "L–Mc" or some other label that helps you find the files you need more quickly. Making use of database indices does have a downside, however; using this method to improve the speed with which a row can be found increases the time it takes to add, delete, or change a row in the table.

The information inside a table can be accessed either directly or as part of a query. The query is a way to retrieve selected information from one or more tables. Remember how you used queries to print letters to selected recipients in Word? A database query is no different. It can almost always be used in place of a table in forms, reports, and charts. Although updating a table is always possible, under some circumstances (namely when a query is run against a form), a query can't be updated. Although this limits a query's usefulness in forms, it isn't a factor in reports and charts that never perform updates.

Anatomy of an Access Application

An application primarily contains forms and reports. Other objects, such as charts, also fall under the application heading. Access stores information about an application inside the database using a series of special tables that you don't access except by using the application. The basic idea is that by enclosing all the information for an application inside the database, you need worry only about a single file.

Parts of a Form

Remember those forms you encountered while working with mail merge? Well, Access has forms, too, but they're a bit more complex. Typically, an Access form contains information from a single row/record from a table that can be edited. Figure 23.1 shows a typical Access form. You can also scroll through the database one row at a time. Another type of form presents the data using a spreadsheet-like format. This type of form is most similar to what you encounter in an Excel data list.

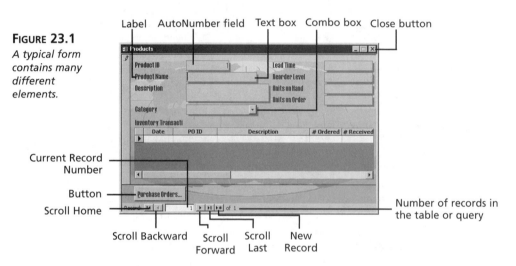

FIGURE 23.1
A typical form contains many different elements.

You can also combine the first two types of forms together to display one row from one table, and multiple rows from another table in the same window. This capability might be helpful in more situations than you first think. For example, if your auto parts store sells both new and used parts, you might present the specifications of a part such as its size, what cars it fits, and so on. Then you could display multiple rows underneath it—one for factory-sealed parts and the quantity available and respective price, one for loose parts with quantity and price, and one for used parts with quantity and price.

A third type of form, called a *switchboard*, is special because it doesn't display any data. It is used to provide menus that can run the various forms and reports that make up the application. It gives you one-click access to the Access elements you want to work with. The switchboard can be likened to a standard Office toolbar in that you simply click a button to go to the element named on the button you clicked.

When you're working with an Access form, as described here, you'll encounter the following buttons or elements. Note, however, that not all of them are present on every type of form.

- A *Close button* closes the current form. Any changes to the current record are then saved. If you are inserting a new record into a table, it is saved unless it's blank. If the form is the main switchboard, clicking this button closes the application.

- A *label* displays a constant value on the form. It is typically used to display a field's name or other nonchanging information.

- An *AutoNumber field* displays the text AutoNumber only while a record is being inserted into the table. When you save the record, the next available number is automatically placed in this field. When you're viewing a record where a number has already been assigned, it is visible in this field.

- A *text box field* contains a blank area where you can enter or edit a value in a database. Despite its name, you can enter numeric or text values into this field.

- A *combo box field* displays the contents of a field that must exist in another table or query. Clicking the down arrow at the right end of the field displays a list of legal values for this field. To add a new value to this list, double-click the field, and a new form is displayed to add the new value. After you enter the required data in the new form, you can close it by clicking the Close button and continue working with the old form.

- A *button* performs a specific function such as opening a new form.

- The *Scroll Home button* displays the first record in the table or query.

- The *Scroll Backward button* displays the previous record in the table or query, unless the first record is being displayed.

- The *Current Record Number field* displays the number for the current record.

- The *Scroll Forward button* displays the next record in the table or query, unless the last record is being displayed.

- The *Scroll Last button* displays the last button in the table or query.

- The *New Record button* moves the current record beyond the last record in the table or query to insert a new one.

- The *Number of Records area* displays the total number of records found in the table or query. It is automatically updated as new rows are added.

You also can invoke a number of functions from the Access toolbar while a form is running (see Figure 23.2). Most of these functions are available via the toolbar only, unless they have been explicitly programmed into the Access application.

FIGURE 23.2

The Access toolbar appears while you're running a form.

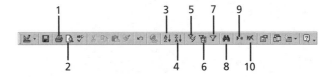

1. Print
2. Print Preview
3. Sort Ascending
4. Sort Descending
5. Filter by Selection
6. Filter by Form
7. Apply/Remove Filter
8. Find
9. New Record
10. Delete Record

So what exactly happens when you click one of these toolbar buttons? If you're brave, you can just click them to find out. Many of the buttons are fairly self-explanatory, but a few could benefit from further explanation. The buttons are as follows:

- The *Print* button sends a copy of the form to your default printer.

- The *Print Preview* button displays the form using the same print preview window used to preview reports. (See the "Parts of a Report" section later in this chapter for more information about the print preview window.)

- The *Sort Ascending* button sorts the records displayed in the form in ascending order based on the field selected before the button was clicked.

- The *Sort Descending* button sorts the records displayed in the form in descending order based on the field selected before the button was clicked.

- The *Filter by Selection* button displays only those records with the same value as contained in the field selected before the button was clicked.

- The *Filter by Form* button displays a blank version of the regular form. Fill in one of the fields with the value you want to see. If you fill in more than one value in the form, only records with all the specified values are selected. By using the Or button at the bottom of the form, you can select a new blank form and specify another set of values. If the record matches the values in any of the Or'ed forms, the record is selected. After you have finished specifying these values, click the Apply Filter button. Any record that matches these values is selected.

- The *Apply/Remove Filter* button applies the form filter or removes either the filter by selection or filter by form filter criteria.

- The *Find* button displays a Find dialog box (see Figure 23.3). Using it, you can search for specific values in a field. You can optionally replace the value with a different value by using the Replace tab. This dialog box looks and works a lot like the Find and Replace dialog boxes found in Word and Excel.

FIGURE 23.3

Using the Find/Replace dialog box, you can find records in the database and optionally update their values.

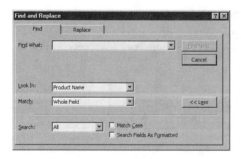

- The *New Record* button moves the current record beyond the last record in the table or query to insert a new one. This button works identically to the New Record button on the form.

- The *Delete Record* button deletes the current record. A dialog box appears, asking you to confirm that you want to delete the record. Clicking Yes deletes the record, whereas clicking No leaves it in the database.

Parts of a Report

Reports create a printed view of the database. You can print the entire contents of the database or just selected items. A preview facility is used to see what the actual output would look like before it is sent to the printer. No sense wasting paper printing a report that doesn't communicate what you want it to! Figure 23.4 shows a typical preview window of a report.

FIGURE 23.4
A typical report contains many different elements.

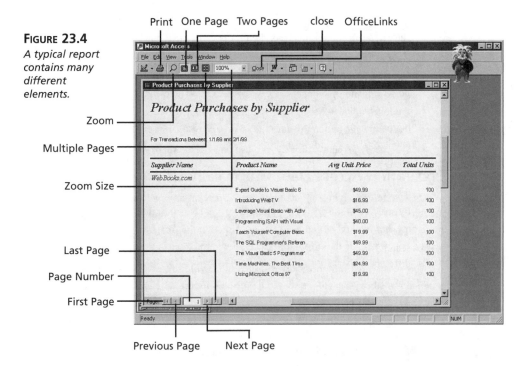

On a report preview screen, clicking a certain button invokes the following actions:

- The *Print* button sends the report to your default printer. You can also choose File|Print from the Access menu bar at the top of the preview window to see the Office 2000 Print dialog box. You can set various print options, such as the name of the printer, the range of pages to be printed, and the number of copies to be printed through this dialog box.

- The *Zoom* button toggles between the best fit and the value specified in Zoom Size.

- The *One Page* button displays one page in the print window.

- The *Two Pages* button displays two pages side by side in the print window.
- The *Multiple Pages* button displays a small window showing six tiny pages. Select any combination of the pages to be shown in the same fashion in the print window.
- The *Zoom size* combo box allows you to select how large or small the page is to be displayed when zoomed. Values range from 200 percent (very large) to 10 percent (very small) and Fit (meaning that the print display is sized to fit in the entire window).
- The *Close* button closes the print window and returns to the switchboard or database window, which displayed the print preview window.
- The *OfficeLinks* button transfers the information into Word or Excel.
- The *First Page* button displays the first page of the report.
- The *Previous Page* button displays the previous page of the report.
- The *Page Number* window displays the current page number in the print preview window. If multiple pages are displayed in the window, the page number of the first page is displayed.
- The *Next Page* button displays the next page of the report.
- The *Last Page* button displays the last page of the report.

Presenting Access Data Graphically Using a Chart

Which has more of an impact—the number 72 percent or a pie chart with nearly three-quarters of it colored in? If you're like most people, you'll find the chart to be a much more powerful method of communication. Although the Access charting tools aren't nearly as powerful as those found in Excel, they are identical in concept.

An Access chart is similar to a report in that information from a table or query is used to produce something that can be sent to the printer. Figure 23.5 shows a simple chart. Unlike a report, a chart must be placed on a form, so it isn't quite the distinct object a report is. However, it is a useful feature of Access.

FIGURE 23.5

A chart presents information from your database in a graphic form.

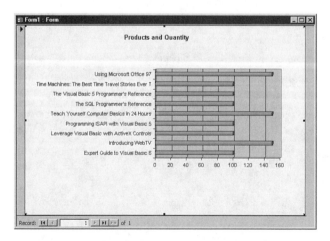

When You Need a Working Database Quickly

If you don't have the time to piece together the perfect application, you might want to consider using the Access Database Wizard.

Access 2000 comes with a set of databases that are designed to perform specific functions such as order entry, inventory control, and time and billing. Each of these databases comes with a wizard that allows you to customize it to fit your needs.

Using a wizard to create your database is a very easy process. You merely respond to a few dialog boxes with some information, and Access automatically creates your database application. Of course, you can always click Finish at any point along the way to accept the default values for the application, but reviewing the various steps is a good idea even if you plan to use the various defaults. There just may be some better choices for you than the default given your needs. Note that clicking Cancel anywhere along the way stops the wizard and deletes any files that might have been created along the way.

1. Start Access 2000, and then click Access Database Wizards, Pages, and Projects, as shown in Figure 23.6.

FIGURE 23.6
Go to Access's list of wizards to select the type of database you need.

2. Select the database you want to create (see Figure 23.7).

FIGURE 23.7
Choose the sample Access 2000 database you want to create.

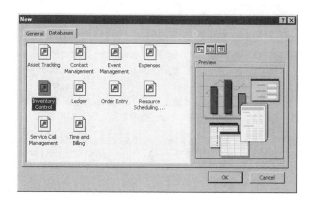

3. You are prompted to choose a filename and locations in which to create your new database using the normal Office 2000 Save As dialog box. Clicking Create creates your database and displays the database wizard.

4. After your database is created, the Database Wizard is displayed (see Figure 23.8). Click Next to continue.

FIGURE 23.8
You can read about the functions available in the database.

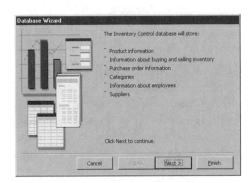

5. The Database Wizard displays the list of tables that will be created for the database with the fields that will be included in each table (see Figure 23.9). Any fields that are displayed in italics are optional and can be added if you choose. All the other fields are required and can't be removed. Click Next to move to the next step.

FIGURE 23.9
Review the tables and the fields in your database.

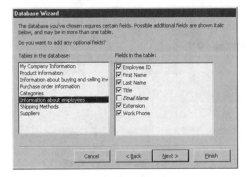

6. Choose the style that will be used for your application (see Figure 23.10). This choice affects the images used in the background of the forms and how the fields are displayed on the form. (You might recall the earlier tip about keeping this option simple to avoid distracting the user.) A preview is displayed on the left side of the form. Click Next to continue.

FIGURE 23.10

Choose a style for your database forms.

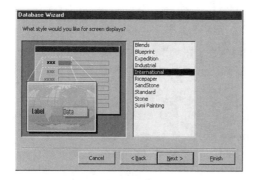

> **Tip: Standard equipment.** The Standard style gives you the most Windows-like display. This style is usually easier to use and read than other styles, and may be less distracting as well.

7. Printed reports use a different style. You can choose one from the dialog box shown in Figure 23.11. Click Next after making your selection.

FIGURE 23.11

Choose a style for your database reports.

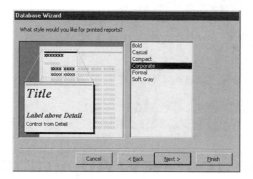

8. You can specify the title of your database application and optionally include a company logo on all reports. Click Next to continue.

9. Click Finish to instruct the wizard to create the database and all the related database objects (see Figure 23.12). You can choose to start the database when the wizard completes it, and you can also display information about how to use a database.

FIGURE 23.12
Review the tables
and the fields in
your database.

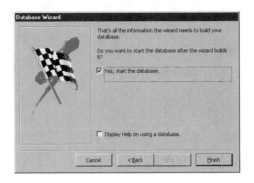

FIGURE 23.12
Review the tables and the fields in your database.

10. The Database Wizard then displays a pair of progress bars that track its activity. This step takes a minute or two to complete, so be patient.

11. If you opted to do so in the last dialog box, Access automatically starts the database after the wizard builds it (see Figure 23.13). Note that you might be prompted to enter some information the first time the database is started.

FIGURE 23.13
Start your application for the first time.

My Company Information	
Enter your company's name and address information here. You will save the information by closing the form.	
Company Name	Just Plane Crazy
Address	1234 JustPC Drive
City	Beltsville
State/Province	MD
Postal Code	20705-
Country	USA
Phone Number	(800) 555-1000
Fax Number	(800) 555-1234

Starting Your New Application

Opening your new application is just as easy as opening any other Office 2000 file. Given that, you have the same wide range of options for opening the application. For an application I run only occasionally, I start Access and choose to open an existing file from the dialog box displayed in Figure 23.14. For databases I work with on a daily basis, I create a special shortcut on my Windows desktop, as I described earlier in the book. Finally, if working with the application is your only responsibility, you might want to program it to launch itself along with Windows when the computer is booted.

FIGURE 23.14

You can choose which database you want to use when Access first starts.

Navigating Through Your Application Using Switchboards

When your application is started, you typically see a special form known as a *switchboard* (see Figure 23.15). A switchboard's purpose is to provide a menu of functions that you can access by clicking a button. Each button moves you to a new location in your application, much like your telephone's speed dial feature lets you call someone by pressing a single button.

FIGURE 23.15

A switchboard allows you to select various features in your application.

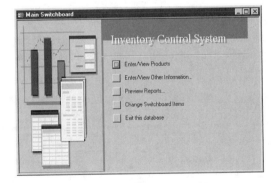

Entering Data in a Form

The information displayed on your form generally represents the data from a single record from a table or a query (see Figure 23.16). On the bottom of the form is a series of scroll buttons that allow you to move through the set of records. You can move to the first or last record in the set, or move forward or backward one record. The current record number is displayed in between the buttons, and the total number of records in the set is displayed to the right of the buttons.

FIGURE 23.16

You can easily change the data in your database by changing the values on the form.

People are always moving, getting new jobs, and so on, so it's inevitable that you'll eventually need to modify an existing entry in your database. You can change any of the information in the record by merely typing the new value in place of the old and then moving to a different record. You save the changes to the database simply by moving to a new record. As always, it's nice to know you have a way out if you make a mistake. If you change your mind and decide not to make the changes, you can click the Undo button while on the current record. You might also be able to restore the record if you've moved to another record as long as you haven't made any changes in the new current record.

When you want to add a new entry, you click the Add button, which enables you to start with a clean slate, so to speak. Clicking the Add Record button basically adds an empty record at the end of the set and makes it the current record. All the fields on the form are blank unless the field is an AutoNumber field, in which case the field contains the text string AutoNumber. The value of an AutoNumber field is generated by Access after the record has been saved.

Back when I managed a small nonprofit organization, we constantly had letters returned and marked undeliverable whenever we did a mass mailing. Because we couldn't afford to waste the postage, I made it a priority to have staff and volunteers physically delete the database entries that were no longer of use. You might find yourself needing to do this too. To delete a record from an Access database, you must locate the record and then click the Delete button on the Access toolbar. Access asks whether you're sure you want to delete the record. Note that after you've deleted a record from the database, you can't get it back.

On some forms, you see a spreadsheet-like grid. This area of the form contains information from another table. You can add, delete, and change records just like you can when only one record is displayed per form. The only difference here is that you need to remember which record is the current record. Access helps makes this clearer by including an arrow in the row header area to mark the current record. Changing a value and moving the current record down one row commits the changes to the database even though the previous row may still be visible on your form.

Previewing and Printing Reports

Viewing a report is easy. Simply click the button beside the report you want to see on the switchboard. For most reports, the print preview window is displayed, letting you scroll through the output before clicking the Print button.

Other reports (typically those that invoke queries) may display a form asking for some information before the preview window is displayed. Providing this information is often helpful because it allows you to reduce the amount of data that is displayed in the report.

Using the Database Window

Your database application is run under control of the database window (see Figure 23.17). Normally, this window is minimized while your application is running. However, if you restore it, you can look at the various objects that make up your application. Many of the objects I've already discussed in this chapter (such as tables, forms, and reports), whereas others (such as queries, pages, macros, and modules) I'll cover in Chapter 24, "Advanced Access 2000 Database Functions."

FIGURE 23.17
The database window allows you to see all the components that make up your database application.

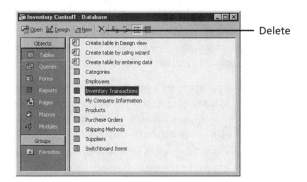

Delete

Ending Your Application

When you are finished working with your application, close all the active reports, tables, and such, and then click the Exit database button, if one is provided, on the switchboard. If one is not provided, simply close the application in your preferred way of closing any other Office application or document.

On Your Own

The only way to really learn how to use a tool such as Microsoft Access 2000 is to dig in and get your hands dirty. Fortunately, Access makes learning easy because you can build one of the sample database applications very quickly. Then you merely need to learn how to use the application.

If you are thinking about building an Access application of your own, you should spend a few minutes and create one of the sample applications. This way, you can get more insight into the benefits and limitations of an Access application.

Can't come up with a good reason to build an Access application? How about one of these?

- Gather all those stray business cards and pencil scrawlings on the back of match-books, and turn them into an address database. Sure, using an Outlook contact list would be easier, but it won't help you get acquainted with Access.

- Help your daughter organize her collection of Beanie Babies by entering information about them into Access. This suggestion has the side benefit of keeping you from wasting money buying Beanie Babies she already has!

- If you have a son, maybe he has a collection you can help with, such as Hot Wheels, comic books, baseball cards, or action figures.

- Catalog all the movies on that pile of videotapes you recorded off the TV.

- Get your audio CDs in order.

- Log all your *Star Trek* novels into Access so that you can easily figure out which ones you're missing.

If you can't think of anything to use for sample data, then you're telling a fib. We all have something we would like to see better organized!

When you open the application, try using the switchboard to move around from one form to another. Remember that closing a form takes you back to the switchboard. Of course, you should also try entering some data into the forms. Try scrolling around and see how the data appears. Change some of the data in a record, move to the next record and then back again, and verify that the changes were made properly. Finally, try previewing some of the reports. Don't expect the reports to be meaningful if you didn't enter the data in the way the application expects.

Finally, try using the main database window to view the various objects in your database. Take a few minutes and look at the database tables and their fields. Look for the same field names in different tables. Try to visualize how this information is used to link the various tables together.

Advanced Access 2000 Database Functions

What do you do when none of the sample applications supplied with Access 2000 meet your needs? You build your own, of course! Unlike most professional development platforms, Access 2000 is very easy to use. Powerful wizards help you build most of the pieces of a database application. All you have to do is supply the answers to the questions the wizard asks of you, and the wizard does the rest.

Looking at Your Needs

Before any database application is built, someone had to have said, "I need…" This need defines the goal that the database application must meet. Without this goal statement, you could end up with an application that generates mailing labels when what you really need is an application that tracks inventory!

Thus, you might say, "I must keep better track of my inventory" or "I want to know which beanbag collector's items my daughter has and which ones she needs to complete her set." I call this the *Problem Statement*. To be successful, the application must solve a very specific problem. All too many times companies are enticed to automate as much of their business as possible although automation, in fact, may be counterproductive.

Peter's Principle: Weigh the pros and cons.

When it comes to automation, there is no perfect answer or obvious solution. When enchanted with a new software product, I often find myself looking to find a way—any way—to put it to use. You may have encountered political powers within your own organization who decided that the organization should be fully computerized whether it made sense or not. When I'm faced with a decision of whether to computerize a given task, I ask myself a few pointed questions. Do I have a specific problem that a computer can help me solve? Can I use software I already know how to use, or will getting up to speed with it take me an eternity? Will others be working with the project under consideration? If so, what are their computer skills? If you ask yourself these questions as I do, you're more likely to make a better decision given your specific circumstances.

Performing a Needs Analysis to Define Your Problem

Part of the decision-making process should involve conducting some kind of needs assessment. Whether it's committed to paper or just bouncing around in your head is irrelevant as long as the process takes place in some fashion.

The *Needs Analysis* is the process of taking the Problem Statement and translating it into a series of statements describing the problem in more detail. These statements help you determine the information you need to store in your database and the functions your application needs to perform.

For instance, "I need to know when to order additional units of each item in my inventory" means that your database must track information about when new orders are received and when items are taken from the inventory. "I need to know the color of the beanbag collector's item" means that your database must track the color of each beanbag.

Also some of your needs may be expressed in terms of actions. For example, "I need to print a report listing all the items in my inventory" is a good example of an action that your application needs to perform. Likewise, "I need to add new beanbag collector's items to the database as they are released" identifies another function that is required of your application.

No one's a mind reader, but try to consider the future as you design your database. An example might be even though your store sells only those beanbag collector's items for now, someday you might decide to trade with customers. In that case, you may eventually want to track which items you would allow to be traded. You might even decide something as complex as "If we have more than five of an item in the inventory, trading will be considered." The more thought you give to what your (or your company's) needs are now and what they might potentially be, the less work you'll have to do on the database down the road.

Designing Your Database Tables

When you understand your needs, designing your database is fairly straightforward. First, you separate the statements that describe tangible pieces of data (such as inventory control number and color) from the statements that describe functions like *report* (produce a printout of certain items) and *add* (to input additional items into the database). Then you separate the data items into groups depending on how each item is related to the others.

> **Caution: There's more to this process than you think.** I don't want you to think that designing databases is a trivial matter. The guidelines I discuss here will work for most of the databases that you will design using Access 2000. Unfortunately, in some situations these guidelines might not be appropriate. As you build more complex databases, you might find that these rules are too simple. If this happens, you should seek the help of an expert—either a more advanced book on Access or a database expert who can help you deal with the problems associated with designing a complex database.

Defining Data Items and Tables

After you've completed an adequate needs assessment and know what you want your database to accomplish, it's time to begin building the database itself. You begin this process by identifying various data items to be included in the database's tables. The easiest way to do so is to look through the data items for keys. Some elements will immediately jump out at you, such as Social Security numbers and inventory control numbers. These items are unique to each specific item. Sometimes you have to combine multiple pieces of data together to make a key, such as the name and color of your collector's items.

When you have a key, you should look for data items that have a one-to-one relationship with the key. This means that for each key value, only one possible value exists for that data item. For example, for each value of an inventory control number, you can have only one value for the year it was purchased, its purchase cost, and its current location. Likewise, for a personal beanbag collection database, you might have the item's name and color, its picture, plus whether you own one, and whether you want one. This information will eventually be formed into a table.

Each key and its associated data items correspond to the columns in a table. Other keys and data items correspond to the columns in their own tables.

Note that sometimes you will find a data item that can fit into more than one group. Having such an item is fine because this data item helps to define other relationships. Typically, these relationships fall into the one-to-many category in which one row in one table can locate multiple rows in another table.

Consider the inventory system for a moment. Each item in the inventory has a unique number, a quantity on hand, a reorder point, and a description. The company orders items from a number of suppliers by sending a purchase order to the supplier with a list of items. Thus, the supplier and the inventory item are related to each other by the purchase order number.

Assigning Data Types

After you have compiled your list of data items, you can begin deciding their data types. In general, your choices of data types fall into one of two basic categories: number values and character values. There are a few other data types besides these, but they are used only for special data such as images and date and time values.

Number values come in two flavors: exact and inexact. Exact numbers are integers or numbers with a fixed number of decimal places. These types are useful in counting things or keeping track of money. Inexact numbers are really floating-point numbers. They are useful when you need to represent a wide range of values or keep track of scientific measurements.

Character values, also known as *string values*, contain sequences of characters such as people's names, descriptions of objects, and so on. They also come in two flavors: fixed size and variable size. Just as their names imply, fixed size strings always take up the same amount of space. They are best suited for values that are always similar in size, such as state abbreviations or United States telephone numbers. Variable length strings, on the other hand, are great for storing information that varies in size, such as names and item descriptions.

> **Tip: Leave room for growth.** When you're using variable length character strings, choose a size that is larger than you need. The extra space might come in handy someday.

Relating Database Tables

If your database requires more than one table, you need to understand how they are related to each other. In general, two tables are related if the records in both tables share some common fields. If they have no fields in common, the tables are said to be unrelated.

In a one-to-many relationship, one row in one table is related to zero or more rows in another table. This relationship is determined by the set of fields that are common to both tables. Typically, you find one field in each table in common. For instance, if you have a database with a table called Songs and a table called Albums, you would see that the AlbumID field is common to both. In the Albums table, AlbumID is used to uniquely identify an album. In the Songs table, AlbumID is used to identify the album containing the song.

Note: Table relationships. Two other possible relationships between tables are the one-to-one and the many-to-many. In the one-to-one relationship, exactly one row in one table is related to exactly one row in another table. In the many-to-many relationship, one or more rows in one table are related to zero or more rows in another table. These types of relationships aren't very common in most simple databases.

Tip: Primary and foreign keys. In a one-to-many relationship, the field or fields that make up the primary key on the "one" table are used to determine the relationship. The fields in the "many" table are often referred to as the *foreign keys*.

Sometimes the field names might be different between two tables, yet the tables are related. Consider a database with two tables, one containing the employees of a company, and the other containing the departments in the company. The employees table holds the employee number, employee name, and a bunch of other stuff associated with an employee. The departments table contains a field called manager, which holds the employee number of the manager for the department. So employees and departments tables are related by the employee number field and the manager field, respectively.

Designing Database Functions

When you have a database, you will want to create various functions in order to make use of it. Queries represent a way of looking at the data in your database. (Remember how we used Web queries back in Excel to extract and look at selected data elements from a Web site?) Forms allow you to browse and update information in the database one item at a time. (You were first introduced to forms in Chapter 10, "Working with Mail Merge.") Reports generate special listings of one or more items, generally on paper. Data pages are Web pages that can be used to collect information from a Web site's visitors using a Web browser.

Tip: If at first you don't succeed, try, try again. Try a few different designs before actually filling a database with live data. Take a look at the sample databases that are supplied with Access. They're pretty good sources of design ideas. And remember to keep it simple. A single table that keeps track of all your information is much easier to build and use than a very complicated database. For databases with fewer than a few hundred records, using a table is often the best solution. And for storing simple tables of data, remember that Excel might be an option, too.

Using Queries to Define How Your Data Is Presented

A *query* is a powerful tool that allows you to create different views of your database. You can use a query nearly anywhere you would use a table. You can use a query to limit the number of fields that are returned on screen or on paper, or to limit the number of rows that are returned. You can also use a query to combine multiple tables into a single view, thus giving you access to the best of all worlds where data is concerned. You can even use a query to create new fields that represent information that can be derived from other fields in the query. For example, you can create a field whose value is dependent on data in another field. To follow through with the beanbag collection example, you might create a field whose value changes from trade to sell depending on how many of a certain item are owned.

> **Caution: All queries are not created equal.** Although you can always view the results of queries, some queries can't be used for updating. You can't update queries that contain summary information or those that use more than one table.

Inputting New Information with Forms

After creating your database, you need a way to enter the information. Although you can open the tables directly and enter the data just like you would in an Excel worksheet, you would be better off having a customized form to enter your data. This is especially true if multiple people will be entering data.

A form generally displays information only about the current record. Access automatically supplies controls that allow you to choose the current record just as the buttons on Word's Mail Merge toolbar enable you to scroll from record to record. There are two exceptions to this rule. The first exception is that a form also might contain a worksheet-like structure that allows you to display multiple rows of information at the same time. You can't arrange the individual fields in this format on the form to make it easier to use.

The second exception is a special kind of form known as a *switchboard*. This form consists of a set of buttons that allow the user to choose various functions in your application. No data from your database tables is displayed on the switchboard.

Typically, you should have one form for each table in your database. However, if you have two tables related to each other by a one-to-many relationship, using a single form makes things easier for the application's user. At the top of the form, you should place all the fields for the "one" table. At the bottom of the form, you should put a grid for the information from the "many" table. The grid should be linked to the information in the top half so that each time you change to a new record in the "one" table, the related records from the "many" table are displayed in the grid.

Communicating Data Results Through Reports

A report is designed to communicate information about the data in your database in a static way. Unlike a form, a report generally contains information from an entire table or query, rather than information from the current record only. A report is also formatted to be printed on paper, with headers and footers, page numbers, and other elements that make the report easier to read and keep track of.

Substituting Data Pages for Forms for Use on the Web

A data page is just like a form; however, it can be accessed over the Internet using a Web browser. For instance, a company might put a data page on its corporate Web site to enable customers to register their products for notification about updates, enhancements, recalls, and such. All the same design issues that apply to forms also apply to data pages. Ease of use and clarity are must-haves if you want to acquire meaningful information. In addition, you need to consider security before you make the data pages public. In many cases, you might not want just anybody entering or modifying data in your database.

Building Your Database Application

Now that you know what you need in an application, it's time to start building it. First, you need to create your database. It will hold all the other objects you create for your application. Next, you create the tables that will hold your data. Finally, you create the forms, queries, and reports that transform your raw data into information.

Creating an Empty Access Database

To create an empty Access database, follow these steps:

1. Start Access 2000, and then select Blank Access database from the Create a New Database Using group box.

2. The normal Office 2000 File dialog box opens with the name File New Database. Select the location and name for your new database.

3. Clicking Create displays the Database window shown in Figure 24.1.

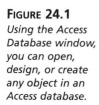

FIGURE 24.1

Using the Access Database window, you can open, design, or create any object in an Access database.

Creating Access Tables

You can create a table in three basic ways. First, you can use a wizard to build it based on some sample tables that are supplied with Access 2000. This method has the advantage of using the work someone has already done to determine which fields are most likely needed for a specific table.

The second way to create a table is to create a table in Design view. This method allows you to directly control the details of fields in the table. You get this same view of the table if you go back to change it later.

In the third approach, you enter some information into a spreadsheet-like grid and let Access determine the data type based on the kind of data you enter. You can then bring up the table layout in Design view and make any changes you want.

Creating Tables with the Table Wizard

To create a table with the Table Wizard, follow these steps:

1. In the Database window, double-click Create Table by Using Wizard. The resulting Table Wizard displays the dialog box containing definitions for many different types of database tables (see Figure 24.2). The tables are arranged in two groups: Business and Personal.

FIGURE 24.2
Using the Table Wizard, you can choose from a number of predefined tables.

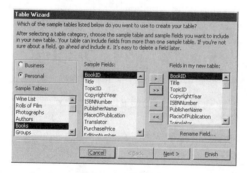

2. You should review the list of tables to find the one that best describes your needs. Then you can select any or all of the fields you want in your own table by clicking the greater than and double greater than buttons. You can even add fields from several different tables. After you've determined the fields you want, click Next. In the following dialog box, you are asked to name your table.

3. After telling the wizard what you want to call the table, you need to tell Access who will determine the primary key for the table. If you choose to create the primary key yourself, the wizard displays the dialog box shown in Figure 24.3. Otherwise, the wizard chooses a key, so you can skip step 4.

Note: Primary key default. When the wizard is automatically determining a primary key for your table, it scans the fields looking for an AutoNumber field. The first one it finds, it uses as the primary key. If the wizard doesn't find one, it creates a new field with the same name as the table but with the letters *ID* appended. Thus, for the Books table, a field called BooksID is created.

FIGURE 24.3

You can choose the field and data type Access should use as the primary key.

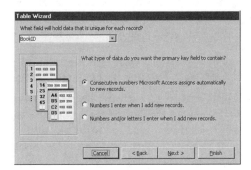

4. The wizard displays a drop-down list of the fields in the table. Select the one that will always have a unique value, and choose its data type. Click Next to continue.

Tip: Key fields. The wizard offers you three choices for the type of data kept in the primary key: an automatic number supplied by Access, a number you supply, or a text string you supply. Unless you have a strong reason for using your own values, let Access supply an automatic number.

5. If your database contains more than one table, the Table Wizard asks you whether it is related to any of these tables. Otherwise, it continues processing on step 7. If it is related, select the name of the table, and click the Relationship button. The Relationships dialog box appears, as shown in Figure 24.4.

FIGURE 24.4

You can specify how one table is related to another in the Relationships dialog box.

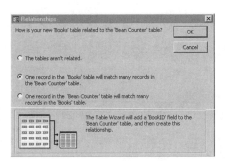

6. Choose the relationship that best describes the two tables. If you decide that the tables aren't related, clicking OK returns you to the previous window. If you choose either of the one-to-many relationships, clicking OK examines the primary key fields in both tables to determine whether they are present in the other table as well. If the key fields aren't found, the wizard automatically adds the primary key fields to the other table.

7. In the concluding Table Wizard dialog box, you can choose to modify the table design using Design view, to enter data directly into the table using a spreadsheet-like view of the data, or to automatically create a form and then enter the data into the table.

Creating and Editing Tables in Design View

If you choose to modify your table after building it with the Table Wizard or choose to create your table directly, you see the Design View window, as shown in Figure 24.5. Three columns describe each field in your table. They are Field Name, Data Type, and Description. Additional information about the current field is displayed in the Field Properties section of the form. Also, a short description of the current attribute of the field is displayed in the comments area.

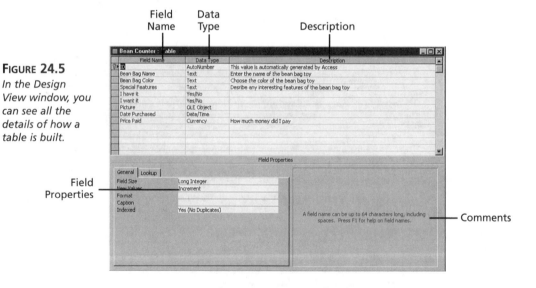

FIGURE 24.5

In the Design View window, you can see all the details of how a table is built.

Note: Naming tables. If you create a new table in Design view, it is named Table1 by default. If a Table1 already exists, the new table is called Table2. When you close the Design View window, you are asked whether you want to save the changes to Table1. Responding Yes opens another dialog box, which asks you to enter a new name for the table. Here, you can change the table name to whatever you want.

Adding a Field Name to a Table

Because a table is merely a collection of fields, all you have to do to add a field to a table is enter a line for it in the Design view. A field name can contain up to 64 characters and can contain any characters except for a period (.), an exclamation point (!), a grave accent (`), and square brackets ([]). Spaces are legal in a field name, but you can't begin a field name with a space.

> **Tip: What's in a name?** The name of a field not only describes the contents of the field, but is also used as a label that describes the field when it is placed on a form or used in a report. Therefore, you should use meaningful field names such as Date Purchased instead of names like PurDate to make your application easier for others to use.

> **Tip: Working backward.** When you're choosing fields for your table, you would be wise to think about how you plan to use this information. The best way to do so is to visualize the reports you would like to see. When you figure out the column headers you would like to see in a report, you have a list of fields that you should add to your table. So, going back to the collection example, you might come up with field names such as Animal, Name, Date Retired, and so on.

Choosing a Data Type for a Field

Choosing the data type for a field is a two-step process. First, you must choose the kind of data you want to store from the list of data types in the Data Type column next to the Field Name column. This data type specifies a general class of data, as listed in Table 24.1. You can find more specific information for Number data types in the Field Size field in the Field Properties section of the Table Design view (see Table 24.2).

Table 24.1 Data Types

Data Type	Description
AutoNumber	Access generates a unique number that is automatically placed in this field when the record is added to the database.
Currency	This data type should be used for monetary values to prevent rounding errors. It has 15 digits to the left of the decimal place and 4 digits to the right.
Date/Time	This data type holds date values ranging from 1 January 1753 to 31 December 9999 and time values accurate to about 3.33 milliseconds.

continues

Table 24.1   Continued.

Data Type	Description
Hyperlink	Fields with this data type are assumed to contain value hyperlinks formatted as URLs.
Memo	This data type holds a sequence of characters and numbers with a maximum length of 65,535.
Number	This data type holds a numeric value. The field size property determines its specific characteristics.
OLE Object	A field with this data type either contains a link to another object such as a Word document or Excel spreadsheet, or the object itself is embedded in the table.
Text	This data type holds a sequence of characters and numbers with a maximum length of 255.
Yes/No	This data type has only two values (yes and no).

Tip: Y2K or not 2K. Entering a date with a two-digit year in the range of 00 to 29 is assumed to be a year in the range of 2000 to 2029. Two-digit years in the range of 30 to 99 are assumed to be in the range of 1930 to 1999.

Table 24.2   Field Sizes for Numbers

Data Type	Description
Byte	A byte value can range in size from 0 to 255.
Decimal	A decimal value can have up to 28 digits of accuracy. The exact number of digits and the placement of the decimal place are controlled by the Precision, Scale, and Decimal Places field properties.
Double	A double value is a double precision floating-point value with about 15 digits of accuracy.
Integer	An integer value ranges in size from −32,768 to 32,767.
Long Integer	A long integer value ranges in size from −2,147,483,648 to 2,147,483,647.
Replication ID	This data type is a special value, also known as a *GUID,* used only with database replication.
Single	This data type is a single precision floating-point value with about 7 digits of accuracy.

If you feel overwhelmed by the number of choices you have, don't worry about it. Most of the fields you will store in your table are Text. The total length of this field is stored in Field Size. You shouldn't choose the largest possible size for this field because this value influences the space reserved for this field on reports and in forms. After all, you wouldn't want a huge, gaping whole for a tiny two-letter state abbreviation! If you need to make this field larger later, then you merely use the Table Design view to increase the field size. The records already in the database are not adversely affected by the change. In fact, it could be argued that, in this instance, increasing a field size as needed is far safer than reducing it later and risking the potential loss of data in a record that was unusually large.

Occasionally, you might want to use a Yes/No value if you want to display a check box on your form. Also, you should always use Date/Time to store any date values. After all, you want your application to be Y2K compliant, right? If you have numeric data, use Currency for any fields that will hold money so that you can preserve the accuracy of any calculations.

By default, a Long Integer field size is used when you select Number as a data type. As long as you don't need to store fractional values in this field, the Long Integer is a good choice because you'll probably never store a number too large in this field. You could easily store a too-large number if you use a smaller field size.

Setting Your Field Properties

The fields listed in the Field Properties part of the form change depending on the Data Type and Field Size chosen. However, many of these properties you will find in all field types:

- Field Size—Determines the maximum size of a Text or Memo value or the specific characteristics of a Number.

- Format—Allows you to specify how a field should be displayed in a report or on a form. This property is most useful when you're dealing with Numbers or Currency.

- Input Mask—Specifies a string of characters that are used to validate the input to the field.

- Caption—Specifies a string that is displayed on a form or report in place of the field name.

- Default Value—Specifies a value that is inserted into the database if the user doesn't fill in this field.

- Validation Rule—Allows you to test a new value for a field to determine whether it's legal.

- Validation Text—Specifies the message that is displayed if the new value fails the validation rule.

- Required—Means that the user must fill out this field before a record can be added to the database. This property is also known as Not Null.

- Allow Zero Length—Means that the field accepts a Text or Memo value without any characters in it.

- Indexed—When yes, means that an index is automatically created and maintained on this field to help speed up searches for information. Note that improving the speed to find a record usually makes adding or changing a record slower.

Note: Empty is not Null. Simply because a field is required doesn't mean that it has a meaningful value. A text field without any characters meets the specification of required; however, it doesn't contain any information. If you set the Allow Zero Length option to No, at least one character must be entered into the field for it to be considered required.

Defining Lookup Fields to Ensure Standard Answers

A useful trick in Access is to define a field as a lookup field. This means that before you can enter a value into the field, it must already exist in the database. This requirement prevents you from entering a bad value into the field. Creating a lookup field is especially useful for fields containing two-letter state abbreviations in which a set standard is used.

To add a lookup to a field on your table, follow these directions:

1. From the Table Design View window, choose the Type column in the data field to which you want to add the lookup, and then select the Lookup Wizard item from the Data Type drop-down list. The Lookup Wizard then launches, displaying the dialog box shown in Figure 24.6. Choose whether you want to use a query against another table or check a list of values that you enter, and then click Next.

FIGURE 24.6

The Lookup Wizard helps you choose a method to perform your lookup.

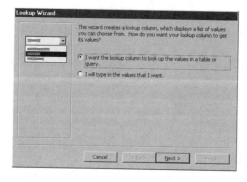

2. If you choose to type in a list of values, you see the dialog box shown in Figure 24.7. You can retrieve more than one column's value into the table using the Lookup Wizard. Then simply list all the possible values that can appear in those fields (such as each of the 50 two-letter state abbreviations), and click Next. The wizard asks you for the label associated with the lookup column. By default, it is the same name as used for the field. Clicking Finish creates the lookup information.

FIGURE 24.7

Enter the possible values for the field in the Lookup Wizard.

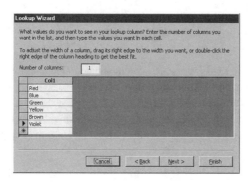

3. If you choose to look for your value in another table, the wizard displays a list of the other tables in your database (see Figure 24.8). You should select the table containing the fields you want and click Next.

FIGURE 24.8

The Lookup Wizard displays all the other tables in your database.

4. The wizard displays the list of fields that will be retrieved from the table (see Figure 24.9). You can choose one or more fields from the table as desired. If you don't choose the primary key from the table, it is automatically added. Clicking Next allows you to set the width of the fields, and then clicking Finish makes the changes permanent.

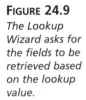

FIGURE 24.9
The Lookup Wizard asks for the fields to be retrieved based on the lookup value.

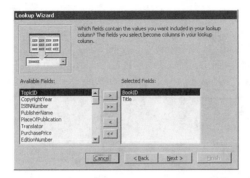

5. If you choose to look up your value in another table, the Lookup Wizard displays a pop-up window with this message: The table must be saved before relationships can be created. Save Now? You should click the Yes button to properly create the relationships. Note that clicking the Yes button also means that you can't undo any of these changes when you close the Design view.

Creating Access Queries

A query is an extremely valuable, timesaving tool. In a single mouse click, a query can return reams of information without your having to fuss over performing a sort or filter each time you want it. This tool lets you see a list of customers in a specific state or inventory items out of stock, even if new information was just entered into the database moments before.

You can create a query either by using the Query Wizard or by using the Query Design view. The Query Wizard prompts you for the information it needs based on the tables in your database. In the Design view, you can build a new query or change an existing query.

Creating Queries by Using the Query Wizard

To create a query by using the Query Wizard, follow these steps:

1. Double-click Create Query by Using Wizard to start the Query Wizard. Select the fields you want the query to return from the list of tables and queries (see Figure 24.10), and then click Next.

2. After you select your tables, the wizard may ask whether you want to create a detail or summary query. A detail query retrieves every record from every table you specify. A summary query allows you to get some statistical information from the numeric fields you retrieve. You can compute Sum, Avg (average), Min (minimum), and Max (maximum). You can also return the number of records retrieved. Select Summary and click the Summary Options button to see the list of fields and their statistical options.

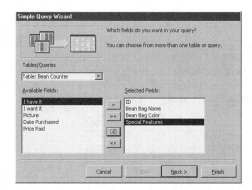

FIGURE 24.10
The Query Wizard asks for the fields it should return.

3. If you chose to create a Summary query in the preceding step, the wizard may ask whether you would like to group your data by dates. One record is returned for each time the date changes. You can group rows by the unique date/time, day, month, quarter, and year.

4. The Query Wizard then prompts you for the name of the query and whether you want to try the query or go to the Design View window to make additional changes. Click Finish to close the wizard.

Refining Queries in Design View

The Query Wizard is limited in its capabilities, so you might want to get familiar with the Query Design view, which can help you refine your query. Figure 24.14 shows the Query Design View window.

Table with fields   Table or query area

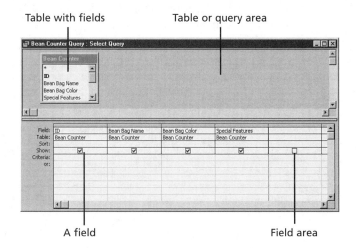

FIGURE 24.11
The Query Design view shows you the fields that your query will return.

A field   Field area

> **Note: There's more than meets the eye.** Queries are powerful tools that allow you to transform your data before presenting the results in a form, report, or data page. You should consider the information in this book only a brief introduction to this subject. You should check out Que's *Special Edition Using Access 2000* for more information about working with queries and creating Access applications.

At the top of the Design View window is a series of small windows containing the fields in each of the database tables or queries that are used in this query.

The bottom half of the window contains the fields that the query will use or return. The Field row contains the name of the field, and the Table row contains the name of the table or query where the field comes from. The Sort row identifies which fields are used to sort the results of the query. When the check box in the Show row is checked, the field is returned in the query's result. The Criteria row begins the set of rows that allow you to select which records will be returned as the result of the query.

To add a new field to the query, simply select the field from the table or query at the top of the window, and drag it down to the bottom half of the form. The values for the Field and Table row are automatically filled in, and the Show check box is checked.

Filtering Records in Design View

One of the best uses of a query is to reduce the number of rows returned. Reducing the number is helpful in a report in which you want to see only certain records. For instance, you might want to print only the list of beanbag toys you want rather than the whole list of beanbag toys available. Likewise, you might want to see only the items in your inventory that need to be reordered.

To select only the rows you want, enter a value in the Criteria row under the field you want to use as the filter. If the row has that particular value in the specified field, it is returned as part of the query. Otherwise, the row is discarded. If you want to return records in which the field can be more than one value, you can list these values one at a time in the Criteria section of the fields area. You can also create an expression that will be true for the values you want to see and false for the values you don't want to see.

For example, if you want to list all the items in your inventory with an ID value of 1, 2, 3, 4, or 5, you can enter those five values into five different rows in the Criteria rows. You can also enter the expression ID <= 5 into a Criteria row under the ID field, and all the rows with an ID value greater than or equal to five are returned.

Tip: Prequel to the SQL (pronounced *sequel*). The Query Wizard and the Query Design view both create a SQL query that is used to perform the work. If you know SQL, then you can view this statement by right-clicking the form and selecting SQL View.

Tip: The cells are too small. When you're entering a complex expression, you might find it difficult to see the entire formula. If you right-click the value and choose Zoom from the pop-up menu, you see a small window displaying your formula. After you make your changes, clicking OK closes the window and saves your changes.

Sorting Records in Design View

Another useful task you might want to perform in the Query Design View window is to sort the records before they are returned. Sorting records is useful when you want to alphabetize the beanbags in your collection or list the items in your store's inventory by item number, for example.

To sort, simply click the field you want to sort by, and choose either Ascending or Descending from the drop-down menu. You can choose (Not Sorted) to stop sorting on that field. You can also choose to sort on multiple fields so that if two or more records have the same value for the first sort field, then the second field is used to determine the order of the records. An example might be a primary sort on a customer's surname and a secondary sort on the first name if you want the query to return an alphabetized list of names.

Tip: Sort first, save problems later. When you're generating reports, sorting your data before you print it is often useful. Sorting data first makes it easier to find information in your report because you don't have to sift through pages of data to find a specific entry; with it presorted, you can find what you want quickly.

Creating Access Forms

Back during one of my stints with a small nonprofit arts organization, I remember the organization's efforts to construct a mailing list. Staff and volunteers alike were scrawling information on scraps of paper. Some pieces of paper had phone numbers in addition to the address, and others did not. Creating a special data entry form is one way to make sure all the data you need is collected in a uniform matter.

Using forms is the basic way to input data into a table. Access offers two ways to create a form: using the Form Wizard or using Design view. The Form Wizard is a flexible tool that helps you build most of the forms you will ever need. If, for some reason, you don't like the form, you can easily change it using the Form Designer.

Creating Forms with the Form Wizard

To create a form with the Form Wizard, follow these steps:

1. Double-click the Create Form by Using Wizard item in the Database window. This action displays the Form Wizard, as shown in Figure 24.12. Select the table and fields you want to include in the form, and click Next to continue.

FIGURE 24.12
Choose all the fields for a table for best results.

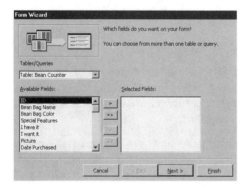

> **Tip: Why not all?** Unless you have a strong reason not to, you should always include all the fields in your table on your form. Otherwise, the data for the missing field on the form never gets collected on a routine basis. Of course, there are always exceptions. For example, in your small collectibles store, you might want any employee to be able to enter information on new items, but you want to retain sole control over the items' prices. In that case, you can leave out the Price field on your form.

2. The next step asks you to choose how you want the fields arranged on your form. You can pick from Columnar, Tabular, Datasheet, and Justified. You can see what the finished forms will look like for each of these choices in Figures 24.13, 24.14, 24.15, and 24.16. Click Next to continue.

FIGURE 24.13
Columnar displays the field names beside the fields along the left edge of the form.

FIGURE 24.14
Tabular displays headings above the datasheet while arranging the fields across the top edge of the form.

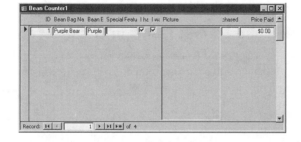

FIGURE 24.15
Datasheet displays multiple rows from your database like a grid.

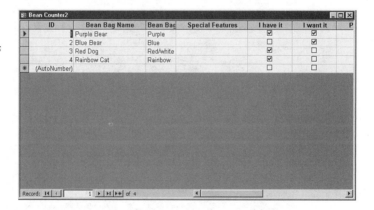

FIGURE 24.16
Justified displays the field names beside the fields along the left edge of the form.

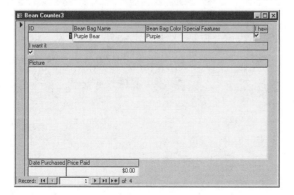

3. The wizard asks you to choose a style for your form. After you select the style you want, click Next to continue.

> **Tip: Pictures are nice and distracting.** Using fancy styles results in a background image that can be distracting for serious work. I suggest that you choose Standard to create a normal windows form.

4. In the final step of the wizard, you are asked to name the form, and to choose to view the form or change its design. After you make your choices, click Finish to build the form and close the wizard.

Creating and Editing Forms in Design View

If you don't like any of the arrangements offered by the Form Wizard, you need to use the Form Design view to build your form on your own (see Figure 24.17). You can use an existing form and change how the fields are arranged on it, add new fields, and remove existing fields.

Form header   Label   Text box   Picture control   Toolbox

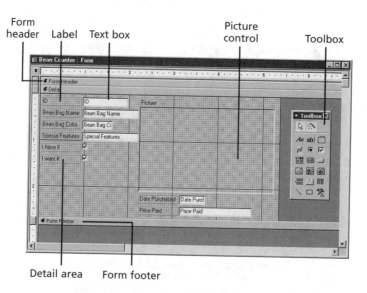

FIGURE 24.17
Build your form on your own by using the Form Design view.

Detail area   Form footer

> **Tip: Modifying is easier than building.** You might find it easier (not to mention faster) to modify a form built by the Form Wizard than to create one from scratch.

Each object on the form is called a *control*. Table 24.3 lists some of the common controls used in an Access form. Note that using some of these controls triggers wizards to help you handle standard situations. Otherwise, you would have to write some code in Visual Basic for Applications to effectively use them.

Table 24.3   Common Controls Available for a Form

Icon	Control	Description
☑	Check Box	Displays a Yes/No value using a box with a check mark (Yes) or without a check mark (No).
	Combo Box	Similar to a text box, but allows a user to click a button to display a list of values he or she can choose from.
	Command Button	Displays a button that, when clicked, causes an action to be performed.
	Image	Displays an image from the database.
Aα	Label	Displays a text value on the form that can't be changed.
	List Box	Displays a list of values.
◉	Option Button	Displays one choice from a set of choices. If you need more than one group of option buttons, each must be placed in an option group.
	Option Group	Identifies an area on the form where you can choose only one value for a set of option buttons.
ab|	Text Box	Displays a text value on the form that can be changed. This control is usually bound to a database table or query.
	Tab Control	Displays a series of tab pages, each of which contains a set of controls.
	Toggle Button	Displays a Yes/No value using the image of a button that is either pressed (Yes) or not pressed (No).

> **Tip: ActiveX to the rescue.** If you find that you need a control that isn't readily available, you can click the More Controls icon in the toolbox to display all the ActiveX controls on your system. If you have Visual Basic installed on your computer, you can choose from a wide range of controls that allow you to send and receive email, display Web pages, and play multimedia files.

Creating Access Reports

After you put your information into your database using a form, you are going to want to get it out in a meaningful way. The best way to do so is to use an Access report. Using an Access report, you can take the information in your database and display it in an easy-to-use format.

At this point, you may be thinking that reports sound a whole lot like queries. So what's the big difference? Think of reports as snapshots of your database, whereas queries are videos.

Creating Reports with the Report Wizard

To create a report in Access, follow these steps:

1. Double-click Create Report by Using Wizard. This action starts the Report Wizard, which asks you to select a table or query and a set of fields that will appear on the report (see Figure 24.18). Choose these values and click Next to continue.

FIGURE 24.18
Choose the fields that you want to include in your report.

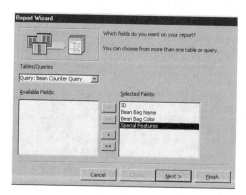

> **Tip: Too many fields spoil the report.** You might be tempted to include several fields in a report, but you probably shouldn't. By selecting a few key fields, you build a smaller, easier-to-use report. Remember, you can always build more reports if you need them.

2. In the Report Wizard, you can define multiple grouping levels for a report, with one grouping level nested inside another (see Figure 24.19). You can change the order of the grouping levels by selecting the grouping level to be moved and then clicking the priority up and down arrows. When you are finished, click Next to continue.

FIGURE 24.19
Choose the grouping levels for your report.

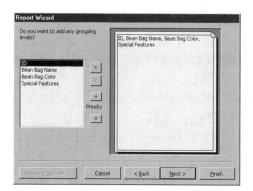

3. In the following dialog box, you can choose how the innermost level of the report is sorted. Click Next to continue.

4. You can choose the report layout that suits your report the best. In general, a tabular report looks the best as long as you don't have too many fields. If you have many fields, you should consider the columnar report, which lists the field names down one column and the field values down a second column. You can also choose to print the report in either portrait mode or landscape mode. Clicking Next moves the wizard to the next step.

> **Tip: Widetrack.** Select landscape mode if you have a lot of fields in the detail records. It makes the report much easier to read.

5. You can also choose a style for your report. The style determines the character fonts and colors used to print the report. After you choose your style, click Next to move to the next step.

6. In the last step of the wizard, you can choose a report name and choose whether to run the report or go to the Report Design view to modify the report. Click Finish to create the report.

Creating and Editing Reports in Design View

Chances are you're going to want to modify the report you just finished in the Design view before you run it, even if all you want to do is change the report's title. You begin working with the report by using the Report Design view (see Figure 24.20).

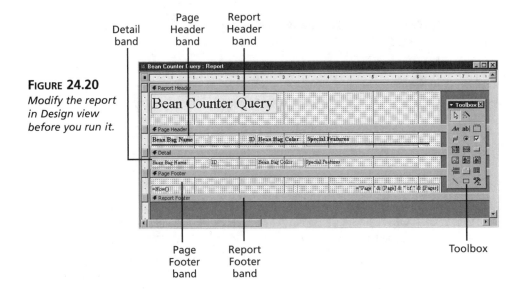

FIGURE 24.20
Modify the report in Design view before you run it.

Detail band · Page Header band · Report Header band · Page Footer band · Report Footer band · Toolbox

Just like in the Form Design view, in Report Design view you have a toolbox with a series of controls that you can put on the report. They are the same controls you found in the Form Design view, but they're not interactive.

The report consists of a series of bands. The Report Header band prints only on the first page at the start of the report. Likewise, the Report Footer band prints only at the end of the report. The Report Footer band is the best place to put grand totals or to display other information that should be done only when the report is complete.

> **Tip: Band on the run.** When you're designing reports, remember that bands are simply areas of the reports where you place controls. You're not restricted to placing everything in a single line. If the band is too small, merely click and drag on the edge of the band to change its size.

The Page Header and Page Footer bands print at the top and bottom of each report page, respectively. The Header band is useful for printing column headers for a tabular report, whereas the Footer band is useful for displaying information such as the page number and the date that the report was generated.

> **Tip: Use the Page Header band for the report title.** Avoid using the Report Header field to include the title of your report. This field is printed only on the first page. Instead, you should use the Page Header band to hold the report's title. That way, when you mix up the printouts of multiple reports, you know which pages belong to which report. Likewise, always put the page number and date generated on each report, either on the Page Header or Page Footer band. This information is also useful when you mix the pages from a set of reports together.

The Detail band holds the part of the report that is printed once for each record. With this band, like the other bands, you can choose to arrange the controls inside the band in any fashion you want. However, remember that this band is printed once for each record in the report, so keeping the Detail band as small as possible is important. Adding a little extra space here can significantly increase the total size of your report.

Creating Access Web Pages

The final Access object I'm going to cover is the *data access page*, one of Access 2000's most touted new features. It is basically a Web page that communicates with an Access database. A data page is kind of a cross between a report and a form in terms of its capabilities. It has most of the features of both. You can group and sort records just like a report, and you can update the data in a table or query just like a form.

> **Peter's Principle: Using Access on the Internet can be hazardous to your data.**
>
> Although Microsoft is pushing data access pages as a big feature of Access 2000, their implementation leaves a lot to be desired. Unless you are very, very careful, publishing data access pages opens up your database to a lot of potential security problems. Failure to properly secure your database and data access pages could give someone the opportunity to access your database and change the data stored there without your permission and/or knowledge. I believe that you shouldn't use data access pages for sensitive data, mission-critical data, or data that can't be re-created after it has been lost. There are just too many risks to using this technology for anyone other than Internet security gurus. If you're certain these pages pose no danger to your data, then go ahead and try them. You might find them very useful.

If you plan to use data access pages, you must keep the following points in mind:

- If you're using the Jet database engine, you must place your database on a public file server or in a Web folder on your intranet so that any user can get to the database.

- You must protect your Jet database with user-level security.

- You must not include the username and password anywhere in your HTML file; that would make it exceptionally easy for experienced eyes to nab.

- All users who need to access your data access pages must have Office 2000 and Internet Explorer 5 installed on their computer.

- If you plan to publish your data access pages to a Web server, make sure that you have the necessary authorizations to save your Web pages onto the Web server.

> **Caution: Evaluate the risk.** Although the tools that you use to develop data access pages work, they aren't as well developed as tools found elsewhere in Office. You should keep in mind that data access pages are first generation tools and will undoubtedly improve with future versions of Access. But for now, enter at your own risk.

Creating Data Access Pages with the Data Access Page Wizard

As is typically the case in Office, Microsoft gives you a wizard to help design data access pages. To create a data page in Access, follow these steps:

1. Double-click Create Data Access Page by Using Wizard. This action starts the Page Wizard, which asks you to select a table or query, and a set of fields that will appear on the data access page (see Figure 24.21). Choose these values and click Next to continue.

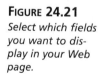

FIGURE 24.21

Select which fields you want to display in your Web page.

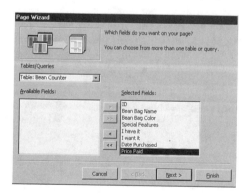

2. The Page Wizard asks you to specify which grouping levels you want to use. You can change the order of the grouping levels by selecting the grouping level to be moved and then clicking the priority up and down arrows. When you are finished, click Next to continue. If you want to display (and edit) only a single record at a time, do not specify any grouping levels.

> **Note: Deja view.** Do these steps look familiar so far? That's because they are, in fact, similar to the ones you need to execute to build a form or report in Access 2000.

3. You can specify how to sort the innermost level of the data if you grouped levels in the preceding step. Otherwise, this step specifies the order in which the records are displayed from the database (see Figure 24.22).

FIGURE 24.22

Choose how the information in your Web page should be sorted.

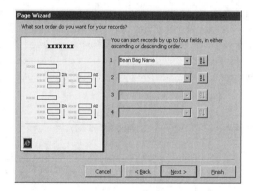

4. In the last step of the wizard, specify a title for the Web page (or use the default value of the table name that the Web page accesses). Choose whether you want to open the page after the wizard has finished, and then check Do You Want to Apply a Theme to Your Page if you want to add a theme to your Web page.

5. Click Finish to create the data access page. If you choose to specify a theme, the Theme dialog box is displayed (see Figure 24.23), and you can choose one of the standard Office 2000 themes.

FIGURE 24.23
Choose a theme
for your data
access Web page.

FIGURE 24.23
Choose a theme
for your data
access Web page.

Creating and Editing Data Access Pages in Design View

As you saw in the Form and Report Design views, you can easily rearrange the controls to get them the way you want them. This is also true of the Page Design view (see Figure 24.24). You have a toolbox filled with controls that you can use on your Web page, although many of the controls are different from what you saw in the previous Design views.

FIGURE 24.24
Edit your Web
page using tools
similar to those in
the Form and
Report Design
views.

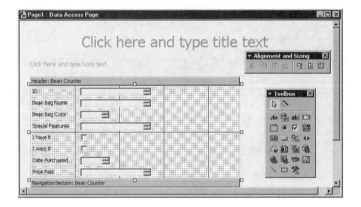

In addition to the toolbox, you also can use an Alignment and Sizing toolbar, which makes it easy to align and size groups of fields on the page. Simply select the fields you want to change, and click the appropriate button.

At the bottom of the form is a small toolbar that is similar to the database navigation bar in an Access form. It also does the same thing. Buttons are available to navigate through the database, insert and delete records, and sort and filter your records. Although Access adds this bar automatically when you run the form, in a data access page, this bar is actually part of the Web page.

Deploying a Data Access Page

After you've created your data access page, you need to save it somewhere that people can access it. Typically, you save it either to a Web folder or a Web server. Saving the data access page to a Web folder or to a Web server is easy; just do the following:

1. Right-click the data access page while in the Database view, and select Save As from the shortcut menu.

2. Specify a filename for the page in the Save As dialog box, and then click OK.

3. Specify the location in which you want to save the data access page using the normal Office Save As dialog box. In the case of a data access page, this location would be the appropriate Web folder or the physical folder where the Web server keeps its files.

4. After you've specified a location, click OK to save the data access page and any other related files to the specified folder.

Accessing Your Database with a Data Access Page

To use a data access page, simply enter the URL for the Web page in your Web browser and press Enter. This action displays a Web page similar to the one found in Figure 24.25. At the bottom of the Web page is a navigation bar similar to the one found on a form. You use this bar to move to different records in the database, add and delete records, and sort and filter records.

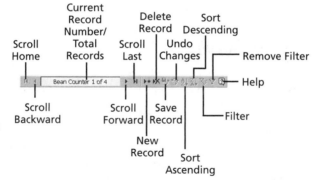

FIGURE 24.25
Use a data access page in your Web browser.

The buttons on the bar perform the following functions:

- The *Scroll Home* button displays the first record in the table or query.

- The *Scroll Backward* button displays the previous record in the table or query, unless the first record is being displayed.

- The *Current Record Number/Number of Records* field displays the number for the current record and the total number of records. It is automatically updated as new rows are added.

- The *Scroll Forward* button displays the next record in the table or query, unless the last record is being displayed.

- The *Scroll Last* button displays the last button in the table or query.

- The *New Record* button moves the current record beyond the last record in the table or query to insert a new one.

- The *Delete Record* button deletes the current record. A dialog box appears, asking you to confirm that you want to delete it. Clicking Yes deletes the record, and clicking No leaves it in the database.

- The *Save Record* button saves the changes you made to the current record.

- The *Undo Changes* button restores the record to the state it was before you changed it.

- The *Sort Ascending* button sorts the records displayed in the form in ascending order based on the field selected before the button was clicked.

- The *Sort Descending* button sorts the records displayed in the form in descending order based on the field selected before the button was clicked.

- The *Filter* button displays only those records with the same value as contained in the field selected before the button was clicked.

- The *Remove Filter* button applies the form filter or removes either the filter by selection or filter by form filter criteria.

- The *Help* button displays the Access help file with instructions on how to use the toolbar.

On Your Own

By now, you should have a fairly good taste of how Access works and what it can do for you. This introduction is sufficient for you to design single-table databases holding data in a straightforward fashion.

Now you should jump in and try to create your own database application. Nearly everyone who buys a computer for the first time tells himself or herself that at least part of the reason for buying it was to organize some aspect of his or her life. In your case, you might want to organize your finances, your recipes, your trading card collection, your music collection, or even your collection of beanbag toys. So pick the application you used as an excuse, and build it now.

You should begin by stepping through the process outlined at the beginning of this chapter under the section titled "Looking at Your Needs." From this, you should be able to determine the data items and the tables you need in your application. I strongly suggest that you try to store everything in one table if at all possible. Using two tables makes your life much more complicated, which is something you definitely don't need when you're just starting out with Access.

After identifying your needs, you can begin building your table. After doing that, use the Forms Wizard to build a form to simplify entering data into your database. Then use that form to enter a dozen or so records into your database. You shouldn't try to enter all your data at this time because you might just start all over again. You do, however, need to enter enough data to understand how to search for information in your database and to see how your reports will look.

Speaking of reports, you should try to design a query and a report that work together to display the information from your database. You should get only the information you want to print in the report using the query, and you should sort the results before trying to print the report.

Finally, if you're brave, you should try to create and publish a Web page. Of course, after you've tested it, you should delete it or at least disable it so that anyone who wants to access your database without your permission can't do so.

Does your newly created application tell you what you want it to? If it doesn't, it might be time to go back to the drawing board.

Part VIII

Advanced Integration

25

The Macro and VBA Primer

Over the years, Microsoft has added so many automatic features to the Office suite of applications that it has almost taken away the obvious need for macro programming, at least for the average user. After all, you don't need to record a macro to create a customized, quickly accessible font style; you can just define your own style. And if you want a block of text inserted on command, you can make it an AutoText entry. Defining shortcut keys is also a breeze in Office, and you're even told which shortcut keys are and are not available. So why, then, would you want to know how to program macros?

In this chapter, we'll take a closer look at a few scenarios in which having a macro might come in handy, and I'll give you step-by-step directions on how to record and make use of those macros. In the following chapter, I'll present some more advanced macros that exploit the power of the Visual Basic for Applications (VBA) macro programming language.

Why Use Macros?

As I stated earlier, the rich palette of Office features has given users fewer reasons to delve into uncharted macro territory. Although these features are often a big help, in just as many instances they fall short of doing what a macro could.

Let's consider Word as an example. You may recall from previous chapters that a Word AutoText entry is limited to 255 characters. That's fine and dandy if all you want to use it for is to add a company name or service mark. But what if you're in charge of writing grants for a small nonprofit animal welfare organization, and you want to be able to call up a wordsmithed mission statement or organizational history? Sure, you could copy and paste it from another document, but wouldn't it be a whole lot simpler (not to mention quicker) if you could pull in the desired text by pressing a couple of keys? No hunting for the document containing the text. No selecting the text. No copy and paste. Look at all those steps you save! If you routinely perform the same set of keystrokes or mouse movements over and over again, that set of steps would be a perfect candidate for a macro.

Excel is also a natural place for writing your own macros. If you routinely enter outrageously long formulas, or if you have a standard but complex formula you regularly use for your business, then designing a macro may be in order. With Excel, you can create functions that return values just like the built-in functions in Excel. For instance, if you run a bookstore that has special discounts for each publisher, you could create a macro that calculates the new price for you. I'll show you how later in the chapter.

With the possible exception of mail merge and PowerPoint presentations, the typical user normally works with Office as an independent set of tools. But sometimes it might be nice to get some information from one tool while using another, such as retrieving information from an Access database and inserting it into your Word document already formatted. Or perhaps you could have Excel perform a scheduled upload of the day's sales statistics to your company's intranet so that the managers could have a look at fresh data first thing in the morning.

Finally, you can create your own applications that are written in Visual Basic for Applications and directly use the facilities available in Office to perform complex tasks. This capability could result in an application that would create custom business proposals, including detailed breakouts of supplies and labor in Excel along with a custom-generated Word cover letter targeted for a specific customer.

Are you convinced that macro programming might be of some use to you after all? I thought so!

Macros and VBA Explained

In the opening paragraphs of this chapter, I referred to the Visual Basic for Applications macro programming language. Don't let the name "programming language" intimidate you. There's a lot of history behind Microsoft's adoption of Visual Basic for Applications as its suite-wide macro programming language.

Believe it or not, in the very beginning, each application had its own way of programming macros. Not only did that make using macros harder to learn, but it made having one application work with another next to impossible. Over the years, as Microsoft became determined to make Office a suite of inter-operating applications as opposed to merely a collection of separate applications, it became clear that a common macro language was needed. That's where Visual Basic for Applications (VBA) comes in. It capitalizes on the ease of use and power of Microsoft's premier programming language, Visual Basic, and pulls it into Office in much the same way that a common tool like the Clip Gallery is shared.

> **Note: A programming language to create a simple macro?** Interestingly, many people perceive macros as being little more than the ability to assign shortcut keys to a task or something equally simple. While you can easily do these things without "getting your hands dirty" with VBA, you now have the power at your fingertips to make Office do even more of your work for you. I'll introduce you to the basics in this chapter, and in the next chapter, you can dig in to see just how much this tool can do to increase and enhance your productivity.

As you work with VBA, you'll discover some subtle differences in the type of information you're asked to provide when you work with each application. That's only to be expected because each application performs a different type of work. And although I can't devote endless amounts of time to macro programming in this book, I will give you everything you need to know to begin creating your own macros in Word and Excel, the two most heavily used Office applications.

> **Note: For more information on VBA...**Check out the book *Special Edition Using Visual Basic for Applications* published by Que.

Recording a Macro in Word 2000

If you want to have Word insert blocks of text that are too large to be stored as AutoText entries, all you need to do is follow the next set of simple steps. To follow through with the grant writing example described earlier, you could create special macros for your mission statement (with an easy-to-remember shortcut of Alt+M), your organization's history (with a shortcut of Alt+H), and so on. You could even place buttons for them on one of your toolbars so that all you would need to do to get the desired text is click the Mission or History macro button.

> **Peter's Principle: Just a thought...**
>
> When I did a lot of grant writing, I actually made a special macro toolbar that displayed all my macro buttons. I could turn my Grants toolbar on and off just as I could any other toolbar. It served the purpose well because I could produce pages of high-quality text in literally seconds. If you think this strategy may be of use to you, you might want to revisit Chapter 3 for a review of working with toolbars.

To begin recording a basic macro in Word, you need to do the following:

1. If you want to apply the macro to a certain document or template only, make sure that document is open so that it's made available in the Record Macro dialog box.

2. Click Tools|Macro|Record New Macro on the menu bar. The Record Macro dialog box shown in Figure 25.1 appears.

FIGURE 25.1

Determine how the macro is activated in the Record Macro dialog box.

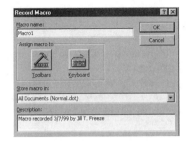

3. In the Macro Name box, type a name that best describes the function of the macro you're about to record. If you feel that further explanation is required, you can enter some information in the Description box as well.

4. Use the Store Macro In drop-down box to select the document or template you want the macro to be made available in. By default, Word 2000 makes the macro available in All Documents (Normal.dot).

5. After you've given the macro a name, it's time to decide how you want to activate the macro. You are given essentially two options: add it to a toolbar or invoke it using a predefined combination of keystrokes.

6. If you clicked the Toolbars button, the Customize dialog box opens. Access the Commands tab, where you'll see the newly named macro listed on the right (see Figure 25.2). To place it on a toolbar, simply click the macro's icon, and drag it into place on the desired toolbar. Click the Close button to begin recording your macro.

> **Tip: Having your cake and eating it, too.** If you want to assign a shortcut key to the macro as well, click the Keyboard button in the bottom-right corner of the dialog box. Clicking this button takes you directly to the Customize Keyboard dialog box described next.

FIGURE 25.2

Click and drag the macro into place on the desired toolbar.

7. If you click the Keyboard button, you see the Customize Keyboard dialog box shown in Figure 25.3. Click inside the Press New Shortcut Key box, press the keys you want to use, and Word enters the shortcut in the proper format. Click the Assign button to assign the shortcut key, and then click Close to exit the dialog box and begin recording the macro.

FIGURE 25.3
Word tells you whether the shortcut keys you chose are available for use.

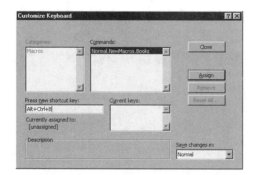

> **Tip: The key to choosing shortcut keys.** Whatever you do, don't replace any key sequence that has already been assigned by Word; fixing it will take a lot of work. Beyond that, you might want to use any of these combinations as shortcut keys because they are not previously assigned in Word 2000: Alt+A through Alt+Z, Alt+Shift+A through Alt+Shift+Z, or Alt+0 through Alt+9.

8. When the Stop Recording button bar shown in Figure 25.4 appears, you can immediately begin using the mouse and/or keyboard to begin recording the macro. You can click the Pause Recording button on the right to suspend recording temporarily, and then click it a second time to resume recording. Clicking the right button concludes the recording of your macro and closes the Stop Recording button bar.

Recording a Macro in Excel 2000

Say you run a small hobby shop that carries all kinds of name brands, and you maintain your inventory in Excel. You have standard discounts for each major brand. Rather than hard-code the discount for each item, you could create a macro that takes each item's list price and automatically calculates your selling price. All this can be done using a standard Excel macro.

Follow these steps to begin recording a macro in Excel 2000:

1. Open the workbook you want to apply the macro to, and then click Tools|Macro|Record New Macro on the menu bar. Excel's Record Macro dialog box (shown in Figure 25.5) appears.

FIGURE 25.4

The mouse pointer turns into a cassette tape to let you know that macro recording is in progress.

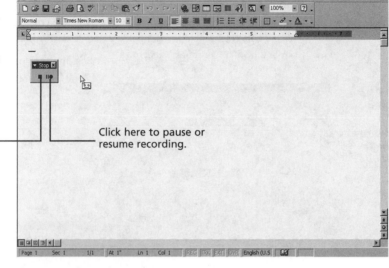

Click here to stop recording.

Click here to pause or resume recording.

FIGURE 25.5

This Record Macro dialog box differs slightly from the one found in Word.

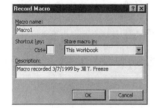

2. Give the macro a meaningful name in the Macro Name box, and then enter additional information in the Description box if desired.

3. In the Store Macro In drop-down box, choose from one of the following:

   - This Workbook (default)—Makes the macro available in the current workbook only

   - Personal Macro Workbook—Makes the macro available whenever you use Excel

   - New Workbook—Launches a new blank workbook and makes the macro available there

Caution: It's now or never. If you think you might want to make the macro available to all worksheets, you need to select that option before you even record the macro because you can't change it after the fact. Macros that are available in all workbooks are known as *global macros*.

4. Notice the Shortcut Key box preceded by a Ctrl+. Click inside the box, and enter the letter you want to use for the macro's shortcut.

Caution: Oops! If you choose a shortcut key for your macro that's an Office standard (such as Ctrl+C for Copy), your macro will be invoked instead of the standard command. To avoid inadvertently overwriting a shortcut, consider pressing the Shift key while you enter the letter in the Shortcut Key box. Doing so results in your needing to press Ctrl+Shift+C (for this example) to invoke the macro. Note the importance of this point because you'll actually see only Ctrl+C in the Record Macro dialog box.

5. Click OK to launch the Stop Recording dialog box shown in Figure 25.6.

FIGURE 25.6

Use this dialog box to take control of Excel macro recording.

Click here to stop recording.

Click here to specify a relative reference.

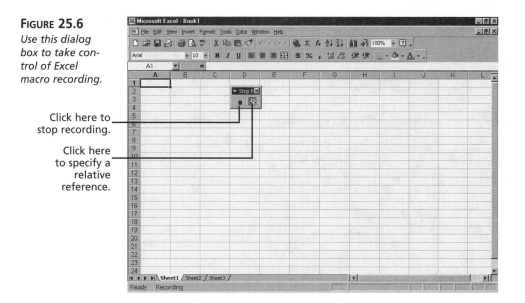

6. Use the mouse and keyboard to begin walking through all the steps that make up your macro. Click the Stop button on the left when you're finished. Clicking this button closes the button bar and saves the macro in the location you specified.

Click the Relative Reference button (see Figure 25.6) to record a macro based on relative cell addresses as opposed to absolute addresses. What does that really mean in the scheme of things? Use relative addresses when you want to refer to cells based on their position relative to the current cell where the macro is invoked. This approach would work well for programming the hobby store discount information I referred to in an earlier example. Use an absolute address when you want the macro to refer to the same exact cell no matter where the macro itself is invoked. For example, say that the hobby store gives a straight 15 percent discount across the board for all brands. You could put 15 percent in a cell and point the macro to that location.

Assigning Excel Macros to a Toolbar or Menu Bar

If others will be working with your worksheets (or if you simply prefer to use buttons or menus to work), you'll appreciate knowing how to create a special button for your new macro on a toolbar or how to add it to a particular menu.

To make your macros more easily accessible, follow these steps:

1. Open the Excel workbook containing the macro you want to assign to a toolbar or menu.

2. Right-click an existing toolbar, and select Customize from the shortcut menu. The Customize dialog box opens.

3. Open the Commands tab, and then scroll down the list of Categories until you see Macros. Click Macros to select it. Custom Menu Item and Custom Button then are listed on the right as the available commands (see Figure 25.7).

FIGURE 25.7
Choose which place you would like to give the macro its own entry.

4. Drag and drop the Custom Button into the desired position on a toolbar. (Or if you prefer, drag and drop the Custom Menu Item text to the desired menu, and drag it down the list until it's stored in the desired location.) Click Close to dismiss the Customize dialog box.

5. Click your new button (or select the Custom Menu Item entry from the menu in which you placed it) to launch the Assign Macro dialog box. There, you will see a list of all the macros available in the current workbook.

6. Click the name of the macro you want to assign to the selected button or menu item, and then click OK. Your macro will then be activated whenever you click the new button or menu entry.

Running a Macro in Word or Excel

How you choose to invoke a macro obviously depends on the various ways you've elected to make the macro available. If you do nothing but record the macro, you can always invoke it by clicking Tools|Macro|Macros. When the Macros dialog box appears, simply select the name of the macro you want to use, and then click the Run button.

Peter's Principle: Do what feels right.

I can't stress this point enough: Don't let anyone tell you there's one best way to make a macro available. Over the years, I've met people who are very much "mouse people" when it comes to using a computer. Going through the steps to define shortcut keys would make little sense for them because they would never use them anyway. Likewise, some people live by the keyboard—the people who think of the Copy command as Ctrl+C, not a button on the toolbar or a menu item. These users need not bother with the niceties of fancy buttons because they would still rely on their favorite shortcut keys. The bottom line is you are the best judge of which method (or methods) you use most. Don't do any more work with this stuff than you have to. Of course, if others will be using your macros, you might want to rethink this position and provide options for every conceivable preference because ease of use is the goal.

Of course, if you followed the proper steps, you can also access the macro via shortcut keys, a special menu item, or a custom macro button on a toolbar.

Deleting a Macro

If the day comes when you no longer need a macro you created, you can easily delete it. After all, why clutter up your hard drive or document's file size if you don't have to, right?

To delete a macro, click Tools|Macro|Macros from the menu bar. The Macros dialog box opens. Simply click the name of the macro you want to delete, click the Delete button, and you're done; the macro is gone for good.

Correcting Typos in a Macro

Say you created a Word macro that automatically inserts the names and titles of your company's board of directors, and you later learn one of the members got married and changed her name. Or perhaps your ma and pa computer store is moving to a bigger, better location, so you want all your address macros to reflect the new information.

Don't panic. You don't have to record all that stuff again; you can update it with minimal hassle. Although it's true that you edit macros by using the Visual Basic for Applications Editor (see Figure 25.8), you needn't be intimately familiar with the programming language to make a simple change in text.

FIGURE 25.8

Look at how much code VBA created for you.

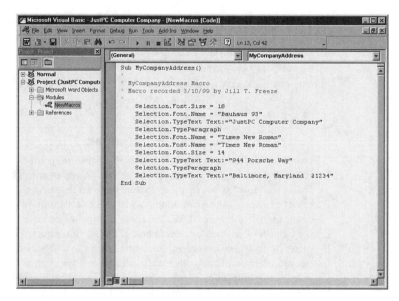

To begin fixing the text of your macro, you need to do the following:

1. Open a file in which you are able to access the macro you want to edit. Being able to access a macro is obviously an issue only when you've chosen to apply the macro to a single file only; otherwise, you can work with any document (including a fresh, blank document in the application that hosts the macro).

2. On the menu bar, click Tools|Macro|Macros to open the Macros dialog box (see Figure 25.9).

FIGURE 25.9

The list of every macro available in the current document appears.

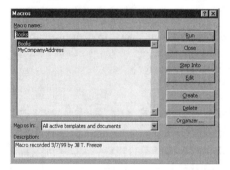

3. Select the name of the macro you want to modify, and then click the Edit button. This action launches the Visual Basic for Applications Editor shown in Figure 25.8.

4. Notice that your macro text is preceded by a VBA statement— `Selection.TypeText Text:=`—and the text itself appears between a set of quotation marks. Anything preceded by that statement and inside quotation marks you can click and edit just as you would in Word.

> **Caution: Simplicity only, please.** Without getting into the thick of VBA, you can make changes only to the words' contents, not to their font characteristics. And whatever you do, don't touch any of those VBA statements. Doing so may very well kill your macro unless you really know what you're doing.

5. When you've made all the necessary changes, close the VBA Editor by clicking the Close (×) button in the upper-right corner.

From that point on, the new text will appear whenever you invoke the macro. If you need to go back and modify a document in which you've already invoked the macro, you must manually delete the obsolete text and then invoke the newly edited macro for the change to take effect.

> **Note: Why can't the macro change past occurrences of the text automatically?** Although it might sound like a good idea in theory, changing old text does pose some logistical problems. For instance, you wouldn't want your new address macro to go in and overwrite the old address that appeared on a letter written three years ago because that information wasn't correct for the time.

Getting Acquainted with the Visual Basic for Applications Editor

Before delving into more advanced macro programming topics, take a few moments to get better acquainted with the Visual Basic for Applications editing window (see Figure 25.10).

FIGURE 25.10

Depending on how your application is set up, you might need to click View | Properties Windows to see the Properties pane.

Project window

Module window

Properties window

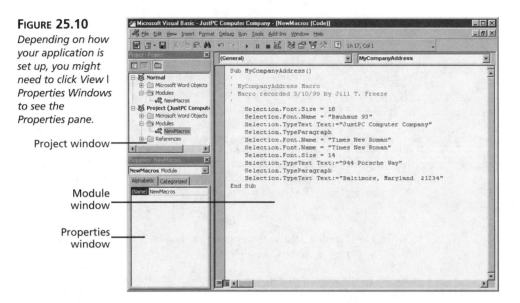

The Visual Basic for Applications Editor contains three major windows, along with a menu bar and toolbar from which you can access commonly used functions. The three windows include the Project window, the Properties window, and the Module window.

The Project window lists all the projects that are currently open in the application from which you launched the VBA Editor. A project can be anything from a Word document to an Excel workbook to a special add-in designed to enhance the application's functionality. All these items are actually considered VBA Projects.

The Properties window may or may not appear, depending on how your system is set up. In this window, you essentially can view and edit the properties of whatever object you've selected in the Project window.

The largest of the windows is the Module window, which displays the contents of your macro. In this window, you do the bulk of your work with the VBA Editor.

Ideas and Tips for Improving Your Macros

Now you can start getting into the thick of Visual Basic for Applications. Up to this point, you didn't really have to know anything about Visual Basic to work with your macros. But in the remaining sections of this chapter, I'm going to give you a VBA quick course as well as provide some tips and tricks for making your macros more powerful.

These sections will prepare you for the next chapter, where I'll walk you through designing some complex macros that you can modify to meet your specific needs. Now on to the tips and ideas...

Including User Input in Your Macros

Remember the company address macro I presented earlier? Well, if you're including that macro as part of a company letterhead template, wouldn't it be neat if each user could enter his or her own name and have it appear in the format specified in the macro? Using the same format ensures complete uniformity in the appearance of your documents, and it gives them a personalized look as well.

You can let users contribute text to your macros on-the-fly by including the InputBox object in your VBA code. Take a look at Figure 25.11 to see just how few lines of code it takes.

FIGURE 25.11
Two lines of code is all it takes to incorporate user input.

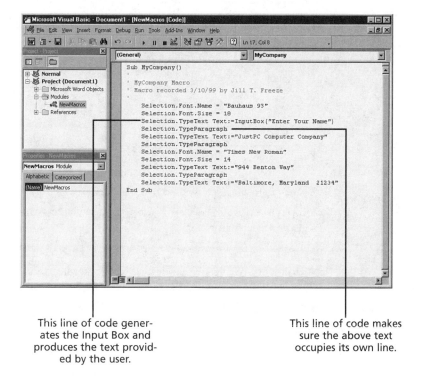

This line of code generates the Input Box and produces the text provided by the user.

This line of code makes sure the above text occupies its own line.

One of the best ways to learn something is by doing it, so let me walk you through the steps you need to follow to generate a macro that incorporates user input:

1. Record a basic Word macro that lists a mock company name and address, as instructed earlier. Don't be afraid to switch fonts as you record to set off the company name from the rest of the information.

2. Open the macro in the Visual Basic for Applications editing screen, as described in the section on correcting macro typos.

3. Under the macro header information, you'll see two lines of Visual Basic code: one line that specifies the name of the font used and a second that specifies its size in points. Right under that, you should see a `Selection.TypeText` statement that contains the company name you recorded.

4. Place the insertion point at the end of the font size line of code, and then press Enter.

5. On the new line, type the following:

```
Selection.TypeText Text:=InputBox("Enter Your Name")
```

Tip: Save your fingers. After you type `Selection.`, a box appears onscreen (as shown in the following figure). Using this IntelliSense box, you can scroll through a list of available objects, so you don't need to type the whole thing manually. Just double-click the one you want to use. Of course, in this example, you still need to key in the InputBox code.

6. Press Enter after you type the close parenthesis.

7. Enter a `Selection.TypeParagraph` statement to make sure the name the user provides occupies its own line.

8. Close the VBA Editor, and the macro is ready to go!

Now when users execute your macro, they'll be presented with a special Input Box like the one shown in Figure 25.12. A user can simply type his or her name, click OK, and the macro text appears personalized with the information the user provided (see Figure 25.13).

FIGURE 25.12

This Input Box lets users customize the output of a macro.

FIGURE 25.13

The polished results ensure consistency throughout your company.

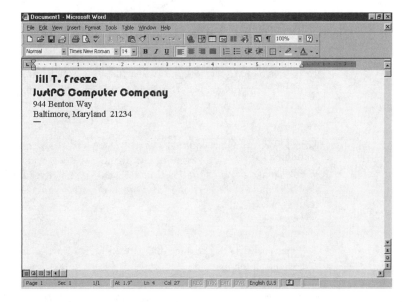

Just think of the possibilities. You could apply the same technique to Excel macros so that the macro's formula could be run against a value supplied by a user. I'll bet you can come up with several ways this capability could help you and/or your company.

Commenting on Your Code

As you get more comfortable using the VBA Editor, your macro code is likely to get longer and more complex. Why? Because you'll find yourself adding message boxes and conditions that must be met for the macro to be executed, for example, and you need to do all this manually, as you'll see in the next chapter.

To help yourself remember which part of the macro does what, you might want to place comments throughout the VBA code to explain why you did things the way that you did then. All you need to do to add a comment is start a new line in the VBA Editor, enter a single quote, and then type your comment. A sample entry might look like this:

```
' Lets the user supply the amount of the item's discount
```

Programming Excel to Compute a Discount Price

Now let's take macro programming a step further and incorporate a bit more VBA. Let's say you want to build something in Excel that computes the discounted price of items after a list price and discount percentage are supplied. Although you begin designing it like a macro, it's really considered creating a new Excel function. To do so, you need to follow these steps:

1. Build a basic Excel worksheet with columns for key information, such as item number, description, list price, discount (which will be expressed as a percentage), and discounted price.

> **Note: Figure out what you really need.** The only three columns that are vital to this macro are list price, discount, and discounted price. You can add as many more columns as your situation warrants, and you needn't refer to the three by the exact names I've given them; it's the information you need, not a certain column header title.

2. Enter your data as I've done in Figure 25.14, but leave your Discounted Price column blank for now.

FIGURE 25.14

For clarity's sake, format the list price and discounted price columns as currency.

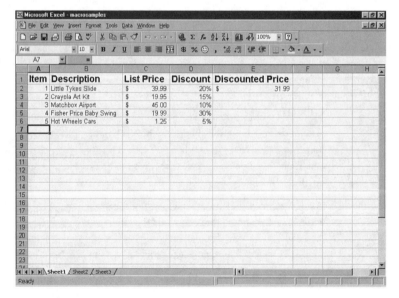

3. Begin designing the function that performs the calculations. Because this step requires editing in VBA as opposed to recording tasks you perform in Excel, you need to create a dummy macro, so to speak. It gives you a framework with which you can begin working. Click Tools|Macro|Record New Macro. Give the macro a name (I chose Discount), and then click OK. When the Stop Recording button bar appears on your worksheet, click the Stop button.

4. Click Tools|Macro|Macros, select the name of the macro you just created, and then click Edit. The Visual Basic for Applications editing screen appears, displaying some macro header information.

5. On the first line, you'll see the word Sub followed by the name you gave the macro and a set of empty parentheses. Delete Sub and type Function in its place.

6. Declare the variables—the items that Excel will look at to return its result. In the case of this project, I used ListPrice and DiscountPercent as the variable names. The variable names should appear inside the parentheses with a comma and a space separating them. The end result of steps 5 and 6 is a first line that looks like this:

```
Function Discount (ListPrice, DiscountPercent)
```

> **Tip: Variably speaking...**For obvious reasons, each variable should have its own unique name. If it doesn't, Excel either returns an incorrect result or an error message. Also note that variable names should appear as single words even if they're made up of two words as you saw previously.

7. Below that first line is a block of information that includes the macro name, when it was recorded, and by whom. You can leave that text untouched. Place the insertion point on the first totally blank line, and then enter the following piece of code:

```
Discount = ListPrice * (1 - DiscountPercent)
```

8. At the bottom of the screen where it says End Sub, change the word Sub to Function. The end result is a VBA screen like the one shown in Figure 25.15.

9. Close the VBA Editor, and return to your Excel worksheet.

10. In the first blank cell under the Discounted Price column, enter the following formula:

```
=discount(C2,D2)
```

This formula calls your new Discount function into action, and C2,D2 references the ListPrice and DiscountPercent variables you declared in VBA. When you press Enter, Excel returns the discounted price for the first item.

11. Because you'll more than likely want to use the same function on more than one item, run your mouse pointer over the right corner of the cell containing the Discount formula you defined. When it turns into a black plus sign, click and drag it down the Discounted Price column through the last row containing data. Excel then computes the applicable discount for each item in the range.

Notice that Excel copies the formula and adds the proper relative cell references for you. That sure beats having to go in and hard-code each line manually!

FIGURE 25.15

It's amazing how much two lines of code can do!

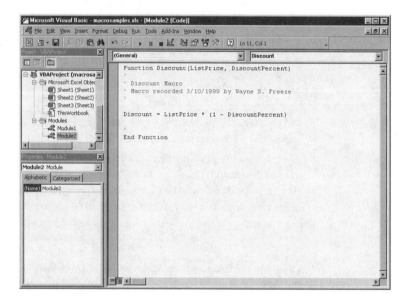

So how else could you use the ability to create your own Excel function? Well, you could build one that would calculate sales tax on items you sell. Or, if you're self-employed, you could design a special function to help you figure out how much estimated tax you owe. The possibilities go on and on, and the best part of all is now that you know how to create a discounted price function, you can easily modify it to meet other needs you may have.

> **Caution: Be prepared.** Whenever you open an Excel workbook with a macro (or user-defined function as the examples before and after this note are often called), Excel will display a message saying that the workbook contains a macro and that macros can contain potentially harmful viruses. If the worksheet contains macros you or someone you know created, chances are you can enable the macros with confidence. If, on the other hand, you downloaded the workbook from somewhere on the Internet, you might want to disable them to protect your equipment until you can verify that the source can be trusted.

Programming Excel to Produce Translation Tables

A translation table is actually a lot less technical than it sounds. It's a custom Excel function that, for example, can take a student's test score and convert it to a letter grade based on a teacher's input. Or it could take the sales of a group of real estate agents and return classifications like Gold Star Producer, or Silver Star Achiever, or whatever special distinctions the real estate company awards.

Although using a translation table may seem like a trivial task to perform manually, it can save you vast amounts of time in having to refer to a grade scale chart or other classification tool. And best of all, if multiple people access the worksheet to add their input, you'll always achieve consistent results.

Peter's Principle: Share the knowledge!

I wish these sophisticated tools were around back when I worked for nonprofit organizations. It would've been great to be able to publish an interactive translation table in Excel to the Web so that others could view the contributions to our organization by the amount donated, the category of contribution (that is, Patron, Supporter, or whatever other special designations we may have had), the supporter's home state, and so on. Consider the potential uses for your translation table as you design it so that you can incorporate all information of value. Pay special attention to who the members of your audience are and what kinds of questions they might want to be able to derive from the data.

Now you can begin creating a translation table. For the sake of these steps, assume that I am building a letter grade translator for my daughter's teachers that would let them enter a student's test results expressed as a percentage and have Excel return the appropriate letter grade. Again, this example is rather elementary, but as I demonstrated earlier, you might find lots of potential uses for this type of function.

Fire up Excel, and then follow these steps to create your own translation table:

1. Build a basic Excel worksheet with columns for key information such as the students' names, student ID numbers, test or project grades (which will be expressed as percentages), and letter grades.

2. Begin entering some sample student data, but leave your Letter Grade column blank for now.

3. Click Tools|Macro|Record New Macro to create the dummy macro as you did in the preceding set of steps. Give the macro a name (LetterGrade in the case of this example), and then click OK. When the Stop Recording button bar appears on your worksheet, click the Stop button.

Note: Macro or user-defined function. Which is it? Although macros and user-defined functions are created in different ways, as you've seen throughout this chapter, Excel treats the two very similarly. In both cases, they are written in Visual Basic for Applications, and you are warned of a potential virus when the workbook is opened. However, they serve different purposes. A macro is designed to be invoked by the user to perform a specific task on a worksheet, whereas a user-defined function enriches Excel's library of functions that can be used in formulas. When it comes to editing the two, however, that's where the similarities stop. You can easily access a macro by clicking Tools|Macro|Macros, selecting the macro's name, and then clicking the Edit button. A user-defined function, on the other hand, requires you to launch Visual Basic for Applications (by choosing Tools|Macro|Visual Basic Editor). You can then typically locate the desired function by clicking the Module1 folder.

4. Click Tools|Macro|Macros, select the name of the macro you just created, and then click Edit. The Visual Basic for Applications editing screen appears, displaying some macro header information.

Caution: There's a first time for everything. If you read the preceding note carefully, you'll recall that I said macros and user-defined functions are edited in different ways. If you took that information to heart, step 4 may have confused you a bit because you were instructed to open the Macros dialog box as opposed to the Visual Basic Editor. The fact is, the user-defined function has not yet been created as of step 4, so it is still treated as a macro. Should you need to edit the user-defined function at a later date, however, you will need to launch the Visual Basic for Applications Editor by clicking Tools|Macro|Visual Basic Editor. You can then typically locate the desired function by clicking the Module1 folder.

5. On the first line, you'll see the word Sub followed by the name you gave the macro (for example, LetterGrade) and a set of empty parentheses. Delete Sub and type Function in its place.

6. Declare the variables—the items that Excel will look at to return its result. In the case of this project, I used Score as the variable name, though another term might be more appropriate given your circumstances. The end result of steps 5 and 6 is a first line that looks like this:

```
Function LetterGrade (Score)
```

7. Leave the macro header text untouched as you did before. Place the insertion point on the first totally blank line, and then type the following pieces of code:

```
If Score >= 0.9 Then
    LetterGrade = "A"
```

```
ElseIf Score >= 0.8 Then
    LetterGrade = "B"

ElseIf Score >= 0.7 Then
    LetterGrade = "C"

ElseIf Score >= 0.6 Then
    LetterGrade = "D"

Else
    LetterGrade = "F"
End If
```

Looking Ahead

Don't get caught up in the code. You'll learn a lot more about `If`, `Else`, and `ElseIf` statements in the next chapter. For now, consider the code the equivalent of a Word template: It gives you the basic format you need, but you can fill in the blanks with whatever information is appropriate. A realtor, for example, might have a statement that looks something like this:

```
If Sales >= 1,000,000 Then
    Club = "Gold Star Producer"

ElseIf Sales > 500,000 then
    Club = "Silver Star Producer"

Else

    Club = "All Star Performer"
EndIf
```

---

8. At the bottom of the screen where it says `End Sub`, change the word `Sub` to `Function`.

9. Close the VBA Editor, and return to your Excel worksheet.

10. In the first blank cell under the Letter Grade column, enter the following formula:

    `=lettergrade(D5)`

    Of course, you might need to change the D5 cell reference to something different, depending on how your worksheet is set up.

    This formula calls your new `LetterGrade` function into action, and `D5` references the `Score` variable you declared in VBA. When you enter a test score and press Enter, Excel returns the applicable letter grade for the first score.

11. Because you'll more than likely want to use the same function on more than one item, run your mouse pointer over the right corner of the cell containing the LetterGrade formula you defined. When it turns into a black plus sign, click and drag it down the Letter Grade column through the last row containing data. Excel then computes the applicable letter grade for each score in the highlighted range.

The large block of code in the preceding steps basically takes the standard 90 percent, 80 percent, 70 percent, 60 percent grading scale and converts it into a letter grade. You can give these statements any name you want and can have them return whatever value you place in the corresponding quotation marks. So, instead of looking at this last exercise as a macro of use to a select few, give it a bit more thought as to how you might be able to modify the function to help you or your company in some way.

On Your Own

Working with macros and Visual Basic for Applications can be intimidating, but not if you look at it in the right light. If you focus on modifying code that already works as opposed to building new code from scratch, you'll spend a lot less time spinning your wheels and trying to second-guess what goes where. Sure, you have a lot to learn about macros and VBA, but I'm here to give you what you need to make the macros work for you, not to give you a condensed summary of everything you need to know in as little space as possible. You've got enough work to do without immersing yourself in the theory of a programming language. If you want to learn more, go for it; but if you want to get the job done quickly, these chapters give you a good start.

Because the next chapter is going to be a real workout (just you wait!), I'm going to go easy on you for this assignment. Create a three-column worksheet that contains the Name, Age, and Label of as many friends and family members you can think of. Fill in the first two columns, and leave the last blank to be filled in by Excel. Next, try writing an Excel function that takes a person's age and returns a special label using the following table as a guide:

Age Range	Label
1–12	Child
13–17	Teen
18–55	Adult
56+	Senior

Apply the new function to all the people you listed.

Now that you've become comfortable with macros and VBA, you're ready for bigger and better things. Get ready, because in the next chapter I'm going to show you how to create your own custom Visual Basic Office 2000 application that will enable you to compress hours of work into minutes.

Building an Office Application Using VBA

So, has your curiosity about macros been sufficiently piqued? Good! Now brace yourself because in this chapter I'm going to give you what you need to become a Visual Basic for Applications (VBA) programmer extraordinaire. You're not a programmer, you say? Don't worry, because you can download everything you need to make the application described in this chapter work. All you have to do is customize the information to meet your specific needs.

In this chapter, I'll show you how to build a mini Office application that creates a business proposal. By making slight modifications, you can apply the case study application to any organization that creates cost-based proposals using standard components. A lawyer's office might use a variant of this application to present clients with a breakdown of their bill. A home improvement contractor might use this technique to help design and cost out a custom deck. A computer consultant might use this application to design a computer network for small business customers. The possibilities are limitless.

Case Study Part 1: Background and Objectives

Samantha's Swing Sets is a small business that builds custom swing sets on its customers' property. A salesperson meets with a prospective customer and develops a list of requirements. These requirements are then entered into an Excel worksheet, which lists all the available components that can be included in a swing set.

Your goal is to calculate the cost of the project and create a business letter outlining the proposal for the customer. My goal is to show you how to accomplish your goal without lifting a finger, using an application you create in VBA.

First, the application verifies that the swing set configuration entered into Excel is correct. After all, you wouldn't want to forget to include the beam that holds the swings or forget one of the end supports! When the configuration is acceptable, you can use the application to print a copy of the worksheet with a customized letter that summarizes the proposal for the potential customer. What a way to save time! After you've entered customer information and an itemized list of the goods or services needed, the letter is written and the total price is calculated for you.

> **Tip: Try it yourself.** Some of the best programmers I know are self-proclaimed "lazy programmers." Rather than redesign each application from scratch, they take bits and pieces from programs they've written in the past and modify them to meet their current needs. Reusing old programs accomplishes two things: It helps ensure that the program code is stable, and it saves hours of work. You can benefit from my hours of work by downloading the sample files for this application from the Internet. Just point your Web browser to www.JustPC.com, and follow the links to *Peter Norton's Complete Guide to Microsoft Office 2000*. Download the files to your hard disk, and follow along as I work my way through the application.

I strongly encourage you to download the files from the Internet as described in the preceding tip. That way, you have a working application at your fingertips, and you can view this chapter as an explanation of how everything works as opposed to a blow-by-blow description of how to build such an application from the ground up. Complex VBA programming can take a long time and is beyond the scope of two chapters in a book, but that doesn't mean I can't give you something complex and of great use to you.

> **Tip: Give me more!** If you're hooked on using VBA by the end of this book, you might want to consult Que's *Special Edition Using VBA* for an in-depth exploration of this powerful programming language.

This application is based around an Excel worksheet that is used to collect information for the proposal. This worksheet includes a series of buttons that help whoever is creating the proposal. These buttons can fill in values for several different standard swing set configurations or clear them out again. After the configuration has been entered, another button can be used to make sure that the swing set is properly designed. When the worksheet has been verified, another button creates a letter to the customer in Word with key information from the worksheet. Finally, the last button prints both the Word document and the Excel worksheet to make the proposal that will be delivered to the customer.

All the VBA code is included in the Excel document, whereas the sample letter is contained as a Word template. These two files comprise the entire application. I chose to work from Excel because most of the programming is against the information in the Excel worksheet. I also did so because I think building programs in Excel is a little easier than building them in Word.

Creating the Worksheet

The first step in this process is to build the basic Excel worksheet. The worksheet has three parts:

- The top half of the worksheet is the place where basic information is entered, such as the customer's name, address, and so on.

- The bottom half contains a big table of each of the available swing set components with list price and installation time.

- The third part of the worksheet is a pair of columns that are adjacent to the big table; they contain information that will be displayed as part of the Word document (or the customized letter that will be generated by the program).

Peter's Principle: Is there a programmer in the house?

If you know how to program, you might wonder why I chose to build the application in this fashion. My goal was to minimize the amount of code you had to write. Also, I tried to build the simplest possible Visual Basic routines. This often meant that I avoided tricks that I would normally use while programming because I thought they would generate more confusion than they were worth. If you are an experienced Visual Basic programmer, you can combine your knowledge of Visual Basic and the information I include in this chapter to create really powerful, custom Office applications.

Entering the Customer's Information

The customer's information is entered into the top half of the worksheet shown in Figure 26.1. (Remember, you can download this worksheet from the Internet and modify it as necessary to save yourself some time.) The worksheet also contains buttons that will be used to perform various tasks with the worksheet, such as verifying the swing set's configuration or creating the proposal document.

Creating this part of the worksheet is straightforward. Simply enter the information into the worksheet. There aren't any formulas here either. These values will be used in the bottom half of the worksheet. Don't worry about the buttons on the worksheet at this point; I'll discuss them later in this chapter.

Note that I make extensive use of borders and merged cells. This way, I can use the same set of columns in the bottom half of the form, while making these input fields wide enough for the data they contain. Otherwise, I would have to create two worksheets—one for the header information and one for the proposal's details.

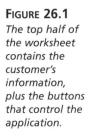

FIGURE 26.1

The top half of the worksheet contains the customer's information, plus the buttons that control the application.

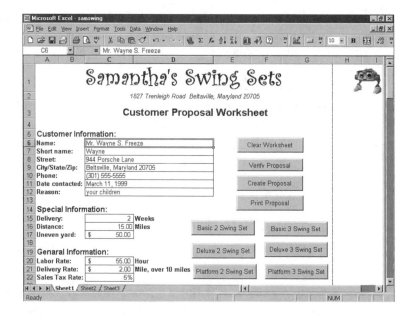

Tip: Monochrome versus color. When I designed this form, I decided not to use color so that it would show up better in the screenshots for this book. However, if I were going to use this form as part of a professional application, I would incorporate color to make the form easier to use. For example, I would use yellow for the background of the cells where information should be entered and light blue for the background of the cells containing values that shouldn't be changed. You should also consider whether you have a printer capable of generating color output before making your decision whether to use color.

Formulating the Proposal's Details

Figure 26.2 shows the bottom half of the form. It is arranged as a list of items, where each line contains the stocking unit number, the quantity, the price, the installation time in hours, the extended cost, and the total time for installation. All the values, except for the quantity, are constants and should not be changed.

Tip: Read-only cells. Information on the worksheet that should not be changed (in this case, the product number, price, and such) should be protected from inadvertent modification. You can do so by formatting the given cells as Locked (choose Format|Cells and then open the Protection tab). You can then choose Tools|Protection and assign a password to ensure that the average user can't change any of these values.

SKU	Qty	Description	Price	Install	Ext. Cost	Tot Time
101	2	Standard swing seat	14.99	0.10	$ 40.98	0.20
102		Deluxe swing seat	24.99	0.10	$ -	-
103		Infant swing seat	19.99	0.10	$ -	-
104		Glider	49.99	0.20	$ -	-
105		Tire swing	38.99	0.10	$ -	-
106		Rope swing	19.99	0.10	$ -	-
201	1	A leg assembly 5' high	49.99	0.50	$ 77.49	0.50
202		A leg assembly 6' high	69.99	0.50	$ -	-
211		2'x3' raised platform 3' high	99.99	1.50	$ -	-
212	1	4'x4' raised platform 4' high	139.99	1.75	$ 236.24	1.75
213		4'x4' clubhouse platform 4' high	199.99	2.50	$ -	-
301	1	Main beam 5' long	49.99	0.25	$ 63.74	0.25
302		Main beam 6' long	79.99	0.25	$ -	-
303		Main beam 8' long	99.99	0.25	$ -	-
311		Ladder beam 5' long	99.99	0.50	$ -	-
312		Ladder beam 6' long	129.99	0.50	$ -	-
313		Ladder beam 8' long	146.99	0.50	$ -	-
401		3' Slide	49.99	0.50	$ -	-
402		4' Slide	79.99	0.50	$ -	-
403	1	4' Tube slide	149.99	1.00	$ 204.99	1.00
		Subtotal			$ 623.44	3.70
		Delivery Charge (over 10 miles)			$ 10.00	$717.61
		Uneven yard charge:			$ 50.00	4 estimat
		Subtotal			$ 683.44	2 estimat
		Sales Tax			$ 34.17	2 total su
		Final Total			$ 717.61	1 total 4'

The calculations for extended cost and total time are straightforward. Total time is computed as

```
total time = install time * quantity
```

whereas extended cost is computed as

```
extended cost = (price + labor * labor rate) * quantity
```

Note that you should use an absolute reference for labor rate to allow you to copy the formula to another cell. This way, the price, labor, and quantity values can change to reference values on the current row while ensuring that the reference to the cell containing labor rate does not change.

At the very bottom of the worksheet is a subtotal field for both extended cost and the total time required to assemble the swing set. Underneath the subtotal of costs are calculations for delivery charge, a charge for assembling the swing set on an uneven yard, and sales tax. These calculations also reference cells in the top half of the form by using an absolute cell reference.

Entering Other Proposal Information

Beneath the total time cells is another series of cells that contain information used elsewhere in the application (see Figure 26.3). I added these cells to save time and effort while writing the VBA application. These values aren't meant to be directly changed by the worksheet user. They are automatically updated as the user enters information into the worksheet. To the right of each of these values is a short description of what they contain.

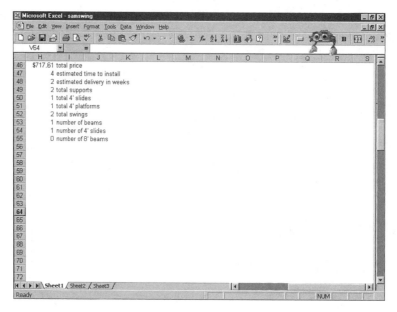

Creating the Letter

Associated with this application is a Word template I created (see Figure 26.4) containing the form letter to be printed with the proposal. It is a relatively straightforward Word document, except that I inserted DOCVARIABLE fields where I wanted the VBA program to insert information from the worksheet. That way, I'm free to rewrite the letter from time to time without affecting my VBA program.

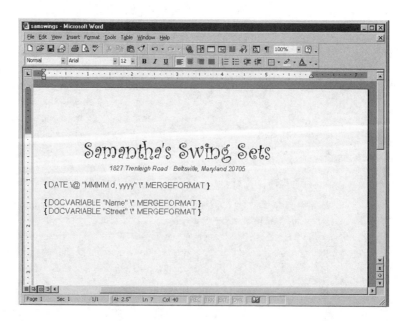

To insert a DOCVARIABLE, follow these steps:

1. Place the cursor in the location where you want the information to appear in your Word document.

2. Choose Insert|Field from the main menu to open the Field dialog box.

3. Select DOCVARIABLE from the Field Names box to display DOCVARIABLE in the Field Codes box.

4. Add the name of the field in quotation marks after DOCVARIABLE in the Field Codes box, and click OK to insert the field in your document. Figure 26.5 shows what the dialog box looks like after I entered the Street field. (Note that I turned on Show Field Codes to show these values. Choose Tools|Options and check the Field Codes check box in the Show section of the View tab.)

In the next section, I'm going to talk a little bit about some Visual Basic for Applications concepts. If you don't know a lot about VBA and the objects available in Microsoft Office, you should take time to read through this material. Otherwise, you can pick up the case study immediately following this discussion.

VBA Primer: From Macros to Programming

To this point, all I've done is essentially record macros. However, Visual Basic for Applications has much more to offer than the simple capability to record and execute macros. In addition to the simple statements you've seen so far, you can use most of the statements that are available in the real Visual Basic programming language. Although I briefly introduce some common Visual Basic statements and concepts here, you don't need to get carried away in trying to understand everything about them. Let them just serve as a guide in helping you interpret what the code you encounter in this chapter does. 'For a more intense VBA experience, you can consult a more comprehensive VBA book, such as Que's *Special Edition Using VBA*.

> **Caution: Halt!** Okay, what I'm about to write really isn't a matter of life or death, but it's an advisable step to take before proceeding with this chapter. Not only should you download the files for this application from the Internet, but I strongly suggest that you open the application inside the VBA Editor so that you can scan through the code as you read as well. That way, what might otherwise seem like boring, out-of-context drivel will have a purpose and will make the pages that follow much more valuable from an educational standpoint. As a challenge, see how many of the statements in the following sections you can find in the code you downloaded.

Assignment Statement

The assignment statement is probably the most used statement in Visual Basic. It enables you to assign an expression to an object or a variable. The expression can be yet another object or variable. It can also be a constant such as the string "Christopher" or the number 4.5. An expression can also be a formula, where multiple objects, variables, and constants are combined with operators such as + (addition), - (subtraction), * (multiplication), / (division), and & (string concatenation). The assignment statement looks like this:

```
<object or variable> = <expression>
```

Dim Statement

When writing programs, you often need places to hold values, much like you hold data in the cells in a worksheet. These places are called *variables*. Like the cells in a worksheet, these values can hold many different types of data. You refer to variables, unlike cells, by assigning them names rather than cell locations.

You can create a variable by using the Dim statement, and then supplying the name of the variable and its data type, as shown here:

```
Dim <variable> As <data type>
```

You can find some of the most commonly used data types in Table 26.1.

Table 26.1 Selected Data Types in VBA

Data Type	Description
String	Holds a sequence of character data
Boolean	Holds a value that is either True or False
Long	Holds an integer value that can range from $-2{,}147{,}483{,}648$ to $2{,}147{,}483{,}647$
Single	Is a floating-point value that can range from $-3.402823E-38$ to $-1.401298E-45$ for negative values and $1.401298E-45$ to $3.402823E-38$ for positive values

You also can use the `Dim` statement to hold references to various objects. You can use any of the objects listed in Table 26.1. After you declare the object, as shown here, you need to use the `Set New` statement (described in the next section) to create a new instance of the object:

```
Dim <variable> As <object>
```

Set Statement

Because object variables are different from normal variables, you need to use the `Set` statement when assigning one object to another:

```
Set <object> = <object>
```

You also can use the `Set` statement to create a new instance of an object:

```
Set <object> = New <object type>
```

Sub Statement

The `Sub` statement is used to define a unit of programming called a *subroutine*, as you can see here. You've seen how the individual steps of a macro are stored in a subroutine. Like a macro, a subroutine is used to hold a frequently used group of statements.

```
Sub <subroutine name> <optional list of parameters>
<list of statements>
End Sub
```

To call a subroutine, simply type the name of the subroutine followed by a list of expressions separated by commas for each of the parameters in the subroutine definition:

```
<subroutine name> <optional list of expressions>
```

Function Statement

You use the `Function` statement, as shown here, to create a special type of subroutine that returns a value. In Chapter 25, "The Macro and VBA Primer," you saw how to create an Excel function that returns a value that can be used in a formula. You can use the same capability inside a VBA program. You might use it to return a value in an assignment statement or evaluate a condition in an `If` statement.

```
Function <function name> <optional list of parameters> <type>
<list of statements>
End Function
```

At least one of the statements in the function definition must be an assignment statement that assigns a value to the function name. This value is returned as the value of the function.

If Statement

The If statement is also important because it enables you to test for a condition or series of conditions. You can use three different forms of the If statement. In the simplest form, shown here, if the condition is True, a list of statements between the If clause and the End If clause is executed:

```
If <condition> Then
<list of statements executed when condition is True>
End If
```

> **Tip: Is Nothing.** One helpful condition takes the form of Object Is Nothing, where Object is the name of an object variable. When this condition is True, the object variable doesn't contain a valid instance of an object, so creating a new object using this variable is okay.

The If statement can also execute a list of statements when the condition is False. These statements fall between the Else clause and the End If clause, as follows:

```
If <condition> Then
<list of statements executed when condition is True>
Else
<list of statements executed when condition is False>
End If
```

In the final form of the If statement, shown here, you can include one or more ElseIf clauses. The ElseIf clause works by evaluating another condition only when the previous condition is False. If this condition is True, then the statements following this clause are executed. You can insert as many ElseIf clauses as you want.

```
If <condition> Then
<list of statements executed when condition is True>
ElseIf <conditionx> Then
<list of statements executed when conditionx is True>
Else
<list of statements executed when all conditions is False>
End If
```

> **Tip: Choose one from many.** You might want to use the If/ElseIf statement to execute a different set of statements based on the value of a single variable.

For Statement

The For statement is useful for repeating a list of statements multiple times, as you can see here. The variable is incremented each time through the loop.

```
For <variable> = <starting value> To <stopping value>
<list of statements executed multiple times>
Next <variable>
```

> **Tip: Long values.** Although the variable used by a For statement can be any numeric data type, you should try to use a Long variable whenever possible. Long variables hold much larger values than Integers, which may be useful when you aren't sure about how large the number will be.

Rem Statement

The Rem statement enables you to include notes in your code. After the Rem statement name, you can type anything you want for the rest of the line. If you need to use more than one line for your comment, you need to begin each one with the Rem statement. Note that you can also use an apostrophe as a shortcut for Rem, as shown here:

```
Rem This is a comment
' This is also a comment
```

> **Note: Green is good.** Comments are displayed using green text in your VBA code. They are ignored by Visual Basic.

With Statement

The With statement, shown next, simplifies using complex objects. It is frequently used in macros recorded in Word where multiple properties are set inside a single object. You can use an object's properties and methods beginning with a period (.).

```
With <object>
<list of statements>
End With
```

> **Note: If it's good enough for Microsoft...**Although I didn't use the With statement in any of the code in this chapter, Microsoft frequently uses the With statement when you record macros.

Understanding Objects and Their Relationships in VBA

The Office 2000 suite of applications is really a collection of objects that can be manipulated by Visual Basic. In Chapter 25, you saw how a macro is really just a Visual Basic routine that performs a series of operations against a set of objects.

An object is a general class of things such as a Word document or an Excel workbook. An object can contain properties that you can set just like you can set the properties of a Word document or an Excel workbook. An object can contain methods that enable you to perform tasks using that object, such as printing a document. An object can also contain other objects; for example, a workbook can contain worksheets. Collections of objects are stored in what's referred to as a *library*.

An instance of an object corresponds to a specific thing such as the Samantha's Swing Sets Excel workbook or Sheet1 inside Samantha's Swing Sets Excel workbook. You need to understand the difference between an object and an instance of an object while writing a VBA program. If the object doesn't exist, you must explicitly create it using the Set New statement (see "VBA Primer: From Macros to Programming," earlier in this chapter).

All the Office applications are built around a complex series of objects. For example, the Excel library contains a Worksheets object, which contains all the Worksheet objects in the workbook. The Worksheet object contains information about a single worksheet and, among other things, contains the Cells object, which contains information about all the cells on the worksheet. This information is contained in a Range object. Inside the Range object are properties such as Value, which contains the value of a cell; Formula, which contains the formula used to calculate the value; and Text, which contains a formatted value. The Range object also contains methods such as Clear, which clears the cells in the range, and Sort, which sorts the cells in the range.

Common Excel Objects

Excel contains a jillion (a technical term meaning too many to count) objects. I've identified a few objects that I used in the application I built in this chapter, plus a few others that you might find useful.

> **Tip: Need an object, record a macro.** The easiest way to find an object and learn how to use it is to record a macro that performs the task you need. Then look at the macro, and you'll see how to access the objects, including parameters and any other information you need.

`Excel.Application` is the most basic object associated with the Excel application. It corresponds to the active Excel session. Because the Samantha's Swing Sets application is created in Excel, this object already exists. Some of the most useful properties, methods, and objects are as follows:

- `ActiveCell`—This object contains a quick reference to the currently selected cell on the currently selected worksheet. All the objects, properties, and methods of the `Range` object, when it refers to a single cell, apply to `ActiveCell`. See "Adding More Useful Buttons" for an example of how you can use `ActiveCell`.

- `ActiveSheet`—This object contains a quick reference for the currently selected worksheet. All the objects, properties, and methods for `Excel.Sheet` also apply to `ActiveSheet`. See "Printing the Proposal" for an example of `ActiveSheet`.

- `ActiveWorkbook`—This object contains a quick reference for the currently selected workbook. All the objects, properties, and methods for `Excel.Workbook` also apply to `ActiveWorkbook`.

- `Range(<cellrange>)`—This method returns reference to the `Range` object for the specified range of cells. This object is used throughout the application. (See the following descriptions for more information about this object.) I often refer directly to this object when looking for the value of a cell because it allows me to directly reference the cells on the currently active worksheet.

- `Selection`—This object contains a quick reference to the currently selected item. The object type returned depends on the currently selected item. It can be a `Range` object if a series of cells is selected, or it can be a `Sheets` object if one or more worksheets and charts are selected. See "A Simple VBA Routine" for an example of this object.

- `Workbooks`—This object contains the collection of workbooks in the Excel session. (See the following descriptions for more information about this object.)

- `Worksheets`—This object contains the collection of worksheets in the Excel session. (See the following descriptions for more information about this object.)

- `Quit`—This method terminates the current Excel session. Any open workbooks are closed, and any tasks are terminated.

- `Visible`—This property determines whether the Excel session appears on the user's display and in the taskbar. By default, this property is `True` because your application is already using Excel.

`Excel.Workbooks` contains the set of workbooks open in the current Excel session. Some of the most commonly used properties and methods are as follows:

- `Add <template>`—This method creates a blank Excel workbook using the specified template and returns a reference to the newly created `Excel.Workbook` object.

- `Count`—This property returns the number of currently open workbooks.

- `Item(<workbook>)`—This method returns the specified `Excel.Workbook` object. `<workbook>` is either a number corresponding to the index of the workbook in the collection or the name of the workbook.

- `Open <filename>`—This method opens the file specified in `<filename>` and returns a reference to the `Excel.Workbook` object containing the document.

`Excel.Workbook` holds information about a single workbook open in the Excel session. Some of the most useful properties, methods, and objects are as follows:

- `Activate`—This method makes the specified workbook the active workbook. You can then reference this workbook by using the `ActiveWorkbook` object.

- `Close <savechanges>`—This method closes the `Excel.Workbook` object and saves any changes to the workbook if requested.

- `Name`—This property returns the name of the workbook.

- `Sheets`—This object contains the list of worksheets and charts in the workbook.

`Excel.Sheets` contains information about the charts and worksheets in the Excel workbook. Some of the most useful properties, methods, and objects are as follows:

- `Add`—This method creates a new Excel worksheet and returns a reference to the newly created `Excel.Sheet` object.

- `Count`—This property returns the number of worksheets in the workbook.

- `Item(<sheet>)`—This method returns the specified `Excel.Worksheet` or an `Excel.Chart` object. `<sheet>` is either a number corresponding to the index of the worksheet in the collection or the name of the worksheet.

`Excel.Worksheet` contains information about a single worksheet in a workbook. Some of the most useful properties, methods, and objects are as follows:

- `Activate`—This method makes the specified worksheet the active worksheet. You can then reference this worksheet by using the `ActiveSheet` object.

- `Cells`—This method returns a `Range` object containing information about all the cells on the worksheet.

- `Name`—This property contains the name of the worksheet.

- `Printout`—This method sends a copy of your worksheet to the printer.

`Excel.Range` contains information about one or more cells in your worksheet. The properties in the following list apply only when you're using a single cell in the worksheet. However, many properties and methods that aren't listed here work on multiple cells like `Clear`. See "Checking Your Worksheet for Errors" for an example of how to use this object.

- `Clear`—This method erases the information from all the cells in the range.

- `Formula`—This property contains the formula used to compute the value using cell addresses in the form of `<rowletter><columnnumber>`.

- `FormulaR1C1`—This property contains the formula used to compute the value using cell addresses in the form of `R<rownumber>C<columnnumber>`.

- `Text`—This property contains the formatted value to be displayed in the cell of the worksheet.

- `Value`—This property contains the raw data value that is stored in the cell.

Common Word Objects

Of the many properties and methods available for Word, I've selected a few key objects, properties, and methods and listed them in this section. Like the Excel objects in the preceding section, about a jillion more objects, properties, and methods are available in the Word library.

> **Tip: Authorized programmers only.** Probably the best tool for finding information about objects is the Object Viewer in the Visual Basic Editor. Choose View|Object Browser from the VBA Editor main menu, and you can see a complete list of the objects available to your program, including their properties and methods. Note that this utility is designed to be used by programmers and may be confusing and cryptic at times. This is especially true because many of the Office 2000 objects are poorly documented in the Object Browser. However, if you're comfortable using objects in Visual Basic, the Object Viewer is an invaluable tool that can often find information about the objects that you can't find anywhere else.

`Word.Application` corresponds to the active Word session. You use this object to create and open documents and manage them when they're active. (See "Creating the Proposal Letter" for an example of how to start the Word session.)

- `Documents`—This object contains the collection of open documents in the Word session. See the following descriptions for more information about the `Word.Documents` object.

- `Quit`—This method terminates the current Word session. Any open documents are closed, and any tasks are terminated.

- `Visible`—This property determines whether the Word session appears on the user's display and in the taskbar.

`Word.Documents` holds the set of Word documents in a `Word.Application` session. Initially, this set is empty. You can use the `Add` or `Open` methods to insert new documents into this collection.

- `Add <template>`—This method creates a blank Word document using the specified template and returns a reference to the newly created `Word.Document` object. (See "Creating the Proposal Letter" later in this chapter).

- `Item(<itemnumber>)`—This method returns the `Word.Document` object that corresponds to the value specified by `<itemnumber>`.

- `Open <filename>`—This method opens the file specified in `<filename>` and returns a reference to the `Word.Document` object containing the document.

`Word.Document` contains information about a Word document. It contains a large assortment of objects, methods, and properties. Some of the most commonly used are listed here. I'll use this object in the application to hold the proposal letter.

- `Close <savechanges>`—This method closes the `Word.Document` object and saves any changes to the document if requested. (See "Printing the Proposal" for how to use this method.)

- `Fields`—This object contains a reference the various special fields in your document. (See the following descriptions for more information.)

- `Paragraphs`—This object contains the set of paragraphs in your Word document. (See the following descriptions for more information.)

- `Printout`—This method sends a copy of your Word document to the printer. (See "Printing the Proposal" section later in this chapter for more information.)

`Word.Paragraphs` contains information about the paragraphs in a Word document. The following are a few key properties, methods, and objects found in this object:

- `Add`—This method adds a new paragraph to the document and returns a `Word.Paragraph` object containing the new paragraph.

- `Count`—This method returns the number of paragraphs in your document.

- `Item(<paragraphnumber>)`—This method returns the specified `Word.Paragraph` object.

- `Item(<paragraphnumber>).Range.Text`—This method returns the text of the specified paragraph.

`Word.Fields` contains information about the special fields in a Word document, including information about `DOCVARIABLE`s and `MERGEFIELD`s. Some of the more interesting properties are listed here. I'll use these properties later as part of the Samantha's Swing Sets application. (See the "Setting Fields" section for more information.)

- Count—This property returns the current number of Field objects in the collection.

- Item(<itemnumber>).Code—This property returns the code string associated with the field, such as DOCVARIABLE, DATE, or MERGEFIELD.

- Item(<itemnumber>).Result.Text—This property returns the value associated with the field specified by <itemnumber>. Note that it uses the Result object to get to the Text property.

Case Study Part 2: Creating Your Worksheet

With a better understanding of objects in Office, now you can begin building the application for Samantha's Swing Sets. I'm going to begin creating some macros that will help the user fill out the worksheet and check the entered values for errors.

A Simple VBA Routine

Obviously, when you begin preparing a proposal for a new client, you want to start with a clean slate, so to speak. To create the macro to erase the cells in the Quantity column, follow these steps:

1. Choose Tools|Macro|Record New Macro from Excel's menu bar. When prompted, specify ClearCells as the macro's name. After you click OK, the Record Macro toolbar is displayed.

> **Note: It's already done for you.** If you have downloaded the sample documents from the Internet, you can view the macro by choosing Tools|Macro|Macros and double-clicking ClearCells. Trying to create the macro generates a message that the macro already exists and asking whether you want to replace the existing macro. Feel free to replace the macro. The contents of the macro are listed in Listing 26.1.

2. Move the mouse pointer to cell B25, which is the top cell in the Quantity column. Press and hold the left mouse button. Drag the cursor to cell B44, and release the left button to select the range of cells B25:B44.

3. Press the Delete key to clear the contents of the cells.

4. Click the Stop button on the Record Macro toolbar to finish recording the macro.

To see what the macro looks like in Visual Basic for Applications, follow these steps:

1. Choose Tools|Macro|Macros to display the Macro dialog box.

2. Select ClearCells and click the Edit button to start the Visual Basic Editor.

3. When the Visual Basic Editor appears, it shows the macro you just created. The code for this macro is shown in Listing 26.1.

The macro listed in Listing 26.1 consists of a Sub statement, four lines of comments, two regular statements, and an End Sub statement. The Sub statement contains the name of the subroutine that will hold the macro and any parameters it contains. In this case, the macro has no parameters, as indicated by the open and close parentheses side by side.

Listing 26.1   The macro uses the Select method to select a range of cells and uses the ClearContents method to erase any values in the cells.

```
Sub ClearCells()
'
' ClearCells Macro
' Macro recorded 3/11/1999 by Wayne S. Freeze
'
'
Range("B25:B44").Select
Selection.ClearContents

End Sub
```

A comment in a Visual Basic program begins with a leading apostrophe. Any characters that follow the apostrophe are ignored by Visual Basic. Comments provide additional information for a Visual Basic programmer or remind you what a specific piece of code does.

The first statement in Listing 26.1 specifies a range of cells and uses the Select method to mark them as selected. You did exactly the same thing in step 2 when you defined the macro.

Likewise, the second statement corresponds to pressing the Delete key to clear the contents of whatever cells have been selected.

> **Caution: The cells changed.** One problem with using cell references in a macro is that when you change the location of the cells in a worksheet, the location of the cells is not automatically updated in a macro. Given that, you shouldn't move cells around on your worksheet without checking your VBA code first to see whether the cells in question would be affected.

Adding Buttons to the Worksheet

Remember the buttons from Figure 26.1? One of the buttons is used to call the ClearCells macro. To add this button to your worksheet, you need to add the Control toolbox to your list of active toolbars. Return to the Excel worksheet, choose Tools|Customize to display the Customize Toolbar dialog box, and select the Control toolbox.

The Control toolbox has a number of different buttons, but only three are important to this application (see Figure 26.6). When the Design Mode button is pressed, you can draw controls on your worksheet by clicking the control in the toolbox and drawing it on your worksheet. You can also move controls around on your worksheet or change their size while the Design Mode button is pressed. Double-clicking a control displays the VBA code that is associated with the control.

FIGURE 26.6

The Control Toolbox helps you add command buttons and other controls to an Excel worksheet.

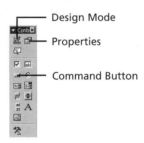

— Design Mode

— Properties

— Command Button

While the Design mode button isn't pressed, the controls are locked into place and can't be changed. Clicking the control calls the subroutine associated with the control. For a command button named CommandButton1, a subroutine called CommandButton1_Click is called.

Just because you added the button doesn't mean that pressing it will make it do anything useful. You have to add some code to the subroutine that will be executed each time the user clicks the button. So, to make the button useful, just follow these steps:

1. Click the Design Mode button on the Control toolbox.

2. Double-click the command button that you just added to display the CommandButton1_Click event in the Visual Basic Editor.

3. In between the Sub and End Sub statements, add the following statement to call to the ClearCells subroutine:

```
ClearCells
```

By default, the text on the button says CommandButton1 rather than something meaningful like Clear Cells. You should follow these steps to change the text displayed on the cell:

1. While you're working in the Visual Basic Editor, press the F4 button or choose View|Properties to display the Properties dialog box for the CommandButton1 control.

2. Change the Caption property from CommandButton1 to Clear Worksheet. This step changes the text displayed on the button to Clear Worksheet (see Figure 26.7).

FIGURE 26.7

Using the Visual Basic Editor to modify your application.

To test the Clear Worksheet button, switch back to your Excel worksheet, and click the Design Mode button. Then enter some test values into the quantity column, and click the Clear Worksheet button. The values you just entered into the worksheet should disappear if the property is set correctly.

Hiding Buttons from the Printout

Unless you specify otherwise, any buttons you add to your worksheet will be visible on any printouts that you make of the worksheet. Although the buttons are tremendously helpful to the data entry person in the pre-proposal generation stage, they can look downright tacky if they are included on the sheet that goes to the prospective customer. Because I plan to include a copy of the worksheet with the letter I generate in Word, I want to hide the buttons when the worksheet is printed. To hide them, you need to follow these instructions:

1. Click the Design Mode button on the Control toolbox.

2. Right-click the button you just created, and select Format Control from the pop-up menu to display the Format Control dialog box.

3. Uncheck the Print Object item on the Properties tab (see Figure 26.8).

FIGURE 26.8

In the Format Control dialog box, you can change various attributes of a button.

Adding More Useful Buttons

You can use command buttons for other things as well. One feature that would be very useful with the kind of worksheet presented here is a button that automatically enters default values for different configurations of swing sets. For instance, if all my swing set configurations are based on six basic designs that feature two or three swings per set—the Basic 2 Swing Set, the Basic 3 Swing Set, the Deluxe 2 Swing Set, the Deluxe 3 Swing Set, the Platform 2 Swing Set, and the Platform 3 Swing Set—I can create one button for each of the designs. After determining which design the customized swing set will be based on, I can click the corresponding button to have the proper quantity of parts entered on the worksheet automatically. Then tacking on any desired options is easy, and I'm spared the time needed to enter the number of parts for each item.

> **Tip: Keep an open mind.** If you don't think you would have a use for such a button, consider these examples. A lawyer might itemize fees for preparing a will, A doctor's office might configure this button to itemize various types of physicals, or a small town pet shop might preconfigure various fish tank setups. The point is, setting some of these parameters ahead of time can pay you back thousands of times over in the amount of time saved down the road.

Now you can create another command button just as you did in the preceding section and then change its caption to Basic 3 Swing. In the CommandButton2_Click event, insert a call to Basic3Swing, as shown in Listing 26.2.

Listing 26.2   Add a call to a subroutine that doesn't exist.

```
Private Sub CommandButton2_Click()

Basic3Swing

End Sub
```

Now create another macro called Basic3Swing using the same basic steps you used to create the ClearCells macro, except this time record a set of steps to create default values for a Basic 3 Swing Set. This means that you need to select the cells and enter values that are appropriate for the swing set. For example, you need to enter the number of swings (3) required for this setup.

Remember, if you make a mistake, just repeat the steps again while you record the macro. You can always delete the unwanted lines of code using the Visual Basic Editor. Listing 26.3 contains the set of steps required to create a swing set with three basic swings, two A leg assemblies, and a main beam.

Listing 26.3   Use the Visual Basic Editor to modify your application.

```
Sub Basic3Swing()
'
' Basic3Swing Macro
' Macro recorded 3/11/1999 by Wayne S. Freeze
'
'
Range("B25").Select
ActiveCell.FormulaR1C1 = "3"
Range("B31").Select
ActiveCell.FormulaR1C1 = "2"
Range("B38").Select
ActiveCell.FormulaR1C1 = "1"

End Sub
```

> **Tip: It isn't defined yet.** You can reference subroutines and functions in Visual Basic before they are created as long as you create them before you try to run the application. I find this trick useful when I know that I want to create a subroutine to perform a specific task, but I'm not quite ready to create it yet.

Cloning a Macro to Save Time

By now, you should be comfortable with recording macros and creating command buttons on your worksheet. However, recording macros is time consuming; you can find much better uses for your time. In your VBA application—like Word, Excel, and the rest of the Office 2000 applications—you can easily cut and paste information to create new subroutines. That means you can produce your Basic 2 Swing Set button with a simple copy and paste and a few edits instead of going through the entire hassle of recording the macro.

A Basic 2 Swing Set has only two differences when compared to a Basic 3 Swing Set—the number of basic swings in the set and the size of the main beam. It's much simpler and more time efficient to create a copy of the Basic3Swing chunk of code and make the necessary changes in the code itself rather than record the macro all over again. Just select the entire subroutine, copy it to the Clipboard, and paste it immediately below the End Sub statement. Then change the subroutine's name to Basic3Swing, and adjust the statements to reflect the new number of swings (3) and the cell reference (B38) for the larger beam.

Listing 26.4 shows the new Basic2Swing macro. Notice that the quantity has been changed to two in the second line of the macro, and the location of the main beam has been changed from cell B38 to B36.

Listing 26.4   Basic2Swing is just a clone of Basic3Swing.

```
Sub Basic2Swing()
'
' Basic2swing Macro
' Macro recorded 3/11/1999 by Wayne S. Freeze
'
'
Range("B25").Select
ActiveCell.FormulaR1C1 = "2"
Range("B31").Select
ActiveCell.FormulaR1C1 = "2"
Range("B36").Select
ActiveCell.FormulaR1C1 = "1"

End Sub
```

Checking Your Worksheet for Errors

Although you can include error checking directly on your worksheet, sometimes adding a VBA routine to do the checking is easier. The routine in Listing 26.5 uses a set of If statements to check various cells on the worksheet for proper values. Any time an error is found, it calls the MsgBox routine to display an error message so that the person inputting the data can take the appropriate action.

Listing 26.5   VerifyProposal ensures that your swing set is configured properly.

```
Sub VerifyProposal()

If Range("H49").Value <> 2 Then
   MsgBox "You must select two supports for the swing set."

ElseIf Range("H53").Value <> 1 Then
   MsgBox "You can only have one beam for the swing set."

ElseIf Range("H50").Value > 0 And Range("H51").Value = 0 Then
   MsgBox "You must have a 4' platform for your 4' slide."

ElseIf Range("B42").Value > 0 And Range("B33").Value = 0 Then
   MsgBox "You must have a 3' platform for your 3' slide."

ElseIf Range("H52").Value > 2 And Range("H54") = 1 Then
   MsgBox "Only two swings are allowed on a five or six foot beam."

ElseIf Range("H52").Value > 3 And Range("H55") = 1 Then
   MsgBox "Only three swings are allowed on an eight foot beam."

Else
   MsgBox "The swingset is configured properly."

End If

End Sub
```

The If statement has a single expression that evaluates to a true or false value. If the expression is True, then the set of statements following the If statement is executed until an Else, ElseIf, or End If statement is encountered.

> **Tip: Just one look...**Take a look back at Listing 26.5. I'm betting you can quickly tell what kind of message the user will get depending on the values he or she enters—even if you aren't an experienced programmer. Programming code is really not as complex and archaic as it might seem at first.

If the expression is False, the expression associated with the next ElseIf is evaluated if it is present. If the ElseIf's expression is True, it works like an If statement. If the ElseIf is False, the next ElseIf, Else, or End If statement is executed. Just look at the code; it'll all make more sense then!

An Else statement is like an ElseIf statement in which the expression is always True. The statements that follow the Else condition are therefore always executed. If an Else statement is present, it must follow any ElseIf statements, or an error occurs. Finally, the End If statement marks the end of the matching If statement. Think of these statements as being similar to a complex set of nested parentheses that almost need to be looked at bit by bit to determine what's what.

To keep this routine simple, I used some cells in the Other Proposal Information section of the worksheet to compute some values. For instance, in cell H49, I used the following formula to compute the total number of supports in the swing set (refer to "Entering Other Proposal Information" earlier in this chapter and Figure 26.3 for more information):

```
=Sum(B31:B35)
```

This formula computes the sum of all the possible swing set support devices, including the different sized A arm assemblies and the various platforms and clubhouses. Because a swing set needs two supports, any value other than two is incorrect.

The same situation occurs for the main beam, where only one beam is allowed. Also, I have the application check to make sure that the user has specified a four-foot high platform or clubhouse for a four-foot slide, and a three-foot platform for a three-foot slide. Finally, I verify that a five- or six-foot beam has a maximum of two swings, and an eight-foot beam has a maximum of three swings.

Power VBA Programming

Are you still with me? Great! Don't let this section header scare you off. Sure, what I'm about to show you is a bit more complicated, but remember that you have the advantage of access to my complete source code for the application. That way, if you encounter a problem and can't quickly determine the cause, you can turn to a working application to get up and running in a hurry.

Everything I've done up to this point has been relatively straightforward. However, to finish this application, I need to add some VBA routines that will create a Word document on-the-fly and insert all the information I want, such as the customer's name, the total cost of the swing set, and such. I chose this approach to be the simplest and most straightforward way to implement this capability. If you are an experienced Visual Basic programmer, you can easily improve this program. But this program works, and it's a whole lot easier for the beginning programmer to understand, so it serves its intended purpose. I limited myself to the fewest possible statements to keep this program as simple as possible.

Adding Word to Your Excel VBA Program to Create a Form Letter

By default, only the objects associated with Excel are included when you record a macro in Excel. Any other objects such as Word, Access, and so on need to be explicitly added to your VBA program. Because the Samantha's Swing Sets application will create a

Word document on-the-fly, you need to add the Word objects to the program. To do so, just follow these steps:

1. In the Visual Basic Editor, click Tools|References to display the References dialog box (see Figure 26.9).

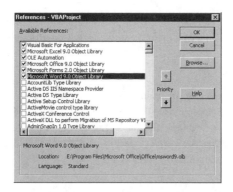

2. Search the dialog box for the Microsoft Word 9.0 Object Library, and place a check mark in its check box.

3. Click OK to add the object library to your program.

Variables and Global Declarations

The code in a Visual Basic program either is associated with an object such as a worksheet or a Word document, or the code is standalone and not associated with any objects. The code for the Command Buttons created earlier is stored in Sheet1, and the macros we entered are stored in an independent location called Module1. I refer to both of these collections of code as *modules*.

Any variables declared at the top of a module are global to all the subroutines and functions that are in the module (see Listing 26.6). Because I plan to use the WordApp and WordDoc variables in more than one subroutine, placing them at the top of the module is the best way to ensure that my application can access them whenever they are needed.

> **Tip: Automatically get into trouble.** VBA automatically creates a variable any time you reference a new one. However, this often allows errors to creep into your program. If you simply misspell the name of a variable, for example, a new variable is automatically created. One thing I highly recommend to every Visual Basic programmer is to include Option Explicit at the start of each program. This statement forces you to declare a variable using the Dim statement before you use it so that your application isn't plagued by illusive spelling error bugs.

`Option Compare Text` ensures that all string comparisons are not case sensitive. Without this statement, two strings are equal only when each character is the same and has the same case. Because you can easily make a mistake when dealing with uppercase and lowercase letters, using the `Option Compare` statement is a good idea. After all, we've all got enough to worry about without having to obsess over whether a certain item's name is capitalized or not!

Listing 26.6 Global declarations are found at the very top of the source code.

```
Dim WordApp As Word.Application
Dim WordDoc As Word.Document

Option Explicit
Option Compare Text
```

Creating the Proposal Letter

Creating the proposal's cover letter involves starting Word, creating a new document based on a previously defined Word template (one with wordsmithed prose and fields for which Excel provides the information), and inserting values from the current Excel worksheet into the `DOCVARIABLE` fields in the new Word document. You can see how I do this in Listing 26.7.

I begin this routine by seeing whether the `WordApp` object contains a valid object. I do so by using the `Is Nothing` test. If the `WordApp` doesn't contain a reference to an object, I create one by using the `Set/New` statement. This automatically starts Word. Setting the `WordApp.Visible` property to `True` displays the Word session on the screen. If you were to remove this statement from the macro, it would still work, except that you would never know that Word is running. It wouldn't be shown on the screen or on the taskbar.

Next, I check to see whether the `WordDoc` variable contains a reference to a valid object. If it does, I assume that I don't need it any longer and use the `WordDoc.Close` method to destroy the document. The `False` parameter instructs the `Close` method to close the document even if it hasn't been saved.

Then I create a new Word document by using the `Document.Open` method. This method opens the specified file and returns a `Document` object that points to the newly created document. Note that both `WordApp` and `WordDoc` are global variables and can be used by any subroutine in this module.

Finally, I assign values for each of the `DOCVARIABLE` fields in the template by using the `SetField` subroutine. This routine takes care of all the dirty work required to assign the value to the specified field name. It has two parameters: the name of the field and the value I want to assign to the field. (The SetField subroutine is discussed in the next section of the chapter.) To get the value for each field, I use the Range object to locate the particular cell I am interested in, and the Text property to retrieve the formatted text value.

Listing 26.7 Creating a proposal requires you to start a Word session and define values for the DOCVARIABLE fields.

```
Sub CreateProposal()

If WordApp Is Nothing Then
    Set WordApp = New Word.Application
    WordApp.Visible = True

End If

If Not (WordDoc Is Nothing) Then
    WordDoc.Close False

End If

Set WordDoc = WordApp.Documents.Add("c:\norton\samswings.dot")

SetField "Name", Range("C6").Text
SetField "ShortName", Range("C7").Text
SetField "Street", Range("C8").Text
SetField "CityStateZip", Range("C9").Text
SetField "ContactDate", Range("C11").Text
SetField "Reason", Range("C12").Text
SetField "Highlights", Highlights()
SetField "TotalPrice", Range("H46").Text
SetField "TotalTime", Range("H47").Text
SetField "DeliveryTime", Range("H48").Text

End Sub
```

> **Note: Something for you to fix.** If you read the code in Listing 26.7 carefully, you'll notice that I've specified the location of the Word template as c:\norton\samswings.dot. If you saved the sample application into a different directory, you need to adjust this statement to reflect the new location of the Word template.

Setting Fields

Sometimes accessing objects can be a little more difficult than you might think because of the way that Microsoft defined them. The Fields collection in a Word document falls into this category.

For the `Fields` collection to work, you must supply the index of the field you want to access. You can't simply specify the name of the Excel worksheet field you want to access. Instead, you need to search for the code value you want to access. It is formatted as the word `DOCVARIABLE`, followed by a space, a double quotation mark, the name of the `DOCVARIABLE`, and another double quotation mark. For example, the `Street DOCVARIABLE` field is as follows:

```
DOCVARIABLE "Street"
```

In the `SetFields` routine (see Listing 26.8), I use two parameters containing the name of the field I want to update and the value I want to assign to it. Because the value stored in the `Code` property is complex, I construct a string called `CompareString` containing the formatted name of the field stored in `DocVarName`. I then use the `Len` function to get the length of this value and save it in the variable called `CompareLength`.

Then I use a `For` statement to loop through each field in the `Fields` collection. I compare only the first `CompareLength` number of characters from the `Code` property with `CompareString`. When I get a match, I set the `Result.Text` property to the new value passed in `DocVarValue`. Because I check every `Code` value in the `Fields` collection, the application can handle the situation in which multiple `DOCVARIABLE`s appear in the document with the same name. Each instance of the `DOCVARIABLE` has an entry in the collection and needs to be updated accordingly.

Listing 26.8   The `SetField` routine makes setting the `DOCVARIABLE` fields easy.

```
Sub SetField(DocVarName As String, DocVarValue As String)

Dim i As Long
Dim CompareLength As Long
Dim CompareString As String

CompareString = " DOCVARIABLE """ & DocVarName & """"
CompareLength = Len(CompareString)

For i = 1 To WordDoc.Fields.count
   If Left(WordDoc.Fields(i).Code, CompareLength) = CompareString Then
      WordDoc.Fields(i).Result.Text = DocVarValue
   End If

Next i

End Sub
```

Picking Highlights from the Worksheet for the Cover Letter

To make the cover letter even more tailored to the customer, I opted to extract the three most important characteristics of the proposed swing set and refer to them by name in the letter. To do so, I needed to make use of the Highlights function.

Although the Highlights function is very long (see Listing 26.9), it isn't very complicated. I begin by defining three temporary strings. These three strings will hold the three most important features of the swing set. I then assign an empty string to each of them.

I use a series of If statements to check specific cells on the worksheet to see whether they have a value greater than zero. If they do, then I know that a particular feature is included in the proposal. When I find a feature, I call the Add3 subroutine with the three temporary variables and a string that describes the feature.

Note that I check the features in order of importance. Checking them this way prevents me from looking unprofessional by highlighting basic information such as the number of A assemblies. Something like a deluxe clubhouse or an installation on uneven ground is far more important (and impressive).

Also to present a variety of features, I group like features together in a single If/ElseIf statement. Thus, only one of the features from each group is selected. This means that I don't return a highlighted phrase that includes both a clubhouse and a platform, or a tube slide and a regular slide.

At the end of the function, I combine the three temporary strings together to make a single coherent phrase. Depending on the features selected, I can end up with one, two, or three features to return. Because the Add3 routine fills the temporary strings in order, I know that I have only one feature if temp2 is empty; thus, I need to return only the first highlight.

Likewise, if the temp3 contains an empty string, then I know that I have to return only the first two strings. So I concatenate temp1, the string " and", and temp2 so that I can return a phrase like a slide and two standard swings.

Finally, if both temp2 and temp3 contain strings, I concatenate temp1, a comma, temp2, the string " and", and temp3. This means that I return a highlight like a clubhouse, a tube slide, and three deluxe swings.

Listing 26.9 The Highlights routine selects the three most important features of the proposal.

```
Function Highlights() As String

Dim temp1 As String
Dim temp2 As String
Dim temp3 As String
```

```
temp1 = ""
temp2 = ""
temp3 = ""

If Range("B35").Value > 0 Then
    Add3 temp1, temp2, temp3, " a clubhouse"

ElseIf Range("B33").Value > 0 Or Range("B34").Value > 0 Then
    Add3 temp1, temp2, temp3, " a raised platform"

End If

If Range("B44").Value > 0 Then
    Add3 temp1, temp2, temp3, " a tube slide"

ElseIf Range("B42").Value > 0 Or Range("B43").Value > 0 Then
    Add3 temp1, temp2, temp3, " a slide"

End If

If Range("B39").Value > 0 Or Range("B40").Value > 0 Or
[ic.ccc]Range("B41").Value > 0 Then
Add3 temp1, temp2, temp3, " a ladder bar"

End If

If Range("B28").Value > 0 Then
    Add3 temp1, temp2, temp3, " a glider"

End If

If Range("B29").Value > 0 Then
    Add3 temp1, temp2, temp3, " a tire swing"

End If

If Range("B30").Value > 0 Then
    Add3 temp1, temp2, temp3, " a rope swing"

End If

If Range("B27").Value > 0 Then
    Add3 temp1, temp2, temp3, " an infant swing"

End If

If Range("B26").Value = 1 Then
    Add3 temp1, temp2, temp3, " a deluxe swing"

ElseIf Range("B26").Value = 2 Then
    Add3 temp1, temp2, temp3, " two deluxe swings"

ElseIf Range("B26").Value = 3 Then
    Add3 temp1, temp2, temp3, " three deluxe swings"

End If
```

continues

Listing 26.9   Continued.

```
If Range("B25").Value = 1 Then
   Add3 temp1, temp2, temp3, " a standard swing"

ElseIf Range("B25").Value = 2 Then
   Add3 temp1, temp2, temp3, " two standard swings"

ElseIf Range("B25").Value = 3 Then
   Add3 temp1, temp2, temp3, " three standard swings"

End If

If temp2 = "" Then
   Highlights = temp1

ElseIf temp3 = "" Then
   Highlights = temp1 & " and" & temp2

Else
   Highlights = temp1 & "," & temp2 & " and" & temp3

End If

End Function
```

Keeping the Top Three Highlights

The Add3 routine is very simple (see Listing 26.10). It merely searches the s1, s2, and s3 strings for the first one that's empty. Then it saves the value in newstr into it. If all three strings are full, then the subroutine merely returns without doing anything.

Listing 26.10   The Add3 routine stores a value in the first available space.

```
Sub Add3(s1 As String, s2 As String, s3 As String, newstr As String)

If s1 = "" Then
   s1 = newstr

ElseIf s2 = "" Then
   s2 = newstr

ElseIf s3 = "" Then
   s3 = newstr

End If

End Sub
```

Printing the Proposal

Of course, what good is a fancy proposal if you can't print it? Instructing the application to print the proposal is very simple (see Listing 26.11). I begin by verifying that I have created the WordDoc object. If the WordDoc Is Nothing, then I know that the WordDoc hasn't been created and I shouldn't do anything. Otherwise, I use the WordDoc.PrintOut method to send the document to the currently defined Windows printer.

Then I use the WordDoc.Close method to close the document. Specifying False as the parameter means that the current document isn't saved when the document is closed. I then close the WordApp by using the Quit method. Along the way, I set the WordDoc and the WordApp objects to Nothing to make sure that they are ready to be used again.

Finally, I send the current Excel worksheet to the printer. I reference the current worksheet by using the ActiveWindows.SelectedSheets object and the PrintOut method to send it to the printer.

Listing 26.11   The last step in creating a proposal is printing it.

```
Sub PrintProposal()

If Not (WordDoc Is Nothing) Then
    WordDoc.PrintOut
    WordDoc.Close False
    Set WordDoc = Nothing

    WordApp.Quit
    Set WordApp = Nothing

    ActiveSheet.PrintOut

End If

End Sub
```

Running the Samantha's Swing Sets Application

Using the Samantha's Swing Sets application is very easy. Simply open the Excel workbook, and begin entering values and clicking buttons. In most cases, you can begin by choosing one of the standard swing set configurations. Simply click the button corresponding to the configuration you want, and the application enters the default values. Then you can modify these values however you want by entering new numbers into the cells. Click Clear Worksheet if you want to enter new values.

You can begin to produce the actual proposal by clicking the Verify Proposal button to ensure that the swing set is configured properly. After you correct any errors in the configuration, click the Create Proposal button to generate the Word document and fill in the information from the worksheet. If you want, after this step is finished, you can edit the Word document to add some personal touches. When you're finished, simply click the Print Proposal button to send both the worksheet and the Word document to the printer and to end the Word session.

On Your Own

The mini application for Samantha's Swing Sets is designed to show you what you can do with a little work and the standard tools that come with Office 2000. However, this is only the tip of the VBA iceberg.

Although Samantha's Swing Sets offers only one proposed configuration for the customer, you could easily use the same techniques to create multiple proposals from which a customer could choose. By simply adding two more quantity columns, you could easily configure three different options. Then you could use another macro to create different worksheets containing the details of each proposal. You could even program the application to suppress any rows that have zero for the quantity so that the customer would see only relevant information on his or her worksheet.

You can expand this application by saving the information collected in the Excel worksheet into an Access database. You could then call up and change this information as needed to reflect the customer's needs. You could also use the Access components to track the proposal as it becomes an order and then use the information for billing purposes.

You could even use the information to help build a PowerPoint slide show that would accompany the proposal. This capability would be especially useful if you want to show the customer the different individual components and how the different completed swing sets might look when finished. Of course, all these capabilities may sound like overkill for a swing set company, but they may be immensely valuable for other types of enterprises.

You could also tie this application into Outlook by saving the customer's information into the Outlook contact list and automatically adding an entry into your Outlook calendar for a follow-up call to the customer to see whether he or she is still interested in the proposal.

So, go ahead and load the application files and experiment. You have nothing to lose (you can always download another copy of the application files if something happens), and oh so much to gain. You know what they say about practice...

Glossary

Access 2000   Microsoft's database application, included with the Office 2000 suite of applications. The application is not included with the Office 2000 Standard Edition, nor is it included with the Small Business Edition.

Answer Wizard   A tool that lets you get help by enabling you to type a question in conversational language. That way, you can find what you need even if you don't know the proper technical terms.

appointment   In Outlook 2000,a scheduled activity that you do not invite others to. An appointment blocks out a chunk of time on your calendar using the standard meeting request form (simply called Appointment). The only difference in function between Outlook meetings and appointments is the fact that appointments do not have attendees.

AutoShapes   Predefined shapes on the Office 2000 drawing tool that can be inserted in place of freehand drawn shapes.

Chart component   A COM Web component that enables a chart published on the Web to change automatically as its corresponding data changes.

Clip Gallery   A shared applet that lets you organize, store, and insert images, movies, and sounds to your work.

Collaboration   A new Web feature in Office 2000 that enables users to comment on and create online discussions in documents that are located on a Web server. Your network server must have the new Office Server Extensions installed for this feature to work.

Collect and Paste   A new Office 2000 Clipboard that lets you gather multiple bits of text or objects and then lets you insert them all at once or one at a time into a document.

COM (Component Object Module)   A technology used primarily to provide application services. Many of the components in Office 2000 are linked together using this technology.

conditional formatting   A type of formatting that tells Access or Excel to format data that meets certain criteria in a way that you define.

database   A collection of data organized in such a way that it can be quickly searched and retrieved.

event   In Outlook, a calendar item that exceeds one work day in length—for example, a conference.

Excel 2000   Microsoft's spreadsheet application that allows you to run calculations on numbers, chart data, and even create a lightweight database.

field   One of the items in a database record, such as first name, city, and so on.

filter   An Outlook and Outlook Express tool to sift out the messages you need to see. For example, you can filter down to messages from a single sender or messages that arrived on a certain day.

First Run Install   A new Office 2000 installation option that prompts you to install an application the first time you try to use it. That way, the entire application is kept on the installation source until you really need it. Using this option can help you save a fair amount of disk space in the short run.

First Use Install   An Office 2000 option that lets Office components (such as themes, extra Office Assistants, and so on) show up on all your menus even if they aren't installed. When you try to use them, you are prompted to install them.

graphical bullets   Images, clip art, or special symbols used as bullets.

HTML (Hypertext Markup Language)   A Web-supported file format that can be understood by all kinds of computers accessing the World Wide Web.

hyperlink   An item or block of text that, when clicked, takes you to another location or resource.

iCalendar   A new scheduling standard that makes scheduling meetings using free/busy data over the Internet possible.

IMAP (Internet Mail Access Protocol)   An alternative mail protocol to POP3, IMAP stores incoming messages on the mail server until you specifically delete them and/or move them to your local machine.

Internet Explorer 5   Microsoft's Web browser that is in large part responsible for powering many of the most notable Office 2000 enhancements, including the Web components, new HTML-based help files, and the ability to see how Office documents will look on the Web before you actually publish them there. Although Office 2000 features are optimized for use with Internet Explorer, any HTML 3.0-compliant browser should work—in theory.

meeting   In Outlook, any event you need to invite other people to or reserve resources for.

message rules   Actions performed on messages that meet given criteria. You can set rules to sort incoming messages into folders, delete junk mail, or even send a return message back automatically.

Multilanguage Pack   An Office 2000 add-in that enables you to work with multiple languages in a single Office 2000 installation.

NetMeeting   An online collaboration application included in the Internet Explorer suite. It is used to collaborate on, brainstorm, or discuss documents over the Internet. NetMeetings can also be scheduled with the help of Outlook.

Office Assistants   Animated characters that offer context-sensitive help onscreen in Office 2000.

Office Server Extensions   Software that runs on a server that enables you to take advantage of many of the Web-related features, such as document discussions.

OLAP (Online Analytical Processing)   A multi-dimensional database that's used for decision support analysis and data warehousing.

Outlook 2000   Office 2000's email client and personal information manager. This application lets you maintain your Address Book/Contact List, helps you organize and schedule meetings, and assists in maintaining your personal calendar, to-do list, and journal entries.

Outlook Express   A lightweight email and news reading client that ships with the Internet Explorer suite of applications. Outlook Express also enables you to maintain a Contact List/Address Book.

personalized menus   When enabled, these menus show the most commonly used commands first, and show the rest of the choices after you wait a few seconds or after you click the double arrows at the bottom of the menu.

personalized toolbars   Similar to the personalized menus, toolbars that place only the most commonly used buttons on the toolbars. You can find the rest of the buttons by clicking the More Buttons drop-down button at the far right end of the respective toolbar.

PIM Only Mode   A setup option whereby you can still use Outlook 2000 as a personal information manager even if you use another application as your email client.

PivotChart   A new Excel chart type that enables you to manipulate chart data right on the chart without having to tweak the worksheet that builds the chart.

PivotTable Component   A tool you can interact with over the Web to analyze multidimensional data in a worksheet-like format.

Places Bar   A button bar on Open/Save As dialog boxes that gives you one-click access to the places you visit most, such as favorite documents, most recently used files, and so on.

POP3 (Post Office Protocol)   The most frequently used mail protocol that pulls down email messages from the mail server as soon as you log on to it (unless you've specifically set options to the contrary).

PowerPoint 2000   A Microsoft application used to create slide shows, online presentations, overhead transparencies or 35mm slides, or even paper handouts. With PowerPoint 2000, you can even broadcast live presentations over the Web.

Present in Browser   An option that lets you view PowerPoint presentations in a Web browser instead of requiring a special viewer.

presentation broadcast   The ability to give live slide shows over the Web with the help of NetMeeting and/or NetShow.

Publisher 2000   Microsoft's desktop publishing application that enables you to produce professional-quality brochures, newsletters, business cards and forms, and the like. Publisher is available with all flavors of Office 2000.

read receipt   A note you receive when an email message is read by the recipient. You must set a special option to be able to request read receipts. Note that not all email clients support the use and generation of read receipts.

SDI (Single Document Interface)   An interface in which each Office 2000 document is easily accessible through its own button on the Windows taskbar.

See-Through view   A new, lighter blue highlighting in Excel that makes it easy to see where you're working. This view replaces the previous version's dark highlighting, which concealed the text underneath it.

self-repairing applications   Applications that run a quick self-repairing script before they are launched.

service pack   A collection of bug fixes available to registered users of an application.

Spreadsheet component   A new Office 2000 Web component that enables Excel 2000 users to take the functionality and interactivity of Excel sorts and such to the Web.

stationery   Outlook 2000's electronic counterpart to fancy paper stationery. You can use a variety of designs and colors to give your email messages a personalized appearance.

template   A special type of document in which formatting and design have been preset; it is used to create a standardized new document.

theme   A way to achieve a consistent look among Web pages, documents, and so on. The theme can contain settings for the background, font, text color, bullet style used, and so on.

Tri-Pane view   A revolutionary new PowerPoint workspace that combines three views into one: Outline view, Slide view, and Notes view.

VBA (Visual Basic for Applications)   A programming language that enables advanced users to further extend their Office 2000 capabilities. It is essentially the new standardized macro programming language.

Web Discussions   A new tool you can use to discuss various Web pages and Office documents with others connected to your LAN. You must be connected to a server running the new Office Server Extensions.

Web folders   Folders that are easily accessible from within any Open or Save As dialog box; they point to the location you are to publish documents or Web pages on your company's server. Consult your network administration for details on setting up these pointers.

Web queries   Excel features that help you define what Web data is to be pulled down for analysis in Excel.

Word 2000   Microsoft's word processing application that's included as part of the Office 2000 suite of applications.

Index

X-Z

Personal Bookshelf

FREE

Get FREE books and more...when you register this book online for our Personal Bookshelf Program

http://register.samspublishing.com/

SAMS

Register online and you can sign up for our *FREE Personal Bookshelf Program*...unlimited access to the electronic version of more than 200 complete computer books—immediately! That means you'll have 100,000 pages of valuable information onscreen, at your fingertips!

Plus, you can access product support, including complimentary downloads, technical support files, book-focused links, companion Web sites, author sites, and more!

And you'll be automatically registered to receive a *FREE subscription to a weekly email newsletter* to help you stay current with news, announcements, sample book chapters, and special events, including sweepstakes, contests, and various product giveaways!

We value your comments! Best of all, the entire registration process takes only a few minutes to complete, so go online and get the greatest value going—absolutely FREE!

Don't Miss Out On This Great Opportunity!

Sams is a brand of Macmillan Computer Publishing USA.

For more information, please visit *www.mcp.com*